Making the Modern South
DAVID GOLDFIELD, EDITOR

Rationing Justice

POVERTY LAWYERS AND POOR
PEOPLE IN THE DEEP SOUTH

KRIS SHEPARD

To Deborah
Kris Shepard

LOUISIANA STATE ✠ UNIVERSITY PRESS
BATON ROUGE

Published by Louisiana State University Press
Copyright © 2007 by Louisiana State University Press
All rights reserved
Manufactured in the United States of America
First printing

Designer: AMANDA MCDONALD SCALLAN
Typeface: WHITMAN
Typesetter: G & S TYPESETTERS, INC.
Printer and binder: EDWARDS BROTHERS, INC.

Library of Congress Cataloging-in-Publication Data

Shepard, Kris.
Rationing justice : poverty lawyers and poor people in the deep South / Kris Shepard.
p. cm. — (Making the modern South)
Includes bibliographical references and index.
ISBN-13: 978-0-8071-3207-4 (cloth : alk. paper)
ISBN-10: 0-8071-3207-1 (cloth : alk. paper)
1. Legal assistance to the poor—Southern States. 2. Legal aid—Southern States.
I. Title. II. Series.
KF336.S52 2007
344.7503'258—dc22

2006014235

The paper in this book meets the guidelines for permanence and durability of the Committee
on Production Guidelines for Book Longevity of the Council on Library Resources.⊗

For Kirby

Contents

ACKNOWLEDGMENTS ix

Prologue / 1

1. A "New Breed of Lawyer" / 16

2. The Lawyers' War on Poverty, 1965–1970 / 37

3. The Lean Years, 1970–1975 / 68

4. "Equal Access to Justice": *LSC and the Expansion of Legal Services in the Deep South, 1975–1981* / 102

5. Low-Income Families, Poverty Lawyers, and the Regulatory State / 132

6. Low-Income Communities, Poverty Lawyers, and Racial Reconstruction / 178

7. Poverty Law, Politics, and the Rationing of Justice, 1981–1996 / 224

APPENDIX:
Political Support for the Legal Services Corporation / 245

ABBREVIATIONS / 255

NOTES / 257

SELECTED BIBLIOGRAPHY / 351

INDEX / 379

Acknowledgments

I am deeply indebted and grateful to a long list of people who made this book possible. My advisors at Emory University, Dan Carter, David Garrow, and Leroy Davis, were especially thoughtful and supportive throughout the project, in particular during the hazy early days as the story told in these pages was coming into focus. Others at Emory, the University of North Carolina at Chapel Hill, and the University of Virginia School of Law provided guidance as well, and I appreciate their input. Some of the brightest people I know took time from their studies to help cure what ailed mine, and for their wisdom and insight I thank them: Andrew Miles Kaye, Brian Luskey, Rob Widell, my fellow Mellon Southern Studies Fellows at Emory (particularly Steve Hahn), and others.

Much of this story was told to me by the people who lived it. Without their having opened up their lives to me, this would have been a very different and far less interesting book. In addition, many people who are or were involved in legal services programs provided me with documents and records from their personal files or the files of their respective institutions. Steve Gottlieb of the Atlanta Legal Aid Society and Phyllis Holmen of the Georgia Legal Services Program deserve special mention, but others provided assistance as well. Their efforts were critical contributions to my work because the records of the Legal Services Corporation are not complete, nor are those of each separate legal services program. Equally important were the librarians and archivists at the National Equal Justice Library at American University in Washington, D.C.; the state archives of Georgia, Alabama, and Mississippi; the federal repository in East Point, Georgia; the Legal Services Corporation's records office; Emory University; the University of Mississippi; the University of Virginia; and the University of North Carolina at Chapel Hill.

Finally, I would not have acknowledged one of my most important sources of support if I failed to mention my family: my father, Adrian Shepard; my mother, Joyce Shepard; and my brothers, Kenny and Kevin. They have never let me down. My wife, Emy, patiently endured my educational career and my own personal foibles, and this book is as much a testament to her as to anyone. She is my life companion, and every day I am amazed to be in her presence. Emy has given me two equally inspiring children, Madeleine and Ava, whose captivating smiles are reflections of their mother. I pray that they will have opportunities like those that I have enjoyed, including meeting the people portrayed in this book and writing their story.

Rationing Justice

Prologue

Law is fine if you get on the good side of it.
—HENRY CHESSER, a tenant farmer

N the spring of 1964, at a Law Day address delivered at the University of Chicago School of Law, Robert F. Kennedy, then attorney general of the United States, chastised his audience of lawyers, professors, and law students for their failure to serve a group of Americans in desperate need of legal counsel: the poor. The occasion was the seventh Law Day commemorated in the United States. President Dwight D. Eisenhower proclaimed the first Law Day in 1958, and in 1961 Congress designated the first day of May as "a special day of celebration by the American people in appreciation of their liberties and the reaffirmation of their loyalty to the United States of America; of their rededication to the ideals of equality and justice under law . . . ; and for the cultivation of that respect for law that is so vital to the democratic way of life."[1] Kennedy used the occasion to lament that the word *legal* had become synonymous with "technicalities and obstruction, not for that which is to be respected." He warned his listeners: "The poor man looks upon the law as an enemy, not as a friend. For him the law is always taking something away." According to Kennedy, poverty was "a condition of helplessness" that resulted, in part, from low-income Americans' inability to assert their rights within the legal system: "The tenants of slums, and public housing projects, the purchasers from disreputable finance companies, the minority group member who is discriminated against—all these may have legal rights which . . . remain in the limbo of the law" because of their lack of legal representation. A "wealthy client can pay counsel to unravel—or to create—a complex tangle" of legal questions, but less affluent persons did not have that luxury.[2] The nation's leading lawyer concluded the castigation of his profession by asserting that "lawyers must bear the responsibility for permitting the growth and continuance of two systems of law—one for the rich, one for the poor."[3]

Within months of Kennedy's Law Day address, Congress passed the Economic Opportunity Act of 1964 to "mobilize the human and financial resources of the Nation to combat poverty in the United States."[4] Using funds appropriated under that act, policy makers developed a Legal Services Program (later known as the Legal Services Corporation) to finance the opening of poverty law offices across the country, including throughout the South, and to employ thousands of "poverty lawyers" to provide free legal counsel to the nation's poorest citizens. The man who drafted Kennedy's Law Day address, Edgar Cahn, and his wife, Jean Cahn, played prominent roles in the development of this federal initiative. When the institution reached its peak in 1981, there were some 6,200 attorneys and 3,000 paralegals working out of 1,450 local offices across the country. That year, poverty lawyers served 1.5 million people.[5] Low-income Americans had access to the legal system where access had not existed, influenced social policy in ways previously not possible, and incorporated legal norms and processes into their lives that were alien to them prior to contact with a poverty lawyer.

Yet, at the time Kennedy spoke in Chicago in the spring of 1964, those developments lay in the future. For the most part the nation's poor did without legal representation, since legal expertise was distributed like any other commodity—through the market—and lawyers made their living by leasing their knowledge to whomever could pay. Small legal aid societies had developed in a few dozen cities, and lawyers occasionally offered pro bono services to the poor, but these were exceptions that proved the rule: access to the legal system was a luxury.[6] Legal counsel for the poor was especially scarce in the Deep South states of Georgia, Alabama, and Mississippi, where small legal aid societies appeared and disappeared sporadically in cities such as Mobile, Savannah, and Birmingham, but only the Atlanta Legal Aid Society forged a steady presence prior to the onset of federal financing in the 1960s.

The first legal aid society in the United States emerged in New York in 1876, when the city's German Society created the *Deutscher Rechtsschutz-Verein,* or German Legal Protection Society, to provide legal counsel to the wave of German immigrants who arrived in the United States during the late nineteenth century. The *Rechtsschutz-Verein* boasted one part-time attorney who helped protect his clients from "the rapacity of runners, boarding-house keepers, and a miscellaneous coterie of sharpers"—translated into less colorful language, unscrupulous employers, landlords, and shopkeepers—"who found that the trustful and bewildered newcomers offered an easy prey."[7] By the 1890s, when the wave of German immigration had subsided, the president of the society, Arthur von Briesen, sought to expand its client base and sources of funding. He cut ties with the German Society and appealed to the city's business elite, capitalizing on their growing fears about mass social unrest that seemed imminent as a depression blanketed the middle years of the decade and violent confrontations such as the Haymarket Riot in 1886, Homestead Strike in 1892, and Pullman Strike in 1894 seemed like harbingers of a Marxian mass revolt. Von Briesen's argument to the city's elite was that legal aid eased unrest among the less affluent: "It keeps the poor satisfied, because it establishes and protects their rights," and, furthermore, "it is the best argument against the socialist who cries that the poor have no rights which the rich are bound to respect." Von Briesen suggested that "communism and socialism have, it seems, lost their grip upon our New York population since our Society has done its effective work in behalf of the poor," and he implied that further support for the organization would ensure social stability.[8] Although von Briesen's conclusions about the impact of legal aid were almost certainly exaggerated, his appeal was successful. With the support of the city's wealthy philanthropists, the New York Legal Aid Society came into being.

Meanwhile, two legal aid societies appeared in Chicago. The first of these, like the *Deutsche Rechtsschutz-Verein,* was directed toward the problems of a specific group of the underprivileged, in this case young women and children. The Chicago Women's Club had become alarmed about "the great number of seductions and debaucheries of young girls under the guise of proffered employment" and sought to counteract such behavior by creating the Protective Agency for Women and Children in 1886. At the time, many Americans were concerned that the vicissitudes of wage labor and the market economy forced countless women to sacrifice their bodies in order to survive, and the agency's caseload reflected this concern, as nearly a quarter of the cases involved claims for unpaid wages (which, if received, might keep women off the streets). The organization soon broadened its scope from protecting female workers to providing a wider range of services for women and children.[9] Two years after the creation of the Protective Agency, the Ethical Culture Society of Chicago established a Bureau of Justice, which became the first organization in the United States to offer legal counsel to the poor regardless of their sex or ethnicity. By 1890 the Bureau of Justice was already three times larger than the Protective Agency as a result of its broader client base.[10]

Charitable organizations and like-minded attorneys began following the lead of the New York and Chicago societies in other cities around the turn of the twentieth century. By 1910 legal aid societies existed in most of the larger cities of the East, and in the years before World War I they emerged in the Midwest, spread to the Pacific

Coast and Southwest, and sprouted, haltingly, in the South. Legal aid lawyers had provided legal advice to over one million low-income persons by the time the nation went to war in 1917, at which point there were forty-one legal aid societies across the country. None were in the Deep South, though local leaders in Atlanta and later Birmingham and New Orleans had made attempts to establish societies in 1904 and 1913, respectively. Atlanta's flourished briefly only to become the first legal aid society in the country to collapse. In Birmingham a group of lawyers established a Lawyers' League to promote social and civic causes, and they opened a legal aid bureau that soon disappeared along with the league itself. Members of the bar also created the legal aid society that operated briefly in New Orleans.[11]

Most legal aid cases involved domestic disputes or wage claims, but lawyers also worked on contract, debt, and other financial claims; landlord-tenant disputes; protection against loan sharks; conflicts over personal property; and a variety of other problems. Resolving domestic disputes was a particularly sensitive topic because legal aid societies were firmly opposed to making divorce easy and inexpensive (and some believed that the poor could not make this decision for themselves). Instead, lawyers guided clients through separation proceedings in cases of physical abuse and helped secure financial support from absent fathers. The societies were careful not to pursue "legal action which breaks up a home forever," opting instead for "action which preserves the home or leaves the path open for reconciliation."[12] Generally, legal aid attorneys refrained from broad, aggressive attacks on social and economic arrangements, partly because their benefactors were among the more powerful and affluent but mostly because they did not believe such action was necessary. Any injustice that existed was a result not of substantive flaws in American law but, instead, stemmed from low-income persons' lack of *access* to the justice system. As an early proponent of legal aid, Boston attorney Reginald Heber Smith, wrote, "The essence of the work of legal aid organizations is the rendering of legal advice and legal assistance to the individual in the individual case." He believed that "the body of the substantive law, as a whole, is remarkably free from any taint of partiality. It is democratic to the core. Its rights are conferred and its liabilities imposed without respect of persons."[13] To eliminate injustice, advocates of legal aid believed, the wealthy and powerful needed only to amend procedural defects in the legal system, especially by extending legal representation to the poor.

Shortly after the end of World War I, Smith published *Justice and the Poor*, documenting what he saw as the failures of the American justice system with regard to the less affluent. Along with lack of access to legal counsel, barriers such as high court costs and fees and prolonged delays in the judicial process limited poor people's ability to utilize the legal system. Smith feared that "the poor come to think of American justice as containing only laws that punish and never laws that help. They are against the law because they consider the law against them."[14] Such antagonism toward the legal system would lead to the disintegration of the rule of law. One solution to this problem, Smith believed, was to expand legal aid, and Smith hoped that *Justice and the Poor* would encourage the growth of such societies. It is no small irony, then, that Smith's study arrived just as the legal aid movement began to stall. The social strife that convinced many elite lawyers and businesspeople to support legal aid societies in the late nineteenth and early twentieth centuries gave way to the relative cohesion of war, many legal aid attorneys (who were predominantly young men) left to fight in Europe, and one of the legal aid community's most prominent figures, Arthur von Briesen, fell victim to the anti-German hysteria that marked the times.[15]

There was little further creation or expansion of legal aid societies until after World War II, with the notable exception of the Atlanta Legal Aid Society. Then, in 1950, Great Britain created its Legal Aid and Advice Scheme, whereby the government began subsidizing legal counsel for lower- and middle-income families. This development alarmed some local bar associations across the United States enough that they created new legal aid societies for fear that the federal government might follow Britain's lead. Nevertheless, even into the 1960s, legal aid existed only in the nation's largest cities, the societies subsisted almost solely on charitable grants, and legal aid lawyers carried enormous caseloads for little pay. About the time of Robert F. Kennedy's Law Day address, there was roughly one legal aid lawyer for every 120,000 potential clients, compared to one private attorney for every 560 paying clients.[16]

Poverty was not the only circumstance that stood between an individual and the remedies of the American justice system. Women in the South and throughout the United States were not well represented within the legal profession, nor were they well represented by the profession.[17] American law reinforced social expectations about women's status and power. Home life lay outside the scope of legal norms, so, if a woman needed protection from an abusive husband, she turned to family and friends, not the courts or law enforcement authorities. Or she resigned herself to the circumstances. Furthermore, a woman generally derived her material well-being from her husband's ability to reap financial rewards in the marketplace, notwithstanding the limited "mother's pensions" offered by state and local authorities beginning around the turn of the twentieth century and federal aid to dependent children, which began during the Depression. Even women's forays into the public sphere were on unequal footing. They initially had no constitutional right to vote; state laws prohibited women from entering certain professions, including the legal profession; and workplace discrimination was licit and quite common.[18] Southern gender relations were idiosyncratic to a point, but women across the United States faced similar legal realities.

In ways more peculiar to the South, racism posed a unique obstacle for poor southerners as compared to poor people outside the region.[19] Conceptions of whiteness and blackness complimented and deepened poverty for southerners of both races. Behind the facade of antebellum mansions were the weatherworn shacks of the slave quarters, and with the end of slavery came sharecropping and its own vortices of destitution. The entire social, political, and legal structure of the South was premised on African Americans comprising a disproportionate share of the lowest-paid, lowest-status workers, as slaves in the "Old" South and sharecroppers and service workers in the "New." Political leaders made sure that African Americans did not gain equal power in the electoral system or equal access to public institutions, lest political power translate into economic might, and mob rule in the form of lynching and race riots reinforced an entrenched social separation. Furthermore, the legal system was an essential cornerstone of the region's social order, imposing segregation and disfranchisement, sanctifying farmers' cycles of debt, and providing a veneer of respectability for "law enforcement" officials who kept a modicum of racial peace.

Pressing African Americans into second-class citizenship not only limited black freedom but also made it difficult for poor whites to alter their economic status because racial animosity, in effect, divided the South's working people. Drawing on the work of historian C. Vann Woodward, Martin Luther King Jr. once explained: "If it may be said of the slavery era that the white man took the world and gave the Negro Jesus, then it may be said of the Reconstruction era that the southern aristocracy took the world and gave the poor white man Jim Crow. . . . And when his wrinkled stomach cried out for the food that his empty pockets could not provide, he ate Jim Crow, a psychological bird that told him that no matter how bad off he was, at least he was a white man, better than the black man."[20] Coupled with racial inequality, poverty became a defining feature of the region for blacks and whites. Despite the New Deal and President Franklin Roosevelt's Depression-era declaration that the South was the nation's preeminent economic problem, followed by the invigoration of industrial development as the nation mobilized for World War II, poor people remained more plentiful in the South than elsewhere in the United States long after the wartime boom. The region's poverty rate was 35.6 percent in 1959 and 20.4 percent in 1969, compared to 22.1 percent and 13.7 percent nationwide in those years.[21] Within the Deep South poverty rates were still higher: 20.7 percent in Georgia, 25.4 percent in Alabama, and 35.4 percent in Mississippi in 1969.[22] Significantly, poverty was more common among blacks than whites. In the South 69.5 percent of African Americans were poor in 1959 and 44 percent in 1969, compared to 26.6 and 14.6 percent of whites.[23]

There was little reason for most poor southerners, black or white, male or female, to believe that they could use the legal system to their benefit. Law had not been an egalitarian force, and the legal regime was even more uncompromising in reality than on paper, since lawyers generally served those who already laid claim to wealth and power. Yet, even in this environment, those engaged in the African-American struggle for freedom and equality began to utilize the legal system to advance the cause of civil rights. The National Association for the Advancement of Colored People (NAACP) created a Legal Defense Fund to chip away at the legal monolith of segregation, and legal strategies became important supports for civil rights activism, such as with the Montgomery bus boycott. Modifying the law was a central objective of the civil rights movement, from the enforcement of constitutional provisions such as the equal protection clause of the Fourteenth Amendment to the framing of new statutes designed to end segregation in public accommodations and racial disparities in voting rights. Martin Luther King Jr. tapped into the powerful symbolism of the American justice system in his first speech as head of the Montgomery Improvement Association, just days after the arrest of Rosa Parks had spurred local African Americans into boycotting the Montgomery city buses. He forcefully defended the boycott strategy designed to force an end to the requirement that blacks begin filling seats from the back of the bus forward and yield seats to white passengers: "We are not wrong in what we are doing. If we are wrong, the Supreme Court of this nation is wrong. If we are wrong, the Constitution of the United States is wrong. If we are wrong, God Almighty is wrong. If we are wrong, Jesus of Nazareth was merely a utopian dreamer that never came down to Earth. If we are wrong, justice is a lie." In King's mind, as in the minds of many African Americans, the concept of "justice" had both legal and religious dimensions, and the system of justice could be an instrument of uplift.

Through their contacts with poverty lawyers as legal services programs spread throughout the region, poor people in the Deep South began to believe that law could be an ally and even a wellspring of power. In seeking representation from a poverty lawyer, the person of limited means used her poverty as a "source of strength."[24] Legal services clients looked to legal counsel to gain some advantage and "anticipate[d] that turning their 'problems' into cases [would] give their matters some respectability and give them some power."[25] Like any of a wide range of behaviors, the act of seeking out a lawyer, asking about one's legal rights, and pursuing those rights was a political act in that it was an expression of need and discontent and an attempt to alter the contours of power within which one lived.[26] Rather than "entering a battlefield unarmed" without a lawyer, having counsel meant that an individual might become aware of her legal rights and be able to employ the "legal language necessary to gain judicial attention."[27] Relying on a poverty lawyer and depending on that lawyer's expertise and judgment paradoxically emboldened and empowered the client.

Having experienced frustration with the legal system in the past, building a relationship with a poverty lawyer and, through that poverty lawyer, with the justice system was an uneasy process. Clarence Cooper, who was the Atlanta Legal Aid Society's first African-American lawyer and worked out of a new poverty law office in a neighborhood near downtown Atlanta, perceived that, although "we try to give poor people a chance to benefit from the law," "poor people have a built-in hatred of the law. They have a hard time trusting me, because they're afraid someone will take advantage of them again." Low-income people "were accustomed to being sued, and not suing." Nevertheless, his clients quickly realized the potential benefits of legal representation in addressing a wide variety of problems. In time Cooper's office, which was located in a dilapidated shopping strip with peeling paint, littered sidewalks, and abandoned stores, was filled with clients. "They started coming," Cooper remembered, and he and his colleagues soon had more clients than they could handle.[28]

The South's poor had many of the same legal problems as low-income people outside the region. Legal services clients introduced their lawyers to a wide variety of tribulations, a large proportion of which were disputes involving housing arrangements, consumer transactions, domestic relations, or claims for public benefits. Poverty lawyers helped their clients win tangible benefits by resolving landlord-tenant disputes and familial crises, preserving personal property from repossession, and enabling eligible clients to obtain public assistance. But poor people's problems did not always come neatly packaged in these categories, whether from the perspective of the client or her lawyer. Furthermore, the lives of the southern poor bore the imprint of the region's history, and thus poverty law practice reflected problems that were to some extent peculiar to the South: widespread and deeply entrenched practices of racial discrimination; welfare policies designed to have a disparate impact on black women; and state and local authorities who were particularly reluctant to embrace mandates that emanated from Washington.

The relationships that developed between poverty lawyers and their clients were, in some ways, like any other lawyer-client relationship. Attorneys took an oath upon their admittance to the bar to uphold the Constitution of the United States and the laws of the state in which they practiced and had to abide by ethical guidelines that, although different in each state, generally required attorneys to be competent counselors and zealous promoters of the client's interest within the country's adversary system. The expectation was that lawyers would follow their client's lead with respect to major decisions, such as whether to go to trial or settle a case. Lawyers were to be conduits for their client to interface with legal institutions. No less than any other lawyer, those who worked for legal services programs were subject to these ethical restraints.

Also, in nearly all lawyer-client relationships, there was some tension between the client's view of her problems and the lawyer's view of the same circumstances. The client naturally saw her problems in the context of her life story, whereas the lawyer constantly reexamined the client's narrative to determine if there was some legal remedy for whatever ailed her. Cultural differences between the lawyer and client contributed to this disjunction. These differences were more profound in poverty law practice than in many other law practices because the lawyers often came from middle- or upper-middle-class backgrounds, unlike their clients, and, at least in the early years of legal services, many of the attorneys were male and a disproportionate number of clients female. In many situations the client's personal experiences were not always easily translated into legal action.[29] In every case poverty lawyers filtered clients' personal experiences to decide whether or not legal action was appropriate, a decision that could have a major impact on a client's life.[30] To borrow an example from later pages of this study, a young male lawyer from outside the South met with a middle-aged southern woman. The client's story was that she had fallen in love and decided to marry two men at different points in her life. Both relationships ended disastrously, and the men were gone. Legal niceties were all but irrelevant to these travails. From her attorney's perspective, however, the woman was a bigamist because she had never obtained a divorce. The details of her relationships were inconsequential; his primary interest was in the legal niceties. Fortunately, her problem had a relatively simple legal solution, and the attorney helped her to obtain two divorces and clean up her legal life.

Social, political, and legal trends on both the regional and national levels also affected the relationships between poverty lawyers and poor people in the Deep South. First, American support for a publicly funded legal services program reflected the shifting political currents of the late twentieth century and revealed the deep imprint of ideological debates on the lives of low-income persons. Poverty lawyers went from being shock troops in Lyndon Johnson's war on poverty to struggling for their existence under the Nixon administration's lukewarm support, from riding a wave of expansion during the Carter years to enduring crushing attacks in the 1980s. The push and pull of liberalism and conservatism within American and southern politics affected the availability of legal services attorneys and, thus, the possibility for the poor people to have access to legal counsel. In the 1960s and 1970s poverty law offices did not spread uniformly across the South, and various sociopolitical factors stunted their growth in much of Georgia, Alabama, and Mississippi until federal funding fueled an expansion during late 1970s. Then, in the 1980s under Reagan and again in the 1990s, an ascendant conservatism imperiled publicly funded legal services throughout the country. After taking control of Congress in 1994, Republicans first sought to eliminate then to emasculate federally funded legal services by slashing the Legal Services Corporation's budget and placing severe restrictions on poverty law practice. These changes, which took place in the midst of broader cuts in social spending, prompted one legal aid lawyer, Jonathan D. Asher, to lament, "The only thing less popular than a poor person these days is a poor person with a lawyer."[31]

In addition, the legal strategies and doctrines available to poverty lawyers in the state and federal courts set the parameters of their representation of the poor. The emergence of poverty law practice expanded those parameters at times, influencing social policy in the South and in Washington. The welfare rights litigation of the 1960s and early 1970s was particularly aggressive in challenging the status quo and resulted in several significant Supreme Court decisions that broadened the rights of the poor.[32] Poverty lawyers involved in formulating law reform strategies generally worked in national law reform units such as the Center for Social Welfare Policy and Law (CSWPL), but legal services lawyers in the Deep South used these appellate decisions to influence public policy and also devised their own methods of advocacy that sometimes relied on state statutes. Through litigation and, to a lesser extent, administrative and legislative efforts, poverty lawyers pushed for legal changes they thought would benefit their clients, and their work altered the legal status of poor in the Deep South and throughout the country. One strategy was to rely on the Supremacy Clause of the

United States Constitution to impress federal rules on state and local authorities. The clause states that the "Constitution, and the Laws of the United States which shall be made in Pursuance thereof . . . shall be the supreme Law of the Land . . . any Thing in the Constitution or Laws of any State to the Contrary notwithstanding."[33] At the same time, legal doctrines and institutional predilections deeply rooted in the American justice system posed sometimes insurmountable obstacles for poverty law advocacy. The courts were willing to go only so far in applying the due process and equal protection clauses of the Fourteenth Amendment, for example, and they generally would not depart from their judicial role to engage in the prerogatives of legislative bodies.

Ultimately, the social, cultural, and legal distinctiveness of the South waned over the course of the twentieth century. The proclivity for racial distinctions so central to southern history came under attack; modern media, transportation, and communication blurred regional boundaries; and the U.S. market economy and culture of consumption seemed to permeate the entire country.[34] American law followed suit. Indeed, the long-term trend of American law has been "to create one legal culture out of many; to reduce legal pluralism; to broaden the base of the formal, official system of law; to increase the proportion of persons, relative to the whole population, who are consumers or objects of the law."[35] Legal services programs in the Deep South were part of that trend: poverty lawyers helped assimilate the poor into American legal culture, even as they did the same for the South itself.[36] That is, poverty lawyers enabled poor people to claim their legal rights and to use the law as an instrument of personal uplift and, in so doing, shaped their clients' expectations about the function of law in U.S. society. Poverty lawyers also forced southern politicians, policy makers, bureaucrats, and private individuals to recognize that their actions were subject to external legal standards; they could no longer treat low-income people as if there were no law. Even though political obstacles would eventually undermine the strength of the federal legal services program and American law itself limited what low-income persons could achieve through legal channels, poverty lawyers nevertheless helped ensure that their clients were consumers, not just objects, of the law.

The expansion of legal services programs into and throughout the Deep South had a profound social impact on the poor. Viewed through ideological lenses, the legal services program was either a product of good intentions and good sense, as policy makers realized that lawyers could be of great benefit to the less affluent by helping the poor deal with a variety of problems,[37] or it was a "giant enabling program for dysfunctional behavior" that harmed the poor by decreasing their incentives to find work and increasing their reliance on public assistance.[38] Framed in less ideological terms, the social impact of poverty law practice on the poor was related to the institutional development of legal services programs and the situation of poverty lawyers within the country's continually changing policy environment.[39] The professionalization of legal services facilitated the persistence of impact litigation into the late 1970s, largely independent of social movements by the poor and their advocates.[40] These litigation strategies produced some benefits for the poor, including "an elaborate body of case law" favorable to them and a "powerful constituency" advocating federally funded legal assistance.[41]

On the other hand, the ultimate value of poverty lawyers' reform litigation was somewhat limited. The "thrust of the most aggressive, innovative, professionally sophisticated work . . . has been to transfer the social organization of poverty from relations in the private economy to relations between citizens and government," the effect being "not to eliminate poverty but to civilize it." Poverty lawyers "promoted the distinctive treatment of the poor by the state" by helping to turn poverty into "an officially sanctioned, routinely administered legal status."[42] Indeed, "the professionalization of reform may have meant a change in the character of reform." Originally "styled 'antipoverty' warriors, their reform activities appeared to have less success in eliminating poverty than in legalizing the state's definition, organization, and maintenance of the poor as a segregated economic class." The mitigation of poverty lawyers' potential impact on poor people's lives "profoundly altered the social meaning of their role," and the "culture of significance" that motivated many of the attorneys disappeared by the early 1980s. Rather than reshaping society on behalf of the poor, poverty lawyers—particularly in conservative political eras—served as "more of an adjunct than an enemy of the state's administration of poverty."[43]

The blunted effect of poverty law advocacy was not necessarily a foregone conclusion. Some legal services activity altered and expanded the rights of poor Americans and challenged existing public policy. Just as it was a political act for the client to contact a poverty lawyer in the sense that clients sought implicitly to criticize or explicitly to modify some power relationship, so could poverty lawyers engage in strategies with the same type of objective. Some poverty law advocacy "involve[d] legal assaults on practices and statuses that have been accepted by the legal world as far back as most people can remember," in particular regarding clients as consumers and as they related to public bureaucracies. Whereas "traditionally, it is the poor who have the obligations and the bureaucrats, landlords, and collection agencies that have the rights and prerogatives," law reform efforts could "convey a sense of efficacy and entitlement" to the poor and also bring them material benefits.[44]

In economic terms "there can be no doubt that legal aid secure[d] real gains for the oppressed," but poverty lawyers did not alter low-income Americans' place within the U.S. political economy. Rather, legal aid arguably fulfilled certain functions in advanced capitalist societies such as the United States, including facilitating the reproduction of labor power and disciplining capital and the welfare bureaucracy.[45] Given that family law constituted much of poverty law practice, legal aid "serve[d] to reconstruct the family, thus ensuring the reproduction of labor," by enabling women to obtain divorces from absent fathers and then claim financial support from either their ex-husbands or the state.[46] Capitalism has an insatiable appetite for more workers, and, "as long as a sexual division of labor continues to characterize the performance of essential tasks of nurturance, state intervention will be a necessary adjunct of social reproduction."[47] In addition, legal aid disciplined both capital and the welfare bureaucracy by easing the effect of market failure on those earning lower incomes. Poverty lawyers protected tenants against landlords, consumers against creditors, and recipients of public benefits against bureaucratic inconsistency. But, even if poverty lawyers eliminated irrational and abusive behavior within the welfare state and low-income consumer markets, they did not fundamentally change either. Market forces continued to shape public assistance programs, housing, and consumer relationships. In effect, then, legal services programs did little more than provide modest protection for low-income Americans within the context of U.S. capitalism.[48]

With respect to the role of the legal system in advanced capitalist societies, the most important result of legal aid programs in the United States and other such societies may have been that, in utilizing the legal system, poverty lawyers and their clients implicitly sanctioned American law by creating the perception that "equal justice" was a reality.[49] Arguably, "legal aid contribute[d] to an image of legal equality in the only sphere where such a myth is credible, just as money conveys the appearance of freedom and equality in the market, and the vote does so in politics, while all three preserve unaltered the central source of inequality—relations of production."[50] Law was not a set of inalienable rights that existed independent of power relationships; it was not "separate from—and 'above'—politics, economics, culture, and the values or preferences" of any individual.[51] Rather, law was a product of the political economy, the "nature of legal aid (as of all law)" was "inherently political," and legal aid served as an enabler for capitalism.[52]

Ultimately, law and legal aid for the poor is culture bound, and, like culture, it is ever changing. Human beings have perpetually molded their legal order to their changing ways of life, and they have argued, compromised, and fought over these changes, often within the legal system itself.[53] While economic factors have dominated cultural and legal developments in the United States, especially in the increasingly market-oriented world of the late twentieth century, alterations in American law were not, and will not always be, a fait accompli as a result of the nation's capitalist orientation. Instead, law is a product of many contentious interests, material and otherwise. Thus, legal aid is not simply an "object of class struggle";[54] it is also an object of gender struggle, racial struggle, and other crucibles of American culture.

Viewing history as more contested than preordained, an examination of the thousands of relationships that developed between poverty lawyers and poor people in the Deep South across nearly two decades enables one to explore the contingencies of the collective relationship between low-income Americans and the nation's legal culture. Through poverty lawyers the low-income clients of legal services programs asserted their interests within the American legal system and, in so doing, raised the possibility of profound social change. They threatened to bend American social policy to the needs of the poor, liberalizing and potentially reshaping the welfare state. They contested their status within the marketplace, confronting private interests that seemed to cause them harm. Because a disproportionate number of poor people were female, legal services clients promoted women's interests, and because so many of the southern poor were black, they challenged the racial customs that shackled them. These were developments of some consequence in the Deep South, demonstrating that change comes to even the most recalcitrant of places.[55] By the 1980s the South's distinctiveness had faded, and the region looked more and more like the rest of the nation. Poverty persisted, but, with the expansion of subsidized legal services, the southern poor experienced American law much as their counterparts in other regions of the United States.[56]

For low-income Americans developing a relationship with a poverty lawyer meant that law became more palpable. If the "language of the law" has long been a "vulgar tongue," even more people began to speak it.[57] One legal services client, George Moore, reflected on how low-income and minority Americans viewed the legal system when he testified before Congress in 1970. As a spokesman for the National Clients' Council, Moore spoke on behalf of millions of legal services clients. "We clients," Moore avowed, "did not start out believing blindly that the law was our friend, that the courts would do justice, and that lawyers were fighters for equal justice for the poor. In fact, we started by fearing the law as the enemy, fearing lawyers and the courts as part of a system which repossessed our furniture, evicted us, garnished our salaries and sent our children to reform schools." In the six short years since Kennedy's Law Day address, however, legal services programs had "won the trust, a precarious trust but a growing trust," of low-income persons and minorities.[58] Long denied a proactive voice in the legal system by reason of poverty, race, gender, or other attribute, low-income and minority Americans began to accept and utilize the law as an ally in a wide variety of personal struggles.[59] Indeed, if Supreme Court Justice Harry Blackmun was correct that confidence in the legal system is the "very foundation of our system of justice,"[60] then the history of poverty lawyers and poor people in the Deep South may be that the justice system stood on firmer, if still unsettled, ground by the end of the twentieth century.

1

A "NEW BREED OF LAWYER"

L EGAL services programs provided a career opportunity that suited the generation of young lawyers graduating from American law schools during the 1960s.
The mid-1960s were uniquely turbulent years in American culture and politics.[1] This was an era of activism, not only in the streets but also among lawmakers and interpreters of law. The Warren Court had called for the desegregation of
southern schools and introduced the one-person, one-vote rule to realign American
politics, even before its liberal majority solidified in the mid-1960s with the addition
of Kennedy and Johnson appointees.[2] Among other constitutional reinterpretations,
the Warren Court broadened the scope of the Fourteenth Amendment's equal protection clause, which prohibits states from denying anyone the "equal protection of
the laws." The Court had long viewed the equal protection clause to require that any
classifications in state statutes "reasonably relate" to a "legitimate legislative purpose."
Chief Justice Earl Warren and his colleagues thought that certain situations involving
"suspect" classifications or "fundamental" rights required more aggressive judicial intervention to determine if states had a "compelling interest" to impose a classification
and to ensure that the classification was "necessary" to achieve that objective. The
Court devoted much of this "strict scrutiny" to racial distinctions in state laws but also
found that individual interests such as voting, criminal appeals, and the right to interstate travel triggered this exacting standard.[3] Apart from the equal protection clause
jurisprudence, Supreme Court decisions upholding the Civil Rights Act of 1964 and
Voting Rights Act of 1965 affirmed Congress's power to fashion broad-brushed legislative remedies for discrimination. The Warren Court's experimentation with new ways
of approaching long-established constitutional principles inspired Archibald Cox to
write of the Court's decisions, "Once loosed, the idea of Equality is not easily cabined."[4]

In similar fashion policy makers in Washington were proposing and implementing
government action to repair the problems they perceived within American society,
many of which also had to do with the "idea of Equality." Having inherited the legacy

of the slain John F. Kennedy, the Johnson administration began to confront some of these ailments. If a politics of desperation had motivated like-minded public servants during the Great Depression three decades before, "optimistic expectations, not despair, lay at the heart of American liberalism in the sixties." President Johnson, after all, declared war on poverty during a time of plenty, rather than economic stagnation, and "shared the contemporary liberal view that the United States, a rich and resourceful country, could afford to do something."[5] Lyndon Johnson's war on poverty was, in part, a response to the manifest material needs of the Deep South and other pockets of poverty including Appalachia, Indian reservations, northern ghettos, and immigrant communities, documented in studies such as John Kenneth Galbraith's *Affluent Society* (1958) and Michael Harrington's *Other America* (1962).[6] Also, civil rights protests had amplified the African-American cry for freedom, drawing attention to racial segregation, the lack of electoral equality, and the economic effect of the South's system of apartheid: widespread black poverty.[7]

Thousands of law students came to the same conclusions as their nation's leaders during this chaotic decade: the United States had yet to fulfill its democratic promise, but it could still do so. Many of these students began their careers as poverty lawyers in a place where this promise seemed most remote, the Deep South. Their personalities—the sum of their predilections, experiences, and motivations—indelibly shaped legal services institutions and poverty law practice. A reporter documenting the emergence of poverty lawyers in the late 1960s suggested that they were nothing less than a "new breed of lawyer," imbued with "a bitter notion that goes back at least to Elizabethan days—that there are two kinds of law, one for the rich, another for the poor."[8] A sense of mission flowed through the Legal Services Program, attracting the altruist, the activist, and occasionally the radical. Poverty lawyers seized the opportunity to make an impact on people's lives, to hasten the coming (they thought) of a more egalitarian society.

Furthermore, the poverty lawyers of the 1960s were far more talented than their legal aid predecessors. Many graduated from distinguished law schools and high in their class, and the Legal Services Program's Reginald Heber Smith Fellowship enticed some eight hundred especially promising students into poverty law practice between 1967 and 1972. Recipients of this fellowship, nicknamed "Reggies," received a financial bonus and special training.[9] Even more than educational achievements, the most consistent characteristic of poverty lawyers was their youth: they were recent law school graduates at the beginning of their legal careers.[10] And many of these young people benefited from their parents' affluence, which enabled them to pursue advanced degrees and devote their early careers to the public interest.[11]

An attraction to poverty law did not derive solely from altruism. A number of legal services lawyers hoped that by entering a public interest career they could save themselves from the war in Vietnam by obtaining a draft deferment. Whereas thousands of young men in their late teens and early twenties were subject to the draft, one earned a deferment if he was enrolled in school or by pursuing certain favored jobs upon graduation.[12] As Robert Dokson, who graduated from the University of Chicago Law School in 1969 and would dedicate more than a decade of his life to Atlanta Legal Aid, explained, "I, at that time, was not terribly dedicated to . . . low-income people; I went into legal services because I got a deferment . . . and there were a lot of us like that in that period of time." Indeed, he had chosen to attend law school more for cultural than philosophical reasons. Dokson later related that he wanted to be a professional, but, because he was not attracted to the sciences, he chose law. The "Jewish boys who can't stand the sight of blood," he quipped, became lawyers. Dokson was not alone in these motivations.[13]

Legal services was also an entry into the legal profession for scores of African-American and female attorneys, for whom it was difficult to break into established law firms throughout the 1960s and 1970s. North Mississippi Rural Legal Services became an especially significant stepping stone to private practice and other careers for black lawyers.[14] Still other young lawyers came to poverty law practice out of no great moral commitment or social consciousness but simply because "it was just a job."[15] Nonetheless, many of these attorneys embraced the mission of legal services programs once they arrived. Dokson, for example, intended to practice just two years and then enter academia, but he found that he enjoyed his work and appreciated its "psychic currency." Except for one year, he remained with the Atlanta Legal Aid Society from 1969 until 1980, serving in its law reform unit, as deputy director, and then as director during the late 1970s.[16] Furthermore, even these self-interested motivations signaled an antiestablishment personality: young men like Dokson were rejecting the nation's agenda in Vietnam, and African-American and women attorneys were changing the complexion of the legal profession itself, trends that were occurring on a much broader scale in American society.[17]

For many law students, such as Jesse Pennington, the path to poverty law practice seemed a natural progression of their personal experiences. Jesse Pennington returned to his home state of Mississippi in 1969, a young graduate of the law school at Howard University. He had resolved to use his newly minted skills for the benefit of poor Mississippians, most of whom were, like Pennington, African-American. "Everybody should have a lawyer," he would say. "My idea was that I wanted every poor person and every black person [in Mississippi] to have an attorney."[18] Pennington had ample reason to believe that having access to the legal system could improve one's circumstances. By the mid-twentieth century the law had become a prime weapon in the hands of various groups seeking social change. Pennington witnessed the *Brown v. Board of Education* decision calling for desegregated schools, the *Gideon v. Wainwright* decision mandating legal counsel for impoverished defendants, and myriad legislative efforts to reduce poverty and discrimination, each of which increased the federal regulatory presence. Moreover, the young lawyer had ample reason to believe that American legal culture had made only limited inroads into the Deep South. White southerners controlled the courts and the jails of Pennington's youth, and law was as much a means of oppressing African Americans, among others, as it was a source of security and power. During the 1940s and 1950s the Deep South, in particular, was a place of rigid racial hierarchy and debilitating poverty.[19] It was also a place where the phrase "equal protection of the laws" had a hollow ring.

Pennington was well aware of the sometimes brutal alignment of racial discrimination and legal authority in the Deep South. Having grown up black and poor in the Mississippi Delta, called the "American Siberia" for its isolation from the country's cultural mainstream,[20] Pennington had more than a passing familiarity with the dynamics of southern society. Walking home from work one evening, not long after the Supreme Court declared segregated schools unconstitutional, three white men pulled their car alongside the teenage Pennington. They jumped out of the car, began pushing him around, and mocked him, saying, "Nigger looks like a monkey." Recognizing one of the men as the county's leading law enforcement officer, Sheriff Freedman, and believing that all three had been drinking, Pennington peppered his responses with copious "yes, sirs" and "no, sirs." But the fifteen-year-old was not defenseless: years of fieldwork had built up his body, and he had been taking boxing lessons from a local prizefighter. When Sheriff Freedman picked up a pile of cow manure and tried to rub it on Pennington's face, Pennington's patience broke. He swung hard, knocking the sheriff down a roadside embankment, and fled toward home.

Fearing retribution, Pennington hid underneath the house in a shallow hole his father had begun digging in order to install an indoor toilet. The sheriff and his friends soon entered and ransacked the place then left abruptly. Assuming they had not seen the last of Sheriff Freedman, the family hastily arranged for an aunt, visiting from Chicago, to carry Pennington up North for a time, but, before she arrived, several carloads returned to search for the sheriff's assailant. The teenager scrambled to find the most secure hiding place he could find: the outhouse the family continued to use in lieu of indoor plumbing. Submerging himself in years of refuse, Pennington heard the scratching and sniffing of the bloodhounds as they traced his scent to the wooden shack above him, but no one imagined that the bloodhounds had actually found their target. After the last of the sheriff's posse left hours later, Pennington climbed out of the hole, cleaned himself, and traveled back roads to meet his aunt, in whose trunk he rode away from Mississippi, through Tennessee, and into Kentucky, on his way to Chicago.[21]

What young Pennington experienced firsthand as an African American living in the South, others of his generation experienced by different means: television, radio, newspapers and magazines, and increasingly within the nation's public discourse. Between 1955 and 1965 Americans witnessed the lynching of Emmett Till in Mississippi, a bus boycott in Alabama's capital, the snarling police dogs and pounding fire hoses of Birmingham's Bull Connor, and the brutality of Alabama state troopers in Selma, events that offended many Americans (and more than a few southerners). They also witnessed the sit-in movement, the March on Washington, Martin Luther King Jr.'s "I Have a Dream" speech, Freedom Summer, and the passage of two civil rights bills.[22] Thereafter, urban riots, war in Vietnam, the "war" on poverty, the deaths of Martin Luther King Jr. and Robert F. Kennedy, and persistent discrimination steeled the resolve of many young people to remake American society. Jesse Pennington, for one, finished high school and began college in Chicago, served in Vietnam during the "advisory" period of the early 1960s, and returned to finish his undergraduate and law degrees at Howard. He then sought to use his skills for the good of society by joining North Mississippi Rural Legal Services, an organization just three years old whose existence was made possible by funding from the newly created Legal Services Program. For Pennington, being a poverty lawyer not only meant battling poverty by helping the less affluent but also joining the African-American struggle for equality not far from his childhood home.[23]

The first African American to work for the Atlanta Legal Aid Society carried a similar sense of responsibility. Clarence Cooper (introduced in the prologue) grew up in Decatur and Atlanta, Georgia, attended the historically black Clark College during the early 1960s, and then matriculated at Howard University's School of Law in 1964. After one year at Howard, Cooper transferred to Emory, where he and Marvin Arrington integrated the law school.[24] This action complemented his motivation for studying law, which was to use his legal talents to further the cause of civil rights, something he had witnessed other African-American attorneys do while growing up. (Cooper was also attracted to law for reasons similar to many young whites: having watched *Perry Mason* as a child, lawyers seemed respectable, even glamorous.) During his final year at Emory, Cooper worked for the Atlanta Legal Aid Society, and, upon graduation in 1967, Nancy Cheves offered him a position in the society's newest office just south of the Capitol and Atlanta–Fulton County Stadium.[25]

In contrast to Pennington and Cooper, for Stanley Taylor and Bill Brennan the civil rights movement was a moral awakening that propelled them into poverty law. Both were white, grew up in the South, and enjoyed relatively affluent childhoods. Taylor's was a sheltered, small-town upbringing in Crosby, Mississippi, a hamlet near the Louisiana border in the southwestern part of the state. Much of his rearing was the responsibility of an African-American nanny. As he matured, however, Taylor's experiences began to deviate from many of his neighbors, in particular those of his parents' generation. He left Crosby for Millsaps College in Jackson, served a couple of years in the navy in Washington, D.C., while on a hiatus from his undergraduate studies, and spent a semester at the University of California at Berkeley. Back at Millsaps, Taylor became involved in an exchange program with the historically black Tougaloo College, where groups from each institution met to discuss current issues. Furthermore, one of Taylor's senior-year political science classes surreptitiously monitored Jackson's television and radio stations to evaluate the racial content of their news and opinion statements. Their findings were startling for a young man coming of age during the early 1960s, when (and where) civil rights activism and violent racial reaction peaked. One television station was particularly open in their anti-black sentiments; on one occasion, for example, the weatherman gave instructions on how to make Molotov cocktails.[26] Also influential on Taylor's developing consciousness was his senior thesis. The same professor who organized the exchange between Millsaps and Tougaloo talked Taylor into writing about the life and recent death of Medgar Evers, a prominent civil rights leader in Mississippi.

The end result of these personal and intellectual experiences was not a certainty about his racial superiority, like many white southerners, but, rather, what Taylor calls a "liberal . . . guilt complex." Rooted partly, perhaps, in respect for his nanny, the influence of an "extremely open-minded" mother, and an inexplicable revulsion against the racial antics of childhood playmates, Taylor grew more and more concerned about racial conflict and oppression. He went to law school at Tulane. Initially, he had no specific plans to address the problems he was witnessing, but during his legal education he became increasingly aware of what he believed were injustices that stemmed largely from poverty: the lack of a support system for the elderly and disabled, an inadequate child support system that left children and mothers abandoned, and a poor person's inability to fight back against a landlord or collection agency. Despite the fact that Tulane was "not in a progressive mode at that time" and he did not benefit from a "steering hand on the faculty," Taylor learned of the Reginald Heber Smith Fellowship at the American Civil Liberties Union (ACLU) office where he volunteered. He applied and won a position at North Mississippi Rural Legal Services in Oxford, turning down jobs with the ACLU and a New Orleans firm. For Taylor, who began work in 1967, poverty law practice in the late 1960s consisted of "mostly doing the nuts and bolts legal services work": administrative advocacy on behalf of clients seeking disability or welfare benefits, along with divorces and other domestic cases. Later he would become involved in more visible cases and become director of a new legal services program in southern Mississippi during the late 1970s, though he never adopted the impassioned personal or professional style of many of his colleagues.[27]

Bill Brennan, on the other hand, was attracted to the confrontational tactics of the Atlanta Legal Aid Society's Michael Padnos, who took over leadership of the organization in 1967. Brennan's family had moved to Atlanta during the 1950s, when Brennan was in the sixth grade, and he attended Catholic school there before beginning to study for the priesthood at a seminary in Alabama. Two years into that preparation Brennan decided he did not want to live the celibate life of a priest, but nevertheless his religious education had left him with a "strong sense of social justice." Despite the Catholic Church's personal "strictures . . . that ended up being repellent," the New Testament, particularly Jesus' teachings in the Sermon on the Mount, appealed to the young Brennan. He decided, under the influence of his parents, to attend law school even though he was unsure that he wanted to practice law. Most of his fellow students hoped to enter private practice, either on their own or with a firm, but Brennan felt drawn to issues of social justice. He remembered taking a political science course focusing on President Kennedy at Emory College during the fall of 1963, when a couple of months into the course Kennedy was assassinated, and recalled more fondly sitting in the front row of a Bob Dylan concert during his first year of law school. There was tumult all around him, in particular the civil rights movement. Even after he earned his law degree, Brennan was uncertain that he wanted to be a lawyer, and he was a school teacher attending a PTA meeting when he learned of Martin Luther King Jr.'s death in 1968. The event crystallized his feeling that he should be doing something, putting his sense of social justice to use. But was he too late? "People my age had already been doing the Mississippi Summer and the Freedom Rides . . . and I really missed that. I later thought . . . that I'd love to get into the civil rights movement somehow. Then it was sort of petering out. I mean, King died and it kind of collapsed."

At that point the Atlanta Legal Aid Society entered the picture. Brennan had already worked for the society as a third-year law student in fulfillment of public service requirements at Emory Law School. While there, he gained an appreciation for the legal aid lawyers' efforts, particularly in the consumer and property rights area. But it was Michael Padnos who convinced Brennan to apply for a position with the society. Listening to the radio, he heard Padnos speaking before the Hungry Club, a forum for discussion about civil rights issues that met at the Butler Street YMCA. The new director was proclaiming that "the biggest enemy of poor people in Atlanta, as far as I can figure having been here for six months, is the Atlanta Housing Authority." Padnos was castigating the establishment.[28] Once Brennan began working for the society, he came to agree with his director: "You put the poor black people over here in public housing, you fence them in; it was like the plantation revisited. . . . The culture today is still over there, where if you spit on the sidewalk you're out. Strict rules. Keep these people in their place. . . . It's just natural that young, idealist, liberal lawyers that want to get into social reform who go to work for legal services will look at the local housing authority and see all these abuses."[29] Brennan had found his niche in the legal profession. Legal services seemed appropriate to different people for different reasons, but the political and cultural atmosphere was a significant influence on them all.

CREATION OF THE LEGAL SERVICES PROGRAM

With the passage of the Economic Opportunity Act in August 1964 and its creation of the Office of Economic Opportunity (OEO), President Lyndon Johnson officially declared an "unconditional war on poverty." Johnson was not a man of modest hopes. In his State of the Union address on 8 January 1964, less than two months into his term, he declared, "Our aim is not only to relieve the symptoms of poverty, but to cure it and, above all, prevent it."[30] This "war," however, was more like a series of tangentially related battles, most of which ended in disappointment. Although the political will existed for an attack on poverty, there was no support for a fundamental restructuring of the U.S. economy or redistribution of wealth, nor was there a national crisis such as the Great Depression to propel Congress into adopting a substantial public works program or other aggressive policies.[31] The Johnson administration's war on poverty was more of a collection of palliatives for financial malaise than a vaccine or cure.

The Economic Opportunity Act and subsequent legislation created a vast array of programs that counteracted the effects of poverty and sought to expand the opportunities of the less affluent. There was financial support for public education, a Job Corps to provide training for unemployed young men and women, a domestic Peace Corps (Volunteers in Service to America, or VISTA), and Head Start, which funded preschool programs. Most controversial among these initiatives was the Community Action Program, which provided support for local communities to establish community action agencies that would, in theory, mobilize and coordinate local resources in a broad attack on poverty. In 1965 Congress created programs of subsidized health care for the elderly and indigent, known as Medicare and Medicaid, respectively. Later in the decade the National Housing Act increased subsidies for low-income housing.[32]

Among these palliatives for poverty was the Legal Services Program.[33] As its first director, Clint Bamberger, stated in 1965, "I ask myself each day—how will lawyers representing poor people defeat the cycle of poverty?" and thereby contribute to Johnson's mission.[34] One method was to provide counsel as legal aid societies had been doing for decades for the wide variety of consumer and family-related problems that faced the poor. But, although the federal government's Legal Services Program was, in part, an offspring of the legal aid movement and its philosophies, legal aid societies were not the only example of lawyers working in the interest of the poor. In fact, by the 1960s many lawyers and legal scholars had come to believe that legal aid societies were not reaching their potential for helping low-income persons. After all, public interest advocacy had become a means to force certain changes on society. For example, legal strategies had long been central to the African-American struggle for equality. The landmark case of *Plessy v. Ferguson* (1896), in which the Supreme Court declared that laws could separate the races if public accommodations were equal, originated as a test case by opponents of the growing number of segregation statutes in the South, but it clearly did not achieve what the litigants had hoped. In the 1930s lawyers working for the NAACP Legal Defense Fund began attacking various segregation statutes in the courts, and their strategy experienced greater success, culminating in the *Brown v. Board of Education* decision barring public school systems from maintaining segregated institutions.[35] Other lawyers had worked to achieve social change through law reform as well. Around the turn of the twentieth century progressive reformers sought to bring about reforms such as limited working days, and women's rights advocate Margaret Sanger utilized test cases to challenge the Comstock Act, which restricted the use of contraceptives. The American Civil Liberties Union, originally established to aid conscientious objectors of World War I, became involved in efforts to protect constitutionally guaranteed rights through litigation, lobbying, and community education.[36] During the civil rights movement new law reform groups emerged, including the Lawyers' Constitutional Defense Committee and Lawyers' Committee for Civil Rights Under Law.

Along with these law reform efforts, several groups of lawyers and legal scholars established "neighborhood law offices" in the early 1960s. These organizations differed from legal aid societies in their sources of funding (mostly foundation grants and small government allocations) and their philosophical directions. The first neighborhood law office opened in early 1963 in New Haven, Connecticut. Under the leadership of Yale Law graduate Jean Cahn, the two-attorney office had little philosophical direction other than the sense that lawyers should work with social workers to solve the legal problems of the poor. The office closed after just seven weeks, when the community became enraged upon Cahn's defense of a black man accused of raping a white woman. It later reopened in 1964. In New York labor lawyer Ed Sparer convinced Mobilization for Youth, an organization designed to combat juvenile delinquency, to create a legal unit in 1964. Under Sparer's leadership the unit began pursuing social change through test cases in the areas of public housing, housing code enforcement, unemployment insurance, and welfare. Rather than placing an emphasis on ensuring access to social services, which presumed that poverty resulted from the personal inadequacies of the less affluent, Sparer and his legal team attacked laws and policies they believed discriminated against low-income persons. Along with the New Haven and New York experiments, the Neighborhood Legal Services Project in Washington, D.C., adopted an approach similar to the New Haven philosophy, offering a broad range of services in decentralized offices located in impoverished communities.[37]

Policy makers built on the traditions of legal aid societies, the activism of reform-minded groups, and the experimentation of the neighborhood law offices to create the Legal Services Program (LSP). This was no small task considering that the initial antipoverty legislation had not provided federal funding for legal services. Rather than a brainchild of Congress, LSP was a product of vague presidential leadership, persuasive bureaucrats, and a cooperative national bar. Even before President Johnson declared war on poverty, two Yale Law graduates, Jean Cahn and her husband, Edgar, planted the seed for a national network of law offices for the poor. While working at the State Department in the summer of 1963, after the inauspicious beginning of the New Haven project, Jean Cahn began circulating a draft of an article she and her husband were writing that addressed the role lawyers could play in alleviating poverty. In its published version the article argued that the administration's efforts to end poverty would be flawed if the potential beneficiaries of social services had no voice in shaping public policy. Lawyers could amplify that voice, exerting influence over government agencies by doing what lawyers do: aggressively pursuing their clients' interests through litigation, lobbying, and other strategies. Instead of suffering an unresponsive social service bureaucracy, lawyers could empower low-income persons in their relationships with new community action programs as well as established agencies.[38]

As the Cahns' article circulated among policy makers, winning increasingly influential converts to the cause of legal services for the poor, Jean's husband made his voice heard as well as a speechwriter for Attorney General Robert F. Kennedy. During the spring of 1964 Edgar Cahn had drafted the Law Day address in which Kennedy called on lawyers to help eliminate the two systems of law that had developed in the United States, one for the rich, one for the poor. Edgar took advantage of the opportunity to incorporate some of his and his wife's notions about the role of the law in the lives of the poor and to raise lawyers' awareness of the unique difficulties the less affluent faced in the legal system. Along with press coverage and publicity within the legal community, one of the most important effects of the speech was that Edgar Cahn soon gained a position in the antipoverty task force formed to plan the war on poverty and subsequently became a special assistant to Sargent Shriver, Johnson's appointee to head the Office of Economic Opportunity.

Shortly after Congress created OEO in August 1964, Shriver created a task force to assess the viability of a legal services program for the poor. The legal services task force had no trouble deciding that OEO should fund legal services programs, but they were not in agreement on the form the program should assume. Some members of the task force argued that federal money should flow into new organizations composed of poor people, concerned citizens, and liberal lawyers, not legal aid societies or local bar associations. Proponents of this viewpoint were particularly concerned about the effect of bar participation in the South, worried that southern bar leaders would not support a program that undertook civil rights cases and other controversial matters. Rather than binding legal services programs to these conservative forces, the federal government should ensure the independence of poverty lawyers so that they could pursue strategies for social change. Other members of the task force believed such a plan would doom LSP from the start. More pragmatic, those supporting bar involvement argued that the support of local lawyers and judges would ensure equitable treatment in the courtroom and in negotiations as well as independence from community action agencies, a central tenet in the Cahns' idea of "civilian" (i.e., low-income people's) involvement in the war on poverty. Ultimately, the majority of the task force became convinced that the participation of local bar associations was a political necessity.[39]

Meanwhile, two influential organizations, the American Bar Association (ABA) and the National Legal Aid and Defender Association (NLADA), came to different opinions about the prospects of federal funding for legal services. The NLADA, representing established legal aid societies, was wary of a legal services program because it feared that OEO would bypass legal aid societies in favor of newly created neighborhood law centers. The organization's opposition, however, removed it from the debate over the creation of the federal program.[40] Conversely, the ABA quickly recognized the necessity of expanding the availability of legal counsel. In his inaugural address as ABA president in August 1964 (before the legal services task force ever met) Lewis F. Powell Jr. spoke of the need for enhanced legal aid and the wider availability of legal counsel. Echoing Robert Kennedy, Powell suggested: "It has been correctly said that respect for the law is at its lowest with under-privileged persons. There is a natural tendency for such persons to think of the courts as symbols of trouble and of lawyers as representatives of creditors and other sources of 'harassment.'" The Cahns' ideas had legs. ABA's support for legal services for the less affluent was not entirely altruistic. Bar leaders realized the damage the American Medical Association had done to its credibility by opposing the proposals for Medicare and were wary of the loss of public image lawyers might suffer should ABA oppose expanded legal services. Lawyers performed a vital public service in using their expertise to sort out clients' legal entanglements, but should lawyers violate the public trust the public could, in theory, revoke the professional monopoly attorneys enjoyed (and for which many were handsomely paid).[41] ABA's support for the creation of a legal services program was partly about lawyers' self-preservation.

Securing the support of the organized bar, at least on the national level, did not resolve the philosophical differences among the supporters of legal services, even as OEO began accepting applications and funding local programs in 1965.[42] There remained the question of mission: were legal services attorneys to ensure that individual clients received legal protections and entitlements from the expanding welfare state?

Or should lawyers seek to initiate structural reform in low-income neighborhoods, public assistance bureaucracies, and economic relationships? This tension became, in part, a tension between "old" legal aid societies and "new" legal services programs, made more palpable as OEO contemplated whether or not to channel federal monies into established legal aid societies. But the tension also existed within the war on poverty and, more broadly, liberalism itself. Should the federal government promote "social change" and, if so, by what means? What should be the limits of that change? No one answered these questions, either within the legal services clique, OEO, or the Johnson administration. Nevertheless, unlike much of the war on poverty, the Legal Services Program would survive despite this initial lack of clarity about its mission, ultimately becoming one of the few successful Great Society initiatives.

That success did not happen uniformly in time or place. Initially, the federal government channeled legal services funding through the Office of Economic Opportunity to existing legal aid societies and newly created legal services programs. In this manner many legal aid societies were able to expand their services, and elsewhere small neighborhood law offices offered legal advice. Just two years after the federal government began funding programs, there were two thousand poverty lawyers working in eight hundred offices throughout the country, about as many personnel as in the Department of Justice.[43] But most of the early poverty law organizations existed outside the South, where there was far more political support for legal services. In Georgia, Alabama, and Mississippi the Atlanta Legal Aid Society was the largest established institution; it began receiving federal funding in 1966. Legal aid societies elsewhere in the region were reluctant to accept legal services funding and did not do so until later in the decade. Apart from these institutions legal services for the poor were limited to North Mississippi Rural Legal Services, which was affiliated with the University of Mississippi School of Law, and a few small poverty law offices sponsored by community action agencies. Indeed, despite the depth and breadth of poverty in the Deep South, legal services programs were slow to emerge there. Between 1965 and 1970 most legal aid efforts found it difficult to thrive in the southern political environment, and only the Atlanta Legal Aid Society and North Mississippi Rural Legal Services forged a significant presence in the region.

CREATION OF LEGAL SERVICES PROGRAMS IN THE DEEP SOUTH

The Atlanta Legal Aid Society was not a product of 1960s liberalism but, rather, of early-twentieth-century progressive reform. Lawyers in Atlanta, like their counterparts in other cities, established a society in 1904, but this effort, the only one in the South at the time, faltered. Twenty years later another group of Atlanta attorneys created a more durable organization. Most of the organizers worked in the city's major law firms, including E. Smythe Gambrell, a recent graduate of Harvard Law School who went on to a distinguished career that included the presidency of the American Bar Association. Convinced of the value of legal aid as a result of his involvement with the Harvard Legal Aid Bureau and other civic affairs, Gambrell provided much of the impetus for this effort and became the society's first chairman and president. In its infancy the Atlanta Legal Aid Society consisted of a general counsel, one assistant counsel, and the donated time of private attorneys. They directed much of their energy toward battling "loan sharks" who provided high-interest, short-term loans to working people, trapping them in a cycle of debt that could last for years. Little more than two years after the society's founding, attorneys had won over two hundred injunctions against such companies, alleging illegal and usurious practices and bringing about the cancellation of many loan contracts. Dozens of these companies ceased operations, while others reduced their interest rates to legal limits (from upwards of 40 percent to 10 percent per month). ALAS's first general counsel left the society in 1928 to continue pursuing such companies and eventually became involved in a major case charging ninety-seven officials with violating federal antitrust laws in a $100 million-a-year usury racket.[44]

The society gained financial security with the beginning of charitable funding in 1926, but its mission was still unclear. Those involved in shaping its activities, especially the board of directors, faced a dilemma that would confound legal services programs in the 1960s and 1970s: was the law itself just? If so, legal aid lawyers could help the poor simply by providing access to the courts, and no major legal reforms were necessary. "Justice" was a problem of the legal process (especially the high cost of legal counsel), not the law's substance. On the other hand, if American law was inherently stacked against the poor, access to the courts would bring only limited benefits, and legal aid lawyers needed to reform the law. The ALAS board resolved this dilemma in 1928 by choosing a second general counsel more interested in reaching a large number of clients than in pursuing law reform. For the next forty years the society would provide individual clients with legal advice regarding a wide variety of problems but refrain from aggressive reform efforts.[45]

The Atlanta Legal Aid Society was not, however, a static institution. In the late 1940s caseloads began to expand rapidly as a result of population growth and a new willingness to prosecute divorces.[46] Underlying these changes were broader shifts in the southern economy. As the region's agricultural base disappeared, thousands of people who had lived in the countryside sought work in the cities. Just as late-nineteenth- and early-twentieth-century immigrants had filled American cities with new bodies and new problems, so this internal migration reshaped urban areas across the country. ALAS caseloads rose from nearly 3,000 in 1948 to 5,156 in 1952 and 8,272 in 1963.[47] After more than twenty years as a two-attorney office, the society added a third lawyer in 1948, a fourth in 1955, and a fifth in 1958. Increased charitable funding and fund-raising among Atlanta lawyers allowed for this institutional growth. Still, when Congress passed the Economic Opportunity Act in 1964, ALAS consisted of just five attorneys working over eight thousand cases with a budget of $55,924. They were overworked and underpaid, even compared to national averages for other legal aid attorneys, and dealt primarily with domestic disputes and minor consumer problems.[48]

Federal funding, like the tasty fruit in the Garden of Eden, was irresistible, but ingesting it brought serious consequences. The Office of Economic Opportunity provided funding for an attorney to work for ALAS in Atlanta's neighborhood service centers beginning in 1965. A larger stream of federal money began flowing into the society the following year, more than doubling the organization's budget and initiating a seven-year period of institutional growth. These financial resources enabled the society to open neighborhood law offices throughout the city and in three surrounding counties (eight by 1972) and to hire more lawyers (forty-four by 1972). With a budget of almost one million dollars, ALAS attorneys handled over fourteen thousand cases that year.[49] More significant than this institutional expansion, however, was how the nature of the society changed. The first manifestation of federal influence was the altered composition of the society's board of directors, which had to include representatives of the poor under OEO guidelines.[50] Also, OEO sent an official to review the work of ALAS in 1966. That official, an attorney named Michael Padnos, reported that the initial wave of federal funding had not altered the work of the Society but, instead, had simply allowed ALAS to provide more of the same services. Poverty lawyers, the national Legal Services leadership believed, should seek not only to provide the poor with access to the system of justice but also should challenge laws that were detrimental to low-income families. The new ALAS board of directors decided, in an effort to abide by these suggestions, to hire someone they believed could take the institution in that direction: the same Michael Padnos.[51]

Padnos remolded the Atlanta Legal Aid Society in his image. He was abrasively idealistic. He sought to use the law as a means of social change, and he did so unapologetically, criticizing the Atlanta Housing Authority for abusing its residents, challenging the welfare department to abide by rapidly developing case law, including Supreme Court cases that broadened a recipient's entitlement to public assistance, and initiating educational campaigns to help low-income individuals recognize loan sharks and extortionate business practices. Perhaps most significantly, Padnos began hiring young attorneys who shared his commitment to battle poverty. Bill Brennan, Steve Gottlieb, Robert Dokson, David Webster, Tom Bowman, George Ellsworth, Tobiane Schwartz, John Paer, Ruby Roy, Jay Loeb, and many others shaped the society into the 1970s and beyond, even after Padnos made his exit.[52] Fortunately for Padnos, he enjoyed the support of the society's board and the freedom to energize the institution as he saw fit. When one of the legal aid lawyers who had worked for ALAS prior to his arrival, Mary Pollota, accused him of being a communist and spread that rumor among local lawyers and judges, hoping to undermine Padnos's leadership, the board kept its faith in Padnos and gave him complete discretion over Pollota, whom Padnos eventually fired.[53] By the time Padnos left the society in 1970, poverty law practice in Atlanta bore the imprint of his sense of mission, and ALAS had established a firm presence in the city.

The formative years of North Mississippi Rural Legal Services had little in common with Atlanta Legal Aid. There was no progressive-era movement to create a legal aid society in Oxford, Mississippi. Instead, professors at the University of Mississippi School of Law established Lafayette County Legal Services, the precursor to NMRLS, in 1966. Just four years earlier, Ole Miss had hosted an eruption of violence when James Meredith, an African American, sought admission to the university. But under the leadership of Joshua Morse the law school began departing from Ole Miss traditions by opening its doors to African Americans and courting graduates of the nation's preeminent law schools to become professors, injecting new blood into the university. Several such figures helped create a legal services program affiliated with the law school.[54] Initially, Lafayette County Legal Services was a combination clinical and "judicare" program, using law students and paying private attorneys to handle much of the caseload (mostly divorce proceedings).[55]

By late 1967 two newly hired professors became convinced that a legal services program could do more to improve the lives of low-income persons in the region. Michael Trister and George Strickler were both Yale graduates whom Morse recruited to teach at Ole Miss. Strickler was born in Louisiana and grew up in Houston; Trister, on the other hand, was not a native southerner, having grown up in New Jersey.

Both joined a faculty advisory board overseeing the activity of the law school's legal services program, and by their second year at Ole Miss they began working part-time in the legal services office. Trister, who taught labor law, also came into contact with the low-income community around Oxford through the activities of his wife, who worked in a local Head Start program. He attended community meetings with his wife, and people often asked him for legal advice. In theory a legal services program could handle many of these problems, but Trister and Strickler realized that Lafayette County Legal Services was not yet equipped to address the legal issues facing Mississippi's poor. Under the leadership of Aaron Condon the law office sought to maintain peaceful relations with private attorneys, who were concerned that federally funded lawyers would siphon off clients. Neither Condon nor Morse promoted the aggressive strategies that characterized other legal services programs across the country. Hoping to alter the nature of the program, Trister and Strickler began devoting more and more of their time to Lafayette County Legal Services beginning in 1967.[56]

Soon thereafter, the activities of the program changed substantially, a fact that local attorneys and state politicians did not fail to notice. Two cases, in particular, sparked the anger of the organized bar and political figures: one challenged Mississippi's residency requirement to be eligible for Aid to Families with Dependent Children (AFDC, commonly known as "welfare"), and another attempted to desegregate the schools in neighboring Marshall County. Critics were incensed that the federal government was funding such activities, and they sought to kill the program, but the route by which funds reached the program made that difficult. Usually, governors had the authority to veto OEO funding in their respective state, but that veto did not apply to programs affiliated with a college or university. Because Lafayette County Legal Services drew its funding through Ole Miss, neither the governor nor state politicians had any direct control over the funding. That did not leave them without a strategy to attack the program. The state legislature held hearings that made it clear it would refuse to use state funds to pay law professors to sue the state welfare department and attack segregation, and the politicians threatened to withdraw financial support for the university if the program continued to exist. Under pressure Chancellor Porter Fortune decided to cut off funding to the legal services program in the summer of 1968 and forced Josh Morse to resign as dean of the law school.

Trister, Strickler, and other professors associated with the program found themselves in a difficult situation. The chancellor instructed them that the university would not allow its law professors to continue legal services work. While other professors decided to accept the prohibition and retain their full-time positions,[57] Trister and Strickler believed that their oral agreement with Morse, in which they were to teach one course each semester during the 1968–69 school year and work part-time for the legal services program, was binding. Disagreeing, the university fired them. Trister and Strickler then filed suit in federal court, claiming that their dismissal was a violation of their constitutional rights. The university could not, they argued, prohibit them from working with the legal services program when it allowed other professors to maintain employment outside the law school. To do so was a violation of the equal protection clause. The university argued, conversely, that it had the prerogative to decide when certain types of employment would make it impossible for a faculty member to fulfill his responsibilities to the university. Trister and Strickler failed to convince the district court judge but won the case on appeal to the Fifth Circuit.[58] Despite their victory, neither remained much longer with the law school: Trister soon left to work full-time with the legal services program, becoming its director; and, after a brief full-time stint with the program, Strickler left to join the Lawyers' Constitutional Defense Committee in New Orleans.[59]

Not only were these academic positions in jeopardy, but so was the existence of the program itself. Expecting Ole Miss to abide by the wishes of state politicians and cut funding to the program, Trister began to entertain other possibilities. Knowing that the governor would use his veto if possible, Trister associated the program, which had changed its name to North Mississippi Rural Legal Services, with the historically black Mary Holmes Junior College in West Point. (Another controversial OEO program, the Child Development Group of Mississippi, was housed at Mary Holmes in order to bypass the gubernatorial veto.) With its path of funding secure, NMRLS began to expand. The program hired its first staff attorney, Stanley Taylor, in 1967 and then John Maxey in 1968. Within two years the program had opened offices in Oxford, Holly Springs, Batesville, Greenwood, and West Point and added several more attorneys. Indeed, the young lawyers Trister hired were fewer in number but as talented as Atlanta's: Jesse Pennington, John Brittain, Alix Sanders, Kent Spriggs, and David Lipman, among others. By the time Trister left in 1970, the program had some fifteen attorneys spread across northern Mississippi.[60]

Elsewhere in the Deep South, legal services attorneys were scarce. A one-attorney office in Clarksdale, Mississippi, offered services under the watchful eyes of the local bar association, and there was a small office on the Choctaw Indian reservation near

Philadelphia, Mississippi.[61] Two groups of lawyers began creating rival programs in Jackson during the late 1960s, but neither was functional before the end of the decade. In Georgia there was little activity outside Atlanta. A small legal aid society existed in Savannah, and others sprouted up in Columbus and Macon, but, until the Georgia Legal Services Program came into being, legal aid was nonexistent in rural areas. Alabama lagged farther behind. The Jefferson County (Birmingham) Committee for Economic Opportunity funded Jefferson County Legal Services beginning in 1968, and later the Birmingham Legal Aid Society received federal funds, as did the Legal Aid Society of Madison County (Huntsville).[62] But neither the predominantly black southern half of the state nor the rural north had a legal services program. Across the entire region (including Louisiana and South Carolina) there were fewer than one hundred poverty lawyers in 1969, more than half of whom worked in the region's cities.[63]

Various factors resulted in the diverse development (or lack of development) among legal services institutions in the Deep South. As was the case with local bar support of the Atlanta Legal Aid Society and the promotion of North Mississippi Rural Legal Services by the Ole Miss law professors, the Legal Services Program relied on local initiative to establish poverty law offices. That initiative simply did not exist elsewhere in the region. In contrast, outside the South community action agencies, local antipoverty organizations, existing legal aid societies, and bar associations often competed for grants.[64] Community action agencies and antipoverty organizations typically wanted aggressive advocates that would seek institutional reform, especially of state bureaucracies, while legal aid societies were concerned for their survival, and private attorneys were hesitant to embrace publicly funded competitors. LSP leaders usually managed to compromise between the competing factions by approving plans whereby each group appointed some members of a program's board of directors. In the Deep South, however, there were fewer legal aid societies and antipoverty organizers, and community action agencies were often under the control of conservative local leaders. Furthermore, southern bar associations were less supportive of free legal services than their counterparts elsewhere in the United States and often expressed open hostility to federally funded legal services.[65] Thus, most southern communities had no one interested in creating a legal services program, much less multiple groups competing for funding.

Several criticisms of the Legal Services Program were common among bar associations in Alabama, Georgia, and Mississippi as well as outside the region. The government should not enter into competition with private attorneys; legal services programs would fall under the control of Washington, D.C., rather than local leaders; poverty lawyers violated professional ethics; and, perhaps most common, legal services programs were unnecessary because private attorneys accepted pro bono cases. After arguing that legal services would amount to the "annihilation" of many private attorneys, an article in the *Alabama Lawyer* in 1966 suggested that poverty lawyers violated professional codes of conduct by fomenting protests, unnecessarily resorting to litigation, and soliciting clients. Furthermore, the authors argued, the virtue of the legal profession was its independence, enabling lawyers to speak freely on behalf of their clients: "When the independent spokesman for the individual is dead so are the rights and safeguards of the individual against overpowering government." A federally funded Legal Services Program would ultimately lead to "socialism and the destruction of the legal profession."[66] Even the voices of support that were audible in Alabama stressed that each local bar association should determine whether there was a need for a legal services program and that, if local attorneys perceived such a need, "each program should . . . be shaped to fit specific local conditions."[67] Mississippi bar leaders were equally suspicious about the prospect of federally funded legal services for the poor. In the midst of the crisis over North Mississippi Rural Legal Services, the state bar association passed resolutions intended to govern all poverty law organizations in the state. The thrust of these regulations was that the bar would have control over the creation of legal services programs and the activities of lawyers working for those programs. Most notably, the regulations prohibited attorneys from filing legal proceedings without the approval of the state bar's board of commissioners.[68] Similar to the Alabama bar, Mississippi's private attorneys favored local over federal control. These notions prevailed among many Georgia lawyers, but the state bar leadership proved markedly more flexible there than in Alabama or Mississippi, as the development of a statewide legal services program by the early 1970s would demonstrate.[69]

The difference in the development of legal services in the Deep South and other areas of the country was attributable in part to a tactical mistake by Legal Services Program bureaucrats in Washington, coupled with the denouement of the initial burst of federal funding as the Johnson administration ramped up funding for Vietnam in 1967 and 1968. LSP leaders had relied on local initiative elsewhere in the country, but this simply did not work in the Deep South. At bottom the dearth of local initiative stemmed from the South's suspicion of federal control and the visceral reaction against "communism" and "socialism" among many southern policy makers. Failing to recognize the political distinctiveness of the South meant that LSP leaders did not utilize the approach used to create California Rural Legal Assistance and Florida Migrant Legal Services. In Florida, for example, LSP had bypassed local attorneys and funded a multi-county program geared toward the state's migrant population by the summer of 1966. After pressure from the state's congressional delegation to suspend the grant, LSP officials negotiated with the congressional delegation, the president of the Florida bar association, and local bar leaders. Local lawyers wanted the program run through the local bar associations, with private attorneys paid to provide counsel to the poor. Ultimately, the compromise reached did not include this structure, but it did allow the bar some influence over the program's board and left the program independent of local bar associations. Notably, five of the six local bar associations refused to accept the plan, but Florida Migrant Legal Services nevertheless remained intact. Nowhere in the Deep South did LSP leaders expend this amount of energy to create a legal services program. By the time they realized such efforts would be necessary if statewide programs were to emerge immediately, the financial spigot was closing, local support was becoming more vital, and thus the conservative bent of southern bar associations and policy makers was even more of an obstacle than it needed to have been.[70]

Even though these political factors limited the growth of legal services programs in the Deep South during the late 1960s, poverty lawyers quickly became an important presence in the shaping of southern social policy. Some of these attorneys worked for national law reform organizations, such as the Center for Social Welfare Policy and Law (CSWPL), which OEO funded to provide support to neighborhood lawyers. Whereas legal services programs attempted to provide comprehensive representation in a wide variety of civil cases, these law reform units focused on specific substantive issues. CSWPL, for example, sought to expand clients' entitlement to Aid to Families with Dependent Children and other social programs. Other support, or "backup," centers specialized in housing, consumer, juvenile, employment, education, health, and elderly law.[71] On many occasions, especially in the Deep South, CSWPL attorneys became involved in litigation seeking to strike down illegal welfare practices. When they were not in the courts, they provided advice to neighborhood lawyers regarding potential law reform issues and changes in welfare law. By 1970 attorneys from the national support centers and local poverty law offices, especially those in Atlanta and northern Mississippi, were beginning to play vital roles in reshaping social policy in the South and across the country. The institutional footholds established in the early years of the Legal Services Program made this work possible and began to open the legal system to the southern poor.

2
THE LAWYERS' WAR ON POVERTY, 1965–1970

POVERTY lawyers and poor people waged a unique war on poverty within state public assistance programs, consumer relationships, and landlord-tenant arrangements, between whites and blacks and other minorities, and even within families. Poor people faced an "ocean of legal needs" in their daily lives.[1] During the late 1960s legal services attorneys enjoyed a great deal of autonomy in formulating legal strategies to ameliorate these problems because there was little bureaucratic oversight during these early stages of institutional growth. Officials within the Legal Services Program were more intent on creating new local programs than on influencing the activities of poverty lawyers. Furthermore, many federal judges were receptive to innovative interpretations of the United States Constitution, federal statutes and regulations, and existing case law that seemed to benefit the poor. Poverty lawyers working for national support centers such as the Center on Social Welfare Policy and Law (CSWPL) were particularly notable for their judicial experimentation, but attorneys in neighborhood law offices were quick to pursue similar strategies and to develop their own.

Although these efforts fell far short of initiating revolutionary changes in the lives of the poor, they nevertheless reshaped certain elements of law and public policy and altered what it meant to be poor in the United States of America. Poverty lawyers aggressively attacked elements of southern social policy and law that seemed to cause their clients harm, including restrictive welfare policies, rigid housing regulations, suspect business practices, and civil rights violations. Although Atlanta Legal Aid and North Mississippi attorneys would quickly join these legal battles, national legal reformers were a step ahead.

WELFARE RIGHTS

The Center on Social Welfare Policy and Law, which was among the earliest legal services grantees, was at the center of the "welfare rights" litigation of the 1960s, and its director, Ed Sparer, became the country's "welfare law guru." A distinguished graduate of Brooklyn Law School, Sparer had been a member of the Communist Party (he became disillusioned when Nikita Khrushchev revealed the extent of Stalin's murderous efforts to maintain authority in the Soviet Union) then, after law school, joined the International Ladies Garment Workers' Union as an associate attorney. In 1963 he left the union to become director of one of the first neighborhood law centers, the Legal Unit of Mobilization for Youth, a comprehensive antipoverty organization in New York City. There Sparer began to attack what he believed were the institutional enemies of the poor, usually state bureaucrats who enforced draconian and arguably illegal housing and welfare policies. He believed that law could and should be an "instrument of social change" on behalf of the poor, similar to the way in which the NAACP Legal Defense Fund and American Civil Liberties Union (ACLU) utilized impact cases to alter political and social arrangements. Sparer wrote that "ultimately, it is hoped that the poor will come to look upon the law as a tool which they can use on their own behalf to vindicate their rights and their interests—in the same way that law is used by other segments of the population."[2] In late 1965 he brought that same sensibility to the Center on Social Welfare Policy and Law, which was based in New York City but created to serve as a support center for legal services lawyers nationwide.

Under Sparer's leadership CSWPL attorneys attacked restrictive welfare policies across the United States and especially in the Deep South, which had more than its share of such policies. Southern states denied welfare benefits to women suspected of "cohabiting" with a man, maintained residency requirements, and could cut payments on a whim, all policies adopted in the wake of World War II, when African-American women began to make up a larger percentage of Aid for Families with Dependent Children (AFDC) recipients. That race played a role in the South's adoption of increasingly restrictive policies is clear: AFDC and other forms of public assistance such as "mother's pensions" had originated as aid for single white homemakers beginning around the turn of the twentieth century, but, because southern policy makers believed that black women were workers and not homemakers, they did not believe it was necessary or even proper to offer these women the same benefits as their white counterparts.[3]

Another factor that attracted Sparer and his CSWPL compatriots to the Deep South was the fact that the region's federal courts were, by 1966, beginning to give effect to changes in federal law that promised to end segregated schools and other public facilities and address voting rights abuses. Sparer believed that some federal judges in the South might be more receptive to "impact" litigation than judges elsewhere because of their exposure to civil rights cases designed to shake the foundations of south-ern apartheid.[4] The theory was that the combination of historical patterns of poverty, racial discrimination, and federal courts with exposure to civil rights claims based on the equal protection and due process clauses of the Fourteenth Amendment made the South's restrictive policies' welfare practices attractive targets. CSWPL attorneys ad-opted what they called an "erosion theory" of litigation: attacking "the worst example of a practice or rule, the gross or excessive form . . . in the most highly suspect social setting," held the greatest potential for law reform.[5] In some ways CSWPL's strategy was counterintuitive. The NAACP's Legal Defense Fund, after all, began its desegre-gation campaign in the border states, where racial discrimination was arguably less entrenched and where Marshall and his colleagues thought there might be less op-position to civil rights litigation.[6]

Sparer and his colleagues believed that, like the Legal Defense Fund's efforts, a well-designed strategy of litigation could alter the legal status of all welfare recipients. They hoped to convince the courts to recognize public assistance as a constitutionally guaranteed right, a "right to live."[7] The phrase was novel to the 1960s and bears no relation to the *right to life* subsequently popularized by anti-abortion activists. Prior to CSWPL's campaign, a Yale law professor named Charles Reich had begun exploring the concept and the ramifications of treating public benefits as a form of personal property. In a *Yale Law Journal* article published in 1964, Reich noted that recipients of government benefits, from families to corporations, held these benefits "conditionally, subject to confiscation in the interest of the paramount state." Governments, then, could use these benefits to coerce recipients. Reich believed that the United States needed a new social compact in which these benefits were considered something more than a gratuity. Welfare and other public benefits should have the legal status of private property, which was protected from government encroachment under the Constitution.[8] So, just as NAACP lawyers had convinced the Supreme Court to declare racial segregation unconstitutional, these poverty lawyers set out to revolutionize the American welfare state and win for the poor a right to live. Unlike the Legal Defense Fund, they began their work in the Deep South.

CSWPL initiated a program to educate recipients and social workers about welfare rights issues, publishing "Welfare Rights Handbooks" for Georgia and Mississippi and conducting a training session in Louisiana for attorneys, community leaders, social workers, and others interested in welfare rights. The attorneys also cultivated relation-ships with civil rights attorneys and antipoverty groups in the region and arranged to review and serve as cocounsel on welfare cases referred to the Legal Defense Fund.[9] These contacts led to CSWPL's involvement in several welfare cases in the Deep South that demonstrated the potential and the limits of litigation, including *Anderson v. Schaefer,* which challenged Georgia's "employable mother" or "suitable work" regulation. That case began in 1966, when several African-American women contacted their NAACP chapter in a small town outside Albany, Georgia, because they felt their local welfare department had discriminated against them on the basis of their race. Caseworkers cut black women—and only black women—off the welfare rolls whenever there was work available in the fields, factories, or as domestic laborers. Local NAACP officials contacted the region's preeminent civil rights lawyer, C. B. King of Albany, who was a veteran of the Albany movement of the early 1960s. King, in turn, contacted CSWPL.

Georgia welfare regulations required that caseworkers cut off payments whenever there was "suitable work" available for AFDC recipients. One of the women who contacted the NAACP, Mary Lee Pressley, received welfare for most of the year, but each harvest season caseworkers cut off her payments because there was fieldwork available. Another, Mary Bell Anderson, was ineligible for AFDC because she worked full-time as a maid at the Sara Ann Motor Lodge in Albany. Even though she earned far less than she could receive in AFDC payments, welfare officials would neither supplement her salary nor allow her to quit working and receive public assistance because to them the fact that she had a job meant there was obviously suitable work for her to do. King, the Legal Defense Fund, and CSWPL filed a complaint on behalf of these women and others in similar circumstances, fashioning a two-pronged argument against Georgia's employable mother regulation.[10] First, they argued that the regulation was unconstitutional because it was so loosely constructed as to allow local caseworkers to discriminate on the basis of race. The plaintiffs presented evidence that made it clear that welfare departments defined *suitable work* differently according to one's race, forcing only black women into fieldwork, domestic labor, and certain factory positions. Second, the regulation created two classes of women—those with full-time employment and those with part-time employment—that bore little relationship to their actual need for financial assistance. Someone in Mary Bell Anderson's position, for example, was ineligible for welfare by virtue of her full-time job but could have received benefits if she worked only part-time but earned the same amount of money. The arguments stressed that Georgia's welfare system denied the women's right to equal protection of the laws under the Fourteenth Amendment.

During court hearings before the three-judge panel created to adjudicate *Anderson*,[11] Circuit Judge Griffin Bell expressed dismay over a system that allowed welfare departments the flexibility to administer programs in a discriminatory manner without allowing recipients to challenge the departments' decisions (such as the determination of whether work was either "suitable" or "available"). Judge Bell began one exchange with Ed Sparer of CSWPL by posing a question: "You say that half the states have a regulation where it is left up to the local welfare director who gets the money. Now, isn't that a terrible thing that a citizen is at the mercy of some agent about whether or not they are going to get any money? They have got unfettered discretion to cut it off or give it to them." Sparer replied, "I do indeed think it is terrible." They continued:

Bell: Do you think it is legal?

Sparer: No, I don't.

Bell: I don't either. I will tell you now, I hope we don't get one like that in Georgia. We don't have one like that now, do we?

Sparer: Your Honor, that is our case.

Judge Bell's concern was not so different from Charles Reich's. He acknowledged the coercive nature of the relationship between social workers and welfare recipients, given that recipients were at the "mercy" of the state authorities, and foresaw that "eventually we will have . . . legal aid in Cairo [Georgia], every place, and when a worker, an applicant is cut off, they will go to the legal aid and say, 'They have cut me off.' . . . The government is getting so complicated now, I guess we are going to have to go to that. There are so many rights now that it is impossible for anybody, the average person to understand all of them. You are liable to lose a right if you are not careful."[12]

Despite Judge Bell's worry, the panel's decision demonstrated the difficulty of translating human experience into a legal remedy. Georgia's employable mother regulation was unconstitutional but not because of its racial implications or even the way it reduced recipients' freedom. The judges were hesitant to delve into the adverse impact on African-American women because the regulation itself did not, on its face, allude to race. They refused to become a "super welfare board" overseeing the individual decisions of hundreds of welfare caseworkers across the state.[13] Indeed, the procedural posture of the case worked to turn the judges away from this approach. Federal law required the formation of a three-judge panel in cases seeking to enjoin the enforcement, operation, or execution of state or federal laws by virtue of their unconstitutionality, but these panels generally did not delve into situations in which state officials were administering a statute in an unconstitutional manner, as opposed to implementing a statute that was unconstitutional on its face.[14] Even if the panel had assessed the constitutionality of the statute as administered by the local social workers, its charge was to determine whether an injunction was warranted that would prohibit officials from implementing the regulation, not to devise a statutory regime that was constitutionally sound (as could federal district courts in school desegregation and other similar cases).

Therefore, the *Anderson* judges limited their holding to the constitutionality of the written provision. With this narrower focus, the three-judge panel concluded that mothers did not have the right to refuse employment in favor of public assistance as long as there were "adequate safeguards" for the mother and her children, such as childcare. Thus, Mary Lee Pressley could not be helped: she would continue to have to go to the fields at harvest time as long as Georgia maintained this policy. In contrast, the judges agreed with CSWPL's argument that Georgia's employable mother provision violated recipients' right to equal protection in that denying benefits to anyone working full-time discriminated between those with full-time and those with part-time employment, since individuals in both groups could be in desperate need of financial assistance. The judges laid that aspect of the regulation to rest, thus helping Mary Bell Anderson win benefits to supplement her wages.[15]

Welfare rights attorneys also found qualified success challenging an Alabama law that removed thousands of women from the welfare rolls each year. Sylvester Smith, a widowed mother of four who lived outside Selma, lost her welfare benefits when the welfare department began suspecting her of cohabiting with a man. That left her and her family with an income of less than twenty dollars per week, which Smith earned working as a cook and waitress on the night shift from 3:30 A.M. until noon each day. Alabama's "substitute father," or "man-in-the-house," rule stipulated that a single mother receiving AFDC could not "regularly and frequently cohabit" with a man or else that man would be deemed responsible for her children's support and render the mother ineligible for welfare benefits. To enforce the provision, caseworkers in Alabama and other states conducted "midnight raids," visiting these single mothers' homes unannounced in anticipation of discovering an illicit relationship. If a woman lost benefits in this manner, she had to get two references from figures in the community that she had not maintained such a tryst. In Smith's case social workers alleged she was having an affair with a "Mr. Williams," a married man and father of nine children and thus in no position to support Smith's family alongside his own. He was not the father of any of Smith's children and had no legal obligation to support them.

CSWPL attorneys learned of Sylvester Smith's situation through their connection to civil rights lawyer Donald Jelinek, who had worked for the Lawyers' Constitutional Defense Committee during the Freedom Summer of 1964 and remained in the South to provide representation to African Americans. Jelinek could not represent Smith due to criminal charges the state of Alabama had filed against him as a result of his work, but he called Sparer to inform him of Smith's circumstances. Among several substitute father regulations CSWPL was contemplating attacking during the fall of 1966, including one in Georgia, Sparer and his colleagues decided that Smith gave them the best chance for victory.[16]

Modeling their complaint on the *Anderson v. Schaefer* case, CSWPL attorneys argued that Alabama wrongfully denied benefits to all "needy Negro mothers and dependent Negro children" in the state. The discriminatory effect on African Americans rendered the substitute father regulation a violation of the constitutional rights of AFDC recipients as a violation of the equal protection clause. Again, however, the federal district court refused to accept this race-based argument, instead declaring the rule unconstitutional because it denied aid to needy children on an irrational basis—whether their mother cohabited—as opposed to assessing their actual need. But the case of *Smith v. King* did not end at the district court. Unlike Georgia in *Anderson v. Schaefer*, the state of Alabama appealed the decision to the Supreme Court, arguing that the rule fell within the prerogative of the state to administer its welfare program and warning that the state's limited resources would require it to reduce AFDC benefits should the rule be lifted.

Martin Garbus, who remained lead counsel even though he no longer worked at CSWPL, responded to Alabama's appeal by reiterating the plaintiffs' race discrimination claims, and he went on to suggest that the substitute father regulation violated Smith's right to privacy by allowing caseworkers to pry into her personal affairs. Garbus also stressed that "the needy have a *right* to receive welfare aid." CSWPL attorneys felt, however, that Garbus's brief failed to question whether the Alabama regulation violated federal statutes, so they fashioned an amicus brief that focused on these issues. Under the Social Security Act needy children were entitled to benefits if a parent was dead, absent, or incapacitated. Alabama's substitute father regulation considered Smith's friend a parent insofar as her AFDC payments were concerned, even though he had not fathered any of her children and had no legal obligation to support them. This determination, said CSWPL attorneys, was inconsistent with federal law because the Social Security Act defined a parent as someone legally responsible for the child, not someone who simply visited the home on occasion.[17]

Ultimately, the Supreme Court passed over Garbus's arguments and the right to live, agreeing with CSWPL attorneys that Alabama's substitute father regulation was inconsistent with federal statutes. Generally, if the Court can decide a case on statutory, rather than constitutional grounds, it will decline to reach the constitutional question. Yet even Justice Douglas, whose concurring opinion would have decided the case on constitutional grounds, rested his conclusion on the equal protection clause and not a right to live, believing that the statute effectively discriminated against the children of mothers deemed "immoral" by law (illegally "penalizing children for the sins of their mother"). In any case, in Alabama alone the decision meant that some twenty thousand children became eligible for AFDC, and, because all the states of the former Confederacy except Florida, but only about a half-dozen other states, had some form of substitute father regulation, *King v. Smith* had a disproportionate impact on southern women and children. Nationwide, as many as 500,000 children became eligible for welfare benefits in the wake of *King v. Smith*.[18]

After *King v. Smith* CSWPL attorneys turned their attention away from the South. Their attempt to link welfare rights to claims of racial discrimination had not convinced judges to move any closer to perceiving a right to live that would protect one's entitlement to public assistance. Also, southern states began altering policies that were under attack to avert lengthy court proceedings. Mississippi, for example, had refused to offer AFDC recipients a hearing prior to cutting their benefits. When poverty lawyers (with CSWPL assistance) filed a case challenging the lack of a prior hearing, officials simply created such an administrative process. This settlement was a victory for welfare recipients in Mississippi, but it created no lasting precedent and provided little monitoring of Mississippi's fair hearing process, which the state subsequently limited to those whose benefits were formally terminated, as opposed to suspended or reduced. The question of welfare recipients' due process rights would soon come before the nation's highest court, but it would not come out of the Deep South.[19]

Despite the strategic retreat of CSWPL lawyers from the South, welfare rights litigation did not cease to be a factor shaping social policy in the region.[20] First, local poverty lawyers offered counsel to clients that enabled the clients to take advantage of changes in welfare policy. Unlike CSWPL, local programs did not concentrate solely on law reform but provided legal counsel on a wide variety of problems. Most clients experienced problems that did not require litigation, so most poverty lawyers provided routine advice and representation. Clients were often unaware of programs of public assistance or felt their caseworker had treated them unfairly or made a mistake in calculating benefits, so poverty lawyers would help resolve such problems by giving advice or calling caseworkers to correct any errors.[21] Prior to having access to a lawyer, a person eligible for public assistance may have gone without or found other sources of advice. Eva Davis, who worked as a housing and welfare rights activist in Atlanta during the 1960s and 1970s (and beyond), recalled that it was difficult for women, especially black women, to obtain welfare prior to the late 1960s. Before ALAS became a prominent institution, Davis got help from a black policeman who happened to know the system.[22] One client at a time, poverty lawyers helped thousands of eligible individuals claim the benefits to which they were entitled.

Second, local legal services programs engaged in law reform litigation as well. Atlanta Legal Aid Society attorneys duplicated the major welfare rights cases that came before the Supreme Court, ensuring that officials implemented these decisions so they became law in Georgia. Along with litigation that brought about the end of Georgia's substitute father rule,[23] ALAS lawyers sued state officials to make sure they abided by *Shapiro v. Thompson*, a 1969 Supreme Court ruling ending residency requirements for AFDC applicants.[24] Likewise, attorneys with North Mississippi Rural Legal Services pressured the state of Mississippi to do away with its residency requirement.[25] These duplicate cases were not coincidental. CSWPL went to great lengths to publicize its activities and the potential role of lawyers in reshaping welfare policies by training poverty lawyers and writing articles for the *Clearinghouse Review*, a national publication that carried news of legal services cases across the country.[26] Moreover, attorneys in local programs contacted CSWPL for guidance in individual cases. Despite the fact that a poverty law hierarchy emerged at the creation of the Legal Services Program, with law reform attorneys such as those with CSWPL enjoying the more respected positions,[27] there was a sharing of knowledge that facilitated the growth of welfare rights litigation across the country.

Most litigation was less about extending constitutional rights than about bringing state regulations in line with federal proscriptions. State bureaucracies were notorious for failing to comply with federal laws and regulations. Filing a case was a way of opening a dialogue between poverty lawyers, their clients, and welfare authorities. In this endeavor poverty lawyers were not always at odds with state officials, some of whom sought to rationalize and even liberalize welfare policy. The director of Georgia's Department of Family and Children Services (DFCS) during the late 1960s and early 1970s, Bill Burson, observed that "more and more people are . . . opening their eyes to the fact that most poor people are not poor because they will not work, but because of human circumstances over which they have no control—that they are poor because they never had a chance; because they are sick, disabled or old; because they never had an opportunity for education or learning employable skills; because they are retarded; or because they are children in poor families who, without help, will face a future that is as hopeless as the present of their parents."[28] Reflecting in its title that the late 1960s and early 1970s was a "Time of Change and Reform," one Georgia DFCS report called for "rational welfare reform" that included narrowing distinctions between the states, meeting a minimum level of need, keeping families intact, offering work and training opportunities, and emphasizing family planning and child development.[29] ALAS attorney Jay Loeb recalled nurturing contacts with caseworkers within the state and county bureaucracies who occasionally called him to complain about a policy that made it impossible for them to grant benefits to a given client. Loeb also reported that he had a contact within the federal social service bureaucracy based in Atlanta who would pass along possible violations of federal statutes by the state of Georgia.[30] Being on opposite sides in a lawsuit did not necessarily mean disagreeing about the optimal result of a lawsuit. Indeed, a legal services lawsuit could provide political cover for welfare bureaucrats who actually hoped the legal services lawyers would succeed.

Just as litigation could alter bureaucratic practices, so could political pressure applied as a result of contacts between poverty lawyers and local organizations. One of the most productive community contacts was between the Atlanta Legal Aid Society and Atlanta's Welfare Rights Organization (AWRO). Established in 1967 and based in an Episcopalian mission near downtown Atlanta called Emmaus House, AWRO varied in size from a few welfare recipients to upwards of one hundred members and another fifty "friends members."[31] Activists in the AWRO, primarily a protest organization, demonstrated against reductions in public benefits, particularly in the state's AFDC program, and other changes they believed were adverse to the interests of recipients of public assistance. Affiliated with AWRO was the Atlanta Poverty Rights Office (PRO), also based at Emmaus House, which provided emergency social services and advice regarding public benefits. Atlanta Legal Aid lawyers, most often David Webster in the early 1970s, met with AWRO activists to discuss developments in welfare policy and listen to problems the members faced in dealing with the welfare bureaucracy. One product of this informal relationship was that the *Poor People's Newspaper*, published by the PRO, carried news of available social programs to thousands of readers and included columns devoted to ALAS activity.[32]

Occasionally, cases grew directly out of these contacts, such as welfare rights leader Carrie Morris's challenge to a state regulation that denied Social Security survivors' benefits to her children because they were the illegitimate progeny of the deceased. Morris was born in 1930 on a farm in Watkinsville, Georgia, the daughter of sharecroppers and a child of segregated schools. She moved to Atlanta in the 1950s and found work as a housekeeper in hotels and private residences and eventually had two children. During the 1960s she became involved in several protest groups that dealt with poor people's issues in an effort to promote their interests but also, perhaps more important, to build up their self-perceptions. Morris saw welfare as "crippling" the recipient because of the way government caseworkers denigrated the poor. Welfare rights activism was largely an effort to overcome this treatment and assert one's worth as an individual regardless of her economic status. Suing the state fit right into this approach. Filed in 1971, Morris's case eventually reached the Supreme Court. Although the Court vacated the lower court decisions because the district court had not properly assumed jurisdiction in January 1973, the parties settled the case less than three months later, when state officials stopped enforcing the relevant portion of the Social Security Act in light of another Supreme Court decision that declared the provision unconstitutional.[33]

Welfare rights was a complex countercultural movement that, at least in part, depended on legal services litigation and informal contacts with poverty lawyers who kept activists informed of impending changes in social policies. In response to such changes, activities engaged in protests that included sit-ins, marches, and one bold display before the Georgia General Assembly. Angered by cuts in welfare benefits, about sixty activists stood up before the assembled politicians and held signs above their heads that read, simply, "SHAME!"[34] AWRO's philosophical underpinning came to reflect this contact with legal aid lawyers. The activists came to believe public assistance was a legal right and demanded that the government recognize poor people's rights to receive welfare, to a "decent job" and "decent house, food and clothes for our family," to a "good education for our children," and "to make important decisions for ourselves."[35] Their perspective reflected the ideas behind the "right to live." This rights consciousness blended with the rhetoric and tactics of the African-American freedom struggle and "Black Power" movements to energize welfare rights activism during the early 1970s. AWRO president Ethel Mae Mathews borrowed freely from Jesse Jackson and other civil rights figures. After traveling to a major welfare rights protest in Washington, D.C., in 1972, Mathews recalled Jackson's declaration of "I Am Somebody!" when she reported back to her constituency through the *Poor People's Newspaper:* "We are welfare mothers, but we are SOMEBODY!"[36] Mathews made "freedom" a common theme of her writing, both personal and public, and also placed her religious faith at the heart of her protest activity.[37] She and other welfare rights activists also utilized the language of the Left and Black Power. Prominent in the *Poor People's Newspaper* were stock phrases such as "Power to all poor people!" Furthermore, a matriarchal sensibility shaped the thinking of welfare rights activists, such as Ethel Mathews's attitude toward women accused of fraud when they illegally supplemented low wages with welfare checks: "I consider them concerned mothers trying to get more bread for their children."[38] This type of attitude was a direct refutation of the underlying assumption of the politics of welfare in the South that black women belonged in the workplace rather than the home.

In contrast to the public stage of welfare rights activism, poverty lawyers used the legal process to advance their clients' interests. ALAS leaders viewed the organization as "primarily a litigation firm," and the extent of public benefits litigation during the early 1970s affirmed that impression.[39] Legal Aid lawyers resorted to litigation when a client could not receive benefits as a result of a bureaucratic error, such as the failure to provide an appropriate or timely administrative hearing;[40] a protracted application process;[41] or the inappropriate denial,[42] calculation,[43] or elimination[44] of benefits. Other cases won AFDC benefits for children aged sixteen and seventeen who were no longer enrolled in public school and kept a Social Security disability recipient from having to repay over seven thousand dollars in unwarranted payments because the statute of limitations had run out.[45] Meanwhile, ALAS lawyers lost efforts to extend AFDC benefits to unborn children and to modify Georgia's method of computing work expenses for the purpose of deciding AFDC eligibility.[46]

The parameters of litigation as a method of altering the rights of the poor became evident as early as 1970. In the spring of that year the Supreme Court gave welfare rights lawyers their greatest victory and, just two weeks later, signaled that welfare rights had reached its legal limits. The first issue before the Court was that in most states, including throughout the Deep South, welfare caseworkers could terminate a recipient's benefits with little or no warning. Many poverty lawyers believed that such terminations violated the recipient's right to due process under the Fifth and Fourteenth amendments. Drawing on Reich's ideas about the "new property," the idea was that the statutory right to receive a welfare payment carried with it a constitutional right under the due process clauses of the Constitution, which prohibit the federal government and the states from depriving anyone of "life, liberty or property, without due process of law."[47] What that language means has been the subject of contentious disputes within the judicial system and has been continually redefined, as it would be again in the Supreme Court's *Goldberg* decision.

As mentioned earlier, CSWPL had attacked Mississippi's failure to provide prior hearings in 1967, but, when the state's welfare department agreed to create a hearing procedure, CSWPL had a victory but no legal precedent binding across the country. The center found such an opportunity not far from home, when John Kelly, who received financial support under the state of New York's "home relief" program, walked into a New York City legal services office and asked for advice after losing his public aid. Poverty lawyers combined his case with those of several other recipients of home relief and AFDC, and their claims eventually reached the Supreme Court in 1969. The Court's decision in *Goldberg v. Kelly*, issued in March 1970, had implications that reached far beyond the legal status of AFDC and home relief recipients.

According to the Court, welfare departments could not terminate benefits without providing adequate due process to welfare recipients. Due process, the Court determined, included the right to a hearing before an independent adjudicator, to present oral evidence, and to cross-examine witnesses. Underlying the reasoning of the five assenting justices was Charles Reich's novel conception of property, an "opportunity theory" prominent in social science and governmental circles during the 1960s, and an appreciation of the financial realities of public beneficiaries. The majority opinion stressed that "welfare, by meeting the basic demands of subsistence, can help bring within the reach of the poor the same opportunities that are available to others to participate meaningfully in the life of the community." Because of the "brutal need" of welfare recipients, to cut benefits without a prior hearing was "unconscionable," stripping recipients of their means of survival and their ability to join American society fully.[48] Welfare had become something more than state charity. No longer did welfare recipients receive benefits simply at the whim of state officials.[49]

The *Goldberg* decision would ripple through poverty law litigation for decades, but it left a major question unanswered. Caseworkers could not terminate benefits without due process, but those benefits were often insufficient to lift recipients out of poverty. Was there a legal basis for requiring states to provide a minimum level of sustenance to the poor? The Supreme Court decided that question forcefully in April 1970. The case, *Dandridge v. Williams*, involved a challenge based on the equal protection clause of the Fourteenth Amendment to Maryland's policy of capping welfare grants at $250 per month for Maryland families ($240 per month for those outside the Baltimore metropolitan area). The litigants were legal services clients from Maryland whose counsel worked for a local poverty law program. CSWPL attorneys tried to prevent the case from moving forward to the nation's highest court by convincing the lead lawyers that the Court was not primed to recognize a right to live or otherwise force states to maintain adequate benefits and that an adverse ruling would create a precedent that would stifle subsequent welfare rights arguments.[50] Given that the Court had recently ignored Martin Garbus's invocation of a "right to live" in *King v. Smith* in favor of CSWPL's statutory argument, CSWPL had reason for concern. Indeed, the majority held that states had broad authority to pay whatever benefits they thought were appropriate. Maryland's maximum grant regulation, which limited the amount a family could receive in AFDC benefits regardless of the size of the family and the family's actual need, was a constitutional display of state power over public assistance programs. Specifically, the state could justify the policy based on its legitimate interests of "encouraging gainful employment," "maintaining an equitable balance between welfare families and those supported by a wage-earner," incentivizing family planning, and allocating public funds to provide for the maximum benefit for the largest number of families.[51]

The following year poverty lawyers in Atlanta who worked for Emory Community Legal Services, a small law reform office that merged with ALAS in the early 1970s, represented several clients in a case with implications similar to *Dandridge*. One plaintiff, Louella Heller, was a single mother of three who, under Georgia law, would lose part of her AFDC benefits when one of her children turned eighteen years of age. Two other plaintiffs, husband and wife Zobe and Carrie Mae Cheley, could not receive welfare payments despite their poverty because their nuclear family was intact. Under Georgia and federal law AFDC benefits were available only if a parent had died, left the family, or become incapacitated. Granting that the Georgia policy that denied benefits to the Cheleys was permitted by federal law, legal services attorney Fred LeClercq argued that Georgia violated the constitutional rights of potential welfare recipients by denying benefits to families with both parents present and at least one employed but which still had incomes below the eligibility levels for single-parent households. The three-judge panel wrote: "By way of commentary on the welfare system, it is an inexplicable anomaly that those who work are denied benefits even when their income is less than the sums nonworking recipients receive under AFDC. . . . The inequity in the system is emphasized here by the fact that the maximum Georgia allowance under the AFDC program is $164 per month while the income of plaintiffs Cheley and Thomas, residents of rural Georgia [and both sharecroppers], is much less." The panel also rejected LeClercq's statutory and constitutional arguments against the policy that promised to reduce Heller's assistance. Relying on the Supreme Court's decision in *Dandridge*, the judges felt that these regulations fell under the state's broad authority to establish benefit levels.[52]

The *Dandridge* and *Cheley* decisions demonstrated the limits of the equal protection clause for advancing the rights of the poor. Although the Supreme Court's 1969 decision in *Shapiro v. Thompson* hinted that a person's welfare benefits or other "necessities" might be a fundamental interest protected by the equal protection clause of the Fourteenth Amendment, *Dandridge* quickly rebutted that possibility.[53] Indeed, the *Dandridge* decision made it clear that the Court's only inquiry would be whether there is a reasonable basis for some classification in state law. The justices would not "impose upon the States their views of what constitutes wise economic or social policy." Harking back to *Goldberg*, the "Constitution may impose certain procedural safeguards upon systems of welfare administration . . . [b]ut the Constitution does not empower this Court to second-guess state officials charged with the difficult responsibility of allocating limited public welfare funds among the myriad of potential recipients."[54] In general the Burger Court would resist additional expansion of the equal protection clause, which the Warren Court viewed expansively, and the *Dandridge* decision was among the earliest that charted this institutional redirection.

Another obstacle to broader welfare rights success was the scope of the due process clause, as an ALAS case revealed in the wake of *Goldberg*. Jay Loeb, the society's preeminent specialist in public benefits law, represented Carolyn Williams, who began receiving Social Security disability benefits in 1963 due to a combination of hypertension and a skin ailment. After she began receiving survivor's benefits following her husband's death in 1971, officials informed her that she was no longer eligible for disability benefits and would have to repay almost a thousand dollars in overpayments. Loeb filed suit in federal court in 1972 when HEW refused to reinstate the benefits and continued to demand repayment without providing Williams with a hearing prior to terminating her assistance. His argument was a regurgitation of the *Goldberg* doctrine, which the district judge embraced: due process demanded that Williams be able to challenge HEW's demands in an administrative hearing.[55] HEW appealed the decision, as it had a similar case from Virginia, but the respective appellate courts affirmed both. For nearly four years *Williams v. Weinberger* and *Eldridge v. Weinberger* made the familiar trek to the Supreme Court, with *Eldridge* always months ahead of the ALAS case. Unfortunately for Williams, the *Eldridge* litigants did not persuade the Supreme Court justices to apply the *Goldberg* holding to disability payments. Instead, the justices believed that recipients of disability benefits did not suffer the brutal need of welfare recipients and that the involvement of medical personnel in the determination of eligibility lessened the chance that a termination would be without reason (and thus without due process of law). Loeb's argument was ruined, and Williams lost the case.[56]

Viewing *Goldberg* and *Mathews* as brackets around a period of change and uncertainty regarding the due process clause indicates that changing personnel on the Court deeply imprinted the rights of low-income Americans. Between 1970 and 1976 four new justices joined the Court. All four were Nixon or Ford appointees and carried different perspectives about the role of the judicial system and different interpretations of the Constitution than their predecessors. In general they were less likely to find constitutional rights where there was no clear textual basis for those rights in the Constitution. They began to qualify the Warren Court's equal protection and due process decisions to narrow the scope of Fourteenth Amendment protections.[57] The contrasting results in *Goldberg* and *Mathews*, just six years apart in time, reflect this growing distance in the Court's interpretive stance. That personnel shifts on the Court affected the *Mathews* holding is apparent from the lineup of justices in the *Mathews* majority and dissent. Of the five justices in the *Goldberg* majority only one, Byron White, joined the majority in *Mathews*. The other four justices were either retired (Douglas and Harlan) or dissented in *Mathews* (Brennan and Marshall). Indeed, even the *Goldberg* decision held the slimmest of margins, with a bare majority of the Court holding that due process required a pre-termination hearing for welfare recipients. Poverty lawyers had no control over these institutional developments, yet their practice and the options they were able to offer their clients reflected the changing faces on the Court.

Poverty lawyers continued to be involved in shaping programs of public assistance, in the Deep South and elsewhere, but after 1970 it became apparent that there would be no revolution in the American welfare state. Courts would treat public benefits as entitlements subject to legal protection, but welfare never became the right many poverty lawyers and others had hoped for. Despite the Supreme Court's appreciation of the brutal need of welfare recipients, state legislatures and welfare departments retained the authority to establish benefit levels. Legal services attorneys began to refocus their attention on law reform measures that were still within reach after 1970. Through litigation and administrative advocacy, poverty lawyers across the Deep South would ensure that states extended the protections granted to AFDC recipients to the beneficiaries of many other government programs. Poverty lawyers also worked to keep state policy consistent with ever-changing federal statutes and regulations. Whenever officials violated federal law to the detriment of the poor, legal services attorneys were quick to seek redress through the courts. Such legal activity did not carry the implications of a right to live or a redefinition of public benefits as a form of private property, but these cases would often bring significant material benefits to legal services clients.

THE ATLANTA LEGAL AID SOCIETY

Although welfare reform was the primary objective of some poverty lawyers, legal services clients sought counsel for a variety of problems that reflected the peculiarities of place so vivid in the Deep South. One's social setting often determined the legal problems one encountered. Low-income city dwellers tended to have more conflicts with landlords, merchants and creditors, and government agencies than low-income individuals who remained in rural settings. As legal services programs developed in the late 1960s, the local social, economic, and political environment shaped the nature of poverty law practice. In Atlanta, as in other urban areas throughout the United States, this meant facing problems that beset the urban poor, in particular disputes over housing.[58]

Bettye Kehrer's first impression of Atlanta's "ghetto" was that on the surface it seemed like a pleasant place to live. Homes and apartments were spread out, and the people were not cramped in high-rise buildings. She soon realized, after becoming the first managing attorney of the society's new office in northwest Atlanta, that there was widespread poverty, little transportation, and few grocery stores or pharmacies. Many people living around her office were dependent on the Atlanta Housing Authority (AHA) for shelter, and Kehrer remembered countless landlord-tenant confrontations that threatened violence. One day, for example, someone ran into Kehrer's office complaining that marshals were trying to evict a pregnant woman who refused to leave her apartment; she was wielding a hammer and threatening bodily harm to the marshals. Kehrer went to speak to the woman, whose anger subsided only when she learned that Kehrer was a legal aid lawyer. Once the woman calmed down, Kehrer convinced marshals to leave the woman in her apartment, and the angry crowd that had gathered dispersed.[59]

The Atlanta Legal Aid Society became deeply involved in housing cases soon after Michael Padnos became director. He believed that the greatest enemy of the poor in Atlanta was the Atlanta Housing Authority, the institution responsible for providing public housing for many of the city's less-affluent citizens.[60] Tenants had long lived in an environment dominated by what some lawyers called AHA's "plantation mentality," referring to the tight reins on tenant behavior and ability to evict tenants at will.[61] ALAS attorneys began to challenge many of the actions of housing authority officials. Such confrontations were not typical of the "old" Legal Aid Society, prior to Padnos's arrival. But, as Padnos attracted more talented, young lawyers to Atlanta, they began to represent their clients more aggressively. The most significant housing case they pursued, *Sanks v. Georgia*, attacked the state's landlord-tenant law, which required tenants to post a bond equal to double their rent in order to challenge an eviction in court. Two reform-oriented attorneys, Bob Newman and John Brent, began attacking the double-rent bond provision in 1968, arguing that it violated the constitutional rights of poor people by making it impossible for a low-income person to challenge an eviction, since few low-income families could afford such a bond and no bonding companies would guarantee it. Filed in 1968, *Sanks* worked its way to the Supreme Court in 1969 and 1970.

Meanwhile, ALAS clients faced other housing issues, some of which hinged on the high court's decision. As in welfare cases, poverty lawyers resolved most housing disputes by giving advice, making a phone call, or assisting clients through an administrative process. Many tenants in Atlanta's public housing paid fees they did not feel were appropriate or faced an eviction for unspecified reasons, problems often solved without resort to litigation. Bill Brennan recalled a client whose toilet had cracked during a cold spell, spilling its water into the bathroom. Although tenants were only required to pay for damages that they caused, the AHA property manager charged the client. When Brennan threatened to sue, the manager waived the fee.[62] Sometimes, especially after Padnos's arrival, attorneys used aggressive nonlegal strategies. In one case Bettye Kehrer represented a woman caring for ten children. They had been evicted from public housing, the father had left, and they had been living in cars for some time. AHA officials told Kehrer that the woman had received too many "demerits" because of her children's behavior and was thus no longer eligible for housing assistance. Padnos decided to alert local television stations and newspapers that the housing authority was denying this family an affordable home, and Kehrer took the family to the AHA director's office and promised to sit there until he relented. He did.[63]

Legal Aid lawyers also represented group clients, most notably public housing tenants who created Tenants United for Fairness (TUFF) in 1968.[64] The tenants urged the Atlanta Housing Authority and city leaders to institute reforms in the city's public housing. TUFF's first public demonstration took place on 8 November, when activists picketed a conference of the National Association of Housing and Redevelopment Officials. Conference participants invited the protesters inside, and Atlanta mayor Ivan Allen promised to hear their grievances, which included criticism of AHA's control over tenants, invasion of tenant privacy, lack of adequate playgrounds, and discouragement of tenant efforts to beautify apartments. The next week TUFF asked ALAS attorneys to serve as the group's legal advisors.[65] Shortly thereafter, Legal Aid attorneys learned that AHA's director, M. B. Satterfield, had written a letter to Economic Opportunity Atlanta (EOA), the community action program through which the society received its federal funds, requesting that financial support for the society be delayed until EOA investigated the activities of ALAS lawyers. Satterfield claimed that the poverty lawyers' activity was a "disruptive influence on the public housing program and serves only to cause friction in the community." EOA nevertheless approved the society's funding for 1969.[66]

Serving as legal counsel to TUFF was the most time-consuming and publicized activity in which ALAS was involved during the first half of 1969.[67] In January TUFF proposed a "Tenants Bill of Rights" to the Atlanta Housing Authority, and members of the AHA board began visiting the city's housing projects. These visits convinced board members that the TUFF grievances were not unfounded. Throughout the winter and spring TUFF leaders, Legal Aid lawyers, and representatives of other community groups negotiated weekly with the authority's board. Meanwhile, ALAS attorneys opened another front against the housing authority, preparing lawsuits related to TUFF's complaints. Occasionally, preparing a lawsuit convinced the housing authority to change its policies, such as when it eliminated its residency requirement and voided a number of contested damage charges.[68]

Public pressure on the authority was significant as well. A mass meeting held on 4 March at the Price High School gymnasium in Atlanta included several hundred people, mostly black tenants of public housing, and revealed that TUFF enjoyed the support of civil rights groups in the city. Early in the meeting several tenants "testified" against AHA. TUFF activists provided a wealth of anecdotal support for their complaints. Perry Homes residents, for example, complained that there was a fence separating the apartments from the community basketball courts but no fence between the apartments and a deep, rock-filled ravine in which six children had drowned. Another horror story became the basis of a lawsuit that ALAS attorney Byron Attridge filed on behalf of Mattie Perryman, a resident of Carver Homes, whose residence, the suit claimed, was "uninhabitable" because of a mysterious, malodorous chemical used to clean the floor. After the testimony against the housing authority, Ralph Abernathy, head of the Southern Christian Leadership Conference following Martin Luther King Jr.'s assassination the previous year, addressed the crowd. He spoke less of specific conditions than about the autonomy of public housing residents. Abernathy preached: "We're sick and tired of the great white father telling poor white folks and poor black folks what to do. We don't need managers from other communities—from Buckhead, Cascade, or Collier Heights." Instead, Abernathy demanded, tenants should run public housing in Atlanta.[69]

This political and legal pressure forced AHA officials to make concessions to public housing tenants. The board announced Satterfield's retirement, and under his replacement, Lester H. Persells, changes seemed to come more quickly.[70] AHA withdrew an eviction notice sent to one ALAS client in Perry Homes whose son had been convicted in a shooting, transferred several people to improve staffing, adopted a new policy allowing tenants to select their own paint colors, rescinded a rent increase imposed on welfare recipients, stopped requiring tenants to buy grass-cutting tools, and agreed to restructure and democratize the tenant associations.[71] The housing authority declared that its "intention" was "to assure each tenant the basic rights of privacy, freedom from harassment and a voice in the making of any decisions that are not contrary to the regulations of the Department of Housing and Urban Development or the Atlanta Housing Authority." AHA also pledged to establish tenant grievance committees "to be open to suggestions, to listen to complaints and at all times to do whatever is possible to better conditions for its tenants," who numbered about thirty-three thousand people.[72] Later in 1969, AHA created a Housing Authority Advisory Board consisting of the presidents of the tenant associations and representatives of six community organizations appointed by the presidents.[73] Public housing in Atlanta still had substantial problems, but tenants were claiming more of a voice in addressing these issues.

While TUFF remained in the press, residents of private rental housing units came to ALAS with similar complaints, and Legal Aid lawyers, in turn, contemplated strategies to address their problems. One strategy they developed, along with tenant groups, was a "rent strike." The legal underpinning of a rent strike was the concept of a "warranty of habitability," a common-law, judge-made doctrine that stipulated that a rental agreement carries with it an implicit obligation for the owner to maintain the premises in a satisfactory manner. This idea was spreading throughout the country in the late 1960s and 1970s, in large part as a result of poverty law advocacy.[74] During the summer of 1968, while working for ALAS after his second year at the University of Pennsylvania Law School, Steve Gottlieb discovered a nineteenth-century Georgia case that allowed someone renting commercial property to pay for necessary repairs and then deduct the expenses from the rent.[75] If the same principle applied to rental housing, tenants might be able to improve their homes even if landlords refused to take the initiative.

Several tenant organizations came to Legal Aid attorneys for advice before and during rent strikes. A prototypical case arose out of a twenty-unit apartment building in Vine City, a predominantly black Atlanta neighborhood, when a tenant wrote ALAS in April 1969 asking how he and his fellow residents could force their landlord to make certain repairs. Legal Aid lawyers inspected the complex and thought that serious repairs were necessary: the rough plaster walls had not been painted in more than five years, each tenant had a unique list of repairs that had not been made, and the landlord had just informed them of a 10 percent increase in rent to take effect on the first of May. The attorneys wrote the landlord demanding the necessary repairs, noting that many tenants had been requesting repairs in vain for months and even years, and they concluded the letter by warning the landlord that the tenants would begin making repairs and withholding rent money to pay for the repairs unless the landlord took action. The landlord's response was rapid. He asked to meet with the Legal Aid lawyers and promised some repairs before the conference. The landlord's lawyer explained that the landlord had employed a management company and was unaware that there were problems at the complex, and he regretted the building's condition. Within a matter of weeks arrangements for the repairs had been made, and the landlord halted the rent increase for six months. [76]

Atlanta's African-American press followed this dispute closely, and soon more complaints began pouring into Legal Aid, so that one of the society's major activities during the second half of 1969 was forcing landlords to repair slum conditions. By the end of the year ALAS had represented at least twenty tenant groups in similar repair cases. The most publicized of the groups was from Bolton Gardens Apartments, where tenants organized a union and decided to withhold their rent in the fall of 1969 after their landlord increased the rent despite worsening conditions at the complex. They complained to Legal Aid attorneys of inadequate maintenance, garbage, rats, roaches, mud, flooding, a lack of play areas for children, and defective facilities such as the "washeteria."[77] Ed Baety, one of the attorneys who worked on the case, responded to the rent increase by informing the landlord that "as legal counsel for the Bolton Gardens Tenant Association I have been authorized to thank you for your offer to raise the monthly rent per apartment from $79.50 to $92.50. . . . In view of the condition of the apartments my clients have directed me to reject your offer."[78] Shortly thereafter, the tenants began their rent strike, and the landlord responded by evicting all those involved in the protest.[79]

Rent strikes have historically been difficult to maintain because they require the activist-tenants to risk losing their homes.[80] Not only was eviction a powerful retaliation for the landlord, but in this case the tenants were relying on the advice of inexperienced lawyers that they had a legal right to protest unsatisfactory conditions by withholding rent.[81] Two Legal Aid attorneys, Bill Brennan and Steve Gottlieb, quickly moved to the forefront of the case. They believed that, given the conditions of the apartments, the tenants could withhold their rent and make necessary repairs on their own. Although the Bolton Gardens case twisted and turned through three courts (two state and one federal) and a variety of procedural developments, the attorneys were never able to present this argument at trial. Exemplifying the difficulty of using litigation as a corollary to protest, the landlord's attorneys maintained that, since the Supreme Court had yet to decide *Sanks,* Georgia law required that the tenants post the double-rent bond in order to challenge the evictions. Because the tenants had not posted that bond, the local judge ignored the tenants' arguments and allowed the evictions to proceed. More than fifty families found themselves on the brink of homelessness.[82] One possibility remained for the Legal Aid attorneys and their clients: federal court. The society's law reform division filed a case mirroring *Sanks,* and the strategy worked, to a point. Hesitant to make a decision about the bond provision of Georgia's landlord-tenant law as *Sanks* was before the Supreme Court, the federal judges tabled the case until the Supreme Court ruled on the constitutionality of the bond provision.[83]

Those familiar with the *Sanks* case, including the opposing attorneys, believed the Legal Aid argument would prevail.[84] As discussed earlier, ALAS attorneys argued that requiring tenants to post a prohibitive bond in order to challenge their eviction was a violation of their due process rights. At trial Judge Osgood Williams of Fulton County Civil Court found that the differential impact on the poor amounted to a denial of the residents' constitutional rights of due process and equal protection under the Fourteenth Amendment, similar to poll taxes. "The real question at issue," wrote Williams, "is whether the defendants are to be granted a hearing before their dispossession. It is the same question asked by St. John, 7:51: 'Doth our law judge any man, before it hear him and know what he doeth?' This Court has no choice but to answer with a pious no."[85]

The Georgia Supreme Court failed to adopt Judge Osgood's reasoning. It is permissible under the Fourteenth Amendment for states to impose distinctions between citizens that are reasonable and related to a legitimate public policy objective. In the court's analysis the Georgia bond provision was reasonable because it guaranteed payment to the landlord for a period in which the tenant had possession and use of the premise. Furthermore, the court viewed the bond provision as a reasonable penalty for the tenant's failure to deliver possession of the premises. The United States Constitution is "no respecter of the financial status of persons" and demands that rich and poor be treated alike, so—in a tortuous twist of logic, given the disparate impact of the provision on the poor—the Georgia bond provision was valid because on its face it applied equally to rich and poor. Handed this defeat, Legal Aid attorneys appealed to the nation's highest court.[86]

The *Sanks* case found the Supreme Court in a period of transition between chief justices, and behind the scenes the case became a point of contention. Chief Justice Earl Warren, who had led the Court during a period of judicial activism that saw segregation undermined, the rights of criminals broadened, voting rights expanded, and a host of other changes, had recently stepped down, and his replacement, Nixon appointee Warren Burger, would lead the Court in a more conservative direction. Nevertheless, after Legal Aid attorneys, led by Michael Padnos, argued the case in December 1969, seven of the eight justices then sitting on the Court believed that Georgia's bond provision was an unconstitutional infringement of the rights of the poor. Paired with *Boddie v. Connecticut,* a case challenging that state's requirement that one pay a fee in order to obtain a divorce,[87] the *Sanks* case held the potential of setting a powerful precedent. Was a law unconstitutional if it had a differential impact on the poor, even if on its face it applied equally to everyone? Alone in his dissent, Justice Hugo Black refused to allow the decision to go forward, believing that the Constitution granted equal access to the courts only in criminal proceedings, not civil cases. As long as the law as written treated everyone equally, it was constitutional. In deference to Black, the other justices refrained from issuing a decision and asked the parties to reargue the case during the next term.[88]

Prior to the November 1970 reargument, there were two crucial developments in the *Sanks* case. First, Atlanta Legal Aid's Robert Dokson drafted and the Georgia General Assembly adopted a new landlord-tenant law that eliminated the disputed bond provision. Fortunately for the society and its clients, the chairman of the ALAS board, Bob Walling, was also a Georgia state senator and head of the Judiciary Committee. Walling introduced the bill and stressed to his colleagues that, should the Supreme Court strike down the Georgia law, there would be no dispossessory process until the subsequent legislative session in 1971.[89] The second development was that the ALAS clients moved. Given these facts, the Supreme Court was left with little to decide.[90] The Court published a decision in which Justice Harlan stated that the Court had accepted the case because it believed the Georgia law might be unconstitutional, but, given that the tenants had moved and the law changed, the case had become moot, and it was no longer prudent for the Court to issue a formal judgment about the law in question. Yet in *Boddie v. Connecticut,* the companion case to *Sanks,* the Court found that the state's court fee denied due process to those who could not afford the court fees necessary to obtain a divorce, suggesting that ALAS had offered a strong argument in *Sanks.* Given the importance of marital status in American society and states' monopolization of the means for legally dissolving the relationship, the due process clause prohibited states from imposing financial requirements that would keep some from obtaining a divorce solely by virtue of their inability to pay.[91]

Although *Sanks* did not set the judicial precedent it might have, the society had effected a major change in Georgia's landlord-tenant law and, it turned out, kept the Bolton Gardens tenants in their homes. Shortly after the General Assembly adopted the new law, the Bolton Gardens landlord and tenants settled the case, and no one was evicted. A victory, to be sure, but there was no decision on the merits of the tenants' initial complaints, and, while the landlord made some improvements, he did so under threat of tenant unrest, not a court order. Many of the tenants simply moved away.[92]

The Atlanta Legal Aid Society remained involved in housing disputes into the 1970s, when many of the same issues emerged anew: conditions in low-income housing, the treatment of tenants in public and private complexes, the ability of tenants to resist eviction proceedings. Of primary concern were evictions, and, though most were resolved outside the courtroom, two cases that ended up before state judges provided greater protections for low-income residents of publicly funded housing. Neither, however, was a clear-cut victory for Legal Aid attorneys. In one case the Buchanan family claimed that its landlord, a nonprofit corporation known as Church Homes, Inc., could not evict them without "good cause." The judge agreed on the law but not on the facts, believing the landlord could show good cause for their eviction. Having failed to convince the judge that the family of five was wrongly evicted, the attorneys nevertheless kept the family in the apartment by doggedly pursuing the litigation, urging Church Homes to dismiss its managerial team, and eventually settling the case.[93] Tenants of Wheat Street Gardens, also owned by Church Homes, likewise found an ambiguous result in a case against their landlord. Because residents of this apartment complex received federal rent subsidies, and because Church Homes had bought the land at a reduced rate with the help of federal financing, the lawyers hoped to convince a superior court judge that, under the due process clause and the *Goldberg* decision, tenants slated for eviction were entitled to an administrative hearing similar to that required for welfare recipients. They were not successful. Relegated to the normal dispossessory process that the Georgia General Assembly established in response to the *Sanks* case, the tenants nonetheless won recognition of their right to remain in the apartment unless the landlord showed good cause to evict them.[94] One year later a third case came before the Georgia Court of Appeals and affirmed that landlords who received federal funding could not arbitrarily evict tenants.[95] Other ALAS housing cases protected a tenant's property, which landlords had previously been able to seize and sell to recoup unpaid rent;[96] won a settlement in a challenge against the Atlanta Housing Authority's condemnation procedures;[97] represented a nonprofit housing corporation in a challenge to Gwinnett County officials' refusal to change zoning ordinances to accommodate a low-income housing complex;[98] and stalled a Department of Housing and Urban Development redevelopment scheme for its failure to produce an environmental impact statement.[99]

These cases did not revolutionize Atlanta's landlord-tenant relationships. Market forces continued to determine the quantity and quality of housing, and Americans were unwilling to initiate major changes in this means of distributing shelter. For low-income families that meant the struggle to obtain affordable housing continued. Nevertheless, legal aid attorneys made it possible for low-income people to challenge landlords' and public agencies' arbitrary and sometimes illegal actions. Such conflicts persisted into the late 1970s and beyond, and the Atlanta Housing Authority, in particular, remained a perennial foe.[100] During their foray into housing law during the late 1960s, poverty lawyers helped their clients win greater access to the courts, some material improvements, and a more substantial voice for residents of public housing. The *Sanks* case, in particular, brought about a significant revision of Georgia's landlord-tenant law that benefited clients and which would not have been possible without the expansion of legal services to Atlanta's poor.

NORTH MISSISSIPPI RURAL LEGAL SERVICES

Low-income people in northern Mississippi and the lawyers working for North Mississippi Rural Legal Services became involved in legal conflicts of a different sort. Whereas welfare and housing cases were early areas of focus for the Atlanta Legal Aid Society, civil rights cases, many involving school desegregation, were prevalent in northern Mississippi in the late 1960s. Before Mike Trister became its director, Lafayette County Legal Services had provided a narrow range of services. Private attorneys and law students helped clients through divorce proceedings, obtained public benefits, and addressed consumer problems. Even after Stanley Taylor and John Maxey joined the program to staff the Holly Springs office, they "started out with fairly traditional legal services, doing divorces" and other individual cases.[101] Such representation continued to dominate poverty law practice for decades to come. Yet, following the lead of poverty lawyers elsewhere in the country, Trister began to guide Lafayette County Legal Services along a more aggressive path.

In this endeavor Trister and his colleagues enjoyed the approval of OEO officials. Mississippi was prominent in the minds of many liberal activists and politicians as the most tenacious stronghold of racial injustice, and the federal government was willing to pour money into the "closed society."[102] Part of the distinctiveness of the civil rights movement in Mississippi was that the state "attracted young activists from all parts of the country simply because of its reputation." Although many major events occurred in Alabama and across the South, "Mississippi remained the standard by which this nation's commitment to social justice would be measured."[103] The same ideas influenced legal services participants as well. One young Ole Miss professor associated with the program recalled, with a degree of sarcasm, "It wasn't hard to shake the Washington money tree and get whatever . . . money you want, because you were a hero out there in the wilderness fighting the forces of evil, and any time Washington could tap in any granting agency, the money just came and came."[104]

Among Lafayette County Legal Services' early law reform cases were several that broadened public benefits for the poor. As mentioned earlier, the Center on Social Welfare Policy and Law had forced Mississippi to adopt a prior hearing procedure for recipients of Aid to Families with Dependent Children, and North Mississippi attorneys began enforcing these rights for individual clients. One of the program's more controversial cases was a successful attack on the state's residency requirement for welfare recipients.[105] Other challenges failed to extend welfare benefits to students older than eighteen[106] or to convince the Mississippi Supreme Court that decisions of the Mississippi Public Welfare Commission were subject to judicial review.[107] North Mississippi attorneys fared better in *Triplett v. Cobb*, when a federal judge forced Mississippi to extend Medicaid benefits to all AFDC recipients in accordance with the Social Security Act. Previously, the state had refused to provide health care for many of the state's poor in violation of federal law.[108] On a smaller scale one of John Maxey's cases forced Marshall County officials to submit their plan to end the county's food stamp program to a countywide vote, a decision that played into the hands of the county's black majority.[109] These cases extended public assistance to thousands of people.

More prominent in the minds of white and black Mississippians was the program's civil rights advocacy. Community groups sought out North Mississippi attorneys for assistance in establishing economic development initiatives, especially agricultural cooperatives. Maxey recalled meetings with groups of mostly African-American farmers to help them pool their produce in order to extract higher prices in the marketplace. Jesse Pennington was particularly interested in such economic development upon joining North Mississippi in 1969. He helped incorporate the Clay County Community Development Program, which ran a day care center, credit union, sewing cooperative (where women made and sold quilts), catfish farms, a cannery, and several supermarkets known as Stuff & Duff. He also used his knowledge of public policy to help clients obtain loans from the Small Business Administration. This type of advocacy was extremely time-consuming; both Maxey and Pennington reported spending many nights meeting with community organizations to seek their legal expertise.[110]

North Mississippi attorneys also represented clients in several significant civil rights cases. One of them, *Anthony v. Marshall County Board of Education*, was the school desegregation case that incensed the Mississippi legislature and cost the legal services program its law school support. Attorneys John Maxey and Stanley Taylor became involved in the case through contacts with a local civil rights organization based in Holly Springs, just north of Oxford.[111] North Mississippi's civil rights caseload grew with the program, as John Brittain, David Lipman, and Kent Spriggs became prominent figures in these struggles. By 1970 North Mississippi lawyers were handling more than two dozen school desegregation disputes, more than any other organization save the Department of Justice and the Legal Defense Fund.[112] Among these cases was an attack on racial segregation in the program's hometown of Oxford, which the attorneys handled with special sensitivity due to widespread displeasure among local whites with both the case and NMRLS. Typically, North Mississippi attorneys officially named only a few plaintiffs in court documents and gained proof of community support by asking local leaders to pass around a petition in support of the action. But in the Oxford case NMRLS carefully guarded against charges that attorneys were using poor clients to advance their own agenda—a claim that followed legal services lawyers throughout the country—by officially naming some one hundred plaintiffs.[113] The result of the case was that District Judge William Keady held Oxford's plan, which would have closed down the historically black high school and run two shifts in the white high school, to be racially motivated and therefore unconstitutional.[114]

Clients won similar school desegregation and other civil rights cases across northern Mississippi, slowly erasing the state's patterns of segregation,[115] but these cases did not proceed without notice from white Mississippians. In the midst of the program's first school desegregation suit in Marshall County, a prominent but intoxicated local lawyer paid a visit to John Maxey and suggested that Maxey and his colleagues were the greatest threat to Holly Springs since Ulysses S. Grant.[116] Hyperbole notwithstanding, there were a variety of ways to debilitate NMRLS. The state's pressure on Ole Miss law school was one tactic. Often, however, resistance to the program stemmed from specific cases, as when Kent Spriggs represented black employees of the Twin County Electric Power Association, a state-chartered public utility, after supervisors coerced them into signing a petition expressing opposition to the local school desegregation suit. Spriggs argued that one employee of the power company lost his job because he was a plaintiff and potential witness in the school desegregation suit.[117] Furthermore, the state bar exerted its authority in opposition to the program, trying to ensure that "outsiders" could not practice law in Mississippi before living in the state for one year. A federal case on behalf of North Mississippi attorney David Lipman overturned this residency requirement in 1971.[118] Around this time bar leaders also financed an investigation of the North Mississippi program.[119]

Furthermore, beginning in the late 1960s, state officials began to monitor the activities of poverty lawyers in Mississippi. White leaders had created the Mississippi Sovereignty Commission to monitor civil rights and other social activists, and the commission's records reveal that it collected information on North Mississippi lawyers through direct surveillance and newspaper reports. Investigators documented Trister's involvement with the program as early as 1967, his suit against Ole Miss and criticism of the law school, and his assessment of the growing white support for "black" causes at Ole Miss, including increased hiring of black faculty and staff and the abandonment of the Confederate battle flag.[120] During the late 1960s and early 1970s Sovereignty Commission investigators followed Alix Sanders when he met with citizens of Belzoni to discuss a local school desegregation suit, John Brittain's battle against charges that he was practicing law in Mississippi without a license, and Thomas Mayfield's representation of civil rights activists jailed for violating Starkville's parade ordinance.[121] In 1971 a Sovereignty Commission report listed the names of the lawyers working for North Mississippi, and another report noted that one attorney, John Brittain, was a board member of the Mississippi chapter of the ACLU.[122]

State authorities did not extend southern hospitality to poverty lawyers, but they could not eliminate the program: North Mississippi's supply line to Washington was secure. By the time Mike Trister left in 1970, the program had established itself as an aggressive advocate for the poor, especially the black poor, of northern Mississippi. It had joined other public interest law firms—the Legal Defense Fund, Lawyers' Constitutional Defense Committee, and the Lawyers' Committee for Civil Rights Under the Law—in expanding the reach of new civil rights statutes and case law, especially regarding school desegregation. One attorney who joined North Mississippi in the mid-1970s (and whose evaluation will seem even more credible by the end of this study) suggested that poverty lawyers "helped ease the transition from segregation to [a] more inclusive society."[123] Legal services attorneys had also made it possible for thousands to obtain public assistance, especially AFDC, and less probable that state officials would cut benefits illegally, and they had begun offering a wide range of legal services in domestic disputes, consumer conflicts, and other problems facing the poor. If poverty lawyers facilitated the shift toward a racially inclusive society, they also contributed to the extension of the welfare state and, more generally, modern legal culture into the Deep South.

The nature of poverty law practice, in Mississippi and elsewhere, depended on the client community. By the late 1960s Mississippi bore the scars of earlier racial conflicts, many of which persisted in the collective memory of the state's African Americans: young Emmett Till's murder in the 1950s, the riot at Ole Miss in 1962 following the admission of James Meredith, Freedom Summer and its concurrent violence. By the time legal services programs began their work in Mississippi, black activism had instigated dramatic changes throughout the Deep South. The Voting Rights Act threatened to reshape Mississippi politics, white resistance to desegregation was waning, and community organizing among the state's black population was likewise declining.[124] Nevertheless, the client community was eager for the legal support that poverty lawyers could provide, in part because Mississippi's African-American community had a long history of grassroots organizing. The lawyers followed their clients into the racial fray, becoming assets for social action.[125]

When Michael Padnos and Mike Trister left their respective programs in 1970, the Atlanta Legal Aid Society and North Mississippi Rural Legal Services were entering a period of great uncertainty for the Legal Services Program and the entire artifice of social programs that the Johnson administration had created. The election of Richard Nixon in 1968 marked a shift to the right in American politics, ushering in a period of Republican dominance that extended in greater or lesser degrees into the twenty-first century. Nixon appointees slowed the pace of school desegregation cases and began to dismantle the bureaucratic apparatus of the war on poverty.[126] Funding for the Legal Services Program, which had stalled as a result of the Vietnam War, now seemed in jeopardy.[127] Yet the liberal tide of the 1960s had not disappeared. Democrats still controlled Congress, preventing the Nixon administration from initiating fundamental changes in the government's social agenda. The Legal Services Program, as well as several other popular programs such as Head Start, survived into the second Nixon administration, which is more than can be said for the Office of Economic Opportunity and most of its creations.

Ultimately, Trister's departure from NMRLS was markedly less tumultuous than that of Michael Padnos from ALAS. After spending four years in Mississippi, the New Jersey–bred Trister and his wife left for Washington, D.C., where he joined the Washington Research Project (later the Children's Defense Fund). They had never intended to make Oxford their permanent home; after all, more than distance separated Mississippi from the Northeast. Moreover, as Trister put it, poverty law practice in Mississippi was "incredibly tense. It's not a normal life." Their social circle was limited to the program itself, and Trister's work, while rewarding, was exhausting.[128] Padnos had other plans as well by 1970, leaving the Atlanta Legal Aid Society to run for local office. After being defeated, he sought to resume his directorship, but the society was not receptive to his return. Padnos had transformed the organization and hired a talented group of lawyers, but most of the staff had come to enjoy his successor's less confrontational leadership style, so Michael Terry took the society into the next decade. Longtime ALAS attorney and director Steve Gottlieb later described Padnos as an "act one" personality. The Legal Aid Society was ready for act two.[129]

3

THE LEAN YEARS, 1970–1975

"**A**CT two" for the Legal Services Program was a period of tepid support from the Nixon administration, which offered only qualified backing and modest budgetary increases throughout Nixon's tenure. The administration's fiscal restraint meant that the growth of established organizations, including the Atlanta Legal Aid Society and North Mississippi Rural Legal Services, stalled, and it became difficult to create new programs. Resourceful local lawyers in Georgia and Jackson, Mississippi, found ways to fund new institutions, but elsewhere in the Deep South legal services programs remained meager if they existed at all. Low-income residents of rural, southern Mississippi and most of Alabama remained without substantial access to legal counsel until the late 1970s, except for small legal aid societies in Birmingham, Huntsville, and Mobile. Nevertheless, even in these lean years the idea of publicly funded legal services for the poor gained support among local leaders and the nation's lawmakers, and poverty lawyers continued to develop new strategies and areas of expertise to address their clients' problems.

Rather than widespread support for the liberalism of the mid-1960s, which fueled the creation and expansion of the Legal Services Program, Americans grew increasingly cautious about governmental activism during the late 1960s and 1970s.[1] A central factor in this shifting political environment was a resurgent philosophical conservatism that championed a wide range of beliefs, including leaving individuals free to pursue their economic interests without government restraint, the efficacy of private property rights, deference to local community values and sources of political power, respect for the role of religion as a defining feature of American life, strict adherence to constitutional limitations on governmental power (especially that of the federal government), and the benefits of meritocracy, among many other sometimes conflicting ideas.[2] These notions had an independent existence in the realm of the mind, free from any taint of political stratagem, but during the 1960s politicians also rediscovered this reservoir of conservative sentiment, winning office by promising to restore these "lost" values to a seemingly errant nation, where many had grown weary of the decade's cultural clashes. Heralding this political agenda was Barry Goldwater's volume *The Conscience of a Conservative,* published in 1960.

Some of these politicians also discovered that another reservoir of political power, one just as deeply rooted in American history, enabled them to forge an equally effective electoral strategy. That reservoir was race, and it added a sharp edge to the conservative resurgence, particularly in the South. White America was becoming satisfied with itself, comfortable that Congress's recent civil rights enactments had solved the problems that plagued the nation and made the South an embarrassment. Many whites were concerned that, as African Americans continued to push for equality, the United States became less livable and less of what had made it a great nation. As they had for generations, opportunistic politicians learned to capitalize on the politics of racial reaction.[3] While overt racist campaigning was becoming obsolete, Alabama governor and presidential candidate George Wallace, among others, articulated a political discourse in which race was embedded, if not explicit. He emphasized states' rights in criticizing civil rights policies such as school desegregation, decried social unrest such as the urban riots of the 1960s, called for "law and order," and hinted that the economic problems of white workers resulted from federal tinkering with the labor market, in particular government efforts to eliminate racial discrimination. Blessed with an astute political sensibility, Richard Nixon learned to speak the language of this conservative "counterrevolution," and during the 1968 campaign he forged an electoral strategy of capturing the South's electoral votes by convincing white southerners that he was an acceptable stand-in for Wallace, whose third-party campaign threatened to throw a plurality of the electoral college to the Democrat, Hubert Humphrey. On school desegregation Nixon expressed his support for freedom-of-choice plans over desegregation mandates. Then, in the weeks before Americans went to the polls, Nixon began warning southerners that their continued support for Wallace would cede the election to Humphrey. To many southerners that was a worse result than turning their back on their native son to embrace Nixon, who won Dixie and, consequently, the White House. By the 1972 election Nixon had refined his "southern strategy" and provided a blueprint for other presidential hopefuls: capture the South with mild racial rhetoric that does not trigger the moral alarms of most Americans but which speaks volumes to a critical contingent of white southerners and more than a few whites elsewhere.[4] In short order, the once solidly Democratic South became, with increasing intensity, a conservative Republican stronghold.

Having found a winning political strategy, Nixon brought his policy predispositions to the White House and lost little time beginning to dismantle his predecessor's "Great Society" agenda. Johnson himself made this task easier by siphoning funds from the war on poverty to pay for the escalating war in Vietnam.[5] Moreover, there were internal cleavages within the liberal coalition that had brought the Democrats to power in the 1960s and bolstered Johnson's domestic agenda. The Office of Economic Opportunity (OEO), which was supposed to coordinate the fledgling social programs, had become an arena of conflict in part because it sought to bypass local and state power structures. Many municipal and state politicians who supported the war on poverty in principle nevertheless believed the federal initiatives, especially the Community Action Program, subverted their leadership by creating a direct link between the national government and the poor.[6] One of Nixon's objectives was to eliminate, or at least reduce, this federal challenge to local and state prerogative.

Nixon's initial approach to the Legal Services Program was to remove it from any connection to the more controversial Great Society programs. Although some politicians had opposed LSP, the conflict over legal services was tame compared to the battles over the Community Action Program. The Legal Services Program was among the most respected products of the war on poverty, not least because it enjoyed the support of the American Bar Association. Thus, even as Nixon eliminated some elements of the Johnson social apparatus, the new president announced plans for the Legal Services Program to be "strengthened and elevated" into a new Office of Legal Services within OEO. Its charge was to "take on central responsibility for programs which help provide advocates for the poor in their dealing with social institutions."[7] Nixon also changed the path of funding for legal services programs. Under LSP legal services grants went through a local community action agency or some other eligible grant recipient, such as an educational institution. ALAS, for example, received its funding through Economic Opportunity Atlanta and NMRLS through the University of Mississippi and Mary Holmes Junior College. This structure could engender political controversy, as in Atlanta Housing Authority director Satterfield's complaints to Economic Opportunity Atlanta or the Mississippi legislature's pressure on Ole Miss chancellor Porter Fortune. In contrast, the Office of Legal Services would make direct grants to local and statewide programs. Federal funding for legal services increased from about $40 million in 1967–68 to over $56 million in 1971, while the number of legal services attorneys rose from about 2,400 in 1968 to 2,660 in 1972. One condition for Nixon's support for federally funded legal services was the appointment of ineffectual and, in two instances, openly hostile directors of the Office of Legal Services.[8] This political context shaped the institutional development of legal services for the poor during the early 1970s and made it difficult, but not impossible, to create new programs or expand existing ones.

Although the early 1970s were lean years with respect to funding and institutional support for legal services programs, several groups of lawyers opened poverty law offices in the Deep South. Low-income residents gained access to free legal counsel in small-town Georgia with the creation of the Georgia Legal Services Program and in Jackson, Mississippi, when attorneys founded Community Legal Services. Alabama programs began to develop as well, although most of the state's poor would have to wait until the end of the decade to have access to free legal counsel.

Local initiative had been vital to the creation of legal services programs since the beginning of the lawyers' war on poverty, and the role of bar leaders and state politicians became even more crucial during the early 1970s. The creation of Georgia's statewide program began in the late 1960s, when four young Atlanta lawyers sought to build a consensus within the state bar association for the creation of a program to cover the 154 mostly rural counties that the Atlanta Legal Aid Society did not serve. Bill Ide, Jim Elliott, Betsy Neely, and Philip Heiner worked in some of the city's most prestigious law firms and were leaders in the Younger Lawyers Section of the Georgia State Bar. They had volunteered their services, on occasion, to the Atlanta Legal Aid Society's Saturday Lawyers Program, through which private attorneys handled a small caseload on a pro bono basis.[9] Sensing that there was a need for free legal counsel outside the Atlanta metropolitan area, they began documenting the legal problems of the rural poor. Their report to the state bar cited national statistics to demonstrate the demand for legal services wherever programs existed and found in Georgia a "distressing disproportion between the actual need for legal services by those who cannot afford them and the present supply of legal services available to them." Legal aid efforts were insufficient, existing only in Atlanta and Savannah. Moreover, even private attorneys were scarce commodities in poor, rural areas: there was an inverse relationship between the number of attorneys and the number of low-income families in a geographic area.[10]

When these Younger Lawyers presented their report to the state bar in 1968, they took aim at the prevalent attitude that private attorneys could provide any legal services the poor should need. "We take care of our own" was the mantra of a good portion of the southern legal profession, but, even if attorneys were so inclined, the dearth of lawyers outside Georgia's cities and towns ensured that few rural residents had access to legal counsel. Some Georgia lawyers explicitly opposed federal funding for legal services as a step toward the "socialization" of the legal profession. These attitudes were predominant in much of the Deep South, particularly among rural and small-town attorneys. Other Georgia lawyers supported the augmentation of pro bono representation, and one group had already created a statewide system of volunteer representation similar to the ALAS's Saturday Lawyers Program, though the Younger Lawyers' report suggested that this was insufficient. Also present within the Georgia bar were "liberally oriented" lawyers who supported the expansion of legal services into rural Georgia, many of whom believed that poverty lawyers should be able to engage in law reform cases. Indeed, by the late 1960s a majority of the Georgia bar's board of governors agreed with the conclusions of the Younger Lawyers' report and supported, in principle, the creation of a statewide legal services program.[11]

Having secured the blessing of the state bar, the major problem facing the Younger Lawyers was financial: how would they fund the program during these lean years? An obvious source of funds was OEO and the Office of Legal Services, but that agency informed the Younger Lawyers that, unless Nixon's policies changed such that funding started to flow more freely, they would have to look elsewhere. That they did, to another federal agency, the Department of Health, Education, and Welfare (HEW). Even before the Supreme Court decided in *Goldberg* that welfare recipients were entitled to a hearing prior to losing benefits, HEW began to set aside funding for states to provide legal advice to beneficiaries of government programs. Ide's group applied for such funding, and the president of the Georgia State Bar, Legal Aid Committee chairman H. Sol Clark (a judge in Savannah who became known as the "father" of legal aid in Georgia), and the director of the state Department of Family and Children Services, Jim Parham, urged Governor Lester Maddox to release matching state funds that would allow the program to open. In some respects this should have been a tough sell. Maddox had become governor on the strength of his vehement opposition to desegregation; he had gained the nickname "Ax Handle" after wielding such a weapon against activists who sought to integrate his Atlanta restaurant. But Maddox was the consummate southern populist: intensely racist but an even more fervent supporter of the "common man." One GLSP founder later remembered: "Lester ate it up. We told him it was for the little people [and we] got our money." Georgia Indigents Legal Services (GILS)—the state bar's board of governors added the word *Indigents* to the title of the organization to underscore that it would serve only the poor—came into being on the strength of just over $200,000.[12]

Bettye Kehrer, the first director of GILS, and the Younger Lawyers quickly realized that the organization would not be able to reach most of Georgia's poor with such meager funding.[13] Kehrer, in particular, had visions of a much larger institution. As Bill Ide recalled, "Bettye was a builder."[14] Even as a young girl growing up in rural Oklahoma, she exhibited an assertive personality. Her father urged her to go to college and on to law school, saying she would be a good lawyer because she could talk so well. As a twenty-year-old, Kehrer was one of five women to begin law school at the University of Kansas City in 1947.[15] Upon graduation she had difficulty finding work in a local law firm but attributed that less to gender discrimination than her alma mater's lack of prestige. Her first job was as a "glorified assistant," and, when she realized that she would not be able to work her way into the courtroom, she began searching for another position. An advertisement in the local paper caught her attention: "Wanted: Lady Lawyer." Most of the other legally trained females in Kansas City interviewed for the job as well, but it was Kehrer who became regional counsel for the International Ladies Garment Workers Union (ILGWU). She soon married and stopped working to care for her children, while her husband worked for the ILGWU. When Kehrer sought to reenter the workforce, ten years had passed, and the family lived near Atlanta, where her husband, Tom, was director of the AFL-CIO's Southern Civil Rights Center. Opportunities for female attorneys were still circumscribed in the early 1960s, but the Atlanta Legal Aid Society employed several women, including general counsel Nancy Cheves. Cheves hired Kehrer and became the first female boss Kehrer ever had. By the time Kehrer started working full-time, war on poverty funding and Michael Padnos (whom Kehrer good-naturedly called a "wild man") had begun altering the society.

Late in the decade Kehrer left the society and began building. First, she received a grant to open a public defender's office in Fulton County Municipal Court that provided legal counsel to anyone arrested for a crime. Despite the Supreme Court's *Gideon v. Wainwright* decision, which stipulated that felony defendants were entitled to free legal counsel if they could not afford an attorney, public defender offices were slow to emerge, particularly in the South. Soon state-funded public defenders took over this task, and Kehrer moved on to create another organization that would make free legal counsel available to the poor. The "time was right," Kehrer believed, for the creation of a statewide legal services program. She had the support of Ide and the

Younger Lawyers and friendly relations with the state welfare director, Jim Parham, who helped convince Governor Maddox to support the grant.

Upon becoming director of GILS, Kehrer began incorporating existing legal aid efforts, including three volunteer networks in Columbus, Gainesville, and Macon, and was pleased to learn that local charities could contribute to the institution, since the United Way was helping to support the Columbus group.[16] The program absorbed the Savannah Legal Aid Society. Along with this expansion, Kehrer continued to seek more public funding, at which point two of OEO's regional leaders entered the equation. Dan Bradley and Hulett "Bucky" Askew, the director and assistant director of Legal Services for the southeast region, respectively, decided to get money to the Georgia program by bending OEO's accounting procedures in a tactic known as "pushing snow," whereby an agency essentially borrows money from anticipated future budgets. They were holdovers from the Johnson administration and strongly supported federally funded legal services, and both would play major roles in the expansion of the late 1970s. After their budget manipulations one major obstacle remained: GILS did not fulfill the federal requirements for client participation on a legal services board, so, in order to receive this funding, GILS leaders had to create a new organization independent of the state bar. Thus came into being the Georgia Legal Services Program. Each institution had a separate board, but their administration and staff were the same and their budgets merged. Ide and his colleagues had to temper bar complaints that they had bypassed it in creating this new institution, but, nevertheless, GILS-GLSP was a half-million dollars richer and began to expand into previously uncovered areas of the state.[17]

Under Kehrer's leadership the Georgia Legal Services Program began establishing branch offices wherever there was sufficient local support.[18] She traveled constantly, cultivating that support and visiting old and new offices to encourage the lawyers to work aggressively on behalf of their clients. By the end of 1971 new offices existed in Albany, Augusta, Brunswick, and Dalton. In each town there was a local bar leader—Tom Dennard in Brunswick, for example, and Bob Bining in Dalton—who, while perhaps in the minority in his locality, embraced the state bar's position that legal services should be extended to the poor. Thirteen attorneys worked in these small towns and, to cover rural areas, had to "circuit-ride" out into the surrounding countryside. They handled 4,535 cases by the end of 1971. The number of attorneys grew to thirty-four in 1972, forty-one in 1973, and sixty in 1974, and there were corresponding increases in the number of cases. Furthermore, GLSP's client base was broader as a result of OEO funding, which allowed attorneys to serve low-income individuals who did not receive welfare, one of the restrictions on HEW funding. This institutional growth was possible because state and federal funding continued to expand. Despite continued opposition from many politicians and lawyers, the General Assembly increased funding for the program so that by 1974–75 GLSP enjoyed a budget of more than $1.5 million. In 1974, once GLSP seemed secure, Kehrer left the program and continued to be a builder, though she never again enjoyed the success she had with GLSP.[19]

Attorneys in Jackson, Mississippi, were also able to create a legal services program during the lean years of the early 1970s. Mississippi's capital was the largest city in the United States without a federally funded legal services program by this time, but legal aid was not entirely new to the city. The Jackson Junior Bar had created the Jackson Legal Aid Society, consisting of one part-time attorney paid by a local charity, in 1952. That one-lawyer office continued to function into the late 1960s.[20] Then, in 1969, several Jackson attorneys founded Hinds County Bar Legal Services (HCBLS), which was closely linked, as its name indicated, to the local bar association. Because local bar leaders appointed the HCBLS board, the organization was not eligible for OEO funds, since OEO regulations required that the board include client representatives. Its financing consisted of local charitable giving and bar support until 1973. Close ties to the local bar association also affected the program's disposition. As one director explained, "We want to represent the individual poor person," not pursue class action challenges, a characteristic of more aggressive advocacy. Nevertheless, the federal government began funding HCBLS in 1973, after which it expanded into neighboring Rankin and Madison counties and changed its name to Mississippi Bar Legal Services (MBLS).[21]

Another group of Jackson attorneys—inspired, in part, by the work of civil rights lawyers based in Jackson and involved, like their Georgia counterparts, in the Younger Lawyers Section of the state bar—hoped to establish a more aggressive institution. Among them was Barry Powell, who had grown up in Vicksburg, Mississippi, attended Yale, and graduated from Vanderbilt's School of Law. Upon his graduation, in 1964, he clerked for a year at the Mississippi Supreme Court, worked in nonlegal positions in the Fiji Islands and Pakistan, then returned to Mississippi to enter private practice in Jackson. While he "had a Christian commitment on issues of race and poverty," he could not recall a specific "turning point" that had led him into involvement with legal aid.[22] Unlike Powell, Francis Stevens was Jackson born and bred, and, given that he worked for his father's prestigious law firm, his effort to establish a legal services program created no small degree of tension within his family and his professional circle. Stevens's mother had been influential in shaping his racial conscience, and he had come to know some of the civil rights lawyers based in Jackson, but it was his representation of Mississippi Action for Progress (MAP), a Head Start grantee, that caused his departure from private practice and in time from his hometown. He refused to honor his firm's request that he stop representing MAP and soon decided to leave the state altogether, giving his career over to public interest work.[23] Also instrumental in the formation of a legal services program in Jackson was another local lawyer with deep roots in the city, Spencer Gilbert.

Before leaving Jackson, Francis Stevens secured a Field Foundation grant that enabled Jackson-Hinds Community Legal Services (CLS) to begin functioning in 1970. The organization hired John Maxey from North Mississippi Rural Legal Services, and for a while Maxey practiced alone. Meanwhile, CLS leaders applied for OEO funding, which arrived in March 1971 and enabled the program to expand to a half-dozen attorneys, including several young African Americans, plus one or two Reginald Heber Smith fellows, or Reggies, each year. Maxey became, in his words, "director by default," as the eldest of the CLS attorneys. He had practiced law for less than three years.[24] Even with federal funding, however, CLS was financially unstable throughout the early 1970s and failed to grow after this initial burst of activity, characteristics that were typical of Deep South programs during the lean years.

Except for the efforts in Jackson and rural Georgia, local initiatives were scarce in the Deep South during these years. Southern Mississippi's low-income citizens had no nearby poverty law offices until the late 1970s. In Alabama only four small programs existed as late as 1974. The Birmingham Legal Aid Society, with nine lawyers, operated out of three offices in Jefferson County and received over half of its funding from the federal government. Another small organization, Jefferson County Legal Services, received funding through the Jefferson County Committee for Economic Opportunity. By 1975 Jefferson County Legal Services had ceased to exist, and the Birmingham Legal Aid Society had split into three units: a criminal indigent defense office, family court practice, and civil legal aid practice. Marvin Campbell, a 1971 graduate of the University of Virginia School of Law who had spent two years with a Birmingham, Alabama, law firm before joining nearby Huntsville's legal aid society for a year, returned to Birmingham to head the civil wing of the newly reconstituted Legal Aid Society.[25] Madison County's Legal Aid Society, located in Huntsville and directed by Norman Bradley, consisted of five lawyers and a staff of ten. Like Birmingham's two organizations, most of its funding came from the federal government. Conversely, the Legal Aid Society of Mobile County survived entirely on private funding from the Junior League and Catholic Social Services. Although Mobile's society predated the war on poverty, it had ceased functioning until the early 1970s, when the revived organization began maintaining a one-lawyer office. Two legal services clinics at the University of Alabama and Cumberland Schools of Law supplemented the work of the poverty law programs.[26]

The lack of legal services programs in Alabama (and elsewhere) was not the result of a lack of need, as some members of the Alabama State Bar had begun to realize. An official bar committee reported that most Alabama lawyers agreed that "there are large numbers of people right here in Alabama today who have legal problems from time to time and are therefore in need of legal services, and who cannot afford to pay even a reasonable attorney's fee for such services."[27] Publicly funded legal services for the poor had not developed, however, because two essential ingredients in the establishment of an influential legal services program were absent in most of Alabama (as in southern Mississippi): a core group of attorney advocates, preferably well connected to the state or local bar association; and substantial federal funding available to those attorneys. A supportive bar association also contributed to, but did not ensure, institutional growth, strength, and stability.[28]

As for the established programs in North Mississippi and Atlanta, they endured significant institutional hardship during the early 1970s. NMRLS and ALAS experienced slowed growth and periodic financial crises as a result of stagnant and unpredictable federal funding combined with an inflationary economy that reduced the buying power of whatever dollars the programs did receive. When Mike Trister left North Mississippi Rural Legal Services, there were some fifteen lawyers assigned to offices in Batesville, Greenville, Holly Springs, Oxford, and West Point who provided legal counsel, in theory, to thirty-nine counties in northern Mississippi, roughly half the state, by circuit-riding throughout the countryside. About the same number worked in the same offices when Legal Services Corporation funding began flowing in five years later.

NMRLS did undergo one notable change during this period. As more African Americans graduated from U.S. law schools, black lawyers made up an increasing proportion of the legal services staff and administration. Many young, black lawyers began their careers in legal services and later moved on to private practice, government positions, and academic careers. Alix Sanders was the first African American to head NMRLS, leading the institution throughout most of 1971 and 1972. Sanders had joined North Mississippi in 1969, opening its Greenwood office the day after he graduated from Ole Miss. He eventually left Mississippi for a position in Washington, D.C., before returning to work with the Lawyers' Committee for Constitutional Rights Under Law (LCCRUL) and, later in the 1970s, entering private practice and local politics back in Greenwood. John Brittain, a Reggie who came to North Mississippi in 1969, left in the early 1970s to join the LCCRUL and eventually moved into academia. When he first arrived in Mississippi, he was one of seventeen black lawyers in the state, only a few of whom lived outside Jackson.[29] Alvin Chambliss, who was NMRLS director for a year in the mid-1970s, worked for the program into the 1980s before also leaving for an academic career. Solomon Osborne, who grew up in Greenwood, returned to Mississippi after law school at Illinois. He later became the first director of Southwest Mississippi Legal Services before entering private practice.[30] In fact, because minorities, like women, were not welcome in the legal fraternity, legal services became a portal for African-American attorneys in the Deep South, where the opportunity to attend law school, much less practice law, had long been constricted.[31] As Leonard McClellan, who joined the program in 1975, pointed out, "Legal services was the only place at that time that a black lawyer could obtain employment and get some experience." He surmised that of his generation of African-American attorneys in Mississippi, including those who entered practice during the late 1960s and 1970s, "practically every one of them got their start working" for a legal services program. Alix Sanders suggested that NMRLS was "the single most influential factor in the development of the black bar in the state of Mississippi."[32]

Overall, however, the early 1970s were difficult years for NMRLS. North Mississippi lost its federal funding for about a year while Alix Sanders was director as a result of an antagonistic OEO. During that period Sanders kept the institution afloat with grants from philanthropic foundations, traveling extensively to nurture such contacts.[33] Moreover, opponents of North Mississippi began to monitor the activity of NMRLS lawyers and later launched one of several investigations of the program in response to North Mississippi lawyers' involvement with civil rights activists in Byhalia. This quasi-official opposition would grow throughout the decade. In terms of institutional development, NMRLS leaders did well to tread water during the early 1970s.

These were particularly lean years for the Atlanta Legal Aid Society as well. Due to static funding, ALAS froze salaries. With inflation that meant Legal Aid lawyers were, in effect, earning less and less money. Many began to leave the society, and a firm of forty-four lawyers shrunk to thirty by 1974. A newspaper article proclaimed the financial strain on the society with the title "Firm for Poor: Legal Aid Size, Punch Shrinking."[34] The same erosion of salaries was taking place across the country. California Rural Legal Assistance submitted data to Congress documenting the problem. In 1968 a CRLA attorney recently admitted to the bar made about $11,000 per year; someone with six years of experience made about $20,000. By 1977 these salaries, adjusted for inflation, were $6,380 and $11,600, respectively. Such remuneration was markedly below that of attorneys working for the federal government, who made roughly $16,255 upon admission to the bar in 1977 and $25,962 with six years of experience, and the salaries were far less than attorneys earned in private practice. The combination of lukewarm political support and dreadful economic forces had placed poverty lawyers among the poorest in their profession.[35] To make matters worse, the demand for legal services grew as a result of the inflationary economy, pressing Legal Aid lawyers into longer hours at their increasingly low pay. Demoralized, six attorneys (one-fifth of the legal staff) left the society unexpectedly between May and July 1975, forcing ALAS to close its doors to new clients and accept only "emergency" cases for a six-week period from mid-July to Labor Day. Although attorneys in private practice devoted time to help the society, the number of clients it served dropped precipitously, from nearly 12,000 in 1974 to 8,269 in 1975.[36] As if to underscore these troubles, a fire, possibly the work of a disgruntled landlord, engulfed the society's Southside office the following year, destroying hundreds of case files, its entire library, office furnishings and equipment, and countless hours of research.[37]

Different problems beset the new programs in Jackson and rural Georgia. Unlike Georgia Indigents Legal Services, Community Legal Services did not enjoy the blessing of the Mississippi State Bar, the Hinds County Bar Association, or Mississippi's governor, John Bell Williams. Governor Williams, who had ascended to office on a wave of resentment over federal desegregation efforts, vetoed the initial OEO grant to CLS in 1971. The state bar's *Mississippi Lawyer* reported that Williams's feeling was that "the Grant is not intended to assist the poor with their legal problems," implying that poverty lawyers were more interested in following their own ideological agenda than in helping the poor.[38] OEO Office of Legal Services director Terry Lenzner subsequently overrode the gubernatorial veto to the dismay of Mississippi's congressional delegation, which pressured Nixon to fire Lenzner. The following year saw the repetition of the same events, minus Lenzner. Then, in 1973, OEO director Howard Phillips refused to override the veto of Governor William Waller, and CLS lost its primary source of funding. The Phillips-led OEO redirected funding earmarked for CLS to Hinds County Bar Legal Services, which had previously operated only on private donations.[39] In response to losing its grant, CLS joined a federal lawsuit against Phillips filed in Washington, D.C., in which several legal services grantees alleged that Phillips acted beyond his legal authority because Nixon had not submitted his name to the Senate for confirmation, as federal law required. A federal judge agreed, forcing Phillips from office and requiring OEO to hold hearings to determine the status of the terminated grants.[40] At the hearing Dan Bradley testified that CLS was doing commendable work, superior to that of Mississippi Bar Legal Services (formerly HCBLS). Largely on the strength of that testimony, OEO restored Community Legal Services' funding.[41]

Office of Legal Services officials then had to decide how to resolve the dilemma of funding two legal services programs in the same city. They commissioned a report that, when issued in 1974, documented the markedly different dispositions of the two institutions. Whereas CLS initiated some substantial reform litigation along with providing basic services, MBLS attorneys were unlikely to pursue law reform cases. MBLS leaders were also adamant in their belief that the bar should control the composition of the board of directors. The report criticized MBLS for failing to utilize fully its financial resources, lacking contact with the client community, and lacking "experience dealing with the wide range of legal problems which most often affect low-income and minority individuals." The quality of work was lower at MBLS, and attorneys saw half the clients whom their counterparts at CLS counseled. Even more troublesome to the investigators was the fact that 56 percent of MBLS clients were white and 44 percent black. Compared to Community Legal Services' clientele, which was 80 percent black and 20 percent white, a ratio much closer to the racial proportions of welfare recipients in Jackson, MBLS's client base was suspect. At the very least it seemed that poor African Americans were less willing to seek the counsel of MBLS lawyers than their CLS counterparts. Furthermore, several attorneys displayed "judgmental attitudes" toward their clients, according to the report, and "the attitude among some of the Bar leadership appears to be that the program is primarily for the benefit of lawyers rather than for the benefit of the low-income community of Jackson."[42] MBLS leaders vigorously disputed the findings of this report and suggested that it was less than impartial. The organization's president, Martha Gerald, stressed that the racial proportions of MBLS clients was comparable to Jackson's population and that the MBLS ratio was more appropriate: "Poverty is no respecter of color and in this City, we have both black and white who are poor and in need of representation." MBLS's official response to the report also rejected the report's finding that only the CLS represented the city's "oppressed elements." Indeed, according to MBLS, there were no "oppressed elements" in Jackson: African Americans served in several state and local government posts, and race relations were reportedly peaceful.[43] Ultimately, despite the report's negative characterization of MBLS, the Office of Legal Services continued to fund both Jackson programs until the Legal Services Corporation forced CLS and MBLS to merge in 1976, at which time CLS basically absorbed its smaller competitor.[44]

Like the other Deep South programs, Georgia Legal Services endured its own crises. The program's funding was never entirely secure. In 1973 HEW contemplated eliminating the optional legal services component through which Georgia Indigents Legal Services received federal money, but then Congress instructed the agency to postpone such action. Meanwhile, Howard Phillips's opposition to legal services seemingly made GLSP's second source of funding unstable. Then the support of the state bar and, consequently, state politicians began to disintegrate in 1974 and 1975. Local bar associations, in particular, resented law reform activities and expressed concern that GLSP lawyers were luring away potential paying clients, especially those seeking a divorce. There was a move on the floor of the General Assembly to end legal services funding in 1975, and GLSP supporters struggled to keep the supply lines open until a Legal Services Corporation came into being. They barely succeeded.[45] In the meantime the growth that had occurred in 1971 and 1972 slowed to a crawl by mid-decade.

POVERTY LAW PRACTICE DURING THE LEAN YEARS

Legal services programs' perpetual financial crises contributed to a siege mentality—Robert Dokson called these the "siege days"—among poverty lawyers in the Deep South and across the country, as administrators struggled to keep their institutions afloat.[46] That they did so is remarkable; that poverty law practice thrived despite these institutional problems is even more so. Indeed, in some ways institutional considerations were ancillary to the experiences of most poverty lawyers. To be sure, the politics of legal services on national, state, and local levels determined the availability of legal counsel for the poor, and the programs provided attorneys with a paycheck (however slender) as well as valuable training and administrative support (equally slender during the early 1970s). Moreover, practicing poverty law within a firm dedicated to low-income clients enabled neophytes to develop personal relationships with more seasoned attorneys, even if *seasoned* meant having practiced two or three years, and from specialists in consumer, housing, public benefits, civil rights, and family law. Nevertheless, if one asks a poverty lawyer to reflect on her legal services career, her mind often turns not to these institutional considerations but, instead, to her clients. The lawyer-client relationship was the central experience of poverty law practice.

Despite the tumult that legal services programs endured as institutions, new attorneys remained talented, committed, and eager to engage in reform initiatives, and federal law remained more generous and protective than state practices. As a result, poverty lawyers were able to utilize legal processes, particularly negotiation and litigation within the federal court system, to bring state practices into line with federal constitutional and statutory precepts. Combined with a vast array of individual client services, these reform efforts integrated low-income individuals into American legal culture and caused regional distinctiveness to diminish. Yet, even as the lawyers assimilated their clients into the legal system—including government regulation of consumer relationships, public initiatives designed to ameliorate poverty, and precepts promising equal rights—they did so without uniformity. Atlanta attorneys, for example, focused on welfare, housing, and consumer protection, while North Mississippi lawyers became more involved in civil rights disputes, and attorneys in Jackson delved into the state's mental health system. There were similarities between programs, such as the prevalence of domestic relations cases, but by and large they constituted a heterogeneous group.

Attorneys working in small legal aid societies or bar-related programs generally became involved in little law reform, or "impact," litigation. Mississippi Bar Legal Services, for example, shied away from class actions in favor of individual client counsel, mostly relating to family law. Other bar-related programs, including the tiny office in Clarksdale, Mississippi, and those in Alabama, had similar personalities. Marvin Campbell, who joined the Madison County Legal Aid Society in 1973 as director of litigation and then a year later became director of the Birmingham Legal Aid Society, explained that the Alabama programs' emphasis on basic client services was partly out of necessity. "We were so swamped with cases," he recalled, "that it was difficult to concentrate in a particular area." The programs simply "did not have the resources to address" many of the systemic problems.[47] That does not mean they never pursued impact litigation. Campbell noted that during his year in Huntsville he attacked a statewide policy of requiring public school students to pay fees to purchase uniforms and filed a case seeking to reform conditions at the Madison County Jail, especially the lack of sufficient medical care for inmates. In Birmingham, Campbell became involved in a case that enjoined public officials from forcing low-income couples to pay certain fees in order to get married and another case that failed to overturn a state requirement that probationers and parolees pay a ten dollar per month "supervision fee" to the board of pardons and paroles. One Birmingham Legal Aid case stipulated that food stamp offices process applications within a set thirty-day period, rather than leaving potential recipients in limbo for much longer periods. But such efforts were the exceptions, not the rule. The vast majority of legal aid practice in these programs involved counseling individual clients in more routine problems such as landlord-tenant and public housing disputes, consumer protection, and claims for public benefits.[48]

Programs with more resources tended to engage in a broader array of activities, supplementing individual client counsel with impact litigation, including class actions. Another valuable tactic that the better-established programs used was community education. Attorneys met with groups such as neighborhood centers, federally funded job training programs, family planning units, youth councils, schools and universities, and the YMCA, among others, to discuss the typical legal problems that low-income persons faced. ALAS cooperated with the *Atlanta Voice* to publish a weekly legal aid column and had a weekly radio program. The hope behind these educational efforts was that low-income people would become more aware of problems they faced and seek out legal aid if necessary. Indeed, educational campaigns and community contacts brought in thousands of clients; for the ALAS in 1972, 5,712 out of 14,513 clients reported visiting a legal aid lawyer as a result of "publicity."[49]

Most of the lawyers working for the larger organizations in Mississippi and Georgia were not unlike their counterparts in the smaller programs. They were "staff attorneys" who carried the bulk of the caseload: divorces and separations, child custody disputes, claims for public benefits, evictions, and a multitude of other problems in the lives of individual clients. Much of this work was tedious and brought little reward to attorney or client. Clients often had no legal recourse or waited too long to seek legal counsel, making it impossible for poverty lawyers to be of any help, and even legal victories usually left clients in poverty. Marian Burge, who served as ALAS's lone Gwinnett County lawyer during the 1970s and later became the society's deputy director, characterized poverty law practice as sometimes "frustrating and frightening," not least because attorneys realized how clients' lives were "so delicately balanced . . . a sense of going from crisis to crisis." It was "easy to get overwhelmed with the clients' lives," especially after "re-meeting a client for the second time with another problem, and realizing, 'I didn't fix this person's life. That's what I wanted to do—make an impact on this person's life.'"[50] What struck Bill Brennan about his early years with ALAS, "being a middle-class . . . person, was meeting and dealing with the poor clients that came into Atlanta Legal Aid. It was such an education to see . . . the misery that they lived in. Your heart just went out to them. It made you angry and it made you think that this system is so unfair."[51] The attrition rate among poverty lawyers was high because many sensed that they were doomed to failure and would in the meantime endure a lifetime of meager material benefits.[52] There were rewards to poverty law practice, of course, but they were primarily psychological: poverty lawyers believed they were making a positive impact in the lives of their clients. Exuding a "missionary" mentality, many poverty lawyers in the South, like others across the country, believed that in serving poor people they were engaged in a moral conflict and were doing what was right. Such beliefs had a self-affirming dimension. As Marian Burge explained, many poverty lawyers felt: "I'm here to do good; this is the side of justice. They need to feel like what they do is right, or else, 'Why should I be doing this for half or a third of the salary that I could use my education to make?'"[53]

Another characteristic of poverty law practice during the early 1970s, particularly within the larger organizations, was the emergence of hierarchies among the attorneys, with some lawyers focusing on law reform litigation and others devoted primarily to basic client services. The Atlanta Legal Aid Society had a law reform division; Georgia Legal Services had specialists based in Atlanta; and the NMRLS, CLS, and the Birmingham programs had several attorneys whose primary work was on impact cases. While these attorneys recognized the importance of "service work" for individual clients, they sought to move beyond the limitations of such advocacy. Robert Dokson, who joined ALAS's law reform division immediately out of law school, noted that a "staff attorney could see ten new clients a week, and have ten dispossessories that they had to stop, and stop all ten, and that was very important to those ten people, but there was still the next week and the next week and the next week. . . . The people who were doing law reform work," he continued, "were really doing better stuff—it was sexier, it was more interesting. I don't know whether it was more important, but it was not nearly the drudge work." Not surprisingly, these internal hierarchies produced a considerable degree of resentment from many staff attorneys.[54]

In any case it was primarily law reform work that distinguished poverty law practice in one locale from that in another. Atlanta Legal Aid attorneys remained focused on housing and public benefits and developed expertise in consumer protection, while

North Mississippi continued much of its civil rights work. Georgia Legal Services joined ALAS in consumer and public benefits litigation, but its lawyers began to represent clients in civil rights disputes as well, much like those in rural Mississippi. Jackson's Community Legal Services handled a variety of issues but became particularly involved in revising the state's justice system and mental health facilities during the early 1970s.

Indeed, lawyers working for Community Legal Services of Jackson quickly made their presence felt in a number of legal areas.[55] Many CLS clients often had difficulty obtaining or retaining public benefits. Two cases enforced federal regulations that required state officials to act upon AFDC applications within thirty days and Aid to the Permanently and Totally Disabled applications within sixty.[56] Another defended a food stamp recipient from accusations of fraud.[57] In yet another case that sought to extend AFDC benefits to unborn children, CLS attorneys convinced District Judge Orma Smith that the state could not refuse assistance to unborn children, and nationwide three other federal judges had come to the same conclusion, but the Fifth Circuit Court of Appeals later overturned a similar Georgia decision.[58] CLS's most significant public assistance case was *West v. Cole*, which expanded Medicaid benefits to children receiving disability benefits (similar to those receiving AFCD, who were automatically eligible for Medicaid benefits after North Mississippi's *Triplett v. Cobb*).[59]

Several CLS cases involved clients' civil rights, though, unlike North Mississippi's civil rights activity, the most prominent CLS cases did not directly involve racial discrimination. CLS attorneys did not feel pressed to pursue claims of racial discrimination because they were located nearby the major civil rights firms in Jackson, including the LCCRUL, LCDC, and LDF. Powell suggested, "The difference between us and North Mississippi, and why we had less controversy than NMRLS, was that the civil rights law groups were located in Jackson, and they basically handled . . . school desegregation . . . reapportionment . . . [s]o we were not drawn into that to much extent at all."[60] Instead, one CLS case filed by Charles Ramberg sought to keep judges from inquiring into the financial status of legal services clients. Critics of legal services often suggested that poverty lawyers were more interested in their own political agendas than the needs of income-eligible clients, and on that theory Mississippi judges sometimes probed the poverty lawyer–client relationship to make sure clients were indeed eligible for free legal counsel and actually suffered the problem of which they complained. In response, Ramberg and his colleagues argued that in making such an inquiry the chancellor in the present case denied the lawyers and the clients their freedom of association and violated the Supremacy Clause of the Constitution by infringing upon the clients' right to benefit from a federal program. A federal judge agreed and forbade the chancellor from treating legal services clients differently than anyone else.[61] CLS attorneys also sought to protect the voting rights of eighteen- to twenty-year-olds and to invalidate Mississippi's four-month registration requirement,[62] and they urged the Mississippi Publishers Corporation, which published two of Mississippi's major newspapers, the *Clarion-Ledger* and *Jackson Daily News*, to stop classifying their employment advertisements by gender.[63] Cases pertaining to the civil and criminal justice systems included one that criticized the living conditions at the Hinds County jail as inhumane and similar litigation seeking to improve living conditions at other jails, the state's training school for juvenile delinquents, and the state mental hospital.[64]

In one of CLS's most significant cases Barry Powell, John Maxey, and Charles Ramberg challenged Mississippi's reliance on justices of the peace, who were elected adjudicators who handled minor criminal and civil disputes. The justices received a fee for each case they handled, and they received higher fees upon convictions in criminal cases and judgments for the plaintiffs (usually creditors) in civil cases. CLS lawyers believed that the fee system impaired the judges' impartiality to the detriment of their clients. Filed in 1972, *Brown v. Vance* would remain active until the early 1980s. CLS attorneys pointed to deep flaws in the system, compiling evidence showing an uneven distribution of cases among justices. One justice explained that creditors pressured him and others to act on their behalf, and, if you refused, "They don't bring you no more business." A Fifth Circuit panel that included the highly respected Judge John Minor Wisdom agreed with the plaintiffs' position that Mississippi's fee system was unconstitutional as a violation of due process. While the court believed that many justices were upright, the fees were their "bread and butter," and "the temptation exists to take a biased view that will find favor in the minds of arresting officers and litigating creditors. This vice inheres in the fee system. It is a fatal constitutional flaw." Indeed, noting the testimony of the justices themselves, the Court held that "possible temptation bloomed into questionable behavior," such as instances of justices advertising their "services" to potential "clients." Even the justice quoted earlier spoke of his cases as "business." The market-like temptation could not exist along with the impartial administration of justice.[65]

During the early 1970s legal services programs began to develop unique areas of expertise as a result of the interests and activities of legal services attorneys and their contact with clients and community leaders. Specialists began to become more prominent in poverty law practice. Community Legal Services, for example, began to focus attention on the rights of mental health patients. The program initiated a Mental Health Project in 1974 and assigned one attorney, Reginald Heber Smith fellow David Michaels, to the project. He and other CLS lawyers became involved in extensive representation and litigation involving the state's commitment procedures and major mental health facility, Whitfield State Hospital. Their litigation docket captured the breadth of issues with which they were involved: they assailed the conditions at the Mississippi State Hospital, attacked the forcible administration of electroshock therapy as abusive, sought to end the summary confinement of patients for alleged violations of unwritten hospital rules, challenged the transfer of inmates from Parchman Penitentiary to Whitfield without a prior civil commitment procedure, and attempted to free numerous individuals confined for years at the hospital who were deemed incapable of standing trial.[66] In one case a client accused of murdering two people and beating four others had been diagnosed with paranoid schizophrenia, judged incompetent to stand trial, and confined to Whitfield for nine years. Michaels and his colleagues convinced the Mississippi Supreme Court that detaining their client for such a lengthy time without a trial violated his constitutional rights to due process and equal protection of the laws. If the state was going to maintain custody, authorities would have to initiate civil commitment proceedings. While there was little hope that this particular client would ever find his way past Whitfield's walls, his was one of many cases that slowly began to expand the rights of the institutionalized in Mississippi.[67]

While CLS was composed of a relatively small group of energetic attorneys by the mid-1970s,[68] North Mississippi Rural Legal Services developed a major legal presence in the northern half of the state, despite little growth during the first half of the decade. As mentioned earlier, an increasing number of African Americans began their careers with North Mississippi, and their personal experiences gave them a unique perspective on the problems among northern Mississippi's poor. Even if they had not been actively involved in the civil rights protests of the 1960s, they had vivid memories of those days. Solomon Osborne, for example, was born in 1948. The murder of Emmett Till—more precisely, the gruesome pictures of Till that *Jet* magazine published in 1955—taught him "that anything could happen to you at any time if you encountered some hostile whites." He recalled "walking along the highways and people would pass and call you 'nigger,'"—"that stands out in your mind." When Freedom Summer shook the state, Osborne was a teenager working on his father's farm, uninvolved in the movement. He nevertheless "wanted to come back" to Mississippi after college because he was "concerned with equal rights, and . . . always wanted to try and do something to bring about equal rights."[69] Johnnie Walls, who grew up in Clarksdale and joined North Mississippi in 1971, recalled his father's resentment against racial discrimination, including his refusal to allow his children to leave school to work in the cotton fields along with most of their counterparts. Just after Congress passed the Civil Rights Act, Walls unsuccessfully tried to order ice cream at a local shop with his girlfriend and another couple, but the clerk was not swayed by their invocation of the new statute that forbade the discrimination to which the young people were being subjected. But, like Osborne, Walls was not deeply involved in civil rights activism. He attended many mass meetings but refrained from open protest for fear of hurting his father's business. This apparent contradiction—resentment toward the status quo but restraint in challenging it—only made Walls more determined to seek racial justice later in life. He pledged to himself, "When I get out of law school, then I will be whatever I have to be to change this system—do whatever I have to do." Upon joining NMRLS, Walls recalled, "It was almost like you were a 'buffalo soldier' given the opportunity to fight the battle."[70] Osborne and Walls were not atypical: memory became motivation for many North Mississippi lawyers.

Recollections of past racial injustices would not suffice, however, to chart a course for the future. Instead, North Mississippi tried to nurture its contacts with the client community by hiring community workers, paralegals, and support personnel with community connections. Unlike the attorneys, most of these employees were black women, such as Annie Burt. She began working for the program in 1967, and her primary role was to help clients obtain public benefits, but Burt also served as a liaison between North Mississippi lawyers and Oxford's African-American community. She was an instrumental figure in the Oxford Improvement Association, which sought to desegregate the city's schools, helped found the Oxford Development Association's credit union and day care (the only black-run day care in the county), and was involved in the local Head Start program. Burt and other support personnel kept the attorneys abreast of problems and perspectives within the client community, as did the program's board of directors. One NMRLS community worker, Dora Adams, reflected client attitudes in expressing that the "system," meaning the local power structure, did not want the poor to have legal representation because then they might be able to force school desegregation or stop police brutality. North Mississippi board chairman and community organizer Wayne Johnson placed poverty lawyers' work in a broader context: "In a capitalistic society, often times what is good for the poor isn't good for the wealthy who indirectly rule the country." Furthermore, the board chairmen who served throughout the 1970s were deeply involved in civil rights struggles: Alfred "Skip" Robinson (1970–72) was head of the United League, Wayne Johnson (1972–77) was a community organizer with NMRLS, and Howard Gunn (1978–80) was also a United League leader.[71]

In many ways North Mississippi's constituency was not only poor Mississippians but also the larger African-American community, and many of the program's cases grew out of its close connection to this constituency. According to a Sovereignty Commission investigator, in 1970 northern Mississippi was quiet except for protests in Starkville, home of Mississippi State University.[72] There black activists, including at least one figure from the Southern Christian Leadership Conference, were marching and boycotting city stores. When city officials arrested two hundred marchers for obstructing traffic that July, North Mississippi attorney Tommy Mayfield, a white, Mississippi-born Ole Miss graduate who would become a prosecutor in Jackson, filed a federal case seeking to protect them against prosecution. Mayfield argued that the city's parade ordinances were an unconstitutional infringement of the protesters' First Amendment rights. The young attorney also defended, unsuccessfully, a protester accused of taking a package from another African American at the local Dollar Store, one of the targets of the boycott.[73] In 1971 North Mississippi attorneys, including director Jim Lewis, attracted the attention of the Sovereignty Commission, investigators watching the organization on behalf of the state bar, and local law enforcement officials in Coffeeville. Although the three legal services lawyers were "not in the column" of marchers, the detective believed the marchers "had been well coached by the Legal Aid group." The sheriff suggested that North Mississippi lawyers posed a law enforcement problem: "These people are always right in the middle of any march or any trouble involving civil rights."[74]

During the early 1970s North Mississippi became involved in several local protests, often in the wake of an alleged incident of police brutality. In Byhalia three white police officers shot and killed a twenty-one-year-old black man, Butler Young Jr., in 1974. The African-American community was enraged, and United League leaders Robinson and Boyd initiated a protest campaign that included marches and a boycott of the town's white-owned stores. Lewis Myers and John Jackson joined in much the same capacity as NMRLS attorneys had in Starkville and Coffeeville but soon became more deeply embroiled in the conflict. A grand jury that had convened to investigate the death of Butler Young instead began investigating the United League. To prevent the grand jury from retrieving United League records, which the activists and attorneys felt would chill the league's ability to nurture community support by publicizing its membership lists, Myers and Jackson filed suit in federal court on behalf of the organization, citing the grand jury's infringement of activists' freedom of speech and assembly. They were successful: the grand jury did not get the records, and the protests continued.[75] So, too, did local and state officials persist in their efforts to undermine the league's activities. They were suspicious, in particular, of North Mississippi's interaction with the United League. The governor filed a complaint with the Office of Legal Services alleging that the program was representing people whose incomes were too high to qualify for free legal counsel, and NMRLS chairman Wayne Johnson had to defend the program formally.[76] North Mississippi was also the subject of an investigation that Community Relations Services (CRS), a branch of the Justice Department, initiated in the midst of the Byhalia protests. CRS was ostensibly in Byhalia to protect the elderly from the "harassing" tactics of the United League's economic boycott, but local African Americans complained that CRS was hiring "local winos" to disrupt community meetings. In response, United League president Skip Robinson sued CRS for gathering information through illegal surveillance methods, prompting the investigators to leave Byhalia.[77] Finally, North Mississippi attorneys filed a wrongful death action on behalf of Butler Young's mother, winning a small monetary settlement. An NMRLS newsletter claimed that the outcome was "heralded by the local poor community as a victory against police abuse."[78] As in other communities, North Mississippi attorneys had protected the right of the United League to protest.[79] This was not the last time they would do so nor the last time that the combination of poverty lawyers and United League activists would draw the attention of white Mississippians and federal officials.

Meanwhile, the school desegregation cases of the late 1960s, many of which remained open under court-ordered plans, gave way to personnel issues. North Mississippi attorneys forced one school district to abandon a policy of denying employment to unwed mothers,[80] and in other cases they protected clients against alleged discrimination in hiring and firing.[81] Employment discrimination cases would become more prevalent in the late 1970s. Another civil rights case charged Marshall County Hospital with failing to admit a pregnant woman due to the fact that she was poor and black. Although she gave birth under conditions that would, the plaintiffs argued, "disgrace a nation of savages" (in the front seat of a car parked in the hospital parking lot), the facts of the case did not persuade District Judge Orma Smith that hospital officials had erred. North Mississippi lawyers used a variety of arguments, claiming that the hospital's actions violated common law, federal statutes, and the constitutional rights of their client. Judge Smith, while expressing mild concern at the hospital's actions, believed that officials had nonetheless remained within the boundaries of the law.[82] Other North Mississippi cases were more of a departure from legal services norms. During the early 1970s, for instance, North Mississippi accepted a number of criminal cases, many of which they guided through lengthy appeals. On some occasions local judges assigned these cases to NMRLS lawyers; on others, alleged criminals or members of their families approached NMRLS. These were not the juvenile misdemeanors that many legal services programs handled during this period but often involved burglary, manslaughter, and murder.[83] North Mississippi lawyers also became involved in a personal injury case against officials at the state's notorious prison, Parchman Farm,[84] and provided research support for *Gates v. Collier*, an LCCRUL case that altered the conditions at the state penitentiary.[85] NMRLS attorneys evidently viewed their role more broadly than other legal services lawyers.

The press of more common problems was also heavy. As elsewhere, most domestic, consumer, and public benefits disputes remained out of court but were no less significant to individual clients. North Mississippi attorneys pursued significant litigation in these areas during the early 1970s.[86] The *Goldberg* doctrine made an appearance, for example, when Stanley Taylor sought to protect an elderly farmer from a home foreclosure. When his client defaulted on a Federal Housing Administration loan due to a severe statewide crop failure, Taylor argued that the federal government should have granted an emergency loan and at least owed him a fair hearing prior to seizing his home. Taylor supported his point by claiming that local officials had discriminated against the farmer on the basis of his race.[87] Finally, while continuing cases begun in the late 1960s and teaming with CLS attorneys in several other cases, North Mississippi attorneys attacked a state regulation requiring a welfare recipient to aid in the prosecution of the absent partner, mostly fathers, for failing to pay child support.[88]

Like North Mississippi Rural Legal Services, the Atlanta Legal Aid Society was no longer experiencing the growth of the 1960s, but the program continued to influence Georgia law and social policy. While continuing to provide basic legal services, ALAS was becoming more conscious of the entrenched problems of its clientele. Along with continuing involvement in public benefits and housing cases, poverty lawyers in Atlanta began to nurture an expertise in consumer law during the early 1970s. Legal services clients confronted a variety of legal problems as consumers: loan sharks charging exorbitant interest rates and fees, merchants attempting to recoup loans, banks seeking to foreclose on homes, and more. ALAS had, of course, long accepted consumer cases. Prior to Padnos's arrival, attorneys for the Atlanta Legal Aid Society often arranged for clients to pay their creditors in installments over a longer period of time, providing them with "breathing room."[89] Under Padnos ALAS attorneys began to look for other means of aiding their clients. The society began a community education campaign, for example, that warned low-income consumers about falling into debt, shopping in stores that charged exorbitant prices, or getting involved in home improvement schemes they could not afford. ALAS placed posters in city buses, community centers, welfare and health department offices, realty companies, and Legal Aid offices that read: "It's a groove to borrow money . . . but a drag to pay it back!"; "I'd rather walk clean across town than pay 45¢ for a bunch of greens!"; and "They fixed my porch, but then they took my house!"[90] Debt and other consumer problems were also common topics in the society's newspaper and radio communications as well as the welfare rights organization's *Poor People's Newspaper*. ALAS produced a fifteen-minute radio show stressing intelligent buying practices and a thirty-minute radio program called *Let's Talk about the Law*.[91] The *Atlanta Voice* ran a column called "Legal Aid Society News" from 1969 to 1973, and the society's director of community outreach, Richard Harris, was the column's first author. Many of his articles provided practical advice for low-income readers, discussing, for example, Bill Brennan's successful action to free a woman from her late husband's debt; salesmen who "will tell a customer almost anything to obtain his signature on a contract," including the failure to disclose various fees; a client whose cemetery lot was sold without his notification; faulty consumer goods with unsatisfactory maintenance service; and various "unscrupulous" business practices. Harris encouraged his readers to seek legal counsel should they find themselves in these types of situations.[92] In the early 1970s Charles Jackson Jr. began writing the column, and the quality diminished, with less practical information and more social criticism. In one article Jackson linked the exploitation of consumers to criminal behavior but provided no evidence to support his claim except his own perceptions about the frustration of "having to slave for 'The Man' and then have 'The Man' take it all away." He wrote that many creditors are "God-Demons," "people who help satisfy your material needs and then force you to spend months and years sweating out payments."[93] Altogether, the society hoped to reach over 400,000 listeners each week through these educational campaigns.[94]

Beginning in the early 1970s, Legal Aid attorneys initiated a more aggressive litigation strategy on behalf of their clients, particularly in their use of the Georgia Industrial Loan Act (GILA). "Loan sharks" had become one of Padnos's major concerns by 1970. Just before leaving the society, he testified before the National Committee on Consumer Finance in Washington about a tactic known as "flipping." Calling it "one of the gravest evils suffered by borrowers in the state of Georgia," Padnos explained how loan companies kept borrowers indebted for years by extending further credit and assessing fees to one's account. One woman borrowed $128.50 in 1965 and four years later had the same amount of debt, despite making regular payments. Another man borrowed $300 and had to pay $340 in fees.[95] To counteract such practices, Legal Aid lawyers began employing a little-used remedy embedded in the GILA. The General Assembly had passed the act in the 1920s, allowing loan companies to offer small loans with interest rates above the rate then considered usurious. In the early 1970s ALAS attorneys discovered that, although the GILA allowed for high rates of interest, it also contained a harsh penalty for companies that violated the provisions of the act: the company would forfeit the entire loan, principal and interest. This penalty provision seemed a remote possibility to these companies until ALAS attorneys began challenging loan contracts they believed to be in violation of the act.

Beginning with *Lewis v. Termplan,* a precedential case before the Georgia Court of Appeals in 1971, ALAS and later GLSP attorneys began pecking away at these illegal contracts, voiding thousands of small loans during the 1970s.[96] The Georgia Legal Services Program brought these legal developments into the Georgia countryside after Harry Pettigrew joined GLSP in 1971 as its consumer law specialist. Pettigrew's contact with the National Consumer Law Center, which provided information to poverty lawyers across the country, enabled him to work closely with staff attorneys at the branch offices throughout the state, sending memoranda and manuals about developing case law and potential legal problems their clients might experience.[97] In time Charlie Baird replaced Pettigrew as GLSP's consumer expert and, by expanding on Pettigrew's efforts, encouraged a wealth of consumer litigation, the foremost of which were Georgia Industrial Loan Act cases.[98] Baird even created a GILA checklist, citing some thirty possible violations of the act, which provided staff attorneys with a guideline for ensuring the viability of loan contracts.[99] Both GLSP and ALAS also provided defense against illegal business practices through enforcement of the federal Truth in Lending Act.[100]

Apart from the thousands of public benefits, housing, consumer, and domestic cases, Atlanta Legal Aid attorneys confronted a wide variety of issues during the early 1970s. Two cases attacked jail conditions in DeKalb and Gwinnett counties, forcing the counties to build new facilities.[101] In another, the Fifth Circuit agreed with ALAS attorneys that a municipal court could not constitutionally jail an indigent defendant for failure to pay a court-imposed fine.[102] Legal Aid lawyers were less successful in challenging Georgia's restriction of ex-felons' voting rights,[103] but they did win a major victory when a federal judge ordered Fulton County election officials to relocate existing polls and establish additional ones in predominantly black neighborhoods. Few cars and a lack of convenient mass transit in these communities, combined with the distant location and geographical separation of the polls, made them inaccessible to much of Atlanta's minority population.[104] ALAS attorneys also represented a Decatur, Georgia, teenager who had been expelled from school after becoming pregnant. Because the father of her child (and other young fathers) could continue to attend school regularly, a federal judge recognized this policy as unconstitutional sex discrimination.[105]

Legal Aid lawyers also became involved in two significant abortion rights cases.[106] The most important was *Doe v. Bolton,* which followed *Roe v. Wade* to the Supreme Court. An ALAS lawyer, Tobiane Schwartz, became one of the lead attorneys in *Doe.* She had come to Atlanta in 1969 from West Virginia and become head of the society's family law division. Elizabeth Rindskopf, then working in the Emory Community Legal Services office, joined Schwartz in taking the case to the Supreme Court. In 1970 the two met with a group of female attorneys, including Georgia Legal Services director Bettye Kehrer, to discuss early case strategy. One of the group's tasks was finding a client. Schwartz's position with ALAS was advantageous because the society saw so many clients, and soon she met a woman whom the group felt would be a sympathetic plaintiff. Schwartz, working with an attorney in private practice, Margie Hames, filed suit, and Rindskopf filed a number of briefs in support of "Mary Doe." Both women would leave their legal services positions during the course of the litigation, but their early legal services work had been a gateway into public interest careers in Atlanta, and the law reform mentality of ALAS and Emory Community Legal Services encouraged their participation in the case.[107] Another abortion rights case remained within ALAS's purview. Jay Loeb and director Michael Terry attacked state Medicaid regulations that denied coverage to women seeking an abortion. Filed in late 1971, they did not meet the resistance that the *Doe* attorneys encountered. Within a few months the state altered its policy to extend coverage to abortion procedures.[108] The impact was immediate. From July 1971 through February 1972 (when the policy change became effective) local hospitals filed twenty-one Medicaid claims for abortion procedures, but the state reimbursed them for none. During this period doctors performed 1,242 abortions (155 per month). Of the 439 abortions performed in March and April 1972, the state reimbursed hospitals for 61 of 66 Medicaid claims and reimbursed private doctors for 6 of 6 claims. Both the rate of abortions (220 per month) and, more significantly, the rate of reimbursement had risen dramatically.[109]

Although the Atlanta Legal Aid Society was the more established program in Georgia, it was not alone in its ability to influence state law and social policy. The Georgia Legal Services Program had not even existed at the turn of the decade, but by 1975 there were nine offices (including the central office in Atlanta), and poverty lawyers circuit-rode to all of Georgia's 154 counties outside the Atlanta metropolis.[110] Many of these attorneys, numbering sixty by 1974, worked on family law cases, which made up the largest single category of cases and sometimes threatened to overwhelm legal services programs.[111] Typically, whatever the law reform activities of ALAS and GLSP, a third or more of their cases involved domestic issues, mostly divorces. During its early years, however, a much higher percentage of the GLSP caseload was made up of domestic disputes: in 1972 nearly 64 percent of the program's cases (10,267 of 16,064) involved family relations (or the lack thereof).[112]

While domestic cases had a great impact on the lives of individual clients, consumer, housing, civil rights, and public benefits cases often involved issues of law and public policy with effects beyond the individual client. Not surprisingly, given the fact that poverty lawyers were making their first forays into rural Georgia, many GLSP cases had racial dimensions. In Macon, for example, the local housing authority utilized an "income range" system whereby it maintained a certain proportion of families from various income brackets. Because there were more applicants in the lower income brackets than their allotted number of apartments, the effect of the system was to exclude the "poorest of the poor." Georgia Legal Services attorneys highlighted the fact that such a policy had an especially detrimental impact on African Americans, who were, on average, less affluent than whites. The parties settled the case before it went to trial,[113] but these types of cases would become more prevalent and more contentious during the late 1970s. Along with housing cases, GLSP lawyers initiated voting rights litigation. One of the program's most significant cases was *Paige v. Gray*, which challenged Albany's at-large election system on the grounds that it diluted African-American votes. GLSP's voting rights specialist, David Walbert, was also involved in an attack on Dublin, Georgia's election scheme and a similar system in Gordon.[114] Most of the voting rights work would come later in the decade, but several of these cases began when Georgia Legal Services was first establishing its foothold in rural Georgia. Furthermore, civil rights went beyond racial discrimination in housing and voting. One case GLSP attorneys pursued during the early 1970s was a challenge, similar to that of Community Legal Services in Jackson, to Georgia's policy of indefinitely confining individuals found incompetent to stand trial. The legal services client was a twenty-three-year-old man accused of molesting a minor in 1970. After declaring him incompetent to stand trial, the state placed him in its mental hospital's maximum-security ward. Not until 1975 did a federal judge require the state to adopt specific guidelines to govern such situations.[115]

Like other legal services programs in the Deep South, poverty lawyers working in rural Georgia also became involved in a significant number of public benefits cases. Most of this activity came in the form of administrative advocacy, with GLSP lawyers and paralegals advising clients about their eligibility for assistance and representing individuals in administrative hearings. According to a GLSP report, most clients suffered some disability that rendered them unable to work. In these endeavors the guidance of Wayne Pressel, the program's public benefits specialist based in Atlanta, proved invaluable. Like Pettigrew and Baird did for developments in consumer law, Pressel sent memoranda to staff members informing them of changes in social programs.[116] Although few law reform cases dealing with such programs emanated from rural Georgia during the early 1970s, that would not always be the case. In 1975, for example, GLSP lawyers filed cases seeking to expand payments to beneficiaries of vocational rehabilitation and to ensure appropriate assistance to legally separated Social Security recipients.[117] Another case, *White v. Butz*, involved claiming food stamps for the plaintiff Ruth White (and others similarly situated), whom the local press dubbed "too poor to get food stamps." A widow, White lived with her daughter and thus was considered part of her daughter's household, rendering her ineligible for food stamps because her daughter already received them. Because of special dietary needs due to her diabetes, she wanted to get her own food stamps. But for the legal services case on her behalf, that would have been possible only if she moved out of her daughter's home, something she could not afford to do.[118]

Considering the small number of impact cases filed during the early 1970s and the low proportion of cases that involved public benefits (6 percent in 1972), it is ironic that a public benefits case nearly brought about the demise of Georgia Legal Services. GLSP's *Crane v. Mathews* typified much of poverty law practice. The case sought to protect Medicaid recipients from an effective cut in services that legal services attorneys argued violated federally established guidelines. In response to its filing, state politicians grew incensed at their apparent lack of discretion over this policy and poverty lawyers' ability to challenge state bureaucrats. Because the state politicians controlled a significant proportion of the GLSP budget, the program's funding was in jeopardy. Poverty law practice in Georgia had generated its own opposition.

In *Crane v. Mathews* GLSP attorneys challenged the state's plan to charge Medicaid patients for each doctor visit. With the support of Governor George Busbee, administrators hoped to offset a budget deficit by requiring Medicaid recipients to pay two dollars each time they visited a hospital or outpatient clinic.[119] Designed to "curtail over utilization in Georgia of 'marginally needed' health care," these fees would save the state an estimated $5.4 million over seven months (until the end of the next fiscal year). After HEW approval, officials were ready to institute the copayment plan on 1 December 1975, before GLSP lawyers won a temporary restraining order.[120] Wayne Pressel, highlighting the damaging effects on his clients' health, argued that HEW had erred in approving the state's plan. The named plaintiffs, Fannie Crane and Evelyn Jackson, were elderly women who received public assistance, and Jackson had three dependents, one of whom was severely retarded. They represented a class that Pressel estimated at 350,000 people.[121]

State politicians and officials, including Governor Busbee, were furious at Georgia Legal Services for initiating the case, not least because the mid-1970s was a period of fiscal crisis for the state government. The Medicaid program was costing Georgia too much money, and Busbee believed this plan would help offset the program's deficit without creating an onerous burden on the recipients. Moreover, state officials and the federal defendant, HEW secretary David Mathews, argued that Mathews had wide discretion to approve experimental plans such as this. Pressel was simply wrong that HEW had acted improperly.[122] District Judge Charles Moye agreed with the defendants on one major point: Mathews, said Moye, had the legal authority to approve of such a plan. The only fault Moye found was that the state had not properly submitted the plan to a review board that would assess its viability. If that board agreed that the copayment plan would effectively cut costs while placing only a minor burden on recipients, the state could institute the plan. Unfortunately for Busbee and state offi-cials, the review board did not cooperate, instead ascertaining that the plan would not effectively curb costs and might have harsh ramifications on Medicaid recipients.[123] Thus, despite an ambiguous result in the judicial skirmish, GLSP won the larger bat-tle, and the state could not implement the plan.

For Georgia Legal Services, however, the legislative backlash against the program imperiled its existence. Opposition to GLSP had been building throughout 1975 in the Georgia General Assembly. During its first session early in the year the Senate Ap-propriations Committee cut the GLSP allocation, which also would have eliminated federal matching funds totaling one million dollars.[124] "If we are not restored to the budget," responded director John Cromartie, "we'll immediately cut off intake. We simply won't take on any new clients. We'll try to serve all our current clients and dispose of their cases before July 1. After that, we'll have to shut the doors." Fortu-nately for the program, most state politicians saw fit to continue funding through the next fiscal year.[125] Furthermore, members of the state bar had grown increasingly suspicious of Georgia Legal Services, not least because of the program's early history, when leaders of Georgia Indigents Legal Services (the bar-sponsored organization) procured separate funding for GLSP. Moreover, the program's second director, Greg Dallaire, did not get along well with state and local bar leaders. His brash personality may have fueled the expansion of the program throughout the state, but it also clashed with the conservative nature of most Georgia lawyers. Dallaire lasted only a year, from 1974 into 1975, before the board fired him under pressure from the state bar.[126]

Meanwhile, a damaging conflict erupted in Savannah, which had a longer his-tory of legal aid support than any other Georgia community, save Atlanta, but also was home to several lawyers who vigorously opposed subsidized legal services. There a simple trover case grew into a legal attack on two GLSP attorneys and the entire Savannah office.[127] The opposing attorney happened to dislike GLSP and convinced his client to file a countersuit claiming that the program's attorneys were practicing law illegally. Georgia Legal Services was a corporation, and under Georgia law cor-porations could not offer legal counsel. Furthermore, he charged Steve Gottlieb and Robert Remar with representing people who were not "indigent," taking frivolous cases, illegally soliciting clients, and engaging in litigation to "harass and fight the estab-lishment." GLSP hired several prominent Savannah attorneys, among them Frank W. "Sonny" Seiler, a former president of the Georgia bar, who removed the case to fed-eral court. There Judge Alexander A. Lawrence dismissed the case against Gottlieb,

Remar, and the legal services program, relying in part on a similar case against the Atlanta Legal Aid Society earlier in the year. Because GLSP was "organized for benevolent and charitable purposes" and was simply "carrying out such objects in the furnishing of legal assistance to the poor and needy," the fact that it was a corporation was irrelevant.[128] The Georgia bar leadership had rallied around GLSP, and Bill Ide and the Younger Lawyers, in particular, worked to ensure that the bar did not abandon the program. Nevertheless, this case was a symptom of a more general distrust with GLSP's work that finally culminated in the elimination of state funding.

Leading the attack on legal services funding in late 1975 and early 1976 was state senator Culver Kidd of Milledgeville. Calling on Governor Busbee to support legislation curbing the activities of legal services attorneys, Kidd argued that "for these attorneys to take Georgia taxpayers' money to file claims against the departments and department heads of our state, costing money in attorney fees and valuable time away from their jobs . . . is disgraceful and unnecessary." Of particular concern to him was GLSP's case against the state's vocational rehabilitation program, which could cost the state millions of dollars. Once legal services attorneys filed the *Crane* case, opposition to GLSP multiplied. Senate Appropriations Committee chairman Paul Broun was "teed off with the whole GILS program" because its lawyers harassed state officials.[129] Apart from the manifest defense of state authority in these arguments, there was an underlying current of federalism, that is, criticism that a federally funded program was the source of these lawsuits against a state. What deepened these politicians' anger was the fact that the General Assembly's grant to GLSP made the federal funding possible because HEW was matching the state's grant: the $250,000 given to GLSP by the state of Georgia became $1 million in the hands of Georgia Legal Services.

Soon after he became director of the program, in 1975, John Cromartie made light of the mounting complaints in a memo sent to the GLSP staff. He recalled that the memo "said you can't do any of the following cases because people are objecting to it: you can't sue retail furniture people, you can't sue housing authorities, you can't sue the government . . . you can't bring divorces because it's taking money out of [private attorneys'] pockets. [I]n short, we've got lots of time on our hands because we can't do any cases because it'd make somebody upset."[130] Advocates of Georgia Legal Services also offered public responses to this criticism. One GLSP attorney told the press, "It seems the more successful we are, the better we do our job, the more opposition we generate from people who are being made to feel the pinch of doing what they were supposed to do all along." State bar president Stell Huie agreed, maintaining that the program "has the enthusiastic and unequivocal support" of the state bar. "It would be a tragedy," he went on, "if through a fit of pique over some wounded wing of some public official, a few controversial lawsuits would result in some 20,000 poor people in Georgia not receiving legal services." Huie continued, "Quite frankly, we feel that it is because the legal services program has been doing an aggressive, effective job that some of the criticism has been leveled at the program."[131] Such was the opinion of many Georgia lawyers: one may not agree with individual cases, but GLSP's broader work was necessary and admirable.[132] Even the head of the Department of Human Resources, a frequent legal services defendant, admitted: "Having these legal aid programs has caused us some problems. But certainly it has meant since the 1960s that people have gone to court many times when they would have gone to the streets for demonstrations and things."[133]

The critical figure in this debate was Governor George Busbee, a longtime supporter of Georgia Legal Services as a leader in the General Assembly. As Cromartie noted, the *Crane* case was not the only GLSP initiative to anger Georgia politicians or the Georgia bar, but "*Crane* did make the wrong person mad . . . the governor." Declaring that some poverty lawyers were "philosophically out of touch with the mainstream of society," Busbee suggested that the program "has been abused" and lamented the "harassment" of the state through GLSP lawsuits. While he said he would not support an elimination of funding, he expressed support for some state control over the activities of GLSP attorneys. Stell Huie attributed the governor's sentiments to "a hangover from the previous director," Dallaire, who "had some different ideas and created some unnecessary controversy" with members of the state bar. But Dallaire did not push Busbee into this critical stance; *Crane* did. One aide reported that Busbee was "as upset as he's been since he's been governor" when he learned that the federal judge had issued an order temporarily restraining the implementation of the Medicaid co-payment plan.[134] During the subsequent session of the General Assembly, the court issued its opinion sending the plan to a review board, and state politicians responded by cutting GLSP funding altogether.[135]

For the Georgia Legal Services Program the elimination of state funding was nearly fatal. The program lost not only $250,000 in state money but also $750,000 in federal matching funds. Understanding that the state cuts might require a dramatically scaled-down version of the program, GLSP leaders instructed attorneys to refuse any new cases and to close as many cases as possible. To make up for the loss of nearly two-thirds of the program's budget, the state bar devised a plan whereby private attorneys would assume some legal services cases, and supporters formed a "Committee to Save GILS," chaired by U.S. representative and civil rights leader Andrew Young, to raise money for the organization. In the event that alternative sources of funding did not develop, Huie encouraged the creation of task forces within each local bar to coordinate pro bono services. Throughout these efforts the most promising cash cow was the recently created Legal Services Corporation, but during the spring of 1976 it was unclear whether that funding would be available by the termination of state funding in June. Administrators actually sent letters laying off some attorneys and retaining others, planning to keep as many offices open as possible while slashing the number of attorneys and support personnel, a plan the majority of the staff approved.[136] To say the least, the first half of 1976 was an unsettled time for the Georgia Legal Services Program.

Likewise, institutional atrophy during the lean years produced uncertainty among other legal services programs in the Deep South. Political and economic trends—that is, lukewarm financial support during an inflationary period—placed strains on legal services staff members and administrators. Even so, the aggressive practice of poverty law among many Deep South legal services attorneys, particularly in Georgia and Mississippi, continued the trend begun in the late 1960s of holding governmental authorities accountable to the law and to the people they were responsible to serve. Poverty law practice continued to bring poor people into the legal system and to seek redress for an expanding array of problems through legal processes. The early 1970s were lean years for legal services institutions but not for the practice of poverty law. Meanwhile, the passage of the Legal Services Corporation Act of 1974 promised increased financial security for legal services programs, including GLSP.[137] No state would be more affected than Alabama, where existing programs served only a small proportion of the state's low-income residents. Like the coming of the first federal dollars in the mid-1960s, the government's renewed commitment to legal services in the late 1970s sparked a rapid expansion of programs across the country, focusing on areas that had little or no coverage, including most of Alabama and much of Mississippi. The lean years were coming to an end.

4

"EQUAL ACCESS TO JUSTICE"

LSC and the Expansion of Legal Services in the Deep South, 1975–1981

T H E Legal Services Corporation Act reached President Richard Nixon's desk during the most tumultuous period of his public life, the summer of 1974. Unable to escape the cloud of the Watergate scandal, Nixon would resign little more than two weeks after deciding the fate of the proposed corporation. The act proposed the creation of a federally funded, nonprofit entity to dispense grants to local legal services programs. Rather than an arm of the executive bureaucracy, LSC would in theory be independent of the executive and legislative branches, "preserv[ing] its strength" by remaining "free from . . . political pressures."[1] Such an institution was necessary, Congress implied, because the traditional means of distributing legal counsel was insufficient. Historically, one characteristic of the U.S. justice system has been the market distribution of legal expertise. Occasional charitable work notwithstanding, elementary economics ensured that the legal profession would serve the interests of affluent America.[2] Congress recognized in the text of the LSC Act "a need to provide equal access to the system of justice" by "provid[ing] high quality legal assistance to those who would be otherwise unable to afford [it]." Such legal aid "will serve best the ends of justice and assist in improving opportunities for low-income persons." A deeper rationale was that, "for many of our citizens, the availability of legal services has reaffirmed faith in our government and laws."[3] In other words, the "ends of justice" should not only be increased opportunity for the poor but also increased stability for society. The creation of the Legal Services Corporation and its expansion during the late 1970s would be the culmination of these ideas, but the central political question was whether Congress and the president could agree on the structure of this new entity. Eventually, they reached a compromise that reflected the political environment of the early 1970s.

CREATING THE CORPORATION

In 1971 a bipartisan group of senators and representatives introduced legislation to create a nonprofit, publicly funded agency called the Legal Services Corporation that would take responsibility for providing grants to local programs and overseeing their activities. Proponents of the corporation were primarily concerned with removing legal services from the executive bureaucracy, in which an antagonistic administration could squash the program. Support for an independent entity, however, reached far beyond the ardent advocates of federally funded legal services. The Senate Committee on Labor and Public Welfare explained: "In our adversary system of law and justice, persons must have access to lawyers in order to obtain a meaningful resolution of problems. Yet many Americans are unable to afford private legal counsel and thus are denied access to decision-making forums. The committee strongly believes that it is in the public interest to encourage and promote the use of institutions (such as the courts, legislatures, and administrative agencies) for the orderly redress of grievances and as a means of securing worthwhile reform."[4] So that low-income persons could have the "same access to justice, subject to the same rights, privileges, and responsibilities . . . available to more affluent Americans," the federal legal services program should be "placed in an institutional setting which will minimize political interference with the provision of legal services." Legal services attorneys should be free to fulfill their ethical responsibilities, and clients must be able to "seek any lawful objective through any legally permissible means." Since the program's inception, poverty lawyers had been unable to provide "full and effective legal representation" as a result of political opposition to legal services.[5] According to the committee, an entity independent of the executive bureaucracy would reduce political pressures on poverty lawyers and thereby enable them to represent the interests of their clients fully.

Much of this political pressure on legal services lawyers stemmed from antagonism between programs and politicians at the state and local levels. Throughout LSP's existence there had been vocal opposition from several governors and their congressional allies, some of whom were hostile to federal funding for legal services in any form. Conflicts raged in several states during the late 1960s and early 1970s,[6] but the most contentious occurred in California. Governor Ronald Reagan urged California senator George Murphy to introduce amendments in 1967, 1969, and 1972 designed to prevent poverty lawyers from pursuing law reform strategies. Reagan had become incensed about the activities of California Rural Legal Assistance (CRLA), whose attorneys represented agricultural laborers in minimum wage disputes, Spanish-speaking residents who could not vote because of the state's literacy requirement, recipients of "Medi-Cal" when the state reduced their health benefits, and welfare recipients and prisoners in a variety of cases.[7] To Reagan these lawyers were the refuse of the legal profession, "a bunch of ideological ambulance chasers doing their own thing at the expense of the rural poor."[8] The conflict between Reagan and CRLA climaxed in 1970, when Reagan vetoed funding for the program. The Office of Economic Opportunity (OEO), in turn, investigated the charges, thought them unwarranted, and then convinced Reagan to withdraw the veto in return for the creation of an experimental "judicare" program utilizing private attorneys to provide legal services to the poor.[9]

There was also opposition to the federal legal services program within the Nixon administration. Vice President Spiro Agnew, for example, was much more critical of poverty lawyers than Nixon, at least in public. In the September 1972 issue of the *American Bar Association Journal* Agnew commended poverty lawyers for "furnishing poor people with legal counsel and effective access to the courts" as well as for "their dedication to the concept of justice and their willingness to sacrifice self-interest in order to help poor people." He explained, "I am very much in favor of providing legal services for the poor." Then Agnew went on to address what he considered a critical failing of the program to date, stating that "throughout this program's existence there has been little serious examination of its philosophical underpinnings." Answering the question "What's wrong with the Legal Services Program?" (the title of the article), Agnew suggested that some attorneys were not "merely reforming the law to rectify old injustices or correcting the law where it has been . . . weighted against the poor" but had instead initiated "a systematic effort to redistribute societal advantages and disadvantages, penalties and rewards, rights and resources." He feared that, without restraints, "we may be on the way to creating . . . a federally funded system manned by ideological vigilantes, who owe their allegiance not to a client, not to the citizens of a particular state or locality and not to the elected representatives of the people, but only to a concept of social reform." The legal services program needed restraints on these "social engineers" in order to reorient poverty law practice toward the needs of individual clients.[10]

As if staunch criticism from the vice president, members of Congress, and several governors was not enough, a conflict erupted within OEO itself that centered on Howard Phillips, who vigorously opposed federally funded legal services (then and later, during the Reagan years). Shortly after Nixon appointed Phillips to direct and, in effect, dismantle OEO, Phillips expressed his vehement opposition to the war on poverty and the federal legal services program in particular. OEO, said Phillips, was based on the "Marxist notion" that "the poor should be treated as a class apart." The agency "has not only failed to help the poor, but we've done positive harm" because legal services had become nothing more than a vehicle to pursue "political ends."[11]

Underscoring the partisan nature of his critique, Phillips suggested that the Legal Services Program "has been run by lawyers who disagree with the President's policies on welfare, on busing, on abortion, on every major social issue, people who have concluded that the only way to serve the poor is by opposing the policies of Richard Nixon."[12] Phillips summed up his approach toward legal services by saying, "I think legal services is rotten and it will be destroyed."[13] To that end he withheld funding from several legal services programs (including Community Legal Services in Jackson, Miss., discussed later) and stipulated that law reform was no longer an appropriate goal. Before irreparable damage was done to any program, however, a federal court forced Phillips from office because Nixon had failed to submit his name to the Senate for confirmation.[14]

Notwithstanding the opposition to legal services programs, proponents of an independent corporation that would fund local programs were easy to locate, and not just on the political Left. The American Bar Association wholeheartedly supported such an institution. ABA president Edward L. Wright told Congress that the "recurring attacks on the Legal Services program have helped shape our view that the Legal Services program should be provided a new and independent home," and the ABA's Standing Committee on Legal Aid and Indigent Defendants issued a report stating that creating a nonprofit corporation would "afford the greatest promise of independence coupled with permanence" and a chance for the nation "to make a lasting unequivocal commitment to the concept of justice for all." Soon the ABA board of governors adopted a resolution supporting the creation of such an entity.[15] Part of the association's concern was ethical: lawyers were obligated to pursue their clients' interests aggressively, and poverty lawyers should be free to do so without fear of political repercussions.

Along with the American Bar Association, the President's Advisory Council on Executive Organization, known as the Ash Council, also supported the creation of an independent corporation to fund legal services for the poor, albeit for somewhat different reasons. Of great concern to the Ash Council was placing poverty lawyers in an "organizational setting" that enabled them to meet the legal needs of the poor without causing the administration "the inevitable political embarrassment that the program may occasionally generate."[16] Just as important was the possibility that a Legal Services Corporation was one "step toward reprivatization of what has traditionally been a function of the private sector." According to the Ash Council, the government should not make a habit of providing legal representation for a "special group" of citizens.[17]

President Nixon soon offered a proposal of his own in the spring of 1971, claiming that he wanted to make legal services "immune to political pressures and . . . a permanent part of our system of justice."[18] The differences between his plan and the congressional initiative were substantial. Nixon wanted the power to appoint every member of the corporation's board of directors, which was important because the board hired staff and set corporation policies and thereby influenced poverty law practice. The congressional plan only allowed the president to appoint part of the board. Furthermore, Nixon's proposal would have restricted poverty lawyers from becoming involved in lobbying, organizing, and other political activities in which they had been free to engage.[19]

When the first LSC bill crossed Nixon's desk in December 1971, he found his power over the board lacking and vetoed the bill. Congress had agreed that the president could appoint all sixteen members of the board but stipulated that eleven of them had to come from lists provided by specified interest groups including, among others, the American Bar Association, American Trial Lawyers Association, and the National Legal Aid and Defender Association.[20] Nixon wanted, instead, a corporation that was "independent and free of politics." The underlying theory was that the president served the "whole American people," not the interest groups that Congress proposed to grant a stake in LSC. His public accountability would result in a board that would "place[] the needs of low-income clients first, before the political concerns of either legal services attorneys or elected officials."[21] The last suggestion—that ideology motivated poverty lawyers as much as it motivated politicians—had been and would remain a persistent critique among conservatives. Nixon's veto message was a reaction against the interest group politics of the Left, and his veto meant the federal legal services program would remain in institutional limbo. For three consecutive years Congress contemplated establishing a Legal Services Corporation, but compromise eluded the administration and congressional advocates of legal services until the last months of Nixon's term in office.

Although congressional liberals initially supported bills that ignored Nixon's demands for unilateral control over the LSC board, they finally conceded these appointments to the president in the 1973 version of the bill after failing to override Nixon's veto in 1971 and abandoning the legislative effort in 1972 under threat of another. The concession, however, was not enough for congressional conservatives, who vigorously opposed the 1973 bill, nor was it enough for many moderates, who were comfortable acceding to various limitations on poverty law practice. In the House critics of federally funded legal services introduced twenty-four amendments to the bill, each attempting to restrict the activities of poverty lawyers. Among them were the Green Amendment, designed to eliminate funding for national support centers such as the National Consumer Law Center and Center on Social Welfare Policy and Law; a ban on "political activity," including voter registration drives, transporting voters to polls, involvement in political campaigns, and encouraging anyone to picket, boycott, or strike; restrictions on lobbying; a prohibition on school desegregation and abortion cases, both of which were prominent in the minds of politicians after the Roe v. Wade and Swann decisions; [22] and a prohibition on the representation of anyone seeking amnesty for evading the draft during the Vietnam War or anyone seeking a personal injury award. Several of the amendments bordered on the absurd, such as a restriction against assisting "indigent, abandoned Watergate defendants," declining counsel to anyone whose poverty resulted from their willful unemployment (as if poverty lawyers could easily make that determination), and an expressed preference for hiring lawyers "who have roots in the community." [23]

The bill inspired similar sentiments from Senate conservatives, whose delaying tactics forced deliberations into 1974. Republican senators Bill Brock of Tennessee and Jesse Helms of North Carolina led a filibuster, claiming that legal services lawyers used taxpayers' money to advance their own political and social causes. Introducing an amendment to cut funding for support centers, Helms offered the opinion that they were engaged in "exotic social reform projects" rather than basic legal research. (In Helms's home state poverty lawyers were controversially representing migrant farmworkers.) Democratic senator James Allen of Alabama believed that the program was an "uncontrollable hydra" run by "legal services fanatics." When he introduced an amendment to protect state and federal laws from challenges on the part of legal services clients, Allen asked, "Why should the taxpayers of this nation be burdened with the cost of paying attorneys to challenge the legality of public policies established by state legislatures?" Senator Russell Long of Louisiana agreed, bluntly suggesting that "no one but an idiot would hire a lawyer to sue himself." These amendments did not pass, despite attracting the support of all the historically conservative Deep South senators, save Herman Talmadge of Georgia (who did not cast a vote) and Ernest "Fritz" Hollings of South Carolina. In all, opponents introduced 120 amendments and survived 2 cloture votes before finally succumbing to a third. Once the filibuster ended, the conservative resistance collapsed under the weight of the substantial support for LSC in the Senate. The bill that eventually emerged from a conference committee passed the Senate 77 to 19 and the House 190 to 183.[24]

The final product reflected the Senate's disposition more than that of the House and was similar to Nixon's proposal. National support centers remained intact,[25] as did the right of attorneys to lobby legislative and administrative bodies on behalf of their clients. While the bill restricted poverty lawyers' political activities and representation of clients in some abortion, school desegregation, selective service, and juvenile cases, most of poverty lawyers' work could continue, though class actions had to be approved by project directors. Even the expressed preference for homegrown attorneys (yes, the amendment survived) would have little effect on the recruitment of attorneys from outside the South. Perhaps most important, the Legal Services Corporation Act gave the president complete discretion over the naming of LSC's board of directors.[26]

Indeed, it was the bill Nixon wanted, and yet he could take little joy in its passage. While a conference committee reshaped the legislation to the satisfaction of both houses of Congress, it became entangled in the politics of impeachment, which was rising to fever pitch during the summer of 1974. Conservative leaders in the House and Senate, as well as several other Nixon advocates, conditioned their continued support of the embattled leader on his promise to veto the Legal Services Corporation Act unless it contained the Green Amendment eliminating (they thought) national support centers. Upon Nixon's threat of yet another veto, the conference committee retained that provision.[27] Compromise thus produced an acceptable bill, which the president signed on 25 July. He left office fifteen days later. Legal services for the poor had seemingly become, as Nixon hoped, "a permanent part of our system of justice."[28] Meanwhile, the Nixon White House passed into history.

Whenever a bill passes through Congress and becomes law at the stroke of the chief executive's pen, a multitude of interests converge in one document. Institutional dynamics within Congress, such as the influence of committees and relations between Congress and the president, shape legislation. Individuals sometimes play critical roles as "policy entrepreneurs," exerting influence far beyond their single vote. Various interest groups affect a politician's vote on a particular measure, either through persuasion or, less directly, financial support. Ideas may have a motivating force independent of these other factors. Often the passage of a particular bill or the outcome of an individual vote reflects strategic behavior on the part of participants in the legislative process.[29] The passage of the Legal Services Corporation Act involved each of these forces. A statistical analysis of several votes on the bill as it moved through the House suggests, however, that one factor had a predominant influence on the process: the ideological stance of each representative.[30] That is, the most influential determinant of support for or opposition to federally funded legal services was how one viewed the proper balance between government intervention in the market and private control of economic power, between federal and state power, and between legislative and executive power.

In advocating the Green Amendment, Edith Green, a Democrat from Oregon, expressed her support for "the right of a poor person to have legal counsel" but criticized backup centers for promoting "cutting edge" social change at government expense, referring to poverty lawyers engaged in school desegregation and busing cases, abortion rights litigation, and lawsuits against policy officers. One exchange is revealing:

> Mr. Koch: Is it not to be preferred that there be a cutting edge for social change applied through the courts rather than through riot and upheaval in the streets, and is it not helpful in terms of testing and changing the law within the framework of the law that those who could not afford lawyers are provided with those legal services?
>
> Mrs. Green: I would respond . . . by saying I think [Koch] oversimplifies the case. Certainly it is better to work through the courts and through the system than out in the streets and through riot. But that is not the issue. The issue is are we going to use Federal tax dollars to finance lobby groups who advocate social changes about which the Congress—the elected Representatives of the people—have taken an opposite or neutral view?[31]

Thus, Green reacted not only against the specific causes poverty lawyers chose to champion but also to their apparent rejection of legislative primacy and embrace of judicial resolutions.

This concern was among the many points of ideological tension in the political haggling over legal services. By the 1970s many liberals had moved away from the old progressive glorification of the legislatures, especially state bodies, toward a belief that the courts, especially the federal courts, provided welcome protection for individual rights. Conservatism had made the opposite journey over the course of the twentieth century.[32] For politicians concerned that poverty lawyers used federal money to pursue a "radical" agenda at odds with the views of elected officials, the national support centers that the Green Amendment targeted were at the forefront of their concern. Echoing Green, Representative Wilmer Mizell, a Republican from North Carolina who introduced the amendment to prohibit poverty lawyers' involvement in school desegregation cases, expressed particular concern with legal services involvement (alongside the NAACP Legal Defense Fund) in the Detroit busing case that eventually ended in defeat, *Milliken v. Bradley*, through its funding of the Harvard Center for Law and Education. Mizell complained that the poverty lawyers' strategy was not majoritarian because most Americans opposed school busing.[33]

Given that the politics of legal services had more to do with ideology than with interest groups, demographic factors, or other common influences on policy making, the legislative process that produced the Legal Services Corporation allowed moderates to play a critical role in shaping the nature of the institution. Moderates threw their support behind the corporation and federally funded legal services but also provided the votes for restrictive measures such as the Green, Quie, and Mizell amendments. This political calculus—moderates siding with liberals to support a federally funded poverty law program but siding with conservatives to limit the autonomy of poverty lawyers—would remain in place throughout the 1980s and 1990s.

"EQUAL ACCESS": THE SEVEN-DOLLAR RULE AND THE DEEP SOUTH

Once national politicians had produced the Legal Services Corporation Act, the real work of institution building began. The act created a nonprofit corporation based in Washington, D.C., "for the purpose of providing financial support for legal assistance in noncriminal proceedings or matters to persons financially unable to afford legal assistance." An eleven-member board of directors, appointed by the president and confirmed by the Senate, was to appoint a president with operational control over the corporation. Part of this operational control included the power to require reports from grantees, prescribe record keeping policies, and require grantees to conduct annual financial audits. The act also gave LSC the authority to provide financial assistance directly to eligible clients or to make grants to entities whose purpose was to provide eligible clients with legal counsel.[34] LSC chose, by force of habit, the latter. Like the Legal Services Program under OEO and Nixon's Office of Legal Services, LSC primarily funded local and statewide legal services programs rather than offering direct financial assistance to the poor for the purpose of obtaining legal counsel. This choice was not inevitable. Other Western democracies and many countries throughout the world have established systems to provide legal services for the poor that utilize private attorneys rather than lawyers dedicated to poverty law practice. In the

United Kingdom, for example, legal aid is available not only to the very poor but also, on a subsidized basis, to much of the population.[35]

While its functions remained similar to that of the Legal Services Program in that LSC was a grant-making and oversight body, LSC leaders signaled a philosophical adjustment from earlier poverty law practice. Rather than financing shock troops for a war on poverty, LSC could set its own agenda. Under the leadership of its first president, Thomas Ehrlich, and executive vice president, Clint Bamberger (who had been the first director of the Legal Services Program), LSC adopted the apparent mandate of the act itself: the guiding principle to provide "equal access to justice" for all Americans.[36] This goal of equal access was a departure from OEO's mission. During the 1960s and the early 1970s poverty law practice was directed explicitly at alleviating the plight of the poor as part of the war on poverty. "Equal access to justice" sounded much less radical.[37] Implicit in the principle of "equal access" was the sense that full access to the legal system *equaled* justice, rendering most law reform unnecessary.[38] The notion harked back to Reginald Heber Smith's *Justice and the Poor* from the early twentieth century. Ehrlich acknowledged that some legal services cases "result[ed] in major decisions . . . protecting the legal rights of the poor far beyond the individual cases being decided," but he asserted that "most of the matters handled by legal services offices involve relatively simple issues that are very important for the particular clients but do not establish important legal precedents."[39] The first chairman of the board, Roger Cramton, went so far as to suggest that "the guy who thought up the 'law reform' label should have been hung by his heels."[40] Law reform continued, to be sure, but concern with equal access focused LSC's efforts on the process of law, rather than its substance.

One manifestation of the "equal access" philosophy was a concrete goal to provide "minimum access" to legal services for all of the nation's poor, which LSC defined as two poverty lawyers for every ten thousand potential clients.[41] LSC leaders realized that there were vast gaps in the provision of legal services to the poor, not least in the South. In some areas—such as southern Mississippi, most of Alabama, and parts of rural Georgia, along with large parts of other southern states, Appalachia, the Midwest, and the Southwest—low-income individuals had virtually no access to legal services. Over 40 percent of the nation's poor fell into this category prior to the coming of LSC funding. Of the 17 million low-income people who lived in areas that were covered by a legal services program, only 1.2 million enjoyed minimum access to legal counsel. Nearly six million had token access (less than one lawyer per poor person), and 10 million had between one and two poverty lawyers available per 10,000 potential clients.[42] In an address to an American Bar Association meeting in Atlanta in 1976, Ehrlich pointed out that in Georgia, the only Deep South state with nominal coverage statewide, each poverty lawyer theoretically served 23,000 low-income people (or two per 46,000 people), far from the standard of minimum access. Based on the number of people living under the poverty line as of the 1980 census, Mississippi needed 153 poverty lawyers statewide, Alabama needed 171, and Georgia needed 185. At mid-decade there were roughly two dozen poverty lawyers in Mississippi, a handful in Alabama, and about three dozen in Georgia to serve as councilors to some 2.5 million poor people.[43] LSC had plenty of work to do.

The "minimum access" objective served not only as a measure of LSC's coverage but also became the linchpin of the corporation's strategy for lobbying Congress to increase its budget. LSC calculated that it needed roughly seven dollars per poor person to finance two lawyers per ten thousand potential clients. As of the creation of LSC, this was an ambitious goal. Legal services programs were unevenly spread across the country.[44] In 1976 the average legal services grant per person below the poverty level was $3.22, and the median grant was $2.29. By 1977 LSC was spending $4.90 per poor person.[45] Moreover, these aggregate figures fail to reflect the situation in the South. Among the eleven former Confederate states the average legal services grant per poor person was just $0.93. Arkansas's per capita legal services grant was the smallest at $0.34 per poor person, compared to Alaska's $21.14, by far the largest. Besides Alaska, only Connecticut ($7.74) and Massachusetts ($8.04) met LSC's seven-dollar rule as of 1976. In the Deep South states of Georgia, Alabama, and Mississippi the grant per poor person was $1.51, $0.35, and $1.43, respectively, reflecting the particular impoverishment of Alabama's programs and the overall lack of development in the region. Furthermore, the general pattern of legal services grants was that the poorest states received the lowest legal services grant per poor person. The quartile of states with the highest poverty rates averaged $1.34 per poor person, while the quartile of states with the lowest poverty rates averaged $4.29 per poor person, with the middle quartiles averaging $3.52 and $3.79.[46]

There was significant room for expansion and, fortunately for LSC, a willing Congress and supportive president. Congress had not significantly altered funding for legal services in five years, so the corporation's budget was $71.5 million for fiscal year 1975 (October 1974 through September 1975). Even before Jimmy Carter assumed office in 1977, Congress allocated budget increases for fiscal years 1976 and 1977, increasing LSC's appropriation to $92.3 and then $125 million. Thereafter, the Carter administration was even more supportive of legal services. Carter offered his opinion on the state of the U.S. justice system in a speech before the Los Angeles Bar Association in 1978. With his typical candor Carter noted that the United States had the highest concentration of lawyers in the world, but, although "we have more litigation . . . I am not sure that we have more justice. No resources of talent and training in our own society, even including . . . medical care, is more wastefully or unfairly distributed than legal skills. Ninety percent of our lawyers serve ten percent of our people." He concluded by saying, "We are over-lawyered and under-represented."[47] Supporting the Legal Services Corporation was one way of remedying this problem. Carter embraced amendments to the Legal Services Corporation Act that altered the composition of the LSC board and local program boards by mandating the inclusion of representatives of eligible clients, the organized bar, legal services attorneys, and the general public. These amendments also liberalized some of the restrictions imposed in 1974, including weakening the Green Amendment. In subsequent years a backlash stemming from political opposition in areas into which LSC expanded during the late 1970s led Congress to return to more stringent limitations on legislative advocacy and the representation of illegal aliens.[48] Still, under Carter's watch LSC's budget rose to $205 million in 1978, $270 million in 1979, $300 million in 1980, and $321.3 million in 1981.[49]

With these welcome increases in hand, LSC began funding new programs in areas where low-income persons had little or no access to legal counsel.[50] In the Deep South this meant increased funding for existing programs as well as the creation of four new programs to cover southern Mississippi and another that covered most of Alabama. First, LSC rushed funding to the Georgia Legal Services Program and saved it from having to shut its doors when the program lost state funding in 1976 during the *Crane v. Mathews* controversy. By 1980 GLSP's budget of $215,000 in 1970–71 and $1.7 million in 1974–75 had exploded to $7.2 million, enabling the institution to expand from eight to twenty-one branch offices.[51] The Atlanta Legal Aid Society's budget more than tripled, from about $500,000 to $1.7 million by the end of the decade. As with other legal services programs, this money fueled institutional growth: ALAS expanded from twenty-two lawyers and a staff of sixty in 1975 to thirty-eight lawyers and a staff of one hundred in 1979.[52] In Mississippi NMRLS operated on less than $1 million prior to

LSC funding, but that amount more than tripled by 1981, to $3.5 million. Thirty-five attorneys, thirty-four paralegals, and forty-three support personnel worked for the program at its peak.[53]

Community Legal Services in Jackson underwent two major institutional changes during this period. First, it merged with Mississippi Bar Legal Services and took on the new name Central Mississippi Legal Services (CMLS). LSC refused to fund two programs in the same geographic area, and the corporation's representatives believed the former would better provide counsel to the region's poor. Neither program was happy about their union. Barry Powell, who had become CLS's litigation director in 1970 and director upon John Maxey's departure in 1975, explained, "Neither one of us wanted to merge because nobody knew who would gain control." If MBLS supporters dominated the new board, Powell might lose his position, and the program would refrain from the impact cases that had become typical under his and Maxey's leadership. Indeed, members of the MBLS board of directors resolved "to bring forward the policies and philosophy of MBLS" through the new CMLS board. Ultimately, CLS supporters maintained their numerical superiority on the board, and class action lawsuits remained in Jackson poverty lawyers' repertoire. The second change for the new CMLS was an improved financial outlook. By 1981 more than a million dollars in LSC funds allowed the program to expand from a half-dozen lawyers to nineteen, with a total staff of forty-five, and to service the ten counties surrounding Jackson (an expansion from the two-county program of the early 1970s).[54]

The coming of LSC funding and consequential regulations precipitated similar crises within the Legal Aid Society of Madison County (Alabama) and Birmingham's Legal Aid Society. These organizations served the two counties of Greater Birmingham and five in the mountainous northeastern corner of the state, leaving sixty Alabama counties uncovered by a legal aid society. In each locale bar leaders refused to abide by new prohibitions on any one group nominating a majority of a legal services program's board of directors and thus controlling the organization. Marvin Campbell, who was director of the Birmingham program during this transition period, explained that the conflict was not overly bitter but, rather, that the bar association simply felt that it had done a good job shaping the society to date and enjoyed the notion that the society was a "feather in its cap." Campbell was not aware of any concern among these private attorneys that their lack of control would somehow allow the legal aid lawyers to engage in outrageous behavior. Nevertheless, they were sufficiently resolute in their rejection of this new regulation that Bucky Askew, LSC's Atlanta regional director, had to withdraw funding from the Birmingham Legal Aid Society and create a new organization known as Birmingham Area Legal Services. Likewise, Askew replaced the Legal Aid Society of Madison County with Legal Services of North-Central Alabama. Both programs had reconstituted boards that included local bar leaders but left them a minority among other community leaders and client representatives.[55]

In the areas where legal services programs did not exist at all, LSC worked with local people to establish them. The corporation's regional office in Atlanta played a critical role in this process, and they did not make the mistakes of Legal Services Program officials in the mid-1960s. Instead, LSC appointed regional staff members to direct the expansion process, and these individuals met with local leaders supportive of creating a legal services program and followed whatever seemed most conducive to meeting the goal of minimum access. This meant different approaches in Alabama and Mississippi that eventually reached the same objective. LSC's Atlanta regional office was headed by Bucky Askew, who had worked for the Legal Services Program's Atlanta regional office since the early 1970s. He and his staff traveled across the South to meet with bar leaders and potential supporters of new programs. In Alabama several lawyers in private practice, community leaders, and leaders of the existing legal services programs, including Marvin Campbell and Norman Bradley, formed a planning group that met with Askew to discuss applying for an LSC grant. With Askew's help they established a nonprofit organization and received a planning grant in 1976. Askew and his colleagues in Atlanta urged the group to create a statewide program similar to GLSP, and Campbell recalled that the planning group believed this was the best way to organize the new institution. Fortunately, the group had the support of the state bar, so members felt that a large, centralized organization would preclude any confrontations with local bar associations. Thus, the Legal Services Corporation of Alabama (LSCA) came into being, consisting of administrative offices and specialist attorneys in Montgomery and several regional offices that enjoyed a great deal of autonomy. LSCA began operations in 1977, opened six offices in 1978, and expanded rapidly over the next couple of years. By the end of 1980 a staff of 203 people, including 84 attorneys and 45 paralegals, provided services across sixty counties, with a budget of $5.2 million. As an LSCA report stated, "Access to legal assistance finally became a reality for thousands of poor Alabamians."[56]

The process of expansion in Mississippi was quite different, although it brought about a similar result. Rather than creating a massive statewide program, Askew, his deputy Clint Lyons, and their contacts in Mississippi—the most important being a former Catholic priest, Michael Raff, who was then head of the Mississippi Council on Human Relations—decided to create four smaller programs to cover the southern half of the state. They believed that opponents of legal services, who were still vocal in Mississippi, would find it more difficult to debilitate six programs (four new ones, plus NMRLS and CMLS) than three. Unlike Alabama, the Mississippi State Bar was openly hostile to federally funded legal services as a result of North Mississippi's aggressive advocacy and the controversy over funding between the two Jackson programs. Moreover, Martha Bergmark, who became the first director of Southeast Mississippi Legal Services in Hattiesburg, explained that local bar associations were often adamantly opposed to legal services and the judiciary was not much more supportive. When Bergmark and her associates attended a local bar meeting to discuss the new program, bar leaders had already written a resolution condemning it, stating that there were plenty of lawyers in Hattiesburg and, furthermore, that it was not even clear that there were any poor people in the area. Other poverty lawyers had similar memories about the opposition of the organized bar in Mississippi.[57] Thus, unlike Alabama, LSC funded four new programs in the state: South Mississippi Legal Services, based in the coastal town of Biloxi; Southeast Mississippi Legal Services in Hattiesburg; Southwest Mississippi Legal Services in McComb; and East Mississippi Legal Services in Meridian. They remained much smaller than NMRLS and CMLS: in 1981 the corporation provided $656,661 for South Mississippi, $646,305 for East Mississippi, $582,323 for Southwest Mississippi, and $568,968 for Southeast Mississippi.[58]

The Legal Services Corporation achieved its minimum access objective by 1980, funding over 300 local and statewide programs and more than 5,000 lawyers and 2,500 paralegals and providing counsel to 1.5 million clients nationwide.[59] From the perspective of the staff and board members responsible for allocating LSC's resources, the late 1970s was a triumphant period. The organization celebrated "5 Years of Progress" with its 1979 *Annual Report,* at which time the chairman of the board was Hillary Rodham Clinton, who had been active with the University of Arkansas Law School's legal aid clinic and helped form the legal services programs in that state. She praised the "significant advancement in the availability of legal assistance for millions of poor people who were previously denied representation," suggesting that "the greatest accomplishment of these past five years has been the development of an equitable funding base to provide legal services in every part of the country." LSC president Dan Bradley remarked that the minimum access plan was nearly complete, bringing closer "the realization of the most basic promise of our free society—equal justice under law." Bradley had worked on behalf of legal services for a decade, and the "growth and progress" he helped achieve during the late 1970s was of great "personal significance" and a testament to legal services workers, whom he commended "for their commitment and effectiveness in improving the lives of millions of poor persons."[60]

In the midst of this expansion of federally funded legal services for the poor, a pressing question emerged for poverty lawyers across the United States: how would LSC, particularly given its philosophical emphasis on equal access, influence poverty law practice? Legal services attorneys were part of a new entity. Whereas poverty lawyers during the 1960s had envisioned themselves as a cadre of autonomous activists on a legal frontier and those of the early 1970s thought of themselves as part of a movement under siege, poverty lawyers in the corporation era came to understand that they were part of a growing, well-supported institution with an ever-increasing bureaucratic appetite that was subtly altering poverty law practice.

THE BUREAUCRATIZATION OF LEGAL SERVICES

The Legal Services Corporation Act not only established LSC and provided a method of funding local programs but also gave the corporation responsibility for enforcing the act's provisions, including various restrictions on poverty law practice. It quickly became evident to local programs that the strings attached to federal funding under the Legal Services Program were minor compared to LSC's oversight.[61] To be sure, the new institutional setting furthered the professionalization of legal services and created a more nurturing environment for young attorneys, who had previously been thrust into the many breaches that existed before the achievement of minimum access. Still, many poverty lawyers chafed at bureaucracy, which they had been fighting on behalf of clients for years. Local programs were responsible for an increasing amount of record keeping and reporting that fed the bureaucratic appetite of the corporation, and LSC personnel regularly visited programs to evaluate their work.[62] Adding to this paperwork was a greater degree of supervision on the part of program directors, litigation directors, and managing and specialist attorneys. Neither the Legal Services Corporation nor its affiliates were democratic institutions, and the established hierarchies within programs grew more pronounced in the early corporation era. As more internal procedures were put in place, if a staff attorney met a client who had a potential class action case, for example, she had to gain the approval of the litigation director or executive director before proceeding. Even if administrators decided to devote resources to such a case, specialist attorneys often assumed responsibility for the litigation. GLSP director John Cromartie praised such structures as creating a "high level of professionalism" (probably an accurate assessment), and LSCA director Marvin Campbell emphasized that LSC was "very supportive" and bureaucracy not a problem,[63] but poverty lawyers undoubtedly became less autonomous during the late 1970s.

Along with increased paperwork and internal oversight, other changes in poverty law practice involved efforts to improve the delivery of legal services through increased institutional support and training, along with case prioritization, and to encourage client input through board membership and clients' councils. Whereas legal services programs had sought to ensure quality legal counsel by attracting much of their personnel from the nation's top law schools, either through individual leadership (such as that of Michael Padnos in Atlanta) or through Reginald Heber Smith Fellowships, during the late 1970s local programs and LSC shifted their focus toward training and oversight.[64] GLSP and ALAS, for example, created joint training programs for attorneys, paralegals, and support staff. Sessions included training in basic substantive areas such as family, employment, consumer, and education law; litigation skills focusing on state and federal courts; and, for paralegals, strategies of advocacy and community education in public assistance and housing cases. The programs also published manuals and training guides so attorneys could further their knowledge on an individual basis and, as part of LSC's Quality Improvement Project, produced videotapes that other programs utilized to train young attorneys.[65] Likewise, Alabama's three programs coordinated their training sessions under the Alabama Consortium of Legal Services Programs, and Mississippi's programs conducted joint training as well. The Legal Services Corporation of Alabama began publishing a bimonthly newsletter, the *LSCA Bulletin,* to share case information among staff members similar to the way the *Clearinghouse Review* provided information about poverty law cases nationwide.[66] This improved training regimen and information sharing eased young attorneys' entry into poverty law practice.[67]

The Legal Services Corporation also required programs to prioritize their caseloads, cutting back on services that administrators and the client community deemed to be less salient. As an LSC report stated, "Funding at the minimum access level cannot meet the volume of need in local communities," and, given that the "legal profession's ethical standards require that attorneys not assume more cases than they can responsibly handle," the corporation urged programs "to set priorities for the types of cases that will be taken."[68] Indeed, amendments to the LSC Act passed in 1977 required programs to adopt prioritization procedures, taking into account client needs.[69] A GLSP report explained that each year branch offices held meetings with clients (through clients' councils and by telephone), private attorneys, representatives from social service agencies, and community leaders to discern the wants and needs of the client community.[70] Although some poverty lawyers were reticent to rank clients' problems, many others were suspicious of the social value of uncontested divorces, name changes, and wills, among others, believing that private attorneys could handle such cases and allow legal services programs to focus on the more peculiar problems facing the poor.[71] Most administrators understood that prioritization was a necessity, and Marvin Campbell recalled that most lawyers greeted prioritization with "a lot of enthusiasm." Realizing that "we have limited dollars, we have limited staff, [and] we were being stretched to the limit," programs asked themselves, "Where should we be focusing our efforts?" LSCA allowed regional offices to establish their own priorities, though the central office provided guidance and an LSC staff member visited each office to help them through this process, which included meetings with and periodic surveys of the client community. In the end "the primary concerns" of each office were remarkably similar: they "were concerns that were related to the basic human needs more than anything else," including public benefits, housing, and consumer problems.[72]

Prioritization amounted to triage, a system for allocating a scarce resource, legal counsel, to the clients who could derive the most benefit from access to a lawyer. From the standpoint of clients this "gatekeeping" function had positive and negative ramifications. On one hand, "without a coherent theoretics of practice, poverty law advocacy degenerate[d] into a discretionary practice of lawyer moral and political judgment." The lack of an adequate theoretical basis for prioritization decisions transferred control from clients to lawyers and effectively stifled the client's voice in the legal process. Even if lawyers had a theoretical basis for these decisions, that basis might ignore the experiences and needs of the poor.[73] On the other hand, if poverty lawyers acted as fiduciaries for low-income persons, they could help make the difficult decisions to allocate resources in ways that maximized the social well-being of the collective client community. The alternative, of course, was to reject any attempt at prioritizing or ranking legal services cases,[74] but this was not an alternative that legal services programs in the Deep South chose or the Legal Services Corporation mandated. Instead, poverty lawyers accepted fewer cases in the hope of maximizing their overall utility to the low-income community.[75]

This selectivity generally enjoyed the approval of the client community. LSC's emphasis on client participation in legal services was a holdover from OEO's effort to ensure the "maximum feasible participation" of the poor in the war on poverty. The corporation required formal client input in programmatic decisions, particularly case prioritization.[76] A GLSP report explained that "clients, members of the private bar, social services agency representatives and community leaders all have a voice" in determining the program's priorities.[77] In 1978, for example, the program's Macon office held a series of meetings to identify areas of focus for the local lawyers. In these meetings legal services personnel; the Macon Regional Client Council; client representatives from the counties served by the Macon office; and representatives of the elderly, the mentally and physically disabled, and the Department of Family and Children Services highlighted three abstract goals: community education, increased client input, and improved access to legal services attorneys. They also made several specific suggestions that included reducing caseloads, spending more time circuit riding to outlying counties, limiting Bibb County intake (where Macon was situated) to "emergency only," reducing the number of cases in which there was little hope for success, and eliminating all domestic, parental rights, auto accident, will, and bankruptcy cases, especially in Bibb County (where, presumably, private attorneys could handle such problems).[78] Such meetings allowed legal services programs across the Deep South to gauge client and community interests.

The most effective formal means for clients to influence legal services priorities was through clients' councils and board membership. As Georgia Clients Council chairwoman Rosita Stanley put it, "Since GLS has limited resources, it can't do everything we would like it to do, so the council helps decide what are the most important problems for the program to deal with."[79] Clients councils did not develop uniformly across the region, despite the fact that these organizations received financial support from the LSC-funded National Clients Council. In Alabama LSCA helped community leaders establish a council that was affiliated with each office, and these regional units selected the client representative for the LSCA board. Where councils were active, usually in towns with an aggressive leader, they served as a liaison between legal services programs and their potential clients, keeping poverty lawyers informed of the various problems that clients faced. Alabama's statewide council vice president,

Gladys Barnes, worked with Gadsden paralegal LaNita Price on community outreach programs, especially tenant organization, because the clients' council had identified housing as a major problem in Gadsden.

Activists such as Barnes and Stanley, however, had no formal authority within legal services programs, unlike client representatives who served as board members. LSC required its affiliates to appoint community representatives to their boards of directors, hoping to balance the interests of attorney representatives, who retained a majority of board seats. Client representatives on the LSCA board came from the Alabama Clients Council, National Association of Landowners, Alabama Migrant and Seasonal Farmworkers Council, Alabama Caucus on the Black Aged, Federation of Southern Cooperatives, Alabama Council on Human Relations, Southeast Alabama Self-Help Association, National Association for the Advancement of Colored People, and Southern Christian Leadership Conference.[80] NMRLS developed close ties with the United League, and that protest organization placed several of its leaders on the NMRLS board. Client representatives were one of several voices on these boards, creating a link between programs and their target populations.

Attorneys and others associated with the oldest Deep South programs were most sensitive to these various bureaucratic changes because many were familiar with the less centralized administration of the 1960s and early 1970s. Community activists for whom NMRLS had been a valuable ally began to criticize the program for becoming too "bureaucratic" during the late 1970s.[81] LSC officials also investigated the program for improprieties during this period, and, although they found no major problems, the investigation sparked changes within the program, and it became clear that North Mississippi attorneys did not enjoy the autonomy of earlier periods.[82] Georgia Legal Services director John Cromartie related that he and his staff had similar "concerns about the fear of an increasing bureaucratization." He suggested that "bureaucracy begins quite innocently, usually in the form of procedures and systems to help us. But slowly, perhaps even unnoticed, the systems or procedures become rigid, stale, or more form than substance." While he "reject[ed] the notion that we can simply not have systems," he admitted that "demand for systems . . . [and] for reducing discretion can lead us down the path of bureaucratic insensitivity, towards encrusting our organization with rigid structures that choke the creativity and life out of our people."[83]

The director of the Atlanta Legal Aid Society since December 1974, Robert Dokson, was more forthright in his criticism of LSC. At first Dokson was pleased with the security that LSC funding brought to the society: "Having been involved in Legal

Services in Atlanta for so long (since 1969), and having been around during the 'siege days' of Legal Services when the Nixon Administration's goal was to drive or starve us out of existence, I am particularly pleased with the state of Legal Services in general, and the Atlanta Legal Aid Society in particular." But, as early as 1977, Dokson recognized the potential problems that a more centralized structure posed. In his annual director's report, a brief synopsis of the year published in the ALAS *Annual Report,* he wrote:

> On the national scene, the Legal Services Corporation has brought about stability, political protection and a great deal more financial support for local programs, but all this has its price. Many people feel the Corporation is having the effect of turning Legal Services into another government bureaucracy—where quantity and not quality will matter, where mediocrity can prevail, where creativity is sacrificed. If we let this happen, the thing that has made Legal Services great—its independence, ingenuity and spark—will die and we will become just another government boondoggle. Indeed, if we let Legal Services become just another HEW or HUD, we become part of the problem instead of part of the solution.[84]

Two years later Dokson had grown "somewhat pessimistic about Legal Services and where we have come," suggesting that poverty law practice had lost its "spirit of mission, of evangelism, of knowing who the enemies of the low-income community were and directing efforts against them." He went on: "A few years ago, I heard one of my colleagues forecast that the legal services community was developing into another bureaucratic morass. . . . Originally designed to aid people, the growth of rules, regulations, etc., he stated, was turning Legal Services into another jungle of red tape." At the time Dokson had dismissed the notion as hyperbolic, but by 1979 he wrote, "I regret to say that I believe that he was closer to the truth than I." The caseload review systems, board reorganization, compliance with various LSC regulations, planning and prioritization, formalized budget procedures, increased training opportunities, and financial management systems could individually help provide higher-quality legal services, but, collectively, they were a burden on legal services attorneys and administrators. For Dokson an overwhelming bureaucracy was a form of narcissism: "We are focusing so much within ourselves that we have lost sight of the real issue," which was "the fact that there are institutional enemies of the poor, and our role is to represent the low income community with these institutions so as to improve our clients' lot."[85]

The bureaucratization of legal services was palpable, and yet much of poverty law practice remained similar to that of the pre-corporation period. Clients experienced many of the same problems, poverty lawyers carried many of the same motivations, and the standards of the legal profession to which all lawyers are expected to adhere were as pervasive among poverty lawyers as ever. Legal services attorneys continued to fulfill their professional duty to provide aggressive advocacy within the context of American law. Some may have been "legal services fanatics," to borrow Alabama senator James Allen's phrase, but they were nonetheless *lawyers* doing what lawyers do. They used a variety of legal strategies on their clients' behalf. Poverty lawyers "gave advice" to nearly all their clients, investigated and researched clients' problems, prepared documents in some 25 percent of their cases, were involved in negotiations in a quarter of their cases, appeared in court or before an administrative agency in roughly one-fifth of their cases, and occasionally engaged in administrative or legislative advocacy. While poverty lawyers resolved much of their caseload, perhaps close to 30 percent, in one day or less, another fifth of all cases lasted up to one month, and roughly one-third more remained open for one to twelve months. Ten percent of the cases lasted more than one year. This time and effort paid off. Although more than 10 percent of legal services clients either withdrew from a case or did not follow up on legal advice and another 10 percent were referred outside the programs, nearly 40 percent of all legal services cases were resolved either through advice or other brief service, some 15 percent reached a conclusion after a court decision, 10 percent ended in a negotiated settlement, and smaller numbers were resolved through an administrative agency decision or other legal services. A small proportion, less than 5 percent, ended because lawyers determined there was insufficient merit to proceed.[86]

Statistics, of course, do not provide sufficient understanding of the human impact of legal services attorneys nor of the varied relationships that developed between lawyers and their clients, as the experiences of Beth McGowin suggest. A native of West Virginia, McGowin attended the University of Rochester before matriculating at Boston College Law School. Upon graduation in 1977, she came south to coastal Georgia, where she circuit-rode out of GLSP's Brunswick office into Appling, Glynn, Jeff Davis, McIntosh, and Wayne counties, meeting with clients at local welfare offices and community centers. When she sat down with a client, she began the interview by listening to the client's story, trying to determine if GLSP could accept the case and whether there was some legal remedy. Most of the problems she saw revolved around social security benefits, public assistance, veterans' benefits, eviction, foreclosure, or some other individual dilemma. "A pretty common case we see," McGowin related, "is when a person comes in, clearly disabled but has been turned down for Social Security benefits because he hasn't had the funds for medical care, thus providing medical records to document the disability." Without legal assistance such a client may never be able to establish such a record of disability—or receive public assistance, win unemployment compensation, or secure their home, be it owned or rented. McGowin's commentary was simple: "Sometimes it's really very sad."[87]

Such a statement hinted that poverty lawyers carried more than their professional prerogatives with them into legal services practice; they also carried psychological baggage. Despite Dokson's fear that poverty lawyers' "spirit of mission" was fading by the end of the decade, most legal services attorneys remained committed to poverty law practice for idealistic, as opposed to self-interested, reasons. For many "equal *access* to justice" was not enough; they sought to achieve Dan Bradley's hope of "equal *justice* under law,"[88] and they rebelled against the vertical pluralism within American law and American life.[89] Poverty lawyers fashioned a moral discourse that rejected the mainstream conceptions of poverty, as is evident in official reports and newsletters published during the late 1970s. They believed they were on the side of "justice," fighting against the enemies of the poor, and the reports implied this through brief narratives that related the experiences of legal services clients. Often these anecdotes were more parabolic than historical. Some revolved around the capriciousness and irony of government bureaucracy, as was the case in GLSP's "A Tale of Two Fannie Maes":

> Fannie Mae Carter didn't have running water in her Hartwell home. To make matters worse, her nearby well was going dry. So, she applied for a 504 grant from [the] Farmers Home Administration [FmHA] to install indoor water service. When her application was denied on the grounds that she wasn't poor enough, she asked GLSP attorney Mary Carden to help her appeal the decision. After losing administrative appeals at the district and state levels, Carden and her client prepared to file suit for relief when the FmHA suddenly agreed to give her almost three times what she had asked for to improve her home.[90]

Other anecdotes portrayed clients as victims of circumstance or even overt abuse and discrimination. "A Mobile woman's husband," one Alabama narrative began, "collected his last paycheck one Friday and never came home. His wife, a mother of three children, waited for two weeks, hoping he would return, before her money ran out. She had no friends or relatives to ask for help, and with her rent overdue, she was about to be evicted." Before divulging the resolution of her problems, the author noted: "The situations differ, but the desperation is the same. Every day hundreds of poor people in Alabama are confronted with what may seem to them insurmountable problems." Several paragraphs later the narrative returned to the "Mobile mother," who "didn't know how to go about getting any benefits" but came to LSCA after hearing about the organization on the radio. Within six weeks of her husband's abrupt departure, paralegal Ellen Laden had helped her obtain Aid for Families with Dependent Children benefits, food stamps, and an emergency grant and helped her delay an eviction procedure until she could find other affordable housing. "Now she's able to live from day to day," said Laden, implying that this was quite an achievement.[91]

Case histories also recorded major class action litigation that had a broader impact on southern law and social policy and often provided a window into poverty lawyers' self-perception. When NMRLS was under investigation during the late 1970s, the program used one installment of its community newsletter, *NMRLS Notes*, to document its present work and its institutional struggles. Communications director Joseph Delaney coupled descriptions of North Mississippi's impact cases with brief historical accounts of the program to describe the beneficial impact poverty lawyers had on the lives of low-income Mississippians. In particular, these descriptions recorded the civil rights litigation that NMRLS attorneys had initiated in conjunction with impoverished African-American communities. Together with the historical accounts, which related the attacks on the program from Trister's tribulations in the 1960s to the ongoing opposition of Mississippi's congressional delegation, the document suggested that whatever NMRLS attorneys had achieved had been done under duress. The first article, for example, was entitled "People's Lawyers under Attack."[92] Similar, if less dramatic, themes were evident in the reports of the Alabama and Georgia programs. Traces of the siege mentality of the early 1970s persisted.

While most Americans continued to view poverty as the product of individual failure or moral turpitude, legal services program reports portrayed poverty as an inevitable, if unfortunate, occurrence or as the result of malevolent social, political, and economic forces. Consequently, those who worked on behalf of the poor generally thought of themselves as virtuous. They sometimes displayed a martial spirit, which Alfred Bragg III exemplified upon his appointment as senior staff attorney in Georgia's

Macon office. Quoting Shakespeare, he wrote: "Once more! Unto the breach, dear friends, once more!"[93] When asked to explain his longevity with the Atlanta Legal Aid Society, Bill Brennan exclaimed, "The outrage, the unfairness of what I see seems to propel me forward to the next thing, whatever it is." Thus, he said, "what makes me want to go to work is to go back to war."[94]

Because their intellectual development had taken place in the world of Vietnam and the antiwar movement, the struggle for women's liberation, the rise and assimilation of the counterculture, and the emerging politics of identity, poverty lawyers who practiced during the late 1970s were not unfamiliar with conflict. For many of them this social strife was their education, and they learned that opposition, not consensus, was a necessary means to a more equitable end. GLSP's Mary Margaret Oliver, for example, recalled being "in the middle of a political environment" characterized by acrimony over the war that culminated in the Kent State University tragedy on 4 May 1970. Although she was not politically active herself at the time—she signed petitions and wore a POW bracelet but did not march or go to Chicago in 1968—she was acutely aware of the world around her and embraced the opportunity for action that legal services practice offered.[95]

Sometimes this oppositional sentiment poured from these personal experiences inward into legal services programs themselves. Noting that many legal services lawyers were "anti-authority," Robert Dokson felt "that worked great when you're directing those efforts toward the welfare department or the housing authority, or a ghetto merchant, but the same personality traits would go toward authority within." Indeed, internal tensions contributed to Dokson's increasing frustration as director of Atlanta Legal Aid and his departure from the program in 1980.[96] GLSP's John Cromartie agreed that "legal services has a way of fighting within itself."[97] In the early years racial and gender tensions among legal services personnel had been largely absent from programs, partly because few minorities and women had held positions as either administrators or staff attorneys, but by the late 1970s African-American and female attorneys became more plentiful and more conscious of their personal status. To varying degrees among Deep South programs, internal groups met to discuss common concerns such as preventing discrimination and broadening affirmative action within legal services. In 1978, for example, during a meeting of thirty-seven GLSP women—including management, lawyers, paralegals, and support staff—members of the support staff highlighted the fact that there was no consistent policy governing job advancement, pregnancy leave, or other personnel decisions. Others complained that the program's insurance policy did not cover maternity benefits for single mothers, and many were particularly interested in GLSP's affirmative action plan.[98] Likewise, African-American attorneys voiced concerns about minority representation among management, attorneys, and support personnel (the latter group being predominantly black). They did not do so uniformly across programs. At NMRLS, to point out the most drastic case, black leadership was predominant during the period, thus precluding much of that debate. But in Georgia GLSP's African-American lawyers, paralegals, and support personnel created an Organization of Black Employees to promote their interests within the program, especially in the wake of budget cuts during the early 1980s. Their primary concern was ensuring that GLSP maintained a vibrant affirmative action policy.[99] Despite these confrontations, racial and gender disputes did not generally rise to the level of disrupting poverty lawyers' professional work, even if such disputes caused periods of anger and discomfort.[100]

Not every law student aspired to work in this environment, and those who did embarked, in many respects, on a countercultural career path. Many identified with underrepresented groups—African Americans, women, the less affluent—and some drew their inspiration from antiwar protests. They tended to embrace diversity and resist traditional ways of thinking.[101] Poverty law practice also held less stringent expectations with regard to personal style, and some poverty lawyers took advantage of this greater flexibility to wear more casual clothing and longer hair than their counterparts in private practice. Perhaps most significantly, material gain was not to be their reward, at least while they remained in legal services. Finally, even as they confirmed some of the legal profession's most respected creeds—"equal access to justice" reinforced the notion of the law as a universal means of settling disputes and maintaining social stability—poverty lawyers constituted a unique segment of the bar. Unlike any other group of attorneys, including those who worked for the government, they received public funds to provide basic legal services. Economic incentives such as billable hours requirements, which were becoming more prevalent during this time period, simply did not affect poverty law practice.[102]

From the perspective of poor people in the Deep South, minimum access to legal services meant that it became easier to obtain legal counsel. With it there simply were more poverty lawyers scattered around the region. Otherwise, new clients faced problems depressingly similar to those faced by legal services clients of the 1960s and early 1970s. These problems revolved around sustenance and consumption: the difficulty of the former and desire for the latter. Since the 1960s most legal services cases fell into one of four categories—income maintenance, housing, consumer, and domestic cases—although civil rights disputes were also prominent in the Deep South. The proportions of each category differed among legal services programs, but by and large poverty law practice was becoming more uniform across the region.

Nevertheless, legal services clients remained members of a distinctive segment of the populace, and the structure of U.S. social policy encouraged Americans to think of public aid recipients as a distinctive group. Legal services itself reflected this reality because eligibility for free legal counsel required a "means test"; that is, only those whose incomes fell below a certain level—specifically, 125 percent of the official poverty level—were eligible for free legal counsel. If the official poverty line was $6,475 per year for a family of four, as it was in 1978, any family of four that earned more than $8,100 was not eligible to seek out a poverty lawyer, even though members of such families probably could not afford a private attorney.[103] Other public policies reinforced this distinctiveness by creating categories of people based on their income (or lack thereof). Aid to Families with Dependent Children, Medicaid, food stamps, and public housing, for example, involved means tests that made these benefits available only to the poorest of the poor. Because there was no guaranteed annual income or comprehensive health insurance available to all Americans, mainstream attitudes toward these means-tested social programs reflected attitudes toward the perceived recipients. In a "land of opportunity," Michael B. Katz proffered in his historical study of welfare in the United States, "poverty has seemed not only a misfortune but a moral failure," in particular for recipients of means-tested public assistance, such that there was a "stigma attached to extreme poverty in America."[104]

The social composition of legal services clients paralleled the Deep South's poor population.[105] Of the clients that the Legal Services Corporation of Alabama served, 59 percent were black and 40 percent white. Half of the GLSP's clients were black, compared to 41 percent white.[106] African Americans made up a larger proportion of North Mississippi's clients and much smaller proportions in northern Alabama and northern Georgia, where whites made up more of the poverty population.[107] Legal services benefited a higher proportion of blacks than whites because a higher proportion of blacks lived in poverty. In 1979, 48.4 percent of Alabama's African Americans survived on less than 125 percent of the poverty line, compared to just 17.2 percent of whites. Mississippi's African-American population was worse off (55.4 and 18.1 percent, respectively), and Georgia's slightly better off (43.3 and

14.7 percent, respectively). Across the South 32.5 percent of blacks and 11 percent of whites lived beneath the official poverty line, whereas nationwide the percentages were 29.9 and 9.4 percent, respectively.[108] Other client characteristics were equally significant. Roughly twice as many women received legal counsel as men, making up about two-thirds of all clients. As late as the 1990s, a disproportionate number of households headed by women were poor. In domestic cases poverty lawyers provided counsel almost solely to women.[109] Furthermore, poverty disproportionately affected children and the elderly, upon whom legal services cases had a significant impact.[110] Legal services clients were also more likely to receive welfare, Social Security, or some other form of public assistance than most Americans,[111] and the client community suffered a higher unemployment rate than prevailed in the rest of the population.[112] By virtue of their existing problems and entitlements, legal services clients had distinctive material interests, a subject explored in the next chapter.

Just as poverty lawyers constructed a self-affirming moral discourse, legal services clients adopted attitudes that expressed their unique material interests and explained their life circumstances. The contours of these beliefs became evident in a statistical study that North Mississippi Rural Legal Services commissioned in 1981. NMRLS personnel conducted a "needs assessment survey," interviewing some twenty-three hundred low-income Mississippians to ascertain the problems their client base felt were most pressing. Significant proportions of the sample group expressed concern about their economic status. More than half had difficulty affording basic necessities (53 percent), paying medical bills (54 percent), and paying utility bills (71 percent). Nearly half said they had difficulty finding work, 55 percent said their bills were typically higher than their income, and 85 percent recognized a need for increased wages. The respondents to the survey expressed an awareness of the public manifestations of economic disparities: less than a third believed there were equal benefits for poor communities when it came to streets, streetlights, fire protection, and sanitation.[113]

Although the survey did not give respondents much opportunity to explain what they thought were the roots of these problems, nearly two-thirds believed there was a "lack of access to justice" for the poor (63 percent), and even more were concerned with the treatment of their children by law enforcement officers (71 percent).[114] Low-income Mississippians also had ideas about potential solutions to these problems. First, expand public assistance: large proportions of the sample supported increased welfare and Medicare payments (69 and 81 percent, respectively), and more than half urged the government to eliminate substandard housing (56 percent). Second, increase political participation: 82 percent expressed the desire for more "citizen participation," 75 percent advocated easier methods of voter registration, 71 percent said they wanted to learn how to draft legislation, and about 67 percent were interested in films on citizen participation and community education.[115] The respondents spoke with a clear voice: ending poverty would have to be a *public* act. By implication poverty did not derive from any moral failure on the part of the poor.

Unfortunately, certain characteristics common among low-income Mississippians would likely make any substantial changes difficult to achieve. Mississippi's poor still lived within a predominantly uneducated oral culture, in which information about government benefits was scarce. For more than half of those interviewed for the survey (52 percent), formal education ended before high school, another 17 percent dropped out prior to finishing high school, and only 18 percent of respondents had earned their high school diploma. That left 13 percent who sought higher education but just half of whom (7 percent of the total) earned a degree. Furthermore, less than half of the respondents (43 percent) reported that their major source of information was through the media, and 38 percent specifically indicated "no source" for information. Information about public assistance, among other things, passed largely by word of mouth, and Mississippi's poor apparently lacked in-depth knowledge of existing social programs. Fewer than one-tenth were aware of the medical care offered by Hill-Burton hospitals, which were federally funded institutions required to offer services to the less affluent. One-third were aware of home weatherization programs sponsored by the Tennessee Valley Authority, and half of respondents knew of emergency energy assistance. Nearly that many said they lacked information about food stamps, more than half reported that they needed information about government benefits, and more than two-thirds of them needed information about programs for the disabled. Just one in ten reported that they understood the distribution of local government expenditures. Finally, even though more than half of the respondents said they knew where a legal services office was located (45 percent did not), only just over a third of them knew what kinds of legal services were available. A major factor in this lack of available information was the fact that northern Mississippi was overwhelmingly rural: two-thirds of those interviewed lived in the countryside, and most of those residing in "urban" areas lived in small hamlets.[116] Elsewhere in the Deep South similar environments likely produced similar social characteristics in the pool of potential clients, especially outside urban areas such as Atlanta, Birmingham, and Jackson.[117]

As subsequent chapters will suggest, the socioeconomic characteristics of legal services clients determined the legal problems they faced and, therefore, the dilemmas that confronted poverty lawyers. Poor people had distinctive material interests, most notably the preservation and expansion of public assistance.[118] Low-income families in the South were also disproportionately African-American, and impoverished African Americans faced not only financial barriers but also racial barriers that persisted into the 1980s. Furthermore, women often confronted problems in the context of their status as wives and mothers for which they sought out legal counsel. Ultimately, the bureaucratization of legal services was a less significant influence on poverty law practice than the problems poor people faced day to day as a result of their distinctive material interests and socioeconomic status. The achievement of LSC's equal access initiative meant that more of these interests entered the legal system during the late 1970s and, as a result, American legal culture became more and more pervasive in the lives of the poor.

5

LOW-INCOME FAMILIES, POVERTY
LAWYERS, AND THE REGULATORY STATE

WITH the expansion of legal services programs, poor people in the Deep South and elsewhere became increasingly integrated into American legal culture. Law became more relevant as rights and entitlements that existed on paper came to shape their lives. For most poor people, joining the legal culture meant interacting with governing entities designed to become involved in the lives of U.S. citizens. Indeed, "for the American poor, the raw material of experience and consciousness is no longer shaped primarily by historical relation to the forces of industry, but by relation to the welfare state."[1] Although the market and the family were primarily private institutions, they became less so during the twentieth century. Laws protected consumers from abuses in the marketplace; extended public assistance to persons in need of housing, health care, and income; and clarified family relationships and responsibilities. The regulatory state affected nearly every aspect of American society, from business practices involving billions of dollars to everyday interactions in the marketplace, workplace, and home. That public apparatus had affected the lives of low-income Americans for some time, in particular since the New Deal. Poverty lawyers brought the regulatory state deeper into the lives of the poor and deeper into southern law and social policy while simultaneously giving their clients more power in their interactions with federal and state authorities as well as private parties.

Governmental regulation of economic and social relationships had increased with the rise of industrial capitalism, taken root during the early twentieth century, and thrived since the New Deal. Rather than the laissez-faire ethos of the nineteenth century, Americans came to accept modest government oversight as the United States became increasingly dense, diverse, and dynamic. By 1920 westward expansion had slowed, the frontier had effectively disappeared, and half of all Americans lived in cities and towns, compared to about 20 percent on the eve of the Civil War. Along with folks leaving the countryside for urban living, millions of immigrants flooded into the United States, settling mostly in cities and augmenting the nation's cultural diversity.

Industrial growth fueled a massive expansion of the U.S. economy; the gross national product jumped fivefold, from $7 billion in 1860 to $35 billion in 1920. Railroads connected East to West, factories provided work for millions of (primarily) city dwellers, and the "captains of industry" became dominant figures in American society. One public response to these trends was increased state regulation of the economy, especially the activities of powerful corporations, through statutes and administrative agencies. The New Deal created a more active, entrenched regulatory structure that emanated from Washington, D.C., and expanded in the aftermath of World War II.[2]

Government attention also turned to social relations. Since the early nineteenth century authorities had sought to curb various forms of "deviance" from middle-class norms.[3] One group that became the subject of public interest because of its alleged deviance was the poor, for whom local governing bodies created the poorhouse, "outdoor relief," and later "mothers' pensions." The federal government joined this relief effort during the Depression, creating several programs of public assistance, including aid to the elderly, the disabled, and families with dependent children. During the 1960s and early 1970s these entitlement programs grew substantially, especially Aid to Families with Dependent Children (AFDC), and the nature of the relief programs changed. Rather than a form of deviance, social engineers began to see poverty as an inevitable by-product of capitalism, and many believed that government should assume some responsibility in ameliorating the conditions of the poor. Yet the growing government aid of the twentieth century was not simply a product of altruism but also an effort to ensure social stability among the less affluent and to regulate the labor market.[4]

Another area of social relations in which government took great interest was the family. As one legal historian has written, "Judicial maintenance replaced patriarchy during the course of the nineteenth century, and the fate of the family, like the fate of the economy, became a matter of public regulation."[5] This included the rules by which mismatched couples could end their marriage as well as judicial oversight of child custody disputes, sexual behavior (including abortion and birth control), and mistreatment within the household. Some state involvement in family life diminished during the twentieth century—especially with the rise of no-fault divorce and the invocation of a right to privacy—but marital status remained a significant legal category and divorce a judicial process. Moreover, in areas such as domestic abuse and neglect, social workers became more prominent actors, as the state was willing to intervene when parents could not or would not care for their children or spouses failed to treat each other according to publicly accepted standards.[6] For legal aid and legal services programs the "dominance of family matters reflect[ed] the growing role of the state within the domestic sphere."[7]

State regulation of economic and social relationships has waxed and waned but has nevertheless remained a prominent feature of the modern American legal order. During the 1970s poverty lawyers utilized some elements of the regulatory state to their clients' benefit, seeking consumer protection and public assistance. They also represented clients in divorce proceedings, believing such advocacy to be beneficial in the context of abusive or otherwise unsatisfying marriages. On occasion, however, state intervention seemed threatening, as when legal services clients stood to lose custody of their children to protective state officials. In any case poverty lawyers enmeshed their clients in the regulatory state and, when possible, bent statutes and public policy to the interests of the poor. That effect was not always possible given the competing interests that poverty lawyers and poor people encountered within the marketplace, welfare state, and family, but, win or lose, poverty lawyers and their clients put their trust in the legal system as an effective ally against and within the regulatory state.

THE MARKETPLACE

Representing low-income consumers made up a large proportion of poverty law practice in the Deep South and throughout the United States. In Alabama nearly one-fifth of all cases during the late 1970s involved consumer disputes,[8] and other Deep South programs handled only slightly lower percentages.[9] Although consumer law existed to protect lenders' capital as much as to protect consumers, poverty lawyers nonetheless used state and federal statutes to protect their clients from abuses in the marketplace. In general abuses went unchecked unless low-income persons faced a financial crisis, the most common being debt delinquency. As GLSP's Rufe McCombs put it, many of her clients were "in arrears," their circumstances complicated because they were often "unemployed, living from domestic job to domestic job, or from laborer job to laborer job, and most often lacking formal education." More than a few had purchased items they really could not afford or signed financing agreements they did not understand.[10] Without access to a lawyer, low-income individuals who defaulted on a debt had no choice but to submit to the garnishment of their wages or, worse, the repossession of personal property or loss of their home, even if the original financing agreement was somehow illegal.

Legal services attorneys adopted a perspective about these disputes that reflected their representation of debtors, rather than creditors. A Georgia Legal Services Program report suggested that debt delinquency was often "the result of an unexpected financial hardship" and not necessarily the client's fault.[11] The newly created Legal Services Corporation of Alabama added that "consumers of all classes need to exercise caution in the marketplace, but the poor are especially vulnerable to exploitation," while another LSCA report offered that such problems were "compounded by a poor person's vulnerability to exploitation and dependence on 'easy credit' for necessities."[12] Poverty lawyers could not claim hardship or gullibility to lighten their client's debt load, but there were legal remedies, notably the federal Truth in Lending Act and, in Georgia, the Industrial Loan Act. Legal services programs in the Deep South adopted, to varying degrees, GLSP's philosophy "that no debt should be presumed legally owing until all aspects of the transaction have been given a strict and thorough scrutiny for possible illegalities."[13]

Attorneys working for the newly established Legal Services Corporation of Alabama, like poverty lawyers elsewhere, represented thousands of low-income consumers faced with a variety of problems. They helped clients file for bankruptcy, enforce contracts and warranties, challenge unfair sales practices, and defend against debt collectors. Attorneys tended to resolve these problems quickly, closing roughly half of consumer cases within a month, more than one-quarter in just a day.[14] Sometimes just the threat of legal action brought the desired results.[15] Yet, even though many of the problems with which they dealt were quite simple to address, "'routine' matters often assume[d] crisis proportions" from the client's perspective.[16] An elderly Dothan couple, for example, ordered cookware by mail one May, paid their last installment by July, but had yet to receive the product that October. After complaining to the state Office of Consumer Protection, they contacted staff attorney Ken Taylor on 1 December; he wrote and called the cookware distributor, and the pots and pans arrived before Christmas.[17]

Many cases required more complex activity. Luvenia Blevins of Selma hired a siding company to make improvements to her home's exterior. She thought the new siding, plus other improvements the door-to-door salesman had promised, would cost thirty-seven hundred dollars, so Blevins was surprised to learn that her payments over seven years would come to nearly six thousand dollars. Nevertheless, she attempted to repay her debt until she became ill and was unable to work; when she fell behind in her payments, the finance company (which had acquired the debt from the home improvement contractor) holding the mortgage on her house began foreclosure proceedings. Blevins then contacted LSCA staff attorney Richard Ebbinghouse, who won a temporary restraining order preventing the sale and then filed a complaint against the finance company. It turned out that Blevins was not alone: the finance company held mortgages on forty-two houses across the state that it had acquired from the siding company. Upon their analysis of these contracts LSCA attorneys found that the initial agreements contained several violations of Truth in Lending regulations, including the failure to disclose interest charges and to notify the buyer of her right to rescind the contract within a three-day "cooling off" period (helpful when companies used high-pressure sales tactics). Blevins had made her own situation worse by signing a contract that did not even list the charges she would incur; those parts of the contract had been left blank. In this and other similar cases legal services clients won financial reprieve, often retaining possession of their home or other personal property.[18]

The Truth in Lending Act became a useful tool to protect low-income consumers. Congress enacted the act in 1968 because, in the words of its authors, an "informed use of credit" would enhance "economic stabilization" and strengthen "the competition among the various financial institutions . . . engaged in the extension of consumer credit." Moreover, a greater openness on the part of lenders would help "protect the consumer against inaccurate and unfair credit billing and credit card practices." The act required creditors to disclose all costs to consumers in the loan contract, lest the contract be considered illegal. Poverty lawyers found that many of their clients had signed contracts to buy furniture, appliances, and other household goods that violated the Truth in Lending Act, and thus, the act became a "potent weapon" in their legal arsenal.[19]

Legal services attorneys had begun utilizing the Truth in Lending Act during the early 1970s. Stanley Taylor pursued alleged Truth in Lending violations while at North Mississippi,[20] and CLS attorneys in southern Mississippi made it possible for debtors to seek damages under the Truth in Lending Act in state courts and forced a Jackson merchant to abide by these regulations.[21] Truth in Lending became such an important part of GLSP's consumer litigation that the program created a manual that correlated each section of the act with all of the corresponding reported cases and administrative decisions.[22] Rufe McCombs, who was instrumental in the creation of the Columbus Legal Aid Society and its subsequent merger into Georgia Legal Services, also began pursuing Truth in Lending challenges during the early 1970s. In one case her client's creditor had charged fees that were not included in the contract; a federal judge awarded her client almost a thousand dollars in penalties.[23] Georgia Legal Services attorneys also represented a group of people who had purchased cancer insurance (called "CancerCare") from a company that failed to disclose all of the terms of the policy. Each won rewards of between one hundred and one thousand dollars. There were numerous such cases throughout the decade.[24]

Prior to her involvement with GLSP, McCombs had attended the University of Georgia School of Law and begun her career in the 1940s with the Department of Agriculture, before entering private practice in 1950. By McCombs's own account her law practice "was not anything to brag about. My gender, while not keeping me from pursuing law, did inhibit me from pursuing high-profile cases. During that time, about the only law cases entrusted to women were divorce cases (of which there weren't many), title searching, deeds, and drafting wills." Later in the decade she left practice to raise a family. When McCombs eventually sought to return to practice in Columbus, a friend and prominent local lawyer advised her that "Columbus is just not ready." Around that time the talk of creating a statewide legal services program had commenced, and McCombs soon "decided that opening an office to serve indigent clients was something I really wanted to do—with or without the funding," so she relied on local charitable contributions to create the Columbus Legal Aid Society. Her organization merged with GLSP during GLSP's expansion of the early 1970s, and McCombs remained with the program until 1975. She went on to become a municipal court and then superior court judge after leaving poverty law practice.[25]

McCombs and her small office, with the help of GLSP specialist Harry Pettigrew, waged a campaign against a local collection agency and several merchants accused of Truth in Lending violations. The agency, owned by one of Columbus's "society women," intimidated debtors into paying illegal fees; several clients had come into her office frightened about having to serve jail time. "Angry over her bully tactics," McCombs "was determined to challenge her image" of gentility. Accordingly, she and Pettigrew filed racketeering charges in federal court claiming that the collection agency's tactics amounted to extortion. The legal action soon put the agency out of business. Meanwhile, during the course of research McCombs and Pettigrew discovered numerous Truth in Lending violations on the part of local merchants who had relied on the agency to collect debts. One merchant, who happened to be McCombs's next-door neighbor, asked her to drop the case against him, saying, "Don't you think they [his customers] ought to pay for the merchandise?" It was a not-so-subtle attempt to appeal to McCombs's class allegiance, which in this case was not as powerful as her adherence to the law.[26]

Like the Truth in Lending Act and other federal statutes, state consumer protection laws provided a means of advocacy for low-income consumers. Georgia's Industrial Loan Act (GILA), for example, enabled lenders to extend small amounts of credit to low-income clients at higher rates of interest than typical loans. The statute included, however, a stiff penalty if loan companies violated its provisions: they would forfeit the entire remaining balance of the loan.[27] Atlanta Legal Aid and Georgia Legal Services lawyers realized during the early 1970s that many GILA contracts contained violations of the act. Once they brought these flaws to the attention of the courts, state judges declared hundreds of loan contracts null and void, meaning that the legal services clients were not required to repay the remainder of the loans.

Atlanta Legal Aid attorneys won the precedential decision, *Lewis v. Termplan*, in 1971. David Webster and his colleagues represented David and Viola Lewis, who were supposed to repay $480 in twenty-four monthly installments of $20. After making eight payments, all late, the loan company initiated legal proceedings against the couple based on a clause in the loan contract that stipulated that the entire loan could be accelerated if the debtor failed to make timely payments. When Termplan attempted to garnish the Lewises' wages, a legal process whereby lenders received payments directly out of the debtor's paycheck, the Lewises contacted ALAS. Legal Aid lawyers not only defended their clients against the garnishment effort but went farther to argue that the entire loan contract violated the Georgia Industrial Loan Act. According to David Webster, Termplan had accelerated the loan but failed to recalculate the interest due on the initial loan; in effect, then, the contract required the Lewises to repay more interest than GILA allowed. The Georgia Court of Appeals agreed, declaring the entire loan contract void. The Lewises, who had already repaid $165, did not have to continue paying off the loan.[28]

Attorneys in Atlanta and, after the creation of GLSP, across the state began examining these loan contracts with attention to detail, exploiting any violation of the GILA. According to several lawyers, virtually every contract contained some violation of the act.[29] If the lawyer could find such a violation, the client did not have to repay the loan. In one case, for example, lawyers argued that a loan contract was void because it extended for a period of two years and fourteen days, while GILA required the loans to be limited to a two-year period.[30] In another case the state Court of Appeals voided a contract that extended for two years and one day.[31] Through the early 1970s consumer lawyers for both ALAS and GLSP became increasingly astute in discovering obscure violations of the loan act.[32]

This effort did not proceed without opposition. Judges across the state were sometimes hesitant to adopt the lawyers' arguments. A state appeals court judge lamented that "the fashion is to look under every rock, comb with a fine tooth comb, place every transaction under an electronic microscope, and find some basis, however miniscule, however lacking in harm, however strained in construction, for declaring void a loan made in good faith by a lawful lender to a borrower, who has utterly failed to repay or keep his obligation." Unfortunately, in the minds of an increasing number of judges, "it appears that an increasing number of people, otherwise thought to be of good judgment, have become overcome by some sort of notion that everyone but a consumer must act responsibly."[33] Soon these sentiments reached the state Capitol in Atlanta and resulted in a legislative backlash.

The case of Buddy and Pauline Peppers represented the peak of poverty lawyers' success in utilizing the GILA on behalf of their clients. The Peppers contacted Georgia Legal Services after the Barrow County sheriff confiscated their truck, car, and furniture to sell at a public auction to repay a debt. According to the Peppers, they had stopped making payments when the loan company closed its Winder office without giving the couple notice of its new address. Attorney Marcus Brown Jr. won a temporary restraining order halting the sale, and two months later a county Superior Court judge gave the property back to the Peppers because he found that the loan agreement contained an illegal overcharge. Several loan companies, realizing that they stood to lose millions of dollars annually in reduced fees and interest payments, hired twenty-three law firms to take their claims to the Georgia Supreme Court against the Peppers and GLSP. The state's highest court, however, left the Peppers's victory intact.[34] The case had an immediate impact on the Peppers family: they did not lose their belongings, and, because the loan contract violated the GILA, they no longer had to repay the debt. Consumer law specialist Charles Baird noted that, as far as other low-income consumers were concerned, "the *Peppers* decision has given GLSP clients a great deal of leverage with small loan companies, and has reduced fees on [GILA] loans by millions of dollars per year." Each individual borrower saved about twenty dollars in fees, but just as significant was the message the decision sent to the loan industry that legal services lawyers would closely scrutinize all loan contracts.

Loan companies were predictably dissatisfied with this turn of events. They began to lobby the General Assembly to change the GILA's penalty provisions, and in 1978 they convinced state politicians to weaken the penalty from nullification of the entire loan to a forfeiture of the interest. When it became evident that these changes did not sufficiently promote the interests of the loan companies, the assembly further weakened the penalty in 1980. Courts quickly adhered to the legislative developments, so legal services lawyers could no longer ask judges to declare a loan contract null and void due to any inherent flaw. Baird's elation over the *Peppers* decision had turned to dismay by the early 1980s, when he left legal services practice. As his colleague David Webster put it, "We killed the golden goose."[35]

Even when poverty lawyers did not find their strategies undermined by such legislative developments, their work on behalf of low-income consumers was filled with frustration. First of all, clients generally did not contact a lawyer until they were faced with a crisis, such as the repossession of their personal property or loss of their home. There was little opportunity for preemptive legal actions. Poverty law practice consisted of putting out fires that had already reached critical proportions. The Peppers, for example, did not feel the need for a lawyer to examine their loan contract until the sheriff confiscated their personal property. Furthermore, deeper economic problems often complicated consumer cases. Luvenia Blevins fell ill, lost her job, and was unable to make payments to the home improvement contractor. Otis Mozley, of Douglasville, Georgia, lost his disability income and fell behind on his car payments.[36] A young mentally retarded Alabama woman found herself the target of harassment by a collection agency after losing her job and failing to make payments on a debt.[37] Poor Americans were part of the United States's culture of consumption, but their place in that economy was less secure because their incomes were less dependable. The apparent neutrality of the contract belied the disadvantages poor people faced in a market economy.[38] Nevertheless, the experiences of the Blevinses and Peppers of the Deep South demonstrated the potential benefits of legal representation for low-income consumers. These were quiet revolts by individuals and families against a threat to their well-being.

THE WELFARE STATE

Like consumer cases, housing disputes were among the most significant cases within poverty law practice.[39] Some government intervention into the low-income housing market was similar to consumer protection statutes, such as the creation of housing codes to regulate the condition of housing maintained by private landlords and laws protecting homebuyers from deceitful lending practices. Poverty lawyers represented clients in a variety of cases stemming from such public oversight of private housing relationships. The Atlanta Legal Aid Society was most active in housing code cases because rural areas typically did not have such codes. Generally, attorneys sought to identify housing code violations when a client faced eviction. In response to an eject-ment proceeding or summary ejectment ruling, which landlords could obtain without contest by the tenant, poverty lawyers often filed counterclaims based on housing code violations in the hope of keeping the client in her home and forcing her landlord to maintain the property properly. Cabbagetown (Atlanta) resident Amy Hewatt, for example, resisted a retaliatory eviction by claiming that her landlord had broken the city's housing code. Such cases were numerous for ALAS during the late 1970s.[40] Legal Aid lawyers attempted to use housing code violations offensively, but Georgia courts rebuffed them by denying monetary damages for a client who lived in substandard housing. After this case it was clear that claims based on housing code violations could only arise as a defensive measure.[41] Apart from litigation, the Legal Aid Society also played a major role in rewriting and strengthening the Atlanta Housing Code when Mayor Maynard Jackson appointed Dennis Goldstein to help in this effort.[42] Back in the courts, other legal services litigation involved evictions from private apartments and foreclosures on homes that low-income individuals had managed to purchase. The latter became a central concern of legal services programs during the 1980s and 1990s, when the Atlanta Legal Aid Society established a Home Defense Program headed by Bill Brennan.[43]

Most governmental efforts in the housing market involved not simply granting protection to renters and homebuyers as consumers of housing but also subsidizing the cost of housing for lower- and middle-income families. A variety of federal, state, and local programs had existed since the New Deal, ranging from tax deductions and federally insured mortgages adopted in the wake of World War II (which benefited middle-class Americans more than the less affluent) to subsidized, semi-private or public housing for the poor. The crucial legal question for poverty lawyers was the extent to which government aid became an entitlement, for, wherever the hand of government went, so also went the constitutional safeguards of due process and equal protection of the laws.[44] This was a stark contrast to the private housing market, in which contractual obligations specified most of the rights that parties enjoyed. Low-income people who took advantage of federal housing subsidies found themselves in a different legal environment. They encountered a variety of dilemmas for which they sought out legal counsel. Clients complained of unfair treatment on the part of local housing authorities and landlords, found themselves evicted without what they considered to be just cause, believed they were not receiving the assistance to which they were entitled, and were faced with home foreclosures at the hands of federal officials ostensibly there to help them. When poverty lawyers contemplated legal action to remedy these problems, they found that housing authorities and other officials throughout the Deep South were violating federal housing regulations, civil rights statutes, and occasionally the United States Constitution. Poverty lawyers were thus able to use the legal process to secure and sometimes improve their clients' shelter.

By the late 1970s public housing authorities had become favorite targets for legal services attorneys. These authorities received federal, state, and local funds to build and maintain apartment complexes that charged little or no rent. Even when public housing officials were sympathetic to residents, housing authorities were notoriously inefficient, sometimes to the level of illegality. Furthermore, some officials simply defied federal statutes and regulations. Legal services programs in Georgia and Alabama conducted especially potent battles against these institutions. A Birmingham case, for example, alleged that the local housing authority's methods of charging late fees and evicting tenants violated federal regulations. After a court order granting an injunction allowed the tenants to remain in their homes pending the outcome of the case, the parties, which included the Department of Housing and Urban Development (HUD) because of its failure to enforce its own regulations, settled the case. The housing authority agreed to refund improperly collected late fees and amend its lease to provide a fourteen- rather than ten-day notice of termination. The settlement also enjoined the authority from adopting policies that did not comply with HUD regulations.[45]

The Atlanta Legal Aid Society represented clients against six different housing authorities in the surrounding metropolitan area. As housing specialist Dennis Goldstein explained, the smaller, suburban housing authorities were "more renegade." They took federal money but operated independently and did not perceive federal requirements as binding, "acting as if they were private landlords" rather than administrators of a public program. One of the most salient issues was whether officials were charging excessive rents. Ultimately, the authorities agreed to bring their practices into compliance with HUD regulations: "When we sued them and beat them it began to change," said Goldstein. Even so, legal actions against Atlanta-area housing authorities did not cease. Steve Gottlieb, assistant director of the society during the late 1970s, described these legal challenges as akin to "hitting a pillow," leaving only a temporary imprint.

Goldstein suggested that the most important factor determining the state of public housing was whether or not housing authority officials could competently manage an unwieldy bureaucracy. Unfortunately for residents of public housing, the level of competence was not consistently high.[46] In many situations, such as a challenge to the Atlanta Housing Authority's utility allowances or rebuff of an eviction despite a grievance committee's contrary recommendation, litigation was the only way for residents to exert some influence over the authorities.[47]

Public housing officials were sometimes blatantly abusive to residents. The atmosphere that dominated the Atlanta Housing Authority during the 1960s, described by some poverty lawyers as a "plantation mentality," persisted in the rural South deep into the subsequent decade. Ayres Gardner, who became a housing specialist for the Georgia Legal Services Program, compared some public housing managers to plantation overseers because of their invasive and brash attitudes toward residents. She graduated from Boston University in 1977 and came south primarily because she had become devoted to poverty law but found that established programs were not hiring new lawyers like the rapidly expanding rural programs were. Although born in east Tennessee, Gardner was a "city girl" at heart, having spent much of her life in Boston, Washington, and New York, so she was hesitant to accept the offer from director John Cromartie. Because there was an available position in the Douglasville office, nearby Atlanta, she decided to join GLSP. What she encountered was a distinctly different world than that served by the Boston Legal Assistance Program (now Greater Boston Legal Services), where she had worked during law school. First of all, she was responsible for circuit riding out to three counties, so she spent much of her time on the road, often seeing clients in local welfare offices. Second, she quickly realized that her clients were worse-off than those she had served in Boston. They were less educated, often completely illiterate and unable to communicate their problems effectively, and their housing and health care were deplorable relative to those of their northern counterparts. Public assistance was so meager that Gardner half-agreed with a local welfare director when he surmised, "You know, all we're really doing is promoting prostitution and bootlegging, because nobody can live on this." The young attorney grew angry whenever her clients, already struggling to survive, became the targets of abuse at the hands of their appointed landlords.[48]

One of Gardner's earliest encounters with such a figure was in Newnan, Georgia, where James Mann ruled with a mixture of intimidation and bureaucratic sleight of hand. The residents Gardner served, who were almost all black, "hated his guts" but nevertheless addressed him by the deferential title "Mr. James." For Gardner it was "like falling into another century." One resident called Gardner after Mann evicted him for failing to get permission before moving additional people into his apartment. Those improper guests were the children of his sister, who had died of ovarian cancer just before Christmas. Gardner's client would have found himself homeless for the holidays if not for the intervention of his attorney.[49] Another case against Mann had broader implications. Gardner discovered that Mann had evicted several residents for falling behind on their electric bills and having their service terminated. When she learned that the Newnan Housing Authority had established an extremely low utility allowance and that Mann was not crediting this allowance directly to the residents' rent payments, she knew there were grounds for legal action. The residents sued Mann, the housing authority, and HUD, forcing the authority to revise its policies and winning nominal monetary relief for the plaintiffs.[50] Most important, they did not have to leave their homes.

Gardner and her colleagues confronted a similar character in Carrollton, Georgia, named Sam Stovall. One client was going through a divorce, and Gardner advised her that her public housing rent would change as a result of her new financial circumstances. The woman, who was middle-aged, white, and illiterate, was afraid to ask Stovall to alter her rent because she did not want him to know her husband was no longer in the household. "He's just really mean to women when they're alone," Gardner remembered her client saying. Because her client's situation was seemingly routine, Gardner nevertheless encouraged her to contact Stovall, who proceeded to prove that the client's fears were warranted. Stovall demanded to know why the woman was getting divorced, forcing her to explain that she had discovered her husband in bed with another woman. Then he wanted to know "what kind of sorry ass lawyer" could not win child support from her husband. (As it happened, the husband was disabled, and his only income was social security, from which the courts could not deduct child support.) Gardner's client called her in tears. Thus was the young lawyer's introduction to Sam Stovall.[51] GLSP lawyers eventually filed a lawsuit on behalf of Carrollton public housing residents alleging that Stovall violated the tenants' rights through his "pattern and practice of intimidation, harassment, and retaliation against tenants." Among the more significant claims was that Stovall interfered with residents' attempts to seek legal representation. The challenge resulted in a settlement whereby the housing authority dismissed Stovall, agreed to new lease and grievance procedures, and promised to support tenant organizations and public forums.[52] Not all public housing officials had the temperament of a James Mann or Sam Stovall, but those that were so disposed could and often did act capriciously until clients confronted them with legal action.

Along with the treatment of public housing residents and their rights relative to housing authorities, poverty law cases also addressed the conditions of these complexes. Compared to the high-rise, concrete towers of northern cities, southern public housing developments were pleasant facilities, at least at first glance. In many small towns housing authorities built ranch-style duplexes with grassy common areas and trees. Even the denser developments, such as those in Atlanta and the larger cities, consisted of two-story apartment buildings in which each apartment had its own private entry. They were not luxurious, with their cement-block walls and linoleum floors, but, with the open spaces available to southern municipalities, there was no need to pile apartment upon apartment, eclipsing the sky. Upon closer inspection poverty lawyers found that their clients often lived in poorly constructed buildings that provided little shelter from heat or cold or from the South's six-legged plague, the cockroach.

Similar conditions afflicted public housing residents, and therefore occupied poverty lawyers' time, across the United States, but the South had one affliction that was unique, if only insofar as the wantonness of its practitioners is concerned. Within a number of public housing authorities there were two distinct sets of complexes. Officials did not publicly label them "White" and "Colored," but racial segregation persisted nonetheless even into the 1980s. Ayres Gardner remembered, for example, driving into McRae, in southeastern Georgia. The "black" project was on the left, just before the railroad tracks that bisected the town. It consisted of two-story buildings with faded, peeling green paint and a dirt yard. Tree roots had wreaked havoc on the sewer system, a common complaint to which the housing authority had not responded. Just across the railroad tracks from the complex was the county jail. In another part of McRae, past the tiny downtown and away from the railroad tracks, there was a pleasant residential neighborhood with spacious lawns, ancient trees, and brick houses. This was the "white" public housing complex, its ranch-style homes blending into the surrounding area.[53]

There was little poverty lawyers could do to improve the conditions of public housing. They could negotiate and litigate but not legislate or administrate. The Atlanta Legal Aid Society and Georgia Legal Services Program were especially active in negotiating with and litigating against housing authorities about facility conditions. Legal services cases made application procedures more open and appealable, enforced federal regulations about one's eligibility for public housing, required housing authorities to charge proper rents, and enabled tenants to criticize and challenge official decisions.[54] During the 1980s GLSP attorneys turned their attention to segregated housing such as that in McRae, settling most cases out of court.[55] These efforts altered public housing administration and the quality of the complexes in piecemeal fashion. Responsibility for running housing projects was dispersed to hundreds of local organizations throughout the region, and, without a central bureaucracy to threaten, poverty lawyers had to tackle McRae, then Tifton, then Alma, then Winder, then College Park, then Bremen, and so on. Reform trickled down from successful legal services cases, as well as HUD directives, but public housing residents never stopped experiencing new problems and introducing them to their lawyers.

Whereas public housing complexes were partnerships between federal and local governments, the federal government also entered into joint ventures with private parties by providing rent subsidies for families living in privately owned developments. Accepting public funding through programs such as "Section 8" housing meant that landlords had to abide by certain federal guidelines, even though the lease agreement itself was basically a private contract. Congress created the Section 8 rent subsidy program with the Housing and Community Development Act of 1974, which amended Section 8 of the Housing Act of 1937. Under Section 8 low-income families applied for a rent subsidy at a local agency (often, but not always, the public housing authority) and, if accepted, searched for a privately owned apartment. The family signed a lease with the landlord agreeing to pay rent in an amount up to 25 percent of their income. The local housing agency paid the remainder of the rent up to the fair market value of the property. In this way Congress hoped to enable low-income families to find decent housing, promote economically mixed communities, and protect the essentially private nature of the housing market.[56]

Clients living in Section 8 and other subsidized housing faced two common problems: eviction and the loss of their rent subsidy (which could, of course, lead to eviction). They brought other problems to poverty lawyers' attention as well, such as a landlord's failure to abide by federal regulations concerning utility allowances (a failure that effectively increased the amount of rent required from the tenant) and several towns' racially motivated refusals to allow such housing to be built or to remain in operation.[57] From a legal perspective the question was the extent to which the government could regulate the relationship between residents of subsidized housing and the owners of such properties. Was this landlord-tenant relationship based on a purely private contract, in which case federal constitutional precedents required the courts to refrain from taking action that would disrupt the contractual relationship between landlord and tenant? Or was there sufficient "state action" to import constitutional safeguards, especially due process, into the landlord-tenant relationship? Only if courts determined that some governing authority played a role in the relationship could they import the constitutional safeguards of due process.

This question was particularly complex when it came to eviction procedures.[58] In purely public housing, tenants could initiate an administrative hearing process if they believed officials had wrongly terminated their lease, similar to welfare recipients' right to a prior hearing before losing benefits, established by the *Goldberg* decision. In contrast, the only protections for anyone living in private housing were embedded in the lease agreement itself or, in some cases, state laws regulating landlord-tenant relations. Rental agreements often stipulated that landlords need only notify tenants thirty days before terminating a lease. The status of Section 8 tenants, who lived in privately owned facilities but received federal rent subsidies, seemed to fall in between. A federal judge recognized the difficulty of discerning the tenants' rights in such a situation: "Where the hand of government is clear, and its path toward contact with the individual unobstructed, the question of state action is easily resolved. Where, however, the hand of government is clear, but its path toward contact with the individual clouded by the action of a private individual, the question of state action is troublesome and fact-specific. 'Only by sifting facts and weighing circumstances can the nonobvious involvement of the State in private conduct be attributed its true significance.'"[59]

Poverty lawyers in the Deep South helped to clarify this issue but not unequivocally in favor of their clients. In *Jeffries v. Georgia Residential Finance Authority* Georgia Legal Services attorneys represented five women, all AFDC recipients, who found themselves without affordable housing when their landlord, seeking to divorce himself from the rent subsidy program, evicted them only a few months into their leases. Under Georgia Residential Finance Authority (GRFA) rules the landlord could evict the tenants without the agency's prior approval. The legal services attorneys argued that such a policy violated their clients' constitutional rights. Not only was there sufficient "state action" to require close scrutiny of eviction procedures because the GRFA received public monies, but the Section 8 tenants also had a reasonable expectation to remain in their home for at least a year (the shortest allowable lease term) unless the GRFA found good cause for their eviction. The federal judge agreed. The tenants essentially had a property interest in their lease separate from, and in addition to, any rights they had under the terms of the lease itself. Without a showing of good cause, the tenants' property interest superseded their landlord's right to terminate the lease in accordance with its terms. Jeffries's landlord, owner of Midtown Apartments in Conyers, had no problem with the residents but only with various GRFA regulations, so there was no showing of good cause, and Jeffries and the other tenants remained in their homes.[60] In contrast, a Mississippi case reached a different result in the same year, 1982, in which *Jeffries* finally came to a conclusion. North Mississippi attorneys' argument paralleled GLSP's, but the federal judges agreed with the owner of Durant, Mississippi's Hartwood Apartments that Section 8 regulations left the landlord with great discretion over the day-to-day administration of the housing development. Landlords with Section 8 tenants "are, in all senses of the word, private owners," and thus there was no state action. The two courts had simply come to different conclusions about the legal status of Section 8 tenants.[61]

Another prevalent type of housing case that raised similar constitutional issues involved clients who received federal subsidies to purchase a home. Deep South legal services programs, especially in Georgia and Mississippi, defended numerous clients against home foreclosures by federal agencies that granted low-income individuals such assistance. Poverty lawyers occasionally helped clients obtain such loans. Kent Spriggs, for example, recalled one client, the diminutive Pink Shaw from the equally diminutive Hickory Flat, Mississippi. Shaw had applied for a Farmers Home Administration (FmHA) loan, but local officials inexplicably passed him by in favor of other applicants. He finally received his loan after Spriggs filed suit against the agency and a federal judge granted Shaw summary judgment. In appreciation Shaw brought what payment he could to the legal services office: a large basket of strawberries.[62]

In examining the plight of Eva Mae Roberts, a Georgia Legal Services client, the Fifth Circuit's Judge Homer Thornberry noted that "the fact situation confronting this court is routine, and probably all too common." Roberts had bought a home in Augusta with a mortgage financed under Section 235 of the National Housing Act, which was designed to encourage private financial institutions to offer mortgages to low-income families by providing (through HUD) mortgage assistance payments.[63] The Cameron Brown Company had offered such a loan to Roberts then sold the mortgage to the Federal National Mortgage Association (known as "Fannie Mae"). Fannie Mae subsequently sought to foreclose on Roberts's home when she failed to make timely payments for several months beginning in January 1974. The company, which Congress had privatized in 1968, conceived of this measure as a purely private act, since

Fannie Mae did not directly receive federal funds. But Roberts contacted Georgia Legal Services, and David Walbert and Bill Cobb understood the foreclosure attempt quite differently. Filing suit to stop Fannie Mae's action, Walbert and Cobb argued that Fannie Mae had denied Roberts her entitlement to mortgage assistance without due process by not offering her an opportunity to dispute the foreclosure in a prior hearing or other administrative process. Just as the *Goldberg* decision protected AFDC recipients' entitlement to public assistance, so did GLSP hope to secure Roberts's entitlement. Roberts's attorneys suggested that, while the foreclosure was, in and of itself, private, the impact of losing her federally subsidized mortgage revealed the hand of the government in their client's life. After several years of litigation, in which a district court found in Roberts's behalf, the Fifth Circuit decided that Walbert and Cobb were wrong. The *Goldberg* case and its progeny did not fit Roberts's circumstances. As the court put it, "The problem for [Roberts was] that those cases generally involved agencies that were quite obviously governmental," whereas FNMA had no direct link to the federal government. The company could continue to foreclose upon federally subsidized homes without affording owners any constitutional protections.[64]

Other beneficiaries of federal mortgage assistance fared better, when government action seemed clearer to the courts. Garney and Margie White, for example, lived in Pontotoc County, Mississippi. The couple received an FmHA loan in 1971 for a house worth $14,600. Garney was forty-six years old and received a veteran's pension equal to $82 per month due to injuries that rendered him unable to work. The better-educated Margie worked as a clerk in a variety store. Their mortgage payments would have been $98 per month but for an interest credit that lowered the payments to $54. Soon after moving into the home, the Whites complained of flaws in the construction. Although federal officials agreed, the builder was predictably not anxious to correct the defects. In response, the Whites stopped paying their mortgage after having paid regularly for eighteen months then later contacted North Mississippi's Stanley Taylor, when FmHA sought to recoup these back payments. FmHA now refused to investigate whether the house met its contract standards and initiated foreclosure proceedings in the spring of 1974, after the Whites had fallen more than a year behind in their mortgage payments. When the family subsequently refused to vacate the property, FmHA began dispossessory proceedings to remove them forcibly. Thus began the case of *United States v. White*.

The central issue in the Whites' case was whether the *Goldberg* doctrine applied to their circumstances. That is, was the government, by foreclosing on their home, depriving them of a property interest without constitutional due process? By the time a district court found against the Whites and the Fifth Circuit affirmed the decision, Alvin Chambliss had taken over the case from Taylor and obtained the assistance of the National Housing and Economic Development Law Project in Berkeley, California. Chambliss asked the Court of Appeals to reconsider the case in light of similar cases litigated by the Georgia Legal Services Program,[65] and the appellate judges remanded the case to the district court because they decided that the foreclosure might have violated due process if the Whites had *unknowingly* waived their right to administrative hearings prior to foreclosure. Then, reversing his previous decision and relying heavily on the *Goldberg* decision, District Judge William C. Keady found this to be the case. The Whites regained the deed to their property, and FmHA would have to conduct hearings before making any subsequent attempt to foreclose on the Whites.[66] Cases involving FmHA loans and other housing subsidies did not always bring such relief to clients, who often had no defensible reason for defaulting on a debt. More often than not, cases ended ambiguously, as was the experience of Bud Law. Law had accepted an FmHA loan to build a swine farm after an FmHA agent convinced him of the plan's virtues. When the project failed, Law nearly lost his home to foreclosure by FmHA. Although Georgia Legal Services attorneys initially lost his case in federal court in 1973, additional proceedings kept Law in his home for several years until the parties settled the case in 1979. The agreement left half of the Law estate intact but not before Bud Law had succumbed to cancer.[67]

As with low-income consumers, poverty lawyers did not revolutionize the legal status of their clients, much less their political clout. To make housing affordable for all Americans would have required a massive coordination of social and political energy. Instead, housing remained a commodity that some could afford and some could not.[68] Nevertheless, thousands of impoverished families benefited from legal counsel, directly and indirectly, as legal services cases reformed the administration of subsidized housing and secured clients' individual entitlements and constitutional rights.

During the twentieth century transformations in the delivery of health care were as remarkable as the scientific and technological advances in the field of medicine. From the late nineteenth century to the 1960s health care delivery was decentralized and health law protected the professional autonomy of individual physicians in private practice. There was little public funding for health care, although some doctors provided pro bono services to less-affluent members of their community.[69] During the post–World War II era, and particularly during the 1960s, a new perspective on health care began to reshape the provision of medical services. Americans came to accept the notion of a "modestly egalitarian" social contract that emphasized not only the rights of health care providers but also the rights of patients and society as a whole. The federal government began to enforce this unwritten contract by creating programs that extended health care to a broader range of the population, notably with Medicare for the elderly and Medicaid for the poor. Doctors, patients, hospitals, and insurance companies had to negotiate the new terrain. More recently, a third ethos has become more prominent in health care, though it has not fully replaced the existing social contract. As early as the 1970s, some scholars and members of the health professions began to argue that free market competition was a more efficient, equitable means of delivering health care than public programming. They argued that private insurance contracts and managed care organizations should replace government regulation and redistributive policies such as Medicare and Medicaid.[70] In representing low-income Americans, poverty lawyers found themselves promoting the second social contract perspective. While many of the lawyers simply agreed with this perspective, the most important factor shaping their work was their clients' material interests. Just as low-income individuals ostensibly benefited from the extension of consumer protections and housing subsidies, government involvement in the market for health care brought them greater access to doctors, hospitals, and restorative medication.

Poverty lawyers employed their typical strategies to open access to health services. Attorneys, paralegals, and other support staff counseled clients about their entitlements and represented them before health care officials and at administrative hearings. In a dramatic example of such representation outside the courtroom, GLSP attorney Phil Merkel, the managing attorney in Savannah, was circuit riding out to rural Claxton, Georgia, when he learned of a woman who had given birth to a child in her home, "a run-down sharecropper's cabin infested with bugs." She was unable to gain admittance to the hospital because she was a Medicaid patient and did not have private insurance, but, when Merkel called the hospital administrator who had denied the pregnant woman's admittance, he was able to convince the administrator to send an ambulance for the woman and her newborn baby.[71] Legal services attorneys also pursued legislative and administrative advocacy when possible. Alabama legal services attorney Will Campbell, then a staff attorney in Florence, testified at an HEW hearing in 1978, for example, in support of heightened regulation of Hill-Burton hospitals. These institutions received federal funding in exchange for promising to provide free or low-cost medical care for indigent patients, but many were not offering these services by the late 1970s. Campbell also convinced Alabama's Medicaid officials to provide disposable syringes for diabetics, suggesting that a failure to do so would violate federal regulations by rendering his clients unable to treat their condition. Georgia Legal Services attorneys urged state officials to expand Medicaid to families with unemployed fathers, unborn children (through prenatal care), and a broadened category of the "medically needy." Atlanta Legal Aid attorneys likewise supported an increase in Medicaid (and AFDC) benefits before the state Department of Human Resources.[72] Many poverty lawyers saw this administrative and legislative advocacy as a critical aspect of their representation of the poor, something attorneys regularly did for wealthy clients.

Poverty lawyers also pressed their clients' interests in a more traditional forum for lawyers, the courts. The health care litigation emanating from legal services programs involved the enforcement of federal Medicaid statutes and regulations, and several of these cases addressed alleged procedural violations by state authorities. GLSP's *Crane v. Mathews* was an early example of such a case, in which poverty lawyers challenged a copayment plan that state officials had adopted without submitting it to a review board to assess its feasibility. Poverty lawyers in Mississippi and Alabama won similar cases during the late 1970s. A federal judge in Alabama agreed with LSCA attorneys, who argued that a two-dollar copayment for doctor visits and increased copayments for prescription drugs violated federal statutes. State officials' attempt to use a portion of nursing home residents' personal needs allowance for prescription drugs was also invalid, according to the court. The judge issued a permanent injunction against these plans.[73] North Mississippi and Central Mississippi attorneys joined to prevent the state from imposing a copayment on prescription drugs in a case that also challenged the composition of the state board that sought to implement the plan, suggesting that it failed to include enough consumer or minority representatives. As a result of this attack, state officials added such representatives to the Medicaid Committee so that it reflected the state's racial composition. Another criticism legal services attorneys levied against the plan was that it eliminated certain drugs from Medicaid coverage, including those used to treat arthritis and circulatory conditions. As would be the result in the *Crane* case, the Mississippi judge decided that the state could impose copayments or cut the drug list, but, before doing so, officials had to provide adequate notice and allow the public to respond to the proposals. Because the state had not done so, the changes were invalid.[74]

Other legal services cases sought to halt decreases in clients' Medicaid benefits. In *Dodson v. Parham*, for example, ALAS and GLSP attorneys attempted to prevent Georgia officials from trimming four thousand of the eleven thousand prescription drugs from the state's list of reimbursable medications. One of the named plaintiffs, a forty-five-year-old paraplegic and mother of three, would have lost Medicaid coverage for herself and her seventeen-year-old son, who needed three prescriptions for his heart ailment. Physicians testified that the proposal would eliminate other useful drugs: a dermatologist suggested that the drugs remaining on the list were either too powerful or not powerful enough; a specialist in internal medicine testified that the most effective drugs for the treatment of muscle inflammation were not on the list; and another physician maintained that there were no efficient prenatal supplements nor effective drugs to treat lead poisoning, tragically too common among Atlanta's Medicaid recipients. Legal services attorneys argued that these cuts violated federal law, which stipulated that the drug reimbursement program "must be sufficient in amount, duration, and scope to reasonably achieve [Medicaid's] purpose, that is, 'the care, mitigation, or prevention of disease.'" Conversely, state officials argued that they could legitimately eliminate some of the drugs covered by Medicaid. They believed that many Medicaid recipients unnecessarily used certain painkillers and muscle relaxers, the most popular reimbursable drugs. A federal judge stopped officials from implementing the plan just before it was to go into effect and, for the most part, agreed with the legal services argument. While he believed that Georgia could restrict its Medicaid drug list and still abide by federal law, in this particular case the state had paid too little attention to medical opinion. Going forward, officials would have to rely more heavily on physicians in cutting the Medicaid drug list in order to ensure that necessary drugs remained available.[75] In *Dodson* the courts interceded to place some parameters on the exercise of power by state officials, but other poverty law cases seeking to prevent benefit decreases were not successful because under federal law the states retained a great deal of autonomy in formulating health policy.[76]

Another strategy was to expand clients' Medicaid benefits, but poverty lawyers found this more difficult than preserving the status quo.[77] Nevertheless, as early as the late 1960s, North Mississippi attorneys had successfully expanded Medicaid coverage to all AFDC recipients in *Triplett v. Cobb*.[78] During the early 1970s Community Legal Services's Barry Powell teamed with North Mississippi's Stanley Taylor to expand Medicaid benefits to the children of recipients of disability benefits. These children were denied access to Mississippi's Medicaid program. The named plaintiff, Larry West, was a ten-year-old boy who had suffered severe brain damage. When the federal government began paying his family disability benefits under the Supplemental Security Income program, he became ineligible for state-subsidized health care under

Mississippi's Medicaid plan. In *West v. Cole* Powell and Taylor sued the state welfare director and every county welfare department, arguing that, because West would be eligible for AFDC and therefore also Medicaid except for the fact that he had begun receiving disability benefits, he should be entitled to Medicaid. District Judge William C. Keady accepted their interpretation of the federal statutes and extended benefits to those in West's position.[79] In the meantime, as discussed earlier, ALAS attorneys had won Medicaid coverage for abortions in a settlement with immediate impact in the lives of impoverished women.[80] Such litigation became less prevalent by the late 1970s, when programs came to rely more heavily on administrative advocacy to influence Medicaid policies.

Along with representing Medicaid recipients, poverty lawyers in the Deep South helped ensure that federally funded hospitals provided services for the poor in accordance with the Hill-Burton Act of 1946. Will Campbell pointed out a major problem with Hill-Burton facilities: "The purpose of this program is to provide access to health care for the medically indigent—but very few of them know about it" because "facilities and state agencies have failed to let the medically indigent in on the secret of this program." One Alabama client, a twenty-two-year-old woman who was seven months pregnant, did not have the sixty dollars that Dale County Hospital required prior to admittance. She heard about LSCA at her church and acquired the assistance of Dothan paralegal Leon Kennedy. Kennedy discovered that the hospital was subsidized under the Hill-Burton Act but had "a history of refusing indigent patients." Nowhere did the hospital make its obligation to the poor public. Indeed, "instead of Hill-Burton signs, they had 'Cash Only' signs all over the place." When Kennedy confronted them, hospital administrators acknowledged that they were not complying with federal law and agreed to admit the pregnant woman without the deposit.[81] As with Medicaid recipients, much legal services representation of potential Hill-Burton beneficiaries took the form of administrative advocacy such as this. Some conflicts, however, required more extensive efforts. Attorneys in Georgia were especially active in utilizing the judicial process to enforce Hill-Burton requirements. ALAS and GLSP attorneys, sometimes working together, forced the DeKalb General Hospital to reassess its provision of uncompensated services to indigent patients, kept Grady Hospital in Atlanta from denying care to anyone except those with a "history" of failure to pay for services rendered, and won a promise from Hutcheson Memorial Tri-County Hospital to accept Medicaid cards as payment for certain services.[82]

There were limits, of course, to the effect poverty lawyers and poor people could have on health care policies. Poverty lawyers worked within the realm of American law; thus, they were dependent on federal statutes and regulations to protect their clients' interests. By the late 1970s constitutional challenges such as *Dandridge* seemed anachronistic, especially with respect to health care, given the increasing interest in market solutions to health care delivery. Legal services attorneys were becoming experts in health law as it related to the poor, but they could not demand expansions in public financing for medical care unless Congress or state assemblies passed laws that made such a demand possible. Many poverty lawyers likely agreed with GLSP specialist David Arnold that "health care is a right" and lamented with him that "lack of access to health care brings home to our clients their status more than anything else. Denial of health care for you or your children is a lot more personal [a] rejection than having your furniture repossessed."[83] These beliefs notwithstanding, poverty lawyers had limited resources for extending health care to the poor.[84]

Consumer protection and housing and health care subsidies were obvious market interventions. Less transparent was the role that public assistance programs played in the labor market. Depending on one's perspective, Aid to Families with Dependent Children, unemployment compensation, and other forms of relief were the products of either a beneficent state or a state intent on controlling its less-affluent ranks. The former argued that public assistance was simply an intelligent response to an obvious social problem: unemployment due to market variability, old age, disability, or the need to care for one's children. After all, the federal government began creating such programs in the midst of the Great Depression, when widespread misery left few to question the proposition that capitalism could fail, at least temporarily if not totally. To the millions of Americans struggling in a stagnant economy, public relief was a godsend. On the other hand, perhaps the government had less than philanthropic motives in creating such programs. Accompanying the economic turmoil of the 1930s was an increase in social tension and radical politics. Hungry people, it seemed, might rebel, so the political elite created programs to pacify the impoverished, to fill their stomachs and thus empty their minds of revolution. Proof that social control was the primary impetus for and result of the government's market intervention lay in the subsequent wax and wane of social programs: during periods of unrest, such as the 1960s, relief efforts expanded; but, when all was quiet among the less affluent, the federal well nearly ran dry. Meanwhile, capitalism thrived.[85]

Ultimately, the experiences of poverty lawyers and poor people in the Deep South reveal the difficulty of perceiving public assistance programs in the context of this debate. Poverty lawyers were not attempting to subject their clients to the control of the state, and their clients were not on the verge of rebellion. The vast majority of law-yers and clients had but one goal: "to put more money in people's pockets."[86] Poverty lawyers could not create jobs, but they could help clients obtain public benefits. Thus, legal services representation was a source of power for low-income Americans, one they used to improve their financial circumstances. Limited as that source of power was, thousands of families nevertheless won public assistance with the aid of a legal services attorney.

Most clients needed only brief consultation about their entitlements or repre-sentation at eligibility hearings, services that paralegals and other support personnel could provide. In a typical case an AFDC recipient asked LSCA paralegal Reggional Southard to help her obtain dental services through the state's Vocational Rehabilita-tion Service. He represented her at an administrative hearing, and welfare officials granted the desired benefits. Another client had more pressing problems. He had ter-minal cancer and, following a surgery that removed part of his lungs, was no longer able to work. When his temporary relief payments ceased pending an official inquiry into his disability, LSCA personnel helped him obtain emergency assistance and then monthly disability benefits.[87]

Sometimes, of course, poverty lawyers resorted to litigation on behalf of individual clients, as was the case when CLS attorneys represented a mother of nine children who had received food stamps for three years before the state accused her of fraud. She had failed to report the income of a male resident of the house, so the state denied her benefits and demanded that she repay three thousand dollars in wrongly issued benefits. Her attorney argued, however, that the termination of her food stamps con-stituted a denial of due process because the state failed to inform her of her right to a pre-termination hearing, which the *Goldberg* decision required. Moreover, the state infringed on the client's right to equal protection and freedom of association by deny-ing her benefits on the basis of her receiving occasional visits from a man to whom she was not married.[88] With the assistance of attorneys and paralegals, thousands of individual clients won AFDC payments, food stamps, social security benefits, and unemployment compensation after being denied such relief.

As with housing and health care policies, poverty lawyers often discovered state officials violating federal regulations.[89] Generally, these bureaucratic failures affected large groups of people receiving public aid. While the lawyers first tried to resolve such problems through administrative advocacy, they often resorted to litigation. These legal actions mirrored those relating to health programs such as Medicaid: poverty lawyers first sought to protect clients from cuts in benefits and occasionally tried to expand the pool of eligible recipients. In *Yearby v. Parham,* for example, Atlanta Legal Aid attorneys attempted to reverse a decrease in AFDC payments when Georgia officials sought to lower grant levels in 1976. The state's argument was a familiar one—that state bureaucracies enjoyed a great deal of discretion in establishing grant levels—but the federal judge agreed with the legal services attorneys' position that this particular decrease in AFDC payments violated federal regulations for revising standards of need.[90] While the challenge effectively halted this decrease in benefits, a notable feature of the legal arguments in the case was that Legal Aid attorneys made no effort to argue for an inherent right to a minimum standard of living, as had the *Dandridge* case earlier in the decade.[91] Poverty lawyers limited themselves to statutory and procedural arguments that were still proving successful in the courts because the more revolutionary constitutional challenges and invocations of a "right to live" had fallen on deaf ears.

Nevertheless, clients often benefited from this pragmatic advocacy. Poverty lawyers won numerous cases in which they represented clients seeking to secure social security disability benefits and other types of assistance. One Alabama client charged that an administrative law judge who had denied her disability claim failed to consider her evidence of disabling pain and did not give her adequate notice that she could obtain legal counsel. Will Campbell twice took her case to the Fifth Circuit Court of Appeals and finally convinced the judges that the initial hearing had been flawed because the client should have had legal counsel and been able to introduce subjective evidence about her painful condition.[92] In Mississippi legal services lawyers helped workers obtain unemployment compensation from the state Employment Security Commission. Many of their clients were women who had been laid off after taking maternity leave and who were applying for unemployment compensation. The jobless women could not receive such assistance if they left work "voluntarily"; to their dismay, the commission often arrived at that very conclusion. In a series of cases that reached the Mississippi Supreme Court, Central Mississippi attorneys protected the right of mothers to keep their jobs during maternity leave and subsequently to receive unemployment compensation should their employer elect to lay them off.[93] Such representation was common among legal services programs in the Deep South.

On several occasions during the late 1970s legal services lawyers represented clients in cases that expanded relief programs by altering public policy. GLSP attorneys, for example, made it possible for workers in the state's Vocational Rehabilitation program to receive "maintenance" payments equivalent to the amount of disability benefits for which they would be eligible if not for their involvement in the rehabilitation effort. The lawyers argued that it was unreasonable for the state to deny them such payments because a lack of funds could potentially drive the worker away from rehabilitation. State attorneys, on the other hand, maintained that Supreme Court decisions such as *Dandridge* gave state authorities discretion to shape programs according to the state's values and financial necessity. Upon reviewing the case, District Judge Newell Edenfield agreed with GLSP attorneys Wayne Pressel, Bob Cullen, and John Cromartie. Recognizing that in *Dandridge* the Supreme Court had "declined to second-guess the social and economic decisions of the states and impose on them its own policy judgments as to what was just and humane," Edenfield held that he was second-guessing state policy because it conflicted with the goal of the Vocational Rehabilitation Act to move disabled individuals back into the workforce.[94] Such results were, however, few and far between by the late 1970s, and legal services attorneys were not always successful in convincing the courts of the propriety of their statutory interpretations to broaden benefits.[95]

The most salient characteristic of public assistance litigation by the late 1970s was its modesty. There was no *Goldberg* nor even a failure on the order of *Dandridge*.[96] Poverty lawyers simply were not pursuing such dramatic law reform strategies. Why was this so? Had there been a shift in the culture of poverty law practice? Perhaps. Some of the high hopes of the 1960s were still evident, but the attorneys understood that they were not part of a larger war on poverty, welfare rights movement, or any other broad-based political struggle.[97] Whatever changes had occurred in the minds and hearts of the lawyers, however, were not nearly as important a factor as the state of American law and the practices of government bureaucracies. The door to radical changes in the legal status of the poor that lay ajar during the 1960s was shut by the early 1970s. Neither welfare nor any other form of public assistance became "property" in the fullest sense, despite the constitutional protections extended to many recipients of relief. Poverty lawyers were left to oversee the policies and practices of federal and state bureaucrats in order to ensure their compliance with established statutes and regulations. These administrations became more dutiful in their compliance in large part because of this oversight, thus eliminating cause for complaint on the part of low-income Americans. Public assistance became more predictable, more secure for the thousands of families eligible for relief, and the legal system became a resource for claiming the entitlements that did exist. Relief programs of the American welfare state never became a constitutional right in and of themselves, as some had hoped, but poverty lawyers nevertheless helped clients exercise certain constitutional and statutory rights under the welfare state apparatus.

FAMILY

Legal services clients were more than the sum of their material interests. They were mothers and fathers, daughters and sons, and husbands and wives. Out of these relationships came some of the most acute problems that low-income people faced. Marriages dissolved, creating not only personal dilemmas but legal ones as well. Child custody disputes were often the most agonizing consequences of these failed unions. Apart from divorce and custody battles, government agencies were becoming increasingly attentive to the ability of mothers and fathers to raise their children.[98] From the perspective of legal services clients this meant public officials scrutinizing their behavior and, in some situations, limiting or terminating one's rights as a parent. On occasion the state actually supplanted biological parents as a child's primary caregiver when children suffered from severe mental disability requiring long-term institutionalization or engaged in delinquent behavior. Poverty lawyers became involved in each of these problems. They guided clients through divorce procedures and child custody hearings, represented parents accused of gross incompetence, and represented children in state mental hospitals and other rehabilitative facilities. Seldom did domestic relations cases promise changes beyond the life of an individual client, but within that individual's life this category of cases may have been more important than any other.[99]

Despite their importance to individual clients, domestic relations cases, especially uncontested divorces, posed a dilemma for legal services programs. At times during the 1960s and early 1970s family problems threatened to overwhelm poverty law practice, and even into the late 1970s such cases constituted a major portion of the legal services caseload. The most drastic example was the Georgia Legal Services Program. In one year, 1972, nearly 64 percent of the program's cases involved family relations. In its infancy GLSP had placed more emphasis on reaching a large number of clients than on prioritizing cases and thus opened itself up to these thousands of divorces.[100] Not even the conservative Mississippi Bar Legal Services had such a high percentage of domestic cases; 46 percent of its cases involved domestic issues, more than a third of those divorce proceedings.[101] For the Atlanta Legal Aid Society domestic relations cases made up over 38 percent of the caseload in 1969 and over 31 percent in 1972. The proportion of divorces among these cases is not always discernible, but, of ALAS's

1969 domestic cases, 2,945 of 6,307 (about 47 percent) involved divorce or annulment.[102] Clearly, there was a demand for legal counsel in such disputes.

Many poverty lawyers believed, however, that their time could be better spent on cases that would help lift their clients out of poverty, not split up families and thereby make it more difficult for them to achieve economic stability.[103] While GLSP's Mike Froman "saw a need for" divorces and other basic services, "a lot of people considered it very unglamorous."[104] This sensibility gained administrative force through the process of prioritization that took place during the late 1970s. Legal services programs sought to devote less time to domestic cases, especially uncontested divorces. The Legal Services Corporation of Alabama, for example, noted that "divorce and family law are not priority issues" but that "family troubles" nevertheless accounted for 9 percent of its 1978 caseload. That percentage rose slowly to over 11 percent in 1980 and 16 percent in 1981.[105] In Georgia the percentage of domestic cases dropped to 28 percent for GLSP during the early 1980s, and there was a slight downward trend at ALAS as well.[106] Moreover, whereas there had been little internal regulation of domestic cases during the 1960s and early 1970s, legal services programs began to categorize domestic problems during the late 1970s. Georgia Legal Services attorney Kay Giese, who worked in Dalton, explained that organization's policy: "Not all offices handle divorces; that's an office decision. But most, like ours, will handle divorce cases for persons in need of immediate protection because of violence." A GLSP receptionist involved in client intake related that "we refer most [divorces] to private attorneys unless there are special circumstances like domestic violence or the family has a lot of children. We don't generally do divorces."[107] Other legal services programs practiced similar methods of categorizing and ranking their clients' problems.

Program reports portrayed the clients whom poverty lawyers elected to serve as victims of peculiar circumstances, especially brutality within the home.[108] GLSP's ten-year anniversary report did not include a section labeled "domestic relations" or "family law" but, rather, a section documenting the program's work with "domestic violence," which claimed that for many legal services clients "'home' is associated with fear and pain and misery," not "warmth, security and stability." The reports told of women (almost exclusively) who suffered from a variety of misfortunes: an ex-husband's failure to pay child support; a mother who won a restraining order and initiated divorce proceedings upon discovering that her husband had severely beaten her two-year-old son; another woman "besieged with extreme difficulties" that included her three-year-old son's terminal cancer along with constant "harassment from her husband and his new girlfriend, who actually shot her at one point."[109] GLSP's Giese related that "each office has its horror stories." Dalton's was of an abused woman whose husband had friends and relatives within the sheriff's department, "effectively cutting her off from police protection."[110] Mary Margaret Oliver's horror story took place during her first year of poverty law practice, when one of her clients was murdered by her estranged husband.[111] In such situations securing a restraining order or processing a separation or divorce—the typical legal activities of poverty lawyers in domestic cases—was for poverty lawyers as much a moral as a legal act. Furthermore, some attorneys realized that there was "a link between the economy and some domestic relations cases," as Albany's Willie Lockette explained. Spousal and child abuse rose along with bankruptcies and unemployment compensation cases during times of financial trouble.[112] For these reasons, in the minds of many poverty lawyers a divorce was not simply the end of a marriage; it was advocacy on behalf of the disadvantaged and oppressed, who were disproportionately female.

Poverty lawyers demonstrated a growing awareness of domestic violence that was consistent with the lessons of the women's liberation movement, which was helping to thrust previously private, personal issues into the public sphere.[113] Representing a battered woman (and perhaps any woman in a domestic case) meant confronting centuries of legal custom that had rendered women subordinate to men in two profound ways. First, American law contained explicit gender distinctions that enabled states to deny women the franchise, excluded them from certain professions or allowed their unequal treatment in the workplace, and regulated their discretion to determine whether and when to bear children. Second, American law historically did not enter the domestic sphere, such that family relations were not a matter of public regulation or even comment. The common law of tort, for example, did not generally apply to injuries inflicted on one family member by another (most often inflicted on the wife by the husband). Legal services representation counteracted the "totality of the law's absence from the private realm" and was part of an opposite trend whereby governments (through legislatures and the courts) inserted public standards into private relationships.[114]

For poverty lawyers, of course, domestic violence was often painfully evident on the faces of their clients, and many were convinced that legal services programs should play some role in halting such abuse. Nancy Spruill, for example, met a Georgia Legal Services attorney circuit riding into Barrow County. She complained of abuse at the hands of her alcoholic husband, who had injured himself five years earlier in an auto accident and subsequently refused to return to work. Spruill provided for their four children by working in a chicken-processing plant. The young woman—she had married at sixteen—endured years of abuse before her husband beat his six-year-old daughter at a family picnic, striking the child in the face repeatedly before relatives pulled him away. Spruill's patience and her hope evaporated. She filed for divorce and won a protective order. In some ways her life did not change: she continued to work at the chicken plant, live in her mobile home, and raise her four children. But her husband was gone, and the violence had ended.[115] Divorce actions of this kind were often, "in themselves, eloquent statements that oppressive, abusive, and offensive behavior was not tolerable."[116]

Believing that existing legal solutions had only limited potential for solving their clients' problems, several legal services attorneys became involved in establishing organizations that provided support for victims of domestic abuse. North Mississippi's Virginia Kilgore explained how this occurred in Oxford. She and several other lawyers working for the program decided to create a shelter for battered women after a client came to the program seeking protection from an abusive husband. The woman planned to leave Oxford and return to her parents' home in Tennessee, but in the meantime the legal services attorneys hid her in their office and collected money so that she could stay in a hotel for the night, until her parents wired enough funds for bus tickets for the woman and her children. This client's experiences propelled Kilgore and her colleagues into action. They worked with others in Oxford to create a shelter, which was first located in a volunteer's home and later received federal funding for a freestanding facility. Kilgore served on its board for several years. Moreover, the connection between North Mississippi and the shelter deepened over time, as the shelter became a source of clients for the legal services program, and vice versa.[117] Like the North Mississippi attorneys, clients' experiences with violence at home moved poverty lawyers and legal services staff elsewhere to action. Kay Giese and another Dalton attorney, Wendy Glasbrenner, helped found the Georgia Network against Domestic Violence, which worked with the Department of Human Resources to ensure that services were available to abused women, and another GLSP attorney, Gloria Einstein, chaired Waycross's Southeast Georgia Interagency Council, an "advocacy group for better human services" geared toward the victims of domestic violence. Upon leaving poverty law practice, Mary Margaret Oliver made fighting domestic violence and child abuse one of the central elements of a political career that took her into the Georgia General Assembly.[118] An attorney working for Southeast Mississippi Legal Services,

Allison Steiner, made domestic violence her primary campaign. She convinced several women who worked for the program and who served on the program's board of directors to establish a battered women's shelter in Hattiesburg and helped draft legislation, later adopted by the Mississippi legislature, that made it easier for a woman to obtain temporary restraining orders against an abusive spouse.[119] Atlanta Legal Aid attorneys also helped formulate legislation that devoted public funds to create shelters, required more police involvement in domestic disputes, and facilitated speedier court intervention in domestic violence cases.[120]

Not all divorces, of course, were responses to acts of violence or even emotional abuse. Many simply marked the end of a dissatisfying partnership or the legitimation of abandonment. For low-income individuals, after all, paying a lawyer to obtain a divorce was often not necessary: "Marriages can rot, love can fade, husbands can slip out the door and never come back, wives can betray; all this can happen without formal divorce, and without any contribution, positive or negative, from the legal system."[121] Indeed, before legal services programs spread throughout the country, this is primarily how low-income couples ended their unions. One client asked Roy Sobelson, who worked in Brunswick, Georgia, to help her obtain a divorce from a man who had left her more than twenty years earlier and another divorce from a second husband who had abandoned her sixteen years earlier.[122] Poverty lawyers often helped sort out such informal dissolutions, in effect legitimating the end of a relationship. "We were cleaning up people's lives," recalled Mike Froman.[123] This "regularization of legal status" was a primary force behind the increasing divorce rates of the nineteenth and early twentieth centuries. A person's legal status often determined rights to property and inheritance, and an uncertain legal status inhibited the operation of the land market by making it more difficult to transfer property. For those without property this regularization of legal status was less of a necessity, but by the late twentieth century property ownership of some sort had extended to many people living below the poverty line. Also, clarity of legal status was important in child custody disputes, adoption proceedings, and for various social programs, such as when one applied for Social Security survivor's benefits because one had to be married legally to receive such benefits. Thus, the very expansion of the welfare state created incentives for low-income Americans to erase legal irregularities. Apart from these legal and economic incentives, divorce simply became easier over the course of the twentieth century, as consensual divorce became possible and the increasing social acceptability of divorce led to an acceleration of the divorce rate beginning in the 1960s.[124] Whether the availability of legal services to the poor brought about a rise in divorces among the poor remains an open question, though clearly Americans in general were becoming more likely to terminate their marriages as compared to earlier times.[125] In any case poverty lawyers helped extend modern legal arrangements and procedures into the family lives of thousands of clients, for better or for worse.

This was also true of poverty lawyers' representation of parents threatened with the loss of their child either to a former spouse or to the state. Bitter disputes over child custody and parental rights had a dramatic impact on the lives of legal services clients. Poverty lawyers could be the difference between a parent losing custody, or even any right as a child's parent, and retaining her child-rearing rights and responsibilities. Few child custody disputes went beyond the trial court level, but those that did reveal the significance of legal representation, given that appellate judges often overturned adverse trial court decisions. Georgia Legal Services attorneys, for example, represented a sixteen-year-old mother who had left her child with her sister-in-law when it was less than three months' old, allegedly commenting that she did not want the baby and considered it an "aggravation." She subsequently lost custody to her husband during divorce proceedings, and he granted custody of the child to his sister. After a trial court formally granted custody to the client's sister-in-law and the sister-in-law began proceedings to adopt the child, legal services attorneys took the case to the appellate level, where they demonstrated that under existing laws their client had not technically abandoned her child. Without "clear and certain proof of abandonment," the child belonged to the biological mother.[126]

Another client filed a citation for contempt when her ex-husband failed to pay child support and found herself losing custody of the children altogether. Bob Cullen, her attorney, recalled that lower courts occasionally granted custody to a child's paternal grandmother rather than its mother on the assumption that young black mothers were incapable of caring for their children. On appeal the Georgia Supreme Court reversed the decision, awarding the client custody and requiring her ex-husband to resume child support payments.[127] In another appellate case Barbara Leyva, who was deaf and mute, retained custody of her children when GLSP attorneys demonstrated her fitness to care for the children despite her having to move repeatedly to find work as a peddler.[128] Elsewhere in the Deep South, poverty lawyers won similar decisions on behalf of their clients, though they were not always successful.[129]

A more drastic form of child custody dispute occurred when government officials attempted to terminate one's rights as a parent. An interventionist state did not always work to the benefit of the poor, as the case of Jerry Elrod made clear. Under a Georgia law passed in 1971, the Division of Family and Children Services (DFCS) could terminate a parent's rights to her child if officials proved that the child was "deprived" and the deprivation was likely to continue.[130] Without these rights a parent had no legal authority to visit the child or play any role in the child's life. Elrod's son, Joey, was born to Jerry and his wife while both were patients in the state's mental hospital in Milledgeville. Jerry had been a patient at the hospital since he had suffered head injuries in two accidents in the late 1960s. After his release in 1971, his wife abandoned the family, and, because Jerry was admittedly unable to care for Joey, that task fell on Jerry's mother in Atlanta and stepfather in rural Yonah, Georgia. They typically shared these duties along with Jerry. If Jerry's mother suffered a financial downturn, Jerry and Joey moved to Yonah; when prospects for Jerry's stepfather soured, father and son returned to Atlanta. But, when both fell into financial troubles, the DFCS placed Joey, then four years old, in a foster home, where he "reacted very favorably to his new environment, including greater cleanliness, more successful toilet training, better manners, increased sociability, improved social inter-relationships, greater emotional stability and other tangible benefits." Because of these improved conditions, state officials decided to terminate Jerry Elrod's rights to his child, and the Georgia Court of Appeals agreed with this decision. Although Jerry and his parents displayed no lack of moral character, according to the court, their economic circumstances inevitably led to neglect and deprivation.[131]

Some clients were not, like Jerry Elrod, sympathetic (albeit unsuccessful) figures before the court. GLSP lawyers represented Kathryn Simms, for example, in an attempt to regain custody of her two children. The Rockdale County DFCS investigated their situation after receiving complaints about possible child abuse and neglect. Upon visiting the home, a caseworker discovered unsanitary conditions, including maggots in the children's dirty diapers; evidence that Simms had severely beaten at least one of her children, pulling his hair out and bruising his head by hitting it against the bathtub faucet; and indications that her husband did "strange things" to the children, including passing gas into a plastic dry-cleaning bag and holding it over the children's heads to punish them. The caseworker also learned that Simms was promiscuous. Shortly after the beginning of this investigation, Simms left Georgia and voluntarily placed her children in foster care. She soon returned and attempted to regain custody, but her efforts were irregular, and Simms was continually unemployed and receiving welfare, so Rockdale County officials did not accede to these requests. Finally, the

Rockdale DFCS sought to terminate Simms's rights to her children. Simms retained the counsel of GLSP attorneys, and her attorneys—a group that included Robert Izzo, Mary Margaret Oliver, Roy Sobelson, Mary Carden, and John Cromartie—pleaded her case primarily on procedural grounds. Ultimately, the facts of abuse and neglect outweighed Simms's claims, and both the juvenile court and state Supreme Court agreed to terminate her parental rights.[132]

Often, however, legal services attorneys were able to convince the courts that, despite the failures of their clients as parents, these shortcomings did not justify the drastic measure of terminating their parental rights. Like Georgia, Mississippi had amended its code during the early 1970s to provide that "whenever the parent or parents of a child have abandoned or deserted such child, or are mentally, morally, or otherwise unfit to rear and train such child, any person, agency or institution may file . . . a petition to have the parental rights of said parent or parents terminated."[133] South Mississippi Legal Services attorney Cecil Jones Jr. and director Stanley Taylor represented a severely retarded mother and educably retarded father whose parental rights to four of their seven children the state Department of Public Welfare sought to terminate. The Mississippi Supreme Court overturned a lower court decision granting custody to the state because the chancellor's rationale for terminating their parental rights was unclear. In fact, there was evidence "that the parents visited with the children while in foster care, that both parents love their children, are concerned about their welfare, and both want custody of the children," and also evidence that the father was able to support them financially.[134] Likewise, Wilma Nix Ray sought to prevent the termination of her rights and regain custody of her children, whom county social workers had placed in foster care shortly after their birth to a sixteen-year-old, unemployed, and admittedly naive Ray. Despite questions about Ray's attentiveness to her children, GLSP attorneys related that she was competently caring for subsequent children, furthering her education, and exhibiting no evidence of bad character. Although a juvenile court had decided to terminate her custody rights, the Georgia Court of Appeals reversed this decision, saying that, although Ray's behavior "had not been exemplary . . . neither had it been so extraordinary that the state should intervene and take her child away from her permanently."[135]

At times disputes over the care of children implicated the South's hostility to interracial intimacy.[136] In *Blackburn v. Blackburn* Georgia Legal Services attorneys represented Kathleen Blackburn, a white woman who lost custody of her son, Nicholas, to her ex-husband's parents. A local judge had ordered Blackburn's parental rights to be terminated after she had an affair with a black police officer and gave birth to the officer's child. Race was not a factor in the decision, claimed the judge, then he declared that "this town just isn't ready for that sort of integration."[137] The case became a minor cause célèbre, as several outside organizations joined the GLSP in arguing that custody cannot be terminated simply because a child might have more advantages with a guardian than with a parent. The Georgia Supreme Court agreed, holding that, while "society may stigmatize Nicholas because his sibling is illegitimate," the sum of the evidence—the grandparents had claimed Blackburn failed to "provide necessities" and was raising Nicholas under "immoral, obscene . . . influences likely to degrade his moral character"—was insufficient to sever the parent-child relationship. Ironically, the grandparents' claims against Blackburn would have been stronger had they also sought custody of the illegitimate child, "but perhaps this is more than one could expect of grandparents even if race was not a motive for their action."[138]

While the facts of these cases are unique, the basic issues are not. State officials with good intentions sought to protect the well-being of children in potentially damaging situations. How they perceived one's child-rearing capabilities depended largely on cultural expectations about the rudiments of the good life, women's proper behavior, and even adherence to imagined racial boundaries. Caseworkers and the courts looked down on promiscuity, carelessness, and an inability to provide material necessities. Because such determinations of unfitness were subjective, legal services lawyers were useful allies, providing a counterpoint to state social workers and alternative custodians.

The judicial system was a means of settling disputes between family members and, from the perspective of the state, enforcing acceptable parental behavior. It was also a means by which government agencies could effectively supplant parents and become a child's primary caregiver and disciplinarian.[139] Officials pursued this course of action when a child's problems overwhelmed his or her parents, as was the case with delinquents and the mentally disabled. In either case the government's solution was some form of structured environment: "training schools" for juvenile delinquents and specialized hospitals for those with mental disabilities. These institutions were by no means new to the United States or the Deep South; indeed, they had emerged in the nineteenth century as a means to exert public control over individual behavior in an increasingly diverse and mobile urban-industrial society. Institutions such as the penitentiary, asylum, reformatory, and almshouse helped preserve order in the midst of rapid social change.[140] Even though Americans found other means of preserving social order during the twentieth century, these institutions remained prominent features of the nation's cultural and political landscape.

The juvenile justice system emerged during the late nineteenth century to provide a rehabilitative, rather than a punitive, environment for young adults convicted of criminal behavior. Juvenile courts and confinement separate from adults were products of the "progressive" concern with child welfare; late-nineteenth- and early-twentieth-century reformers had envisioned these courts as "child-saving" institutions that would recommend treatment for young people who committed crimes and promote a stable, salubrious home environment.[141] Indeed, it was in juvenile courts that government officials attempted to terminate parental rights and legal services lawyers attempted to defend them. Legal services lawyers occasionally found themselves defending juvenile defendants in the same courts.[142] Furthermore, Central Mississippi attorneys litigated several significant cases seeking to reform the state's juvenile justice system. In two cases CMLS attorneys failed to keep their client's trials in the juvenile courts, demonstrating that, even if one was a minor, a prosecutor might still try him as an adult, and in another they failed to convince a federal court that juveniles could not "intelligently and competently" waive their right to counsel in a juvenile delinquency proceeding.[143] They were successful in keeping one of their clients out of the state's Oakley Training School because the facility did not have a regimen appropriate to his condition. In the opinion of the court he needed a residential treatment center with individual and group psychotherapy, and the state had either to release him or provide such services.[144] The young man was lucky to avoid Oakley, since a subsequent CMLS case won a federal order requiring Mississippi officials to remedy various constitutional violations at the Oakley Training School, including the lack of a rehabilitative treatment program; conditions that amounted to "cruel and unusual" punishment, especially in the Intensive Treatment Unit; negligent medical and dental care; and a failure to provide adequate access to legal counsel. The judge accepted the theories propounded by CMLS attorneys Charles Ramberg and Barry Powell, finding that, "where, as in Mississippi, the purpose of incarcerating juveniles in a state training school is treatment and rehabilitation, due process requires that the conditions and programs at the school must be reasonably related to that purpose." That was not the case at Oakley, where "punishment" had become the raison d'être.[145] Elsewhere in the Deep South, poverty lawyers were less aggressive with regard to reforming juvenile justice systems,[146] but they nevertheless represented individual clients in cases before juvenile court judges. The fact that such representation continued to be a part of poverty law practice revealed the bifurcation of the adult and juvenile justice systems and the links between juvenile justice and other state involvement in family life.

Like juvenile justice reform cases, those involving the institutionalization of children and young adults were few in number but nevertheless held the potential for drastic changes in public policy and were, at the very least, deeply symbolic. Two GLSP cases, in particular, displayed for poverty lawyers the dangers of an intransigent, obfuscatory, or incompetent bureaucracy. In *Dutton v. Lamb* Bill Cobb represented two parents, Jackie and Geraldine Dutton, in their attempt to find their daughter within "the institutional maze" of the Department of Human Resources' Youth Services Division.[147] Robbie Dutton, who was seventeen years of age, ran away from home and was apprehended as a runaway and confined to the state's Youth Development Center in Rome. Officials did not attempt to reunite the family and even counseled Robbie that she did not have to return home. Meanwhile, they moved her to a smaller residential facility, from which Robbie, "fearing for her physical well-being," ran away again. Officials found her and sent her to another group home, where she attempted to commit suicide, after which she was moved to an Atlanta hospital. During this time state officials did not notify the Duttons about their daughter's movements or condition, seek to reunite the family, or allow the Duttons to communicate with Robbie. Why administrators behaved in this manner was not clear from the state's response to complaints filed by the Duttons, as the state made only procedural arguments and claimed government immunity from the lawsuit. These arguments were unpersuasive to the courts, and GLSP attorneys were able to win concessions from the Department of Human Resources, including a monetary reward and a legally binding promise to rewrite the *Youth Services Manual* to make "family unity" the agency's top priority and provide extensive training for its employees. The changes may have come too late for the Duttons, however, whose daughter Robbie remained alienated from them throughout the course of the legal battle. Bill Cobb optimistically pointed out that the case would "help ensure that this kind of thing doesn't happen again," but the legal victory was likely little solace to the Duttons or to their troubled daughter Robbie.[148]

The Georgia Legal Services Program's most complicated and long-lasting litigation involved its representation of children similarly lost within the state bureaucracy. In *J.L. and J.R. v. Parham* a team of legal services attorneys headed by David Goren sought to reform the process by which children became institutionalized in Milledgeville Central State Hospital, the largest mental health facility in Georgia. Their argument was simple: the state law that permitted parents to commit their children to mental hospitals without an initial hearing or any subsequent hearings violated the constitutional due process rights of the children so committed. The children should have access to counsel independent of their parents. As a basis for litigation, however, that conceptual simplicity failed to foreshadow the complex issues at stake in resolving the question of whether the state was illegally depriving the children of their liberty by keeping them confined in the state's mental hospitals without access to counsel or the judicial process.

Goren first met Joey Lister, the "J.L." for whom the case was named, during one of his routine visits to Milledgeville. Like poverty lawyers elsewhere, in particular those with Central Mississippi Legal Services, Goren had learned that many inmates in state mental facilities were unable to challenge their continued confinement due to a lack of administrative hearings and legal representation. Children were particularly vulnerable to such bureaucratic neglect. J.L. had lived at the hospital for almost six years, committed by his adoptive mother. "J.R." had similarly found himself at Milledgeville when his guardian, the Georgia Department of Human Resources, committed him. Both young men remained confined despite the recommendation of their chief therapists that institutionalization was unnecessary. Goren's team found other children in similar situations and believed that many of them were not even mentally ill. A "large number of children . . . were forced to remain in institutions for long periods of time simply because there were no other alternatives available or because officials simply didn't make the effort to discover such alternatives."[149] With financial help from the Southern Poverty Law Center, a civil rights firm based in Alabama, GLSP filed suit against the state and began the discovery process to support its claims.

After a lengthy period of investigation that included visits to the state's mental hospitals and amicus briefs filed by the National Juvenile Law Center and the ACLU's Child Advocacy Project, a three-judge federal court sitting in Macon decided that Georgia's juvenile commitment procedures were unconstitutional. Under Georgia law parents (or, as in J.R.'s case, state agents) could request that their child be admitted to a state mental facility, at which time the child entered a period of "observation and diagnosis" that lasted a minimum of five days. If this psychiatric evaluation suggested that institutionalization might help the child, he became a resident of one of the state's mental hospitals. In theory hospital administrators would release a patient once his illness subsided and institutionalization was no longer advisable. But in practice "the absence of parents ready, willing and able to again accept their child [was] unfortunately a normal situation," in which case state agents had to find foster care for the child. Such care was difficult to locate, so children often unnecessarily remained in the hospital. Several factors exacerbated these systemic problems, including the inconsistent and conjectural nature of psychiatric evaluations and the fact that "there are a lot of people who still treat [mental hospitals] as dumping grounds."[150]

One of the named plaintiffs, J.R., put a sad face on the problems the trial judges believed existed in the Georgia commitment statutes. District Judge Wilbur D. Owens Jr. related the boy's experiences in the panel's published decision. A juvenile court judge had removed J.R. from his parents' home when he was three months old due to signs of "severe parental neglect." During the next seven years he lived in seven different foster homes, until state officials committed him to Central State Hospital. "In each foster home," Owens wrote, "it seemed that he lost his place to a more favored child." Hospital personnel found J.R. to be "unsocialized, aggressive" and mildly retarded. In 1973, after three years at Milledgeville, J.R.'s doctors suggested that he be placed in a long-term foster or adoptive home. They "felt that efforts to obtain a foster placement should be primary at this time, lest he become a permanently institutionalized child." But state officials could not locate a foster home, and J.R. was still a Milledgeville patient when Georgia Legal Services filed its lawsuit in 1975. Of the thirteen years and two months of his life, J.R. had been a resident of the state mental hospital for over five years.

Viewing J.R.'s life through constitutional lenses, Owens pointed passionately to the crux of the court's finding:

> This case raises the most important question of every child's constitutional right to liberty, not only the liberty that includes freedom from bodily restraint . . . but also the liberty that includes the freedom of an ordinary, every-day child in these United States of America—the freedom to live with mothers, fathers, brothers and sisters in whatever the family abode may be; the freedom to be loved and to be spanked; the freedom to go in and out the door, to run and play, to laugh and cry, to fight and fuss, to stand up and fall down, to play childish games; the freedom to go to school and to frolic with school mates; the freedom to go to Sunday school and church; the freedom to watch and listen or not to watch and listen to television; the freedom to buy candy at the corner store; the freedom to be a normal child in a normal household cared for by normal parents.

This sentimental view of childhood contrasted sharply with the realities of institutional life. Placing a child in a mental hospital was not only a deprivation of that freedom, the court contended, it was a fundamental alteration of the child's existence. The child's "world becomes a building with locked doors and windows, regimented routine and institutional hours." Instead of relatives and friends, "his world is peopled by psychiatrists, psychologists, social workers, state employees and children who are to a greater or lesser extent, also emotionally disturbed." Relying on legal precedents emanating from the Supreme Court, Owens concluded that "it would be extraordinary if our Constitution did not require the procedural regularity and the exercise of care implied in the phrase 'due process' . . . for children to be confined and detained under Georgia's voluntary admissions statute." According to the three-judge panel, the state was not acting as *parens patriae* (i.e., as the children's legal guardian), "merely assist[ing] parents in the performance of their traditional parental duty of providing for the 'maintenance, protection and education of their children,'" in which case due process safeguards did not apply. Rather, the courts could, and should, protect children from the "arbitrary action of government."[151]

The solutions to these problems were not self-evident. Acceding to prevailing psychiatric opinion, the judges maintained that the "plaintiff children could be cared for in a less drastic, non-hospital environment if such an environment were available." They ordered the state to provide such facilities as small group homes, specialized foster care programs, and private child care agencies and "to place these children in such non-hospital facilities as soon as reasonably appropriate." Furthermore, by declaring the present procedures unconstitutional, the judges forced the state to adopt a commitment process that did not violate a child's right to due process and to revisit the commitment of those already in institutions. Within sixty days government officials would have to provide hearings for patients to determine whether they should remain institutionalized and begin similar adversarial hearings for any future patients in the state's juvenile courts.[152] Not surprisingly, given the far-reaching implications of the court's decision, the state won a stay of the court order and, because the trial had been before a special three-judge panel convened to hear allegations of constitutional violations by state officials, appealed directly to the Supreme Court.[153]

Georgia Legal Services director John Cromartie twice argued the case before the Supreme Court along with GLSP attorney Gerald Tarutis. Their claims fell on less sympathetic ears but ones that understood the difficulty of balancing the interests of individuals, families, and the state. More than three years after the three-judge panel found in favor of GLSP's young clients, the Supreme Court reversed nearly every aspect of that decision. Four of the justices joined Chief Justice Warren Burger in delivering the majority opinion, holding that, while a child's "liberty interest," that is, his interest in remaining free from government bondage, was a vital concern for the Court, so was the interest of the state, "including . . . the fiscal and administrative burdens that the additional or substitute procedural requirement would entail." Specifically, Georgia could confine the use of costly mental health facilities to cases of genuine need, refrain from imposing unnecessary procedural obstacles that could discourage citizens from seeking needed assistance, and place priority on diagnosing and treating patients rather than on time-consuming pre-admission procedures. Most important, however, the Supreme Court emphasized the role of "experts"— psychiatrists and other hospital officials—in finding that Georgia's existing commitment procedures did not violate a child's right to due process. If parents tried to use mental hospitals as a "dumping grounds" for rambunctious offspring, these experts would refuse to endorse such an action. In fact, an adversarial hearing in juvenile court prior to a child's commitment might serve to obfuscate or exacerbate the child's problems because judges, not doctors, would be responsible for determining the proper course of action and the antagonistic nature of the hearing would pit parent against child.[154]

The legal relationship between parents, their children, and governing authorities was at the center of the Supreme Court's deliberations. "In an earlier day," Burger suggested, "the problems inherent in coping with children afflicted with mental or emotional abnormalities were dealt with largely within the family." Although families increasingly turned "for assistance to local, public sources or private charities . . . most of the states did little more than provide custodial institutions for the confinement of persons who were considered dangerous." But, "as medical knowledge about the mentally ill and public concern for their condition expanded, the states, aided substantially by federal grants, have sought to ameliorate the human tragedies of seriously disturbed children." Burger concluded the opinion by recalling the objective of Georgia's mental health policy: to provide care for anyone who could not afford private treatment. In the Court's view Georgia officials resisted the district court's prescriptions because they were unnecessary, threatened to divert public funds from health care to judicial proceedings, and might aggravate tensions between parents and children or discourage parents from seeking help for their children.[155]

In his concurring opinion Justice Potter Stewart, joined in part by Justice William Brennan, placed more emphasis on the legal responsibilities borne by parents on behalf of their children than on the role of experts in Georgia's statutory scheme. Stewart recognized that "for centuries it has been a canon of the common law that parents speak for their minor children" and a presumption of American jurisprudence that most parents act in the "best interests" of the child. Commitment to a mental institution was not a *governmental* loss of liberty, then, and did not require due process protections. Rather, such a commitment was an acceptable parental prerogative because, "under our law, parents constantly make decisions for their minor children that deprive the children of liberty." The justices concluded that, "if the [institutionalized children] in this case were adults who had voluntarily chosen to commit themselves to a state mental hospital, they could not claim that the State had thereby deprived them of liberty in violation of the Fourteenth Amendment. Just as clearly . . . children on whose behalf their parents have invoked these voluntary procedures can make no such claim."[156] In his partial dissent Brennan, joined by the two remaining justices, Thurgood Marshall and John Paul Stevens, took these conclusions a step farther to argue that the state of Georgia could not constitutionally commit its wards, such as J.R., without a judicial hearing prior to the child's confinement. Government agents—in this instance social workers who sought to commit a child to a state mental facility—could not be trusted to act in the child's best interest. Likewise, children already accepted as mental patients should also be accorded an adversarial hearing when it becomes evident that their "supposed protectors," that is, their parents, have abandoned them.[157] By and large, however, the Georgia statute should remain intact as long as parental authority was apparent. The sum of these overlapping opinions was that decisions regarding the mental health of children were best left to experts and parents, not lawyers and judges.

The Supreme Court did leave several issues for the lower court to decide, including individual claims that initial admissions were improper, whether the periodic review process sufficiently protected children voluntarily committed, and whether the procedures for reviewing a child's need for continuing care should be different for a ward of the state, as opposed to a child with natural parents.[158] Five years later GLSP and government attorneys settled these issues. Mental health officials agreed that young patients had the right to an attorney whenever they lacked "active parental involvement" in their treatment or were wards of the state. Furthermore, the medical panels that conducted periodic reviews into whether continued hospitalization was necessary for these children would inform GLSP whenever they determined that a patient should remain in the facility; GLSP would then provide counsel to children who wished to challenge such decisions. In 1984, for example, the year the case was settled, legal services lawyers represented twenty-five children in review hearings, many of whom were released to less-restrictive treatment facilities.[159] Thus, even in defeat at the Supreme Court legal services attorneys helped reshape social policy.

Because domestic relations had become socialized—that is, placed under the purview of the state—poverty lawyers were faced with perplexing legal questions. As the *J.L.* case and others demonstrated, government agencies had taken a more active role in family life, especially the lives of poor mothers and fathers and their offspring. To what extent could poverty lawyers protect their clients' constitutional rights without damaging state-sponsored programs designed to help them? Particularly sensitive, as the *Crane v. Mathews* case had proven during the mid-1970s, was political support for social programs when it appeared that beneficiaries were "biting the hand that fed them." Furthermore, legal services lawyers realized that a "serious barrier to helping troubled children" remained because Georgia simply lacked "sufficient treatment environments to serve as alternatives to hospitalization." What they and most psychiatrists believed to be the most effective means of treating young mental patients was not possible because the state was reluctant to devote sufficient funds to the state's mental facilities.[160]

Poverty lawyers had long been cognizant of such frustrations, of course, given that their dependence on litigation, not legislation, limited their efforts to protect and expand other social programs. Nothing symbolized the limits of legal strategies more than the tragic experiences of Joey Lister, or J.L. About a year after GLSP attorneys filed the case, Central State Hospital released Joey to his adoptive father, a dentist in Thomasville by the name of Joe Mack Lister. A GLSP report related the story: Joey had been an "emotionally troubled" child when his adoptive mother, recently divorced from Dr. Lister, brought him to Milledgeville for treatment. "Forced to live in the confinement and deprivation of an institution, Joey suffered through five years of learning how 'crazy' people behave and became more unstable." Just six months after his release, this instability led to a tragic end to Joey's life. He committed suicide, and a subsequent investigation found that Lister had abused Joey by "forcing him to do excessive exercise, leaving him out in the sun without food or water, and tying him on the bed on occasion." Although Lister received a prison sentence of five years, the GLSP report blamed state officials for Joey's death. Director John Cromartie stated: "There are still many unanswered questions about the lack of supervision by the state over his placement. Good supervision would undoubtedly have uncovered the problems Joey was having in the new setting."[161] This sense of outrage was ironic, if understandable, given that the objective of the case that bore Joey's name was to remove him from the care of the state and place him in the care of his family.

The rise of the regulatory state altered the relationships between American citizens and their government. Government became a larger part of everyone's life during the course of the twentieth century. For the poor there was a coercive dimension to the expansion of the regulatory state. Poor southerners, like low-income Americans everywhere, now "share[d] the common experiences of state sanctioned poverty," which "are characterized by governmental regulation and surveillance."[162] This was particularly true of government involvement in social institutions such as the family. At the same time, there was a participatory dimension to poor people's contact with the American welfare state. The poor derived material benefits as a result of their election to take advantage of public housing, income supplements, and government-sponsored health care. Poverty lawyers helped their clients assert rights within the context of the regulatory state that enabled them to participate in a more assertive, proactive way and to push state actors to be more responsive to their needs. Ultimately, joining the regulatory state had an ambiguous effect on the poor: they often lost autonomy even as they gained material benefits. They lost some of that autonomy to their lawyers, who became intercessors between the poor and legal authorities. They also lost autonomy to the state. The 1960s and 1970s saw an increase of "dependent individualism," in particular among many low-income, urban dwellers. Recipients of public relief came to depend on government for economic sustenance even as they asserted control over their personal lives.[163] Indeed, notions of American liberty had begun to shift as early as the turn of the twentieth century, as Americans came to believe that "individual liberty depended upon state protection," even though "protection of liberty came at a cost to individual autonomy."[164] This belief became more pervasive throughout the course of the twentieth century. Legal services cases reveal this tension between liberty and dependence. The ability to provide one's family with security based on the material benefits of a regulatory state came at a price to the poor.

Poverty lawyers also helped reduce the differences between how the southern poor and their counterparts elsewhere in the United States experienced the expanding regulatory state. Southern policy makers had long resisted encroachments by federal initiatives that sought to modify southern realities, be they racial, economic, or other social realities. The region's power brokers pragmatically accepted federal aid during the Great Depression without subscribing to the ethos that drove the New Deal. They resisted attempts by national entities, whether Congress or the Supreme Court or the chief executive, to enter the debate over race in southern life. When the Johnson administration proposed programs of both economic uplift and racial reform, southerners were among his most vociferous opponents. Even when southern states adopted programs—from AFDC to Social Security to public housing—that emanated from Washington, southern policy makers often gave them limited support compared to policy makers in other states, and they often administered the programs to reduce their impact in the region or to impose onerous requirements on recipients of public aid. The effect of poverty law strategies was to cut against these regional differences by forcing compliance with national legal and regulatory standards. By ensuring that the administration of social programs in the South was consistent with that in the rest of the country, poverty lawyers enabled low-income southerners to access social programs available to poor people throughout the United States.

Although legal services programs contributed to the percolation of the regulatory state throughout the South and to poor people across the country, that effect was not the primary motivation of poverty lawyers or their clients. Clients were primarily concerned with improving their material condition, and poverty lawyers were doing what lawyers do: pursuing their clients' agenda insofar as the law would allow. Poverty lawyers did not pass the laws, but they did help enforce them. While many poverty lawyers believed that government bore a responsibility to low-income families, their philosophical predilection was less significant than their professional ethic, which bound them to promote their clients' interests with whatever legal means they could devise. That meant utilizing law to protect and benefit clients and to resolve disputes but also resisting governmental action when that action worked to their client's detriment.[165] They were not simply and blindly devoted to expanding the welfare state, but they were devoted to their clients. In any case, whether poverty lawyers were inviting in the regulatory state or keeping it at arm's length, they were always integrating their clients into U.S. legal culture. If "the raw material of [poor people's] experience and consciousness" was their "relation to the welfare state,"[166] that experience and consciousness increasingly involved American law and the legal process.

6

LOW-INCOME COMMUNITIES, POVERTY
LAWYERS, AND RACIAL RECONSTRUCTION

DURING the 1960s the South experienced a racial reconstruction. The African-American freedom struggle thrust civil rights onto the national agenda and created a moment of political triumph that began to undermine entrenched patterns of discrimination. In the judicial and executive enforcement of constitutional and statutory precepts, particularly the Civil Rights Act of 1964 and the Voting Rights Act of 1965, federal authorities played a major role in reshaping the southern racial order. Southern politics also underwent several transformations that were still in progress as the 1960s ended. The "massive resistance" that erupted after the *Brown* decision, with politicians across the South decrying the Supreme Court's meddling in southern affairs, had largely run its course after much grandstanding by the likes of George Wallace and no small degree of associated violence, such as the Ole Miss riot of 1962. There would be no more literal standing in the schoolhouse door to block the entry of African-American applicants. The race mongering that became the language of southern electioneering around the turn of the twentieth century, and which experienced a revival in the midst of the civil rights movement, faded into subtext and innuendo. Also, as Nixon's "southern strategy" signaled the beginning of Republican dominance of presidential politics in the South, state politics also began to reflect partisan competition and the decline of Democratic solidity. By the mid-1970s much had changed in the South: blacks and whites were nominally equal under law, publicly sponsored segregation had disappeared, African Americans who wanted to vote could, and mass violence toward blacks was becoming a thing of the past.[1]

Nevertheless, race persisted as a perplexing facet of southern culture, and southern race relations came to lie "somewhere between old-fashioned strict segregation, on the one hand, and complete racial integration, on the other."[2] To begin with, racial reconstruction was uneven across the South, with many rural areas untouched by civil rights activism even into the 1970s and the *Brown* decision but a distant echo. Even where change had come, racial inequality often remained, though its sources became less apparent, given the curious connection between race and class in the region. One of the major catalysts of racial reconstruction, the civil rights movement, was multifaceted and disorganized by the 1970s (if it can be said to have continued at all into that decade), and it lacked the powers of persuasion symbolized by Martin Luther King Jr.'s "I Have a Dream Speech" at the Lincoln Memorial back in 1963.[3] Even though blacks had gained the right to vote, they often struggled to wield political power; workplace discrimination was illegal but remunerative employment still difficult to come by; and white violence toward blacks had certainly not disappeared. Despite the manifest public victories of the 1960s, private tribulations still faced many African Americans in the Deep South.

Increasingly, African Americans turned to lawyers and to the courts to remedy these persistent problems, not least because the executive and legislative branches of government were growing less willing to act on their behalf in the midst of a mounting white backlash. Various proponents of civil rights had legal teams active in the South, but poverty lawyers were uniquely situated to represent clients who were both black and poor, and their work reveals the perplexities of the struggle for freedom and equality in the wake of the civil rights movement of the 1960s. They found that there was substantial demand for representation in civil rights disputes, especially in rural areas. That is not surprising, considering the racial proportions of their clientele and the persistence of racial discrimination in the South. North Mississippi Rural Legal Services had the largest proportion of black clients compared to other southern legal services programs, perhaps nine out of every ten people served. Central Mississippi's clientele reached roughly four blacks for every one white.[4] More than half of LSCA's clients were black, as were roughly half of GLSP's clients.[5] In predominantly white areas legal services clients were overwhelmingly white, but by and large the clientele mirrored the racial proportions of people living in poverty, more than half of whom were black.[6]

For poverty lawyers altering the status of their African-American clients proved difficult. Generations of white southerners had inherited presumptions of racial superiority; entrenched patterns of discrimination placed disproportionate economic resources in the hands of wealthy whites; and U.S. federalism, the sharing of power by national, state, and local officials, made it impossible for any central authority to control the actions of individuals and institutions across the country. However powerful the president and executive bureaucracy, the legislators on Capitol Hill, and the justices that decided the nation's highest law, none could extend freedom to every out-of-the-way hamlet in the United States. Only the residents of those hamlets could do that, and some were just beginning their struggle even as the national civil rights movement was becoming a memory.[7]

Legal services programs were not the only public interest firms working on behalf of black southerners during the 1970s. The NAACP Legal Defense Fund (LDF) had been involved in civil rights disputes for decades and remained so into the 1970s. The Lawyers' Constitutional Defense Committee (LCDC), Lawyers' Committee for Civil Rights Under the Law (LCCRUL), American Civil Liberties Union (ACLU), and United States Justice Department continued to employ resources to dismantle racial discrimination. Also, private lawyers began to take civil rights cases on a pro bono basis or when they could win attorneys' fees, and Morris Dees and Joseph Levin established the Southern Poverty Law Center, a firm devoted to civil rights practice, in Montgomery, Alabama, in 1971. The Southern Poverty Law Center became involved in some representation of low-income individuals that resembled the advocacy of legal services attorneys (such as cases broadening medical services for the poor), but, despite its moniker, the organization's principle focus was on civil rights, not poverty law, including cases challenging segregation and employment discrimination, representing death penalty inmates and other inmates complaining of prison conditions, and combating the Ku Klux Klan and other white supremacist groups.

Even with all these civil rights litigators in the Deep South, there was more work than they could handle, and thus legal services programs joined numerous local struggles. Whereas most poverty law practice dealt with the problems of individual clients, civil rights disputes typically involved community groups. These were often class action, "law reform" cases. They constituted only a minor proportion of the legal services caseload but drew more than their share of attention from antagonistic public figures as well as from young lawyers looking for interesting work.[8] Fortunately for poverty lawyers and their clients, they inherited the legal changes of the 1960s, most notably the Civil Rights Act of 1964 and Voting Rights Act of 1965. Those statutes, plus the increased willingness of the federal courts to extend constitutional protections to African Americans, created a legal environment in which their civil rights litigation was quite successful, especially in the types of cases that were plentiful throughout the South, such as voting rights claims. After the *Brown v. Board of Education* decision in 1954, southern courts had not rushed to implement the decision, in part because the Supreme Court invited delay with its ambiguous phrase in *Brown II* mandating school desegregation "with all deliberate speed."[9] Yet in the 1960s civil rights litigation gained momentum in the context of school desegregation efforts and, subsequently, cases promoting voting rights and equal employment. Furthermore, in voting rights cases civil rights litigants had possible claims under not only the equal protection clause and Voting Rights Act but also the Fifteenth Amendment, which provides that American citizens' right to vote cannot be "denied or abridged" by the United States or by any state "on account of race, color, or previous condition of servitude."[10] Despite the conservative turn of the courts beginning in the 1970s, many remained open to civil rights claims. Taken together, poverty lawyers' voting rights, jury discrimination, equal employment, First Amendment, and criminal justice cases, among others, facilitated black political and economic activity at the local level.

Ultimately, grassroots pressure by proponents of change and the often debilitating counterforce applied by their opponents were more important factors than litigation in shaping the course of the African-American freedom struggle. Yet poverty lawyers proved to be helpful allies to grassroots activists, and, together with their clients, poverty lawyers altered many of the communities in which they worked. As resources for community leaders and local organizations, poverty lawyers became instruments for attacking existing power structures when other forms of persuasion had failed.[11] Furthermore, because of the geographic spread of legal services programs by the end of the decade, this became true more uniformly across the Deep South, as places such as McIntosh County, Georgia, and Tupelo, Mississippi, faced the long-term trend of allowing U.S. law "to create one legal culture out of many."[12] Racial reconstruction permeated the Deep South (though not completely), and the region's distinctiveness from the rest of American society diminished.

One community that drew poverty lawyers into its racial struggles was sparsely populated McIntosh County, along the Georgia coast. The turbulence of sit-ins, marches, boycotts, and other civil rights activism did not disrupt relations between McIntosh County's white and black citizens during the 1960s. Although nearly all African Americans of voting age in the county were registered to vote by the early 1970s, blacks wielded little political power. McIntosh County and its county seat, Darien, had never elected an African-American mayor, county commissioner, city council member, or school board representative. No African American had served on a grand jury, trial jury, or county governing board, and none had been elected to state office outside of McIntosh County since Reconstruction. Black laborers occupied the lowest-paying jobs in the McIntosh County economy, as maids, cooks, and unskilled workers, and black children rode buses to an all-black school, where they used outdated textbooks and secondhand supplies.[13] Power, political and economic, resided predominantly in one man: Sheriff Tom Poppell. Outsiders, including state law enforcement officials, viewed Poppell as "the last of the old-time political bosses in Georgia"; one local lawyer claimed that the sheriff was "judge, jury, and monarch." Poppell's control relied less on threats and violence than on paternal persuasion. On one occasion, for example, two trucks collided on Highway 17, leaving hundreds of pairs of shoes scattered across the county's major thoroughfare. The sheriff averted his eyes when nearby residents, all African-American, sorted through the wreckage and left with new footwear. The event was not an isolated one; Tom Poppell made a habit of granting such rewards in return for allegiance to his rule.[14] Thus were maintained peace *and* inequality.

The events that led McIntosh County's African-American community to challenge Sheriff Poppell and the racial status quo were often repeated in the Deep South. African Americans were not oblivious to their second-class citizenship. Most, if not all, had personally experienced racial discrimination. Thurnell Alston, for example, the man who would become the most visible black leader in the county, remembered back to his teenage years in the 1950s, when Sheriff Poppell had refused to find food for African Americans out of work due to a severe rainy season. Poppell's response, according to Alston, had been to remark, "Only way you can control the Negroes is to keep them hungry."[15] Memories such as this festered and created fuel for action.

The "season of great change," a chronicler of these events has suggested, began with the shooting of Ed Finch in March 1972. In the midst of a tussle with a police officer, Finch found himself at the wrong end of a .38 caliber revolver. The officer, Chief of Police Guy Hutchinson, had placed the gun into his mouth and fired when Finch reached for a hoe lying nearby. Hutchinson then dragged Finch across the street to the city jail, placed him in a cell, and charged him with aggravated assault, drunk and disorderly conduct, and obstructing the work of a law enforcement officer. That night Finch lay "in jail with a fresh bullet in his jaw, choking on blood in his throat, blood drenching his clothes, and spitting fragments of teeth." No one called a doctor.[16]

Word of the shooting and Finch's medical state spread quickly through the black community, reaching Thurnell Alston late that night. He was unsure why the people came to him, except that "every time I went to church, I was telling people about some of the things we should do. So I guess they were just thinking maybe I would be the one could start some kind of reaction." They guessed correctly. Early the next morning Alston led some two or three hundred people to city hall demanding that Finch receive medical treatment. By the time they left Darien, Finch was in a hospital, the city had agreed to pay his expenses, and Hutchinson was removed from office pending an investigation. Although these informal agreements did not survive long—Finch was convicted on the criminal charges, the city council reappointed Hutchinson to his post, and Finch lost a civil suit against the city—the Finch shooting and its aftermath demonstrated for McIntosh County's blacks the potential power of community mobilization.[17]

Not long thereafter, the lone African American on the county's board of education, Chatham Jones, lost his position in May 1975. The board that had appointed Jones, an entity known as the McIntosh County Grand Jury, replaced him with a white man who happened to be the jury foreman's brother. Although the grand jury had the authority to make such a change, the county's black population believed the move was an instance of racial discrimination because Jones had begun to spread word that the board of education was funneling money to the private, all-white Oglethorpe Academy. Shortly after Jones's removal from office, Alston and a friend, Nathaniel Grovner, resurrected the local NAACP and created the McIntosh County Civic Improvement Organization (MCCIO) to organize protests. That summer African Americans congregated daily in the tiny churches spread across the county. In sermons and speeches black leaders urged their listeners to join together to challenge white dominance, and the collections went to the NAACP and MCCIO. Alston, Grovner, and another old friend, Sammie Pinkney, joined regularly with several other leaders to discuss strategy. The atmosphere "had gotten so heated in Darien," related Pinkney, "that white folks felt they had to call in the Ku Klux Klan. They marched more than once. The last time they came, we came so close to having bloodshed it was unbelievable." Movement had come to McIntosh.[18]

It was Sammie Pinkney who contacted Georgia Legal Services attorneys in nearby Brunswick. During the summer of 1975 the Brunswick office consisted of four attorneys, three paralegals, and one administrative assistant. Thomas Affleck, just two years out of Georgetown University Law School, was the managing attorney, and his compatriots were no more seasoned in the profession. Mark Gorman had come to Georgia from the University of Texas School of Law, class of 1974, and Ed Zacker was a 1975 graduate of American University Law School. Those who arrived soon thereafter, like those who had preceded this group, were similarly young and inexperienced. Practicing poverty law in Brunswick did not, as of 1975, include much law reform work. Instead, the attorneys circuit-rode hundreds of miles and met clients in county welfare offices. Most of the cases involved domestic relations, but the Brunswick attorneys also helped clients obtain AFDC, food stamps, and other public benefits. Their practice was uncontroversial. Even Sheriff Tom Poppell had contacted Affleck, asking him to send an attorney over because "some folks over here in McIntosh need some divorces." Until they became involved in McIntosh County's racial conflicts, these young lawyers engaged in little impact litigation. But McIntosh County's black activists forced their hand.[19] "What I remember about the summer of 1975," Gorman recalled, "is that these people from McIntosh County showed up in our office, and that suddenly there was a lot of commotion . . . about the situation there, about the discharge of the black member of the school board by the grand jury. What the McIntosh people wanted the most was to get at the school board selection process."[20] The lawyers, they believed, could help them do that. That summer the Brunswick staff worked with Pinkney, Alston, and Grovner to fashion a legal challenge to the grand jury system.

They received invaluable assistance from GLSP's Atlanta-based civil rights specialist, David Walbert, who had embraced law reform with missionary zeal. "I just loved to go out and sue people," Walbert once said, belying his conservative upbringing.[21] That he was an aggressive public interest lawyer expending much of his efforts in rural Georgia was somewhat surprising, given his sheltered youth in Cleveland and academic interest in physics. As he later reflected, "Lord knows, if it weren't for the civil rights movement and Vietnamese War—just being a twenty-one-year-old kid at that point in time . . . I'm not sure if my life ever would have changed direction." But he did live at a unique time and soon found that life in academia did not suit his growing awareness of the problems around him. Thus, Walbert decided to begin law school in 1969, though, even after finishing three years at Case Western Reserve, he did not want to practice law. A year clerking for a federal judge changed his mind. He became intrigued with the dynamics of the courtroom and sought to merge that interest with his social conscience. Georgia seemed like a good place to do that, given the persistence of racial discrimination there in the early 1970s. After joining Georgia Legal Services as a housing specialist in 1973, Walbert became involved in dozens of voting rights suits and other civil rights complaints across the state. He was getting his opportunity to "change the world," or at least small parts of it.[22]

In attacking McIntosh County's grand jury system, Walbert and the Brunswick lawyers faced a significant obstacle: most of the county's black population was registered to vote, and thus there was little evidence of discrimination in voter registration. McIntosh County's voting-age population of 4,251 people was 45 percent white and 54 percent black, 53 percent female and 47 percent male. The list of registered voters from which the grand jury and trial jury members were drawn was 56 percent white and 44 percent black, 52 percent female and 48 percent male. While somewhat disproportionate, there were still substantial numbers of blacks registered to vote. Yet this was not the entire story. McIntosh County jury commissioners created a jury list from the voter registration rolls and from which they selected trial juries. That jury list consisted of only 398 people: 87 percent were white, 13 percent black, and 92 percent of the eligible jurors were male. The grand jury list, containing just 156 names, was 90 percent white and 92 percent male. The lines of power were clear, and so was the legal services argument: the board of education was the product of an unlawful grand jury, one that failed to represent all the people of McIntosh County.[23] Federal District Judge Anthony Alaimo was receptive to this argument, urging county officials to settle the case, and the parties soon agreed to a consent order that required that McIntosh County include blacks and women on its juries.[24]

Not long after initiating this case, black leaders turned to the polls. Thurnell Alston had unsuccessfully run for a seat on the county commission in 1973. When he decided to make a second attempt in 1975, Alston realized that he needed more than the support of the African-American community, so he sought and won the support of Sheriff Poppell. Victory should have been easy: there was a black majority among those of voting age, and African Americans made up a large proportion of the voting population; add Poppell's approval, and Alston seemed secure. But Poppell changed his mind. At the last minute he instructed his allies to support Alston's opponent, who defeated Alston by three votes. With GLSP's Tom Affleck, Alston contested the election, but a judge ruled that there was not enough evidence of fraud, even though GLSP lawyers had discovered that some 137 black voters had been turned away from the polls because they were "improperly registered." Fraud aside, the major obstacles to African-American success at the polls were Sheriff Poppell and McIntosh County's at-large, or county-wide, electoral system. In that system the entire county voted for each commissioner, as did the entire town of Darien for its city council members. Since African Americans made up only 44 percent of those registered to vote, no black politician could win without white support (i.e., without Poppell's support).[25] Fortunately for Alston and McIntosh County's African-American community, Walbert and his colleagues had a solution: attack the system of at-large voting as an unconstitutional dilution of the black vote.

Challenging at-large, multi-member election systems was the next phase of voting rights litigation after initial efforts to register African-American voters under the Voting Rights Act of 1965.[26] Across the South African Americans found that voter registration did not translate immediately into electing black leaders where blacks constituted less than half of the voting population in a county or city, because white majorities tended to elect white leaders. Dividing larger political units such as cities and counties into separate districts that each elected a representative would disperse local-level political power and in some places create majority-black political subdivisions. The problem for civil rights lawyers such as Walbert was how to fashion an argument to achieve that result.[27] He tested the judicial waters in Albany, a small city in the southwestern portion of the state that had seen more than its share of civil rights activity.[28] During the early 1960s NAACP, Student Nonviolent Coordinating Committee (SNCC), and Southern Christian Leadership Council (SCLC) activists, including Martin Luther King Jr., had helped organize the black community to protest its lack of political power. They had won some concessions from city officials but few tangible rewards.[29] Georgia Legal Services attorneys hoped to do better when they filed a case known as *Paige v. Gray* challenging Albany's at-large election system.

Albany adopted an at-large election system to select its mayor and city commission in 1947, replacing a system in which five wards had elected their own commission representatives. The timing was not uncalculated. Three years earlier the Supreme Court had declared all-white Democratic primaries unconstitutional.[30] In the subsequent primary the black majority in Albany's Fifth Ward proved decisive in the selection of Democratic candidates for city offices. Responding to this show of political will, white leaders decided to alter the electoral arrangement by stipulating that all city officials be elected at-large, and not by smaller political subdivisions.[31] Thus, despite being able to vote in the Democratic primary, which was critical to enjoying political power at that time in much of the South, blacks lost a substantial degree of power over the outcome of citywide elections. This system remained intact for three decades.

Georgia Legal Services attorneys argued on behalf of Grady Caldwell, Fanny Paige, Erma Moss, and Mary Young, representing Albany's black community, that the at-large system diluted the voting strength of Albany's black residents because more than 60 percent of the city's residents were white. Between 1947 and 1975 several black candidates had sought seats in municipal government, and, while many enjoyed majorities in the ward in which they resided, they failed to win the citywide election.

For District Judge Wilbur D. Owens Jr. these statistical incongruities were sufficient to hold the at-large system unconstitutional. Under a 1960 Supreme Court decision the plaintiffs did not have to prove that those who framed the 1947 law had intended to discriminate against African Americans (though that does appear to have been their objective). Rather, the city's at-large system violated the Fifteenth Amendment to the Constitution because it had the "inevitable effect of depriving Negro citizens of their votes and of the consequent advantages that the ballot affords them."[32] The Fifteenth Amendment proved decisive for Owens, while he was less convinced that the scheme was unconstitutional on other grounds.[33] As a result, Judge Owens ordered the city to utilize the long-dormant ward system to elect its officials during the fall of 1975.

Interestingly, both the legal services clients *and* the defendant city officials appealed the decision. Both sides believed that Owens had applied the wrong legal precedents and therefore failed to address a more critical issue of whether or not there were tangible repercussions from an obviously diluted vote. If not, that is, if Albany officials represented black residents equally, then the system was permissible. But, if one could prove that the dilution of the black vote resulted in discriminatory treatment at the hands of elected officials, a fact the plaintiffs were certain they could substantiate, then the courts would not only have to strike down the at-large system, but also civil rights litigators would have a broader legal precedent to apply in future cases.[34] Both plaintiffs and defendants hoped to draw attention to the present, not the past—the city in order to win this case, the GLSP attorneys in order to set a precedent that they could carry to places such as McIntosh County. The Fifth Circuit Court of Appeals agreed, sending the case back to Owens with instructions to analyze the Albany scheme under recent Fourteenth Amendment cases, dismantle the at-large voting system, and assess the validity of an at-large election for the mayor.[35]

When Walbert and two legal services attorneys in Albany, Mary Young and Alfred Bragg III, documented the effects of diluted black political power, Judge Owens only grew firmer in denouncing the at-large system as it operated in Albany. In his subsequent decision Owens reiterated how the 1947 changes had decimated the emergent African-American vote. Then he documented the historical and current effect of that dilution. Albany maintained its municipal services and facilities on a segregated basis. Schools, police and fire departments, street construction and maintenance, garbage collection, parks, swimming pools, tennis courts, the municipal auditorium, the airport, a municipal library, and an open-air stadium all reflected the persistence of apartheid in the Deep South. All African-American residents had to vote in one precinct at the city auditorium. Albany's public housing authority, the board members of which were appointed by the mayor and all white, operated its projects on a segregated basis. Of the twenty-six boards or authorities that carried out the work of the city, sixteen had no black representatives; blacks constituted just 13 percent of the overall appointees, compared to 40 percent of the population, and twenty-five of the thirty-nine black appointees served on just two boards. One proof of the adverse effects of vote dilution was that civil rights leaders had already initiated several lawsuits to attack these policies, including the city's persistent policy of discrimination against its own employees on the basis of their race.[36]

For Georgia Legal Services attorneys and their clients the decision was an overwhelming victory: Judge Owens required Albany to establish six wards, two of which had black majorities, though the city would still choose its mayor in a citywide election.[37] Reflecting on the case soon after its conclusion, lead attorney David Walbert was optimistic about Albany's future and the potential for lawyers to contribute to community well-being. He believed that the results benefited both blacks and whites because they began working together as African Americans elected their own representatives. The mayor, a major target of the lawsuit, seemed to have "softened his segregationist attitudes," and in the future white and black children would "know the governing body of their city is integrated and that will have a long-term salutary effect on that community." As far as the legal profession was concerned, "The most worthwhile thing lawyers can do is help bring real democracy to those who haven't experienced it since Reconstruction."[38] They had helped to do that in Albany and in a manner that contrasted sharply with the Albany movement of the 1960s.

Georgia Legal Services lawyers adopted a similar strategy in Burke County, some thirty minutes south of Augusta. Bob Cullen, who had become interested in poverty law as a law student at Boston College and began his legal career in GLSP's Augusta office in 1974, established extensive contacts with African-American leaders in Waynesboro, the county seat, most notably with Herman Lodge. He met Lodge even before being admitted to the bar, when Lodge walked into the Augusta office and told Cullen "he was real sick of white lawyers who never did anything for all these people" in Burke County. Later, in his first court appearance after being admitted to the bar, Cullen watched the court conduct three consecutive capital murder trials while he waited in court to defend a client against a furniture repossession. All three of the capital defendants were black, all three trials were complete by the court's afternoon session, and all three defendants received the death penalty. Cullen's furniture repossession case occupied the court the balance of the afternoon and took longer to resolve than the three capital cases combined. The young lawyer was "enraged" at what he had witnessed, not least because there were "absolutely no . . . blacks on the jury panel."[39]

Cullen's lay counterpart in Burke County, Herman Lodge, was typical of local civil rights leaders in the Deep South. He had grown up in rural Burke County, where he attended high school, and graduated from Fort Valley State College, a historically black institution, in 1951. Subsequently, Lodge was drafted into the army during the Korean War. Upon his release from military service, Lodge returned to Burke County, worked for a year as a teacher in the still-segregated schools, and then joined the Veterans Administration hospital as a physical therapist. He still worked there in the 1970s. In 1961 Lodge and other black leaders established the Burke County Improvement Association (BCIA), one of countless such organizations across the region modeled on the Montgomery Improvement Association, and Lodge became its executive secretary. Although the creation of the BCIA coincided with the broader sit-in movement, the catalyst for its creation was local. A young black man had entered the Piggly Wiggly supermarket to buy a pack of cigarettes. He and the clerk, a white female, had a misunderstanding about which cigarettes he wanted and the amount of his change. She threw the cigarettes and change at him and called her manager, who then contacted the police; they threw the young man in jail. Distressed and angry, twenty African Americans, including Lodge, met and created the BCIA soon thereafter.[40]

In the words of Herman Lodge they formed BCIA "for the welfare of the people in Burke County." During the 1960s the organization focused on "selective buying" strategies, which Lodge thought produced "better results" than marches, and it later received grants through President Johnson's war on poverty to run programs such as Head Start and an emergency food service. In the late 1960s BCIA turned to the courts, seeking an end to segregated trial juries and segregated schools. Such efforts countered the inertia of generations of discrimination. African Americans had played virtually no part in Burke County politics prior to the Voting Rights Act, and even then participation was problematic. Many blacks lived far from polling places, had little education, and feared economic reprisal, including the possibility of white officials terminating their welfare checks or other benefits. GLSP attorneys would also later argue that the county's at-large election system diluted the black vote. Like many southern towns, roads were paved in white sections but not in black parts of town. Yet changes did begin to occur in Burke County. The drugstore shut down its lunch counter when it became evident that the Civil Rights Act would open it to African

Americans, and the movie theater agreed to end its segregationist policies after a tense weekend during which an angry crowd tried to prevent several young activists from moving downstairs from the balcony and state troopers spent the weekend in Waynesboro to prevent further violence. In contrast, the city gave away some of its properties, including the public swimming pool, to prevent their integration.

Litigation was one means of propelling and influencing such change, though African Americans did not blindly embrace the justice system. As Herman Lodge indicated, "We consider the courthouse a symbol of injustice . . . [;] when I walk in the courthouse, I still have some anxiety."[41] Nevertheless, during the mid-1970s improving the welfare of the people of Burke County led Lodge and BCIA to initiate two cases that mirrored those down in McIntosh County. One challenged the process whereby grand juries were formed, the other Burke County's at-large system of elections. In *Sapp v. Rowland* Bob Cullen and his colleagues, including David Walbert and an ACLU attorney, Laughlin McDonald, argued that racial and sex discrimination in the grand jury selection process rendered those bodies invalid. Similar to McIntosh County's grand juries, those in Burke County were 89 percent white and 99.8 percent male, even though the county's voting-age population was 53 percent black and 55 percent female. The plaintiffs were particularly concerned that grand juries appointed school board members, making it impossible for any African American or woman to serve in such capacity without the support of white males. Little more than a year after filing the case, Judge Anthony Alaimo gave the legal services clients a resounding victory, using the McIntosh County model to require Burke County jury lists to reflect the demographics of the community.[42]

The Burke County voting rights case, like those in Albany and in McIntosh County, took much longer to resolve. With Laughlin McDonald, GLSP attorneys filed *Lodge v. Buxton* in April 1976, a month before filing *Sapp v. Rowland*. Yet the case persisted well into the 1980s because white authorities were reluctant to relinquish their advantages in the at-large system of elections. According to the plaintiffs, such a system diluted the black vote, so that, even if African Americans were able to vote in Burke County, they were relatively powerless in local politics. The defendants, on the other hand, disagreed that the at-large system had the intentional effect of diluting the black vote and refused to concede that there was a history of official racial discrimination in Burke County. In one telling rebuttal to the black community's complaint, white officials denied that the "plaintiffs desire[d] to participate in the electoral and political process equally with other citizens of Burke County and to have their votes counted

on an equal basis with those of white citizens of Burke County."[43] This was an odd
argument considering that black citizens had filed a lawsuit to achieve that very result.
Over the next six years the attorneys guided the case through the district court (where
Judge Alaimo found in favor of Burke County's black citizens) and the appellate process. During the appeals the Supreme Court permitted white authorities to delay
implementing Alaimo's decision, but the Fifth Circuit later affirmed the lower court's
judgment on the grounds that, although racially neutral on its face, the at-large system was "created or maintained for the purpose of preventing minority groups from
effectively participating in the electoral process." After the Supreme Court refused to
overturn this decision and then denied the defendants' motion for a rehearing, Judge
Alaimo could finally implement his initial decision. By this time the year was 1982.
Alaimo had found white officials "unresponsive" to the black community and sought
to remedy this "insensitivity" and "callous indifference" by forcing the county to abandon its at-large system. He ordered special elections for the fall of 1982, a decision that
the Fifth Circuit and Supreme Court upheld.[44]

Even before these elections, black mobilization had begun to bring change to Burke
County. The county opened satellite sites for voter registration and a transportation
system for the elderly, and two African Americans gained seats on the Waynesboro city
council. Herman Lodge believed that local public policy reflected these early changes
in representation: the county had added fifty units of public housing, a food processing center to help thousands of poor residents, a new training center for the mentally
ill, and infant-maternal care programs to reduce the county's high infant mortality
rate.[45] With the resolution of Lodge v. Buxton, change came more quickly. By 1984
three of the five members of the Burke County Commission were African-American;
the county was only the second in Georgia to have a majority-black commission. Two
of the plaintiffs, Herman Lodge and Woodrow Harvey, were among the three elected
to the commission, and Lodge was its vice chairman. (Lodge also became president
of the GLSP Board of Directors in 1983.) The presence of a third black commissioner,
Ellis Godbee, was evidence that race relations were truly in transition: his district was
65 percent white. Lodge explained the impact of this new leadership by saying that
he and his colleagues were "trying to run [the county] like a business should be run,"
adopting formal job descriptions, salary schedules, and personnel policies and adding
a retirement program for county employees. They created a department on aging,
provided support for a new nutrition center for senior citizens, and sought to establish
a health department. Furthermore, black leaders worked with GLSP attorneys in two

other cases in the mid-1980s, one seeking to end discrimination against low-income residents in one of Waynesboro's Section 8 housing complexes and another compelling Burke County to build a new jail.[46] Neither the courthouse nor the county commission remained a "symbol of injustice" for Burke County African Americans.

Back in McIntosh County, the combination of community activism and litigation was similarly altering power relations between whites and blacks. Not long after Thurnell Alston narrowly lost his bid for the county commission, African-American leaders turned to a new protest strategy: the boycott. In January 1976 Darien's new mayor dismissed all seven African Americans who worked for the city, including six sanitation workers and one police officer. None of them were given notice or severance pay. Days later the black community visited City Hall en masse, as they had when Ed Finch lay bleeding in the city jail, and they demanded that the workers be rehired and threatened to initiate a selective buying campaign if they were not. Legal services attorneys Mark Gorman and David Walbert drove up for the event. Gorman later related: "My perception of David's and my role was that we were sort of the six-guns strapped in the belt of the black community. . . . But neither of us said a word that night." They did not need to. After several leaders had spoken before the city council, the council adjourned briefly, while the activists began singing "We Shall Overcome" and other traditional protest hymns. The council soon returned and agreed, reluctantly, to reinstate the dismissed employees. Later that night Walbert and Gorman realized that they had not fully understood the racial dynamics in McIntosh County. They accompanied Alston, Grovner, Pinkney, and other male leaders to a black-owned gas station across the highway from City Hall. Both lawyers were surprised when, with a sheriff's cruiser passing back and forth in front of the station, everyone else pulled out a gun. "I hadn't realized they were armed," said Walbert. "When I saw all those guns, I remember thinking, 'Jesus Christ, no wonder the city council rescinded.'" Gorman added that he "came to realize during my years in south Georgia, that one of the principal reasons for relative peace between the races was that both were equally armed and each side knew it." When the lawyers left for Brunswick later that night, their clients escorted them through the McIntosh County swamps back to the Glynn County line.[47]

Their victory before the city council did not keep the African-American community from initiating a boycott against the county's white businesses. In doing so, they hoped that public officials would work to end job discrimination, especially within government agencies. After three weeks officials agreed to establish a biracial committee to implement an affirmative action program in the county, but a year and a half later there had been little progress. At that point black leaders turned back to the courts and GLSP, filing separate voting rights suits against the city of Darien and McIntosh County.[48] The cases mirrored Albany's *Paige v. Gray* (which the courts decided the same year in which attorneys filed the McIntosh County actions) and Burke County's *Lodge v. Buxton* as well as several other cases in rural Georgia. Like them, the cases attacking Darien and McIntosh County voting procedures were successful, although McIntosh County's peculiarities made the path more difficult. Initially, the same district court judge who had dismantled Burke County's at-large system, Anthony Alaimo, dismissed the suit against Darien because black voter registration was high and a black man, Chester Devillers, was a city councilman. On appeal the Fifth Circuit reversed Alaimo's decision, citing evidence of racial discrimination that included blacks' lower educational levels, the purge of 137 voters during Alston's previous attempt to win a commission seat, the forty-dollar fee required to become a candidate, and evidence that a small group of whites wielded disproportionate power in city government.[49] Soon thereafter, GLSP and city attorneys settled the case against the city of Darien, dividing it into districts, including a majority-black district, just as they had partitioned the county.[50] The impact of these voting rights cases was immediate, especially for Thurnell Alston. He ran for county commissioner for a third time in 1978, and this time he won.[51]

Poverty lawyers proved to be resourceful allies elsewhere in Georgia and not only on behalf of African Americans. GLSP's slate of voting rights cases had an enormous impact on black communities across the state,[52] and civil rights cases also attacked the unequal distribution of municipal services and racial discrimination in public housing.[53] Other legal services cases brought benefits to other underrepresented groups. During the early 1970s, for example, Atlanta Legal Aid attorneys sought to extend equal voting rights to convicted felons (they were unsuccessful), improve the distribution of polling places, and ensure that low-income individuals could afford to run for public office.[54] They also made it possible for convicted criminals to receive the necessary licenses to drive a cab and to sell real estate.[55] During the early 1980s ALAS attorneys provided representation for Cuban refugees detained in the federal penitentiary in Atlanta, people whom the Immigration and Naturalization Service had detained upon their entry into the United States because they had prior criminal records. ALAS attorneys initiated habeas corpus proceedings to seek their release.[56] GLSP attorneys helped an allegedly homosexual soldier regain his position in the army,[57] prevented an emotionally disturbed student from being suspended as a result of his disability,[58] and protected the voting rights of senior citizens in a Blue Ridge, Georgia, nursing home.[59] Attorneys in Albany forced the city court to change its policy of imprisoning those who were unable to pay their court-imposed fines upon their conviction on misdemeanor charges. Instead of placing these people in jail, the city would allow them to pay their fines in installments.[60]

Atlanta Legal Aid and Georgia Legal Services attorneys became involved in cases designed to reform the state's penal institutions, most notably the Georgia State Prison at Reidsville. The increased rights consciousness that pervaded American society during the 1960s and 1970s drew attention to the plight of inmates in U.S. jails. Even the state of Georgia expressed official concern by establishing the Governor's Jail Standards Study Commission, which released a proposal for minimum standards among Georgia prisons in 1979. This commission reported that, of the state's 294 jails, only one met health care standards adopted by the American Medical Association, 40 percent failed to meet fire safety standards, 41 percent were run by jailers with no relevant training, 40 of the 294 jails were more than a half-century old, and 10 percent had no shower facilities. Although poverty lawyers quickly realized that major reforms would require much more than litigation, they also understood that impact cases could initiate the process of reform. Not only were legal services programs able to confront these issues as a result of healthy funding during the late 1970s, but many legal services attorneys were philosophically inclined to advocate such efforts. One GLSP report introduced its jail conditions cases with the following pronouncement: "If, as Dostoevsky said, 'The degree of civilization in a society can be judged by entering its prisons,' then ours is still groping about in the Dark Ages."[61] Poverty lawyers hoped to encourage the "enlightenment" of the Georgia penal system.

Yet in many ways legal services attorneys remained "six-guns strapped in the belt" of clients who had other weapons. Legal challenges were but one of several means by which inmates sought to alter their environment, the most dangerous, from the perspective of both inmates and prison authorities, being collective violence.[62] Inmates of the DeKalb County Jail decided to pursue nonviolent strategies first and eventually reached out to lawyers for help. A group of inmates became angry at their treatment while awaiting trial: overcrowded, unsanitary conditions; a lack of visitation rights; no reading material; a lack of exercise opportunities; meager medical care (particularly after a bout of food poisoning at the jail); and arbitrary discipline. One inmate, nineteen-year-old Marion Beacham, testified that two local policemen took a man named "Supersonic" from the jail: "As he walked out, the fat cop hit him over the head with a blackjack. He fell down, and the little policeman hit him. The big one hit him again, and then he was put back in the cell. No one ever knew why Supersonic was beaten." In response to these problems, the inmates first circulated a petition to jail authorities, which the authorities ignored, and then attempted to send letters to Governor Lester Maddox and a local television station that never made it out of the facility. Finally, they smuggled a letter out to the newspaper and a television station. Soon thereafter, they began receiving media publicity and, as a result, the attention of Legal Aid attorneys. With Andrew Sheldon taking a lead role in the subsequent litigation, along with director Michael Terry and Victor Geminiani, the inmates challenged the jail's conditions on constitutional grounds. Two years later DeKalb County had built a new facility, and ALAS attorneys asked that the case be closed.[63] A similar combination of legal pressure and adverse publicity achieved the same result in Gwinnett County during the early 1970s.[64]

Later in the decade the Georgia Legal Services Program became involved in numerous suits against local, state, and even federal penal institutions and by 1979 saw the need to create a Jail Litigation Task Force. On occasion GLSP attorneys worked alongside their ALAS counterparts, such as in cases against the federal penitentiary in Atlanta, Fulton County Jail, and Cobb County Jail.[65] Most often, however, Georgia Legal Services attorneys were busy in the smaller towns across the state. GLSP's jail conditions litigation dated back to 1977, when attorneys filed cases against correctional facilities in Bibb, Chatham, and Richmond counties. As a result of these challenges, each county had to construct a new jail. In Richmond County, where District Judge Anthony Alaimo agreed with legal services attorneys that the jail conditions were inhumane and therefore unconstitutional as a violation of the Eighth Amendment, the court entered a consent order stipulating changes to address overcrowding, staffing, access to reading and law materials, classification and segregation of prisoners, exercise and other physical amenities, discipline, and visitation. Also, the jail was to comply with American Medical Association Standards for the Accreditation of Medical Care and Health Service in Jails and HEW regulations regarding architectural accessibility and nondiscrimination against the handicapped.[66] Similar decisions followed throughout the state.[67] Sometimes prisoners complained not only about physical conditions but also about mistreatment at the hands of authorities. Such was the allegation of Terry Kelsey, the named plaintiff in GLSP's suit against the Bleckley County Jail. Each time Sheriff Coley or his deputies beat Kelsey, he wrote a letter to either his wife or his girlfriend (for Kelsey's sake, hopefully neither read his deposition), asking them to convince his mother to approach the local NAACP president for help. Among the most salient problems facing inmates there was the sheriff's determination to limit their contact with attorneys. In one instance he refused to allow GLSP attorney Camille Hope to see a client because he disapproved of her "unladylike" behavior. Eventually, these allegations became the centerpiece of a GLSP lawsuit that reformed the Bleckley County Jail.[68]

None of the cases was as complicated, far-reaching, or long-lasting as *Guthrie v. Evans,* which pitted convicted criminals and their lawyers against the most notorious penal institution in the state, the Georgia State Prison at Reidsville. Again, a group of inmates initiated the case by filing a "crudely written" complaint in 1972.[69] Arthur S. Guthrie, Joseph Coggins III, and fifty other inmates signed the document, which fell (fortunately, for the inmates) onto Judge Anthony Alaimo's docket. Alaimo had been born in Italy and immigrated to the United States as a child. During his service in the United States Army in World War II, Germans captured the young soldier and held him in a prison camp before Alaimo escaped, disguised as an Italian worker. After the war he returned to college and earned his law degree from Emory University in 1948. When faced with the inmates' allegations, Alaimo had been a federal judge for only a year, having been appointed by Richard Nixon in 1971. During the course of the litigation Alaimo would preside over several prison conditions cases, most emanating from GLSP's Augusta office and the desk of Bob Cullen. He also proved decisive in several civil rights cases, including those in McIntosh and Burke counties, with which GLSP attorneys were involved. In fact, it was through Alaimo that Bob Cullen and GLSP became involved, somewhat reluctantly, in *Guthrie v. Evans.*

After the inmates filed their initial complaint, one of the leaders, Joseph Coggins, contacted the NAACP Legal Defense Fund and requested assistance. The Legal Defense Fund asked a Columbus, Georgia, attorney, Sanford D. Bishop, to investigate the inmates' claims and soon thereafter became deeply involved in the case. Their first objective was to desegregate the prison, which the federal court had ordered in 1974.[70] Then attorneys sought to remedy the conditions at Reidsville. In a later decision Judge Alaimo outlined these problems, noting that "testimony covered the gamut typical of these cases: substandard environmental conditions; inadequate medical and psychiatric care; unconstitutional disciplinary practices; summary punishments and guard brutality; failure to protect from harm; racial discrimination in work assignments, imposition of discipline, and other prison practices; racially motivated verbal abuse; infringements on the rights of Muslim inmates; inadequate law library; lack of educational and vocational activities; interference with correspondence."[71] A GLSP report was more graphic in its descriptions, calling the conditions at the State Prison "horrendous" and "unbearable": "Some prisoners were fed only once every third day. The level of light in some cells was so dim—only five foot-candles—that it was considered torture. There was no heat and, worse in South Georgia, no cooling and poor ventilation. Prisoners were routinely segregated. Open dormitories were overcrowded with 110 inmates each, and there were not enough bunks for all inmates. Human waste not only accumulated in cells but also caked on the bars through which food was passed. Even worse, fresh water and sewer lines were interconnected so that sewage often flowed from water faucets."[72] Legal Defense Fund attorneys guided the litigation through the discovery period and trial, which ended in 1977. Because of the complexity and breadth of the case, Alaimo appointed a special master to oversee the discovery and settlement process; that person would report back to Alaimo regarding developments in the case. Like other prison conditions cases, the court's role was to supervise and encourage the parties to resolve disputes themselves, rather than to issue numerous opinions. The trial, then, which itself took place before the special master, was not the alpha and omega of the litigation but only allowed the sides to clarify their arguments and marshal evidence on their behalf.

Once LDF attorneys saw the *Guthrie* case through discovery and trial, they decided to abandon it largely for financial reasons. At that point Judge Alaimo asked Bob Cullen and Georgia Legal Services to enter the fray. Alaimo, who had presided over the Richmond County jail conditions case, which Cullen litigated in 1977 and 1978, knew and respected Cullen. But GLSP director John Cromartie was not enthusiastic about assuming responsibility for the case because he realized that its resolution was years away and would require an enormous sacrifice on the part of Cullen and other legal services attorneys. After meeting with Alaimo, however, Cromartie acquiesced, and Cullen became the inmates' primary advocate.[73] When Cullen replaced the lawyers of LDF, there was an evident shift in the relationship between opposing attorneys. Whereas they had previously been "fierce adversaries," after 1978 their interaction was more cooperative. This change was partly a result of personality, but there were other factors involved. Not least among them was that Alaimo had made it clear in other jail conditions cases that he was supportive of the inmates' efforts. Furthermore, the trial was the most antagonistic segment of the litigation, after which it was clear that the court was determined to reshape Reidsville's state prison. Cullen was, in a sense, riding a wave of court-ordered reform. In any case, after 1978 the parties began to resolve many of the disputes between inmates and prison authorities.[74]

Meanwhile, the inmates themselves had become less involved in the litigation. Shortly after LDF answered their requests for help, "events in this and later phases of *Guthrie* were dominated by attorneys, with the plaintiff-inmates as quiet and some-times silent partners." Yet, if they were not filing their "crudely written" complaints and seeking legal counsel, the Reidsville inmates as a whole were not at all silent during the 1970s. First, Cullen met regularly with an advisory council of inmates that raised issues of importance to them. Second, after the court's 1974 desegregation order "incidents of physical abuse and verbal threats escalated," such that one No-vember day a group of inmates went on strike during work detail. Guards responded by firing on them "without provocation," killing one and wounding others. Violence remained prevalent throughout the decade, even as Cullen took over for the depart-ing LDF attorneys.[75] During the summer of 1978 some two hundred black prisoners rebelled against their predominantly white guards and white inmates, and six of them would face the death penalty for killing one of the guards.[76] The legal dilemmas fac-ing the lawyers were, in some ways, far removed from the daily dilemmas facing the inmates.

Prison life at Reidsville began to change perceptibly, however, once Cullen be-came involved in the case. Of forty-one separate issues up for debate in 1978, the inmates won relief on forty.[77] The state agreed to lower the permanent prison popu-lation by half until it erected two new wings that contained individual cells rather than dormitories. No longer could authorities use corporal punishment to enforce discipline, nor could they summarily punish inmates by segregating them from other inmates. State officials improved the quality of food (including pork-free diets for Muslim inmates), installed fans to improve ventilation, provided opportunities for daily recreation, and complied with fire safety requirements. Along with constructing two new wings, the prison added new classrooms and activity areas and made library materials more readily available. Other agreements provided for improved medical services, religious liberty for Muslim inmates, policies concerning the distribution of coveted jobs for inmates (specifically those in the hospital), and an inmate griev-ance procedure.[78] None of these changes happened overnight. There was a consider-able amount of noncompliance with court orders, and long into the 1980s Cullen and other attorneys continued to refashion the remedies when necessary. Once the court-appointed monitor withdrew in 1984, a state-funded monitor took responsibility for ensuring compliance, with GLSP continuing to review developments at Reidsville. A GLSP paralegal traveled to the prison twice weekly to hear inmates' complaints and guide them through the newly established grievance procedure. Violence had not disappeared, to be sure, but the outbreaks of the 1970s had ended. By 1986 the state estimated that it had spent between $55 and $100 million on the prison as a result of the *Guthrie* case, most of the expenses going toward structural changes. Georgia Legal Services, which had only reluctantly joined the inmates' effort, received $3 million in attorneys' fees over the course of the litigation.[79]

Despite the effectiveness of litigation, however halting and cautious, Cullen and other legal services attorneys realized that an exhaustive reformation of Georgia's penal institutions required more than judicial action. Many correctional facilities reflected the needs and philosophies of bygone eras or simply the inevitable decay of time. As a federal judge in one GLSP case noted, "When you say the jail was built in 1914, you don't have to identify what the problem is."[80] Many public officials, including those who presided over the jails, welcomed increased budgets and new facilities that were the product of many a legal services case. Bob Cullen suggested that the most important change within Georgia prisons was a shift from a balkanized system, in which each institution was autonomous, to a more uniform system with a larger, more professional staff, standard operating procedures, more health care, and less violence. As Warden Lansom Newsome of the Georgia State Prison related, "If you'd asked me a year ago, I might not have said this, but *Guthrie* is the best thing that could have happened."[81] Others were less than enthusiastic about such litigation.[82] Most Georgians fell into the latter category: there simply was not sufficient public sentiment to bring about revolutionary change in the state's penal institutions. Such was the lesson of much of poverty lawyers' civil rights work.

Only in North Mississippi were legal services attorneys more involved in civil rights disputes than poverty lawyers in rural Georgia. During the late 1970s NMRLS attorneys represented clients in voting rights, jail conditions, employment discrimination, and other civil rights cases but most notably served as legal advocates for northern Mississippi's most active civil rights organization, the United League. Elsewhere in the state, Central Mississippi attorneys pursued some civil rights litigation, but the four new programs covering southern Mississippi directed their attention primarily toward institutional development and basic client counsel. Poverty lawyers in Alabama, especially with the statewide Legal Services Corporation of Alabama, also engaged in civil rights advocacy but were less active than those in Georgia and North Mississippi. Even in Georgia, legal services lawyers did not become involved in racial disputes uniformly across the state, as they did public benefits, housing, consumer, and domestic cases.

What explains this lack of uniformity? The most important ingredient in civil rights litigation was, as the experience of GLSP attorneys suggests, community mobilization. That is, poverty lawyers became involved in civil rights conflicts only where local activists had already begun some form of protest and requested legal representation. Scholars have long sought to identify the underlying currents that shaped each community's unique pattern of social change. While this inquiry lies beyond the scope of the present study, clearly there was great diversity in the South, and each locale found its own means of resolving racial tensions and reshaping racial relationships (or not).[83] Legal services programs happened to become entangled in only some of these local struggles. Whether or not poverty lawyers became involved was not, however, solely dependent on the internal dynamics of each individual community. Rather, the established, predominantly rural programs—Georgia Legal Services and North Mississippi Rural Legal Services—were more likely than other programs to become involved in local civil rights disputes. Some of the lawyers working for these organizations had begun their careers earlier in the decade, which placed them closer in time to the civil rights movement of the 1960s. Also, these programs had a longer institutional history in the communities they served. North Mississippi, for example, had a relationship with the United League that began during the early 1970s; when United League activists began pressuring Tupelo and other northern Mississippi towns later in the decade, it was not the first time that poverty lawyers assisted their struggle. Younger legal services programs were more concerned with survival and institutional stability during the late 1970s. LSC was not pushing law reform to the extent that legal services leaders of the 1960s had and in fact was encouraging programs to prioritize their work, leading to an emphasis on public benefits cases (most pronounced with LSCA).[84] Stanley Taylor, the NMRLS attorney who became the director of South Mississippi Legal Services in Biloxi, noticed that under LSC each local program was "being transformed into a service oriented institution," as opposed to the reformist bent of programs in the 1960s and early 1970s.[85] Indeed, Martha Bergmark, the first director of Southeast Mississippi Legal Services, believed that "in terms of the program's core activities . . . it was our political salvation that we maintained a very large caseload of just routine cases." Local judges and private attorneys, who initially resisted the creation of legal services programs, came to see poverty lawyers as a necessary component of the justice system, providing counsel to people who would otherwise go without representation.[86] Finally, there were other civil rights firms based in Montgomery (the Southern Poverty Law Center and ACLU) and Jackson (ACLU, LCCRUL, LCDC, and LDF) that had been working on behalf of African Americans prior to the expansion of legal services. Where these organizations were still active, there was little need for poverty lawyers to engage in civil rights work.

Nevertheless, the younger programs became involved in civil rights disputes that reflected the same range, if not the same volume, of legal activity present in rural Georgia. In its first annual report LSCA noted that, "as the 1980s draw nearer, the struggle for racial equality of the sixties may seem distant and remote. Much was accomplished in that era, but much remains to be done before equal rights is a reality for everyone." Only a small proportion of the organization's caseload was devoted to civil rights—1.4 percent in 1979 and 2 percent in 1980—but LSCA lawyers worked on a wide variety of disputes. They helped African Americans in Gadsden obtain Community Development money for sewer and water lines in a neighborhood in which dozens of black families had no such services. Dothan staff members helped the black community acquire recreational facilities commensurate with their white neighbors.[87] On occasion poverty lawyers turned to the courts, handling cases involving voting rights,[88] jail conditions,[89] housing,[90] employment discrimination,[91] and the treatment of African Americans and disabled students in the public schools.[92] The other Alabama programs, based in the city of Birmingham and the predominantly white northeastern corner of the state, were less involved in civil rights cases.[93]

As in Alabama, to say that Mississippi's new programs were less confrontational than the GLSP and NMRLS does not mean that they were not confrontational at all. Many of the figures who became prominent leaders in the new programs had begun their careers with either NMRLS or CMLS, where they were involved in law reform litigation. Bergmark, for example, grew up in Mississippi and worked for a Head Start facility during the tumultuous summer of 1964. When she left Mississippi for Oberlin College in 1966, she thought she would never want to return. Soon thereafter, however, she decided to go back to Mississippi because "there was so much to do there" in those "exciting times." After matriculating at the University of Michigan School of Law, Bergmark returned during the summer of 1971 as an intern with North Mississippi Rural Legal Services. That summer, marking the beginning of her legal career, she traveled to Parchman Penitentiary to work on habeas corpus pleadings and researched a Tate County jury discrimination case. Bergmark returned the following summer and, upon graduation, won a Reginald Heber Smith Fellowship to practice with Community Legal Services in Jackson. She left poverty law practice briefly to join her law school classmate and, later, husband in a private civil rights firm in Hattiesburg, but, when LSC funds became available, she was one of a group of attorneys who helped plan the expansion process and became the first director of the new program based in Hattiesburg. She retained the position for nine years, from 1978 to 1987.[94] Other legal services lawyers moved directly from NMRLS and CMLS into the new programs emerging in southern Mississippi: Harrison McIver, Solomon Osborne, and Stanley Taylor, to name a few. Like all poverty lawyers, they had spent much of their time providing basic counsel to individual clients but had also been involved with civil rights cases early in their careers. Taylor became proficient in consumer advocacy, and McIver would recall doing the "meat and bread" cases, including divorces. At the same time, Taylor worked on school desegregation cases as well as other law reform efforts during the 1960s and early 1970s, McIver was involved in numerous impact cases involving HUD and Hill-Burton regulations and joined civil rights protests while working for NMRLS, and Osborne similarly lent his expertise to North Mississippi's civil rights agenda.[95] They were not unaware of the potential of poverty lawyers to encourage and occasionally force change.

Although the newly created southern Mississippi programs were less likely to engage in law reform litigation than their more established counterparts, these leaders pursued such strategies when they seemed appropriate. Martha Bergmark described some of the cases that were more controversial in the minds of the same local attorneys who had only recently come to accept the program. Southeast Mississippi lawyers brought two jail conditions cases against the Forrest and Jones county jails; in each case the parties settled the cases, and the counties fell under a consent order to improve their facilities. They handled a voting rights case in Jefferson Davis County in the wake of redistricting after the 1980 census that sought to increase black political power in the county. Other cases with racial implications involved Section 8 housing, utility rate regulation, and the Mississippi Employment Security Commission's job referral practices.[96] Some civil rights cases did not directly involve racial issues. Harrison McIver, then with Southwest Mississippi Legal Services, remembered representing a pregnant high school student, for example, in her successful attempt to force the system to readmit her and allow her to earn her diploma.[97] Likewise, Central Mississippi Legal Services attorneys engaged in civil rights advocacy that, rather than augmenting black political power (as many GLSP and NMRLS cases promised to do), challenged local jail conditions and sought to prevent discrimination against clients with mental and physical disabilities.[98] Ultimately, however, North Mississippi became the hot spot for poverty lawyers' civil rights activity during the 1970s.

North Mississippi Rural Legal Services attorneys worked in an environment that was remarkably different from that of their Deep South counterparts, even those in rural Georgia. Like no other legal services program in the region, and few in the country, black lawyers dominated the institution from the early 1970s, both numerically and as leaders, and were more connected to local black activists and African-American organizations. While North Mississippi carried a heavy caseload of domestic, public benefits, and consumer cases, its leaders were aggressive in their use of legal strategies to support civil rights activism and African-American interests. Correspondingly, local activists were well aware of the potential of the law as an instrument of social change and thus welcomed impact litigation. Some even came to hold prominent positions within NMRLS, the most significant being Alfred "Skip" Robinson, the head of the United League, who became chairman of the NMRLS board of directors. One community organizer suggested that NMRLS was "a positive program for the grass root and community people," and those associated with North Mississippi saw it as a "people's program" and its legal staff as "people's lawyers."[99] The intimacy between North Mississippi and its client community carried a price that became evident in time, but during the late 1970s the relationship enabled legal services attorneys to play vital roles in northern Mississippi's racial struggles.

North Mississippi's director throughout this period, Wilhelm Joseph, had a history of community activism. Joseph was not a native Mississippian but, rather, had come to the United States from Trinidad on a track scholarship. He matriculated at Mississippi Valley State College in the spring of 1966, and a good part of his education was learning the ways of the American South. Joseph remembered: "It didn't take me very long to be . . . incensed by what was all around me . . . . I was surprised by the gap between what the law at the time said life should be about and what in fact was happening on the street." Vestiges of segregation were ubiquitous. "There were still signs up: 'Black' and 'White.' . . . blacks were still going to the black part of restaurants; doctors' offices were still segregated." When he traveled to Vicksburg during Christmas vacation, he noticed that blacks were still riding in the back of city buses. Joseph grew even angrier when the president of Mississippi Valley State refused to offer the school's facilities to marchers who took up James Meredith's solitary march across the state after a bullet felled the activist. The young man came to believe that the school itself was part of the problem, perpetuating an oppression of the mind, if not of the body.[100]

Joseph became a student organizer, traveling to both predominantly black and predominantly white colleges across the state to recruit others to join civil rights protests. Along with hundreds of fellow students, Joseph marched and picketed in small Mississippi towns throughout his years at Mississippi Valley State, urging public officials and businesses to hire more African Americans. Student organizers also encouraged other young people to vote and to pressure their parents to vote, especially in the election of 1968. By his senior year Joseph won election as student body president and from that position directed his attention toward school administrators. He asked them to adopt more courses in black history, buy more books by black authors, and schedule more black speakers on campus. Mississippi Valley State students protested in support of these demands, leading to the arrest of fifteen students and the temporary expulsion of nearly two hundred more. Officials within and outside the school targeted Joseph for his activities. Governor John Bell Williams asked Mississippi senator James Eastland to help deport Joseph, and a police officer arrested him en route to a protest in the town of Marks just two days before graduation. It was this arrest that gave Joseph his first major contact with North Mississippi Rural Legal Services: attorney Bill Joiner represented him in court.[101]

Rather than leaving Mississippi, either willfully or by force, Joseph decided to enter law school at the state's flagship university, the University of Mississippi, known as "Ole Miss." Under Dean Joshua Morse the law school had begun admitting African-American students, though the first black student, Cleveland Montgomery, found administrators all too eager to withdraw their invitation. As Joseph recalled, "His gun fell out of his briefcase on the law school steps, and within two weeks he was expelled." During Joseph's first year Ole Miss "was not a place that was socially friendly on the whole," though not only for African Americans. Poor whites also lived "on the fringe" of university activities, which revolved around fraternities and sororities populated by the sons and daughters of Mississippi's elite. Nevertheless, Joseph promised himself that, by the time he left Ole Miss, everyone would know that "change was coming."[102] From the perspective of the chief of campus security and, it turned out, the Mississippi Sovereignty Commission, Joseph was one of the state's "troublesome Negroes." But Joseph's primary objective was that of all law school students: to graduate, which he did in 1972. As one of a steadily growing number of African-American graduates, Joseph's success evidenced the shifting racial environment at the university. Nevertheless, he remained dissatisfied that vestiges of racism persisted. In an editorial published in the school newspaper just months before leaving Ole Miss, Joseph lamented that "the racist Confederate flag (which incidentally makes fair though not fine toilet tissue) is a symbol of school spirit here." He signed the letter, "Wilhelm Joseph, Just another nigger." The last Sovereignty Commission report to mention Joseph read: "Chief Popernik (of Ole Miss) stated Wilhelm Joseph has finally finished at the University and was, at present, in New York City. Chief further advised everything has been extra quiet on the campus this summer."[103]

Yet Wilhelm Joseph was not finished letting Mississippians know that "change was coming." He spent two years as national director of the Law Students Civil Rights Council, an organization created in the wake of Freedom Summer to recruit minorities into law school and provide them with summer internships in public interest and civil rights firms. In 1974 he returned to Oxford as a staff attorney, then an administrator, and, by the end of 1975, director of North Mississippi Rural Legal Services. It was an auspicious time to join a legal services program because Congress had recently passed the Legal Services Corporation Act and LSC soon began offering "equalization" funds to make sure that northern Mississippi's poor had at least "minimum access" to legal counsel. The organization more than tripled in size and more than doubled its number of offices. Joseph recalled little opposition to this expansion, other than the occasional hesitancy of landlords to rent them office space. His major dilemmas were logistical: where to open new offices, whom to hire to fill those offices, and how to retain attorneys in small-town Mississippi.[104]

North Mississippi's lawyers faced enmity from locals as they began working in these new communities. "There was hostility in those towns once we got there," Joseph recalled, "hostility toward the work we did because . . . back then, legal services in Mississippi, by necessity, became a kind of civil rights practice." First of all, northern Mississippi was predominantly black, especially the Delta counties. Second, African Americans had experienced only marginal success finding jobs in municipalities and businesses in which whites predominated, many counties were reluctant to allow blacks to serve on juries, there were few African-American police officers and public officials, and schools remained heavily segregated.[105] Potential clients faced countless problems that were a direct result of their race. While North Mississippi attorneys did not adopt a focused reform strategy, as had the NAACP Legal Defense Fund when it targeted segregation itself throughout the 1930s, '40s, and '50s, poverty lawyers hoped that, case by case, community by community, their presence would help transform the racial status quo.

These racial struggles revolved around employment, education, and political activism. At first glance, based only on the holdings in reported judicial decisions, NMRLS lawyers were distinctly unsuccessful during the late 1970s and early 1980s. Of nineteen reported employment discrimination decisions, North Mississippi lawyers won seven;[106] of four reported cases dealing with school students allegedly denied due process, they won just one;[107] of six reported actions on behalf of convicted criminals, they won two;[108] and in three other discrimination claims against a hospital, school district, and utilities cooperative, they lost all three decisions.[109] North Mississippi attorneys enjoyed a better record in voting rights cases, winning five of six decisions,[110] and cases involving First Amendment freedoms, winning at least partial victories in three of four published decisions.[111] Such a statistical breakdown is, of course, an incomplete means of comprehending the influence of North Mississippi's civil rights activity. Most of the decisions dealt with procedural claims or resolved cases involving individual clients rather than broad, reform-minded class actions. Even victories could be ambiguous, giving partial but not categorical relief to legal services clients. None of the cases threatened major alterations of racial relationships in Mississippi, with the possible exception of one, *Ayers v. Fordice*.[112] That is, there was no *Brown* or *Swann* or *Bakke* decision upon which rode the legal status of all African Americans.

Nevertheless, North Mississippi Rural Legal Services began to reshape the legal status of low-income African Americans in their corner of the South, which was not an insignificant corner, considering that it encompassed the Mississippi Delta. Many legal services cases resulted in settlements favorable to legal services clients, rather than in published decisions. Of the cases that NMRLS counted among its most significant as of late 1978, just four of eleven resulted in published decisions. (All but two of the eleven cases involved civil rights disputes.) North Mississippi attorneys negotiated agreements that allowed Muslim inmates of Parchman Penitentiary the freedom to practice their religion, forced officials to improve living conditions at the Panola County Jail and other facilities, won a small monetary award in a wrongful death action against two Byhalia policemen charged with brutality, won concessions from the city of Oxford regarding the equalization of municipal services, protected the rights of citizens to march and assemble in Tupelo by overturning two city ordinances, and required the city of Greenwood to adopt an affirmative action program and compensate those previously denied city employment in the amount of $115,000.[113]

North Mississippi attorneys later recalled a wide variety of civil rights disputes. Leonard McClellan explained the NMRLS strategy with regard to employment discrimination cases, which they began focusing on shortly after he joined the program in the summer of 1975. Since "we didn't have the resources or the staff for us to sue all" the counties, towns, and banks in northern Mississippi, "we decided to select certain key cities in different parts of our service area, figuring that if we filed lawsuits against those that some of the others would get the message." As it turned out, "It worked pretty much as planned": the target institutions opened up positions to African Americans, and other local leaders approached North Mississippi to help the organization formulate an affirmative action policy so that they would avoid litigation.[114] Wilhelm Joseph returned to Ole Miss by filing a case against its law school alleging racial discrimination in its treatment of black law students, and he also recalled confronting numerous locales about their various methods of diluting black voting power.[115] Harrison McIver, who began his career with NMRLS in 1977, related that he and McClellan represented a client in a lawsuit against the sheriff of Quitman County. They were unable to convince a jury of the sheriff's misconduct, but McIver maintained that "we really took him to task for what he had done."[116] By themselves these cases were small strikes against the status quo; together they were helping to remake Mississippi.

What made North Mississippi Rural Legal Services unique from other civil rights firms was its flexibility and the volume of legal challenges that federal funding made possible during the late 1970s and early 1980s.[117] As Harrison McIver pointed out, NMRLS attorneys had a "deep pocket theory": "Because I wasn't on billable hours," he explained, "I would just work the hell out of a lawyer" during the course of litigation, and "many times they would settle." Unlike most public interest lawyers, poverty lawyers were not bound by any specific agenda. Theirs was the broad goal of providing "equal access" to the legal system. Individual programs were responsible for deciding what that meant and could set their own priorities within the context of federal regulations. During this period North Mississippi decided, in effect, that the most pressing problem facing their clients was racial discrimination. They would quickly discover that they were not as free as it seemed but not before they had used those deep pockets to advance a civil rights agenda across northern Mississippi.

On one of its major legal fronts North Mississippi was allied with the United League, which by the mid-1970s had become the most prominent activist organization in Mississippi.[118] NMRLS's association with the United League dated to the late 1960s, when legal services attorneys represented black residents of Holly Springs in a school desegregation case. Early in the 1970s NMRLS lawyers provided legal support for United League protests in Starkville and Coffeeville, such that law enforcement officials accused NMRLS lawyers of "coaching" the marchers because they were "always right in the middle of any march or any trouble involving civil rights." Later that decade North Mississippi's lawyers were similarly "in the middle" of three major engagements in Lexington, Okolona, and Tupelo, so much so that local and state officials called for LSC to investigate the program's activities.[119]

The United League came to expect and rely on the program's legal support. On one hand, league leaders expressed cynicism about the ability of legal authority to eliminate inequality. Skip Robinson, for example, declared that a major motivation for his protests was "to spread the news that the progress we thought we made in the 1960s is only a dream and not a reality." Much like earlier decades, *law enforcement* often meant the suppression of African-American activism, not the fulfillment of equal rights. During one late-1970s conflict Robinson suggested that "law and order has completely broken down in Okolona. It has gotten to the point where you can't tell law officers from the Klan—they're one and the same!"[120] Moreover, United League leaders dismissed the inherent virtues of nonviolence and an exaggerated reliance on legal processes. They utilized nonviolent tactics but advocated fighting violence with violence if necessary. Howard Gunn, an Okolona United League leader who became chairman of the NMRLS board in 1978, justified a shootout with Klan members by saying: "If any person fires upon us, we aren't going to tuck our tails and run. We're going to retaliate with every available resource we have. If any person ever fires upon any Black person in this community, we're going to blow their doggone head off." And, again, Robinson: "We still believe very deeply in what Dr. King meant when he said that love and understanding can overcome hate and killing. But we don't feel he meant that we should be cowards. If the Klan moves into my neighborhood and shoots at my neighbor, shoots into my house, I'm not going to fall on my knees and say 'O Lord, stop him.' God stops man through man. If the Klan shoots into my home, if I do anything I'm going to say 'O Lord help me to aim straight.'"[121] On the other hand, Robinson and the United League hoped that North Mississippi lawyers could help them achieve their goals by using the legal system. They encouraged litigation and depended on legal services attorneys to protect their constitutional rights. Symbolic of their precarious trust in the law was a United League T-shirt that featured the slogan JUSTICE FOR ALL beside a picture of a gavel.[122]

Like United League protests elsewhere in the state, such as those in Byhalia in 1974, the organization's engagement in Tupelo began with allegations of police brutality. Located in the majority-white northeastern quadrant of the state, the small industrial city had a reputation for peaceful race relations. Yet early in 1978, when city officials refused to fire two police officers found guilty of beating a confession out of jail inmate Eugene Pasto, the black community seethed. Four days later another black prisoner up the road in Holly Springs was found hanging in his cell, his hands and feet bound. This succession of events propelled the United League into action. Under the leadership of Skip Robinson the organization began street protests and demanded the termination of the two Tupelo policemen. Linking these acts to broader racial injustices, the league also initiated a boycott of white-owned businesses beginning on 24 March, Good Friday, and urged public officials and local business owners to end discriminatory hiring practices.[123] Later that year similar acts of violence toward black prisoners brought United League protests to Lexington, Okolona, and other northern Mississippi towns.

North Mississippi lawyers were never far behind. They helped activists navigate local ordinances governing marches, represented activists jailed on various misdemeanor charges associated with violating these ordinances, and negotiated with local officials regarding their clients' demands, especially with regard to employment practices. In the midst of the spring of 1978 protests Lewis Myers Jr. and other NMRLS lawyers filed suit against the city of Tupelo, alleging that officials had discriminated against three African-American applicants for jobs as police officers and firemen. The officials had claimed that there were no job openings but subsequently moved the two policemen charged with beating Eugene Pasto into positions in the fire department. In another suit in federal court NMRLS lawyers represented a United League activist who claimed that Tupelo law enforcement authorities had intimidated him and arrested him illegally. They also planned to file suit against two major Tupelo retail stores charging them with employment discrimination.[124]

Meanwhile, United League activists conducted numerous marches and a selective buying campaign against Tupelo merchants, and a rejuvenated Ku Klux Klan met these protests with marches of its own, creating tense standoffs in the streets of the now turbulent city. On one occasion in early April, 450 United League marchers listened to Skip Robinson vow to continue battling local authorities and profess his lack of fear of the Klan and recent threats to his life: "If God takes my life for freedom," he exclaimed, "then so be it. Long live America." At the same time, in a local motel, the Grand Dragon of the Mississippi Knights of the Ku Klux Klan, Douglas C. Coen, was telling his audience that "the white man has ruled this earth for 5,000 years, not because they are stupid, [but] just the opposite." He urged the seventy people in attendance (a number that included several reporters and policemen) to unite in racial solidarity. Failure would mean that "you won't have Tupelo in three years[;] it will be a mass ghetto." Fortunately, such fiery language had not, as of yet, led to massive violence, though it had led to a number of arrests.[125]

These activities drew the attention, indeed the ire, of local and state authorities. On 9 May 1978 Tupelo's board of aldermen authorized Mayor Clyde Whitaker to file a formal complaint against North Mississippi Rural Legal Services with the Legal Services Corporation, which was responsible for overseeing local programs and ensuring their compliance with federal law.[126] By filing the complaint, the mayor initiated a bureaucratic process that would culminate in an LSC investigation of the program and drive a wedge between North Mississippi and the United League. Whitaker's initial letter to Arlo Temple, an attorney in private practice who served as chairman of the State Advisory Council for legal services, consisted of vague allegations that NMRLS attorneys, most notably Lewis Myers, had violated various LSC regulations. Whitaker related that NMRLS attorneys "originally came into the picture under the guise of representing the United League, but in the past six weeks they have been most active in encouraging, organizing and giving active leadership to marches, demonstrations, boycotts and picketing." Moreover, "when the marchers have reached the Lee County Courthouse in downtown Tupelo, these attorneys have joined in the demonstration and have made highly inflammable speeches as a part of the demonstration." They similarly took the lead in organizing the boycotts and placing pickets in Tupelo's business district. "These illegal activities on the part of the Legal Services attorneys have resulted," Whitaker suggested, "in counter measures by the Ku Klux Klan and [have] brought about a condition which threatens the law and order of our City and the safety of all of our citizens." Not only had North Mississippi attorneys engaged in prohibited political activism, but they were also guilty of "failing to act in a manner consistent with attorneys' professional responsibilities," "instituting legal action solely for the purpose of harassment of the City of Tupelo," and misusing federal funds.[127]

Subsequently, the City of Tupelo's attorney, Guy Mitchell Jr., embellished these complaints in a letter to an LSC official, Hulett Askew. First, NMRLS attorneys had violated the LSC Act by "engaging in and encouraging others to engage in public demonstrations, picketing and boycotting." On 10 June Lewis Myers made a speech from the Lee County Courthouse steps to a United League assembly, exhorting his listeners to continue their protests. During the previous three months there had been eleven similar marches, and each time Myers and other NMRLS attorneys had been present. Myers was allegedly the "second most vocal person" at these demonstrations, behind Skip Robinson. On occasion he "personally stationed the pickets." Deborah Jackson, another NMRLS attorney, had recently spoken at a United League rally in Holly Springs, where she urged those present to support the protests and suggested that public school teachers encourage their students to join the United League. Furthermore, Robinson was head of the United League and a member of the NMRLS board of directors, and United League leader Howard Gunn was then chairman of the board of directors. Mitchell supported these claims with newspaper articles and five affidavits from a local merchant, three reporters, and Tupelo's chief of police.[128] The attorney's second claim was that North Mississippi lawyers had failed to abide by professional standards in their use of media outlets to publicize their litigation. Lewis Myers, for example, regularly called news conferences to announce lawsuits, sometimes before he had actually filed suit.[129] These legal actions were designed primarily to harass the City of Tupelo, contrary to standards of professional conduct. Furthermore, North Mississippi attorneys violated professional ethics by "actively solicit[ing] clients and . . . the filing of class actions." The news director for two local radio stations, Chuck Connor, attended a United League meeting at a Tupelo church where a North Mississippi attorney told of the opening of a new office in Tupelo and urged those present to contact the program "if any of them felt they had been discriminated against in any way." Connor quoted the attorney: "We particularly love class action suits, and we like to sue cities, hospitals, schools, factories and banks."[130] Mitchell also charged that North Mississippi had failed to solicit the advice of local bar leaders and to attempt to hire local lawyers before making hiring decisions, most recently by placing Sentwali Aiyetoro, who was from Kansas City, in the new Tupelo office.

The most damaging allegation of wrongdoing on the part of North Mississippi Rural Legal Services was Mitchell's claim that the program had misused federal funds by committing them to United League activities. North Mississippi had become, in effect, the "alter-ego of the United League," financing the league's activities in Tupelo and elsewhere. Tupelo authorities believed that NMRLS printed and distributed United League literature, including a communist newspaper that advocated the overthrow of the United States government and state "confiscation of all means of production."[131] Further evidence of the intimate relationship between the two organizations was that Skip Robinson had declared that the United League would continue its protests until Tupelo officials abandoned their calls for an investigation of NMRLS. In essence, Mitchell suggested, North Mississippi Rural Legal Services had become "a black racist organization rather than a responsible law office."[132]

LSC responded to these complaints by initiating an investigation of North Mississippi, in part because Mississippi's congressional delegates, including archconservatives John Stennis and James Eastland, along with a young Trent Lott, were demanding such an inquiry.[133] Those responsible for documenting the program's activities were the architects of the expansion of legal services in the South during the late 1970s, Hulett "Bucky" Askew, Clint Lyons, and Michael Terry, the last of whom had joined LSC's Atlanta Regional Office from the Atlanta Legal Aid Society.[134] Later LSC hired a consultant to review the competing claims and offer an opinion about the legality of NMRLS's relationship with the United League. For its part North Mississippi procured the counsel of a former NMRLS lawyer, John Brittain, then living in Connecticut, and vigorously disputed the claims of Tupelo authorities. Wilhelm Joseph later reflected, "We felt the investigations were unjustified and were simply a political response to these politicians in Washington," and "we did everything we could to fight . . . LSC." The corporation was, in his mind, "caving in to political pressure. We can't afford to do that. We are here locally, on the ground. And we're going to organize even if it's against you [LSC], because we know we are on the right track here morally, spiritually, legally, everything."[135]

In their communication to the LSC investigators Brittain and Joseph professed their intent to cooperate with the investigation but also emphasized their belief "that NMRLS has represented its clients 'zealously within the bounds of the law' in providing 'high quality legal assistance to those who would otherwise be unable to afford adequate legal counsel.'"[136] They related a brief history of the organization's "ten years of existence under the most hostile and antagonistic conditions." "What looms at stake here," suggested the authors, "is the strength of the program to be kept free from the influence of political pressure and the freedom of its attorneys to protect the best interests of their clients." They believed that the program had "been singled out here not for any violation of the statutes or regulations of the Corporation or the Code of Professional Responsibility, but because of the program's long-standing vigorous and successful representation of northern Mississippi's poor people." Brittain and Joseph then discussed the Tupelo protests, noting that "Tupelo escaped the brunt of the civil rights movement" because "the people lacked a unifying catalyst for action," which appeared in the controversy surrounding the beating of Eugene Pasto. Defending North Mississippi's involvement in Tupelo and the other instances of NMRLS attorneys representing the United League, they characterized the organization as an "association of people working together to alleviate the problems associated with their poverty" and stated that roughly 70 percent of league members were poor enough to be eligible for free legal counsel.[137]

Concerning specific allegations against the program, Brittain and Joseph pointed out that the prohibition on political activity applied only to employees of legal services programs, not board members Robinson and Gunn. The attorneys alleged to have engaged in illegal activities were only present "for the purpose of providing legal assistance to a qualified client," the United League, and only "advised their clients about legal alternatives to litigation." Only if North Mississippi attorneys "usurp[ed] or invade[d] the rightful authority of a client to determine what cause of action to follow" would they be guilty of violating LSC regulations. On the contrary, NMRLS affidavits maintained that United League members marched and boycotted "on their own free will."[138] The charge that Lewis Myers "stationed" pickets was essentially true: he had "counseled demonstrators regarding the law on blocking the ingress and egress of passageways." Whereas Tupelo's complaint argued that Myers had urged people to boycott, NMRLS responded that he only "counseled and affirmed the right of his client and their member-supporters to exercise their volition by engaging in constitutionally protected activity." Myers's rhetorical flourish in delivering such counsel "merely reflects the intimacy with which he identifies with his client's plight"; "an attorney need not surrender his First Amendment rights of expression when employed by Legal Services."[139]

The allegations of irresponsible professional behavior on the part of Myers and other North Mississippi lawyers were, in the opinion of Brittain and Joseph, equally unwarranted. Not only were the city's claims "vague and nebulous," but they also asked LSC to enforce codes of conduct that only state bar associations and the courts, not LSC, were entitled to enforce.[140] Regarding NMRLS's placement of attorney Sentwali Aiyetoro in Tupelo, Brittain and Joseph admitted that in filling staff positions it had solicited the recommendations only of those private attorneys who supported legal services in Mississippi; such people were few and far between. In any case Aiyetoro was not really an "outsider" anyway because he "only ended up in Kansas City after fleeing the racism and discrimination of the Mississippi Delta where he was born and raised." Finally, Brittain and Joseph responded to the suggestion that NMRLS was the "alter-ego" of the United League and helped to finance league activities. Tupelo's claim, they argued, "has absolutely no basis in fact." Betraying the growing tension between the organization and city officials, they contended that the "NMRLS is just as vigorous in representing the United League in combating racial discrimination practiced by the City of Tupelo as Mr. Mitchell's steadfast maintenance of the white racist status quo in Tupelo." NMRLS had "uncovered no evidence" that anyone used federal funds for league activities, other than the authorized payment of court costs incurred in litigation, nor did they print or distribute league literature.[141]

Brittain and Joseph filed a second response to the Tupelo complaint in which they elaborated on their conception of North Mississippi's responsibilities to their clients.[142] NMRLS "represents a vanguard legal entity in the struggle by the poor people of Northern Mississippi to relieve the pressure of oppression and achieve a moderate degree of human equality." Citing the actions of local and state bar associations, municipal governments, school boards, and state officials, Brittain and Joseph argued that "history is replete with concrete examples of interposition and nullification" that effectively abrogated the "laws providing for equal rights for all persons." North Mississippi attorneys "have every right, indeed an obligation, to apprise its clients of legitimate alternatives that they might use as a weapon to bring a measure of racial justice to Tupelo," and they had "a professional responsibility to inform the public of the evils within and without the profession of law and to address" themselves "to those evils that affect the daily lives of poor citizens in Mississippi." Examples of such efforts to address those "evils" were North Mississippi's cases against Tupelo,[143] along with other litigation against Mississippi municipalities.[144] These and other cases "resulted in a measure of change for Black employment in the respective towns," though "employment discrimination remain[ed] a rampant problem throughout every county in Mississippi." Indeed, the persistence of racial discrimination was, according to Brittain and Joseph, a major factor in the persistence of poverty in Mississippi.[145] Because of the critical role legal services lawyers had assumed in helping low-income Mississippians, many of them African-American, improve their economic status, LSC "must treat complaints filed by a municipality with extreme suspicion and caution so as not to align itself with interests directly in conflict with the poor Black clients" whom NMRLS represented.[146]

While LSC mulled over this information during the summer and fall of 1978, the streets of Tupelo brimmed with protest. As Tupelo officials initiated the LSC investigation, they also asked United League and Klan members to end their public demonstrations. Neither group was willing to comply with this request. KKK Exulted Cyclops Gary Wilson vowed that the Klan would maintain its presence in Tupelo: "I am a white citizen of Tupelo and I stand for the white citizens of Tupelo," Wilson stated. Echoing George Wallace, he promised, "The Klan is here today, tomorrow and forever." Klan members would, however, abide by the city's resolution that banned both groups from using public facilities for marches or rallies.[147] United League leaders were not so cooperative. The resolution, adopted on 18 May, called for a ninety-day moratorium on protests for fear of a planned 10 June confrontation between league and Klan marchers. District Judge Orma Smith, however, agreed with NMRLS attorneys that the resolution was unconstitutionally broad, saying that public facilities should be open "for peaceful demonstrations or peaceful discussions." Smith then implored city officials and league leaders to negotiate, believing that Tupelo's racial controversy should be settled by "people sitting down at the conference table."

When negotiations broke down,[148] the voiding of the city's moratorium meant the 10 June marches could proceed, which they did with much tension but only minor outbreaks of violence. An estimated seven hundred United League protesters and three hundred Klansmen took turns exclaiming their beliefs from the steps of the Lee County Courthouse, with Tupelo police officers in riot gear separating the two groups.[149] By early fall the combination of protests and legal challenges brought city officials back to the negotiating table. With Mississippi NAACP leader Charles Evers mediating, Skip Robinson and Mayor Whitaker met in Jackson and agreed to an affirmative action plan. While Whitaker believed the agreement would bring an end to the United League protests, Robinson sensed an opportunity to broaden the league's victory. He orchestrated further protests during the fall of 1978, including a major march during the last weekend in November, but little more than a week later the city's affirmative action plan took effect, Robinson's attempt to win further concessions from the city was unsuccessful, and calm finally descended on Tupelo.[150]

Even as Tupelo cooled, the United League and its legal services allies moved into other Mississippi communities, most notably Lexington and Okolona. As in Tupelo, incidents of alleged police brutality were catalysts for black protests. NMRLS attorneys performed similar functions in these locales, representing jailed activists and challenging parade ordinances that limited their clients' ability to march. Also like Tupelo, the Klan was ever present.[151] At the height of this nascent movement North Mississippi's Lewis Myers announced that he was sending a list of demands to each city in the thirty-nine counties of northern Mississippi. His demands detailed how these municipalities could "clean their houses" by adopting affirmative action plans to end discriminatory hiring practices. If local United League members felt their home-towns were not meeting the demands, the league would visit those towns with protest marches.[152] The plan was bold but short-lived. By the summer of 1979 the campaigns in Lexington and Okolona had weakened internally,[153] and the United League had lost its most valuable ally, North Mississippi Rural Legal Services.

Ironically, the split between North Mississippi and the United League did not result, at least directly, from the LSC investigation of the program. Prior to issuing its findings, LSC had faced its own hostile protesters and complaints from other legal ser-vices programs concerned about the corporation's investigation of North Mississippi. In November 1978 NMRLS sponsored a conference of some one hundred civil rights attorneys, most from NMRLS and the National Conference of Black Lawyers (NCBL), to discuss the investigation.[154] One of the attendees, Lennox Hinds of the NCBL, ex-pressed the fear that they would experience continued pressure on their right of free expression as a result of their professional status.[155] Early in 1979 about four hundred persons demonstrated in front of LSC's Washington, D.C., offices and near the White House took part in a protest sponsored by the National Organization of Legal Ser-vices Workers, National Lawyers Guild, United League, Delta Ministry, and NCBL. Held "to protest the Corporation's actions and to support the legal services workers at North Mississippi Rural Legal Services and their work with the United League," they criticized any attempt to limit the First Amendment rights of legal services attorneys simply because the programs received federal funding.[156]

In response to the demonstrations LSC released a statement to defuse the conflict. The corporation stated, "We regret that lack of familiarity with the Act and Regula-tions has led many—both in legal services and outside—to believe the restrictions to be more repressive than is the fact." Furthermore, "neither the Act nor its implement-ing regulations are designed to interfere with an attorney's right to participate in any lawful public demonstration, picketing, boycott or strike, while the attorney is not en-gaged in legal assistance activities supported by the Corporation." LSC then clarified its role in a 23 January letter in which President Thomas Ehrlich expressed his "concern that legal services workers not be deterred from vigorously representing their clients" but reiterated the corporation's responsibility to investigate complaints.[157]

The following month LSC's consultant presented his findings to the corporation, and soon thereafter LSC issued its final report. Neither found substantial violations of the statutes and regulations governing legal services practice. Indeed, once the LSC investigators met with city officials and clarified the regulations, the officials themselves agreed that NMRLS was in compliance. North Mississippi's only transgressions were a "technical violation" of the LSC Act's requirement to consult with local bar leaders before hiring new attorneys, an error "mitigated . . . by the apparent lack of interest shown by those bar associations in legal services," and a lack of clarity regarding the program's accounting procedures. Without admitting any wrongdoing, NMRLS pledged to ensure that sufficient procedures existed to prevent any abuses in the use of federal funds. The investigation had no immediate effect on the program, its work, or its most aggressive attorney, Lewis Myers.[158]

Nevertheless, the relationship between North Mississippi Rural Legal Services and the United League soured during 1979 and 1980. This time director Wilhelm Joseph moved to the center of controversy. Despite LSC's exoneration of the program, Joseph began taking steps to differentiate the two organizations, a task that proved difficult. By 1979 North Mississippi was intertwined with the United League from its leadership ranks to its secretarial pools. As mentioned earlier, Skip Robinson had served as chairman of the board during the early 1970s and had been a board member since the program's infancy, and Okolona's United League leader Howard Gunn became chairman in 1978. North Mississippi's Lewis Myers and paralegal June Johnson, a veteran of the Mississippi civil rights movement of the 1960s, served on the United League's board of directors. For years North Mississippi had given jobs to United League members as paralegals and other support staff. Two such employees were Walter Stanfield, head of the Lee County chapter of the United League, and Henry Boyd, second in command to Robinson.[159] Furthermore, the links between the program and the activist organization were not simply institutional. This was a relationship rooted in the African-American struggle for equality and forged in the streets of Byhalia, Holly Springs, Okolona, Tupelo, and other towns as well as in the courthouses of northern Mississippi.

Joseph was under pressure from LSC, however, to limit the program's devotion to United League activities. He later recalled that in the wake of the Tupelo investigation "they kept their eyes on us very closely."[160] An internal corporation report issued in

1979 suggested that North Mississippi, and Lewis Myers in particular, had expended too much energy on Tupelo and other protests and reminded the program that it was prohibited from representing clients in criminal cases.[161] Shortly thereafter, NMRLS stopped representing some three hundred United League protesters facing misdemeanor charges stemming from a march in Okolona, and about this time Myers decided to leave the program, a move that chairman Howard Gunn believed would damage North Mississippi's connection to its client community. Health problems were reportedly the primary reason for Myers's departure,[162] but he and Joseph had a difference of opinion over the program's continued representation of the United League, with Joseph wanting to create a clearer distinction between the two organizations and Myers advocating "business as usual."[163] The following year Skip Robinson sharply criticized Joseph's leadership, suggesting he had "wasted more than $100,000" in hiring new attorneys rather than filling other staff positions. Robinson believed Joseph was "wasting taxpayers' money to set up a dictatorship that is used to by-pass the needs of the client community it is designed to service." Joseph, on the other hand, was "very surprised and confused" at Robinson's outburst, noting that the longtime board member had not raised these concerns during any NMRLS meetings.[164] In any case the alliance between the two organizations was no more, and by 1981, after some fifteen years of existence, the United League no longer existed as an effective protest organization.[165]

While they were valuable allies, North Mississippi lawyers could not follow a long-term civil rights agenda because of their status within the federally funded legal services program. Unlike the NAACP Legal Defense Fund and other civil rights firms, NMRLS was *not* a civil rights practice by design. Many of its lawyers and support staff worked on civil rights issues because they perceived that many of their clients' problems were rooted in race.[166] But, when the program became too enmeshed in the political activism of its clients, the regulatory apparatus that governed legal services practice became an obstacle to North Mississippi attorneys.

Poverty lawyers faced other boundaries more deeply rooted in law and the American political order. Even as the judicial system remained a powerful weapon against overt racial discrimination, the courts began to be increasingly less kind to civil rights litigants during the 1980s. Issues became more complex and the sources of and solutions to inequality less clear. One federal district judge, for example, recognized that claims of racial discrimination against the town of Cochran, Georgia, did not exactly match the facts of life there. Georgia Legal Services attorneys were trying to convince Wilbur D. Owens that officials had discriminated against Cochran's black citizens by refusing to extend municipal services such as paved roads, working fire hydrants and streetlights, and a modern sewer system into black neighborhoods. There were inequalities, to be sure, but Owens suggested they were as much economic as racial: "I imagine if we rode around town, we've got a lot of white areas that are neglected, too. Most communities have. I think we're dealing with economic power. The tax dollars seem to go to the areas that are economically more prosperous than others, and I think it unfortunately happens in the traditional South that we've had a greater percentage of our black population on that level than we have of the white population."[167] Owens was right, but that was little comfort to the legal services attorneys, whose arguments revolved around claims of racial discrimination. GLSP still won Owens's support and various concessions from officials in Cochran,[168] but they were not as successful in other disputes.

In a series of cases addressing elements of racial inequality in the public schools, Georgia Legal Services attorneys found federal and state courts reticent to embrace their arguments. The state Supreme Court, for example, dismissed a complaint against the Sumter County School Board in which GLSP asked the courts to order the state superintendent of schools to take over the local system. According to the GLSP attorneys and their clients, the school board was denying their children an "adequate education." Board members sent their children to private, all-white academies while only lukewarmly supporting improvements in the county's predominantly black public school system. Most notably, the board failed to support a bond referendum that would have funded new school construction. But from the perspective of the Supreme Court justices:

> Courts are ill-equipped to make such fundamental, legislative and administrative policy decisions as how much local supplement to teachers' salaries should be paid in order to attract qualified teachers, how many levels of English or math should be taught, whether a system of pupil ability grouping shall or shall not be used, whether buildings shall be constructed and, if so, where, and the myriad other matters involved in the everyday administration of a public school system which the courts would face were they to embark upon

the course of judicial activism desired by the school patrons [GLSP's clients]. Resolutions of these discretionary policy determinations best can be made by other branches of government.[169]

Other GLSP cases attacked educational practices that seemed rife with racial discrimination, especially the tracking of students into ability groupings. Such policies, which many Deep South school boards adopted when they were forced to desegregate in the late 1960s and early 1970s, resulted in the re-segregation of black and white students within schools that were technically integrated. While the legal services clients received some relief on a smaller scale in Tattnall County,[170] a statewide case fell short of dismantling this ubiquitous practice. In the latter litigation the Eleventh Circuit Court of Appeals found that neither tracking nor the classification of students into special education programs was sufficiently "racial" to amount to any constitutional violation but, rather, was based on sound pedagogical theory that students learned most effectively when placed among students of similar intellectual abilities.[171] As GLSP attorney Jonathan Zimring recalled, the state's "defense to the race claims [was] that it was class. Anything but race." In other words, rather than race being the determinative factor in tracking students, the state argued that it was discriminating on the basis of "ability," which Zimring saw as closely linked to socioeconomic status.[172]

The potential for change and the limits of litigation were powerfully displayed in North Mississippi's most notable case, *Ayers v. Fordice,* which sought to equalize the state's institutions of higher learning. Like its elementary and secondary schools, Mississippi had maintained segregated colleges and universities: five predominantly white and three predominantly black. In *Ayers* the plaintiffs, represented by North Mississippi's Alvin Chambliss, sought to erase that tradition of separateness and inequality. Chambliss had become involved in the case during the mid-1970s, along with other NMRLS attorneys including Jesse Pennington and Solomon Osborne. They had joined other African-American attorneys to form a group known as the Mississippi Council on Higher Education. At the initial stages civil rights attorney Isaiah Madison was the primary lawyer on the case, but he soon left Chambliss in charge. Chambliss was to remain involved in the *Ayers* case far longer than he anticipated: the case was not settled until 2001.[173] In the meantime Chambliss and his colleagues were able to win several major victories, the most salient being the Supreme Court's decision in *United States v. Fordice* (1992), which Chambliss argued against the federal government's solicitor general, Kenneth Starr. The decision acknowledged that Mississippi's colleges were still effectively segregated and required the state to take steps to erase the imprint of race on its institutions of higher learning.[174]

In the aftermath of this apparent victory, the parties could not agree on an adequate remedy for the age-old problems that plagued the system. The Supreme Court demanded that there be equality among the institutions, but with a goal of racial integration, not a throwback to the separate-but-equal days of *Plessy v. Ferguson.* This meant the possible disestablishment of the historically black colleges and forced integration of the remaining schools. One scholar has characterized the *Fordice* decision as "eerily anticlimactic" because "it seemed to resolve so little and to offer so little instruction and direction about the future. *Fordice* was, at best, inconclusive."[175] That conclusion was borne out over the next decade, as the state continued to grapple with these dilemmas and made only halting progress.[176]

The connections between race and poverty and the lack of sufficient legal remedies for these problems has long frustrated poverty lawyers.[177] Bob Cullen recognized that "racial and poverty issues . . . were intertwined" and that "you could never attack the root causes of poverty until you attacked the racial issues, because no matter what you did on one, the one's going to impact the other."[178] As David Walbert explained, within the U.S. legal system it had become easier to alter racial inequalities than economic ones:

> I used to be a real purist: I didn't want to approach the law from a racial point of view. When I went into legal services in '73, my feeling was, my thesis, my perception, was to try and bring the law to bear to help the poor. . . . [But] that was really hard. The law just provided so little remedies there that [were] pertinent to one's poverty status. . . . It's almost like giving up, in a way, doing traditional civil rights on a race basis. It was obviously a good thing, but it was a realization that from the point of view of somebody who wants to file a lawsuit . . . [that] race was still enough alive in civil rights and in the Constitution where you could effect some change in Georgia.[179]

Jonathan Zimring came to the same conclusion in litigating the education cases of the late 1970s and 1980s: he used claims of racial discrimination as a proxy for more complex social problems.[180] This meant, of course, that, as activists and litigators defeated the most overt examples of racial discrimination, they were left with a declining array of arguments to tackle poverty by proxy. One strategy for dealing with this deficit of legal remedies was to help community groups mobilize their economic resources, something poverty lawyers had been doing since the 1960s. Jesse Pennington and many of his North Mississippi counterparts, for example, worked with community organizations to establish credit unions, day cares, cooperatives, and other institutions that spurred economic growth and independence for African Americans.[181] But these efforts were time-consuming and difficult and not nearly numerous enough to alter the economic status of low-income southerners significantly.[182]

Ultimately, the successes poverty lawyers in civil rights litigation enjoyed were in spite of the limitations of litigation as a catalyst for creating a more egalitarian political culture. Indeed, some scholars have suggested that civil rights advocates became too comfortable in the courts, failing to realize the limits of American law. Litigation was a reactive strategy and courts reactive institutions. Judges cannot simply exclaim legal doctrines. They require a vehicle, the lawsuit, which might not arise when and where it is most needed. Furthermore, procedural rules promised few swift resolutions, and procedural errors or obstacles might derail a case altogether. Litigants also ran the risk that they were seeking results in the courts that might be impossible for the justice system to deliver. One scholar bluntly questioned the efficacy of "using litigation as a surrogate for political power," arguing that "judges cannot compel society to do what it lacks the political will to do." Focusing on school desegregation and other claims based on the Civil Rights Act, his conclusions are applicable to poverty lawyers' efforts: "The litigation strategy asks too much of the courts and the legal process and too little of ourselves as citizens of a democratic political order."[183] President Dwight D. Eisenhower was correct, if cowardly, when he responded to the Supreme Court's *Brown v. Board of Education* decision by saying, "It is difficult through law and through force to change a man's heart."[184]

Historically, the justice system has been no more likely than other elements of the American political order to provide an arena in which minorities could advance their interests. The Supreme Court was something of a trailblazer with its *Brown* decision, and the Warren Court led the nation through the "rights revolution" of the 1960s. But the courts do not inevitably persist in the vanguard of social change. Quite the contrary, they are often bastions of social order.[185] Poverty lawyers' civil rights advocacy revealed the possibilities and the limits inherent in American law. Among their most significant effects was, as Leonard McClellan suggested, to "ease the transition from segregation to [a] more inclusive society."[186] Litigation and other forms of legal activism were far more peaceful than street protests, massive marches, or concerted violence. Which tactic held the most potential for social change is debatable,[187] but there is no doubt that the availability of poverty lawyers and other civil rights attorneys energized, even as they channeled, African-American activism. As North Mississippi's Solomon Osborne put it: "There were people in the community, say here in Greenwood, that knew that something needed to be done. They . . . didn't have the resources to do these things, and they probably didn't know what direction they should be going in. But they knew something needed to be done. I think when legal services came in it probably provided some focus and brought some needed resources to the community. . . . [But] some things you could litigate and fashion into a legal remedy; some things you couldn't."[188] Poverty lawyers resorted to race claims because that was often how they and their clients understood the problems they faced and because at the time such claims were the most promising avenues available within American law.

Yet, the racial peculiarities of southern law faded along with the structural distinctiveness of the southern political economy during the second half of the twentieth century.[189] Within the nation's modern, market-oriented society, in which the South was increasingly enmeshed, encoding racial distinctions in law was not necessary for wealth creation nor to secure social stability. The central problem for poverty lawyers and low-income minorities, as well as other civil rights litigants, was that racial discrimination was expendable in a consumer culture, but poverty was not. Poverty lawyers' success in supporting the expansion of minority civil rights in the South simply uncovered the harsh reality that it remained perfectly legal to discriminate on the basis of socioeconomic status.[190] Racial discrimination did not disappear altogether, to be sure, but, through the advocacy of poverty lawyers and other proponents of civil rights, race had a weaker hold on southern minds and was less intertwined with southern interests by the turn of the twenty-first century. In contrast, socioeconomic stratification was as robust as ever and as firmly embedded in American law as racism had been in the laws of the American South for nearly four centuries.[191] More and more, the experiences of the black southern poor became those of the white southern poor, and the statement that "poverty is no respector of color" became increasingly true.

7

POVERTY LAW, POLITICS, AND THE
RATIONING OF JUSTICE, 1981–1996

STEVE Gottlieb had unfortunate timing: he became director of the Atlanta Legal Aid Society two weeks before the election of Ronald Reagan. The day after the election an ALAS board member glumly predicted, "I don't think you're going to survive." For Gottlieb, who had been with ALAS since the late 1960s through the turbulence of the Nixon years and the expansion of the late 1970s, "the handwriting was on the wall." Like many within the legal services community, he believed that Reagan's vehement opposition to California Rural Legal Assistance while governor of that state prefigured his approach to legal services as president. According to Bucky Askew, then working for LSC in Washington, Reagan's election "sent shockwaves through the legal services community," from the local programs to LSC headquarters.[1]

There were various sources of opposition to federally funded legal services programs in the early 1980s. Many critics were being sued or otherwise found themselves opposite a legal services attorney, giving them an immediate reason to malign poverty lawyers. Whether it was the mayor of Tupelo, the Atlanta Housing Authority, a retail furniture company, a financial institution, or one of many landlords, each expressed dismay that a portion of their tax dollars had come back to haunt them.[2] Such sentiments were part of a more generalized, but no less vehement, opposition to federally funded legal services that lamented poverty lawyers' litigious nature, their egocentric radicalism, and the irony of the federal government financing lawsuits against itself as well as against state and local governments. One Augusta, Georgia, official granted poor people's need for representation but suggested that "it's ridiculous for the federal government to run housing or community development programs and then hire lawyers to harass them. They constantly harass people implementing federal programs with lawsuits. It's an absolute waste of taxpayers' money. . . . I hope President Reagan does eliminate it." Augusta's mayor called Georgia Legal Services a "harassment agency." A common complaint was that lawyers were more self-serving than servants of the poor: "They answer to no one. They prostituted a good idea and now serve the ends of the agency rather than serving the needy."[3]

As it turned out, poverty lawyers and their supporters had reason for concern upon Reagan's election. Since 1975 the Legal Services Corporation's annual budget had risen from $71.5 million to more than $321 million, most of that increase occurring under the Carter administration. Programs across the country, but especially in regions lacking full coverage, such as the Deep South, sprouted and expanded rapidly during the late 1970s, and by 1981 LSC had achieved its goal of ensuring "minimum access" to legal counsel for all of the nation's poor.[4] Reagan, however, was not a friend of legal services. As governor of California in the 1960s and early 1970s, he had become engaged in a bitter struggle with California Rural Legal Assistance, and his distaste for poverty lawyers had not dissipated by the 1980s. During the presidential campaign Reagan expressed his intention to "explore possible alternatives to the monolithic federal approach to the legal problems of the poor," suggesting that "there is room for increased activity on the part of local government and local bar associations."[5] He also echoed the claims of legislative primacy heard in the debate over the Legal Services Corporation Act, arguing that federal money should not pay for lawsuits that "are in reality attempts to enforce a judicial resolution of political and public policy issues properly left to the electorate."[6] More generally, Reagan promised to usher in a new era of American politics, one in which government would do less but expect more of its citizenry. He would leave the "safety net" intact but trim unnecessary and dysfunctional social programs.[7] Advocates of legal services worried that LSC would be one of his targets.

They were right. Not long after Reagan's inauguration, the new administration announced plans to abolish the Legal Services Corporation. Reagan pursued two means of eliminating LSC. First, the administration sought to revoke congressional authorization for the corporation. Many federally funded institutions have to go through a two-step process, often annually, in order to have the resources to function: Congress must authorize the institution's existence, and then separately appropriate funds for the institution's operation. Failure to achieve either objective means the entity disappears. LSC's authorization technically expired in 1980, but, because the Legal Services Corporation Act contained no sunset provision, LSC continued to exist in limbo.[8] Shortly after taking office, in early February 1981, Reagan vowed to veto any bill reauthorizing the corporation, including one that was before the House. In Congress supporters of legal services offered to accept restrictions on poverty law practice in return for reauthorization, but opponents, notably senators Orrin Hatch of Utah and Jeremiah Denton of Alabama, prevented these bills from moving forward. In lieu of this conditional reauthorization, which would have secured LSC's existence for some time to come, subject to Congress's continued assent, the administration proposed to abolish LSC altogether and allow states to fund legal services programs through federal block grants given to each state for social services programs. This block grant proposal never picked up inertia, but neither did a consensus coalesce around reauthorization.[9]

Given the stalemate over reauthorization, debate over LSC reemerged during the appropriations process. Consistent with his ultimate goal for LSC, Reagan proposed to eliminate its funding, which would effectively kill the corporation regardless of any reauthorization. Congress eventually agreed to a compromise, ignoring the administration's proposal to eliminate funding and also dismissing another proposal to reduce it to $100 million. Instead, lawmakers temporarily settled the budget conflict with the president by passing a continuing resolution that left LSC with a budget of $241 million for fiscal year 1982, a 25 percent decrease from 1981. The following year another continuing resolution left that funding intact for 1983, before Congress increased LSC funding slightly to $275 million in 1984.[10]

Beginning in 1982, these budgetary resolutions also included restrictions on poverty law practice, which opponents imposed on LSC by attaching riders to the appropriations bills. The continuing resolution passed in late 1982 (providing funding for fiscal year 1983) incorporated a prohibition on the representation of illegal aliens, legislative lobbying, and unrestricted class actions against government agencies, and it required greater bar involvement in appointing local program boards. When Congress passed the appropriations bill in 1983, it maintained these restrictions and added two more, seeking to prevent training programs from advocating specific public policies and making it more difficult for programs to appeal an LSC decision to withdraw funding.[11] Reagan had not achieved his goal of eliminating LSC, but he nevertheless won the significant concessions of reduced funding and increased restrictions on poverty lawyers.

The administration also found other means of limiting poverty law advocacy. In late 1981, after inexplicably leaving the Carter-appointed LSC board intact for nearly a year, Reagan made six recess appointments to the board. The new members quickly signaled their opposition to the status quo. On New Year's Eve, one day after their appointments, they conducted a conference call and passed a resolution to prevent the dispersal of program funding for 1982, unaware that the corporation had already released this money.[12] Then, in March 1982, the newly constituted board elected a new chairman, William Harvey, who unequivocally announced his opposition to "law reform" strategies. Relations between the existing LSC staff and the new LSC board deteriorated, as did relations between LSC and its grantees.[13] Many LSC personnel, including longtime advocates such as Bucky Askew, Dan Bradley, and Clint Lyons, began to leave the corporation.[14] The Reagan board and the staff that it hired sought less to facilitate the provision of legal counsel to the poor than to monitor and restrict poverty lawyers through bureaucratic procedures. Askew, the last holdover from the pre-Reagan LSC, recalled that "there was no effort at technical assistance; no effort to try and improve the programs; no effort to try and assist them in meeting their goals. It was simply an effort to police them."[15] The problem was not lost on supporters in Congress, who were able to place a rider on the continuing resolution for fiscal year 1983 that sought to prevent the LSC board of directors "from taking adverse action against legal services programs." Local programs, such as North Mississippi Rural Legal Services during the Tupelo conflict, had often resisted the encroachment of Washington officials, who sometimes seemed overly zealous in enforcing LSC regulations and preventing political controversy. Yet under the Reagan administration LSC became the distant Leviathan that some, like Robert Dokson, had feared.[16]

Before leaving LSC, holdovers from the Carter era such as Askew, Bradley, and Lyons began organizing to ensure the perpetuation of legal services and, preferably, the corporation itself even before Reagan took office. Alan Houseman, an architect of this "survival campaign," later summarized the efforts of the LSC staff and the larger legal services community by saying that proponents "developed an effective affirmative lobbying effort."[17] National staff members held regional meetings in which they suggested ways that programs could survive severe budget cuts or even the annihilation of the program, and they cultivated relationships with LSC supporters, including the American Bar Association, state and local bars, civil rights groups, and business and labor leaders, to encourage such groups to express their support openly for publicly funded legal services. The American Bar Association, whose support traced back to the presidency of Lewis Powell (by now a Supreme Court justice), lobbied Congress on behalf of LSC. Under the leadership of ABA president Reece Smith, the ABA conducted a "March on Washington" (comprised of about two hundred influential lawyers) and held a news conference expressing its support of LSC on the same day, 10 March 1981, that Reagan delivered his request to Congress that LSC funding be eliminated. The National Legal Aid and Defender Association and other groups within the legal services community helped mobilize existing allies, and coalitions of supporters outside the legal services orbit emerged. One such group, Advocates of Legal Services, was cochaired by former vice president Walter Mondale and former United States senator James B. Pearson of Kansas. The group published a booklet entitled *An American Institution: The Legal Services Corporation*, documenting and defending the program's work on behalf of the poor.[18] LSC staffers also initiated a media campaign that resulted in positive portrayals of legal services in the nation's newspapers.[19] These efforts helped solidify congressional support during a critical period, preventing the wholesale abandonment of federally funded legal services.

In time, however, LSC's campaign to cultivate political support drew the attention and ire of legal services opponents. For congressional conservatives the survival campaign confirmed their sense that poverty lawyers worked less in the public interest than in their own. In the spring of 1983 two prominent critics, senators Orrin Hatch and Jeremiah Denton (both Republicans), initiated a congressional investigation of the corporation. Over an eighteen-month period the Senate Committee on Labor and Human Resources, aided by Reagan-appointed LSC board members, collected documents that demonstrated, in the minds of opponents of LSC, that legal services staff members in Washington, regional offices, and local programs had engaged in illegal political activity when, in the wake of Reagan's election, they attempted to invigorate support for the program lest the new administration seek to dismantle it. Specifically, Denton and Hatch argued that the corporation's staff had illegally funneled millions of tax dollars into a grassroots campaign to preserve federally funded legal services.[20] Senator Denton described this effort as a "political campaign" that was not "part of the mainstream of American politics" and that was, indeed, "hatched and carried out in the murky backwaters of a rogue federal program." These "rogue" elements hoped "to assure the survival of a radical philosophy of social engineering" that was, in effect, "rejected by a large majority of Americans" when they elected Ronald Reagan in 1980 and 1984 and, in 1980, gave Republicans control of the Senate. Denton feared that "LSC was to become the taxpayer-funded fulcrum for the left to leverage a national political agenda in the Reagan era."[21] Ultimately, the results of the investigation were inconclusive, though the senators claimed victory by suggesting that their diligent oversight had brought an end to whatever transgressions had taken place: "The rampant abuse of the early 1980s has been stopped."[22]

After the end of the Senate investigation Denton and Hatch, along with three legal scholars, published a collection of essays documenting their investigation of the LSC staff's survival campaign. These essays revealed the underlying reasons that Denton, Hatch, and many of their colleagues opposed continued funding for the Legal Services Corporation. The authors were concerned that the LSC staff had violated the spirit, if not the letter, of the LSC Act. But their criticism of the corporation and its grantees ran much deeper than these allegations of wrongdoing. Indeed, conservative opposition to federally funded legal services had more to do with ideology than with ensuring the sanctity of federal laws. Hatch believed that "the majority of programs are attempting to help the poor with their legal needs, but that a well-funded, vocal minority has attempted and is still trying to turn the program back into a federally financed political machine." That machine, fueled by the "political ambitions" of the LSC staff, was pursuing a "liberal Democratic political agenda." [23] Both Denton and Hatch quoted Alan Houseman, a leader within the legal services community, in seeking to portray LSC as antagonistic to conservative goals. Houseman had suggested in a January 1981 speech: "What is at stake is not solely the survival of the Legal Services program. What is at stake is the survival of many social benefits—entitlement programs that we struggled, since 1965, to make real for poor people. . . . What is at stake is a number of other kinds of programs like affirmative action, civil rights programs. . . . Those, in the end, are far more important than legal services. Legal services is a tool to get them." [24] So went the debate over legal services: supporters clamored for more funding and freedom for poverty lawyers so that they could help ameliorate poverty by helping the poor obtain access to public assistance as well as various private legal remedies; opponents criticized poverty lawyers as foot soldiers in a defunct "war on poverty," underground supporters of a liberal agenda. Poverty lawyers have been, in the eyes of politicians and academes, of the Left and of the Right, agents of the American welfare state and also products of it. As Lucie White put it, legal services have generally been "defined as a commodity, like education, housing, health care, child care, and the like, that was to be 'delivered' to low-income persons through a quasi-public state bureaucracy that was funded through tax transfers." [25]

Portraying poverty lawyers as agents of the welfare state impoverished the debate over legal services, drawing attention away from the role these programs had played in reinforcing the U.S. legal system and the rule of law, that is, to nurture the precarious trust between low-income Americans and the law. Arguing that legal services lawyers helped create dependence on government assistance deflected attention from the underlying social policy. Those who did not agree with the underlying social policies could have addressed their concerns directly to those policies but, instead, targeted poverty lawyers as scapegoats for what they conceived to be failed initiatives. Poverty lawyers, after all, were simply doing what lawyers do: pursuing whatever advantages they believed were possible for their clients within the legal system. Trying to undermine the welfare state by making it impossible for potential beneficiaries to claim their legal entitlements was a cynical solution, reflecting and perhaps breeding disrespect for the law. Moreover, viewing poverty lawyers as agents of the welfare state made it difficult for policy makers, especially liberals, to consider alternatives to the staff-based model that existed in the United States.

Other Western democracies have established distinctly different systems to provide legal services for the poor. Great Britain was the first of these countries to create a state-supported scheme with the Legal Aid and Advice Act of 1949, which replaced a volunteer network of lawyers and special procedural provisions for the poor with a legal aid program administered by Britain's Law Society, a corollary to the bar association in the United States. The program subsidizes services provided by private attorneys, rather than full-time staff members of government-funded entities, as in the United States. This subsidy has historically been available to most of the population (over 80 percent in 1950, 50 percent as of the late 1980s), though more wealthy clients must pay a portion of the legal fees that they incur.[26] Legal aid models throughout the West fall somewhere along the spectrum between the British and American models.[27] Alternative means of delivering legal counsel to the poor may or may not be more effective but in any case have rarely even been contemplated in the United States because the legal services program is embedded in the ideological sparring between "liberal" and "conservative" policy makers.[28]

In the midst of the tense, if stultifying, debate over legal services, local programs were ultimately more concerned with their own evolution and survival. Directors such as Steve Gottlieb had to adapt to a new legal and political environment because the election of 1980 ushered in dramatic changes in American political culture. Under Reagan the federal government's willingness to fund social programs waned, and the vilification of the "undeserving" poor became of staple of political discourse. For Gottlieb and his colleagues the budget cuts and practice restrictions of the early 1980s were body blows from which legal services programs across the United States, and especially in the Deep South, found it difficult to recover.

ADAPTATION

For legal services programs throughout the United States the political events of the early 1980s had drastic consequences. Nationwide, the number of neighborhood law offices dropped from 1,406 to 1,121. That was a minor blow compared to the effect of budget cuts on legal services personnel: the number of lawyers and paralegals plummeted from 9,416 to 4,766.[29] Similar changes swept through Georgia, Alabama, and Mississippi, where fiscal retrenchment forced programs to close offices and lay off or decline to hire new lawyers and support staff. North Mississippi Rural Legal Services closed six of its eleven branch offices and eliminated twenty-five positions.[30] The Atlanta Legal Aid Society closed its Westside office by the end of 1981 and another soon thereafter, lost numerous attorneys, and laid off support staff, including paralegals.[31] With director John Cromartie warning that "this may be the most difficult period we have faced," Georgia Legal Services closed three offices but, more critically, lost nearly half of its staff after program personnel decided that it was more important to maintain a presence in a greater number of communities than to maintain a larger but more centralized staff.[32] In Alabama, by contrast, LSCA leaders froze salaries and thereby retained much of its staff, but that choice led to future problems within the organization.[33] North Central Alabama Legal Services, on the other hand, lost more than half of its legal staff, dropping eight of its fourteen attorneys while retaining most of its support staff.[34] In some of the younger programs the cuts halted expansion but did not require any layoffs because these programs were still in the process of growth; others experienced difficulties similar to their elder counterparts.[35]

One consequence of this fiscal contraction was that many of the most talented, experienced poverty lawyers left legal services, sensing that their careers might be in jeopardy. North Mississippi's Leonard McClellan, who became the program's director during the late 1980s, suggested that the budget cuts and subsequent restrictions initiated an "experience drain."[36] Steve Gottlieb's perception was that the Atlanta Legal Aid Society "didn't lose either our worst or our best" lawyers. Rather, those who left were those who had been thinking of leaving anyway; the budget cuts simply made leaving more appealing.[37] Whether or not Gottlieb's impressions were accurate or applicable to other programs, there were fewer poverty lawyers in the Deep South after the cuts, and many of those who left took with them years of accumulated expertise.

The decision to leave poverty law practice was often complex for individual attorneys. Consumer law specialist Charlie Baird, who left Georgia Legal Services in the early 1980s, explained, "I was very discouraged about the whole situation. . . . The Reagan cuts came around about the same time the law was being gutted," specifically the federal Truth in Lending Act and Georgia Industrial Loan Act. In any case he had always "oscillated," to use his word, between the legal profession and his other lifelong loves, literature and linguistics. So, in the midst of this adverse environment, Baird left the legal profession to study linguistics.[38] Longtime Alabama poverty lawyer Marvin Campbell was also a casualty of the budget cuts. Not only was he disturbed by the cuts themselves, but his relationship with LSC's Atlanta regional office became strained over a disagreement with the formula the office was using to decide how much funding to eliminate from each program. Campbell felt that other states were receiving undue preference to Alabama's detriment. Ultimately, however, this dispute was but one aspect of a growing disillusionment with national developments that threatened to undermine publicly funded legal services for the poor. His energy spent, Campbell left for private practice in 1981.[39]

The political environment of the early 1980s also made poverty law practice less attractive to graduating law students, for a variety of reasons. Budget cuts signaled a lack of stability among programs; salaries for law graduates in private firms were on the rise, as were law school tuitions and, hence, educational debts; and the growing restrictions and lessened emphasis on "law reform" made the legal activism of the 1960s and 1970s seem quaint.[40] Not insignificant was the failure of most legal educators to help students to see the provision of legal services to the poor as a professional responsibility, a failure that lessened the chances of students taking public interest jobs and undercut pro bono efforts.[41] The long-term impact of these trends remains to be seen, but it is clear that, at the very least, the Reagan cuts (and later cuts during the 1990s) exacerbated the "turnover problem" among legal services programs and decreased the availability of poverty lawyers to the poor.[42]

Changes that occurred within the Atlanta Legal Aid Society provide further insight into the impact of fiscal retrenchment on legal services programs in the Deep South. Steve Gottlieb has suggested that the most dramatic adjustment the society made under his leadership was to move, in his words, "back to our roots" with the private bar. ALAS became the first program in the South to initiate a fund-raising campaign among local attorneys and won a grant from LSC to finance its own project as a model for other legal services programs. Not only did this campaign provide an alternative source of funding, but it also cultivated the bonds between Legal Aid lawyers and the Atlanta legal community. By the late 1990s this financial support was sufficient enough to enable the society to depend on LSC for only one-third of its funding. Other Deep South programs were neither as resourceful nor as fortunate as Gottlieb and Atlanta Legal Aid.[43] Despite occasional tension, the Georgia Legal Services Program was able to win substantial bar support during the 1980s and 1990s, decreasing its LSC funding to 71.3 percent of its budget by 1996.[44] Most Deep South programs could not hope for or simply failed to cultivate such support, and, as a result, programs in Mississippi and Alabama still received 95 and 92 percent, respectively, of their funding from LSC in the late 1990s.[45] Such a heavy reliance on federal funding limited the stature of these programs compared to those in Georgia and made them particularly sensitive to political events at the national level.

The Atlanta Legal Aid Society, like other programs, also began implementing new methods of providing counsel to clients. Attorneys began offering advice over the phone, which was not typical of poverty law practice prior to the 1980s. Later, in the 1990s, the society joined with GLSP to establish a landlord-tenant hotline available to low-income people across the state.[46] ALAS also created special units to focus attention on certain groups of clients. This trend began in 1976 with the Senior Citizens Law Project but accelerated in the 1980s and 1990s with the formation of an AIDS Legal Project, Home Defense Program, Mental Health Law Project, and Cancer Legal Initiative.[47] Other legal services programs created focused projects. North Mississippi, for example, began receiving grants for an Elder Law Project in the mid-1980s. Virginia Kilgore, who had been with the program since 1977, headed the initiative, providing counsel to individual clients in person and via a telephone hotline as well as conducting dozens of community education seminars annually.[48]

Finally, legal services programs sharpened their prioritization policies in response to the budget cuts. Gottlieb explained that retrenchment forced Legal Aid attorneys to "cut back on what we did and forced us to be much more focused on the kinds of cases that we were willing to take." The society, for example, no longer accepted all eviction cases but, instead, categorized evictions on the basis of the impact on the client's family, whether the client had a reasonable defense and a good chance of winning, whether the client could defend herself with some brief guidance, whether a volunteer from the private bar could take the case, and whether there were law reform issues involved, especially regarding the Atlanta Housing Authority's treatment of its residents. Divorces became high priorities only if the client suffered a violent spouse or if there was a dispute over child custody or child support. Public benefits cases remained high priorities—Gottlieb pointed out that with "welfare issues, everybody's very poor" and often desperate for help—but Legal Aid lawyers did begin to refer Social Security cases to private attorneys because these attorneys could take fees from awards of unpaid benefits.[49] Marian Burge echoed Gottlieb's assessment in commenting on the distinctions and similarities between poverty law practice in the 1970s, when she joined ALAS, and the 1980s and 1990s. Burge recalled that during the 1970s, when she was the lone Legal Aid lawyer in Gwinnett County, "anything that walked through the door that was income-eligible and wasn't criminal, I handled. . . . There was no screening." By the 1980s prioritization became a fact of life at ALAS, as the program became "more and more selective in what we actually end up taking as on-going representation. . . . We've got so many more cases than we've got staff to handle them well, so we spend a lot more time sifting through what we really want to take." She noted, however, that, despite efforts to prioritize problems, "the basic priorities stay the same because poor people have the same needs: they need income, they need housing, they need something to eat, they need protection from the 'sharks,' they need access to the array of government benefits that are supposed to be there to help them."[50] However persistent the problems of the poor, prioritization became imperative in the wake of the budget cuts.

After adapting to the budget cuts, local programs had to learn how to survive the increasingly antagonistic bureaucratic environment. Even in the 1970s ALAS director Robert Dokson had complained about the increasing paperwork and internal oversight of the Legal Services Corporation. "Management and accountability," he said, were the prices Congress extracted for the fourfold increase in funding under the Carter administration. Dokson suggested that he and other legal services leaders became "paralyzed by our caution" as they handled rapidly growing budgets. "What Nixon, Agnew and Reagan (as governor of California) could not do to Legal Services explicitly, that is, to reduce our efficiency and effectiveness in aggressive advocacy for the poor, we have done to ourselves." Looking back on the fate of legal services and ALAS after his departure in 1980, Dokson realized that his earlier sentiments seemed histrionic, given that the LSC staff had at least been friendly to local programs.[51] By the mid-1980s the Reagan-appointed board had hired an entirely new staff bent on curbing the perceived excesses of legal services attorneys.[52] LSC began to "increase substantially the amount of information it sought from field programs," partly in response to the Denton-Hatch inquiries into the corporation. Enduring corporation monitoring and filing grant applications became more of a chore,[53] and some new regulations and instructions aimed to limit the scope of poverty lawyers' activities beyond what the LSC Act and appropriation riders required.[54] By the time McClellan left NMRLS in 1990, he lamented, "most of the programs—not just North Mississippi Legal Services, but other programs in Mississippi and other states, too—had been literally relegated to doing . . . primarily domestic relations and consumer type cases."[55] Askew, who left LSC to join the National Legal Aid and Defender Association and help local programs navigate the increasing bureaucratization, felt that the monitoring had a "chilling effect" on some programs.[56] Just as the investigation but ultimate exoneration of Lewis Myers was symbolic of the increasing bureaucratization of legal services during the late 1970s, the experience of Alvin Chambliss was representative of the atmosphere of the 1980s: Chambliss lost his job at North Mississippi because he refused to relinquish the *Ayers* case.[57]

Despite these changing institutional dynamics, legal services programs continued to bring low-income Americans in the Deep South within the purview of U.S. law. Admittedly, practicing poverty law in the 1980s and 1990s felt as if there were "too many battlefronts and not enough resources," according to Tom Keith, and some programs became timid, afraid that overly aggressive advocacy might draw the unwelcome attention of the corporation.[58] Even these programs, however, provided basic client representation that had not existed prior to federally funded legal services. The bulk of poverty law practice, as always, dealt with the thousands of problems for which individual clients sought the assistance of legal services personnel each year. Just as before, a simple act could set off a major legal conflict, as was the case when Christine Grier enrolled her six-year-old child, Mark, in school. Grier did not have official custody of the child, whom an acquaintance had left with her when he was an infant. When a juvenile court ruled that Grier had no right to Mark and state officials took custody, GLSP lawyers pursued the case to the Georgia Supreme Court, which decided in Grier's favor.[59] Conversely, a major event could set off what seemed to be many minor problems, as happened to numerous south Georgians when the state's most devastating floods in five hundred years hit during the summer and fall of 1994. GLSP's Albany office was itself only inches from Flint River floodwaters, and staff members spent hours stacking sandbags to prevent further damage to the town. Once the waters began to recede, they turned to the problems of their clients. They joined private attorneys in staffing the State Bar of Georgia's Hotline for disaster victims and trained volunteer attorneys to provide assistance to victims of the floods. Of the cases that GLSP lawyers handled themselves, most involved evictions, denials of unemploy-

ment compensation, or questions regarding federal disaster assistance. Poverty lawyers represented clients seeking to replace lost housing, as they did an elderly couple,
Rufus and Mary Medlock, who paid a contractor ten thousand dollars only to learn
that he had fled town after being charged with writing bad checks. A legal services
attorney helped them get out of that contract and retrieve their lost funds, then super-
vised the Medlocks' subsequent agreement with a contractor who followed through
with the repairs.[60]

Moreover, legal services programs, most notably ALAS and GLSP, continued to
represent clients in law reform initiatives. They did so by providing an institutional
environment in which attorneys with unique areas of expertise could pursue issues
on behalf of individuals or groups of clients.[61] In the 1980s Bill Brennan and Dennis
Goldstein of the Atlanta Legal Aid Society represented the Atlanta Community Re-
investment Alliance in its attack on several banks' mortgage lending practices for ignoring poor, predominantly African-American parts of the city. Subsequently, Brennan
began focusing on defending homeowners from predatory lenders and home improvement scams, while Goldstein continued to represent community groups, especially
low-income tenants.[62] Another ALAS attorney, Sue Jamieson, navigated a case to the
United States Supreme Court that required the Georgia Regional Hospital to place
mentally disabled patients in less restrictive, community-based treatment programs.[63]
Other legal services programs continued to engage in reform litigation as well.[64] Poverty lawyers found it increasingly difficult, however, to initiate change through litigation. The judiciary became more conservative, and the federal government sought to
decentralize and privatize its functions. Because much of the success of legal services litigation depended on enforcing federal statutes and regulations, these changes
proved critical to poverty law practice.[65]

Yet, even if the legal and political environment of the 1980s and 1990s damaged
legal services programs' ability to provide counsel to the poor, poverty lawyers continued to believe that their work was somehow blessed. They were, in a metaphorical
sense, helping to stack sandbags for their clients, keeping the floodwaters of poverty
at bay. Whatever frustrations, old and new, came with poverty law practice, the attorneys, perhaps more than ever, thought they were morally and spiritually justified.
One attorney, Vicky Kimbrell, found inspiration in the tragic story of a mother who
was wrongly denied Medicaid benefits (a problem Kimbrell could have repaired) and
who was unable to afford private health insurance. When the woman's two-year-old
child contracted pneumonia, the mother had no means of obtaining medical care,

and the child died. Poverty lawyers may not have been able to erase poverty, but they could, Kimbrell believed, prevent such tragedies from occurring if presented with the opportunity. As Dennis Goldstein suggested, "people here . . . work more for the satisfaction through what they do than for the money, because the money's not very good."[66] When GLSP director John Cromartie reflected on poverty law practice during the 1980s, he realized that, for many attorneys, representing the poor was imbued with spirituality. He would "tell people that one good thing about legal services [is] when you wake up in the morning, you know it's going to be a good day because you're doing what's right. When you go to bed at night, you know that you've done something worth doing. It's a great feeling." Cromartie left GLSP in 1990 to become a Methodist minister and related that he saw no discontinuity moving from poverty law practice to the pulpit: "They're both about the healing process, a helping process. The church at its best is about the underdog, and legal services is about the underdog, so I didn't see a great disconnect between being a legal aid lawyer and being a pastor—still don't."[67]

"YEAR OF CRISIS"

From the mid-1980s to the mid-1990s the ideological sparring within Congress was less potent that it had been during the early Reagan years, and Congress slowly increased funding for the Legal Services Corporation. For the time being, opponents and supporters reached an unsteady compromise whereby legal services programs lived with lower funding and greater restrictions than before but enjoyed modest annual increases in funding. Legal services programs in the Deep South maintained a stable, if weakened, presence during these years, with fewer offices, fewer lawyers, and fewer support personnel. That truce came to a halt, quite abruptly, after the election of 1994, when Republicans seized control of both houses of Congress for the first time in four decades. The new majorities took charge in 1995, and by fiscal year 1996 LSC and local legal services programs faced a crisis comparable to that of the Reagan years.

As LSC's *Annual Report* noted, "1996 was a year of crisis": opponents in Congress attempted to dismantle the corporation and replace it with block grants, though they succeeded only in winning another round of budget cuts and adding new restrictions on poverty law practice. The variety of reasons expressed for opposing LSC echoed those of the Denton-Hatch committee. As Texas senator Phil Gramm put it, legal services was a "major impediment to meaningful welfare reform," which was one of the primary objectives of Speaker of the House Newt Gingrich's "Contract with America" and thus atop Republicans' agenda after the 1994 elections. Gramm said of poverty lawyers, "They're being advocates for the existing welfare bureaucracy, and while they may have a right to do it, they don't have a right to do it with taxpayers' money."[68] Other Republicans added more general commentary, such as California congressman Ron Packard's claim that LSC "is more focused on advancing grand social causes than on helping the poor with ordinary legal problems."[69] Also mobilized against federally funded legal services was the grassroots organization at the forefront of the religious Right, the Christian Coalition. A coalition spokesman summarized that organization's opposition by criticizing poverty lawyers' "lobbying to expand the welfare state, to increase the number of people on the welfare rolls and to block welfare reform" and arguing that they "contributed to the break-up of the family by using tax money to help people get divorces." Christian Coalition head Ralph Reed was more succinct, suggesting that poverty lawyers were undermining American values by "subsidizing divorce and illegitimacy."[70] The conjunction of these cultural and ideological perspectives with the Republican Party's congressional ascendance placed LSC in a position as precarious as that of the early Reagan years.

Given the nature of poverty law practice, it is not surprising that fiscal and social conservatives rebelled against continued federal funding for LSC. They viewed legal services programs as a component of the American welfare state and thus believed that poverty lawyers adhered to a political agenda antagonistic to their ideals and goals. In fact, poverty lawyers, like most attorneys, essentially adopted the interests of their clients. Had legal services programs provided counsel to a larger proportion of the working poor or even the lower middle class, those with higher incomes who still had difficulty affording legal counsel, poverty law practice would have seemed far less radical. That is not to suggest that legal services attorneys had no political perspective or that they served as poor people's legal weapons without somehow reshaping or even distorting their clients' objectives,[71] but it is to assert that poverty lawyers were less motivated by their own beliefs than by the problems of their clients and the potential solutions that existed within American law. By categorically limiting the legal services clientele to those living near or below the poverty line, Congress itself established poverty lawyers' agenda as that of advancing the interests of the least affluent. In so doing, Congress effectively built opposition to legal services into public policy.

For legal services programs in the Deep South and across the country, the fiscal retrenchment implemented in 1996 was more severe than that of the early 1980s.[72] Congress decreased LSC funding by over 30 percent, from $400 million to $278 million. Nationwide, legal services programs lost some nine hundred attorneys and closed three hundred offices. They also served, predictably, fewer clients. Legal services attorneys handled 1.7 million cases in 1995, then 1.4 million in 1996, a decrease of nearly 20 percent.[73] As they had after the budget cut of 1981, local programs in the Deep South adapted to the new fiscal realities by decreasing cases and services and, in some cases, reaching out for alternative sources of funding. The Atlanta Legal Aid Society, under the leadership of Steve Gottlieb, became particularly adept at fundraising among the private bar.[74] In spite of such efforts, retrenchment affected all local programs, and the cuts proved devastating for programs that relied heavily on LSC funding, such as those in Mississippi and Alabama. More drastic than the budget cuts, however, was the new slate of restrictions on the types of cases poverty lawyers could handle. Conservative opponents finally achieved their long-sought goal of restricting representation to individual clients, rather than groups of low-income Americans, by making it illegal for legal services attorneys to participate in class action lawsuits, which had been central to poverty lawyers' "law reform" strategies since the 1960s. Other restrictions ended legal services advocacy of many aliens and all prisoners as well as strengthened limitations on lobbying. Furthermore, the same Congress that ended the federal entitlement to welfare made it illegal for poverty lawyers to challenge these reforms.[75] To be sure, legal services lawyers confronted many of the same issues they had for three decades,[76] but the legislative events of the mid-1990s promised to reshape poverty law practice once again.

Within the context of post-1960s American politics the history of legal services for the poor reflects the dwindling of the liberal social agenda in the midst of a conservative resurgence.[77] To be sure, compromise had always been part of the calculus of federal funding. Lyndon Johnson's Office of Economic Opportunity had, after all, sought the approval of the American Bar Association, thereby reassuring the established legal community that government involvement in the market for legal services would be limited.[78] Significantly, poverty lawyers could serve only the poorest of the poor and not more affluent segments of the population that nevertheless found it difficult to afford legal counsel. Governmental activism extended only so far. Compromise became even more crucial during the Nixon years, when advocates of legal services traded some of poverty lawyers' autonomy for the security of the corporation. Finally, compromise became necessary for survival under Reagan and the Republican-controlled Congress of the 1990s. Advocates of legal services accepted further restrictions on poverty law practice and lesser financing, but LSC managed to persevere. Indeed, the budget cuts of the 1990s typified the new political order that President Bill Clinton ushered in: the federal government would continue to fund legal services for the poor, but only halfheartedly.

It is unclear thus far what President George W. Bush's tenure will ultimately mean for the Legal Services Corporation and local legal services programs. If financial support is any indication, the federal commitment to publicly funded poverty law practice is waning. As compared to other developed countries in the West, the United States devotes far less public money to legal services for the poor. The annual per capita government expenditure for civil legal assistance in the United States is roughly $2.25; in England the amount is $32, over fourteen times the U.S. per capita expenditure. Furthermore, the budget for LSC increased by less than 3 percent during Bush's first term, from roughly $329 million in fiscal year 2001 to roughly $339 million in fiscal year 2004. This is just a few thousand dollars more than the amount appropriated for LSC for fiscal year 1981 even without adjusting for inflation. The corporation reached its minimum access goal of two poverty lawyers per 10,000 eligible clients two decades ago, but, as of 2004 there was a single lawyer for every 11,500 low-income persons. Accounting for inflation, to match the $321.3 million budget in 1981 would require Congress and the president to increase LSC's budget to roughly $700 million. To match the $7 per poor person goal reached in 1981, LSC would need to spend $14.91 per person; its 2004 budget provided enough to spend $7.88. Numerous studies have indicated that the result of these financial realities is that millions of low-income people, perhaps as many as eight of every ten, do not have access to a lawyer for necessary legal counsel.[79] Bush's second term may or may not result in another shift in the political calculus that has kept LSC treading water for two decades.

Ultimately, Americans have yet to reach a lasting consensus regarding the provision of legal services to the poor. There are those who place their faith in the market and in private initiatives, who argue that whatever legal needs the poor have can be addressed without significant government funding. Others consent to federal funding, but at the price of severe restrictions on poverty law practice. These restrictions are designed to ensure that poverty lawyers neither interfere with policy initiatives (such as the welfare reform measures of the 1990s) nor embarrass public officials by utilizing federal funds to pursue controversial cases. There also exists, to be sure, substantial political support for a well-financed Legal Services Corporation, largely as a result of the American Bar Association's continuing endorsement.[80] In the early twenty-first century policy makers seem to have reached a tentative compromise based not on the notion of "equal access," much less the notion of poverty lawyers as agents of a war on poverty, but, rather, on qualified and limited support for individual client services.[81] Yet the history of legal services in the United States suggests that any turn in national politics could alter the status of the Legal Services Corporation and its grantees, just as political shifts from the 1960s to the 1990s led to the creation, expansion, and near demolition of the program.

Realizing that the future of federal funding is unclear and even insecure, advocates of legal services continue to experiment with various methods of funding programs and offering counsel to the poor. Former ABA president Talbot "Sandy" D'Alemberte has suggested that there are many "tributaries of justice," and another proponent and historian of legal services, Earl Johnson, has offered that there is a "multi-lane high-way," or several routes, to equal access. Among his "tributaries" D'Alemberte included federally funded legal services; state-based funding (through mechanisms such as a filing fee surcharge or special tax on for-profit legal services); the distribution of a portion of punitive damage awards into a fund for civil legal services, requiring government agencies deemed to have erred to pay for litigation expenses and attorney's fees; comprehensive pro bono plans; diverse local initiatives; and funding from Interest on Lawyers' Trust Accounts (IOLTA). D'Alemberte cited IOLTA funding, in particular, as "one of the most remarkable innovations in legal services."[82] These plans, which forty-nine states had adopted by the mid-1990s, took interest earned from trust accounts created by lawyers from pooled client payments (such as retainer fees) and directed it to public service projects, including legal services programs. While IOLTA funding has become embroiled in litigation that could undercut these plans, either IOLTA or similar funding mechanisms will likely survive.[83] Other tributaries may include the provision of legal services by faith-based organizations,[84] integrating legal services into school-based social service delivery systems,[85] and the distribution of residual funds from class action settlements under the *cy pres* doctrine, which could allow these funds to be put to their "next best use."[86] At the local level many legal services programs continue to nurture pro bono programs, and some, notably both Georgia programs, have also excelled in cultivating the financial support of state and local bar associations. State (and perhaps federal) judicial authorities can also promote legal aid, as they have in D'Alemberte's home state of Florida, where the state Supreme Court recently adopted guidelines that turn volunteerism into a professional expectation: attorneys in that state must report their contributions of time and money for the provision of legal services. While not a requirement, the Court has emphasized the importance of these expectations. In adopting the plan, Justice Ben F. Overton emphasized that "for this justice system to maintain credibility . . . it must be available and affordable to all segments of society."[87]

Given this continued experimentation and adjustment, drawing broad conclusions about legal services is difficult, fleeting, and perhaps misleading. Yet the history of poverty lawyers and poor people in the Deep South does provide some insight into the role of law in American life, including the lives of the poor. First, despite the salience of internal elements of change, in particular the professionalization of legal services during the 1970s and its independence from social movements, the reality is that legal services programs are part of a larger political arena. Political developments from Washington, D.C., to Jackson, Mississippi, and all points in between, influenced the size and shape of local programs in the Deep South. Institutional developments affected not only the number of clients served but also the nature of that service. Furthermore, political change affected the law itself, so that the legal avenues available to the poor changed over time. Since law is but a reflection of society, including the contours of power that exist within society, legal services is necessarily a political institution caught up in contemporary political discourse.

Ultimately, poverty law practice was less about earth-shaking, class action, "impact" litigation than about everyday problems that were intensely personal. Marvin Campbell, who grew up in the mountainous reaches of northern Alabama, explained, "Having grown up in a rural area, I fully understood the isolation of a rural community from the urban centers and the sense that you were not part of the decision-making process that affected your everyday life." Access to a lawyer, or even the knowledge that you could have access should a need arise, helped change that feeling of helplessness, not only in the mountains of northern Alabama but also the impoverished streets of southern cities and the rural pine woods and plantation country that dominated the southern landscape. For most poor people, Campbell concluded, such a connection to the larger legal culture came not through class action litigation but through individual client counsel dealing with "day-to-day" problems. "We were doing more than just putting Band-Aids on legal problems," but, nevertheless, "I would say that the . . . most important impact [of poverty lawyers] was the daily service work that we were doing."[88] Whenever politicians voted to cut legal services funding, then, the effects fell primarily on individual clients and their families. In the wake of the budget cuts of the mid-1990s Hillary Clinton suggested that retrenchment meant that "somewhere a couple and their young children will have to sleep in an unheated car or on the street because of an unlawful eviction; a woman will be forced to cower in her bedroom, a victim of domestic violence; and a child will go to school hungry because his father refuses to pay child support."[89] Maudlin rhetoric notwithstanding, Clinton was correct in drawing attention to individual client problems, not the relatively rare controversial cases that opponents kept citing as evidence of poverty lawyers' too-generous leash.

Then again, focusing solely on individuals, one could miss the broader significance of legal services programs. That broader significance was that poverty lawyers assimilated their clients into American legal culture. They made it possible for low-income individuals to utilize the legal system to their apparent advantage: "Law is a toolbox of practical instruments,"[90] which poverty lawyers placed in the hands of the poor. Indeed, poverty lawyers enabled the poor to attempt to "dismantle the master's house with the master's tools."[91] Having legal representation did not always mean increasing one's power over her life, though that was sometimes true. It did mean that millions of low-income people accepted—implicitly, in their actions, if not explicitly, in their minds—the potential advantages and inevitable limitations of working within the legal system. Whenever a client brought her problem to a poverty lawyer, she was asking for an ally in some personal power struggle, and that is what she got, but she was also accepting the parameters of U.S. law. While working within the legal system could instigate and encourage social change, it could not ensure it or achieve it independently of other elements of American culture. Much as the apparatus of the welfare state served to diminish the possibility of revolt by the poor against the foundations of American society,[92] so did operating within the legal system make it impossible to seek anything but glacial change in socioeconomic relations. Even as poverty lawyers helped keep the floodwaters of poverty at bay, they also strengthened the barriers to decisive disruptions of American life. The metaphorical sandbags had multiple functions. They stemmed the catastrophic tide, but, as the Egyptians have learned, to their dismay, by their damming of the Nile, a damaging flood may also be a rejuvenating one. "Civilizing" poverty by extending legal services to the poor made such a transformation all but impossible.[93]

Many poverty lawyers understood the conservative implications of extending legal counsel to the poor. John Cromartie noted that the program was based on the "very conservative notion of resolving disputes in the traditional legal system."[94] Harrison McIver suggested that, at least conceptually, there was "nothing more conservative" than legal services: "It perpetuates the system, you function within the system, and you're seeking redress within the system. So how is that radical?"[95] Whether the poor might have turned to other weapons of protest had poverty lawyers been unavailable is impossible to discern, but many did, without a doubt, turn to the legal system when faced with dilemmas large and small. McIver's colleague Leonard McClellan recalled that "people felt that if they had a grievance they could seek some redress . . . through legal means, and . . . if people had not had that option, I don't know what would have happened, what they would have done."[96] Ironically, then, "liberal" supporters of legal services pursued the more conservative public policy, at least from the perspective of preserving existing social institutions. By broadening "access to justice," they made it more likely that the poor would seek recourse within existing legal channels. One consequence was that, as the Legal Services Act of 1974 suggested, "for many of our citizens, the availability of legal services . . . reaffirmed faith in our government and laws."[97]

Yet that faith is not unshakable. It is a conditional, even precarious, trust that people living under the rule of law cannot take for granted.[98] Learned Hand, one of the country's eminent jurists, recognized this fact some five decades ago. Speaking before the New York Legal Aid Society, Judge Hand emphasized the importance of an equitable rule of law in a democratic society, saying, "If we are to keep our democracy, there must be one commandment: Thou shalt not ration justice."[99] Legal services for the poor is only one facet of America's system of law, but the history of poverty lawyers and poor people in the Deep South cautions that, if rationing justice is fatal to democracy, the American experiment in democracy must continue.

Appendix

Political Support for the Legal Services Corporation

Logistic regression is a commonly accepted method of analyzing the effect that several explanatory variables have on a categorical dependent variable (that is, a variable that has only two responses, such as a vote for which the response is either "aye" or "nay"). Specifically, logistic regression suggests how a change in an explanatory variable affects the odds that the dependent variable will equal one, that is, the odds that a particular representative would vote "aye." Logistic regression also allows one to compare the effects of the explanatory variables to determine which factors most influenced the votes in question. The explanatory variables used in the models below include: political variables, such as the party affiliation of individual representatives and the percentage of votes cast for the Democratic candidate in a given district (an indicator of the degree a district supports the Democratic or Republican Party); demographic variables, such as the percentage urban population, percentage rural nonfarm and rural farm, percentage living in metropolitan area, population density, median age, and median years of schooling completed in a district; variables indicating the degree of wealth in a particular congressional district, such as median family income and the percentage of population below poverty; racial and ethnic variables, including the percentage of people classified as "black" for census purposes, percentage nonwhite, and percentage classified as "foreign stock"; indicators of social dislocation, such as the percentage change in population and mobility (person has moved within the previous five years); employment variables, such as the number of persons employed in manufacturing, agricultural, or professional jobs; measures of interest group influence, including the ratio of lawyers in a state's population, the per capita legal services grant (a proxy for the influence of the legal services community), and the percentage of the population receiving welfare payments; an important personal characteristic, whether a representative had legal training; and, finally, the statistical models include a variable measuring a representative's ideology, or political philosophy, by using ideological ratings published by the American Conservative Union (ACU).[1]

The American Conservative Union ratings are based on roughly two dozen critical votes the ACU selects each year, and, on a scale from 0 to 100, a score of 100 reflects a member's unanimity with the ACU's preferred selections. These preferences reflect the ACU's principles of strict limitations on the power of government in order to protect individual liberties and support for capitalism and the private control of economic power. Perusing the vote preferences used to calculate a member's rating also reveals a social agenda antagonistic to abortion rights, the National Endowment for the Arts, expanded rights for homosexuals, and gun control—a social agenda that is not explicit in the ACU's statement of principles.[2] When applied to the debate over legal services, these principles suggest two arguments against federally funded legal services: there is no need for the government to become involved in the market distribution of legal expertise; and legal services lawyers seek to expand social programs or lend support to parties with interests that conflict with a conservative worldview.

The statistical models presented here use these variables to explain the outcome of votes on three amendments introduced during the House debate in 1973 as well as the penultimate vote as the bill, H.R. 7824, emerged from the House (but before the conference committee revised it). Each of these amendments reflected major concerns among opponents of legal services and therefore reflected the politics surrounding the act. Also, from a statistical standpoint, as a general rule, the greater the number of dependent variables, the more accurate the model. Thus, the House makes a better case study than the Senate. The Green Amendment was designed to eliminate funding to national support centers that conducted research and formulated law reform strategies, communicating these ideas to local programs across the country (see table 1).[3] A second amendment, offered by Republican representative Albert Quie of Minnesota, restricted legal services programs from lobbying activity, which may be considered beyond simple legal advocacy and especially problematic when directed toward state legislatures (see table 2).[4] Finally, the Mizell Amendment prohibited poverty lawyers from becoming involved in school desegregation cases (see table 3).[5] Each of these amendments passed the House and eventually became part of the Legal Services Corporation Act. With these compromise measures intact, the act easily passed the House by a vote of 276 to 95 (see table 4).

While several explanatory variables appear statistically significant in one or more models, ideological rating was consistently the greatest determinant of one's vote. The more conservative the representative, the more likely she was to favor the Green, Quie, and Mizell amendments and the less likely she was to favor passage of the act.

Specifically, a one-point increase in one's ACU ideological rating meant an increase of 6 to 12 percent in the odds that one would vote in favor of the amendments, depending on the amendment and the statistical model. A one-point increase in one's ACU ideological rating meant a decrease of roughly 6 percent in the odds that one would favor the passage of the act. This conclusion is based on two elements of the models. First, one must determine the significance of a variable (this is presented on the top line in each cell of the tables). A variable is deemed to be statistically significant if this number is less than 0.05. Second, one looks at the bottom line in each cell for the "odds ratio." If this number equals 1.000, the variable has no effect on the odds that the dependent variable equals one. If the number is greater than 1.000, the variable has a positive effect; if the number is less than 1.000, the variable has a negative effect. In table 1 dealing with the Green Amendment, the odds ratio of ideological rating ranges from 1.093 to 1.103. This indicates that a one-point increase in the explanatory variable increased the odds of voting in favor of the amendment by between 9.3 and 10.3 percent. One should note, however, that these models are most useful as a means of comparing the effect of various explanatory variables rather than determining the precise effect of a particular variable. The measure of significance, as well as the consistency of a variable's effect, indicates that it is a major influence on the dependent variable.

All one hundred representatives in the most conservative quartile (based on ACU ratings) voted in favor of the Green Amendment, 99 percent favored the Quie Amendment, and 94 percent favored the Mizell Amendment. Of representatives slightly right of center (with ACU ratings between 50 and 75) 85 percent favored the Green Amendment, 80 percent favored the Quie Amendment, and 77 percent favored Mizell's. In contrast, representatives slightly left of center (with ACU ratings between 25 and 50) were less likely to support these changes; 46 percent voted to adopt the Green Amendment, and just 31 percent supported Quie's, while a slight majority favored Mizell's. The most liberal quartile had a more pronounced opposition to these measures: just 7 percent supported the Green Amendment, none favored the Quie Amendment, and 11 percent supported the Mizell Amendment. On the final vote on H.R. 7854 a majority of representatives with ideological ratings between 0 and 75 supported the bill: 96 percent of the most liberal, 92 percent of those slightly left of center, and 76 percent of those slightly right of center. Just 31 percent of the most conservative representatives voted to pass the bill, a number that still represented a decent measure of support for the creation of the Legal Services Corporation even within this cadre of politicians.

The bill attracted substantial votes from both parties, but Democrats were more likely than Republicans to favor the final product by 84 to 62 percent.

Along with ideology another predictor of support for these amendments was whether a representative had undergone legal training. Representatives who studied to become lawyers were less likely to support the Green and Mizell amendments than those without legal training. In contrast, this characteristic did not have a statistically significant impact on one's vote on the Quie Amendment. One explanation for this discrepancy may be that lawyers tended to be more concerned with congressional limitations on what was uniquely lawyers' work, litigation, which was at issue in the Green and Mizell amendments. Quie's amendment, on the other hand, sought only to limit lobbying activity, with which the lawyer-representatives may have been more comfortable because lobbying was not done solely by lawyers. An exchange on the floor of the House between Quie and California representative Alphonzo Bell supports this conclusion. As Quie explained, lawyers were not necessary to the legislative process because legislators were directly available to constituents. "Poor people are no different than . . . other individuals, nonpoor, who usually do not secure an attorney to represent them before the legislatures" but, instead, contact the representative directly by telephone, in writing, or in person. In contrast, Bell, an opponent of the amendment, argued that "the proper function of an attorney in our complex industrial society is not and cannot be limited to activity in the courts."[6] Yet that is essentially what Quie hoped to do.

In any case, no other variable had as consistent an effect on one's vote as ideological predilection and legal training, including the various interest group indicators. A state's per capita legal services grant, a proxy for the size of the legal services community, and the percentage of a state's population receiving welfare payments appeared to be significant in at least one model for the Green Amendment, reflecting some interest group influence. Similarly, the percentage of a representative's district that was nonwhite may have had a small negative impact on one's vote on the bill itself.[7] These variables, however, only inconsistently seemed to exert influence.

Two other variables not included in the tables deserve mention. First, party affiliation had an impact on one's vote (see table 3), but this impact was less than that of ideology. Since party affiliation and ideology are highly correlative variables, including both in the models would have obscured their effect and reduced the efficacy of the models. Second, whether or not a representative was from the South (defined as the states of the former Confederacy) did not have a statistically significant impact in any of several alternative models prepared by the author but not included here.

TABLE 1. OUTCOME OF VOTES ON THE GREEN AMENDMENT

Explanatory variable		Model 1	Model 2	Model 3	Model 4
Persons per lawyer	Significance	.603	—	.120	—
	Odds ratio	.999	—	.999	—
Per capita legal services grant	Significance	.045	.078	.079	.530
	Odds ratio	.846	.880	.881	.939
Percentage of population receiving welfare payments	Significance	—	—	—	.031
	Odds ratio	—	—	—	.731
Per capita expenditures on public assistance	Significance	—	—	.182	—
	Odds ratio	—	—	.995	—
Percentage classified as "low-income"	Significance	.008	—	.434	—
	Odds ratio	1.085	—	1.024	—
Percentage population "nonwhite"	Significance	—	.749	—	.687
	Odds ratio	—	.995	—	.994
Percentage population classified as "foreign stock"	Significance	.929	—	.002	.950
	Odds ratio	1.002	—	.954	1.001
Median age of voting-age population	Significance	—	.650	—	—
	Odds ratio	—	1.028	—	—
Median years of school completed	Significance	—	.001	.115	.000
	Odds ratio	—	.420	.690	.353
Percentage living in metropolitan area	Significance	.794	.859	—	.663
	Odds ratio	.998	.999	—	1.003

(*Continued on next page*)

TABLE 1. (*continued*)

Explanatory variable		Model 1	Model 2	Model 3	Model 4
Legal training indicator	Significance	.009	.008	.027	.005
	Odds ratio	.416	.409	.580	.381
Ideological rating	Significance	.000	.000	—	.000
	Odds ratio	1.093	1.099	—	1.103
Party affiliation	Significance	—	—	.000	—
	Odds ratio	—	—	8.045	—

Model summary

	Model 1	Model 2	Model 3	Model 4
No. of observations	411	411	410	411
c^2	301.001	308.630	140.230	313.323
Significance of change in c^2	.000	.000	.000	.000
Pseudo-R^2	.701	.713	.391	.720
Goodness of fit	.502	.974	.099	.796

Note: The table reports the marginal effect of a one-unit change in each explanatory variable on the odds that a House member votes in favor of the proposal. An explanatory variable is considered statistically significant if the number labeled "significance" is less than 0.05. The c^2 statistic represents the change in the -2 log-likelihood from a model containing no explanatory variables; if the number indicating the significance of this change is less than 0.05, the explanatory variables added to the model explain a statistically significant portion of the outcome. The Pseudo-R^2 statistic varies from 0 to 1, with numbers approaching 1 indicating that the model better explains the outcome; this model summary provides the Nagelkerke R^2. "Goodness of fit" is taken from Hosmer and Lemeshow's Goodness of Fit Test; numbers above 0.05 indicate that the model explains the outcome at an acceptable level. Pseudo-R^2 and goodness of fit are useful measures for comparing models. The number of observations may change as a result of nonvotes or missing statistical data.

TABLE 2. OUTCOME OF VOTES ON THE QUIE AMENDMENT

Explanatory variable		Model 1	Model 2	Model 3	Model 4
Persons per lawyer	Significance	.590	—	.393	—
	Odds ratio	1.001	—	.999	—
Per capita legal services grant	Significance	.553	.614	.348	.975
	Odds ratio	.936	1.049	.932	.996
Percentage of population receiving welfare payments	Significance	—	—	—	.118
	Odds ratio	—	—	—	.789
Per capita expenditures on public assistance	Significance	—	—	.250	—
	Odds ratio	—	—	.996	—
Percentage classified as "low-income"	Significance	.229	—	.061	—
	Odds ratio	1.041	—	1.059	—
Percentage population "nonwhite"	Significance	—	.995	—	.961
	Odds ratio	—	1.000	—	1.001
Percentage population classified as "foreign stock"	Significance	.047	—	.042	.044
	Odds ratio	1.047	—	.967	1.048
Median age of voting-age population	Significance	—	.064	—	—
	Odds ratio	—	1.141	—	—
Median years of school completed	Significance	—	.121	.985	.029
	Odds ratio	—	.653	.996	.537
Percentage living in metropolitan area	Significance	.107	.499	—	.195
	Odds ratio	.989	.996	—	.991
Legal training indicator	Significance	.251	.356	.256	.232
	Odds ratio	.663	.716	.752	.649
Ideological rating	Significance	.000	.000	—	.000
	Odds ratio	1.114	1.115	—	1.121
Party affiliation	Significance	—	—	.000	—
	Odds ratio	—	—	11.847	—

Model summary

	Model 1	Model 2	Model 3	Model 4
No. of observations	381	381	380	381
c^2	314.480	317.554	134.193	319. 577
Significance of change in c^2	.000	.000	.000	.000
Pseudo-R^2	.750	.755	.397	.758
Goodness of fit	.133	.745	.004	.538

Note: See note to table 1.

TABLE 3. OUTCOME OF VOTES ON THE MIZELL AMENDMENT

Explanatory variable		Model 1	Model 2	Model 3	Model 4
Persons per lawyer	Significance	.324	—	.748	—
	Odds ratio	1.001	—	1.000	—
Per capita legal services grant	Significance	.052	.142	.069	.358
	Odds ratio	.863	.906	.873	.930
Percentage of population receiving welfare payments	Significance	—	—	—	.206
	Odds ratio	—	—	—	.856
Per capita expenditures on public assistance	Significance	—	—	.551	—
	Odds ratio	—	—	.998	—
Percentage classified as "low-income"	Significance	.048	—	.752	—
	Odds ratio	1.055	—	.991	—
Percentage population "nonwhite"	Significance	—	.051	—	.057
	Odds ratio	—	.971	—	.972
Percentage population classified as "foreign stock"	Significance	.414	—	.024	.878
	Odds ratio	1.014	—	.966	1.003
Median age of voting-age population	Significance	—	.866	—	—
	Odds ratio	—	1.009	—	—
Median years of school completed	Significance	—	.000	.029	.000
	Odds ratio	—	.327	.586	.302
Percentage living in metropolitan area	Significance	.948	.205	—	.183
	Odds ratio	1.000	1.006	—	1.008
Legal training indicator	Significance	.011	.009	.007	.007
	Odds ratio	.478	.450	.516	.442
Ideological rating	Significance	.000	.000	—	.000
	Odds ratio	1.064	1.069	—	1.071
Party affiliation	Significance	—	—	.000	—
	Odds ratio	—	—	3.852	—

Model summary

	Model 1	Model 2	Model 3	Model 4
No. of observations	371	371	370	371
c^2	192.939	210.083	87.972	211.669
Significance of change in c^2	.000	.000	.000	.000
Pseudo-R^2	.548	.584	.286	.587
Goodness of fit	.014	.303	.760	.509

Note: See note to table 1.

TABLE 4. OUTCOME OF THE FINAL VOTE ON H.R. 7824

Explanatory variable		Model 1	Model 2	Model 3	Model 4
Persons per lawyer	Significance	.573	—	.519	—
	Odds ratio	.993	—	.999	—
Per capita legal services grant	Significance	.636	.510	.605	.634
	Odds ratio	.959	1.050	.957	.950
Percentage of population receiving welfare payments	Significance	—	—	—	.278
	Odds ratio	—	—	—	1.136
Per capita expenditures on public assistance	Significance	—	—	.894	—
	Odds ratio	—	—	1.001	—
Percentage classified as "low-income"	Significance	.577	—	.301	—
	Odds ratio	1.015	—	.968	—
Percentage population "nonwhite"	Significance	—	.020	—	.080
	Odds ratio	—	.965	—	.972
Percentage population classified as "foreign stock"	Significance	.069	—	.000	.116
	Odds ratio	1.047	—	1.104	1.042
Median age of voting-age population	Significance	—	.186	—	—
	Odds ratio	—	.932	—	—
Median years of school completed	Significance	—	.132	.059	.133
	Odds ratio	—	.677	.599	.666
Percentage living in metropolitan area	Significance	.244	.012	—	.085
	Odds ratio	1.006	1.013	—	1.009
Legal training indicator	Significance	.537	.571	.333	.602
	Odds ratio	1.202	1.186	1.294	1.170
Ideological rating	Significance	.000	.000	—	.000
	Odds ratio	.946	.940	—	.945
Party affiliation	Significance	—	—	.000	—
	Odds ratio	—	—	.325	—

Model summary

	Model 1	Model 2	Model 3	Model 4
No. of observations	371	371	370	371
c^2	141.998	143.592	75.508	146.509
Significance of change in c^2	.000	.000	.000	.000
Pseudo-R^2	.468	.472	.271	.480
Goodness of fit	.214	.632	.174	.465

Note: See note for table 1.

Abbreviations

MANUSCRIPT COLLECTIONS AND OFFICIAL RECORDS

ALAS	Records of the Atlanta Legal Aid Society, Atlanta
ALAS, AHC	Atlanta Legal Aid Society Collection, Atlanta History Center
BF, NEJL	E. Clinton Bamberger Files, National Equal Justice Library
CLASP	Center for Law and Social Policy Documents
DFCS, GDAH	Department of Family and Children Services, Georgia Department of Archives and History
FRC	Federal Records Center, East Point, Ga.
GDAH	Georgia Department of Archives and History, Atlanta
GLSP	Records of the Georgia Legal Services Program, Atlanta
LANS, ALAS	Legal Aid News Scrapbook, Atlanta Legal Aid Society Collection
LSC	Records of the Legal Services Corporation
LSCA	Records of the Legal Services Corporation of Alabama, Montgomery
MSBA	Mississippi State Bar Association Records, Mississippi Department of Archives and History, Jackson
NCS, ALAS	Newspaper Clippings Scrapbook, Atlanta Legal Aid Society Collection
NEJL	National Equal Justice Library, Washington, D.C.
NM, LSC	North Mississippi Rural Legal Services Files, Legal Services Corporation Archives, Washington, D.C.
NMI, LSC	North Mississippi Investigation Files, Records of the Legal Services Corporation Archives
NMRLS	Records of North Mississippi Rural Legal Services, Oxford, Miss.
PRO, AHC	Muriel Lokey Poverty Rights Office Collection, Atlanta History Center
SCR	Sovereignty Commission Records, Mississippi Department of Archives and History

JOURNALS AND NEWSPAPERS

ABAJ   *American Bar Association Journal*
  AC   *Atlanta Constitution*
ADW   *Atlanta Daily World*
   AJ   *Atlanta Journal*
  AJC   *Atlanta Journal and Constitution*
   AL   *Alabama Lawyer*
  AV   *Atlanta Voice*
  CA   *Commercial Appeal* (Memphis, Tenn.)
  CL   *Clarion-Ledger* (Jackson, Miss.)
 CQA   *Congressional Quarterly Almanac*
  CR   *Clearinghouse Review*
   DJ   *Daily Journal* (Tupelo, Miss.)
GLSN   *Georgia Legal Services Newsletter*, BF, NEJL
 GSBJ   *Georgia State Bar Journal*
   JA   *Jackson Advocate*
   JD   *Juris Doctor*
  JDN   *Jackson Daily News*
 LAN   *Legal Aid News* (ALAS), located in ALAS, AHC
  MLJ   *Mississippi Law Journal*
  NYT   *New York Times*
  PPN   *Poor People's Newspaper* (Atlanta)
  WP   *Washington Post*

Notes

The fictional tenant farmer's entire legal commentary: "Law is a good thing but how you look at it makes a difference, and which side you're on, and how people look at what you've done. Law is fine if you get on the good side of it. It's all owen to which party gets the law on his side. But once you get it on the contrary side, why you might see a sight of worry from it." Elizabeth Madox Roberts, *The Time of Man* (New York: Viking Press, 1926), 281.

1. 36 U.S.C. § 113 (2005). The quoted language is from the 1961 designation; Congress modified the provision slightly in 1998.

2. At the time of Kennedy's speech the Supreme Court had recently recognized that indigent defendants had a right to counsel in certain criminal proceedings, *Gideon v. Wainwright*, 372 U.S. 335 (1963), and Kennedy pointed out that lawyers might secure an indigent person's acquittal "only to abandon him to eviction notices, wage attachments, repossession of goods and termination of welfare benefits." The Supreme Court has not recognized a constitutional right to legal counsel in civil cases or in criminal cases in which personal liberty is not at stake. See *Lassiter v. Department of Social Services*, 452 U.S. 18 (1981), which holds that the Fourteenth Amendment's due process clause requires legal counsel in civil cases only when the balance of the private interest at stake, the government interest at stake, and the risk of erroneous deprivations in the absence of counsel, weighed against each other, favor appointing counsel.

3. An excerpt from Kennedy's "Address on Law Day," 1 May 1964, at the University of Chicago Law School, can be found in Edgar S. and Jean C. Cahn, "The War on Poverty: A Civilian Perspective," *Yale Law Journal* 73 (July 1964): 1336–37. President Lyndon Johnson soon arrived at much the same conclusion. Defending the legal services program against congressional attacks, he said, "To be poor is to be without an advocate—in dealing with a landlord, a creditor, or a government bureaucrat. It is to be subjected to the hostility or indifference of society, without redress. It is to be exposed to frustration and delay, without relief." "Text of President's Message on Urban, Rural Poverty," 14 March 1967, *CQA* 23 (1967): 102–8.

4. The quotation is from the act's preamble. Public Law 88-452, *United States Statutes at Large* (Washington, D.C.: Government Printing Office, 1965), 78:508–16.

5. Earl Johnson Jr., *Justice and Reform: The Formative Years of the OEO Legal Services Program* (New York: Russell Sage Foundation, 1974), 71; LSC, *Annual Report, 1981* (Washington, D.C.: LSC, 1981); and *Annual Report, 1980;* Alan W. Houseman and John A. Dooley, "Legal Services History," MS, November 1985, chap. 3, 10. Poverty lawyers actually served many more people because most of their clients had families that were directly affected by one member seeking legal counsel.

6. Friedman referred to this as "vertical pluralism" within American law. Lawrence M. Friedman, *A History of American Law*, 2nd ed. (New York: Simon and Schuster, 1985), 677–78. "Elite" lawyers "preserved

social and economic inequality" by offering their expertise to the country's industrial giants." Jerold S. Auerbach, *Unequal Justice: Lawyers and Social Change in Modern America* (New York: Oxford University Press, 1976), 12. Upon examining the influence of these powerful business interests on American law, Friedman suggested that "Justice was a whore of the rich." Friedman, *History*, 513.

7. Reginald Heber Smith, *Justice and the Poor: A Study of the Present Denial of Justice to the Poor and of the Agencies Making More Equal Their Position before the Law with Particular Reference to Legal Aid Work in the United States*, 3rd ed. (1919; rpt., Montclair, N.J.: Patterson Smith, 1972), 135. Smith's study was originally published in 1919. See also Ronald M. Pipkin, "Legal Aid and Elitism in the American Legal Profession," an introductory essay in Smith, *Justice*, xi–xxvi.

8. Quotations from von Briesen's annual reports of the legal aid society are in Pipkin, "Legal Aid and Elitism," xxi.

9. The agency handled 349 claims for wages among 1,455 cases in 1890. Smith, *Justice*, 135–36. For the larger historical context, see Amy Dru Stanley, *From Bondage to Contract: Wage Labor, Marriage, and the Market in the Age of Slave Emancipation* (Cambridge: Cambridge University Press, 1998), esp. chap. 6: "The Purchase of Women."

10. Smith, *Justice*, 136.

11. Ibid., 140–48.

12. Ibid., 152–55 (quotation at 155).

13. Ibid., 150, 13.

14. Ibid., 10.

15. Pipkin, "Legal Aid and Elitism," xxiii–xxv.

16. Johnson, *Justice and Reform*, 9. Four hundred legal aid lawyers theoretically served almost 50 million Americans who could not afford an attorney, while 250,000 lawyers served the remaining 140 million Americans. Johnson took his statistics from Emery Brownell, the head of the National Legal Aid and Defender Association and author of *Legal Aid in the United States*, published initially in 1951 and again, with a supplement, in 1961. Houseman and Perle relate that by 1965 there were some 157 legal aid societies, including one in virtually every major city in the United States, and their aggregate budget was nearly $4.5 million. Alan W. Houseman and Linda E. Perle, *Securing Equal Justice for All: A Brief History of Civil Legal Assistance in the United States* (Washington, D.C.: Center for Law and Social Policy, 2003), 3.

17. Jerold Auerbach argues that economic factors were not the only determinants of one's access to legal counsel or ability to excel in the legal profession. Wealthy white men had advantages of race, ethnicity, and gender as well. Auerbach, *Unequal Justice*, 12.

18. See Nadine Taub and Elizabeth M. Schneider, "Women's Subordination and the Role of Law," in *The Politics of Law: A Progressive Critique*, ed. David Kairys, 3rd ed. (1982; rpt., New York: Basic Books, 1998), 328–55.

19. Historians of the American South have long highlighted the economic manifestations of power relations in the region and how race and gender complicated class relationships. See, generally, Eric Foner, *Reconstruction: America's Unfinished Revolution, 1863–1877* (New York: Harper and Row, 1988); Elizabeth Fox-Genovese, *Within the Plantation Household: Black and White Women of the Old South* (Chapel Hill: University of North Carolina Press, 1988); Eugene Genovese, *Roll, Jordan, Roll: The World the Slaves Made* (New York: Vintage Books, 1976); Steven Hahn, *The Roots of Southern Populism: Yeoman Farmers and the Transformation*

of the Georgia Upcountry, 1850–1890 (New York: Oxford University Press, 1983); and Stephanie McCurry, *Masters of Small Worlds: Yeoman Households, Gender Relations, and the Political Culture of the Antebellum South Carolina Low Country* (New York: Oxford University Press, 1995).

20. "Address at the Conclusion of the Selma to Montgomery March," in *A Call to Conscience: The Landmark Speeches of Dr. Martin Luther King, Jr.*, ed. Clayborne Carson and Kris Shepard (New York: Warner Books, 2001), 124. See, generally, Edward L. Ayers, *The Promise of the New South: Life after Reconstruction* (New York: Oxford University Press, 1992); Pete Daniel, *The Shadow of Slavery: Peonage in the South, 1900–1969* (Urbana: University of Illinois Press, 1972); George Tindall, *The Emergence of the New South: 1913–1945* (Baton Rouge: Louisiana State University Press, 1967); C. Vann Woodward, *Origins of the New South: 1877–1913* (Baton Rouge: Louisiana State University Press, 1951); and Woodward, *The Strange Career of Jim Crow*, 3rd rev. ed. (New York: Oxford University Press, 1974).

21. U.S. Bureau of the Census, *U.S. Census of Population: 1980*, vol. 1: *Characteristics of the Population*, pt. 1: *United States Summary*, table 96: Poverty Status in 1979, 1969, and 1959 of Families and Persons by Race: 1960 to 1980 (Washington, D.C.: Government Printing Office, 1973). The "poverty rate" is a term of art used by the federal government that refers to the percentage of persons living in households that earn less than an established "poverty level," which is the amount of income a household must earn to provide for a nutritionally adequate diet designed by the Department of Agriculture. Poverty income cutoffs are revised annually to allow for changes in cost of living as reflected in the consumer price index but do not account for regional differences. In 1969 poverty thresholds ranged from $1,487 for an unrelated female individual sixty-five years old and over and living on a farm to $6,116 for a nonfarm family with a male head and seven or more persons. The average poverty threshold was $3,745 for a family of four headed by a male. See *U.S. Census of Population: 1970*, vol. 1: *Characteristics of the Population*, pt. 1: *United States Summary* (Washington, D.C.: Government Printing Office, 1973), app. 39. It probably goes without saying that such statistical measures are, at best, rough approximations of a family's ability to survive.

22. U.S. Bureau of the Census, *U.S. Census of Population: 1970*, vol. 1: *Characteristics of the Population*, pt. 12: *Georgia*, table 58: Poverty Status in 1969 of Families and Persons by Race and Urban and Rural Residence: 1970 (Washington, D.C.: Government Printing Office, 1973); *U.S. Census of Population: 1970*, vol. 1: *Characteristics of the Population*, pt. 2: *Alabama*, table 58: Poverty Status in 1969 of Families and Persons by Race and Urban and Rural Residence: 1970 (Washington, D.C.: Government Printing Office, 1973); *U.S. Census of Population: 1970*, vol. 1: *Characteristics of the Population*, pt. 26: *Mississippi*, table 58: Poverty Status in 1969 of Families and Persons by Race and Urban and Rural Residence: 1970 (Washington, D.C.: Government Printing Office, 1973).

23. U.S. Bureau of the Census, *U.S. Census of Population: 1980*, vol. 1: *Characteristics of the Population*, pt. 1: *United States Summary*, table 96: Poverty Status in 1979, 1969, and 1959 of Families and Persons by Race: 1960 to 1980 (Washington, D.C.: Government Printing Office, 1983).

24. Abel, "Law without Politics," 613. Abel's entire phrase is that "the poor use[d] their only resource, their poverty, as a source of strength," but this understates poor people's other "resources," such as their identities as women, African Americans, or another minority or the threat of violence, protest, boycott, or political participation that could be sources of strength regardless of one's economic status.

25. Rosalie R. Young, "The Search for Counsel: Perceptions of Applicants for Subsidized Legal Assistance," *Brandeis Journal of Family Law* 36 (Fall 1997–98): 553.

26. Robin Kelley has expanded our understanding of "politics" to include a wide variety of behaviors of seemingly little social consequence but which nonetheless are meaningful to an individual or small group. He uses the term *infrapolitics* to describe these typically unseen actions (unseen by most Americans as well as most scholars). See Robin D. G. Kelley, *Race Rebels: Culture, Politics, and the Black Working Class* (New York: Free Press, 1994); and *Yo' Mama's Disfunktional! Fighting the Culture Wars in Urban America* (Boston: Beacon Press, 1997).

27. Young, "Search for Counsel," 553, 558.

28. Cooper, interview by author; Maxine Rock, "An Even Break for Poor at Law," *AJ*, 25 October 1967, in LANS, ALAS; "Clark Grad Employed as First Negro Legal Aid Attorney," [*ADW*], n.d., NCS, ALAS; Harmon G. Perry, "Howard High Graduate Named Fulton Assistant Prosecutor," [*ADW*], n.d., NCS, ALAS.

29. Asymmetries between a poverty lawyer and her client often resulted in misperceptions of the client's personal experiences, as the lawyer had first to understand the problems apparent in the client's narrative of events and then to translate those problems into legal solutions (if possible). Alfieri explains:

> Situated outside lawyer-told client story is an alternative client story composed of multiple narratives, each speaking in a different voice of the client. The different voices of client narratives imbue client story with normative meanings associated with values such as selfhood, family, community, love, and work. In this view, client story presents a rich text of interwoven voices and narratives. In poverty law advocacy, the integrity of client story stems from the revelation and integration of client voices and narratives in lawyer storytelling. When the client's voices are silenced and her narratives are displaced by the lawyer's narratives, client integrity is tarnished and client story is lost.

Indeed, Alfieri maintained that the "historical price of poverty law" was "the image of the unspeaking client." Anthony V. Alfieri, "Reconstructive Poverty Law Practice: Learning Lessons of Client Narrative," *Yale Law Journal* 100 (May 1991): 2119, 2147. Some of the stories related in the present study confirm this view, but others do not. Clients could and often did "speak" quite perceptibly, and in any case Alfieri overstates the extent to which "silencing" within the legal process equated with client disempowerment.

30. Paul R. Tremblay, "Rebellious Lawyering, Regnant Lawyering, and Street-Level Bureaucracy," *Hastings Law Journal* 43 (April 1992): 947. Tremblay notes that commentators have proposed two basic models to deal with these tensions: "rebellious" lawyering emphasizes mobilization of the poor and the deprofessionalization of legal services programs; "regnant" lawyering relies, instead, on the traditional methods of the legal profession and on the expertise and dominance of lawyers, even as they seek the client's best interests. He suggests that increased client centeredness actually leads to regnant lawyering, despite the possibility that rebellious lawyering may, in some instances, promote the long-term best interests of the low-income community. See also Paul R. Tremblay, "Toward a Community-Based Ethic for Legal Services Practice," *UCLA Law Review* 37 (August 1990): 1101–56, which suggests that poverty lawyers have to take a more assertive role in decision making than their counterparts in private practice because legal services for the poor are more scarce and because poverty lawyers should consider community needs, not just individual client objectives.

31. Qtd. in Robert Pear, "As Welfare Overhaul Looms, Legal Aid for Poor Dwindles," *NYT*, 5 September 1995, 1A. Asher worked for a legal aid society in Denver, Colo.

32. Martha F. Davis, *Brutal Need: Lawyers and the Welfare Rights Movement, 1960–1973* (New Haven,

Conn.: Yale University Press, 1993); Susan E. Lawrence, *The Poor in Court: The Legal Services Program and Supreme Court Decision Making* (Princeton, N.J.: Princeton University Press, 1990); and Elizabeth Bussiere, *(Dis)entitling the Poor: The Warren Court, Welfare Rights, and the American Political Tradition* (University Park: Pennsylvania State University Press, 1997). Other studies of welfare rights include Mimi Abramovitz, *Under Attack, Fighting Back: Women and Welfare in the United States* (New York: Monthly Review Press, 1996); Lawrence Neil Bailis, *Bread or Justice: Grassroots Organizing in the Welfare Rights Movement* (Lexington, Mass.: Lexington Books, 1974); Larry R. Jackson and William A. Johnson, *Protest by the Poor: The Welfare Rights Movement in New York City* (Lexington, Mass.: Lexington Books, 1974); Nick Kotz and Mary Lynn Kotz, *A Passion for Equality: George A. Wiley and the Movement* (New York: Norton, 1977); R. Shep Melnick, *Between the Lines: Interpreting Welfare Rights* (Washington, D.C.: Brookings Institution, 1994); Jacqueline Pope, *Biting the Hand That Feeds Them: Organizing Women on Welfare at the Grass Roots Level* (Westport, Conn.: Praeger, 1989); Guida West, *The National Welfare Rights Movement: The Social Protest of Poor Women* (New York: Praeger, 1981).

33. U.S. Constitution, art. 6, cl. 2.

34. See, generally, Numan V. Bartley, *The New South, 1945–1980* (Baton Rouge: Louisiana State University Press, 1995); and David R. Goldfield, *Black, White, and Southern: Race Relations and Southern Culture, 1940 to the Present* (Baton Rouge: Louisiana State University Press, 1990).

35. Friedman, *History,* 662. This study contends that the history of legal services programs in the United States is best viewed in the context of this "long-term trend of American law." Most surveys of U.S. legal history, including Friedman's, mention legal services programs (if at all) within the context of law reform strategies that became prominent during the 1960s, a perspective that understates the significance of the less confrontational but more plentiful cases in which low-income clients utilized alternative legal remedies for more common problems. Friedman, e.g., suggested that poverty lawyers and others within the legal profession "were in open revolt against vertical pluralism in American law and life," i.e., the disadvantaged place that low-income persons held in the legal system. Friedman wrote that poverty lawyers were "charged with helping poor clients against their enemies," which often included governmental bodies. "Poverty lawyers," he continued, "stepped up pressure on the system for far-reaching change." Friedman, *History,* 677–78. His more recent book, Lawrence M. Friedman, *American Law in the 20th Century* (New Haven, Conn.: Yale University Press, 2002), 471–72, perpetuates the same analysis, discussing poverty lawyers primarily within the context of the welfare rights movement.

36. Friedman defines *legal culture* generally to mean "people's ideas, attitudes, values, and expectations with regard to law." He also suggests that legal change emanates from legal culture, which itself is closely linked to broader social developments. Friedman, *American Law,* 589. Friedman, in *American Law,* and others have related that Americans in the late twentieth century expected a lot of "law" and developed a tendency to take a multitude of problems before the courts, legislatures, and other legal arenas. Through poverty lawyers this became true of poor people as well.

37. Johnson, *Justice and Reform,* and Alan Houseman's writings are the best examples of this perspective. See Alan W. Houseman, "Political Lessons: Legal Services for the Poor: A Commentary," *Georgetown Law Journal* 83 (April 1995): 1669–1709; and Houseman and Dooley, "Legal Services History." Legal scholars have produced a wealth of articles on the practical flaws that debilitated poverty law practice, but most of them still supported the basic mission of legal services for the poor. See, e.g., Joel F. Handler, Ellen Jane

Hollingsworth, and Howard S. Erlanger, *Lawyers and the Pursuit of Legal Rights* (New York: Academic Press, 1978); Mark Kessler, *Legal Services for the Poor: A Comparative and Contemporary Analysis of Interorganizational Politics* (Westport, Conn.: Greenwood Press, 1987); Douglas J. Besharov, ed., *Legal Services for the Poor: Time for Reform* (Washington, D.C.: American Enterprise Institute, 1990).

38. The quotation is from Rael Jean Isaac, "War on the Poor," *National Review,* May 15, 1995, 36. See also Kenneth F. Boehm, "The Legal Services Corporation: Unaccountable, Political, Anti-Poor, Beyond Reform and Unnecessary," *Saint Louis Public Law Review* 17 (1998): 321, whose title leaves little to the imagination. See, generally, Charles Murray, *Losing Ground: American Social Policy, 1950–1980* (New York: Basic Books, 1984).

39. Jack Katz, *Poor People's Lawyers in Transition* (New Brunswick, N.J.: Rutgers University Press, 1982), is the most comprehensive analysis of legal aid within a particular social context, the city of Chicago during the 1960s and 1970s. Katz's primary objective was to analyze how institutional dynamics nurtured or discouraged attorneys' law reform activities. Katz recognized that "the history of legal assistance to the poor cannot be explained fully by an institutional analysis" but suggested that "the influence of economic and political events has been neither so direct nor so decisive as to render spurious an institutional analysis of civil legal assistance" (5–6).

40. Katz offers a theory of "involvement," whereby legal aid attorneys in Chicago affirmed their own "significance" by engaging in law reform work. This explains how law reform work could exist independent of an external push for social reform. His conclusion is generally accurate, but this study will suggest that poverty lawyers' work and the development of legal services institutions were sometimes linked to an external social movement. See ibid., chap. 6.

41. Ibid., 6.

42. Ibid., 12–13, 182–83. Katz's conclusions need qualification. First, he exaggerates the causal link between the professionalization of reform and the changing character of that reform. As this study will demonstrate, poverty lawyers worked within legal and political limitations that became increasingly evident during the 1970s and 1980s, and these factors had a greater impact on poverty lawyers' reform activities than their own professionalization. Second, Katz's analysis is focused somewhat narrowly on poverty lawyers' litigation activities within the context of American social policy and their social impact on the poor. As another scholar, Richard L. Abel, has written, "a frequent pitfall in assessing legal aid is the tendency to focus on the periphery rather than the core—on law reform litigation and community organization rather than routine servicing of individual cases." Abel, "Law without Politics: Legal Aid under Advanced Capitalism," *UCLA Law Review* 32 (1985): 607. This is a pitfall within the political discourse over federally funded legal services in the United States; in particular, opponents of such funding have tended to focus on more controversial cases that are outliers, unrepresentative of the bulk of poverty law practice. Katz's relatively narrow focus caused him to gloss over two major areas of legal services work that were more integrative than segregative and less likely to involve law reform strategies: domestic relations and consumer law. Also, in the Deep South poverty lawyers helped extend constitutional and statutory rights to African Americans, thus dismantling a pattern of segregation along racial lines. There was even a way in which improving clients' access to public benefits was integrative, if one accepts the arguments of Piven and Cloward. They suggest that the state used welfare programs to regulate the labor market: in times of turmoil among the poor, the state expanded benefits, but, when this turmoil subsided and there was a need for labor, the state

decreased benefits. If this was the case, then poverty lawyers helped integrate their clients into the labor market and welfare state in all its regulatory functions. Piven and Cloward's seminal work is Francis Fox Piven and Richard A. Cloward, *Regulating the Poor: The Functions of Public Welfare,* updated ed. (New York: Vintage Books, 1993).

43. Katz, *Poor People's Lawyers,* 8, 190–94. Katz points out that in the larger context of American history legal aid "played only a peripheral role in the transformation of poverty from a sporadically prosecuted crime to a bureaucratically maintained legal status" (190). A major influence on his assessment of legal aid was Michel Foucault, who had recently written that in capitalist societies the state utilized prisons and asylums to discipline "deviant elements of the working classes." Katz suggested there was a "chilling plausibility" that "poor people's lawyers in conservative political epochs" might play an analogous role, given that in "1981 reactionary national policies tried to sharpen the state's administrative segregation of the poor" and that "liberal humanitarianism appear[ed] less likely to help indigents by pressing for class-integrated administrative formats than by continuing to dramatize the need for a greater differentiation of the poor" (193–94). See also Michel Foucault, *Discipline and Punish: The Birth of the Prison* (New York: Pantheon, 1978); and David J. Rothman, *The Discovery of the Asylum: Social Order and Disorder in the New Republic* (1971; rpt., Boston: Little, Brown, 1990).

44. Stuart A. Scheingold, *The Politics of Rights: Lawyers, Public Policy, and Political Change* (New Haven, Conn.: Yale University Press, 1974), 183–84. Scheingold warns that much of poverty law practice did not represent engagement in a "politics of rights" that sought to alter poor people's legal and economic status but, instead, simply accepted the "myth of rights" that pervaded American legal culture and American society. That myth is essentially the assumption that our rights already exist and, if we do not presently enjoy them, they need only be claimed through the legal process. "Legal assistance," by which Scheingold refers to the passive role of the attorney simply responding to the needs of her client without framing problems in a broader context, relies and reinforces the myth of rights. See Mauro Cappelletti and James Gordley, "Legal Aid: Modern Themes and Variations," *Stanford Law Review* 24 (January 1972): 347–421, which emphasized that legal aid reflected contemporary conceptions of the role of states and the rights of citizens and suggested that in the modern era Western nations have moved toward a conception of legal aid as a right requiring state action. Thus, efforts to implement publicly funded legal aid programs were themselves part of a politics of rights.

45. Abel, "Law without Politics," 607–8. Abel included a third function, "mitigating state coercion," drawing attention to criminal defense work by legal aid lawyers, which in theory protects the rights of the accused but arguably is only a pretense of protecting those rights (611–12). Although significant, this subject lies outside the scope of the present study.

46. "Absent" in terms of their productive capacity, either physically or through indifference or abusive behavior. Ibid., 592, 588–89. Many conservatives have criticized legal aid for promoting just the opposite—i.e., the breakdown of the family—by offering representation through divorce proceedings.

47. As Abel suggested: "All societies must devise ways to support those members who are not directly involved in production because they are too young, too old, or too disabled, or are caring for such a person, and who therefore cannot appropriate the resources they need. Most societies rely on kinship obligations for this purpose, but private relationships no longer perform that function adequately under advanced capitalism." Ibid., 608.

48. Ibid., 609–10.

49. The starkest version of this perspective argues that poverty lawyers have done more damage than good because they have failed to "inculcate consciousness of class among the poor," thus leaving the hegemonic function of the law intact. Anthony V. Alfieri, "The Antinomies of Poverty Law and a Theory of Dialogic Empowerment," *New York University Review of Law and Social Change* 16 (1987–88): 659–712, 680. Instead, poverty lawyers have operated under two disempowering assumptions: the myth of legal efficacy, i.e., "that the law—in its constitutional, statutory, and decisional forms—and legal institutions—courts, government agencies, and advocacy organizations—can be marshaled into an effective instrument to alleviate poverty"; and "the belief in the inherent isolation and passivity of the poor—the inability of the poor to interconnect and exercise shared control over their own lives and communities" (673). Alfieri's solution: "By developing hegemonic alternatives and oppositional discourses in collective relational contexts, the poor enter the transformational process of breaking free from the subordinate role and identity assigned by the dominant hegemony. With the splintering of dominant hegemony, the poor may converge as a class-for-itself around an alternative vision of reality" (682). Similarly, an unwillingness to appreciate the political implications of legal aid led to "value incoherence," according to Abel. Advocates of legal aid have variously stressed its ability to reduce social conflict, to enhance "access" to law, to pursue substantive goals rather than simply "procedural justice," to address problems peculiar to specific groups (women, minorities, children, the elderly, the disabled), and to promote collective action. They have failed to develop a uniform strategy to address the problems of the poor. Abel, "Law without Politics," 485–98.

50. Abel, "Law without Politics," 614.

51. David Kairys, "Introduction," in *The Politics of Law: A Progressive Critique*, ed. D. Kairys, 3rd ed. (1982; rpt., New York: Basic Books, 1998), 1. See Morton J. Horwitz, *The Transformation of American Law, 1870–1960: The Crisis of Legal Orthodoxy* (New York: Oxford University Press, 1992), for a discussion of what he termed "classical legal thought," which dominated the nineteenth century, and the rise of "progressive legal thought" during the early twentieth century. With this intellectual shift the notion of law as apolitical faded in favor of "legal realism," but tension remains between these competing perceptions of the law.

52. Abel, "Law without Politics," 476. Such critical views of legal aid have improved our understanding of these institutions, but there are flaws with perspectives that too narrowly emphasize the influence of the political economy on human behavior and on our legal regime. They often fail to explain the specific timing of institutional development, the diverse motivations of legal services attorneys and their advocates, or the vehement opposition to publicly funded legal aid. Also, they tend to underappreciate the historical contingencies that shaped poverty law practice and do not adequately acknowledge the meaning and impact of legal aid in the lives of legal aid clients. About the latter point, note the work of Robin Kelley, discussed earlier.

53. As Friedman suggests, "History of law is not—or should not be—a search for fossils, but study of social development, unfolding through time." He emphasizes law as an element of "culture," uniquely suited to each society. Friedman, *History*, 19. Hall studies "the interaction of law and society," using law as a means of inquiry (a "magic mirror," a phrase proposed by Justice Oliver Wendell Holmes Jr.) into American culture and finding that law has been constantly transformed ("more like a river than a rock," he concludes). Kermit L. Hall, *The Magic Mirror: Law in American History* (New York: Oxford University Press, 1989), vii, 3, 333.

54. Abel, "Law without Politics," 592.

55. Focusing on the Deep South states of Georgia, Alabama, and Mississippi encourages an examination of the intersection of law, poverty, and race, among other things, at a particularly tumultuous time and place. Legal services programs emerged in the midst of rapidly changing race relations and, as it turned out, a civil rights movement in transition. Also, a regional study allows for the documentation of institutional development over a longer period of time and a deeper exploration of poverty law practice than a study of a broader geographic area, without sacrificing a comparative analysis. Because legal and institutional developments in the Deep South were closely linked to national politics, this study explores relevant national events in some detail, but the story remains situated in the unique history of the region.

56. The Supreme Court's decision in *Boddie v. Connecticut* put this in the broadest possible terms: Perhaps no characteristic of an organized and cohesive society is more fundamental than its erection and enforcement of a system of rules defining the various rights and duties of its members, enabling them to govern their affairs and definitively settle their differences in an orderly, predictable manner. Without such a "legal system," social organization and cohesion are virtually impossible; with the ability to seek regularized resolution of conflicts individuals are capable of interdependent action that enables them to strive for achievements without the anxieties that would beset them in a disorganized society. Put more succinctly, it is this injection of the rule of law that allows society to reap the benefits of rejecting what political theorists call the "state of nature." *Boddie v. Connecticut*, 401 U.S. 371 (1971)

57. This was the conclusion of Alexis de Tocqueville, that the "language of the law" had long been a "vulgar tongue," meaning that it had long penetrated "into the bosom of society, where it descend[ed] to the lowest classes, so that at last the whole people contract[ed] the habit and tastes of the judicial magistrate." Tocqueville, *Democracy in America*, 4 vols. (1835; rpt., New York: Vintage Books, 1959), 1:290.

58. George Moore, representing the National Client's Council, in testimony before the Subcommittee on Employment, Manpower, and Poverty on 9 October 1970, qtd. in Congress, Senate, Committee on Labor and Public Welfare, *Economic Opportunity Amendments of 1971*, 92nd Cong., 1st sess., 1971, Report No. 92-331, 28.

59. Eric M. Uslaner has suggested that low-income and minority Americans may be less likely to trust the legal system and to trust people in general than more affluent, white Americans. He argues that the increase in economic inequality in the United States contributed to a decline in "interpersonal trust" between Americans during the late twentieth century and that low levels of interpersonal trust contribute to low levels of trust in institutions such as the legal system. Uslaner, *The Moral Foundations of Trust* (Cambridge: Cambridge University Press, 2002), 46–47.

60. *Georgia v. McCollum*, 505 U.S. 42, at 49–50 (1992).

1. A "NEW BREED OF LAWYER"

1. One historian called "the 1960s a modern Great Awakening which ignited a 'Burned-Over Decade' of cultural change akin to the turbulent 1840s." Patterson, *Grand Expectations*, 442, and chaps. 15 and 18; Arlene Skolnick, *Embattled Paradise: The American Family in an Age of Uncertainty* (New York: Basic Books, 1991), 89–99. See also William Braden, *Age of Aquarius: Technology and the Cultural Revolution* (Chicago:

Quadrangle Books, 1970); Morris Dickstein, *Gates of Eden: American Culture in the Sixties* (New York: Basic Books, 1977).

2. Chief Justice Earl Warren called the latter decision—*Baker v. Carr*, 369 U.S. 186 (1962)—the most important of his tenure. Earl Warren, *The Memoirs of Earl Warren* (New York: Doubleday, 1977), 306. See Morton Horwitz, *The Warren Court and the Pursuit of Justice* (New York: Hill and Wang, 1998); Lucas A. Powe Jr., *The Warren Court and American Politics* (Cambridge, Mass.: Belknap Press, 2000).

3. Gerald Gunther, "Foreword: In Search of Evolving Doctrine on a Changing Court: A Model for a Newer Equal Protection," *Harvard Law Review* 86 (1972): 1–48.

4. Archibald Cox, "Foreword: Constitutional Adjudication and the Promotion of Human Rights," *Harvard Law Review* 80 (1966): 91.

5. Patterson, *Grand Expectations*, 534–35. See also Peter H. Irons, *The New Deal Lawyers* (Princeton, N.J.: Princeton University Press, 1982).

6. John Kenneth Galbraith, *The Affluent Society* (New York: Houghton Mifflin, 1958); Michael Harrington, *The Other America: Poverty in the United States* (New York: Macmillan, 1962).

7. Eric Foner, *The Story of American Freedom* (New York: Norton, 1998), 284: "the black [civil rights] movement succeeded in placing the question of economic freedom back on the nation's political agenda." Fred Siegel suggests that the social programs of the 1960s and 1970s were largely responses to a "riot ideology," i.e., "the assumption that the violence of the sixties riots and their criminal aftermath were both justified and, to a considerable extent, functional in rectifying the sins of racism." One must keep in mind, however, that the origins of these programs predated the wave of riots that plagued American cities from 1965 (Watts) to 1968 (after the King assassination). Fred Siegel, *The Future Once Happened Here: New York, D.C., L.A., and the Fate of America's Big Cities* (New York: Free Press, 1997), xii.

8. "New Breed of Lawyer Serving the Poor," *NYT*, 30 August 1969, 11, LANS, ALAS. Nicholas deB. Katzenbach, who succeeded Robert F. Kennedy as attorney general, used the phrase in a speech at a Department of Health, Education, and Welfare conference in June 1964, when Katzenbach was deputy attorney general. He referred respectfully to the work of legal aid societies but stated that "we cannot translate our new concern [for the poor] into successful action simply by providing more of the same" and that a "new breed of lawyers is emerging, dedicated to using the law as an instrument of orderly and constructive social change." Qtd. in Houseman and Perle, *Securing Equal Justice*, 5.

9. Johnson, *Justice and Reform*, 179, 189.

10. See Katz, *Poor People's Lawyers*. Nearly all of the attorneys interviewed for this study began their legal careers immediately or within a few years of attending law school. Johnson notes that comparative increases in salaries helped attract people into legal services as well. Federal funding had allowed for an approximately 40 percent increase in salaries: the average salary of legal aid attorneys in 1959 was less than $6,000 in larger cities and less than $5,300 in smaller ones; in 1965 an NLADA figure estimated the average to be approximately $6,500. In 1967, however, the average salary of OEO funded attorneys was $9,500. Johnson, *Justice and Reform*, 189 and 337 n. 15; Emery A. Brownell, *Legal Aid in the United States : A Study of the Availability of Lawyers' Services for Persons Unable to Pay Fees* (Rochester, N.Y.: Lawyers Cooperative, 1951), 48.

11. Patterson, *Grand Expectations*, chap. 11: "The Biggest Boom Yet."

12. The draft began to increase substantially after 1964, but never did a large percentage of men of draft age serve in Vietnam when compared to earlier conflicts. Of the 26.8 million men aged eighteen through twenty-five, 2.1 million went to Vietnam, and 1.6 million of those saw conflict (though 11.7 million served somewhere in the armed services during the ten years of major American involvement in Vietnam). During World War II some 80 percent of draft-age men served in the military, and 50 percent served during the Korean War, compared to 40 percent during Vietnam. Of those who served in the armed forces, they were disproportionately less affluent, less educated, and minority. This was largely because of the Selective Service deferment policies. Those who attended college or graduate school did not have to serve until Congress changed these policies in 1967 and Johnson implemented them in 1968. After 1968 graduate students not studying divinity, dentistry, or medicine who had not completed two years of study would be eligible for the draft, as would college seniors graduating in 1968. James Patterson points out that these changes did not have a dramatic impact on the draft, but they "greatly unsettled students and their parents. For the first time, it seemed, the college-educated sons of the middle classes might have to face the terrors of the bush." Significantly, much of the opposition to Vietnam emanated from the nation's elite campuses. There were other means of avoiding the draft as well, including getting married and having children, joining the military reserves or the National Guard, convincing a physician that one was too sick (sometimes mentally) to be inducted, or claiming to be homosexual. Patterson, *Grand Expectations*, 598–99, 629–32.

13. Dokson recalled that Dan Bradley, who was then in charge of the Reginald Heber Smith Fellowship program and would later hold several positions within the legal services bureaucracy, sold Dokson on poverty law by telling him that accepting the Reggie scholarship would win a deferment. Robert Dokson, interview by author, 2 December 1998, Atlanta, audiotape in author's possession (unless otherwise noted, interviews by author are audiotaped and in the author's possession). Others who have mentioned this motivation include David Webster and Tom Bowman; Webster, interview by author, 18 February 1999, Atlanta; Bowman, interview by author, 10 December 1998, Conyers, Ga. Bowman was from Mississippi and joined ALAS in 1969. His draft board granted him a deferment but required him to serve his two years in Mississippi, so he worked for NMRLS before returning to Atlanta in the early 1970s.

14. See chap. 3 for further discussion.

15. Tom Royals, interview by author, 6 July 1998, Jackson, Miss. Royals worked for North Mississippi Rural Legal Services in the late 1960s.

16. Dokson, interview by author.

17. Patterson, *Grand Expectations*, chaps. 19 and 21; Friedman, *American Law*, 457–59 (on the changing demographics of the bar nationwide).

18. Jesse Pennington, interview by author, 8 July 1998, Jackson, Miss.

19. See, generally, Bartley, *New South*.

20. David Oshinsky, *"Worse than Slavery": Parchman Farm and the Ordeal of Jim Crow Justice* (New York: Free Press, 1996), 55.

21. Jesse Pennington, interview by author.

22. For an insightful example of how the events of the 1960s entered the consciousness of persons far removed from the Deep South, see Henry Louis Gates Jr., *Colored People: A Memoir* (New York: Vintage Books, 1994).

23. Pennington, interview by author.

24. Clarence Cooper, interview by author, 28 January 1999, Atlanta. The previous year another African American had begun attending Emory's less prestigious night law school.

25. Cooper remained in poverty law for less than a year, leaving to become the first black assistant prosecutor in Fulton County. After serving as assistant prosecutor for only a few months—which he hoped would open opportunities for other African Americans in public service—Cooper was drafted into the army. Although he had legal training, the military resisted placing him in the Judge Advocate General's Corps (JAG), the specialized legal branch of the armed services. Only after the National Association for the Advancement of Colored People (NAACP) and National Urban League contacted the army on his behalf—Georgia senators Richard Russell and Herman Talmadge had done nothing—did Cooper win his JAG placement. He served in Vietnam for two years, after which he returned to a position in the Georgia Attorney General's office from 1970 to 1975. Cooper then moved behind the bench, holding several local judgeships before Governor Joe Frank Harris appointed him to the Georgia Court of Appeals in 1990. Four years later President Bill Clinton appointed him to the federal bench, and he remains a federal judge in Georgia's Northern District in Atlanta. Cooper, interview by author; Maxine Rock, "An Even Break for Poor at Law," *AJ*, 25 October 1967, in LANS, ALAS; "Clark Grad Employed as First Negro Legal Aid Attorney," [*ADW*], n.d.; and Harmon G. Perry, "Howard High Graduate Named Fulton Assistant Prosecutor," [*ADW*], n.d., both in Newspaper Clippings Scrapbook, ALAS.

26. Taylor reported that, as a result of this study, the federal government revoked the television station's license. Stanley Taylor, interview by author, 1 July 1998, Biloxi, Miss. See *Office of Communication of United Church of Christ v. F.C.C.*, 359 F.2d 994 (D.C.Cir. 1966); and substantial subsequent administrative history beginning with *In re Applications of Lamar Life Broadcasting Co. for Renewal of License of Television Stations WLBT and Auxiliary Services, Jackson, Miss.*, 3 F.C.C. 2d 784 (1966).

27. Taylor, interview by author.

28. Brennan, interview by author, 6 November 1998, Decatur, Ga.; Michael Padnos, interview by author, 11 January 2001, Vauvenargues, France (by telephone). The quotation is Brennan's recollection.

29. Brennan, interview by author.

30. Qtd. in Robert Dallek, *Flawed Giant: Lyndon Johnson and His Times, 1961–1973* (New York: Oxford University Press, 1998), 62. See also Doris Kearns Goodwin, *Lyndon Johnson and the American Dream* (New York: Harper and Row, 1976).

31. American political discourse steadily narrowed beginning around the turn of the twentieth century with the demise of the Populist movement, and again during the New Deal era, as policy makers passed over, and seemingly forgot forever, the most radical reform possibilities. See Lawrence Goodwyn, *Democratic Promise: The Populist Moment in America* (Oxford: Oxford University Press, 1976); and Alan Brinkley, *The End of Reform: New Deal Liberalism in Recession and War* (New York: Vintage Books, 1995).

32. Allen J. Matusow, *The Unraveling of America: A History of Liberalism in the 1960s* (New York: Harper and Row, 1984), chaps. 8 and 9. See also Daniel P. Moynihan, *Maximum Feasible Misunderstanding: Community Action in the War on Poverty* (New York: Free Press, 1970), for a similar assessment.

33. The Economic Opportunity Act of 1964 did not expressly create the Legal Services Program, but the program was specifically added in the Economic Opportunity Act Amendments of 1966 and made a

special emphasis program in the Economic Opportunity Act Amendments of 1967. Houseman and Perle, *Securing Equal Justice*, 7.

34. Address by E. Clinton Bamberger, National Legal Aid and Defender Association's Annual Meeting, Scottsdale, Ariz., 18 November 1965, qtd. in Cappelletti and Gordley, "Legal Aid," 411.

35. See Mark Tushnet, *Making Civil Rights Law: Thurgood Marshall and the Supreme Court, 1936–1961* (New York: Oxford University Press, 1994); and Richard Kluger, *Simple Justice: The History of* Brown v. Board of Education *and Black America's Struggle for Equality* (New York: Knopf, 1976).

36. See, e.g., *Muller v. Oregon*, 208 U.S. 412 (1908); Hall, *Magic Mirror*, 238–46, 161–62, 260–64.

37. Johnson, *Justice and Reform*, chap. 2; Daniel H. Lowenstein and Michael J. Waggoner, "Note: Neighborhood Law Offices: The New Wave in Legal Services for the Poor," *Harvard Law Review* (February 1967): 805–50.

38. Johnson, *Justice and Reform*, 32–35; Cahn and Cahn, "War on Poverty."

39. Johnson, *Justice and Reform*, 40–43. See Scheingold, *Politics of Rights*, for a discussion of the "myth of rights" and the "politics of rights." This internal debate within the legal service task force reflected a tension between these two conceptualizations of the potential role of poverty lawyers.

40. Johnson, *Justice and Reform*, 48–49.

41. Ibid., 43–70, quote at 56. For a discussion of Powell's role in the formation of the Legal Services Program, see John C. Jeffries Jr., "Lewis F. Powell, Jr. and the Birth of Legal Services," *Virginia Lawyer* (December 1998): 7–9. Richard Nixon appointed Powell to the Supreme Court in 1972.

42. Johnson, *Justice and Reform*, 70.

43. Ibid., 71.

44. "Atlanta Legal Aid Society History," ALAS, AHC, 1–11.

45. Ibid., 7, 12–14. Most of the charitable funding was from the local Community Chest.

46. Ibid., 14.

47. Ibid.; ALAS, *Annual Report, 1963*.

48. "Atlanta Legal Aid Society History," 14–16; Luther Rosser Shelton, interview by author, 16 December 1998, Atlanta; Virginia Bips, interview by author, 23 November 1998, Atlanta (by telephone), handwritten notes. Bips guessed that roughly half of the domestic cases were divorces.

49. "Atlanta Legal Aid Society History," 17–20; ALAS, *Annual Report, 1966*; ALAS, *Annual Report, 1972*.

50. "Atlanta Legal Aid Society History," 18.

51. Padnos related that he initially suggested that the ALAS board hire a new director. Then he decided to get out of Washington, D.C., and wanted head his own legal services program, so he informed the board that he was available. Thus did Padnos become director of ALAS. Michael Padnos, interview by author.

52. Padnos later saw this as one of his great achievements in Atlanta. Padnos, interview by author. In 1969 alone, the society added four VISTA lawyers, six Reggies, and seven new staff attorneys, to make thirty-two lawyers, including at least one each from Yale, Chicago, and Pennsylvania. ALAS, *Annual Report, 1969*; LAN, August 1969.

53. Padnos, interview by author.

54. See Nadine Cohodas, *The Band Played Dixie: Race and the Liberal Conscience at Ole Miss* (New York: Free Press, 1997), 118–22.

55. Aaron Condon was hired to organize the efforts of law students and local lawyers. Also, during the summer of 1966 Professor Michael Horowitz, recently graduated from Yale Law School, arranged for several Ole Miss law students to practice in legal services programs across the country. Michael Trister, interview by author, 28 May 1998, Washington, D.C.; Aaron Condon, interview by author, 15 July 1998, Oxford, Miss.; Michael Horowitz, interview by author, 28 May 1998, Washington, D.C.

56. Condon, interview by author; Trister, interview by author; George Strickler, interview by author, 2 July 1998, New Orleans, La.

57. Luther McDougal, interview by author, 2 July 1998, New Orleans, La.

58. Several documents relate these events: *Trister v. University of Mississippi*, 420 F.2d 499 (5th Cir. 9 October 1969); Trister, interview by author; Strickler, interview by author; and Joseph Delaney, *NMRLS Notes*, September 1978, NM, LSC (hereafter *NMRLS Notes*).

59. Trister, interview by author; Strickler, interview by author.

60. Trister, interview by author.

61. Coahoma Legal Aid, Inc., was funded in 1966 to cover only Coahoma County. Based in Clarksdale, the program was a recipient of local community action agency funds and later began receiving funds directly from OEO. Initially a one-lawyer office, the program hired a second attorney later in the decade. The majority of the caseload was basic legal services, and, as a Mississippi State Sovereignty Commission reported (approvingly), the lawyers were wary of offending the local bar association. One board member traveled to Atlanta for an OEO Legal Services conference at which they discussed "pushing cases involving welfare"; Mr. Roberson wanted no such activity, and "such a practice was not then and isn't now followed in the operation of the Legal Assistance Program." Greek Rice, former attorney general of Mississippi and sheriff of Coahoma County, conveyed to Sovereignty Commission investigators that he "personally, does not like the program but he cannot say anything bad about it." "Memorandum: Legal Assistance Program," 16 February 1971, in Stanley Taylor File, SCR. The program in Philadelphia, Choctaw Legal Services, was affiliated with the Choctaw community action agency and provided legal services for some four thousand members of the Mississippi Band of Choctaw Indians. A one-lawyer office, the program suffered from unstable funding.

62. Johnson, *Justice and Reform*, 99, 318 n. 72; Alabama State Bar Committee on Group and Prepaid Legal Services and Legal Services to the Poor, "Group and Prepaid Legal Services and Legal Services to the Poor," *AL* 36 (1975): 380–81. Attorneys working for the JCCEO's Jefferson County Legal Services were involved in a few significant cases. They represented a predominantly black women's organization known as the Poor People's Action Committee in a challenge against, ironically, the JCCEO. The women were protesting what they felt were discriminatory practices within the JCCEO's Concentrated Employment Program, which was placing black women in a chicken-packing plant rather than human relations positions for which the program had trained them. Moreoever, these women complained that the white director and black assistant director threatened and intimidated them for protesting these placements. They won the case, the director of the employment resigned, and the JCCEO disciplined the assistant director. Kelley, *Race Rebels*, 96. See also *Morris v. Alabama Department of Industrial Relations* (N.D. Ala.), reported in *CR* 4 (June 1970): 92; *Morris v. Jefferson County Committee for Economic Opportunity* (5th Cir.), reported in *CR* 4 (December

1970): 378. Also, JCLS attorney Demetries Newton represented African-American residents of Fairfield, Alabama, in a challenge to that city's urban renewal program, which was allegedly relocating them without providing for alternative housing as well as providing municipal services for whites but not for blacks. With the help of NAACP Legal Defense Fund attorneys, Newton convinced the Fifth Circuit Court of Appeals that the city was violating HUD regulations regarding racial discrimination in housing. *Arrington v. City of Fairfield, Alabama* (N.D. Ala.), reported in *CR* 2, no. 13 (November 1968): 19; *Arrington v. City of Fairfield, Alabama* (5th Cir.), reported in *CR* 3 (October 1969): 140–41.

63. Piven and Cloward, *Regulating the Poor,* 319, based on statistics provided by OEO.

64. LSP published the *Legal Services Guidelines* and later *How to Apply for a Legal Services Program* to facilitate this process and notify applicants of some of the salient elements of OEO regulations, such as the requirement that low-income people be represented on program boards of directors. Houseman and Perle, *Securing Equal Justice,* 8.

65. Johnson, *Justice and Reform,* 190–91. Outside the South, OEO usually managed to compromise between the competing factions by approving plans whereby each group appointed some members of a program's board of directors.

66. Billie Bethel and Robert Kirk Walker, "Et Tu, Brute!" *AL* 27 (1966): 17–31.

67. "Committee on Law and Poverty Recommendations," *AL* 27 (1966): 142–43; Paul Johnston, "Legal Services to the Poor—Where Does the Alabama Bar Stand?" *AL* 27 (1966): 144–51.

68. "Memorandum on the Validity of a Set of Rules and Regulations Adopted by the Mississippi State Bar Purporting to Restrict the Formation of Group Legal Services Programs in Mississippi," n.d., NEJL. This document, dated approximately mid-1969, was an OEO report detailing the actions of the Mississippi state bar and explaining why those actions were contrary to federal statutes and the American Bar Association's guidelines governing professional ethics and legal services programs.

69. Bill Ide (interview by author, 5 March 1999, Atlanta) and James Elliott (interview by author, 6 April 1999, Atlanta) discuss the Georgia bar's reaction to federally funded legal services.

70. As Johnson put it: "When the money was there, the applications were not. When the applications finally came in, the money was gone. Had we started to form regional organizations sooner, the South undoubtedly now would have hundreds of poverty lawyers instead of a few score." *Justice and Reform,* 93–94, 191–92.

71. Ibid., 181. Earl Johnson, the second director of LSP, was a strong supporter of backup centers and "established 'law reform' as the chief goal of OEO legal services." Houseman and Perle, *Securing Equal Justice,* 11.

2. THE LAWYERS' WAR ON POVERTY, 1965–1970

1. Tremblay, "Acting 'A Very Moral Type of God,'" 2481.

2. Mobilization for Youth Legal Unit Report, November 1965, 3, qtd. in Davis, *Brutal Need,* 30, and 22–35.

3. See Premilla Nadasen, "The Welfare Rights Movement, 1960–1975" (Ph.D. diss., Columbia University, 1999), which expertly makes this connection between the increase in the percentage of AFDC recipients who were African-American women and the creation of restrictive policies in the South. On the origins of AFDC and other forms of relief for women, see Joanne L. Goodwin, *Gender and the Politics*

of *Welfare Reform: Mothers' Pensions in Chicago, 1911–1929* (Chicago: University of Chicago Press, 1997); Linda Gordon, *Pitied but Not Entitled: Single Mothers and the History of Welfare, 1890–1935* (New York: Free Press, 1994).

4. Davis, *Brutal Need,* 56. See Jack Bass, *Unlikely Heroes* (New York: Simon and Schuster, 1981), which documents the prominent role of southern federal judges in the civil rights movement, in particular several distinguished jurists who sat on the Fifth Circuit Court of Appeals. The hierarchical structure of the American courts meant that these individuals had significant influence even beyond cases that came before them, since appellate judges often reviewed and could reverse decisions made by federal district court judges, a possibility of which these "lower court" judges were constantly aware and which they generally tried to avoid.

5. Lee Albert, "Choosing the Test Case in Welfare Litigation: A Plea for Planning," *CR* 2 (November 1968): 4–6, 28. Ironically, the phrase *erosion theory* better fits the NAACP strategy; with each welfare rights case, the CSWPL sought a knockout punch.

6. See Mark Tushnet, *The NAACP's Legal Strategy against Segregated Education, 1925–1950* (Chapel Hill: University of North Carolina Press, 1987).

7. Davis, *Brutal Need,* 37–38; Edward V. Sparer, "The New Legal Aid as an Instrument of Social Change," *University of Illinois Law Forum* (1965): 57–62; Sparer, "The Role of the Welfare Client's Lawyer," *UCLA Law Review* (1965): 361–80; Sparer, "Social Welfare Law Testing," *Practical Lawyer* (April 1966): 13–31; Sparer, "The Right to Welfare," in *The Rights of Americans,* ed. Norman Dorsen (New York: Pantheon, 1971), 65–93; "Guarantee of 'Right to Live' Is Urged," *NYT,* 28 September 1969, 40.

8. Charles A. Reich, "The New Property," *Yale Law Journal* 73 (1964): 768, 779, 787; Davis, *Brutal Need,* 83–86. See also Reich, "Individual Rights and Social Welfare: The Emerging Legal Issues," *Yale Law Journal* 74 (1965): 1245–57.

9. *Anderson v. Schaefer,* Case File No. C.A. 10443 (N.D. Ga.), FRC; Davis, *Brutal Need,* 56–57; Greenberg, *Crusaders,* 438–39.

10. Complaint, 20 September 1966, in *Anderson v. Schaefer,* Case File, FRC. This was a talented group of lawyers, including the head of the LDF, Jack Greenberg, along with other LDF attorneys; Howard Moore Jr. of Atlanta and C. B. King; and Edward Sparer (who presented most of the argument before the court), Martin Garbus, Stephen Wizner, and others from CSWPL.

11. Under then-existing civil procedure, in order to speed the appellate process for cases challenging the constitutionality of a state law and seeking an injunction restraining the enforcement, operation, or execution of the law, such cases had to be argued before a three-judge panel consisting of one federal circuit and two district judges. Appeals from these panels went directly to the Supreme Court. 28 U.S.C.A. § 2281 (repealed by Public Law No. 94-381, 12 August 1976, 90 Stat. 1119); 28 U.S.C.A. § 1253.

12. Transcript of proceedings, 25 April 1967, in *Anderson v. Schaefer,* Case File, FRC.

13. Transcript of proceedings, 25 April 1967, in *Anderson v. Schaefer,* Case File, FRC.

14. The law regarding three-judge courts was not decisive at the time, and concern over this lack of clarity and the relatively quick road to the Supreme Court caused Congress to repeal the statute in 1976. Some three-judge courts did assess laws as applied to plaintiffs, but other judicial decisions suggested that three-judge courts were not appropriate where a constitutional statute was being administered in a manner that violated one's constitutional rights. Regardless, the "great majority" of suits before a three-judge panel

alleged facial unconstitutionality, so the courts were not used to requests for analysis of statutes as administered. See Leland C. Nielsen, "Three-Judge Courts: A Comprehensive Study," *Federal Rules Decisions* 66 (1975): 495–526.

15. *Anderson v. Burson,* 300 F. Supp. 401 (N.D. Ga., 5 April 1968); transcript of proceedings, 15 November 1967, in *Anderson v. Schaefer,* Case File, FRC.

16. Davis, *Brutal Need,* 60–61.

17. Ibid., 62–66.

18. Ibid., 68. The case is reported at *King v. Smith,* 392 U.S. 309 (17 June 1968); and *Smith v. King,* 277 F. Supp. 31 (M.D. Ala., 8 November 1967). An estimated sixteen thousand children became eligible for AFDC in Georgia. Jack Nelson, "State Rolls Would Add 20,000," *AC,* 5 October 1967, in Atlanta Legal Aid Society clipping file, ALAS. For the disposition to decide cases on statutory, rather than constitutional, grounds, see, e.g., *Harmon v. Brucker,* 355 U.S. 579 (1958).

19. Davis, *Brutal Need,* 68–69.

20. Davis suggests that welfare rights lawyers reached an "impasse" in the South. Ibid., 69. While this is correct from the perspective of CSWPL attorneys, it downplays the impact of subsequent litigation in the region, pursued primarily by local legal services programs.

21. ALAS attorneys, e.g., handled 1,301 "administrative" cases dealing with public assistance programs in 1969; 426 dealt specifically with AFDC payments. Few of the cases resulted in litigation. ALAS, *Annual Report, 1969.*

22. Eva Davis, interview by author, 6 March 1997, Decatur, Ga., handwritten notes.

23. *Thomas v. Burson* attacked Georgia's "substitute father" regulation and earned a federal injunction. ALAS, *Annual Report, 1969;* "U.S. Court Enjoins 'Sub-Father' Law," *AC,* 23 March 1968, 10. The United States Supreme Court later dismissed the case for want of jurisdiction after the policy was changed. *Thomas v. Burson,* 398 U.S. 934 (1970).

24. *Bryson v. Burson,* 308 F. Supp. 1170 (N.D. Ga. 1969) (making permanent a preliminary injunction prohibiting Georgia from refusing welfare benefits to potential recipients who had not resided in the state for at least one year); ALAS, *Annual Report, 1969.* The Supreme Court decision that rendered these residency requirements unconstitutional was *Shapiro v. Thompson,* 394 U.S. 618 (1969).

25. See *NMRLS Notes,* September 1978, NM, LSC, for a discussion of *Jackson v. Winstead.* The case was not reported.

26. Edward Sparer, e.g., lectured to a group of recent law graduates who had won the inaugural Reginald Heber Smith Fellowship in 1967. The fellowship, recipients of which were known as "Reggies," was intended to attract talented young lawyers into legal services programs across the country. One week of their five-week training sessions was devoted to welfare litigation. Davis, *Brutal Need,* 58.

27. Davis discusses this developing hierarchy (ibid.).

28. Georgia Department of Family and Children Services, *Adding Hope to Help II: Annual Report of the Georgia Department of Family and Children Services* (Atlanta: Department of Family and Children Services, 1969), 6–7, DFCS, GDAH.

29. Georgia Department of Family and Children Services, *Time of Change and Reform: Annual Report of the Georgia Department of Family and Children Services* (Atlanta: Department of Family and Children Services, 1971), 5, DFCS, GDAH.

30. Jay Loeb, interview by author, 18 January 1999, Atlanta.

31. *Poor People's Newspaper* (August 1970), PRO, AHC. AWRO's constitution limited formal member-ship to those receiving AFDC or social security or living beneath the poverty line. See *Constitution: Welfare Rights Organization, Local Atlanta Chapter*, art. 3, located in Ethel Mathews's personal papers, copies of which are in the author's possession. David Webster reported that between thirty and fifty people typically attended meetings during the 1970s. Webster, interview by author, 5 March 1997, Atlanta, handwritten notes.

32. Editions of the *Poor People's Newspaper* are located in PRO, AHC. According to a handwritten note by Muriel Lokey, located in the "PRO Stuff" folder in that same collection, the first edition of the newspaper went out to more than seven thousand recipients who had requested that the paper be sent to them. The PRO published the newspaper until 1993. This history of the AWRO is based on Ethel Mathews, interview by author, 27 February 1997, Atlanta, handwritten notes; Austin Ford, interview by author, 6 March 1997, Atlanta, handwritten notes; Muriel Lokey, interview by author, 26 February 1997, Atlanta (by telephone), handwritten notes; David Webster, interview by author, 5 March 1997; and the *Poor People's Newspaper*. For a discussion of the National Welfare Rights Organization and the welfare rights movement, see Frances Fox Piven and Richard A. Cloward, *Poor People's Movements: Why They Succeed, How They Fail* (New York: Random House, 1977), chap. 5, 288–89; Nick Kotz and Mary Lynn Kotz, *A Passion for Equality: George A. Wiley and the Movement* (New York: Norton, 1977). Piven and Cloward, "The Weight of the Poor . . . A Strategy to End Poverty," *Nation*, 2 May 1966, 510–17, was the seminal intellectual piece of the movement. See also Nadasen, "The Welfare Rights Movement, 1960–1975" (Ph.D. diss., Columbia University, 1999).

33. Carrie Morris, interview by author, 21 February 1997, handwritten notes; *Morris v. Richardson*, 346 F. Supp. 494 (N.D. Ga. 1972), 455 F.2d 775 (4th Cir. 1972), and 409 U.S. 464 (1973), reported in *CR* 6 (November 1972): 451; complaint, 8 October 1971, and Consent Order, 5 April 1973, in *Morris v. Richardson* Case File No. 15733 (N.D. Ga.), located at FRC. The critical Supreme Court decision was *Davis v. Richardson*, 342 F. Supp. 588 (D. Conn. 1972), *aff'd, Richardson v. Davis*, 409 U.S. 1069 (1973).

34. Austin Ford, interview by author, 6 March 1997, Atlanta, handwritten notes.

35. *PPN* (August 1970); "Goals of the National Welfare Rights Organization," a flyer in Director's Subject Files, DFCS, GDAH.

36. *PPN* (May 1972), PRO, AHC.

37. These themes were prominent in the civil rights movement of the 1960s. See Richard King, *Civil Rights and the Idea of Freedom* (Athens: University of Georgia Press, 1992). On one occasion, Mathews wrote explicitly of her notions of freedom: "In my opinion nobody knows what freedom really is, but to the black people freedom is everything. The white man says that we have freedom but we don't because if we did have freedom we wouldn't have to get the less paying job because of our color. And what about homes—we can't live where we want to. And if we have freedom we would have a freedom of speaking, clothing. In my opinion that's freedom. I really don't know what freedom is because I'm black and that play[s] a great part in my life." Ethel Mathews, "Freedom," handwritten document, 17 November 1970, located in Ethel Mathews's personal papers, copies of which are in the author's possession. Within three years, during which time the AWRO was engaged in several prominent protests, Mathews had a different conception of herself as a "free" person: "I am black and I am free. I am determined, at all costs and regardless of what happens, to stay free." Qtd. in Jones and Massey, "'Things Have Happened I Never . . . Thought Would Happen': A

Conversation with Mrs. Ethel Mae Mathews," *New South* 28 (Summer 1973): 54. See also Ethel Mathews, interview by author, 27 February 1997, Atlanta, handwritten notes.

38. Jones and Massey, "'Things Have Happened,'" 55. Columbus Ward mentioned the influenced of Black Power discourse on welfare rights activism in Atlanta (interview by author, 25 February 1997, Atlanta, handwritten notes).

39. Quotation is from the director's report of Robert Dokson, then the director of the society, in ALAS, *Annual Report, 1975.*

40. *Dailey v. Cawthon*, No. 14546 (N.D. Ga. 1971), reported in *CR* 5 (June 1971): 116, forced Georgia to provide AFDC administrative hearings within sixty days of request, an HEW requirement. *Davis v. Caldwell*, No. 14973 (N.D. Ga. 1971), reported in *CR* 5 (February 1972): 621, declared Georgia's workmen's compensation program unconstitutional because it failed to provide a hearing prior to the termination of benefits.

41. *Fiquette v. Harden* (N.D. Ga.), noted in ALAS, *Annual Report, 1975,* challenged the state's failure to act on an appeal within the required sixty days.

42. *Martin v. Saucier*, No. 16955 (N.D. Ga. 1973), reported in *CR* 7 (December 1973): 504, held Georgia's application and appeal process for Aid to the Aged, Blind, and Disabled (AABD) to be a denial of due process and held that the state's denial of disability benefits to homemakers still able to work in the home was improper. *Trice v. Weinberger*, No. 74-208 (N.D. Ga. 1974), reported in *CR* 7 (April 1974): 759–60; and 392 F. Supp. 1193 (N.D. Ga. 1975), reported in *CR* 9 (September 1975): 357, required an administrative law judge to reconsider his decision to deny Social Security disability payments in light of factual discrepancies regarding the claimants' ability to work. In *Jones v. Caldwell*, No. B-81520 (Fulton Co. Super. Ct. 1973), reported in *CR* 7 (July 1973): 173, a state court found that the Legal Aid client had been wrongly denied unemployment compensation.

43. One early case failed to convince the federal courts that Georgia's income determination scheme for potential Medicaid recipients was in error. A Legal Aid client hoped to receive Medicaid and would have been eligible if the state ignored the fifty dollars per month of his income he spent on medical care. The district and circuit court rejected the plaintiffs' arguments, finding that under the federal statutory scheme taking such expenses into consideration was optional. *Freeman v. Parham*, No. 15877 (N.D. Ga. 1973), reported in *CR* 5 (June 1971): 98, and *CR* 7 (August 1973): 213–14; dismissal *aff'd*, 475 F.2d 185 (5th Cir. 1973). In *Adams v. Parham*, No. 16041 (N.D. Ga. 1972), reported in *CR* 6 (December 1972): 619, and noted in ALAS *Annual Report, 1972,* the district court enjoined the state from maintaining a policy that limited work expense allowances to AFDC recipients. The effect of this limitation had been to decrease the amount of legal aid clients' benefits, who won retroactive benefits to December 1971. State policy was inconsistent with the Social Security Act. *Barron v. Bellairs*, No. 17237 (N.D. Ga. 1973), reported in *CR* 7 (December 1973): 508, previously reported as *Spellers v. Saucier* (N.D. Ga.), in *CR* 6 (December 1972): 522, and *aff'd* in part, vacated in part, 496 F.2d 1187 (5th Cir. 1974), forced Georgia to drop a method of calculating the income of potential recipients by averaging the individual's income from the previous six months. The ALAS client had received a child support payment but was not expecting further payments. Nevertheless, state officials included that payment in calculating her income, rendering her ineligible for AFDC. Under HEW regulations such a scheme was inappropriate. After ALAS attorneys appealed the decision, hoping to win retroactive benefits as well, the Georgia General Assembly passed the Child Support Recovery Act, rendering the case moot, according to the appellate judges. *Barron v. Bellairs*, 496 F.2d 1187 (5th Cir. 1974).

In *Carr v. Saucier*, No. 16704 (N.D. Ga. 1973), reported in *CR* 7 (June 1973): 117–18, the district judge agreed with Legal Aid attorneys that the state's method of including lump-sum payments in calculating income to discern one's eligibility for Aid to the Aged, Blind, and Disabled violated HEW regulations. The client was a man who received a lump sum Social Security payment because he had been wrongly denied benefits, and the state then included that large payment with his monthly income and found that he was not eligible for further disability benefits. HEW regulations required that states only consider income that was available on a regular basis for immediate use. This case was, however, vacated as moot by the 5th Circuit. *Carr v. Saucier*, 582 F.2d 14 (5th Cir. 1978).

44. *Simmons v. Parham*, No. 15244 (N.D. Ga. 1971), reported in *CR* 5 (October 1971): 334, argued that a temporary reduction of AFDC payments in the June checks was a violation of HEW regulations requiring "adequate and timely" notice of such a reduction.

45. *Adams v. Parham*, No. 16042 (N.D. Ga. 1971), reported in *CR* 5 (April 1972): 773, and noted in ALAS *Annual Report*, 1972. *U.S. v. Dimeo*, No. 19021 (N.D. Ga. 1974), reported in *CR* 7 (April 1974): 760. (The ALAS client has received benefits over sixteen years but not during the eight years before the government action.)

46. *Parks v. Harden* (N.D. Ga. 1975), reported in *CR* 6 (March 1973): 713, *CR* 7 (September 1973): 314, and *CR* 9 (October 1975): 434. *Finch v. Weinberger*, Case File No. 75-592A (N.D. Ga. 1975), reported in *CR* 9 (August 1975): 288–89, and *CR* 9 (November 1975): 511. See discussion of *Finch* in chap. 6.

47. U.S. Constitution, Fifth Amendment (applying to the federal government) and Fourteenth Amendment (applying to the states).

48. *Goldberg v. Kelly*, 397 U.S. 254 (1970); Davis, *Brutal Need*, chaps. 7–8. The five justices in the majority included two appointees of Kennedy and Johnson, Thurgood Marshall and Byron White, along with Brennan, Douglas, and Harlan. The three dissenters were Black, Stewart, and Burger, the last being the first Nixon appointee. The ninth seat on the Court had been vacated by Fortas and was yet to be filled by Blackmun.

49. See, generally, William W. Van Alstyne, "The Demise of the Right-Privilege Distinction in Constitutional Law," *Harvard Law Review* 81 (May 1968): 1439–64.

50. This type of tension existed in the NAACP Legal Defense Fund's litigation strategy as well, with local lawyers often operating outside the Legal Defense Fund's control. See, generally, Kluger, *Simple Justice*.

51. *Dandridge v. Williams*, 397 U.S. 471, quotation at 483–84 (1970); Davis, *Brutal Need*, chap. 9. Justice Potter Stewart wrote the majority opinion. Compared to *Goldberg*, Harlan and White are the only two justices who were in the majority in both cases. The district court, in finding for the plaintiffs, had acknowledged these interests but held that the Maryland statute constituted "overreaching" in conflict with the equal protection clause. The Supreme Court rejected this application of the "overbreadth" concept to Fourteenth Amendment claims, stating that the concept was limited to claims under the First Amendment involving laws that, because of their expansive language, infringed on the free speech and assembly rights granted in that amendment.

52. *Cheley v. Burson*, 324 F. Supp. 678 (N.D. Ga. 1971). This case is distinguished from *Anderson v. Schaefer* in that *Cheley* dealt with households with both parents present.

53. See *Shapiro v. Thompson*, 394 U.S. 618 (1969).

54. *Dandridge*, 397 U.S. at 487.

55. Complaint, 11 September 1972, in *Williams v. Richardson* (original defendant), Case File No. 17128 (N.D. Ga.), FRC; *Williams v. Weinberger,* 360 F. Supp. 1349 (N.D. Ga. 1973). Loeb often worked closely with David Webster; see Loeb, interview by author; and Webster, interview by author, 18 February 1999.

56. *Mathews v. Eldridge,* 424 U.S. 319 (1976). The Supreme Court decision, which was six to two with one justice not participating, did not use the phrase *brutal need.* Numerous subsequent cases would cite *Mathews v. Eldridge* as a precedent for a narrower conception of due process. The progression of the *Williams* and *Eldridge* cases can be followed in the published decisions of both: *Williams v. Weinberger,* 360 F. Supp. 1349 (N.D. Ga., 22 June 1973); *Williams v. Weinberger,* 494 F.2d 1191 (5th Cir., 31 May 1974); *Eldridge v. Weinberger,* 361 F. Supp. 520 (W.D. Va., 9 April 1973); *Eldridge v. Weinberger,* 493 F.2d 1230 (4th Cir., 1 April 1974). The Supreme Court vacated and remanded *Williams* in 1976; *Mathews v. Williams,* 424 U.S. 951 (1976). See also "Stipulation for Dismissal," 30 August 1976, in *Williams v. Richardson* (original defendant), Case File No. 17128 (N.D. Ga.), located at FRC. See also *Williams v. Weinberger* (N.D. Ga.), reported in *CR* 7 (August 1973): 236; *Weinberger v. Eldridge* (U.S.), reported in *CR* 9 (May 1975): 64; and *Mathews v. Eldridge* (U.S.), reported in *CR* 9 (April 1976): 913–14.

57. See Gunther, "Foreword."

58. One author suggested that a new area of law had emerged, which he called "urban law." Frank J. Parker, *The Law and the Poor* (New York: Orbis Books, 1973).

59. Bettye Kehrer, interview by Sharon Rowen, n.d., Atlanta, videotape in Rowen's possession.

60. Brennan, interview by author, 6 November 1998; Padnos, interview by author.

61. Dennis Goldstein, interview by author, 21 January 1999, Atlanta; Brennan, interview by author, 6 November 1998.

62. Brennan, interview by author, 6 November 1998.

63. Kehrer, interview by Sharon Rowen; Padnos, interview by author.

64. Padnos related that Legal Aid lawyers were deeply involved in putting this group together. Padnos, interview by author.

65. An *Atlanta Daily World* article, "Legal Aid to Serve as Advisor for Tenants United for Fairness," 3 December 1968, 6, related a specific list of grievances that included tenant participation in public housing governance, the creation of a prior hearing before sanctions, the establishment of a Tenant's Fair Hearing Panel to hear tenant complaints, and the issuing of authority-wide rules governing evictions, punishments, and fines. According to newspaper reports, TUFF's formation was a response to the AHA's "backsliding" regarding promises made to be more responsive to tenant grievances. Newspapers reported that the demonstrators on 8 November were a biracial group of about thirty people and that it was Mayor Allen who invited them inside for lunch at the Marriott. TUFF, however, was much larger. A 19 November mass meeting at Central Presbyterian Church in downtown Atlanta brought two hundred representatives from all but two of the city's public housing complexes. "Mayor Invites Pickets to Lunch," *AJ,* 9 November 1968, LANS, ALAS; "Tenants Picket Housing Meet," *AC,* 9 November 1968, LANS, ALAS; "Pickets Point to Trouble in Public Housing," *AC,* 11 November 1968, LANS, ALAS; *LAN,* October 1968, ALAS, AHC.

66. During this period TUFF chairwoman Mandy M. Griggs testified before a Georgia General Assembly committee that subsequently voted to open a formal investigation of TUFF's charges against AHA. *LAN,* December 1968, ALAS, AHC; "EOA Asks Legal Aid, Defying Objections," *AC,* 19 December 1968, LANS, ALAS; "Full Housing Investigation is Ordered," *AC,* 19 December 1968, LANS, ALAS.

67. According to Padnos in ALAS, *Annual Report, 1969*, 3.

68. AHA had denied anyone housing if they had not lived in Atlanta for twelve out of the previous thirty-six months. *Jones v. Atlanta Housing Authority*, complaint drafted but not filed, reported in *CR* 3 (July 1969): 79. See ALAS, *Annual Report, 1969*, 7; *LAN*, June 1969, ALAS, AHC. According to "Public Housing Residency Rule Is Hit," *AC*, 16 April 1969, C10, LANS, ALAS, Padnos and Sondra Goldenfarb requested that AHA drop its one-year residency requirement as the *Shapiro v. Thompson* decision was about to be released (on 21 April 1969). *Legal Aid News* editions in June 1969 (there were two editions published that month) reveal that AHA resisted this request until late June, when it finally abolished the rule just before the ALAS case attacking it was filed. Black politicians also pressured AHA from within the Georgia legislature. John Hood promised to introduce a bill that would change the composition of the AHA board and reduce the terms of board members from ten to four years. "Negro Legislators Urge Housing Board Changes," *AC*, 14 January 1969, 10, LANS, ALAS.

69. *LAN*, March 1969, ALAS, AHC; "Abernathy Demands Tenant-Run Housing," *AC*, 5 March 1969, 27, LANS, ALAS; "Negro Legislators Urge Housing Board Changes," *AC*, 14 January 1969, 10, LANS, ALAS.

70. Goldstein, interview by author, 19 January 1999, suggested that AHA leadership was a critical determinant of the quality of life in Atlanta's public housing, and he complimented Persells's work during the early 1970s.

71. ALAS, *Annual Report, 1969*, 7.

72. "Opening the Door," *AC*, 20 March 1969, 4A, LANS, ALAS. On at least one occasion AHA could not respond to legal and political demands because its hands were tied by federal statute. Joe Boone, an Atlanta minister and activist, accused AHA of "living a lie" by preaching progress while allowing Palmer House for the aged to remain all-white. Persells, head of AHA, said the federal government would not allow the AHA to create a new waiting list, but, instead, the authority had to retain the old one from pre-integration days. "AHA Said Lagging in Integration," *AC*, 21 July 1969, LANS, ALAS.

73. ALAS, *Annual Report, 1969*, 7.

74. Perhaps the most influential case was *Javins v. First National Realty Corporation*, 428 F.2d 1071 (D.C. 1970). Friedman suggests that the civil rights movement and "legal services movement" contributed mightily to the dispersion of the warranty of habitability throughout the United States. Friedman, *American Law*, 407.

75. Steve Gottlieb, interview by author, 4 December 1998, Atlanta.

76. ALAS, *Annual Report, 1969*.

77. The society's 1969 annual report discusses these conditions (ibid.), as do court documents in *Kates v. Motz*, Case File No. B-50919 (Fulton Co. Civil Court). See, in particular, "Petition for Declaratory Judgment and Injunctive Relief," 26 November 1969, in *Kates v. Motz*, Case File, which also discusses the landlord's failure to build a shopping center and pool, as promised.

78. Baety to Motz, 3 October 1969, in *Kates v. Motz*, Case File. See also Edward Baety, interview by author, 15 January 1999, Atlanta.

79. See *Kates v. Motz*, Case File; Brennan, interview by author, 11 November 1998, Decatur, Ga.

80. On the role and benefit of tenant protest in altering the housing market, especially the availability of affordable housing for low-income persons, see John Cowley, "The Limitations and Potential of Housing Organizing," in *Critical Perspectives on Housing*, ed. Rachel G. Bratt, Chester Hartman, and Ann

Meyerson (Philadelphia: Temple University Press, 1986), 398–404, points to a variety of concrete and abstract problems: the ability of the landlord to evict the tenants, the spatial relationships of housing, and the "secondary" nature of housing relationships ("second" to the capital-wage relationship, which Cowley believes is the most immediate of human relationships). In the same volume Kathy McAfee, "Socialism and the Housing Movement: Lessons from Boston," 405–27, relates that activists accepted profit incentives as inevitable. McAfee suggests, critically, that profit motives and decent, affordable housing cannot coexist. Despite these limitations of housing organizing, other scholars assert that the mobilization of tenant groups has been and will be essential to increasing the stock of "decent, affordable" housing for the poor. See, in the same volume, Emily Paradise Achtenberg and Peter Marcuse, "The Causes of the Housing Problem," 4–11; and John Atlas and Peter Dreier, "The Tenants' Movement and American Politics," 378–97.

81. Gottlieb, interview by author, 4 December 1998; and Brennan, interview by author, 11 November 1998.

82. The number of families under eviction notices varied during the course of the rent strike as some voluntarily moved away from Bolton Gardens and others decided to join the rent strike, which took place primarily during the winter of 1969–70, or escape the threat of eviction by paying rent. Although there was broad support for the rent strike in the complex—apartment dwellers in 160 of the 168 units signed a petition in favor of the protest—there were initially just 37 tenants who refused to pay their rent to the landlord. They paid it, or were supposed to pay it, to the tenant association. Within a couple of weeks the number of tenants withholding rent rose to 57 but then decreased to 45 when eviction seemed imminent. As more tenants' rent came due, the number grew to 77 by the middle of December. In early 1970 the number of strikers was at 58 when the Fulton County Civil Court ruled against them, and it remained above 50 while the case sat in federal court. See "Apartment Tenants Protest Rent Hike," AV, 2 November 1969; "Eviction Faces Rent Holdouts," AC, 13 November 1969; "45 Evictions Fought Here," AC, 19 November 1969; "Rent Strikers Challenge Law on Eviction," AC, 13 December 1969; "Throw Out Rent Strikers, Local Civil Judge Rules," AJ, 28 January 1970; "Eviction Law Due Rehearing," AC, 30 June 1970, all LANS, ALAS.

83. Honorable Frank A. Hooper to Honorable Griffin Bell and Honorable Newell Edenfield, 4 May 1970, in Atkinson v. Motz, Case File No. C.A. 13344 (N.D. Ga.), FRC. This case file contains numerous documents that detail the procedural twists of the Bolton Gardens cases.

84. John Brent, one of the ALAS attorneys who worked on Sanks, recalled that while in Washington for oral arguments, the state's lead attorney expressed his feeling that the ALAS would win the case. Brent, interview by author, 18 November 1998, Atlanta.

85. Unpublished Decision of Fulton County Civil Court, 2 October 1968, in Georgia v. Sanks, Case File Nos. 24992 and 24993 (Ga. Sup. Ct.), GDAH. The ALAS's Legal Aid News, June 1968 and September 1968, in ALAS, AHC, discuss the early efforts in the case.

86. State v. Sanks, 225 Ga. 88 (1969).

87. Boddie v. Connecticut, 401 U.S. 371 (1971).

88. This behind-the-scenes deliberation is detailed in Bob Woodward and Scott Armstrong, The Brethren: Inside the Supreme Court (New York: Simon and Schuster, 1979), 89–91. The Supreme Court noted probable jurisdiction, Sanks v. Georgia, 395 U.S. 974 (1969), restored the case to the calendar for reargument, 399 U.S. 922 (1970), and, after the law was changed, the Court dismissed the appeal and remanded the case back to the Georgia Supreme Court, 401 U.S. 144 (1971).

89. Dokson, interview by author; Brent, interview by author; Hugh Merrill, "Bill Seeks Aid for Tenant, Eviction Law Favors Landlord," *AJ*, 7 January 1970, LANS, ALAS; *Sanks v. Georgia,* reported in *CR* 2, no. 13 (November 1968): 11; *CR* 2, no. 16 (March 1969): 15; *CR* 4 (April 1971): 609. See also Padnos, interview by author.

90. *Sanks v. Georgia,* 401 U.S. 144 (1971).

91. *Boddie v. Connecticut,* 401 U.S. 371 (1971). The Court made it clear that its holding was limited to the facts of the present case. As applied to *Sanks,* this holding would have required that the Court see the landlord-tenant relationship as closely akin to the marital relationship and that the state imposed exclusive procedures for dissolving the landlord-tenant relationship. Neither of these qualifications was necessarily the case in *Sanks.*

92. "Motion to Dismiss," 24 July 1970, in *Atkinson v. Motz,* Case File No. C.A. 13344 (N.D. Ga., filed 1969), FRC. This document points out that the landlord agreed to abandon the dispossessory proceedings. Many Bolton Gardens tenants had already moved away from the complex, as evidenced by the Atlanta *City Directory* of 1969, 1970, and 1971. The major figures in the three cases, the Wheats, Kateses, and Ms. Atkinson, had all left Bolton Gardens.

93. Complaint, 27 October 1969; "Brief in Support of Defendant's Motion to Dismiss for Failure to State a Claim," 18 November 1969; "Brief of Plaintiff and Response to the Motion to Dismiss of Defendant Q. V. Williamson," 25 November 1969; "Plaintiff's Response to the Motion to Dismiss of the Defendant Atlanta Housing Authority," 9 December 1969; "Order," 23 March 1970; Elizabeth Rindskopf to Judge Sidney O. Smith, 6 April 1971; "Order," 16 December 1971, in *Buchanan v. Wheat Street Three, Inc.,* Case File No. 13183 (N.D. Ga.), FRC. Rindskopf was a local public interest lawyer associated with Emory Community Legal Services; she was the lead attorney in this case but was joined by Michael Padnos and Michael Terry.

94. "Petition for Declaratory Relief," 19 February 1971; "Order," 19 February 1971, granting temporary restraining order; "Motion to Dismiss," 22 March 1971; "Order," 22 March 1971, in *Anthony v. Wheat Street Gardens,* Case File No. B-62717 (Fulton Co. Civil Court, Atlanta); Loeb, interview by author.

95. *Jenkins v. Allen Temple Apartments,* 127 Ga. App. 61 (Ga. App. 1972), discussed in ALAS, *Annual Report, 1972.* The critical question in these cases was the extent of government involvement in these housing projects and whether state action required greater procedural protections for tenants. Each of these complexes received funding under the National Housing Act (see 12 U.S.C. § 1715[d][3] and, more broadly, 42 U.S.C.S. Chapter 8, also known as "Section 8"), which provided rent subsidies for low-income families. They were not owned by any government agency but, rather, by private nonprofit corporations such as Church Homes. Church Homes was affiliated with local African-American churches; Williams Holmes Borders, one of Atlanta's preeminent ministers, sat on the corporation's board. The *Jenkins* case resolved this issue, requiring "good cause" for such landlords to evict tenants.

96. *Blocker v. Blackburn,* No. 26728 (Fulton Co. Super. Ct., Atlanta, 1971), reported in *CR* 4 (January 1971): 443; and *CR* 5 (February 1972): 606.

97. *Atlanta Housing Authority v. Jones,* No. 61041 (Fulton Co. Super. Ct., Atlanta, 1971), reported in *CR* 5 (November 1971): 413.

98. *Gwinnett Nonprofit Housing Corporation v. Pruitt,* No. 17602 (N.D. Ga. 1973), reported in *CR* 7 (July 1973): 162–63.

99. *Freeman v. Lynn,* No. 18901 (N.D. Ga. 1973), reported in *CR* 7 (December 1973): 488. HUD and

the Atlanta Housing Authority were seeking to acquire and clear 279 acres of inner-city property populated primarily by low-income African Americans; they planned to resell the land to private interests with the alleged effect of transforming a black, urban ghetto into an upper-income white residential and commercial community.

100. ALAS, e.g., initiated several cases against the AHA and other local housing authorities in 1975, litigation that would last through rest of the decade. See chap. 6.

101. John Maxey, interview by author, 8 July 1998, Jackson, Miss.; Taylor, interview by author.

102. James W. Silver, *Mississippi: The Closed Society* (New York: Harcourt, Brace and World, 1964).

103. John Dittmer, *Local People: The Struggle for Civil Rights in Mississippi* (Urbana: University of Illinois Press, 1994), 425.

104. Horowitz, interview by author.

105. *NMRLS Notes*, September 1978, discusses this case, known as *Jackson v. Winstead*. See also Trister, interview by author. It did not go to trial.

106. Whether or not one remained in school, one lost benefits upon turning nineteen. *Williams v. Winstead* (N.D. Miss., filed 1970), in *CR* 4 (July 1970): 170.

107. The commission had denied disability benefits to a legal services client. Because the state's highest court understood disability benefits to be a state charity similar to aid to the blind and aged, recipients did not enjoy any "right" to such benefits. Thus, the Public Welfare Commission's own administrative hearing procedures were sufficient to protect against errors on the part of caseworkers, and there was no need for the courts to oversee these actions. *Winstead v. Kirkwood*, in *CR* 2 (January 1969): 19; and *CR* 5 (May 1971): 53–54; *Winstead v. Kirkwood*, 246 So.2d 557 (Miss. S.C., 1971).

108. *Triplett v. Cobb*, in *CR* 4 (July 1970): 157, and *CR* 6 (May 1972): 60; *Triplett v. Cobb*, 331 F. Supp. 652 (N.D. Miss. 1971).

109. *Gill v. Woods*, 226 So.2d 912 (Miss. S.C. 1969); Maxey, interview by author, 8 July 1998.

110. Maxey, interview by author; Pennington, interview by author.

111. *Anthony v. Marshall County Board of Education*, 409 F.2d 1287 (5th Cir. 1969). The Fifth Circuit remanded the case to the district court for the adoption of a more effective desegregation plan. See Francis B. Stevens and John L. Maxey II, "Representing the Unrepresented: A Decennial Report on Public-Interest Litigation in Mississippi," *Mississippi Law Journal* 44 (1973): 348–54.

112. Stevens and Maxey, "Representing the Unrepresented," 348–54; Spriggs, interview by author, 29 June 1998, Tallahassee, Fla.

113. Trister explained this strategy in Trister, interview by author. See also Spriggs, interview by author.

114. *Quarles v. Oxford Municipal Separate School District*, in *CR* 3 (February 1970): 272; *Quarles v. Oxford Municipal Separate School District*, 366 F. Supp. 247 (N.D. Miss., 1972), regarding court action to enforce Judge Keady's 1970 desegregation order; *NMRLS Notes*, September 1978. John Brittain was the lead attorney on this case.

115. *Pickens v. Okolona Municipal Separate School District*, No. EC6956-K (N.D. Miss. 1971), in *CR* 5 (December 1971): 470. Not all civil rights cases involved claims of racial discrimination. In one NMRLS case, e.g., attorneys lost a challenge to the practice of imprisoning indigents for failure to pay fines. *Wade v. Carsley*, 221 So.2d 725 (Miss. S.C. 1969). Some civil rights cases based on racial discrimination involved

complicated problems. John Brittain, e.g., represented three black teachers in Okolona fired due to alleged incompetence, along with ten black teachers challenging the school board's adoption of the National Teachers Examination as a prerequisite for re-employment in the newly desegregated system. When Brittain convinced the court that the school board began using the test because it knew white teachers generally scored higher than black teachers, the court ordered the black teachers to be reinstated and ordered hearings to allow the other three teachers to defend themselves.

116. Maxey, interview by author.

117. *Brown v. Twin County Electric Power Association*, No. GC69-35S (N.D. Miss. 1969), in *CR* 3 (November 1969): 174. At this point the court refused a motion to dismiss, saying it was inclined to ensure that no witness in a federal suit was the subject of such intimidation.

118. *Lipman v. Van Zant*, 329 F. Supp. 391 (N.D. Miss. 1971), in *CR* 6 (October 1972): 348. In *Kline v. Rankin*, 352 F. Supp. 292 (N.D. Miss. 1972), two NMRLS attorneys argued that the state's new ninety-day residency requirement was also unconstitutional; they were unsuccessful. A few years later several legal services and civil rights attorneys challenged Mississippi's policy of not requiring University of Mississippi graduates to take a bar exam nor attorneys admitted to practice in states with a reciprocal agreement with Mississippi. They also attacked the bar examination itself but lost on all fronts. *Shenfield v. Prather*, 387 F. Supp. 676 (N.D. Miss. 1974).

119. "Memorandum: Rural Legal Assistance Program," 16 December 1971, in Stanley Taylor File, SCR.

120. Trister supported the Association of American Law Schools' investigation of Ole Miss, expressing his hope that the law school would remain on probation, and in another article discussed a meeting between white and black students and faculty in the wake of the arrest of sixty African-American students after a quiet protest during a campus concert. See, generally, Mike Trister File, SCR, and specifically, "Hearing Is Due on Law School," *CA*, 17 February 1970; "Ole Miss: Black Militancy, White Support," *Southern Patriot*, March 1970; "Ole Miss Hearings Bring Protests," *CA*, 6 March 1970; and "Campus Unit Joins Forces to Seek Ole Miss Accord," *CA*, 6 March 1970, in Mike Trister File, SCR.

121. Toby Wood to State Sovereignty Commission, 20 March 1970, in Alix Sanders File, SCR; Fulton Tutor, "Weekly Report, 3/23–3/28/70," 28 March 1970, in John Brittain File, SCR; "Marchers Plan to Stay in Jail," *CA*, 10 July 1970, in Thomas Mayfield File, SCR.

122. "Memorandum: North Mississippi Legal Services," 12 February 1971, in Stanley Taylor File, SCR; "ACLU of Mississippi State Board," [20 November 1971], in John Brittain file, SCR.

123. Leonard McClellan, interview by author, 8 July 1998, Jackson, Miss.

124. See Charles M. Payne, *I've Got the Light of Freedom: The Organizing Tradition and the Mississippi Freedom Struggle* (Berkeley: University of California Press, 1995); and Dittmer, *Local People*, for excellent studies of the Mississippi freedom struggles. Payne, in particular, documents the decline of what he calls the "organizing tradition" in Mississippi by the late 1960s.

125. This assessment is based primarily on interviews with poverty lawyers (especially Mike Trister, Stanley Taylor, John Maxey, Alix Sanders, and Kent Spriggs) and my reflections on legal services cases, which often required community mobilization to be effective (I am thinking, in particular, of school desegregation cases).

126. On school desegregation cases, see Stephen C. Halpern, *On the Limits of the Law: The Ironic Legacy*

of Title VI of the 1964 Civil Rights Act (Baltimore: Johns Hopkins University Press, 1995), 81–91. For a broader analysis of the rise of conservatism see Dan T. Carter, *The Politics of Rage: George Wallace, The Origins of Conservatism, and the Transformation of American Politics* (New York: Simon and Schuster, 1995).

127. The *Congressional Quarterly Almanac* cited the Vietnam War, adverse political reaction to the urban riots, and the lack of administration pressure as reasons for Congress's low level of funding for OEO for fiscal year 1967. Congress did, however, earmark funds for the Legal Services Program in the amount of twenty-two million dollars. "Antipoverty Funds Reduced and Earmarked," *CQA* 22 (1966): 250–65.

128. Trister, interview by author.

129. Gottlieb, interview by author, 17 December 1998.

3. THE LEAN YEARS, 1970–1975

1. See Patterson, *Grand Expectations,* chap. 25.

2. Charles W. Dunn and J. David Woodard, *The Conservative Tradition in America* (Lanham, Md.: Rowman and Littlefield, 1996).

3. Historians have traced racial politics back at least to Bacon's Rebellion in late-seventeenth-century Virginia. In order to quell rebellious lower-class whites, the colony's white elite began to stress slavery as a racial condition, placing all whites in a caste above their black neighbors. Lower-class whites became, the argument goes, psychologically connected to the white elite, rather than to black slaves, with whom they shared economic interests. See Edmund S. Morgan, *American Slavery, American Freedom: The Ordeal of Colonial Virginia* (New York: Norton, 1975); as well as C. Vann Woodward, *The Strange Career of Jim Crow,* 3rd rev. ed. (New York: Oxford University Press, 1974).

4. See Dan T. Carter, *From George Wallace to Newt Gingrich: Race in the Conservative Counterrevolution, 1963–1994* (Baton Rouge: Louisiana State University Press, 1996), chap. 2; and Carter, *Politics of Rage.*

5. "Antipoverty Funds Reduced and Earmarked," *CQA* 22 (1966): 250–65; Dallek, *Flawed Giant,* chap. 6, which is entitled "Retreat from the Great Society."

6. Moynihan's *Maximum Feasible Misunderstanding* is a particularly forceful criticism of the "war on poverty." See also Matusow, *The Unraveling of America;* Jill Quadagno, *The Color of Welfare: How Racism Undermined the War on Poverty* (New York: Oxford University Press, 1994); and Michael L. Gillette, *Launching the War on Poverty: An Oral History* (New York: Twayne Publishers, 1996), chap. 17.

7. Qtd. in Johnson, *Justice and Reform,* 162.

8. Johnson, *Justice and Reform,* 188; Houseman and Dooley, "Legal Services History," chap. 1, 11.

9. See ALAS, *Annual Report, 1967,* ALAS, AHC; *Legal Aid News,* April 1968, ALAS, AHC; R. William Ide III, "Atlanta Legal Aid Society—Saturday Lawyers Program," draft of article, n.d., GLSP; Padnos, interview by author.

10. The number of persons per lawyer ranged from 2,638 in the rural Patuala circuit to a low of 298 in the Atlanta judicial circuit. The number of poor families (with incomes of three thousand dollars or less) per lawyer ranged from 382 in the Patuala circuit to 19 in Atlanta. R. William Ide III and Lawrence L. Thompson, "The Organized Bar—Yellow Brick Road to Legal Services for the Poor," *Vanderbilt Law Review* 27 (1974): 667–70. Ide and Thompson took these statistics from a "Report of the Younger Lawyers Section of the State Bar of Georgia Committee on Legal Aid Programs," written and presented in 1968. In 1969 the Committee on Legal Aid Programs consisted of the four attorneys mentioned previously as well as Michael

Padnos. See "Younger Lawyers Section of the State Bar of Georgia Legal Aid Programs Committee Report, 1968–69," n.d., GLSP.

11. Ide and Thompson, "Organized Bar," 668 n. 5.

12. Quotation in ibid., 674, from the *AC,* 3 January 1972, 10A. This discussion is an oversimplification of the process of winning funding for the GLSP. Once OEO officials rebuffed the Younger Lawyers seeking to establish the program, they went to HEW, where they thought they had funding under that agency's mandatory legal services program. That plan would have provided for one-to-one matching federal-to-state funds. HEW dropped the mandatory program, however, in May 1970, after GILS had been incorporated that March. Funding seemed fleeting, until proponents of GILS discovered that HEW had created an optional program with three-to-one federal-to-state funds. They convinced Maddox to support this plan, and the program began with a budget of $216,000 rather than $108,000. There were other benefits to receiving funding through the optional program. Whereas the mandatory program had limited the activities of attorneys to helping welfare recipients with public benefits issues, the optional program carried only the requirement that the clients be welfare recipients. Attorneys could provide an array of services to these clients. As the reader will see, the bureaucratic confusion did not end there. Ibid., 672–75; GLSP, *The First Decade: A Special Report* (Atlanta: GLSP, 1981), 4–12; Kehrer, interview by Rowen; Ide, interview by author; Elliott, interview by author.

13. Ide, interview by author; Kehrer, interview by Rowen.

14. Bill Ide, interview by Sharon Rowen, n.d., videotape in Rowen's possession, Atlanta.

15. Now the University of Missouri at Kansas City.

16. The federal government also matched local funds, three-to-one. Ide and Thompson, "Organized Bar," 675–76.

17. The first OEO appropriation was $250,000 for a six-month period, but the annual appropriation was $500,000. Ide interview, 5 March 1999; Ide and Thompson, "Organized Bar," 675–77; GLSP, *First Decade,* 16; Hulett "Bucky" Askew, interview by author, 4 March 1999, Atlanta.

18. Hereafter I will refer to GILS-GLSP simply as GLSP, for the sake of brevity. GILS funding—i.e., state support for the program and matching HEW funds—did not end until 1975.

19. Kehrer tried to obtain funding for a statewide public defender program, but this effort turned out to be her greatest defeat; Georgia politicians were not prepared to stake their political lives on such a controversial institution. She then accepted a position with the National Legal Aid and Defender Association, which put her in a national leadership role, and later went into private practice, working with labor unions and workers. Once again, in the late 1970s and early 1980s her creative instincts emerged in an effort to establish a prepaid legal services plan that would have served middle- and working-class clients. As many in the legal profession realized, once legal services programs came into being, those with the least access to legal counsel were those whose incomes made them ineligible for free services but who could not afford to pay for services either. Such plans were similar to health insurance: clients would pay a periodic fee and then contact their legal services provider when necessary. This effort was not a success, primarily because the state bar opposed the plan. Kehrer, interview by Rowen. See GLSP, *Annual Report, 1972,* for a record of the expansion process. By the end of 1974 there were nine GLSP offices including the central office in Atlanta. This number remained stable until the coming of LSC funding.

20. Maxey, interview by author; A. Spencer Gilbert (of CLS) to Bucky Askew, 5 July 1974, MSBA.

21. "Legal Services Gets New Title," *CL*, 24 January 1974, 8B, MSBA. See also Stevens and Maxey, "Representing the Unrepresented," 346–47. The funding level was about $200,000 per year.

22. Barry Powell, interview by author, 6 July 1998, Jackson, Miss.

23. Francis and Ann Stevens, interview by author, 2 June 1998, Bethesda, Md. Stevens initially joined the faculty of Antioch Law School, founded by Jean and Edgar Cahn, then from 1972–74 was director of North Mississippi Rural Legal Services. That his career turned on his representation of MAP was ironic, considering the rather conservative origins of that program. MAP competed with the Child Development Group of Mississippi (CDGM) for OEO money during the 1960s, and, although several NAACP leaders were involved in MAP, many black Mississippians criticized OEO's preferencing that organization over CDGM. Still, as John Dittmer points out, those involved in MAP were genuinely interested in alleviating poverty, and, as Stevens's account reveals, even a relatively conservative antipoverty program was controversial in Mississippi's political environment. CLS's first staff attorney and first director, John Maxey, noted that the CLS board members "were pretty conservative from my point of view, but they were pretty progressive from the bar's point of view." See Dittmer, *Local People*, 377–82; Maxey, interview by author.

24. See Maxey, interview by author; Powell, interview by author; Stevens, interview by author.

25. The previous director of the Legal Aid Society remained head of the criminal and family law practice, the latter focusing not on divorces but on child custody and other disputes before the local family court. All the legal aid offices reported to the same board composed primarily of members of the Birmingham Bar but which also included representatives from JCCEO, Catholic Social Services, and other agencies. Marvin H. Campbell, interview by author, 1 August 2000, Montgomery, Ala. (by telephone).

26. Summary Report by the Alabama State Bar Committee on Group and Prepaid Legal Services and Legal Services to the Poor, "Group and Prepaid Legal Services and Legal Services to the Poor," *AL* 36 (1975): 380–81. To clarify the status of the Southern Poverty Law Center: SPLC was founded in 1971 as a private civil rights law firm by Morris Dees and Joseph Levin. It was based in Montgomery and did some poverty law work but focused on civil rights in the 1970s and anti-white supremacist activity in the 1980s and 1990s.

27. The authors noted that more than 25 percent of the state's residents were poor, and, of persons over age sixty-five, over 45 percent lived below the poverty level. Ibid., 378–79.

28. Noticeably absent from this equation was any form of social movement or protest organization. Jack Katz, in *Poor People's Lawyers*, seems to agree that legal services programs were, at least in terms of institutional development, largely independent of social movements. To be sure, the civil rights movement encouraged the Johnson administration to initiate the war on poverty, but there was no grassroots movement to create the federal Legal Services Program nor any of the legal services programs in the Deep South.

29. As *NMRLS Notes*, September 1978, pointed out, African-American attorneys made up 1 percent of the legal profession of the state but 43 percent of its population.

30. Alix Sanders, interview by author, 10 July 1998, Greenwood, Miss.; Solomon Osborne, interview by author, 10 July 1998, Greenwood, Miss.

31. Unfortunately, the records of NMRLS are insufficient to document the racial and gender proportions of staff attorneys and those in leadership roles. The discussion here is based on oral interviews with Trister, Sanders, Stevens, Joseph, Pennington, McClellan, Askew, Maxey, and others.

32. Leonard McClellan, interview by author, 8 July 1998, Jackson, Miss.; Sanders, interview by author.

33. Alix Sanders, interview by author.

34. Jim Gray, "Firm for Poor: Legal Aid Size, Punch Shrinking," *AC*, 25 December 1974, 4B.

35. California Rural Legal Assistance, Statement before the Senate Committee on Human Resources, Subcommittee on Employment, Poverty and Migratory Labor, on the Legal Services Corporation Reauthorization Bill (1977), printed in Hearings before the Senate Committee on Human Resources, Subcommittee on Employment, Poverty and Migratory Labor, 95th Cong., 1st sess., 25–26 April 1977, 261.

36. ALAS lawyers handled 8,269 cases in 1975, but that caseload was down drastically from previous years: 13,696 in 1971; a peak of 14,513 in 1972; 12,119 in 1973; and 11,814 in 1974. Jim Gray, "Firm for Poor: Legal Aid Size, Punch Shrinking," *AC*, 25 December 1974, 4B, based primarily on an interview with the new director, Robert Dokson; Dokson, interview by author; "Atlanta Legal Aid Society History," 28–30; ALAS *Annual Report, 1972*; ALAS, *Annual Report, 1975*, particularly Dokson's director's report; Craig R. Hume, "Legal Aid Cuts Services to Ease Financial Crunch," *AC*, 31 July 1975, 2C; Chet Fuller, "Legal Aid May Get Help Soon," *AJC*, 3 August 1975, 4A; "Bar Association Volunteers Easing Legal-Aid Case Load," *AC*, 12 November 1975, 8A; Lee May, "Changes, Changes," *AC*, 1 September 1976, 5A.

37. ALAS's Dennis Goldstein became convinced that an opposing landlord was to blame for the blaze. Goldstein was representing tenants of Primrose Gardens in a rent strike, and the landlord, to use Goldstein's word, was "crazy." Faced with losing the complex, the landlord refused to relent to tenant demands, and Primrose Gardens closed. About this time the building in which Goldstein worked caught fire, his office burned, and the Primrose files were gone. A witness claimed to have seen the landlord there just before the fire. Goldstein, interview by author, 21 January 1999; Warren Clayton, "Legal Aid Office Hit by Blaze," *AC*, 31 December 1976, 2A; Editorial, "Help Legal Aid," *AC*, 11 January 1977," 4A; ALAS, *Annual Report, 1976*.

38. Williams is quoted in Stevens and Maxey, "Representing the Unrepresented," 346–47, which cited *Mississippi Lawyer* (May 1971). Maxey was, at the time this article was published, director of CLS. See also Stevens, interview by author.

39. "Funding of Legal Aid Project Expected to Stir Opposition," *CA*, 17 January 1971, in Mike Trister File, SCR; Lyman, "Overview Report: Community Legal Services and Mississippi Bar Legal Services Programs, Jackson, Mississippi," 7 May 1974, MSBA. Lenzner and his assistant director, Frank Jones, lost their jobs as a result of this and other similar controversies. See Johnson, *Justice and Reform*, 333 n. 41; and Houseman and Dooley, "Legal Services History," chap. 1, 10–11, for specific mention of Lenzner in the context of these controversies. Lenzner, incidentally, was not unknown in Mississippi. He had traveled to the state as a federal civil rights lawyer to investigate the deaths of three civil rights workers, James Chaney, Michael Schwerner, and Andrew Goodman, in Neshoba County during the Freedom Summer of 1964. Later, not long after he became head of the OEO Office of Legal Services, he returned to Mississippi bearing a fifty thousand dollar emergency grant to aid victims of Hurricane Camille. Lenzner had pushed the grant through in a matter of hours, a minor miracle in the federal bureaucracy. Jack Rosenthal, "Advocate for the Poor," *NYT*, 29 August 1969, LANS, ALAS.

40. See *Williams v. Phillips*, 360 F. Supp. 1363 (D.D.C. 1973); and *American Federation of Government Employees, Local 2677 v. Phillips*, 358 F. Supp. 60 (D.D.C. 1973), discussed later.

41. Maxey, interview by author; Lyman, "Overview Report."

42. Lyman, "Overview Report." One of the people hired to investigate the conflict between these two programs was Bettye Kehrer, recently departed from the GLSP.

43. Martha Gerald (MBLS president) to Bucky Askew, 5 July 1974, in Mississippi State Bar Association Records, MDAH; MBLS, "Response to the Overview Report," [5 July 1974], MSBA. It probably does not need to be said that, in fact, poverty was a "respector of color" in the Deep South, as discussed earlier. For its part CLS was not entirely pleased with the government report, resisting the investigators' suggestion that the CLS withdraw from one section of Hinds County to allow MBLS to focus there. A. Spencer Gilbert (of CLS) to Bucky Askew, 5 July 1974, MSBA.

44. See chap. 4.

45. Ide and Thompson, "Organized Bar," 676–80, covers the period up to 1974, with no reference to the increasing opposition among state politicians and the bar. (The article was published in 1974.) Ironically, Ide and Thompson were extolling the "yellow brick road of bar support," even as that support began to decline. See GLSP, *First Decade*, 20–28, for coverage of the growing anti-GILS sentiment; as well as Kehrer, interview by Rowen; John Cromartie, interview by author, 16 March 1999, Cumming, Ga.

46. ALAS, *Annual Report, 1977*, 9.

47. Campbell, interview by author.

48. Ibid.; *Land v. Cockrell*, No. 75-P-0234-S (N.D. Ala. 1976), reported in *CR* 9 (March 1976): 777; *Tinker v. Ussery*, No. 203-060 (Ala. Cir. Ct. 1977), reported in *CR* 10 (March 1977): 1077–78; *Thomas v. Clements*, No. CA75-M-0525 (N.D. Ala. 1975), reported in *CR* 9 (February 1976): 721.

49. ALAS, *Annual Report, 1972*.

50. Marian Burge, interview by author, 21 January 1999, Atlanta.

51. Brennan, interview by author, 11 November 1998. During the 1980s and 1990s, Brennan developed a more coherent political philosophy that grew out of his Legal Aid experiences. As he said in the interview cited here: "I see that so much of what we've been doing in legal services has been right. It's been an effort on behalf of equality and fairness in the face of this overwhelming capitalism that has just been so destructive to so many people's lives. And that keeps me going. . . ."

52. Marc Feldman, "Political Lessons: Legal Services for the Poor," *Georgetown Law Journal* 83 (April 1995): 1529–1632.

53. Burge, interview by author. See Melissa Faye Greene, *Praying for Sheetrock: A Work of Nonfiction* (New York: Fawcett Columbine, 1991), esp. chap. 9, for an excellent portrayal of the mentality of poverty lawyers.

54. Dokson, interview by author; Brennan, interview by author, 6 November 1998; Sanders, interview by author; Baird, interview by author, 27 March 1999. There has long been a debate within the legal services community about the relative value of law reform and basic client counsel. See Marie A. Failinger and Larry May, "Litigating against Poverty: Legal Services and Group Representation," *Ohio State Law Review* 17 (1984): 1–56.

55. One of these areas was consumer law, not covered here; see discussion in chap. 6. See Maxey, interview by author; Powell, interview by author.

56. Stevens and Maxey, "Representing the Unrepresented," 383–84, reports *Hayes v. Mississippi State Department of Public Welfare* (S.D. Miss. 1973); and *Benton v. Mississippi State Department of Public Welfare*

(S.D. Miss. 1972). Stevens and Maxey also report a case known as *Thomas v. Mathews* (S.D. Miss. 1972), which extended AFDC benefits to all children aged sixteen or seventeen, regardless of their attendance at school.

57. *Jones v. Mississippi*, No. H925 (S.D. Miss. 1971), reported in *CR* 5 (September 1971): 247.

58. The CLS case was *Harris v. Mississippi State Department of Public Welfare*, 363 F. Supp. 1293 (N.D. Miss., 1973). The other three cases were *Parks v. Harden*, 354 F. Supp. 620 (N.D. Ga., 1973); *Wilson v. Weaver*, 358 F. Supp. 1147 (N.D. Ill. 1973); and *Green v. Stanton*, 364 F. Supp. 123 (N.D. Ind. 1973). Unfortunately for CLS and ALAS, the Fifth Circuit vacated the Georgia decision the following year at *Parks v. Harden*, 504 F.2d 861 (5th Cir., 1974), in light of *Burns v. Alcala*, 420 U.S. 575 (1974).

59. *West v. Cole*, 390 F. Supp. 91 (N.D. Miss. 1975).

60. Powell, interview by author. Another difference, increasingly pronounced, was the extent to which African-American attorneys and local civil rights figures pervaded NMRLS by the mid-1970s.

61. *Ramberg v. Porter*, No. 72 J-43(N) (S.D. Miss. 1973), reported in *CR* 6 (June 1972): 101. The named plaintiff, Charles Ramberg, was a CLS lawyer. He also served as counsel on the case, along with director John Maxey, Barry Powell, and Geraldine Carnes.

62. When the Twenty-sixth Amendment to the Constitution was ratified on 30 June 1971, enabling all eighteen-year-olds to vote, Mississippi's voter registration deadline for the November elections was two days away. Many eighteen- to twenty-year-olds were unable to register during that time frame, and CLS attorneys became involved in this case in an attempt to ensure that they were able to vote in the elections. Regarding Mississippi's four-month registration requirement, they argued that the time period was un-constitutionally lengthy. Initially, a federal judge declined to accept the CLS argument, but the Supreme Court reversed and remanded the case, and the judge altered his opinion, suggesting thirty days as a more appropriate deadline for registration. *Ferguson v. Williams*, 330 F. Supp. 1012 (N.D. Miss. 1971); *Ferguson v. Williams*, 405 U.S. 1036 (1972); and *Ferguson v. Williams*, 343 F. Supp. 654 (N.D. Miss. 1972). See Stevens and Maxey, "Representing the Unrepresented," 362; Maxey, interview by author.

63. *Morrow v. Mississippi Publishers Corporation*, 5 Fair Empl. Prac. Cas. (BNA) 287 (S.D. Miss. 1972). Mississippi Publishers classified their employment advertisements by gender as such: "Help Wanted—Female," "Help Wanted—Male," "Wanted—Male, Female." Morrow's position was that, because of the importance of the corporation's publications in the Jackson job market, it should be subject to the Civil Rights Act of 1964's prohibition against employment discrimination on the basis of sex. This published decision was not a final stipulation by the federal judge, but he strongly urged Mississippi Publishers to revise its policy before trial on the merits. The case is listed in Barry Powell's "CMLS Decrees, 1971–1983," in author's possession.

64. *Obadele v. McAdory*, No. 72J-103N (S.D. Miss. 1973), reported in *CR* 7 (September 1973): 306, was a class action brought on behalf of all those awaiting trial who, although still presumed innocent by law, were allegedly deprived of their freedom and subjected to "inhuman" conditions at the Hinds County jail. The court issued a declaratory judgment setting forth specific guidelines to correct overcrowding, unsanitary conditions, nonhygienic toilet and cleansing facilities, a lack of light and air, inadequate and often complete lack of health and dental care, a lack of recreation, restrictive visitation policies, the denial of communica-tion and association privileges, punitive and unlawful detention practices, and numerous other conditions present in the Hinds County jail. Defendants were also ordered to end racial segregation and discrimina-

tion. Another case related to the criminal justice system was one in which CLS attorneys sought to keep the trial of a client in youth court, rather than having him tried as an adult. *In re Randy Joe Watkins*, 324 So.2d 232 (Miss. Sup. Ct. 1975). See Barry Powell, "CMLS Decrees, 1971–1983," in author's possession. See also Barry Powell, "Director's Report—1975, CLS," n.d., MSBA.

65. *Brown v. Vance*, 637 F.2d 272 (5th Cir. 1981); *Brown v. Vance*, 1981 U.S. App. LEXIS 19148 (1981) denied rehearing. See *Brown v. Vance*, No. 72-591(N) (S.D. Miss., filed 1972), reported in *CR* 6 (November 1972): 432–33; in *CR* 7 (July 1973): 150; and in *CR* 15 (June 1981): 178. The case was combined with *Boone v. Dennis*, No. 72J-118(N) (S.D. Miss., filed 1972). There had been earlier litigation against Mississippi's justice of the peace system, but attorneys lost that challenge, *Melikian v. Avent*, 300 F. Supp. 516 (N.D. Miss. 1969). CLS filed *Brown v. Vance* in 1972, the same year the Supreme Court's decision in *Ward v. Village of Monroeville*, 409 U.S. 57 (1972), promised a different result than *Melikian*.

66. Litigation Docket through 20 December 1974, CLS Mississippi Mental Health Project, [20 December 1974], MSBA. See also Lyman, "Overview Report: Community Legal Services and Mississippi Bar Legal Services Programs, Jackson, Mississippi," 7 May 1974, MSBA, which explains that one of CLS's "Reggies" spent 80 percent of his time at Whitfield State Hospital. See Barry Powell, "Director's Report—1975, CLS," n.d., MSBA, for a brief discussion of many of these cases. Most were settled, there were a few outright victories, and a couple of outright defeats, including an effort to protect Whitfield inmates out on convalescent leave from the summary termination of that leave. *Hooks v. Jaquith*, 318 So.2d 860 (Miss. Sup. Ct. 1975), reported in *CR* 9 (September 1975): 352; and *CR* 9 (January 1976): 657.

67. *Brown v. Jaquith*, 318 So.2d 856 (Miss. Sup. Ct. 1975), reported in *CR* 9 (November 1975): 499. A diagnosis of paranoid schizophrenia meant that doctors at Whitfield had little hope for Brown ever gaining the ability to stand trial, much less leave the institution. There were many cases that followed *Brown*, more than a dozen out of the CLS Mental Health Project. See Litigation Docket through 20 December 1974, CLS Mississippi Mental Health Project, [20 December 1974], in MSBA.

68. They accepted 3,815 cases in 1975. See Powell, "Director's Report—1975, CLS," n.d.

69. Osborne, interview by author.

70. Johnnie Walls, interview by author, 13 July 1998, Greenville, Miss.

71. *NMRLS Notes*, September 1978.

72. Fulton Tudor, "Weekly Report, 3/23–3/28/70," 28 March 1970, in John Brittain File, SCR.

73. SCLC's Rev. R. B. Cottonreader was among those arrested. "Marchers Plan to Stay in Jail," *CA*, 10 July 1970, Thomas Mayfield File, SCR; "Negro Convicted in First Boycott Trial," n.p., 9 November 1970, part of a report from Fulton Tudor, Thomas Mayfield File, SCR; Tom Royals, interview by author, 6 July 1998, Jackson, Miss.

74. Memorandum, W. Webb Burke to Honorable Herman Glazier, 16 February 1971, John Brittain File, SCR.

75. *Ealy v. Littlejohn*, 569 F.2d 219 (5th Cir. 1978), contains a lengthy narrative of the events in Byhalia as well as the final resolution of the case. By that time, of course, the protests had ended. Nevertheless, the decision relates the role of the federal courts in preventing local authorities from undermining the United League's protests through investigations such as the grand jury's.

76. Wayne Johnson to Rhett Dawsom (acting chief, Operations Division, Office of Legal Services), 12 May 1975, NMI, LSC.

77. See *NMRLS Notes,* September 1978, esp. discussion of *Robinson v. Ensley,* which was not reported. See also "United League: Can It Destroy Stable NAACP?" *Capital Reporter,* 14 September 1978, 2, United League Subject File, MDAH; "Blacks in Tupelo Protest City Action," *CL,* 12 March 1978, Tupelo Boycott—1978 Subject File, MDAH.

78. *NMRLS Notes,* September 1978. The case was *Henretta Young v. Morris Hanna et al.*

79. See Stevens and Maxey, "Representing the Unrepresented," 354–55, for a discussion of litigation protecting freedom of speech and assembly.

80. *Andrews v. Drew Municipal Separate School District* (N.D. Miss. 1973), reported in *CR* 7 (September 1973): 286–87; and *Peacock v. Drew Municipal Separate School District,* 433 F. Supp. 1072 (N.D. Miss. 1977). The plaintiffs won damages against the school board.

81. *Pickens v. Okolona Municipal Separate School District,* 380 F. Supp. 1036 (N.D. Miss. 1974), grew out of litigation begun by NMRLS lawyers in the late 1960s, wherein they challenged Okolona's policy of using the National Teachers Examination to determine whom to hire and retain as teachers. While that case was successful, they did not convince the federal judge that the present plaintiff, Lagrone Pack, was dismissed as a result of racial discrimination. In another case the wife of former NMRLS employee and Sunflower County civil rights activist Carver Randle retained employment in the Indianola public schools when a court found that the school board had denied her a position as a result of her husband's activities. *Randle v. Indianola Municipal Separate School District,* 373 F. Supp. 766 (N.D. Miss. 1974). Carver Randle, a schoolteacher himself, was involved in the Indianola Development Association and in founding the local NAACP chapter, which boycotted the town's schools in the late 1960s, before working with NMRLS during the early 1970s.

82. *Campbell v. Mincy,* 413 F. Supp. 16 (N.D. Miss. 1975).

83. Reported cases include *Crosby v. State of Mississippi,* 270 So.2d 346 (Miss. Sup. Ct. 1972); *Holloway v. State of Mississippi,* 261 So.2d 799 (Miss. Sup. Ct. 1972); *Evans v. State of Mississippi,* 273 So.2d 495 (Miss. Sup. Ct. 1973); *Tate v. State of Mississippi,* 290 So.2d 263 (Miss. Sup. Ct. 1974); *Collier v. State of Mississippi,* 299 So.2d 203 (Miss. Sup. Ct. 1974); *Bradford v. Byars,* 302 So.2d 503 (Miss. Sup. Ct. 1974); *Daniels v. State of Mississippi,* 315 So.2d 443 (Miss. Sup. Ct. 1975); *Rustin v. State of Mississippi,* 338 So.2d 1006 (Miss. Sup. Ct. 1976). Of these reported cases NMRLS attorneys won two and lost six. They fared better in other criminal cases that did not reach the appellate level. Later in the decade NMRLS attorneys handled (and lost) at least one capital murder case, *Irving v. State of Mississippi,* 361 So.2d 1360 (Miss. Sup. Ct. 1978).

84. *Bogard v. Cook,* 60 F.R.D. 508 (N.D. Miss. 1973), 405 F. Supp. 1202 (N.D. Miss. 1975), and affirmed at 586 F.2d 399 (5th Cir. 1978).

85. Martha Bergmark, interview by author, 22 May 1998, Washington, D.C. See also *Gates v. Collier,* 349 F. Supp. 881 (N.D. Miss. 1972) and 501 F.2d 1291 (5th Cir. 1974); David M. Oshinsky, *"Worse than Slavery": Parchman Farm and the Ordeal of Jim Crow Justice* (New York: Free Press, 1996), chap. 10.

86. E.g., Stanley Taylor's consumer litigation, specifically his use of the Truth in Lending Act. North Mississippi attorneys also litigated child custody disputes. Two such cases reached opposite results for legal services clients. In one a young mother won custody of her child, despite evidence of neglect and inexperience; in another the NMRLS client had abandoned her child, and the court declared her morally unfit for

parenthood, awarding custody to the child's father. *Cook v. Conn.*, 267 So.2d 296 (Miss. Sup. Ct. 1972); *Bowen v. Neal*, 277 So.2d 433 (Miss. Sup. Ct. 1973).

87. *Robinson v. McAlister*, 310 F. Supp. 370 (N.D. Miss. 1970), in *CR* 4 (February 1971): 501–2.

88. *Saddler v. Winstead*, 332 F. Supp. 130 (N.D. Miss. 1971), in *CR* 5 (December 1971): 486; Stevens and Maxey, "Representing the Unrepresented," 380–84. NMRLS attorneys teamed with CLS in the *Harris* and *West* cases; see chap. 2. NMRLS was also still working to resolve *Triplett v. Cobb*, begun under the Trister regime. *Triplett v. Cobb*, 331 F. Supp. 652 (N.D. Miss. 1971).

89. Bips, interview by author; Shelton, interview by author. See chap. 1 for discussion of more confrontational Legal Aid cases of the 1920s and 1930s.

90. ALAS, *Annual Report, 1969*, 17–18; *Legal Aid News*, April 1968. The Atlanta Chamber of Commerce sponsored this campaign.

91. See *Legal Aid News*, April and June 1968, ALAS, AHC; Achsah Nesmith, "Legal Aid Plan Aims at Consumer Guards," *AC*, 20 July 1968, 12; "Urban Law," *Time*, 7 March 1969, 47.

92. Richard Harris, "Legal Aid Society News," *Atlanta Voice*, 2 February 1969, 6; Harris, "Legal Aid Society News," *Atlanta Voice*, 30 March 1969, 5; Harris, "Legal Aid Society News," *Atlanta Voice*, 6 April 1969, 8; Harris, "Legal Aid Society News," *Atlanta Voice*, 20 April 1969, 5; Harris, "Legal Aid Society News," *Atlanta Voice*, 13 April 1969, 5.

93. Jackson, "Legal Aid News Column," *Atlanta Voice*, 15 May 1971, 5.

94. Nesmith, "Legal Aid Plan Aims at Consumer Guards," *AC*, 20 July 1968, 12; "Urban Law," *Time*, 7 March 1969, 47.

95. "Loan 'Flipping' Hit by Legal Society," *AJ*, 22 June 1970, LANS, ALAS. Indignation about this practice spread beyond the ALAS and legal community. A cartoon in the *Atlanta Journal*, 26 June 1970, in LANS, ALAS, demonstrates a broader recognition of the problem. The drawing shows two vicious sharks labeled "Georgia's Loan Sharks" attacking a man suspended upside down in the air above the water. On one shark, it is written, "'FLIPPING' READJUSTMENT OF EXISTING FINANCE CHARGES" and, on the other, "AND ADDED ON TO CURRENT OUTSTANDING LOAN." Above the scene a bird is saying, "Poor little sucker!" and the caption reads, "IT AIN'T THE FRIENDLY 'FLIPPER' ON TV, FOLKS!" See also Bob Hurt, "State Loan Law Is Called among Worst in Nation," *AC*, 24 June 1970, LANS, ALAS; Hurt, "Borrow $229, Pay $495," *AC*, 28 June 1970, LANS, ALAS.

96. *Georgia Laws, 1920 Session*, 215–22; amendments at *Georgia Laws, 1955 Session*, 431–45; *Lewis v. Termplan*, 124 Ga. App. 507 (1971); Gottlieb, interview by author, 4 December 1998; Webster, interview by author, 18 February 1999.

97. Mark Budnitz, interview by author, 9 March 1999, Atlanta, handwritten notes.

98. Charles Baird, interview by author. Baird worked in GLSP's Columbus office before coming to Atlanta late in 1973.

99. Baird, interview by author; *Belton v. Columbus Finance and Thrift Company*, 127 Ga. App. 770 (1972); *Mason v. Service Loan and Finance Company*, 128 Ga. App. 828 (1973); *Lee et al. v. G. A. C. Finance Corporation*, 130 Ga. App. 44 (1973); *Sellers v. Alco Finance, Inc.*, 130 Ga. App. 769 (1974); *Georgia Investment Company v. Norman*, 231 Ga. 821 (1974); *Allen v. Alco Finance Inc.*, 131 Ga. App. 545 (1974). See also chap. 5.

100. In other consumer cases legal services clients received assistance through bankruptcy proceedings and protection against unlawful repossession. *In re Christian*, No. 19368 (M.D. Ga. 1973), reported in

CR 6 (April 1973): 746, protected a client against unlawful acceleration of a loan agreement. *Herring v. B. H. Moore and Son, Inc.*, No. B-8155 (Ga. Super. Ct. 1973), *CR* 7 (May 1973): 28, declared the defendant's repossession of the plaintiff's personal property unconstitutional since there had been no court judgment or notice of repossession. See chap. 5 for a more lengthy discussion of the GILA litigation.

101. *Freeman v. Martin* Case File, No. 15877 (N.D. Ga., filed 1971, settled 1973), FRC; *Hodge v. Dodd* Case File, No. 16171 (N.D. Ga., 1972), FRC, and reported in *CR* 6 (September 1972): 287.

102. *Frazier v. Jordan,* 457 F.2d 726 (5th Cir. 1972); Richard Roesel, interview by author, 1 June 1998, Washington, D.C.

103. *Kronlund v. Honstein,* No. 14103 (N.D. Ga. 1971), reported in *CR* 4 (January 1971): 450–51, and *CR* 5 (September 1971): 271; Dokson, interview by author. Dokson recalled plans to appeal *Kronlund,* but his client, a reformed drug addict, went back on drugs and effectively withdrew from the case.

104. *Davis v. Graham,* No. 16891 (N.D. Ga. 1972), reported in *CR* 6 (December 1972): 518.

105. *Farley v. Reinhart,* No. 15569 (N.D. Ga. 1971), reported in *CR* 5 (February 1972): 620, and *CR* 6 (June 1972): 114; Loeb, interview by author. The ALAS had pursued another case, *Houston v. Prosser,* the previous year. See ALAS, *Annual Report, 1972.*

106. Padnos noted that the program's lawyers enjoyed the support of the ALAS board in contributing its resources to *Doe v. Bolton.* Padnos, interview by author.

107. After the justices issued their opinions in January of 1973, women could no longer be denied an abortion in the early stages of pregnancy. *Roe v. Wade,* 410 U.S. 171 (1973); *Doe v. Bolton,* 410 U.S. 179 (1973). See discussion of both cases in David J. Garrow, *Liberty and Sexuality: The Right to Privacy and the Making of* Roe v. Wade (New York: Macmillan, 1994), esp. 424–28, 444–50. Further biographical information on Schwartz is in ALAS, *Annual Report, 1969;* and *Legal Aid News,* August 1969, box 9, ALAS, AHC.

108. *Doe v. Venable,* Case File No. 15862 (N.D. Ga., filed 1971), FRC; Loeb, interview by author. The state changed these policies effective February 1972, but certain aspects of the case remained open until 1974.

109. See "Defendant's Answers to Plaintiff's Second Interrogatories of Defendant," 3 July 1972, in *Doe v. Venable,* Case File. Loeb reported that ALAS achieved the same result for kidney transplants, winning Medicaid coverage for such procedures. Loeb, interview by author.

110. GLSP, *20th Anniversary* (Atlanta: GLSP, 1991), 3. The program's second director, Greg Dallaire (1974–75) urged circuit riding to every Georgia county.

111. Feldman, "Political Lessons," criticized the time demands of domestic cases (divorces in particular) on poverty lawyers.

112. GLSP, *Annual Report, 1972,* 34. Consumer cases made up just over 18 percent of the caseload; housing over 5.75 percent; welfare over 6 percent; and "other" 6 percent. Mike Froman and Roy Sobelson spoke of the preponderance of divorces in their circuit riding experience. See Froman, interview by author, 23 March 1999, Atlanta; Sobelson, interview by author, 23 March 1999, Atlanta.

113. Notably, eight of the ten housing projects in Macon were still completely segregated, one of the other two was mostly black and the other was mostly white. See Complaint, 31 August 1973; "Federal Defendants' Answers to Plaintiffs' First Set of Interrogatories," 20 December 1973; and other documents in *Scott v. Housing Authority of Macon,* Case File No. 2899 (M.D. Ga.), FRC. Another housing case without these obvious racial implications ended in defeat for GLSP attorneys. In *Winningham v. HUD,* No. 3237 (S.D. Ga.),

reported in *CR* 7 (February 1974): 619–20, and *CR* 9 (June 1975): 127, *aff'd*, 512 F.2d 617 (5th Cir. 1975), the Fifth Circuit upheld a district court decision that declared a HUD regulation constitutional that rendered a recently divorced resident of public housing ineligible for rent supplements because she had not previously lived in "substandard" housing.

114. *Paige v. Gray*, No. 74-50-ALB (M.D. Ga. 1975), reported in *CR* 9 (October 1975): 421; *Sheffield v. Cochran*, No. CV 374-14 (S.D. Ga. 1974), reported in *CR* 9 (June 1975): 115; *Ivey v. Garner*, No. 74-200-MAC (M.D. Ga.1975), reported in *CR* 9 (June 1975): 115–16.

115. The court-ordered policy stipulated that someone sent to the state mental hospital due to his incapacity to stand trial must be evaluated within forty-five days. If he was still considered incompetent to stand trial, the hospital could wait ninety days to evaluate the individual and determine whether there was a substantial probability that he would become competent in the foreseeable future. If he was found to be incompetent without a substantial probability of becoming competent in the foreseeable future, the hospital now either had to release the individual or initiate civil commitment proceedings. If he was found to be incompetent but with a substantial probability that he would become competent in the fore-seeable future, the hospital had to report that finding to the trial court and could retain the individual for an additional treatment period not to exceed nine months. At end of this period, if the individual was still considered incompetent, the hospital had to release him or initiate civil commitment proceedings. *Pate v. Parham*, No. 75-46-MAC (M.D. Ga. 1975), reported in *CR* 9 (July 1975): 212; and *CR* 9 (November 1975): 499. These changes were in accordance with the Supreme Court's decision in *Jackson v. Indiana*, 406 U.S. 715 (1972).

116. GLSP, *First Decade*, 16; Don Samuel, interview by author, 25 March 1999, Atlanta.

117. *Scott v. Parham*, No. C75-614A (N.D. Ga., filed 1975), in *CR* 9 (June 1975): 121; *Ellison v. Wein-berger*, No. C75-497A (N.D. Ga., filed May 17, 1975), in *CR* 9 (June 1975): 153, *CR* 9 (January 1976): 667, and *CR* 10 (April 1977): 1085.

118. See GLSP, *First Decade*, 16.

119. The plan was actually more complicated than this statement suggests. The district court decision outlined the details of the plan at *Crane v. Mathews*, 417 F. Supp. 532, 537 (N.D. Ga. 1976):

The state proposes to impose co-payments for some, but not all, types of mandatory medical care—certain inpatient and outpatient hospital services and physicians' services. Certain pre-ventive services are to be exempted from the co-payments. . . . Moreover, co-payments are not required for children eligible under the Child Welfare or Aid to Families with Dependent Chil-dren foster care programs. The amount of the co-payment is $2.00 for all other office and home physicians, outpatient hospital, emergency room, psychiatric, and physical medicine services. A co-payment of 50% of the state's payment for each day of care up to a maximum of $25.00 is to be made on inpatient hospital services except those resulting from EPSDT referrals. A refund would be made to the recipient of all co-payments when those payments exceeded six physician or outpatient visits over a continuous six-month period or when inpatient hospitalization was in excess of a continuous twelve-month period. One co-payment would be required for each program of care. A "Recipient Special Services" function would be created within the Medicaid program to provide a mechanism for recipients to appeal cases in which co-payment created a special financial difficulty.

120. Quotation at *Crane v. Mathews*, 417 F. Supp. 532, 537 (N.D. Ga. 1976). The plan required a waiver from HEW for Georgia to implement an "experimental" plan, since copayments were generally not allowed under federal Medicaid law. See "Complaint—Class Action," 1 December 1975; and "Order," 3 December 1975, in *Crane v. Mathews*, Case File No. C75-2317A (N.D. Ga.), FRC. See also Claudia Townsend, "Legislators May Try to Kill Georgia Legal Aid," *AC*, 8 December 1975, 2A.

121. Pressel's argument, in "Complaint—Class Action," 1 December 1975, was that HEW (in the person of Mathews) had acted beyond the scope of its authority by granting a waiver for a plan that was not an "experiment, pilot project or demonstration" and failing to "give potentially adversely affected Medicaid recipients timely notice of the Georgia co-payment waivers and opportunities to object and seek administrative review."

122. "Federal Defendant's Memorandum of Points and Authorities in Support of His Motion for Summary Judgment and in Opposition to Plaintiffs' Motion for a Preliminary Injunction," 23 December 1975, in *Crane v. Mathews*, Case File.

123. *Crane v. Mathews*, 417 F. Supp. 532 (N.D. Ga. 1976), in *CR* 9 (March 1976): 787, and *CR* 10 (August 1976): 284; GLSP, *First Decade*, 13–14.

124. Technically, this funding was earmarked for GILS, not GLSP.

125. Chuck Bell, "Budget Cut to End Legal Assistance?" *AC*, 20 March 1975, 8A; Editorial, "A $250,000 Mistake," *AC*, 19 March 1975, 4A; GLSP, *First Decade*, 20–21.

126. Cromartie made a point of crediting Dallaire with centralizing GLSP and thereby allowing lawyers and staff in the Atlanta headquarters to support attorneys in the local offices more effectively. He suggested that the organization had been little more than a confederation of these offices before Dallaire. One important result of this increasing centralization was that local offices were less dependent upon local bar leaders, something those local leaders did not appreciate. It was partly for that reason that Dallaire become such a controversial figure in the eyes of the state and local bar associations. Cromartie, interview by author.

127. An action in "trover" is a legal action whereby an individual seeks to regain property that, allegedly, he rightfully owns. In this case a woman sought to win back property from her former mother-in-law after divorcing the woman's son.

128. *Dixon v. GILS*, 388 F. Supp. 1156 (S.D. Ga. 1974). For further information on the *Dixon* case, see GLSP, *First Decade*, 23–24; Holmen interview, Gottlieb interview, Cromartie interview, Kehrer interview, Remar interview; and several letters, court documents, and newspaper clippings on file at the Georgia Legal Services Program, Atlanta. The case actually lasted into 1975 because the attorney filed another, identical case, which was similarly dismissed. The Atlanta Legal Aid Society fought off a similar legal challenge in *Wehunt v. Atlanta Legal Aid Society*, No. B-94519 (Fulton Co. Super. Ct., decided 23 May 1974). Judge Osgood Williams presided over that case, to an identical result.

129. Townsend, "Legislators May Try to Kill Georgia Legal Aid," *AC*, 12 December 1975, 11A.

130. Cromartie, interview by author.

131. Townsend, "Legislators May Try to Kill Georgia Legal Aid"; Townsend, "Legal Aid Chief Defends Program," *AC*, 12 December 1975, 11A; editorial, "Legal Aid Jeopardy," *AC*, 9 December 1975, 4A; GLSP, *First Decade*, 32.

132. As Huie, e.g., acknowledged, "we [Georgia Bar leaders] fully recognized that some of the criticism may well be legitimate, because nothing is perfect and there is no institution—whether within or without the government—which cannot stand refinement and improvement." GLSP, *First Decade*, 32.

133. Joe Brown, "Parham Fights Cutback in Legal Services Funds," *AC*, 6 January 1976, 2A.

134. Cromartie, interview by author; Townsend, "Legislators May Try to Kill Georgia Legal Aid"; Townsend, "Legal Aid Chief Defends Program."

135. The *Crane v. Mathews* decision was issued on 5 February 1976; the House Appropriations Committee deleted GLSP funding on 13 February, and the Senate quickly followed suit. GLSP, *First Decade*, 32.

136. Ibid., 32–42; "Lawyers Band to Aid GILS Caseload," *AC*, 14 March 1976, 21A; Michael A. Doyle, "Let's Pull Together," *Georgia State Bar Journal* 12 (April 1976): 167–69; Stell Huie, "President's Page: A Higher Calling," *Georgia State Bar Journal* 12 (April 1976): 165–66; Cullen, interview by author, 30 March 1999, Atlanta; Cromartie, interview by author. Cullen and Cromartie reported that the GLSP staff was more concerned with maintaining a "presence" in a greater number of communities than in retaining a larger number of lawyers.

137. There was a delay in the corporation becoming fully operable because it took nearly a year for Gerald Ford to appoint and the Senate to confirm the first LSC board of directors, as opponents of LSC urged President Ford to appoint several critics of federally funded legal services. Houseman and Perle, *Securing Equal Justice*, 20.

4. "EQUAL ACCESS TO JUSTICE"

1. Legal Services Corporation Act of 1974, Public Law 93-355; 42 U.S.C. Sec. 2996 et seq.

2. Friedman, *History*, chap. 12, 687–95; and Auerbach, *Unequal Justice*.

3. Legal Services Corporation Act of 1974, Public Law 93-355, 88 Stat. 378; see 42 U.S.C. Sec. 2996 et seq.

4. Congress, Senate, Committee on Labor and Public Welfare, *Economic Opportunity Amendments of 1971*, 92nd Cong., 1st sess., 1971, Report No. 92-331, 27.

5. Ibid., 28–29.

6. See Johnson, *Justice and Reform*, chap. 4; Houseman and Dooley, "Legal Services History," chap. 1, 11.

7. Jerome B. Falk Jr. and Stuart R. Pollak, "Political Interference with Publicly Funded Lawyers: The CRLA Controversy and the Future of Legal Services," *Hastings Law Journal* 24 (March 1973): 607.

8. Qtd. in Houseman and Dooley, "Legal Services History," chap. 1, 12.

9. See Falk and Pollak, "Political Interference"; Michael Bennett and Cruz Reynoso, "California Rural Legal Assistance (CRLA): Survival of a Poverty Law Practice," *Chicano Law Review* 1 (1972): 1–79; Houseman and Dooley, "Legal Services History," chap. 1, 12–13.

10. Specifically, Agnew suggested that law reform activities be limited to the national office and backup centers; national leaders adopt policies regulating poverty lawyers' activities and priorities; "professional control" be instituted on the local level; and "basic attitudes within this program . . . be changed." Spiro Agnew, "What's Wrong with the Legal Services Program," *American Bar Association Journal* (September 1972): 930–32. Agnew had recently grown angry over a lawsuit filed by Camden Regional Legal Services against the City of Camden, N.J., challenging its urban renewal program. Houseman and Dooley, "Legal

Services History," chap. 1, 14. According to Johnson, the vice president made similar comments to the National Governors' Conference on 23 February 1972 as well as to a national Mayors' Conference and the Texas State Bar. See Johnson, *Justice and Reform*, 281, 377 n. 58.

11. "OEO Director Says Program Was Based on Marxist Notion," *ADW*, 6 February 1973, 1.

12. Qtd. in Mark Arnold, "The Knockdown, Drag-Out Battle over Legal Services," *Juris Doctor* (April 1973): 5.

13. Congress, House, Representative Heinz, speaking during debate over Legal Services Corporation Act, *Congressional Record*, 21 June 1973, 119:20696. The quotation was entered into the *Congressional Record* and reported in Houseman and Dooley, "Legal Services History," chap. 1, 14–15. See Arnold, "The Knockdown, Drag-Out Battle over Legal Services," *Juris Doctor* (April 1973): 4–10; Arnold, "The Odyssey of Legal Services and the Games Politicians Play," *Juris Doctor* (October 1974): 23–28; "Making Peace with Poverty: Legal Services under Fire," *Legal Services Reporter*, 30 March 1972, 55–60; and Warren E. George, "Development of the Legal Services Corporation," *Cornell Law Review* 61 (June 1976): 681–730.

14. Houseman and Dooley, "Legal Services History," chap. 1, 14–15; *Williams v. Phillips*, 360 F. Supp. 1363 (D.D.C. 1973); *American Federation of Government Employees, Local 2677 v. Phillips*, 358 F. Supp. 60 (D.D.C. 1973).

15. Houseman and Dooley, "Legal Services History," 29–30.

16. Ibid., 30.

17. Ibid., chap. 1, 13, quoting the Ash Council's report to the president.

18. President's Message to the Congress Proposing Establishment of the Independent Corporation, *Weekly Compilation of Presidential Documents* 7 (5 May 1971): 727, qtd. in Houseman and Dooley, "Legal Services History," chap. 1, 13.

19. Houseman and Dooley, "Legal Services History," chap. 1, 13. These restrictions were in neither the Economic Opportunity Act nor the congressional plan for an independent corporation. See Warren E. George, "Development of the Legal Services Corporation," *Cornell Law Review* 61 (1976): 681–730.

20. Houseman and Dooley, "Legal Services History," chap. 1, 15; note, "The Legal Services Corporation: Curtailing Political Influence," *Yale Law Journal* 81 (1971): 231–86.

21. Houseman and Dooley, "Legal Services History," chap. 1, 15–16, which cites "Veto of Economic Opportunity Amendments of 1971," *Weekly Compilation of Presidential Documents* 71 (9 December 1971): 1634–35.

22. *Roe v. Wade*, 410 U.S. 171 (1973); *Swann v. Charlotte-Mecklenburg Board of Education*, 402 U.S. 1 (1971).

23. "Legal Services Program Transfer Stalled," *CQA* 29 (1973): 581–85; Houseman and Dooley, "Legal Services History," chap. 1, 15–17.

24. "Legal Services Corporation Established," *CQA* 30 (1974): 489–95; Houseman and Dooley, "Legal Services History," chap. 1, 17–18. This final Senate vote came on 18 July 1974. The initial LSC Act containing more substantial curbs on poverty law practice passed the House by a vote of 276 to 95, including the support of a healthy majority of the Deep South's representatives.

25. The support centers survived because Representative Green's amendment was ineffective. The act empowered LSC to "undertake directly and not by grant or contract" various activities, including research,

training and technical assistance, and providing an information clearinghouse. Green's amendment simply inserted the phrase "not by grant or contract" into the act, leaving LSC with the authority to finance backup centers directly. Legal Services Corporation Act of 1974, Public Law 93-355, Sec. 1006(A)(3); 119 *Cong. Rec.* 20717-23 (1973).

26. Legal Services Corporation Act of 1974, Public Law 93-355, 88 Stat. 378.

27. Recounted in Houseman and Dooley, "Legal Services History, chap. 1, 17–18; and based on Arnold, "The Odyssey of Legal Services and the Games Politicians Play," *Juris Doctor* (October 1974): 23, 27. The Green Amendment actually failed to exclude funding for the national support centers, which remained intact until the 1990s.

28. President's Message to the Congress Proposing Establishment of the Independent Corporation, *Weekly Compilation of Presidential Documents* 7, 5 May 1971, 727, qtd. in Houseman and Dooley, "Legal Services History," chap. 1, 13. For an examination of Nixon's politics, see Alonzo L. Hamby, "The Flawed Challenger: Richard M. Nixon," in *Liberalism and Its Challengers: From F.D.R. to Bush,* 2nd ed. (New York: Oxford University Press, 1992), 282–338; Herbert S. Parmet, *Richard Nixon and His America* (Boston: Little, Brown, 1990); and Stephen E. Ambrose, *Nixon: The Triumph of a Politician, 1962–1972* (New York: Simon and Schuster, 1989). The title of Dan Carter's chapter on Nixon in *From George Wallace to Newt Gingrich* is revealing: "The Politics of Accommodation." However vilified was Nixon by the Left, Democrats still dominated Congress, and thus his presidency was marked by considerable compromise. Carter, "Politics of Accommodation," in *From George Wallace to Newt Gingrich,* 24–54.

29. See William N. Eskridge Jr., Philip P. Frickey, and Elizabeth Garrett, *Legislation and Statutory Interpretation* (New York: Foundation Press, 2000), 67–114.

30. See appendix for discussion of this statistical analysis.

31. Edith Green, Testimony before the House of Representatives, 21 June 1973, 119 *Cong. Rec.* 20718.

32. See Edward A. Purcell Jr., *Brandeis and the Progressive Constitution: Erie, the Judicial Power, and the Politics of the Federal Courts in Twentieth-Century America* (New Haven, Conn.: Yale University Press, 2000).

33. *Milliken v. Bradley,* 418 U.S. 717 (1974); Wilmer Mizell, Testimony before the House of Representatives, 21 June 1973, 119 *Cong. Rec.* 20746.

34. Legal Services Corporation Act of 1974, Public Law 93-355, 88 Stat. 378.

35. Joan Mahoney, "Green Forms and Legal Aid Offices: A History of Publicly Funded Legal Services in Britain and the United States," *Saint Louis University Public Law Review* 17 (1998): 223, 226–29; Abel, "Law without Politics," 540–45. A Delivery System Study that LSC conducted between 1976 and 1980 indicated that the staff attorney model performed better than alternative delivery models. Houseman and Perle, *Securing Equal Justice,* 23.

36. See LSC's first annual report: LSC, *Annual Report, 1976* (Washington, D.C.: LSC, 1976), 5, esp. the foreword by Ehrlich and Bamberger.

37. Katz made the observation that "ever since its creation . . . the Legal Services Corporation has steered clear of indignant commentary on the social reality of poverty in the United States." Antipoverty rhetoric within the legal services community faded during the 1970s. Katz, *Poor People's Lawyers,* 179.

38. This notion was typical of what some scholars have termed "liberal legality." For those who sub-

scribe to this view, law's substance is unassailable; once the legal process is opened and equal, "justice" is secured. There are others, of course, who believe that inequality is rooted not only in unequal access but also substantive inequities. See Austin Sarat, "Going to Court: Access, Autonomy, and the Contradictions of Liberal Legality," in *The Politics of Law: A Progressive Critique,* 3rd ed. (New York: Basic Books, 1998), 97–114.

39. LSC, *Annual Report, 1976,* 5.

40. Houseman and Dooley, "Legal Services History," chap. 2, 2–6, quotation at 6.

41. Even meeting this goal would provide only modest access to legal counsel for the poor, since there were 11.2 private attorneys per 10,000 persons. Askew and Gilbert, "A History of the Legal Services Corporation's Expansion Efforts," n.p., December 1982, 6, in author's possession. See Thomas Ehrlich, "Giving Low-Income Americans Minimum Access to Legal Services," *ABAJ* 64 (1978): 696–98. For potential budgetary and delivery alternatives, see Congressional Budget Office, *The Legal Services Corporation—Budgetary Issues and Alternative Federal Approaches* (Washington, D.C.: CBO, July 1977).

42. Houseman and Dooley, "Legal Services History," chap. 3, 16–17, and chap. 2, 9–10; Len Goodman and Margaret Walker, *The Legal Services Program: Resource Distribution and the Low-Income Population* (Washington, D.C.: Bureau of Social Science Research, 1975). Houseman and Dooley's statistics are based on a report financed by the Office of Legal Services and conducted by the Bureau of Social Science Research in 1975. By 1976 the number of low-income persons enjoying "minimum access" had increased to 9.4 million of an estimated 29 million poor people nationwide, still leaving more than two-thirds without minimum access. LSC, *Annual Report, 1976,* 15; Askew and Gilbert, "History," 1.

43. GLSP, *First Decade,* 42; *U.S. Census of Population: 1980,* vol. 1: *Characteristics of the Population,* pt. 2: *Alabama Summary* (Washington, D.C.: Government Printing Office, 1983), table 82; pt. 12: *Georgia Summary,* and pt. 26: *Mississippi Summary.* According to LSCA, *First Year,* 6, a 1974 American Bar Association survey indicated that each year one in four poor people encountered a need for legal counsel. In Alabama alone that would create an enormous demand: 275,000 people in 1978, when LSCA served some 2,450 clients.

44. The legal services grant per person below the poverty level is derived from data from LSC, *Annual Report, 1976* (the legal services grants per state); and U.S. Bureau of the Census, *Statistical Abstract of the United States, 1974* (1974). Since these sources are not from the same year and the *Statistical Abstract* provides the estimated number of persons below the poverty line, the statistic discussed here, legal services grant per person below the poverty level, is necessarily an estimation.

45. Askew and Gilbert, "History," 10; Houseman and Dooley, "Legal Services History," chap. 3, 16–17, and chap. 2, 9–10; LSC, *Annual Report, 1976.*

46. LSC, *Annual Report, 1976* (the legal services grants per state); and U.S. Bureau of the Census, *Statistical Abstract of the United States, 1974.*

47. Qtd. in LSCA, *First Year,* 6.

48. Legal Services Corporation Act Amendments of 1977, Pub. L. 95-222, 91 Stat. 1615 (1977); Houseman and Dooley, "Legal Services History," chap. 3, 1–10. Exemplifying the backlash was a congressman's addition of a rider to the legal services appropriations bill in 1978 that prohibited the use of LSC funds for legislative advocacy. It passed by a vote of 264 to 132. Houseman and Perle, *Securing Equal Justice,* 27.

49. Askew and Gilbert, "History"; Houseman and Dooley, "Legal Services History," chap. 3, 16.

50. Such policy choices should not be taken for granted. LSC could have focused on successful existing programs, especially by increasing salaries for poverty lawyers, the stagnation of which during the early 1970s had led thousands of legal services attorneys to leave poverty law practice. Nearly one thousand attorneys left legal services programs each year during the early 1970s; when LSC began operating, there were thirty-three hundred attorneys nationwide, so roughly 30 percent of the programs' legal staff changed each year. LSC attributed this high turnover rate to the gap between legal aid salaries and salaries paid attorneys in other public agencies, not to mention the gap between legal aid and private attorney salaries. LSC, *Annual Report, 1976,* 12–13.

51. GLSP, *First Decade,* 20–42.

52. ALAS, *Annual Report, 1978.*

53. NMRLS, *30th Year Reunion,* May 1997, in author's possession; Wilhelm Joseph, interview by author, 26 May 1998, Baltimore, Md.

54. Members of the MBLS board of directors were concerned that the state bar "may not be able to endorse CMLS and may in fact be tainted by the association." They continued to resist merger into July 1976, when they realized that merger had become inevitable. Minutes of Board of Directors of Hinds County Legal Services, Inc., 13 July 1976, MSBA. According to the Minutes of Board of Directors of Hinds County Legal Services, Inc., 23 July 1976, MSBA, MBLS was to lose funding in August 1976, so its board supported the merger to ensure that MBLS assets were conveyed to CMLS. Bucky Askew had made it clear that LSC would only fund CMLS, so MBLS either had to merge or simply cease to exist. Powell, interview by author; David J. Lillesand, "Memorandum: Technical Assistance to Central Mississippi Legal Services, Inc.," 30 June 1977, in Barry Powell's personal files (see esp. 7); Guy Lescault, "Program Report for Central Mississippi Legal Services, Jackson, Mississippi," prepared for the Legal Services Corporation, 19 March 1981, in Barry Powell's personal files; Minutes of Board of Directors of Hinds County Legal Services, Inc., 21 August 1975, MSBA; Minutes of Board of Directors of Hinds County Legal Services, Inc., 29 April 1976, MSBA; Legal Services Corporation Prehearing Conference between MBLS and CLS, 25 May 1976, MSBA; Bucky Askew to Jimmy Miller (director of MBLS), 29 July 1976, MSBA.

55. Campbell, interview by author; Tom Keith, interview by Ken Cain, 26 July 1992, St. Petersburg, Fla.; Guy Lescault, interview by Bucky Askew, 3 September 1991, Atlanta, videotape at NEJL; Askew, interview by author, 4 March 1999; LSC, *Annual Report, 1976, Annual Report, 1977,* and *Annual Report, 1978.* Birmingham Area Legal Services is now known as Metro Birmingham Legal Services.

56. LSCA, *First Year,* 1979; LSCA, *What You Should Know about Legal Services,* 1980; LSCA, *A Report* (Montgomery, Ala.: LSCA, 1980).

57. Bergmark, interview by author; Michael Raff, interview by author, 7 July 1998, Jackson, Miss.; Clint Lyons, interview by author, 1 June 1998, Washington, D.C. Barry Powell reported that he and the chairman of the CMLS board, Spencer Gilbert, believed that if CMLS tried to expand to cover the southern part of the state, the bar might be able to retake control of the organization, as it had controlled Mississippi Bar Legal Services prior to its merger into the CMLS. Thus, they chose not to seek expansion funding to open CMLS throughout southern Mississippi. Powell, interview by author.

58. LSC, *Annual Report, 1981,* 27.

59. LSC, *Annual Report, 1979*, 8; and *Annual Report, 1980*, 5.

60. LSC, *Annual Report, 1979*, 4–5; Hillary Rodham Clinton, interview by Victor Geminiani, 21 July 1991, videotape at NEJL, Washington, D.C.

61. See Gary Bellow and Jeanne Kettleson, "From Ethics to Politics: Confronting Scarcity and Fairness in Public Interest Practice," *Boston University Law Review* 58 (1978): 337.

62. Houseman and Dooley, "Legal Services History," chap. 3, 18–21.

63. GLSP, *First Decade*, 11–12; Campbell, interview by author.

64. See LSC, *Annual Report, 1976*, 19, for discussion of LSC's Office of Program Support, which offered training.

65. GLSP, *First Decade*, 8.

66. LSCA, *Report*, 6.

67. Many of those who began poverty law practice during the 1960s and early 1970s expressed their feeling of being thrust into the front lines with little training or oversight immediately out of law school. That was less of a theme among the interviews of lawyers who came along in the late 1970s. Feldman has criticized the legal services program for these and other shortcomings. Feldman, "Political Lessons," was an explication of the shortfalls of the Legal Services Program and Legal Services Corporation by a former poverty lawyer. He discussed the "randomness" of cases—i.e., the failure of programs to organize cases into a larger reform framework; insufficient substantive knowledge; and the lack of sustained litigation, accountability to clients, and enforcement of decisions. These embedded weaknesses, Feldman argued, stemmed from OEO's compromising with the American Bar Association in allowing that organization significant influence over the composition and function of legal services programs. As a result, legal services lawyers have not effected the reforms possible through legal strategies. Two articles that accompanied Feldman's criticized his findings. Gary Bellow and Jeanne Charn, "Paths Not Yet Taken: Some Comments on Feldman's Critique of Legal Services Practice," *Georgetown Law Journal* 83 (April 1995): 1633–68, suggested that Feldman's link between early decisions within OEO and subsequent problems with the program are "questionable" (1633). Bellow and Charn perceived many of the same problems but suggested that they arose developmentally, not necessarily as a result of early OEO decisions. Moreover, they took issue with Feldman's methodology, arguing that many of his points are based solely on anecdotal evidence from his own experience in poverty law. The second critique of Feldman's work was Alan W. Houseman, "Political Lessons: Legal Services for the Poor: A Commentary," *Georgetown Law Journal* 83 (April 1995): 1669–1709. Houseman portrayed OEO's compromise with the ABA as a necessary tactic to ensure ABA support for the Legal Services Program and then went on to cite numerous instances in which poverty lawyers had a positive impact on the legal status of their clients.

68. LSC, *Annual Report, 1979*, 37.

69. Legal Services Corporation Act, as Amended 1977, §1007(a)(2)(C); 42 USC §2996f(a)(2)(C); Houseman and Dooley, "Legal Services History," chap. 3, 23. The amendment required LSC to "insure that (i) recipients, consistent with goals established by the Corporation, adopt procedures for determining and implementing priorities for the provision of such assistance, taking into account the relative needs of eligible clients for such assistance (including such outreach, training, and support services as may be necessary)."

70. GLSP, *20th Anniversary*, 9.

71. The Atlanta Legal Aid Society stopped taking uncontested divorces and name changes during its fiscal crisis of 1975. See ALAS, *Annual Report, 1972; Annual Report, 1978, Annual Report, 1979;* and *Annual Report, 1980;* and Burge, interview by author.

72. Campbell, interview by author.

73. Alfieri is critical of poverty lawyers' "gatekeeping" function in the absence of what he calls a "theoretics of practice." Anthony V. Alfieri, "Impoverished Practices," *Georgetown Law Journal* 81 (August 1993): 2568. See also Anthony V. Alfieri, "Reconstructive Poverty Law Practice: Learning Lessons of Client Narrative," *Yale Law Journal* 100 (1991): 2107. See also Lucie White, "Paradox, Piece-Work, and Patience," *Hastings Law Journal* 43 (April 1992): 853–59, arguing that the theoretical basis should be derived from the experiences and needs of the poor, not simply emanate from the minds of theoreticians.

74. Tremblay, "Acting 'A Very Moral Type of God': Triage among Poor Clients," favored poverty lawyers acting as fiduciaries. Cf. Justine A. Dunlap, "I Don't Want to Play God—A Response to Professor Tremblay," *Fordham Law Review* 67 (April 1999): 2601–16, who rejects Tremblay's hierarchy of problems and any system of triage, advocating instead the provision of maximum access to the legal system.

75. The Atlanta Legal Aid Society's prioritization had a dramatic impact on the organization's caseload during the late 1970s. Even as the society expanded, its caseload grew smaller, from a peak of 14,513 in 1972 to 7,082 in 1976, 5,773 in 1977, 5,267 in 1978, 4,776 in 1979, and 4,195 in 1980. See ALAS, *Annual Report, 1972, Annual Report, 1976, Annual Report, 1977, Annual Report, 1978, Annual Report, 1979,* and *Annual Report, 1980.* I am fortunate to have access to all of the Atlanta Legal Aid Society's annual reports from the late 1970s; unfortunately, the documentary record of the other Deep South programs is not so complete. And, of course, such statistics would not be as revealing in any case for programs such as LSCA, which was still in the process of massive expansion during the late 1970s.

76. See Houseman and Dooley, "Legal Services History," chap. 3, 25–27.

77. GLSP, *20th Anniversary*, 9.

78. *GLSN*, May 1978, 26–29.

79. Qtd. in GLSP, *First Decade*, 53.

80. LSCA, *First Year*, 14–15; LSCA, *Report*.

81. *NMRLS Notes*.

82. See chap. 6 for a discussion of this investigation, which was a reaction to the involvement of NMRLS lawyers in civil rights activity during the late 1970s.

83. *GLSN*, April 1978.

84. ALAS, *Annual Report, 1977*, 9.

85. ALAS, *Annual Report, 1979*, 4–8. In later years Dokson downplayed the restrictive nature of LSC regulations in comparison to the drastic budget cuts and political attacks on legal services during the early 1980s and 1990s. He recalled that during the late 1970s he became increasingly burned-out, and he soon left ALAS for that reason, coupled with a desire to provide better financially for his family. Dokson, interview by author.

86. LSC, *Annual Report, 1979*, 17, 20.

87. Jamie Denty, "Legal Service," *Jesup Press Sentinel*, 19 March 1978, reprinted in *GLSN*, April 1978.

88. This is not a pedantic distinction. Rhetorically, the goal of "equal access to justice" reflects the "myth of rights" discussed in Scheingold, *Politics of Rights*, whereas the phrase "equal justice under law" (which is, incidentally, emblazoned on the facade of the Supreme Court's building in Washington, D.C.) potentially invokes Scheingold's "politics of rights." Whether poverty law practice actually shifted its philosophical mooring is a separate question.

89. See Friedman, *History*, 677–78.

90. GLSP, *First Decade*, 21.

91. LSCA, *First Year*, 5–6.

92. *NMRLS Notes.*

93. *GLSN*, April 1978. The quote is from Shakespeare, *Henry V*, act 3, scene 1, line 1. Interestingly, the exclamation points are Bragg's additions.

94. Brennan, interview by author, 11 November 1998.

95. Mary Margaret Oliver, interview by author, 10 March 1999, Decatur, Ga.

96. Dokson, interview by author.

97. Cromartie, interview by author.

98. *GLSN*, April 1978, 12–13.

99. Cromartie reported that the Organization of Black Employees sought to ensure that no African Americans lost their jobs during the round of budget cuts in the early 1980s. Also, the organization raised complaints about black lawyers' greater difficulty passing the state bar exam (there was unsuccessful litigation against the exam dealing with this issue). Cromartie, interview by author.

100. This was a consistent response in the author's interviews with poverty lawyers.

101. A GLSP newsletter carried the story of Harry and Joan Stoddard. While Joan finished law school at Boston College, Harry, who had graduated from Harvard Law, practiced with a distinguished corporate firm in Boston. Upon Joan's graduation in 1977 she obtained a job with the Georgia Legal Services Program, and the couple moved south. A child, John, was on the way, and Harry and Joan decided that Harry would remain at home with the children. Admittedly, Harry's job "had gotten boring," but such a decision was only then becoming more common among American families. See "Who Does What? Who Cares!" (Gainesville, Ga.) *Times*, 9 April 1978, reprinted in *GLSN*, April 1978, 30.

102. See Friedman, *American Law*, 467–68, on the rise of the billable hour.

103. LSC, *Annual Report, 1978*, 8. The LSCA set a slightly lower standard, 55 percent of the state's median income. That meant clients living in a family of four had to make less than $7,673 per year to be eligible for legal services. LSCA, *First Year*, 6.

104. Michael B. Katz, *In the Shadow of the Poorhouse: A Social History of Welfare in America* (New York: Basic Books, 1986), xi–xii. See Katz for a discussion of the distinctions between public assistance and social insurance programs, which have "bifurcated social welfare along class lines," with public assistance benefiting the poorest segments of society. He suggests that social insurance programs, such as social security, enjoy "a strong, articulate middle-class constituency" and thus it "carry no stigma." No "stigma," perhaps, but such programs are still directed toward specified groups—in this case the elderly—with unique economic problems.

105. Comparing the racial and gender composition of clients served to the pool of potential clients—i.e., those with incomes less than 125 percent of the official poverty level—has proven difficult. The closest

comparison possible is on the national level, but peculiarities in the reporting of census data make exact comparison impossible. Nationally, in 1979, 29.7 percent of legal services clients were black, 56.9 percent white, 10.1 percent Hispanic, and 3.2 percent "other." Of those below the poverty level (not 125 percent of the poverty level, which was not reported by race), 27.9 percent were black and 63.3 percent white. See LSC, *Annual Report, 1979*, 14; and *U.S. Census of Population: 1980*, vol. 1: *Characteristics of the Population*, pt. 1: *United States Summary*, table 96. These differences seem inconsequential, and none of my research, including my interviews with former poverty lawyers, has given me reason to believe that legal services programs somehow preferenced minority clients, wittingly or unwittingly. On the state level comparisons between legal services clients and the pool of potential clients is more difficult due to the lack of consistent (and in some cases extant) reporting among legal services programs. Fifty-nine percent of the LSCA's 1979 clients, e.g., were black, while statewide just 49.2 percent of those receiving less than 125 percent of the poverty level were black. But LSCA served Alabama's "black belt," and, without the racial breakdown of the Huntsville- and Birmingham-based programs (the former serving the predominantly white northeastern section of the state), the source of this disparity is impossible to discern. See LSCA, *What You Should Know about Legal Services*; and *U.S. Census of Population: 1980*, vol. 1: *Characteristics of the Population*, pt. 2: *Alabama* (Washington, D.C.: Government Printing Office, 1983), table 82. It is possible that poverty lawyers served a slightly higher proportion of African Americans than their proportion of the pool of potential voters, but I have no reason to believe that such preferencing was either dramatic or widespread, if it existed at all.

106. LSCA, *What You Should Know about Legal Services*; and GLSP, *Georgia Legal Services Program: 20th Anniversary*. GLSP's statistics are based on 1990 percentages, which may have been slightly different than those of the late 1970s.

107. See chap. 6 on NMRLS. Statistics for the Mississippi programs, as well as ALAS, are lacking.

108. Of all Americans 12.4 percent lived beneath the official poverty line in 1979. See *U.S. Census of Population: 1980*, vol. 1: *Characteristics of the Population*, pt. 2: *Alabama* (Washington, D.C.: Government Printing Office, 1983), table 82; *U.S. Census of Population: 1980*, vol. 1: *Characteristics of the Population*, pt. 26: *Mississippi* (Washington, D.C.: Government Printing Office, 1983), table 82; *U.S. Census of Population: 1980*, vol. 1: *Characteristics of the Population*, pt. 12: *Georgia* (Washington, D.C.: Government Printing Office, 1983), table 82; *U.S. Census of Population: 1980*, vol. 1: *Characteristics of the Population*, pt. 1: *United States Summary* (Washington, D.C.: Government Printing Office, 1983), table 96.

109. In Alabama 63 percent of clients were women in 1979 and 65 percent in 1980. Nationwide 67.8 percent of clients were women in 1979. See LSCA, *What You Should Know about Legal Services*; LSCA, *Report*; LSC, *Annual Report, 1979*. Phyllis Holmen discussed the disproportionate poverty among households headed by women—over one-third of such households in the 1990s—in her article "Georgia Legal Services: Quality Justice for All," *Georgia Bar Journal* (August 1997): 11.

110. Holmen, "Georgia Legal Services," 11.

111. Nationwide, sources of income for legal services clients were as follows: welfare or Supplemental Security Income (SSI), 33.9 percent; social security, 15.8 percent; unemployment compensation, 3.6 percent; employment, 21.7 percent, and "other," 25 percent. LSC, *Annual Report, 1979*, 14. I have not been able to locate such statistics for Deep South programs.

112. In northern Mississippi, e.g., 37 percent of the client base was unemployed as of 1981. See NMRLS Office of Planning and Development, *An Analysis of the Attitudinal, Socioeconomic, County Expenditure and*

Federal Grant Characteristics of the North Mississippi Rural Legal Services Needs Assessment Survey (Oxford, Miss.: NMRLS, 1981), table 1, located in NM, LSC (hereafter cited as NMRLS, *Analysis*).

113. The percentages who answered yes when asked whether they perceived equal benefits when it came to streets, streetlights, fire protection, and sanitation were 23 percent, 30 percent, 32 percent, and 29 percent, respectively. More than half expressed concern with public sanitation (57 percent) and road conditions (77 percent).

114. NMRLS, *Analysis*.

115. Ibid. See table 18, 94–98, for statistical summaries.

116. Ibid. See table 18 and table 1, 5.

117. Unfortunately, I have been unable to locate equally detailed studies of the client community elsewhere in the region. One survey of 535 ALAS clients does reveal some similarities—notably, the predominance of oral means for the distribution of information about the society—and some differences. Of the 535 respondents 171 had heard of the society from friends or speaking events; 145 from the radio, 93 from social workers within the government bureaucracy, 48 from welfare caseworkers, and 61 from television; and just 11 from posters, 5 from housing code notices, and 2 from newspaper articles, the only written forms of communication listed in the survey. *LAN*, December 1968.

118. Scholars should be cautious not to assume that distinctive material interests determined cultural life among the poor or created a "culture of poverty." As the NMRLS study suggested, many low-income persons subscribed to the same ideas and desires as their more affluent counterparts. They valued family, economic stability, and good health. See NMRLS, *Analysis*, table 18, which reports that those interviewed for the study reported that their "first priority among social issues" was "family" (25 percent of the 2,300 respondents), "income" (20 percent), or "health" (14 percent).

5. LOW-INCOME FAMILIES, POVERTY LAWYERS, AND THE REGULATORY STATE

1. Alfieri, "Antinomies," 667. See also Katz, *Poverty Lawyers in Transition*.

2. Barbara Young Welke, *Recasting American Liberty: Gender, Race, Law, and the Railroad Revolution, 1865–1920* (Cambridge: Cambridge University Press, 2001); Hall, *Magic Mirror*, chap. 10; Peter H. Irons, *The New Deal Lawyers* (Princeton, N.J.: Princeton University Press, 1982). Horwitz, Hall, and others have pointed out that local, state, and federal governments have long been encouraging and influencing economic growth.

3. See David J. Rothman, *The Discovery of the Asylum: Social Order and Disorder in the New Republic* (Boston: Little, Brown, 1990).

4. Piven and Cloward, *Regulating the Poor*. Others place less stress on the "social order" function of public assistance. See Patterson, *America's Struggle against Poverty, 1900–1994*, 3rd ed. (Cambridge, Mass.: Harvard University Press, 1994); Walter I. Trattner, *From Poor Law to Welfare State: A History of Social Welfare in America*, 5th ed. (New York: Free Press, 1994); Linda Gordon, *Pitied but Not Entitled: Single Mothers and the History of Welfare, 1890–1935* (New York: Free Press, 1994), which places more emphasis on gender as a determining factor shaping social policy.

5. Hall, *Magic Mirror*, chap. 8, 167.

6. Friedman has written, "If there was one constant in the twentieth-century history of the family, and family law, it was that parents were losing control over their children." *American Law*, 455.

7. Abel, "Law without Politics," 608. Many feminist scholars have criticized the role of the state in women's lives, arguing that the state simply replaced male dominance with a "social" or "public patriarchy." Even those who have recognized the benefits of public power for women express ambivalence about becoming "dependent" on the state, though Piven and Cloward have suggested that "the main opportunities for women to exercise power today inhere precisely in their 'dependent' relationships with the state." After all, "all social relationships involvement elements of social control, and yet there is no possibility for power except in social relationships." See Francis Fox Piven and Richard Cloward, "Women and the State: Ideology, Power, and the Welfare State," in *The Breaking of the American Social Compact*, ed. Piven and Cloward (New York: New Press, 1997), 214.

8. LSCA, *First Year*, 18, notes that consumer problems made up 18 percent of the LSCA's 1978 caseload; that percentage remained constant in 1979 (18 percent, according to LSCA, *What You Should Know about Legal Services* (LSCA, 1980) and 1980 (19 percent, according to LSCA, *Report*).

9. The ALAS, *Annual Report, 1979*, reported that 825 of the organization's 4,776 new cases (17 percent) involved consumer problems; the percentage was 14.4 percent in 1980 (ALAS, *Annual Report, 1980*). The GLSP reported that consumer cases made up 13 percent of its 1984 caseload, a percentage that was probably representative of the late 1970s; GLSP, *Toward Justice* (Atlanta: GLSP, 1985). These proportions were only slightly higher than national averages. The LSC reported that consumer cases constituted 12.1 percent of legal services cases in 1979 and 13.7 percent in 1980. LSC, *Annual Report, 1979* (LSC, 1980); and LSC, *Annual Report, 1980* (LSC, 1981).

10. Rufe McCombs, with Karen Spears Zacharias, *Benched: The Memoirs of Judge Rufe McCombs* (Macon, Ga.: Mercer University Press, 1997), 133; Baird, interview by author.

11. GLSP, *First Decade*, 36.

12. LSCA, *First Year*, 18; LSCA, *Report*.

13. GLSP, *First Decade*, 36.

14. It is likely that most of these one-day cases were resolved through advice or brief services or referral to a private attorney. This assumption is based on statistics LSC used to document the duration of legal services cases by the major reason the cases were closed. Client withdrawals and closure due to insufficient merit rarely happened within one day. See LSC, *Annual Report, 1979*, 19. For a nationwide breakdown of consumer cases, see LSC, *Annual Report, 1979*, 15, 18. Bankruptcy cases constituted 2 percent of the entire caseload, enforcing contracts and warranties 2.2 percent, and defending against collections 3.1 percent.

15. McCombs mentioned that, when violations of the Georgia Industrial Loan Act "came in, I would draft a letter informing the said company that they were violating Georgia law, that they had so much time to refund all of the overcharged interest and to write up a new contract for my client or I would pursue the case." Most companies would cut the refund check. McCombs, *Benched*, 133.

16. LSCA, *First Year*, 5.

17. Ibid., 19.

18. Ibid., 18–19; LSCA, *Report*.

19. 15 U.S.C. §1601; last quotation at GLSP, *First Decade*, 36. See *Jones v. Consumer Remodeling Service, Inc.* (M.D. Ala., 1981), reported in *CR* 15 (February 1982), 861–62; see also an East Mississippi Legal Services case, *White v. World Finance of Meridian*, 653 F.2d 147 (5th Cir. 1981). Friedman points out that the Truth in Lending Act and other consumer protections were the result of an increasingly persua-

sive consumer movement that was gaining momentum in the late 1960s and 1970s. Friedman, *American Law*, 380.

20. See, e.g., *Williams v. Land-Hurst Furniture Company*, No. EC 71-79-S (N.D. Miss. 1971), reported in *CR* 5 (February 1972): 602.

21. *Lewis v. Delta Loans, Inc.*, 300 So.2d 142 (Miss. Sup. Ct., 1974); *McFall v. Helton Enterprises of Jackson, Inc.*, No. 72J-120 (C) (S.D. Miss., 1972), reported in *CR* 6 (March 1973): 681. CLS attorneys also convinced a federal judge that Mississippi's replevin statute was unconstitutional because it allowed creditors to seize property without affording the debtor adequate notice or a pre-seizure hearing. *Turner v. Colonial Finance Corp.*, No. 4821 (S.D. Miss., 1972), reported in *CR* 6 (January 1973): 556.

22. GLSP, *Annual Report, 1972*.

23. *Johnson v. Johnson*, No. 74-11 Col. (M.D. Ga. 1975), reported in *CR* 9 (August 1975): 255.

24. The case, begun at the circuit level in 1973, dragged on through appeals until 1979. *Cody v. Community Loan Corporation of Richmond County*, 606 F.2d 499 (5th Cir. 1979); reported in *CR* 9 (September 1975): 327; and *CR* 10 (June 1976): 129. Other Truth in Lending cases included *Eady v. General Finance Corporation of Augusta*, No. 1726 (S.D. Ga. 1972), reported in *CR* 6 (March 1973): 677; *Kilgore v. Kennesaw Finance Company of Douglasville*, No. 47586 (Ga. App., filed 1973), reported in *CR* 6 (March 1973): 675–76; and *Hodges v. Community Loan and Investment Corporation*, No. 29643 (Ga. 1975), reported in *CR* 9 (June 1975): 108.

25. McCombs, *Benched*, 68–71, 125–31.

26. Ibid., 140–43.

27. *Georgia Laws, 1920 Session*, 215–22; amendments at *Georgia Laws, 1955 Session*, 431–45.

28. *Lewis v. Termplan*, 124 Ga. App. 507 (1971); Gottlieb, interview, interview by author, 4 December 1998; Webster, interview by author, 18 February 1999.

29. Webster, interview by author, 18 February 1999; Gottlieb, interview by author, 4 December 1998; and Charles Baird, interview by author.

30. *Abrams v. Commercial Credit Plan, Inc.*, 128 Ga. App. 520 (1973).

31. *Gray v. Quality Finance Company*, 130 Ga. App. 762 (1974). Two judges dissented, arguing that the last payment due would have fallen on a Sunday had the loan company not extended the contract an extra day. The presiding judge, Eberhardt, wrote: "The borrower has defaulted in the payment of substantially the entire loan, but the majority, refusing to give the recognition which the law does to the practicalities of an obligation maturing on Sunday, proclaims a forfeiture of the whole of the loan, because, forsooth, the debtor is to be afforded an extra day in which to meet his obligation!"

32. *Reese v. Termplan, Inc.*, 128 Ga. App. 527 (1973); *Southern Discount Company v. Cooper et al.*, 130 Ga. App. 223 (1973); *Cullers v. Home Credit Company*, 130 Ga. App. 441 (1973); *Frazier et al. v. Courtesy Finance Company*, 132 Ga. App. (1974). See later discussion of the GLSP's GILA cases.

33. *Lawrimore v. Sun Finance Company*, 131 Ga. App. 96 (1974).

34. The Georgia Supreme Court refused to rule on the case, which was argued by Kendric Smith. *Consolidated Credit Corporation of Athens, Inc. v. Peppers*, 144 Ga. App. 401 (1977); GLSP, *First Decade*, 39–40.

35. GLSP, *First Decade*, 39–40; Baird, interview by author; Webster, interview by author, 18 February 1999; *Georgia Laws, 1920 Session*, 215–22; amendments at *Georgia Laws, 1955 Session*, 431–45; *Georgia Laws 1978 Session*, 1033–34; *Georgia Laws 1980 Session*, 1784–87; *Southern Discount Company of Georgia v. Ector*, 152

Ga. App. 244 (1979), 246 Ga. 30 (1980), 155 Ga. App. 521 (1980); *Moore v. Beneficial Finance Company of Georgia*, 158 Ga. App. 535 (1981). Congress similarly weakened the Truth in Lending Act during the early 1980s with the Truth in Lending Simplification and Reform Act, Pub. L. No. 96-221, Title VI § 601, 94 Stat. 168 (31 March 1980). Baird, interview, interview by author.

36. The case of *Otis Mozley v. Ford Motor Credit Company*, related in GLSP, *First Decade*, 40.

37. Related in LSCA, *First Year*, 18.

38. Peter Gabel and Jay Feinman, "Contract Law as Ideology," in *The Politics of Law: A Progressive Critique*, ed. David Kairys, 3rd ed. (New York: Basic Books, 1998), 497–510. Gabel and Feinman argue that in the nineteenth century contract law conveyed an imagery—"freedom of contract"—that denied "the oppressive character of the market and the lack of real personal liberty experienced by people in their personal and work lives." During the twentieth century that imagery has changed to reflect the regulated competition of contemporary capitalism, with a stress on "good faith" agreements. "In sum," write Gabel and Feinman, "people are conceived to be partners in a moral community where equity and the balancing of interests according to standards of fair dealing have supplanted the primitive era, when every moral tie was dissolved in 'the icy waters of egotistical calculation.'" The image of the state is "as active enforcer of the newly conceived notion of the general welfare." Such imagery does not, in their minds, represent the reality of competing class interests within an advanced capitalist framework.

39. Housing made up 11 percent of LSCA cases in 1979, 11.5 percent in 1980, and 12 percent in 1981, according to LSCA, *First Year*, LSCA, *What You Should Know about Legal Services*, and LSCA, *Report*. The percentages were somewhat higher in Georgia. Of the ALAS's cases in 1978, 18 percent involved housing; in 1979, 21.7 percent. See ALAS, *Annual Report, 1978*; and ALAS, *Annual Report, 1979*. GLSP attorneys handled slightly fewer cases: 15 percent in 1984, according to GLSP, *Toward Justice*.

40. According to ALAS annual reports: ALAS, *Annual Report, 1976*; and *Annual Report, 1978*. The *Poor People's Newspaper*, June 1981, PRO, AHC, documents the Hewatt case. Friedman, *American Law*, 407.

41. *Kaplan v. Sanders*, 136 Ga. App. 902 (1975), 237 Ga. 132 (1972), and 139 Ga. App. 624 (1976); reported in *CR* 9 (December 1975): 576, and *CR* 10 (September 1976): 379–80; *Kaplan v. Sanders*, Case File No. 30851 (Ga. Sup. Ct.), GDAH. The trial court and Court of Appeals initially allowed the defendant to seek exemplary damages, but the Georgia Supreme Court disagreed.

42. Goldstein, interview by author, 21 January 1999; ALAS, *Annual Report, 1978*.

43. Brennan, interview by author, 11 November 1998.

44. The U.S. Constitution generally limits governmental conduct, not the conduct of private individuals. Therefore, for constitutional principles to be relevant in a dispute there must be some "state action." The courts have viewed a variety of situations as involving state action when government involvement is not immediately apparent, including when a government turns over certain traditional public functions to private parties, when judicial enforcement is necessary to implement private discrimination, and when public and private action is so intertwined that the action complained of can be attributed to the government. See *Evans v. Newton*, 382 U.S. 296 (1966); *Shelley v. Kraemer*, 334 U.S. 1 (1948); and *Burton v. Wilmington Parking Authority*, 365 U.S. 715 (1971), respectively, as well as the more recent case of *Edmonson v. Leesville Concrete Company*, 500 U.S. 614 (1991).

45. *Nunn v. Harris*, No. CA 78-MO 1765 (N.D. Ala. 1978), reported in *CR* 11 (April 1978): 1014–15; and *CR* 12 (July 1978): 191. The attorneys were from the Birmingham Area Legal Services Corporation. Another

Alabama case, which came out of the Legal Services Corporation of Alabama, unsuccessfully attacked the Auburn City Housing Authority's eviction procedures. *Echols v. Auburn City Housing Authority*, No. CV 79-035 (Ala. Sup. Ct. 1980), reported in *CR* 13 (September 1979): 409; and *CR* 13 (April 1980): 993.

46. ALAS, *Annual Report, 1975* and *Annual Report, 1976;* Gottlieb, interview by author, 4 December 1999; Goldstein, interview by author, 21 January 1999.

47. *Glaze v. Atlanta Housing Authority*, No. C79-246A (N.D. Ga. 1979), reported in *CR* 13 (May 1979): 48, litigated along with the GLSP; *Sagoes v. Atlanta Housing Authority*, No. C76-1171A (N.D. Ga. 1976), reported in *CR* 10 (October 1976): 466.

48. Ayres Gardner, interview by author, 10 March 1999, Decatur, Ga.

49. Ibid.

50. *Leslie v. Mann*, Case File No. C77-49N (N.D. Ga., filed in 1977), FRC, reported in *CR* 11 (March 1978): 946–47, *CR* 12 (May 1978): 62, *CR* 13 (May 1979): 47–48, *CR* 14 (November 1980): 776, and *CR* 14 (April 1981): 1286; Gardner, interview by author.

51. Gardner, interview by author; Holmen, interview, interview by author, 4 March 1999, Atlanta.

52. Complaint, 27 October 1981, and "Consent Order and Judgment," 1 November 1982, in *Grier v. Stovall*, Case File No. C81-113N (N.D. Ga.), FRC, reported in *CR* 15 (February 1982): 875; Gardner, interview by author; Holmen, interview by author.

53. Gardner's trip to McRae occurred in the mid-1980s. Gardner, interview by author. The GLSP represented clients of McRae's public housing complexes in a challenge to the authority's utility allowances. *Brown v. Housing Authority of McRae*, 784 F.2d 1533 (11th Cir. 1986), 804 F.2d 612 (11th Cir. 1986), 820 F.2d 350 (11th Cir. 1987).

54. See earlier mention of the Atlanta Legal Aid Society's housing authority litigation during the mid- to late 1970s. GLSP cases included *Billington v. Underwood*, 613 F.2d 91 (5th Cir. 1980); *Boykin v. Bremen Housing Authority* (N.D. Ga.); *Clark v. Housing Authority of Alma* (S.D. Ga., settled 1979); *Lake v. Winder Housing Authority* (N.D. Ga., settled 1979); *Lewis v. Housing Authority of Augusta* (S.D. Ga.); *Scott v. Housing Authority of Macon* (M.D. Ga.). See GLSP, "Directory of Reported Decisions and Unreported Decisions with Ongoing Impact," December 1988, on file with GLSP, Atlanta. CMLS, "Decrees," [1984] notes that Central Mississippi attorneys challenged the Jackson Housing Authority for discriminating against a mentally handicapped client; *Middleton v. Jackson Housing Authority* (S.D. Miss.).

55. GLSP's "Directory of Reported Decisions and Unreported Decisions with Ongoing Impact," December 1988, lists the following cases involving the desegregation of public housing authorities: *Crumbley v. Housing Authority of Winder* (N.D. Ga.); *Freeman v. Rogers* (N.D. Ga., settled 1978); *Holmes v. Housing Authority of Brunswick* (S.D. Ga.); and *In re Wrightsville Housing Authority* (Wrightsville Housing Authority Board Resolution). Ayres Gardner discussed the case against the Wrightsville Housing Authority, suggesting that it began the process of forcing officials to desegregate public housing complexes across the state. This case occurred during the early 1980s. Gardner, interview by author. The *Freeman v. Rogers* case, however, pre-dated *Wrightsville;* the settlement in that case included an agreement to refrain from racially discriminatory placement of applicants. See Complaint, 18 October 1976, and Consent Order, 2 May 1978, in *Freeman v. Rogers*, Case File No. C76-141R (N.D. Ga.), FRC.

56. See 42 U.S.C. §1437ff.

57. See *Glaze v. Atlanta Housing Authority*, No. C79-246A (N.D. Ga. 1979), reported in *CR* 13 (May

1979): 48, and in ALAS, *Annual Report, 1979* and *Annual Report, 1980; Boyd v. Harris,* Case File No. CV 178-250 (S.D. Ga., settled 1979), FRC; *Lambert v. Waynesboro Properties, Inc.,* Case File No. CV 181-71 (S.D. Ga., settled 1982), FRC, and reported in *CR* 15 (July 1981): 285; *Russell v. Savannah Housing Authority,* No. CV477-254 (S.D. Ga. 1978), reported in *CR* 12 (September 1978): 313. CMLS's Barry Powell and Alison Steiner represented clients in a challenge against the Mississippi Regional Housing Authority, which administered the state's Section 8 housing, and officials in two cities that were refusing to adopt the Section 8 program. They alleged that the officials' actions were racially motivated, i.e., that the effect of their action (or inaction) was to prevent African Americans from having access to affordable housing in their locales. The suit did not ignore potential white applicants but simply noted the disproportionate effect on blacks. The parties settled the case when officials agreed to implement Section 8 programs in the two cities in question. *Hammond v. Russell,* No. J77-0408(N) (S.D. Miss. 1978), reported in *CR* 11 (March 1978): 946; and *CR* 12 (October 1978): 365. The ALAS brought a similar action against the city of Fairburn, arguing that municipal leaders sought to end the Section 8 program in order to make it impossible for the beneficiaries, who were predominantly black, to remain in the city. Like the CMLS case, the parties settled this case when city officials agreed to maintain the program; plaintiffs won monetary damages and attorneys' fees in both cases. *Williams v. City of Fairburn,* No. C78271A (N.D. Ga., filed 1978), reported in *CR* 11 (April 1978): 1015; *CR* 13 (June 1979): 118; *CR* 15 (July 1981): 284; ALAS, *Annual Report, 1978, Annual Report, 1979,* and *Annual Report, 1981.*

58. Another major issue, more easily resolved in the courts, was whether Section 8 tenants should be able to challenge a housing agency's determination that they were no longer eligible for rent subsidies. Since the housing agency received federal funds and was thus a "state agency," state action was obvious, thereby requiring constitutional due process. Arthur Madden, a staff attorney in Mobile, Alabama, brought one of the earliest cases to substantiate this point. See *Watkins v. Mobile Housing Board,* No. 79-0067-P (S.D. Ala. 1979), reported in *CR* 13 (September 1979): 398–99, and *CR* 13 (March 1980): 901; LSCA, *First Year,* 20–21.

59. *Jeffries v. Georgia Residential Finance Authority,* 503 F. Supp. 610 (N.D. Ga. 1980). The judge quoted from *Burton v. Wilmington Parking Authority,* 365 U.S. 715, at 722 (1961), a case involving racial segregation.

60. GRFA appealed the case to the Eleventh Circuit, which affirmed the district court decision, and then to the Supreme Court, which denied certiorari. One result of the case was to invalidate the GRFA's regulations governing eviction procedures, requiring the agency to become involved in such procedures, and to invalidate the HUD regulations that had allowed the GRFA to formulate their errant policies. *Jeffries v. Georgia Residential Finance Authority,* 503 F. Supp. 610 (N.D. Ga. 1980), 90 F.R.D. 62 (N.D. Ga. 1981), 678 F.2d 919 (11th Cir. 1982), 459 U.S. 971 (1982), reported in *CR* 14 (July 1980): 375–76, *CR* 14 (November 1980): 775, *CR* 15 (July 1981): 285, and *CR* 16 (October 1982): 452; GLSP, *First Decade,* 18–19.

61. *Miller v. Hartwood Apartments, Ltd.,* 689 F.2d 1239 (5th Cir. 1982). It would be easy to attribute the Mississippi results to the conservatism of that state's Southern District, a characteristic several poverty lawyers noted in their interviews. The federal judges referred to two recent rulings, however, in making the crucial decision that there was insufficient state action to warrant constitutional scrutiny. In one, *Blum v. Yaretsky,* 457 U.S. 991 (1982), the Supreme Court held that, because the state regulations did not "dictate the decision to discharge or transfer" of a particular nursing home patient, state action was not implicated. They also referred to a Fifth Circuit decision, *Taylor v. St. Clair,* 685 F.2d 982 (5th Cir. 1982). By this

time the Deep South was divided between the Fifth and Eleventh circuits, and these circuits' precedents could diverge, at least temporarily. One possible reason for the divergent results in *Jeffries* and *Miller* was that NMRLS attorneys did not challenge any action of the Mississippi Regional Housing Authority, which administered the state's Section 8 program, whereas by suing the GRFA, Georgia Legal Services attorneys drew attention to the regulatory structure of the program, as opposed to the conflict between the landlord and tenants.

62. Spriggs, interview by author.

63. See 12 U.S.C.S. § 1715z (2000).

64. Walbert and Cobb faced greater legal hurdles than they had anticipated when they initiated the case because, after they won at the district court level, the Fifth Circuit rejected the argument that FNMA foreclosures violated due process in a case it decided in 1975, *Hoffman v. HUD*, 519 F.2d 1160 (5th Cir. 1975). For documentation of the Roberts case, see *Roberts v. Cameron Brown Company*, 410 F. Supp. 988 (S.D. Ga. 1975), 72 F.R.D. 483 (1975), and 556 F.2d 356 (1977); Walbert, interview by author.

65. Most important was *United States v. Wynn*, 528 F.2d 1048 (5th Cir. 1976), in which the court decided against GLSP's clients but nevertheless recognized that *Goldberg* applied to the foreclosure of government-sponsored loans by government agencies. The Wynns, however, waived their right to a judicial foreclosure, so the court found that the government did not have to conduct administrative hearings prior to foreclosing on their home.

66. *United States v. White*, 543 F.2d 1139 (5th Cir. 1976), and 429 F. Supp. 1245 (N.D. Miss. 1977); reported in *CR* 11 (July 1977): 259–60.

67. *Law v. United States Department of Agriculture*, 366 F. Supp. 1233 (N.D. Ga. 1973); GLSP, *First Decade*, 20–21; reported in *CR* 7 (January 1974): 557. Other legal services cases involving FmHA loans included the CMLS's *Ramage v. Shell*, 493 F. Supp. 718 (N.D. Miss. 1980), and 644 F.2d 33 (5th Cir. 1981); *United States v. Henderson*, 707 F.2d 853 (5th Cir. 1983). NMRLS's *Hannah v. Butz*, 445 F. Supp. 503 (N.D. Miss. 1977); *Hudson v. Farmers Home Administration*, 654 F.2d 334 (5th Cir. 1981), also reported in *CR* 15 (February 1982): 888; *United States v. Garner*, 567 F. Supp. 313 (N.D. Miss. 1983). GLSP's *United States v. Wynn* and *Law v. United States Department of Agriculture* are mentioned earlier; *Williams v. Butz*, No. CV 176–153 (S.D. Ga., filed 1976), reported in *CR* 10 (November 1976): 640–41, and *CR* 12 (June 1978): 132, and discussed in GLSP, *First Decade*, 19–20; *Curry v. Block*, 541 F. Supp. 506 (S.D. Ga. 1982), 738 F.2d 1556 (11th Cir. 1984), and 608 F. Supp. 1407 (S.D. Ga. 1985); *Cash v. United States*, 571 F. Supp. 513 (N.D. Ga. 1983); see also "A Tale of Two Fannie Maes," in GLSP, *First Decade*, 21.

68. See, e.g., Michael E. Stone, "Housing and the Dynamics of U.S. Capitalism," in *Critical Perspectives on Housing*, ed. Rachel G. Bratt, Chester Hartman, and Ann Meyerson, eds. (Philadelphia: Temple University Press, 1986), 41–67.

69. Matusow, *Unraveling of America*, 231–32. See Rand E. Rosenblatt, "Health Law," in *Politics of Law*, 149–50, for a discussion of the "three models" of health law since the late nineteenth century.

70. Rosenblatt, "Health Law," 149–50. See the work of Clark Havighurst for an early exposition of the benefits of market competition in health care: e.g., "Health Maintenance Organizations and the Market for Health Services," *Law and Contemporary Problems* 35 (Autumn 1970): 716–95; "Government's Increasing Involvement in the Health Care Sector: The Hazards of Regulation and Less Hazardous Alternatives," in *The Changing Role of the Public and Private Sector in Health Care*, ed. Neil Hollander and Robert G. Joyce (New

York: National Health Council, 1973), 34; *Health Care Choices: Private Contracts as Instruments of Health Reform* (Washington, D.C.: AEI Press, 1995).

71. GLSP, *First Decade*, 54.

72. LSCA, *First Year*, 24; *In re Cooper* (hearing before the Alabama Medical Services Administration, 1980), reported in *CR* 14 (November 1980): 773; GLSP, *First Decade*, 31–33; ALAS, *Annual Report, 1978*, 47–51.

73. *Potter v. James* (M.D. Ala. 1980) and (5th Cir., filed 1981), reported in *CR* 14 (July 1980): 371, *CR* 14 (February 1981): 1112, and *CR* 15 (November 1981): 606. Another major issue in the case was the process by which the state had attempted to impose these higher copayments. Legal services attorneys argued that officials had not given recipients adequate notification; the court agreed, and the state Department of Human Resources formulated new policies to provide such notification and the opportunity for public hearings prior to any future changes in Medicaid.

74. *Addison v. Holiday*, No. G76-163-K (N.D. Miss. 1978), reported in *CR* 11 (May 1977): 44; and *CR* 12 (January 1979): 567.

75. *Dodson v. Parham*, 427 F. Supp. 97 (N.D. Ga. 1977), reported in *CR* 10 (March 1977): 979; ALAS, *Annual Report, 1976*, and *Annual Report, 1977*; GLSP, *First Decade*, 35.

76. See, e.g., *Norman v. St. Clair*, 610 F.2d 1228 (5th Cir. 1980), reported in *CR* 11 (August 1977): 387, and *CR* 14 (May 1980): 55; *Williams v. St. Clair*, 610 F.2d 1244 (5th Cir. 1980), reported in *CR* 11 (December 1977): 740–41; Complaint, 6 January 1977, and "Stipulation for Dismissal," 23 September 1977, in *Milton v. Busbee*, Case File No. C77-18A (N.D. Ga.), FRC.

77. ALAS, e.g., failed to win a challenge to Georgia's policy of deducting medical expenses from a person's income when deciding whether or not they were eligible for Medicaid assistance. *Freeman v. Parham*, 475 F.2d 185 (5th Cir. 1973), affirming unreported district court decision; case reported in *CR* 5 (June 1971): 98, and *CR* 7 (August 1973): 231–34. The district court dismissed the case, and the Fifth Circuit and Supreme Court affirmed this decision. In another ALAS case Kenneth Levin tried to win Medicaid coverage for sex changes. Levin represented Carolyn Rush, whose only masculinity resided, her doctor believed, in her genitalia. The legal question centered on whether transsexual surgery was "experimental"; if so, the state did not have to provide Medicaid coverage. Although successful in the district court, Rush lost her claim at the Fifth Circuit, and that decision was upheld in further deliberations. Sex changes, according to the courts, were "experimental" medical practices. *Rush v. Parham*, 625 F.2d 1150 (5th Cir. 1980), and 565 F. Supp. 856 (N.D. Ga. 1983); see also coverage in ALAS, *Annual Report, 1977, Annual Report, 1978, Annual Report, 1979*, and *Annual Report, 1980*.

78. *Triplett v. Cobb*, 331 F. Supp. 652 (N.D. Miss. 1971). See discussion in chap. 1.

79. *West v. Cole*, 390 F. Supp. 91 (N.D. Miss., 1975). The federal judge did not accept the plaintiffs' argument that Medicaid should be extended to all children receiving SSI disability benefits but ruled, instead, that only those who otherwise would be eligible for AFDC could receive Medicare benefits.

80. "Defendant's Answers to Plaintiff's Second Interrogatories of Defendant," 3 July 1972, in *Doe v. Venable* Case File. See discussion of *Doe v. Venable* in chap. 2.

81. LSCA, *First Year*, 24. The hospital continued to demand payment from the woman and actually refused to give the mother her newborn child until her husband signed an agreement to pay the costs. Kennedy set out to overturn this agreement, but it is unclear from the record whether or not he was successful.

82. *In re DeKalb General Hospital* (Ga. Dept. of Health and Human Services), reported in *CR* 15 (December 1981): 678; *Cloud v. Regenstein,* Case File No. C77-599A (N.D. Ga. settled 1981), FRC; *Crowe v. Heckler,* Case File No. C84-355R (N.D. Ga. settled 1985), FRC. See also ALAS, *Annual Report, 1978,* and *Saine v. Hospital Authority of Hall County,* No. 1478 (N.D. Ga.), reported in *CR* 7 (October 1973): 342, *CR* 7 (March 1974): 680, and *CR* 8 (n.d.): 563. See also GLSP, *Toward Justice* (GLSP: [1984]), 18.

83. Qtd. in GLSP, *First Decade,* 33.

84. Although mental health cases involved extremely significant "health care" issues, they had less to do with encouraging public funding than with protecting clients from overzealous officials and flawed institutions. (See later discussion of mental health cases.)

85. See, e.g., the work of Piven and Cloward.

86. GLSP, *First Decade,* 16, describing legal services lawyers' perspective on public assistance cases.

87. LSCA, *First Year,* 18.

88. *Jones v. Mississippi,* No. H925 (S.D. Miss. 1971), reported in *CR* 5 (September 1971): 247. This last point was similar to the argument of poverty lawyers in *King v. Smith* (1968).

89. Friedman distinguished, wisely, between "official law" and "living law," saying that they "are not, and never have been, the same in this country, or even close to it." He could not have been more accurate than with respect to low-income Americans and the welfare state. Friedman, *History,* 663.

90. "Defendant Parham's Memorandum of Authorities," 14 January 1976, in *Yearby v. Parham,* Case File No. C75-2532-A (N.D. Ga.), FRC; *Yearby v. Parham,* 415 F. Supp. 1236 (N.D. Ga., 1976), reported in *CR* 9 (March 1976): 811, *CR* 9 (April 1976): 920, and *CR* 10 (August 1976): 305.

91. Complaint, 29 December 1975, and "Motion for Temporary Restraining Order," 29 December 1975, in *Yearby v. Parham,* Case File, FRC. The federal statute in question, 42 U.S.C. Sec. 602(a), stipulated that states adjust their standard of need for AFDC payments according to rising costs of living. Georgia had done so in 1971 but sought to reduce this standard of need beginning in 1976, despite the fact that costs of living had actually risen significantly.

92. *Benson v. Schweiker,* 638 F.2d 1355 (5th Cir. 1981) and 652 F.2d 406 (5th Cir. 1981), reported in *CR* 14 (October 1980): 600–601, *CR* 15 (July 1981): 300, and *CR* 15 (February 1982): 890. Similar cases included *Harrell v. Harris,* No. 79-2935 (5th Cir. 1980), reported in *CR* 14 (May 1980): 70; *McLemore v. Schweiker* (N.D. Ala. 1981) and (5th Cir. 1981), reported in *CR* 15 (October 1981): 533. Poverty lawyers were not always successful, of course. See *White v. Harris,* 605 F.2d 867 (5th Cir. 1979), a CMLS case, and *Brantley v. Califano,* 478 F. Supp. 613 (M.D. Ga. 1979), a GLSP case.

93. *Smith v. Mississippi Employment Security Commission,* 344 So.2d 137 (Miss. Sup. Ct. 1977); *Whitehead v. Mississippi Employment Security Commission,* 349 So.2d 1048 (Miss. Sup. Ct. 1977); *Williams v. Mississippi Employment Security Commission,* 395 So.2d 964 (Miss. Sup. Ct. 1981). See also *Cane v. Mississippi Employment Security Commission,* 368 So.2d 1263 (Miss. Sup. Ct. 1979); and *Tate v. Mississippi Employment Security Commission,* 407 So.2d 109 (Miss. Sup. Ct. 1981). An Alabama case allowed illiterate workers some leeway in appealing unemployment compensation denials; they had not applied for an appeal within the seven-day period. *Malone v. Ventress,* No. CA-75G-1858-NE (N.D. Ala. 1976), reported in *CR* 10 (September 1976): 402. The GLSP filed a suit on behalf of three women who had lost their jobs for the same offense (clocking in two or three minutes late on several occasions) but been unequally penalized when they ap-

plied for unemployment compensation. Georgia's Employment Security Agency withheld from seven to nine weeks of benefits because they had been fired and not simply laid off. The agency established allowable penalty ranges for specific offenses, thereby limiting the arbitrariness of the penalties. *Fantroyal v. Caldwell* (S.D. Ga. 1980), reported in *CR* 14 (February 1981): 1136; GLSP, *First Decade*, 49.

94. *Scott v. Parham*, 69 F.R.D. 324 (N.D. Ga. 1975) and 422 F. Supp. 111 (N.D. Ga. 1976), reported in *CR* 9 (June 1975): 171, *CR* 9 (February 1976): 720, and *CR* 11 (July 1977): 254. As discussed earlier, another GLSP case resulted in a settlement whereby a class of potential food stamp recipients—people the local press lamented were "too poor to get food stamps"—were able to receive assistance. *White v. Butz*, Case File No. C75-1511A (N.D. Ga.), FRC, reported in *CR* 9 (January 1976): 645; and discussion of the case in GLSP, *First Decade*, 16.

95. The ALAS's Webster, Kramer, and O'Donnell, e.g., brought a case seeking to force Georgia to count unemployment benefits as "earned income" in determining AFDC eligibility, a change that would have expanded the pool of AFDC recipients. They were not successful. *Finch v. Weinberger*, 407 F. Supp. 34 (N.D. Ga. 1975), reported in *CR* 9 (August 1975): 288; see *Finch v. Weinberger*, Case File No. 75-592A (N.D. Ga.), FRC.

96. Poverty lawyers did continue to enforce the *Goldberg* doctrine, such as in CMLS's case forcing the state to provide hearings prior to cutting off food stamps; *Williams v. Butz*, No. J75-24(N) (S.D. Miss. 1976), reported in *CR* 10 (September 1975): 375.

97. See Jack Katz, *Poor People's Lawyers*, for a discussion of the changing atmosphere of poverty law practice, even in the midst of continuing impact litigation.

98. On developments in family law generally, see Friedman, *American Law*, 430–56.

99. See Peter Margulies, "Political Lawyering, One Person at a Time: The Challenge of Legal Work against Domestic Violence for the Impact Litigation/Client Service Debate," *Michigan Journal of Gender and Law* 3 (1996): 493–514.

100. GLSP, *Annual Report, 1972*, 34; Michael Froman, interview by author, 23 March 1999, Atlanta; Roy Sobelson, interview by author. Froman recalled the most domestic cases were uncontested divorces. Consumer cases made up just over 18 percent of the GLSP caseload; housing over 5.75 percent, welfare over 6 percent, and "other" 6 percent.

101. Mississippi Bar Legal Services, *Annual Report, 1975*, MSBA.

102. ALAS, *Annual Report, 1969*; and *Annual Report, 1972*.

103. Southeast Mississippi Legal Services, under the leadership of Martha Bergmark, was an exception to this rule. As Bergmark explained, "My program happened to have in it . . . an attorney [Allison Steiner] . . . for whom [domestic violence] was her passionate interest. . . . So my program never had what many legal services programs did, which was sort of a sense of devaluing the domestic cases as a potential divorce mill that was going to just kill any sense of program spirit or interest in the so-called bigger, higher-profile case." Bergmark, interview by author, 1998. Likewise, Virginia Kilgore expressed her sense of the value of domestic relations cases to clients, saying that clients always expressed an interest in keeping them a high priority. But she recalled much sentiment within NMRLS to limit these cases. Virginia Kilgore, interview by author, 14 July 1998, Oxford, Miss.

104. Froman, interview by author. See also Burge, interview by author.

105. LSCA, *First Year*, 22; LSCA, *What You Should Know about Legal Services*; LSCA, *Report*. Some offices had higher percentages of domestic cases, such as Gadsden's 26 percent; see LSCA, *First Year*, 22.

106. Domestic cases made up 31.4 percent of the ALAS caseload in 1972 and 33.5 percent in 1975. Once LSC funding began, the percentages dropped to 26.7 percent in 1976, 24.9 percent in 1977, 25.6 percent in 1978, 22.4 percent in 1979, and rose to 27.3 percent in 1980. See ALAS, *Annual Report, 1972; Annual Report, 1975; Annual Report, 1976; Annual Report, 1977; Annual Report, 1978; Annual Report, 1979; Annual Report, 1980*. For Georgia statistics, see GLSP, *Toward Justice*.

107. GLSP, *First Decade*, 27; English, "Legal Services Crisis," *AC*, 5 April 1981, mag. 26–34.

108. Interestingly, these program reports give less coverage to domestic cases than other types of cases, reflecting their status within the programs.

109. LSCA, *Report*; LSCA, *First Year*, 22; GLSP, *First Decade*, 29 (see discussion of *Brackett v. Brackett*). Marian Burge, among others, recalled that the vast majority of clients in domestic relations cases were women. This was reinforced by prioritization, which put an emphasis on domestic violence (most victims were women) and child custody disputes (women usually had custody of the children in the event of a marital separation). Burge, interview by author.

110. GLSP, *First Decade*, 27.

111. Oliver, interview by author.

112. GLSP, *20th Anniversary*, 11.

113. Peter Margulies, "Representation of Domestic Violence Survivors as a New Paradigm of Poverty Law: In Search of Access, Connection, and Voice," *George Washington Law Review* 63 (August 1995): 1071–1104, criticizes poverty lawyers and legal scholars for failing to recognize the significance of domestic violence cases. "Poverty lawyers have a major role to play in fighting domestic violence. The efforts of individual legal services attorneys demonstrate this potential, but also heighten the sense of missed opportunity attendant on the lack of a major institutional commitment in poverty law offices to the struggle against woman abuse." The source for this overall neglect has been the "failure of poverty theory and poverty law to adequately integrate gender" into conceptions of poverty (1103).

114. Taub and Schneider, "Women's Subordination," 328–55.

115. GLSP, *Toward Justice*, 17. While he did "not wish to underrate the importance of redressing sexual inequalities," Richard Abel suggested that "providing women with legal representation in family matters at most effects a horizontal or intraclass transfer of resources without altering class differences." Abel, "Law without Politics," 609.

116. Roderick Phillips, *Untying the Knot: A Short History of Divorce* (Cambridge: Cambridge University Press, 1991).

117. Kilgore, interview by author. Kilgore mentioned that there was a young organization called the Coalition against Domestic Violence in Mississippi, which held monthly meetings; she and some other NMRLS attorneys began attending these meetings.

118. GLSP, *First Decade*, 27–28; Oliver, interview by author; and "Mary Margaret Oliver Biography," in author's possession.

119. Bergmark, interview by author; Kilgore, interview by author.

120. ALAS, *Annual Report, 1980*. See Oliver, interview by author, for discussion of domestic violence as increasingly visible problem and political issue.

121. Lawrence M. Friedman, "Rights of Passage: Divorce Law in Historical Perspective," *Oregon Law Review* 63 (1984): 649.

122. Roy Sobelson, interview by author. Barbara Ehrenreich has argued that the breakdown of the traditional two-parent family resulted from male "emancipation" from the burdens of family support—both women's greater ability to enter the workforce and men's capitalizing on the material advantages of marital separation. Men, Ehrenreich and others have pointed out, grew richer in the aftermath of a divorce, while their ex-wives suffered a declining standard of living. Barbara Ehrenreich, *The Hearts of Men* (New York: Anchor Books, 1983); Lenore J. Weitzman, "The Economics of Divorce: Social and Economic Consequences of Property, Alimony, and State Support Awards," *UCLA Law Review* 28 (1981): 1181–1268.

123. Froman, interview by author. For child legitimation, see, e.g., *In re Pickett*, 205 S.E.2d 522 (Ga. App. 1974), in which the father of a child born to a woman not his wife petitioned the courts to legitimate that child, which was possible under Georgia law. Legal services cases also dealt with typical property disputes that arose in divorce proceedings. See, e.g., the Central Mississippi cases of *Hodges v. Hodges*, 346 So.2d 903 (Miss. Sup. Ct. 1977), in which the Court stipulated that judges could not impress a lien on one's state retirement funds in a divorce decree; *Murray v. Murray*, 358 So.2d 723 (Miss. Sup. Ct. 1978), involving a property dispute; and *Callahan v. Callahan*, 381 So.2d 178 (Miss. Sup. Ct. 1980), which stipulated that bigamy was grounds for a divorce.

124. Friedman, "Rights of Passage"; Kilgore, interview by author.

125. Friedman wrote that rising divorce rates during the late nineteenth century stemmed from "people want[ing] *formal* acceptance of the fact that their marriages were dead," not from some broader declension of family life. Furthermore, he noted that "divorce became much more a woman's remedy" for a husband's adultery or abuse. Friedman, *History*, 500–501. These themes are relevant to twentieth-century domestic relations and to the family law cases of legal services programs. Conservative opponents of legal services later used the prevalence of divorces in poverty law practice to argue that poverty lawyers were encouraging familial disunity among the poor. Such arguments were, at best, without proof and, at worst, patronizing in that they assumed that low-income people could not decide for themselves whether they wished to end their marriage. Most important, such arguments failed to recognize the extent to which legal services clients needed simply to legitimize their de facto familial status. That said, at least one serious scholar has suggested that legal aid decreased the real costs of divorce and therefore made divorces easier to obtain. Phillips, *Untying the Knot*, 239.

126. *Owens v. DeLoach*, 134 Ga. App. 783 (1975).

127. *Young v. Young*, 221 S.E.2d 424 (Ga. 1975); Bob Cullen, interview by author. The Georgia Supreme Court also dismissed *Horton v. Horton*, 235 Ga. 227 (1975), on a technicality, leaving custody of the child to the legal services client. Poverty lawyers also helped clients win such financial support in disputes that occasionally reached the courts. See, e.g., the CMLS's *Palmer v. Mangum*, 338 So.2d 1002 (Miss. Sup. Ct. 1976), *Rias v. Henderson*, 342 So.2d 737 (Miss. Sup. Ct. 1977), reported in *CR* 10 (April 1977): 1058, and *Quarles v. St. Clair*, 711 F.2d 691 (5th Cir. 1982), which dealt with the amount of child support payments that could be retained by the state from AFDC recipients; and the GLSP's *Woodes v. Morris*, 247 Ga. 771 (Ga. Sup. Ct. 1981), and *Foy v. Lewis*, 248 Ga. 234 (Ga. Sup. Ct. 1981). GLSP lost a claim for child support when the state's highest court refused to uphold a contempt citation against a husband who refused to pay his ex-wife's mortgage; *Ramsey v. Ramsey*, 231 Ga. 334 (1975). In *Lanning v. Mignon*, 233 Ga. 665 (1975), the Georgia

Supreme Court provided that a mother seeking support for her minor children after having entered into an agreement waiving child support could at a later time petition the court for child support. Upon remand the lower court required child support. ALAS, *Annual Report, 1975.*

128. *Leyva v. Brooks, et al.,* 244 S.E.2d 119 (Ga. App. 1978); and *Brooks et al. v. Leyva,* 249 S.E.2d 628 (Ga. App. 1978). The GLSP was active in child custody cases, and usually successful. See *Huff v. Moore,* 144 Ga. App. 668 (1978); *Nelson v. Taylor,* 244 Ga. 657 (Ga. Sup. Ct. 1979); *Diggs v. Diggs,* 158 Ga. App. 277 (1981); *Prescott v. Judy,* 157 Ga. App. 735 (1981). One GLSP case reached the highest appellate level in the land, the Supreme Court, in an interstate dispute, although that Court dismissed its writ of certiorari after learning that the federal claims were not raised in Georgia state courts. *Webb v. Webb,* 451 U.S. 493 (1981) and *Webb v. Webb,* 245 Ga. 650 (Ga. Sup. Ct. 1980); see also *Dropkin v. Dropkin,* 237 Ga. 768 (Ga. Sup. Ct. 1976), an earlier loss in a similar interstate dispute.

129. See, e.g., two NMRLS cases from earlier in the decade: *Cook v. Conn,* 267 So.2d 296 (Miss. Sup. Ct. 1972), a victory, and *Bowen v. Neal,* 277 So.2d 433 (Miss. Sup. Ct. 1973), a loss. An interesting twist on child custody disputes occurred when an East Mississippi Legal Services attorney representing a child's mother and grandmother requested a chancery court to enjoin the father from pursuing his custody claims in the Choctaw Indian tribal court near Philadelphia, Mississippi. Unfortunately for the legal services clients, the Indian Child Welfare Act of 1978 had reserved such issues for the tribal courts. *King v. Johnson* (Miss. Chancery Court, Neshoba County, 1980), reported in *CR* 15 (May 1981): 96.

130. *Georgia Laws 1971,* 709 et seq.

131. *Elrod v. Department of Family and Children Services,* 136 Ga. App. 251 (1975).

132. *In the Interest of M.A.C. et al.,* 261 S.E.2d 590 (Ga. Sup. Ct. 1979).

133. Mississippi Code Annotated (1972), sec. 93-15-1–93-15-11. The petition was to be filed in the chancery court of the county in which the parents were residing or the child was found.

134. *Reyer v. Harrison County Department of Public Welfare,* 404 So.2d 1023 (Miss. Sup. Ct. 1981), reported in *CR* 15 (June 1981): 187.

135. *Ray v. Department of Human Resources,* 270 S.E.2d 303 (Ga. App. 1980). See also *R.C.N. v. State of Georgia,* 233 S.E.2d 866 (Ga. App. 1977), an earlier case involving Ray's parental rights. Other reported cases included *Crews v. Brantley County Department of Family and Children Services,* 146 Ga. App. 408 (1978); *Chancey v. Department of Human Resources,* 156 Ga. App. 338 (1980). Also, one Atlanta Legal Aid case that reached the Georgia Court of Appeals stipulated that the state could not place a child in foster care without proving that both parents were unfit. *Gay v. Gay,* 149 Ga. App. 173 (1979); ALAS, *Annual Report, 1979.*

136. This hostility was not limited to the South but had a deep history in the region. See Randall Kennedy, *Interracial Intimacies: Sex, Marriage, Identity, and Adoption* (New York: Pantheon Books, 2003).

137. *Blackburn v. Blackburn,* 249 Ga. 689, 292 S.E.2d 821 (1982); *Newsweek,* 17 May 1982, 105; Derrick Bell, *Race, Racism and American Law,* 3rd ed. (Boston: Little, Brown, 1992), 96–97.

138. Bell, *Race,* 96–97.

139. This could also be true of adults, as GLSP client Reece Benton discovered. Benton's brother had him committed to the State Mental Hospital in Milledgeville, where Benton remained for eighteen years until GLSP attorney David Goren discovered him and initiated habeas corpus proceedings on his behalf. GLSP, *First Decade,* 34.

140. See Rothman, *Discovery of the Asylum*. Among Rothman's most important arguments is that these public institutions shifted from a focus on rehabilitating inmates to simply containing them over the course of the nineteenth century.

141. Hall, *Magic Mirror*, 182–83. Hall relies on Anthony M. Platt, *The Child Savers: The Invention of Delinquency*, 2nd ed. (1969; rpt., Chicago: University of Chicago Press, 1977).

142. Juvenile cases made up only a small portion of the legal services caseload: 1.3 percent nationwide in 1979. Of Mississippi Bar Legal Services's cases some 20 percent were juvenile cases in 1975, much higher than elsewhere. See LSC, *Annual Report, 1979*; and Mississippi Bar Legal Services, *Annual Report, 1975*, MSBA. Most program reports did not report the percentage of juvenile cases nor give descriptions of them. Clearly, however, poverty lawyers did bring such cases, as is evidenced by their mention in the ALAS, *Annual Report, 1972*; and Brent, interview by author. I have not found any mention of them in LSCA reports or other documents.

143. See *Carter v. State of Mississippi*, 334 So.2d 376 (Miss. Sup. Ct. 1976) and *In the Interest of Randy Joe Watkins*, 324 So.2d 232 (Miss. Sup. Ct. 1975); *McLemore v. Cubley*, 569 F.2d 940 (5th Cir. 1978). A GLSP case, *Hardwick v. Parham*, 141 Ga. App. 318 (1977), involved the state's "aftercare or alternative plans" for rehabilitating juvenile delinquents, specifically whether Department of Human Resources hearing officers could obtain evidence and prescribe different care for those who violated the conditions of their existing program.

144. *In re R. R.* (Miss. Youth Ct., Hinds Co. 1976), reported in *CR* 9 (April 1976): 899.

145. *Morgan v. Sproat*, 432 F. Supp. 1130 (S.D. Miss. 1977).

146. Based on my inability to find any reported decisions comparable to those of Central Mississippi Legal Services and the failure of legal services program reports to record specific cases.

147. The quote is from the text describing the case in GLSP, *First Decade*, 30.

148. Complaint, 5 April 1978, and Consent Order and Judgment, 18 August 1980, in *Dutton v. Lamb*, Case File No. C78-582A (N.D. Ga.), FRC, reported in *CR* 12 (May 1978): 67, and *CR* 15 (May 1981): 93; GLSP, *First Decade*, 30. It is unclear from the court records what became of Robbie Dutton, though she was not immediately returned to her parents. Some of the records remain sealed by order of the court. A later GLSP case, however, strengthened the rights of low-income parents against state intervention. In *J.J. v. Ledbetter*, Georgia Legal Services attorneys helped a mother regain custody of her son and forced the state Division of Family and Children Services to develop a plan to help reunite families and give parents the right to challenge such plans. See GLSP, *20th Anniversary*, 6.

149. GLSP, *First Decade*, 15.

150. *J.L. and J.R. v. Parham*, 412 F. Supp. 112 (M.D. Ga. 1976).

151. Ibid. The judges referred to *In re Gault, supra*, 387 U.S. 1 (1967).

152. Ibid. The plaintiff children numbered forty-six, according to the court, forty-seven according to GLSP reports.

153. *J.L. and J.R. v. Parham*, 412 F. Supp. 141 (M.D. Ga. 17 March 1976); *Parham v. J.L. et al.*, 425 U.S. 909 (5 April 1976). See also *Parham v. J.L. et al.*, 427 U.S. 903 (28 June 1976), in which the Supreme Court denied the GLSP request to expedite the consideration of the case; *Parham v. J.L. et al.*, 431 U.S. 936 (31 May 1977), granting appellees permission to proceed *in forma pauperis*, noting probable jurisdiction, and

directing the parties to brief and argue the question: "Whether, where the parents of a minor voluntarily place the minor in a state institution, there is sufficient 'state action,' including subsequent action by the state institution, to implicate the Due Process Clause of the Fourteenth Amendment?"; and *Parham v. J.L. et al.*, 434 U.S. 962 (28 November 1977), granting permission to the solicitor general to file a brief as *amicus curiae.*

154. *Parham v. J.L. et al.*, 442 U.S. 584, at 597, 599–600 (20 June 1979).

155. Ibid., at 598–99, 620.

156. Ibid., at 621–24.

157. Ibid., at 625–39.

158. Ibid., at 617–19.

159. GLSP, *Toward Justice,* 7; *First Decade,* 15; *20th Anniversary,* 6. The voluminous case file for this case is still on file with the Middle District of Georgia in Macon. GLSP's 1984 report, *Toward Justice,* made it clear that GLSP lawyers were not backing down even after the settlement. They filed a motion for contempt against the state for failure to extend the same protections to all children—basically the same argument the Supreme Court had rejected five years before. Subsequent reports do not suggest that they were successful. See GLSP, *20th Anniversary,* 6. See also Jonathan Zimring, interview by author, 10 March 1999, Atlanta, regarding the changing commitment statutes and GLSP representation of mental health patients during the late 1970s and 1980s.

160. See GLSP, *Toward Justice,* 7; GLSP, *20th Anniversary,* 6.

161. GLSP, *First Decade,* 15.

162. Alfieri, "Antinomies," 667.

163. Siegel, *Future Once Happened Here.* This was perhaps not only true of public beneficiaries but also of their ostensible benefactors. Christopher Lasch's work suggests that many liberals, too, had come to depend on the growing state bureaucracy to confront social problems. See Lasch, *The Culture of Narcissism: American Life in an Age of Diminishing Expectations* (New York: Norton, 1979), 385–91.

164. Welke, *Recasting American Liberty,* xiv. Welke tied the shifting notions of American liberty to Americans' response to the social impact of railroads. Americans came to accept greater limitations on their personal behavior in return for public regulation of railroads, among other industries, in order to promote safety and security in modern life.

165. There were some instances of this apparent contradiction in the welfare rights cases of the 1960s and 1970s, especially *King v. Smith.* In that case the Supreme Court declared that a woman's decision to have a "substitute father," i.e., a man who slept over periodically, was irrelevant to the material needs of her children. While courts generally did not portray such decisions as a protection of civil liberties, the result of such decisions was to limit the extent to which states could make eligibility contingent on "good behavior." Meanwhile, however, welfare rights cases sought to expand benefits to low-income families. This tension reflected the contradictions within liberalism and conservatism: "liberals" tended to support government programs to help certain groups of people, notably the less affluent, but also to support civil liberties; "conservatives" tended to resist government intervention in the marketplace but also to support government limitations on personal decisions based on their embrace of cultural precepts.

166. Alfieri, "Antinomies," 667.

6. LOW-INCOME COMMUNITIES, POVERTY LAWYERS, AND RACIAL RECONSTRUCTION

1. See Earl Black and Merle Black, *Politics and Society in the South* (Cambridge, Mass.: Harvard University Press, 1987), 276–316.

2. Ibid., 293.

3. See, generally, Goldfield, *Black, White, and Southern*, 227–55; Black and Black, *Politics and Society*, 292–316; Charles M. Payne, *I've Got the Light of Freedom: The Organizing Tradition and the Mississippi Freedom Struggle* (Berkeley: University of California Press, 1995); Taylor Branch, *Parting the Waters: America in the King Years, 1954–1963* (New York: Simon and Schuster, 1988); Branch, *Pillar of Fire: America in the King Years, 1963–1965* (New York: Simon and Schuster, 1998); David J. Garrow, *Bearing the Cross: Martin Luther King, Jr., and the Southern Christian Leadership Conference* (New York: Morrow, 1986).

4. These are approximations. Unfortunately, data is not available for every program across the time period in question; in fact, there are only a few documents that reported the precise racial proportions of the clientele. This should suffice as at least an approximation of these proportions, since other sources, especially oral interviews, have given no indication that there were major shifts in the clientele during the late 1960s and 1970s. That was not the case beginning, most likely, during the 1970s and especially the 1980s, as Leonard McClellan pointed out in an interview with the author. Once the NMRLS opened offices in predominantly white areas, such as Tupelo, and the racial conflicts of the late 1970s subsided, more whites began seeking legal counsel from NMRLS lawyers. See Leonard McClellan, interview by author; NMRLS, *Analysis*, table 1; Lyman, "Overview Report."

5. LSCA, *What You Should Know about Legal Services*; GLSP, *Toward Justice*.

6. In 1980, 46 percent of Alabama's poor families (those whose incomes were less than 125 percent of the official poverty level) were black; in Georgia that percentage was 50.2 percent, and in Mississippi 58 percent. Unfortunately, it is in the areas of the Deep South that had predominantly white populations that such data is not available. *U.S. Census of Population: 1980*, vol. 1: *Characteristics of the Population*, pt. 2: *Alabama Summary* (Washington, D.C.: Government Printing Office, 1983), table 82; pt. 12: *Georgia Summary*; and pt. 26: *Mississippi Summary*.

7. One of the most enduring points of contention within civil rights historiography has been the relative influence of charismatic leaders such as Martin Luther King Jr., organizations such as the Student Nonviolent Coordinating Committee and the Congress of Racial Equality, and "local people," or indigenous community organizing. Charles Payne's *I've Got the Light of Freedom* and John Dittmer's *Local People* are recent works stressing the impact of grassroots efforts to effect change. Ideally, scholars should recognize the complex interactions between these people and groups. For an excellent discussion of this debate, see Payne, *I've Got the Light*, 413–41.

8. While the percentages were certainly higher for NMRLS, only 1.4 percent of LSCA's cases and 3 percent of GLSP's cases involved civil rights issues in 1980 and 1984, respectively. See LSCA, *What You Should Know about Legal Services*; and GLSP, *Toward Justice*.

9. *Brown v. Board of Education*, 347 U.S. 483 (1954); and *Brown II*, 349 U.S. 294 (1955).

10. U.S. Constitution, Fifteenth Amendment.

11. This interpretation of legal services programs' civil rights cases suggests that community activism was an essential impetus for litigation. Katz, in *Poor People's Lawyers*, 5–6, has argued that poverty law

was not contingent on social movements. In general I agree: much law reform work happened outside the context of any well-defined effort for social change. That was not the case, however, with civil rights cases in the Deep South, which generally were contingent on community activism.

12. Friedman, *History*, 662.

13. Greene, *Praying for Sheetrock*, 8.

14. Ibid., 1–6, 234.

15. Ibid., 38.

16. Ibid., 117–27.

17. Ibid., 127–38; Alston qtd. at 128.

18. Ibid., 140–46, 169.

19. Ibid., 168, chap. 9; Affleck, interview by author; Samuel, interview by author; Froman, interview by author; Sobelson, interview by author.

20. Greene, *Praying for Sheetrock*, 173.

21. Ibid., 172.

22. Walbert, interview by author, 9 March 1999, Atlanta.

23. Greene, *Praying for Sheetrock*, 177–78.

24. Ibid., 190–91. They settled the case in early 1976.

25. Ibid., 192–94.

26. See, generally, Frank Parker, *Black Votes Count: Political Empowerment in Mississippi after 1965* (Chapel Hill: University of North Carolina Press, 1990).

27. Frank Parker, e.g., has noted that "no clear constitutional precedent existed" regarding the dilution of the black vote as of the late 1960s. The critical case in which the Supreme Court recognized that vote dilution could be as damaging to black political interests as the outright denial of the right to vote was *Allen v. State Board of Elections*, 393 U.S. 544 (1969), which arose out of Mississippi. Ibid., 78–101.

28. Albany's was the first such legal services case that went to trial and set an important precedent for future voting rights cases, but one of the first challenges filed was against the city of Dublin, Ga. The opposing parties settled the Dublin case prior to trial. Walbert, interview by author.

29. Garrow, *Bearing the Cross*, chap. 4, esp. 217–19.

30. *Smith v. Allwright*, 321 U.S. 649 (1944); *Chapman v. King*, 154 F.2d 460 (5th Cir. 1946) applied this precedent in Georgia.

31. These events are documented in *Paige v. Gray*, 399 F. Supp. 459 (M.D. Ga. 1975), 538 F.2d 1108 (5th Cir. 1976), and 437 F. Supp. 137 (M.D. Ga. 1977), reported in *CR* 9 (October 1975): 412; *CR* 10 (November 1976): 628; and *CR* 11 (January 1978): 807. See also *Georgia Laws 1947*, 725.

32. *Paige v. Gray*, 399 F. Supp. 459, 464 (M.D. Ga. 1975). Owens was relying on the Supreme Court's decision in *Gomillion v. Lightfoot*, 364 U.S. 339 (1960).

33. Specifically, Judge Owens hesitated to accept the plaintiffs' arguments that the 1947 statute violated the equal protection clause because such a holding would have required a retroactive application of precedents that had emerged since the act was passed. Because he believed the 1947 provision clearly violated the Fifteenth Amendment at the time of its passage, he rested his analysis on that amendment rather than the equal protection clause. *Paige v. Gray*, 399 F. Supp. 459.

34. Both sides argued that the controlling decisions were *White v. Regester*, 412 U.S. 755 (1973) and

Zimmer v. McKeithen, 485 F.2d 1297 (5th Cir. 1973), not *Gomillion v. Lightfoot*. In these cases at-large electoral systems were not inherently flawed. Rather, "to establish that a plan impermissibly dilutes, the plaintiff must show more than a mere disparity between percentage of minority residents and percentage of minority representation. The proof must affirmatively demonstrate that the affected group has less opportunity to participate in the political process."

35. *Paige v. Gray*, 538 F.2d 1108 (5th Cir. 1976). The standard for the Fifth Circuit was outlined in the *Zimmer* case: "Where a minority can demonstrate lack of access to the process of slating candidates, the unresponsiveness of legislators to their particularized interests, a tenuous state policy underlying the preference for multi-member or at-large districting, or that the existence of past discrimination in general precludes the effective participation in the election system, a strong case is made."

36. *Paige v. Gray*, 437 F. Supp. 137 (M.D. Ga. 1977).

37. Ibid.

38. Quotation in GLSP, *First Decade*, 25; Walbert, interview by author.

39. Cullen, interview by author.

40. Trial Transcript, 22 June 1978, in *Lodge v. Buxton*, Case File No. CV176-55 (S.D. Ga.), FRC; Cullen, interview by author.

41. Trial Transcript, 22 June 1978, in *Lodge v. Buxton*, Case File No. CV176-55 (S.D. Ga.), FRC.

42. According to Transcript of Hearing, 18 May 1977, in *Sapp v. Rowland*, Case File No. CV176-94 (S.D. Ga.), FRC. See Preliminary Statement, 12 May 1976, and Order and Judgment, 20 May 1977, in *Sapp v. Rowland*, Case File No. CV176-94 (S.D. GA.), FRC; Cullen, interview by author; GLSP, *First Decade*, 23.

43. Complaint, 5 April 1976, Amended Complaint, 26 April 1976, and Defenses of Defendants, 28 April 1976, in *Lodge v. Buxton*, Case File No. CV176-55 (S.D. Ga.), FRC.

44. David Walbert argued the case on appeal to the Supreme Court and was joined on the brief by Bob Cullen and the ACLU attorneys. *Lodge v. Buxton*, 639 F.2d 1358, 1363 (5th Cir. 1981), *aff'd, Rogers v. Lodge*, 458 U.S. 613 (1982), rehearing denied, 459 U.S. 899 (1982). See material in *Lodge v. Buxton*, Case File, esp. Trial Brief, 14 June 1978, Judgment, 2 October 1978, Order (from the Supreme Court), 3 November 1978, and Order, 7 October 1982, in *Lodge v. Buxton*, Case File No. CV176-55 (S.D. Ga.), FRC; and Cullen, interview by author.

45. GLSP, *First Decade*, 23.

46. GLSP, *Toward Justice*, 8. *Lambert v. Waynesboro Properties, Inc.*, was a suit against a Section 8 housing project in which GLSP attorneys argued that Waynesboro Properties violated federal regulations by refusing to admit applicants whose incomes were so low that they would become "negative rent tenants" if admitted. See *Lambert v. Waynesboro Properties, Inc.*, Case File No. CV 181-71 (S.D. Ga.), located at FRC; *Lambert v. Waynesboro Properties, Inc.*, reported in *CR* 15 (July 1981): 285. The case was filed in 1981. See also Pat Powers, "New Political Order Reigns in Burke County," *Augusta Chronicle*, 5 June 1983, reprinted in *GLSP Newsletter*, July 1983, 7.

47. Greene, *Praying for Sheetrock*, 195–203, quotes at 201–3; Walbert, interview by author.

48. Greene, *Praying for Sheetrock*, 203–11.

49. *McIntosh County NAACP v. City of Darien*, 605 F.2d 753 (5th Cir. 1979), reported in *CR* 13 (February 1980): 787.

50. Greene, *Praying for Sheetrock*, 211–19.

51. Subsequent events would demonstrate that litigation was but one agent of change and not nearly the most significant. First, McIntosh County remained among Georgia's poorest, notwithstanding the efforts of Alston and other black leaders. The great changes the county experienced were not the result of the county commission, much less one of its members. Interstate 95, which replaced Highway 17 as the major thoroughfare through the county and completely bypassed the soon-to-decay hamlet of Darien, began to alter the demographics of McIntosh County business. Meanwhile, law enforcement officials from the state of Georgia and the federal government were focusing their attention on Sheriff Tom Poppell's extracurricular activities, especially as head of an illicit drug ring. They were never able to convict him for any crime, but he departed McIntosh County nonetheless, passing away in 1979. Thurnell Alston had his own departure, ignominious, if temporary. The commissioner was convicted for accepting a bribe for which Alston promised to support the business interests of a prospective nightclub owner and, as it turned out, drug dealer. He was sentenced to seventy-eight months in federal prison. Law had enabled Alston to win his seat on the county commission, and, as it turned out, law proved his undoing. In his wake other black leaders assumed positions of leadership in McIntosh County, suggesting that, despite the limitations of litigation, eliminating at-large systems of election had enabled African Americans across Georgia to assume a greater role in local politics. See ibid., 219–32; chap. 13, 267–8; and chap. 16.

52. See, e.g., *McRae v. Board of Education of Henry County*, 491 F. Supp. 30 (N.D. Ga. 1980); the city of Gordon's *Ivey v. Garner* (M.D. Ga. 1975), reported in *CR* 9 (June 1975): 115–16; the city of Dublin's *Sheffield v. Cochran* (S.D. Ga., filed 1974), reported in *CR* 9 (June 1975): 115; Meriwether County's *Harris v. Levi*, 416 F. Supp. 208 (D.D.C. 1976), *aff'd* in part, *rev'd* in part, *Harris v. Bell*, 562 F.2d 772 (D.C. App. 1977), reported in *CR* 10 (November 1976): 628–29; the city of Moultrie's *Cross v. Baxter*, 604 F.2d 875 (5th Cir. 1979), reported in *CR* 13 (February 1980): 787.

53. According to GLSP attorney Al Bragg, *Kelsey v. Killebrew* was "the first case in the state of Georgia in which a whole city has been shown denying municipal services in a discriminatory manner." The case went to trial, but the judge did not render a decision; the parties presumably resolved the dispute, although the case file is incomplete. The judge was pressing the parties to negotiate, according to the Partial Transcript of Non-Jury Trial, 13 August 1980, in *Kelsey v. Killebrew*, Case File No. 78-33-MAC (M.D. Ga.), FRC. Other documents in the case file include Transcript of Pretrial Conference, 19 March 1980, and several depositions. Like other civil rights cases in Georgia, the local NAACP chapter was instrumental in bringing this lawsuit, according to the Deposition of Elisha Freeney, 26 June 1978; and Deposition of Lizzie Kelsey, 26 June 1978. See chap. 4 for a discussion of the public housing cases, especially *Grier v. Stovall*.

54. See *Legal Aid News*, August 1970, in Box 9, ALAS, AHC, and *Kronlund v. Honstein*, No. 14103 (N.D. Ga.), reported in *CR* 4 (January 1971): 450–51, and *CR* 5 (September 1971): 271; *Davis v. Graham*, No. 16891 (N.D. Ga. 1972), reported in *CR* 6 (February 1972): 518; *Mathews v. Little*, No. 18241 (N.D. Ga., filed 1973), reported in *CR* 7 (August 1973): 238.

55. *Lane v. Inman*, 509 F.2d 184 (5th Cir. 1975), reported in *CR* 7 (October 1973): 340, and *CR* 9 (May 1975): 40; *In re Holmes* (Ga. Real Estate Commission), reported in *CR* 13 (January 1980): 694.

56. Gottlieb, interview by author.

57. *Doe v. Secretary of the Army*, reported in GLSP, *First Decade*, 26.

58. *Myers v. Douglas County Board of Election*, No. C78-1837A (N.D. Ga. 1978), reported in *CR* 12 (February 1979): 735. This was not an isolated case. GLSP's Bob Cullen and Bill Cobb, aided by the Children's

Defense Fund, successfully represented a student expelled after an angry outburst in school. The student, Jamie Davis, was retarded, and his Burke County teachers had required him to cross his arms and lay his head on his desk for four months prior to the outburst. Under the Rehabilitation Act of 1973 the school system had to provide a special education program for such students. *Davis v. Wynn*, reported in GLSP, *First Decade*, 45. The GLSP was involved in a number of cases involving students with civil rights complaints, such as Raiford Stanley and Al Bragg's efforts to force the Peach County school system to allow pregnant students to attend class with the other students (the county had previously sent such young women to a separate school) and Phil Merkel's representation of a black student expelled from school after a cafeteria brawl in which both whites and blacks were involved. See *Linda Hill v. A. B. Johnson* and *Braboy v. Chatham County School Board*, reported in GLSP, *First Decade*, 44–45. GLSP attorney Gloria Einstein advised the Pierce County NAACP in its complaint to the Office of Civil Rights regarding persistent racial discrimination in the public schools. See *Westbrooks v. Gainesville City Schools' Board of Education*, reported in GLSP, *First Decade*, 44.

59. *Republican Party v. The City of Blue Ridge*, reported in GLSP, *First Decade*, 25. In the *Republican Party* case those who lost the local election charged that forty-five absentee ballots representing the votes of the nursing home residents were invalid because members of the winning ticket and nursing home administrators had "helped" the residents with their ballots. In so doing, they had explained that a vote for them was a vote against "dirty movies" at the local drive-in theater, the issue at the heart of the campaign. It so happened that residents could view the drive-in's movie screen from their facility. Although a judge ordered new elections, the GLSP ensured that the residents would still be able to cast their ballots in the new contest.

60. *Moore v. Stewart*, reported in GLSP, *First Decade*, 25.

61. GLSP, *First Decade*, 45. For information about the prison reform movement in Alabama, see Larry W. Yackle, *Reform and Regret: The Story of Federal Judicial Involvement in the Alabama Prison System* (New York: Oxford University Press, 1989).

62. See Eric Cummins, *The Rise and Fall of California's Radical Prison Movement* (Stanford, Calif.: Stanford University Press, 1994), for an analysis of the variety of strategies prisoners used to press for reform. Cummins describes what he calls a "highly developed radical convict resistance movement inside prison walls."

63. Affidavit of Marion Beacham, 30 November 1971, in *Freeman v. Martin*, Case File No. 15877 (N.D. Ga., filed 1971, settled 1973), FRC. See also Affidavit of James H. Kirby, 30 November 1971; Affidavit of Chester Vendable, 1 December 1971; Affidavit of Arthur Roy Freeman, 1 December 1971; Affidavit of William Bryant Cook, 30 November 1971; Affidavit of James Haynes, 30 November 1971; Complaint, 15 November 1971; Answer of Defendants, 8 December 1971; and Motion to Dismiss, 12 December 1973, in *Freeman v. Martin*, Case File.

64. Complaint, 4 February 1972; Order, 1 May 1972; Order, 2 March 1973; and Order, 8 March 1974, in *Hodge v. Dodd*, Case File No. 16171 (N.D. Ga., 1972), FRC, and reported in *CR* 6 (September 1972): 287.

65. The case against the federal penitentiary was *Loe v. Smith*, Case File No. C79-1176A (N.D. Ga., filed 1979), FRC; the case against the Fulton County Jail was *Fambro v. Fulton Co.*, Case File No. C82-2136 (N.D. Ga., filed 1982), FRC. As with the earlier Atlanta-area jail cases, the prisoners at the federal penitentiary initiated the legal challenge. They filed a complaint and numerous briefs and motions; these documents

were all handwritten in pen on thin, blank paper, in blocky, capital letters. A private attorney, Billy Spruell, became involved with the case, and then ALAS attorneys and the GLSP's Bob Cullen joined Spruell. Both case files are extensive, and the litigation stretched into the early 1990s; during much of this time a special magistrate oversaw the institutions' compliance with court orders. The case against the Cobb County Jail was *Yinger v. Hutson*, closed after the county erected a new jail; see *Yinger v. Hutson*, Case File No. 1:CV-81-785-MHS (N.D. Ga., filed 1981), FRC, esp. Complaint, 28 April 1981, and Order, 9 December 1987. Cullen was also the GLSP attorney involved in this case.

66. *Brown v. Beck*, No. 177-56 (S.D. Ga.), reported in *CR* 12 (August 1978): 253. GLSP attorneys failed to extend medical benefits further in *Brown v. Beck*, 481 F. Supp. 723 (S.D. Ga. 1980), more than a year and a half after the initial consent order. See also GLSP, *First Decade*, 47.

67. These included *Holland v. Steele*, 92 F.R.D. 58 (N.D. Ga. 1981); *Armour v. England*, No. C79-32G (N.D. Ga., filed 1979), reported in *CR* 13 (April 1980): 1002; *Reece v. Evans*, Case File No. 1:CV-82:0001251 (N.D. Ga., filed 1982), FRC; *Brown v. Cantrell* (N.D. Ga.), reported in *CR* 14 (December 1980): 881; *Crane v. Davis*, No. C79-56G (N.D. Ga., filed 1979), reported in *CR* 13 (April 1980): 1004, and *CR* 15 (December 1981): 688. See GLSP, *First Decade*, 45–47.

68. Complaint, 14 August 1979; Order, 21 November 1979; Deposition of Terry Kelsey, 9 October 1979; and Order, 4 February 1979, in *Kelsey v. Holder*, Case File No. 79-CV-196-MAC (M.D. Ga.), FRC. See also GLSP, *First Decade*, 47. Interestingly enough, the NAACP president was Rev. Hosea Blackshear of Cochran, who also figured prominently in the GLSP case of *Kelsey v. Killebrew*, which attacked discrimination in the town's distribution of municipal services (see earlier discussion). Lizzie Kelsey was the named plaintiff in that case.

69. Much of this discussion is based on Bradley Stewart Chilton, *Prisons under the Gavel: The Federal Court Takeover of Georgia Prisons* (Columbus: Ohio State University Press, 1991), quote at 1. See also GLSP, *First Decade*, 47; Cullen, interview by author; Cromartie, interview by author.

70. The Georgia State Prison and all other state prisons were supposed to have been desegregated by court order in *Wilson v. Kelley*, 294 F. Supp. 1005 (N.D. Ga., 1968).

71. *Guthrie v. Evans*, 93 F.R.D. 390 at 391–92 (S.D. Ga. 1981). This decision reconfirmed the eventual settlement of the case. See also Chilton, *Prisons*, 33.

72. GLSP, *First Decade*, 47.

73. Chilton, *Prisons*, 47; Cromartie, interview by author; Cullen, interview by author. Cullen reported that one of Cromartie's stated reasons for not wanted to assume the case was that it was not a priority of the Clients Council, to which Judge Alaimo replied that he had thirty-six hundred clients who, in Cullen's words, "would all make it their first priority"—the prisoners at Reidsville.

74. Chilton, *Prisons*, 47–49; Cullen, interview by author. Chilton places more stress on "personnel changes," i.e., Cullen's involvement, which brought about a shift in the "style" of the case.

75. Chilton, *Prisons*, 27, 31, 35–40; Cullen, interview by author.

76. *PPN*, June 1979, PRO, AHC. Outside organizations were well aware of the events at Reidsville. The Atlanta Welfare Rights Organization, e.g., a group with ties to Georgia's legal services programs, helped arrange bus trips to the prison for Atlanta residents with relatives confined there. The group's monthly publication, the *Poor People's Newspaper*, was highly critical of prison authorities and supportive of the legal efforts to reform the institution. Ethel Mathews, the welfare rights organization's president, spoke out

against capital punishment in an editorial about the state prison. She urged society to "end the concentration camp system for the poor," suggesting that "capital punishment, throughout our history, has meant that the people without the capital receive the ultimate punishment—death." Mathews asked, rhetorically: "How can our children respect the LAW when they see the LAW killing people, in their names? How can our children believe in justice and equality under the LAW when they see who is on death row and who is not?" "At a certain point," she wrote in another editorial about Reidsville and the criminal justice system, "the judge becomes the criminal and the law becomes his stick-up gun." See *PPN*, February 1980, and *PPN*, November 1978, PRO, AHC.

77. According to GLSP, *First Decade*, 47, the state was able to convince the court that the prison's punishment procedures were not racially discriminatory.

78. Chilton, *Prisons*, 49; GLSP, *First Decade*, 47.

79. None of this, of course, went directly to the lawyers involved. The state had spent $5 million total to defend the case by 1981; after that, more public funds went to the GLSP and to fund the special monitor to report on the prison's compliance with court orders. That monitor cost $15,000 per month, and the total costs to the state were already approximately $61 million by 1981, according to GLSP, *First Decade*, 47. Chilton reports the state's later approximation of $55 to $100 million (*Prisons*, 72). See also GLSP, *Toward Justice*, 9; GLSP, *20th Anniversary*, 6.

80. District Judge Wilbur Owens, presiding over the Bleckley County Jail case of *Kelsey v. Holder*, qtd. in GLSP, *First Decade*, 47.

81. Cullen, interview by author; Newsome qtd., reportedly speaking to a newspaper reporter, in GLSP, *Toward Justice*, 9.

82. In his case against the Dougherty County Jail, the GLSP's James Finkelstein faced vehement opposition from the county sheriff and negative press in the local newspaper, the *Albany Journal*. That newspaper called Finkelstein a "harassment-type, underpaid attorney." The sheriff, for his part, maintained that inmates were treated fairly at his facility. "Finkelstein Attacks Sheriff; Complains to Washington," *Albany Journal*, 7 April 1978, and "Sheriff Denies Charges," *AC*, 6 April 1978, both included in the *GLSN*, April 1978, in BF, NEJL.

83. See, e.g., Robert J. Norrell, *Reaping the Whirlwind: The Civil Rights Movement in Tuskegee* (New York: Knopf, 1985); Glenda A. Rabby, *The Pain and the Promise: The Struggle for Civil Rights in Tallahassee, Florida* (Athens: University of Georgia Press, 1999); Glenn T. Eskew, *But for Birmingham: The Local and National Movements in the Civil Rights Struggle* (Chapel Hill: University of North Carolina Press, 1997).

84. Recall, too, that the LSC Act of 1974 made it illegal for legal services attorneys to become involved in school desegregation cases.

85. Taylor, interview by author.

86. Bergmark, interview by author.

87. LSCA, *First Year*, 25; LSCA, *What You Should Know about Legal Services*; and LSCA, *Report*.

88. LSCA, *First Year*, 26, mentions one voting rights case in Lowndes County. The town of Hayneville had incorporated itself in 1968 but zoned black neighborhoods out of the city limits, contrary to principles mandated by the Voting Rights Act of 1965. The Justice Department ruled that the city was not in compliance and forced it to reshape its boundaries. Another voting rights case, mentioned in LSCA, *Report*, dealt with the town of Clio's illegal annexation of two sections of Barbour County.

89. LSCA attorneys handled two jail conditions cases in 1978. Litigation forced the Choctaw County Jail to close its isolation cell (which purportedly was used to hold livestock as well as inmates); to provide nurses once a week; to improve its food standards; to make various physical improvements to the facility; and to establish disciplinary guidelines. The parties settled this case in 1978. *Nicholson v. Choctaw County,* 498 F. Supp. 295 (S.D. Ala. 1980), reported in *CR* 12 (November 1978): 429; and *CR* 14 (April 1981): 1307. Another jail conditions case addressed problems in the Marshall County Jail. See LSCA, *First Year,* 27. A later report mentioned three more jail conditions cases; in two of them a federal court appointed LSCA attorneys to represent the inmates (LSCA, *Report*).

90. LSCA reports noted that housing was a major problem for low-income African Americans. Poverty lawyers sought to remedy this problem by helping clients get into public housing and, in one instance, seeking to force the federal government to open up a closed Air Force base to house African Americans. See LSCA, *First Year,* 25; *Alabama Cooperatives Association v. Solomon,* No. 78-1936 (D.D.C., filed 1978), reported in *CR* 12 (January 1979): 567. Lawrence Gardella filed an amicus brief in a case on behalf of the Montgomery Improvement Association charging the city with an improper use of Housing and Community Development Act funds. See *Montgomery Improvement Association, Inc. v. HUD* (M.D. Ala., filed 1977), reported in *CR* 11 (November 1977): 653, *CR* 13 (October 1979): 462, *CR* 15 (August 1981): 372, and *CR* 15 (February 1982): 874.

91. Some, but not all, of these cases involved racial discrimination. Poverty lawyers represented clients before the Equal Employment Opportunity Commission as well as the National Labor Relations Board and with reference to the Comprehensive Employment and Training Act. Employment issues made up a larger proportion of the LSCA caseload and were considered separately from civil rights cases; they constituted 6 percent in 1979 and 1980. See LSCA, *Report;* LSCA, *What You Should Know about Legal Services.*

92. An LSCA paralegal helped several black students in Selma who were suspended or put back a grade after the desegregation of the city's schools. The school system had not offered them a hearing or notified their parents. In another education case a Dothan attorney represented the parents of a retarded girl for whom they sought to force the Headland school system to provide an appropriate education. See LSCA, *First Year,* 27; LSCA, *Report.*

93. That is not to say that civil rights violations were nonexistent or that these programs pursued no civil rights cases. In general, however, fewer civil rights cases originated either in urban areas or predominantly white regions. Birmingham poverty lawyers had, as early as the 1960s, engaged in some civil rights work (see chap. 1). During the 1970s the Legal Aid Society of Birmingham lost a case that sought to force the city's transit authority to provide more accessible buses for disabled persons. *Snowden v. Birmingham-Jefferson County Transit Authority,* No. 75-G-330-S (N.D. Ala. 1975), reported in *CR* 9 (September 1975): 336–37. Birmingham Area Legal Services, which took the place of the Legal Aid Society of Birmingham, challenged a local technical school's denial of admittance to probationers, parolees, and ex-convicts in *Vincent v. Payne* (N.D. Ala.), reported in *CR* 15 (August 1981): 363. Attorneys working for the Legal Aid Society of Madison County challenged Huntsville city policies of suspending or terminating nonprobationary employees without due process in *Mason v. Davis,* No. 75-G-0348-NE (N.D. Ala.), reported in *CR* 9 (January 1976): 642.

94. Bergmark, interview by author.

95. McIver, interview by author; Taylor, interview by author; Osborne, interview by author.

96. Bergmark, interview by author. Regarding utility rate regulation, see *Mississippi Public Service*

Commission, et al v. Mississippi Power Company, 429 So.2d 883 (Miss. Sup. Ct. 1983), in which Bergmark, Stanley Taylor, and former CMLS director John Maxey were involved. Bergmark made a point of saying that none of these was the most controversial case that southeastern Mississippi attorneys ever brought. The most controversial was actually a parental rights case in which the state had taken away a woman's child due to allegations that her boyfriend abused the child. A SEMLS lawyer represented the woman and won custody of the child. Subsequently, the boyfriend killed the child, and the presiding judge was furious at the legal services attorney (not least because the judge would soon be up for reelection).

97. McIver, interview by author.

98. See Barry Powell, "CMLS Decrees, 1971–1983."

99. *NMRLS Notes*, September 1978; Alix Sanders, interview by author.

100. In Joseph's words, "to me, to move beyond segregation was not just a physical thing, but moving to a state of mind that everybody is equal in terms of their opportunities . . . and they are supposed to be treated that way." For this reason Joseph recalled that his "struggle actually began within the school itself." Joseph, interview by author.

101. Joseph was arrested for reckless driving and resisting arrest. He allegedly attempted to outrun the law enforcement officer. A court later found him guilty on three counts, fining him a total of thirty dollars. "Patrol Arrests 15 Students, Buses Away 198 Protesters," *CA*, 10 February 1969; "Officers End MVS Love-In," *Clarion-Ledger*, 10 February 1969; W. Webb Burke to James O. Eastland, 28 March 1969; James M. Mohead, "Weekly Report, 5/19/69–5/24/69," 24 May 1969; and "Memorandum," 27 February 1970, all in Wilhelm Joseph File, SCR. See also Joseph, interview by author.

102. Joseph, interview by author.

103. W. Webb Burke, "Memorandum," 8 March 1971; W. Webb Burke, "Memorandum," 30 August 1971; Wilhelm Joseph, letter to editor, "Racism Is Still in Mississippi," *Daily Mississippian*, 6 March 1972; and Fulton Tudor, "Weekly Report, 7-3-72—7-7-72," 7 July 1972, all in Wilhelm Joseph File, SCR. See also Joseph, interview by author.

104. Joseph, interview by author; NMRLS, *30th Year Reunion*, May 1997, in author's possession.

105. Joseph, interview by author.

106. The cases included *Pickens v. Okolona Municipal Separate School District*, 380 F. Supp. 1036 (N.D. Miss. 1974) and 527 F.2d 358 (5th Cir. 1976); *Stewart v. Bank of Pontotoc*, 74 F.R.D. 552 (N.D. Miss. 1977); *Clark v. Emerson Electric Manufacturing Company*, 430 F. Supp. 216 (N.D. Miss. 1977); *Smith v. Community Federal Savings and Loan Association of Tupelo*, 77 F.R.D. 668 (N.D. Miss. 1977); *Carpenter v. Herschede Hall Clock Division, Arnold Industries*, 77 F.R.D. 700 (N.D. Miss. 1977); *Heath v. D. H. Baldwin Company*, 447 F. Supp. 505 (N.D. Miss. 1977); *Quarles v. North Mississippi Retardation Center*, 455 F. Supp. 52 (N.D. Miss. 1978); *Flora v. Moore*, 78 F.R.D. 358 (N.D Miss. 1978) and 461 F. Supp. 1104 (N.D. Miss. 1978); *Wooley v. Mississippi Employment Security Commission*, 368 So.2d 840 (Miss. Sup. Ct. 1979); *Pinson v. Hendrix*, 493 F. Supp. 772 (N.D. Miss. 1980); *Burt v. Ramada Inn of Oxford*, 507 F. Supp. 336 (N.D. Miss. 1980); *Langdon v. Drew Municipal Separate School District*, 512 F. Supp. 1131 (N.D. Miss. 1981); *Blair v. City of Greenville*, 649 F.2d 365 (N.D. Miss. 1981); *Russell v. Harrison*, 562 F. Supp. 467 (N.D. Miss. 1983) and 736 F.2d 283 (5th Cir. 1984); and *Redditt v. Mississippi Extended Care Centers, Inc.*, 718 F.2d 1381 (5th Cir. 1983).

107. The cases included *Mitchell v. Board of Trustees of Oxford Municipal Separate School District*, 625 F.2d 660 (5th Cir. 1980); *Gaston v. Calhoun County Board of Education*, 88 F.R.D. 356 (N.D. Miss. 1980);

McClain v. Lafayette County Board of Education, 673 F.2d 106 (5th Cir. 1982); and *Keough v. Tate County Board of Education,* 748 F.2d 1077 (5th Cir. 1984).

108. The cases included *Jackson v. State of Mississippi,* 311 So.2d 658 (Miss. Sup. Ct. 1975); *Daniels v. State of Mississippi,* 315 So.2d 443 (Miss. Sup. Ct. 1975); *Rustin v. State of Mississippi,* 338 So.2d 1006 (Miss. Sup. Ct. 1976); *Evans v. Liberty Cash, Superintendent, Mississippi State Penitentiary,* 429 F. Supp. 681 (N.D. Miss. 1977); and *Irving v. State of Mississippi,* 361 So.2d 1360 (Miss. Sup. Ct. 1978), a capital murder case in which NMRLS Leonard McClellan was able to convince a federal court in *Irving v. Hargett,* 518 F. Supp. 1127 (N.D. Miss. 1981), to reduce Irving's sentence from death to life in prison.

109. The cases included *Campbell v. Mincy,* 413 F. Supp. 16 (N.D. Miss. 1975), dismissing a claim that the Marshall County Hospital violated Campbell's civil rights by refusing to admit her, forcing her to give birth in the hospital parking lot; *Taylor v. Coahoma County School District,* 581 F.2d 105 (5th Cir. 1978), in which a team of attorneys, including NMRLS, Legal Defense Fund, and other civil rights attorneys, lost their attempt to prevent the county from closing a historically black elementary school; and *Givens v. Delta Electric Power Association,* 572 F. Supp. 555 (N.D. Miss. 1983), denying that black members of the Delta Electric Power Association were victims of discrimination.

110. The voting rights cases included *Smith v. Granberry,* 349 So.2d 555 (Miss. Sup. Ct. 1977); *Jackson v. Riddell,* 476 F. Supp. 849 (N.D. Miss. 1979); *Dotson v. City of Indianola,* 521 F. Supp. 934 (N.D. Miss. 1981) and 551 F. Supp. 515 (N.D. Miss. 1982); and *Tucker v. Burford,* 603 F. Supp. 276 (N.D. Miss. 1985). In *Jordan v. City of Greenwood,* 711 F.2d 667 (5th Cir. 1983), the Court of Appeals forced the district court to revisit its decision regarding an at-large voting system. See *Jordan v. City of Greenwood,* 534 F. Supp. 1351 (N.D. Miss. 1982); and 541 F. Supp. 1135 (N.D. Miss. 1982). Prior to the involvement of NMRLS attorneys in the case of *Jordan v. City of Greenwood,* former NMRLS attorney and director Alix Sanders had litigated the case; see *Jordan v. City of Greenwood,* 450 F. Supp. 765 (N.D. Miss. 1978) and 477 F. Supp. 885 (N.D. Miss. 1979). In *Jordan v. Winter,* 604 F. Supp. 807 (N.D. Miss. 1984), and *Jordan v. Allain,* 619 F. Supp. 98 (N.D. Miss. 1985), NMRLS attorneys Alvin Chambliss and Willie Perkins joined other civil rights attorneys, including the legendary Frank R. Parker, in forcing the state to revise its congressional districts to prevent the dilution of the African-American vote. The primary named plaintiff in the latter three cases was David Jordan of the Greenwood Voters League. See Payne, *I've Got the Light,* for discussion of the Jordan family.

111. These included *Ealy v. Littlejohn,* 569 F.2d 219 (5th Cir. 1978); *Pickens v. Okolona Municipal Separate School District,* 594 F.2d 433 (5th Cir. 1979), involving the same Pickens from the unsuccessful employment discrimination lawsuit; and *Robinson v. Stovall,* 473 F. Supp. 135 (N.D. Miss. 1979), later overturned at 646 F.2d 1087 (5th Cir. 1981).

112. A case filed in 1974 seeking to equalize the historically white and historically black colleges in Mississippi (to be discussed later).

113. *NMRLS Notes,* September 1978. NMRLS lawyers attempted a far-reaching jail conditions suit attacking all of Mississippi's eighty-two county jails. Ultimately, the Fifth Circuit upheld the district court's dismissal of the suit on the grounds that there must be a cause of action against each individual jail. *Steward v. Winter,* 669 F.2d 328 (5th Cir. 1982), reported in *CR* 15 (October 1981): 529; and *CR* 16 (October 1982): 459. See also June Johnson interview, for a discussion of her case against Greenwood, Miss. *NMRLS Notes* also reports successful litigation against the Tippah County Jail, where officials agreed to improve the fa-

cility's conditions and their treatment of the inmates. See *NMRLS Notes,* September 1978; Virginia Kilgore, interview by author, for discussion of representation of Muslim inmates at Parchman Penitentiary.

114. McClellan, interview by author.

115. Joseph, interview by author.

116. McIver, interview by author.

117. Unfortunately, the documentary record is incomplete; I have been unable to locate official reports that document either the total number of cases or their breakdown into categories.

118. United League president Alfred "Skip" Robinson claimed more than sixty thousand members (some, but not all, of whom paid one dollar in membership dues) across the thirty-nine counties of northern Mississippi. "United League: Can It Destroy Stable NAACP?" *Capital Reporter* 14 September 1978, 2, in United League Subject File, MDAH. The Student Nonviolent Coordinating Committee, which had led the protests during Freedom Summer of 1964, was no longer active in Mississippi (or elsewhere) by the 1970s. See Clayborne Carson, *In Struggle: SNCC and the Black Awakening of the 1960s* (Cambridge, Mass.: Harvard University Press, 1981), esp. chap. 18; Payne, *I've Got the Light;* Dittmer, *Local People.* Likewise, the Mississippi branches of the NAACP were less significant by the late 1970s than they had been previously, not in the least because of a lawsuit against the statewide organization. White merchants in Port Gibson, Mississippi, claimed that the NAACP had engaged in a "secondary boycott" and were asking the courts to grant them $1.25 million in damages. When Skip Robinson announced plans to expand the United League from northern Mississippi throughout the state, NAACP leader Aaron Henry welcomed the move, mentioning the NAACP's restraint while the Port Gibson lawsuit progressed and noting that the United League's greater flexibility (it was unincorporated) would make it more difficult to attack in the courts. The civil rights veteran stated that "Skip has been a dutiful member of the NAACP and there is no conflict between us. It's certainly a welcome and refreshing wind that's blowing that encourages him to step up efforts for human rights." In some communities, however, most notably in Tupelo, the United League seemed to be replacing the NAACP entirely. See "Black United League Fills Void Left by Tupelo NAACP Chapter," *CA,* 14 May 1978, 4A, NMI, LSC; Henry qtd. in "NAACP Leader OKs Statewide United League," *CL,* 2 July 1978, 3A, in United League Subject File, MDAH; "Henry Welcomes Statewide Expansion of United League," *JDN,* 3 July 1978, in Aaron Henry Subject File, MDAH; "United League."

119. The Jackson *Clarion-Ledger* published an editorial cartoon in the fall of 1978 that pictured a knife embedded in the state of Mississippi. Upon the knife was the word *Racism,* and upon the map were three cities: Tupelo, Okolona, and Lexington. At the bottom was the following quote from Jonathan Swift: "We have just enough religion to make us hate, but not enough to make us love one another." "Racism," *CL,* 11 October 1978, 3B, in Race Relations 2 Subject File, MDAH. See chap. 2 for discussion of NMRLS involvement with United League protests during the early 1970s.

120. Leon Rubis, "March in Okolona Hot, Peaceful," *CL,* 10 June 1979, 3A; and "Jail Shooting Fans Flames in Okolona," *JA,* 7 June 1979, 1A, in Okolona Subject File, MDAH.

121. "A Tale of Two Cities," *JA,* 21 December 1978, 3A, in United League Subject File, MDAH. There was tension between the United League and the NAACP that revolved around the comparative militancy of the two organizations. Responding to the possibility that Mississippi NAACP leaders might help mediate between the league and Tupelo authorities, NAACP field director Emmett Burns feared the league "would

attack us as Uncle Toms if we try to mediate": "When you mediate you have to compromise and the league doesn't compromise." Robinson was also quoted as saying that the NAACP may not be the best mediator. Some NAACP chapter presidents, he suggested "are not willing to take a stand. The NAACP is not militant enough, half the chapters in the state are not functioning—they just won't take a stand." "League, NAACP at Odds in Mediating Dispute," *CL*, 8 September 1978, 3A, in United League Subject File, MDAH. See also "Emerging Civil Rights Groups Dispute 'Docile' NAACP Tactics," *CL*, 10 July 1979, 3A, in NAACP Subject File, MDAH.

122. See, e.g., the picture of United League spokesman Arnett Lewis in Anne Wetzel, "4 Nuns among 11 Protesters Arrested in Lexington Boycott," *CL*, 27 August 1978, 1B, in Lexington, 1970 Subject File, MDAH.

123. Along with the incident of police brutality, a white grocer just outside of Tupelo had reportedly shot and killed a black man he said had insulted his wife, leading to dismay within the black community. Thomas A. Johnson, "Below Tupelo's Calm, a Residue of Tension," *NYT*, 30 January 1979, 10A. The events that occurred in Tupelo during 1978 are well documented in newspaper reports, internal LSC files, and correspondence between the NMRLS, public officials, and LSC. See, e.g., Bill Drew, "Visit to a Town Divided," n.p., [1978]; "Rights Struggle, Klan Rallies . . . Tupelo," *Indianapolis Star*, 20 August 1978, 4, sec. 5, all in NMI, LSC.

124. Fredric N. Tulsky, "Legal Services Launches Suit," *CL*, 14 April 1978, NMI, LSC; Joseph Shapiro, "Suit Seeks to Reduce Tupelo Federal Funds," *CA*, 14 April 1978, NMI, LSC; Wilhelm Joseph, interview by author.

125. Walter B. Stanfield (chairman of the United League of Lee County) to mayor and Board of Aldermen of Tupelo, 21 February 1978, NMI, LSC, announcing upcoming lawsuits and demonstrations; Lewis Myers Jr. to Mayor Clyde Whitaker, 3 April 1978, NMI, LSC; Fredric N. Tulsky, "Klan, League Hold Opposing Tupelo Rallies," *CL*, 8 April 1978, NMI, LSC. See also Fredric N. Tulsky, "Racial Tension Mounts in Tupelo," *CL*, 24 February 1978, 1A, in Tupelo Boycott, 1978 Subject File, MDAH; Tulsky, "Blacks in Tupelo Protest City Action," *CL*, 12 March 1978, in Tupelo Boycott, 1978 Subject File, MDAH; "Tupelo Blacks Will Continue Protest, Maybe Pickets," *JDN*, 27 March 1978, 1C, in Tupelo Boycott, 1978 Subject File, MDAH; "Marchers' Spirits Not Dampened," *CL*, 30 March 1978, 1C, in United League Subject File, MDAH; Tulsky, "Klan Calls for White Unity; Cross Burning Event Climax," *CL*, 10 April 1978, NMI, LSC; Joe Rutherford and Michael Kerr, "Small Group Hears Klan Praise Racism; Blast Carter, Metrics," *DJ*, 10 April 1978, NMI, LSC; Kerr, "Cross-Burning Said Held on City Property," *DJ*, 11 April 1978, NMI, LSC; Kerr, "United League Wants Federal Monitoring of Saturday March," *DJ*, 4 May 1978, NMI, LSC; Joseph Shapiro, "Community Foundation Blasts Klan; Defends Tupelo's Record on Race," *CA*, 5 May 1978, NMI, LSC; Kerr, "Unrest Continues to Rumble in Tupelo," *DJ*, 8 May 1978, NMI, LSC; David Crary, "A Hard Rain Doesn't Cool Down Tensions in Tupelo," *CL*, 8 May 1978, 3A, in Tupelo Boycott, 1978 Subject File, MDAH; cartoon: "Make Way for a Patriot," *CA*, 4 May 1978, NMI, LSC.

126. Board of Aldermen of the City of Tupelo, "Resolution Concerning Illegal Activities of Attorneys for North Mississippi Rural Legal Services Office," 9 May 1978, NMI, LSC; Michael Kerr, "Aldermen Issue Race Resolutions," *DJ*, 10 May 1978, NMI, LSC; "Aldermen Issue Racial Resolution," *DJ*, 10 May 1978, NMI, LSC (reprints text of resolution); Michael Lollar and Joseph Shapiro, "Tupelo Step Angers League Leadership," *CA*, 11 May 1978, NMI, LSC. According to "Tupelo Step Angers League Leadership," the Board

of Aldermen also passed a resolution condemning the United League and the Ku Klux Klan, saying that the "radical" groups "are not needed in Tupelo, are not welcome in Tupelo, and are not wanted in Tupelo. There are hereby officially asked to stay out of Tupelo."

127. Clyde Whitaker to Arlo Temple, 11 May 1978, in NMRLS Investigation Files, LSC. Whitaker ended the letter by criticizing the antics of NMRLS attorney Sentwali Aiyetoro, who was representing two protesters when a city judge charged him with contempt of court and threw the young attorney in jail. He made no specific charges, however, about this incident. See "Defense Lawyer Sent to Jail," *DJ*, 11 May 1978, NMI, LSC; Joseph Shapiro, "League Ends Talks with Tupelo," *CA*, [11 May 1978], NMI, LSC.

128. Guy Mitchell, Jr. (Tupelo city attorney) to Hulett Askew (LSC, Atlanta Regional Office), 14 June 1978, NMI, LSC. Affidavit of Felix Black, 13 June 1978; Affidavit of Chuck Connor, 15 June 1978; Affidavit of Nathan Duncan, 15 June 1978; Statement of R. Michael Kerr, 15 June 1978; Affidavit of Edward L. Crider, 15 June 1978, NMI, LSC. Among the portions of newspaper articles included as exhibits was one that quoted Myers encouraging a crowd: "We've already won the boycott. In 10 more days we're going to win the town. That's what we're going for." See Exhibit F, in NMI, LSC, which included portions of articles from the *CA*, 2 April 1978; and *Lee County News*, 13 April 1978.

129. See Exhibit G, Exhibit H, and Exhibit I, in NMI, LSC—an article, "Myers Sets Conference," *DJ*, 13 April 1978; Excerpts from News Conference Called and Held by Lewis Myers Jr., 13 April 1978; and press release, 11 May 1978. At that news conference Myers announced that the NMRLS had filed an employment discrimination suit against the City of Tupelo involving the two policemen transferred to the fire department as well as a complaint filed with the U.S. Treasury Department seeking to terminate the city's federal revenues. He defended these actions, saying that, "since the City of Tupelo has refused to negotiate with black citizens who have been peacefully admonishing them to change their ways in connection with racial discrimination in employment in city government, we have exercised our rights and our alternatives to file a federal action against them." He also suggested that program attorneys might file more lawsuits in the immediate future. Asked if the filing of the lawsuits signaled a shift from demonstrations to legal action, Myers promised that the boycott and demonstrations would continue. In his Press Release, 11 May 1978, included as Exhibit I, Myers decried Tupelo officials' plans to file the complaint with the LSC. He concluded: "I will not be deterred by the racist, coercive, intimidating and repressive tactics of the Mayor or Police Chief in Tupelo. I've resolved to work even harder to defend and protest the rights of my people in that city. The Mayor, Chief of Police and Board of Aldermen should know that they will not run Lewis Myers out of Tupelo. I'll be there to haunt them for as long as they are there to preach the gospel of racism and ignorance." See also "United League Lawyer Accused of Violating Professional Ethics," *American* (Hattiesburg, Miss.), 22 June 1978, NMI, LSC.

130. Guy Mitchell Jr. to Hulett Askew, 14 June 1978; Affidavit of Chuck Connor, 15 June 1978, NMI, LSC.

131. Mitchell included this newspaper, the *Call*, as exhibits J and K, in NMI, LSC.

132. Guy Mitchell Jr. to Hulett Askew, 14 June 1978, quote at 6, NMI, LSC.

133. The earliest correspondence in the NMRLS Investigation Files, LSC, is a letter from Guy Mitchell Jr. to Senator John Stennis, 15 May 1978. This was followed shortly thereafter by two letters from B. T. Mitchell, a Tupelo attorney: B. T. Mitchell to Griffin Bell (U.S. attorney general), 17 May 1978; and Mitchell to Stennis, 19 May 1978. Dennis Carlisle also wrote to Stennis; Carlisle to Stennis, 30 June 1978.

Stennis soon wrote to the LSC, noting that "I have received complaints about this organization (NMRLS) and its personnel over the years." Stennis to Thomas Ehrlich (LSC president), 21 July 1978; Ehrlich to Stennis, 31 July 1978. Also included in NMI, LSC, are Trent Lott (representative, Fifth District, Miss.) to Thomas Ehrlich, 30 June 1978, mentioning Lewis Myers's activities in particular; Ehrlich to Lott, 5 July 1978; James O. Eastland (U.S. senator) to Ehrlich, 6 July 1978; Ehrlich to Eastland, 11 July 1978; Eastland to Ehrlich, 15 August 1978; Ehrlich to Eastland, 31 August 1978. Eastland included letters from a constituent and Guy Mitchell Jr.'s son and associate, Guy Mitchell III. Guy Mitchell III to Eastland, 7 August 1978; Dennis Carlisle to Eastland, 30 June 1978. Ehrlich forwarded this information to LSC general counsel Alice Daniel, who relayed it to Bucky Askew in Atlanta and Wilhelm Joseph. Daniel to Askew, 18 July 1978; and Daniel to Joseph, 25 September 1978.

134. See Clinton Lyons to Wilhelm Joseph, 27 June 1978; and Alice Daniel (LSC General Counsel) to Hulett Askew, 17 May 1978, NMI, LSC.

135. Joseph, interview by author.

136. They quoted from the ABA Code of Professional Responsibility, canon 7; and 42 U.S.C. §2996(2), Congress's declaration of purpose for the LSC. Brittain and Joseph to Askew, 7 August 1978, NMI, LSC.

137. Brittain and Joseph to Askew, 7 August 1978, NMI, LSC.

138. The quoted regulation was C.F.R. §1612.2(a)(2). See Brittain and Joseph to Askew, 7 August 1978; Affidavit of Alfred "Skip" Robinson, 30 August 1978; Affidavit of Alfred "Skip" Robinson, September 1978; Affidavit of George Pritchard, 12 September 1978; Affidavit of John Thomas Morris, 18 September 1978; Affidavit of Walter Stanfield, 18 September 1978, all in NMI, LSC. In his September affidavit Robinson said: "It insults our integrity to suggest that NMRLS attorneys have encouraged or exhorted us to boycott and demonstrate. Our decisions regarding tactics are made collectively by the people. No one has invaded the process and the ultimate authority of our membership to select the best course of action to accomplish or demands for equality."

139. Brittain and Joseph to Askew, 7 August 1978, NMI, LSC.

140. Ibid. See 42 U.S.C. §2996(e)(3), which restrains the corporation from "abrogat[ing] . . . the authority of a state or other jurisdiction to enforce the standards of professional responsibility generally applicable to attorneys in such jurisdiction." Brittain and Joseph also pointed out that holding press conferences or issuing press releases was not a violation of professional codes of conduct unless they created "prejudicial publicity." The city's attorney had not made such a claim. As far as the allegation that NMRLS attorneys initiated improper class actions, Brittain and Joseph related that all class action suits had the approval of the project director, Joseph, in accordance with federal guidelines at 42 U.S.C. §2996(d)(5).

141. Brittain and Joseph to Askew, 7 August 1978, NMI, LSC.

142. Clint Lyons, who had become director of the LSC Office of Field Services, requested that they send further information. Lyons to Joseph, 15 August 1978, NMI, LSC. They responded to Lyons with Brittain and Joseph to Michael Terry (acting Atlanta regional director), 25 September 1978, NMI, LSC.

143. The cases included *Turner v. Crider*, No. EC 78-67-S (N.D. Miss., filed 1978); *Jackson v. Tupelo*, No. EC 75-159-S (N.D. Miss., filed 1975); and *Warren v. Tupelo*, No. EC 78-71-K (N.D. Miss., filed 1978).

144. Brittain and Joseph named *Johnson v. Greenwood*, the employment discrimination suit that settled for $115,000; *Williams v. West Point*, in which the city settled and began hiring blacks; *Bell v. Anderson*, another employment discrimination suit against the city of Aberdeen; *Pegues v. Oxford*, a suit recently dis-

posed of by consent decree that attacked HUD and Oxford for racial discrimination in the city's urban renewal plan; *Stewart v. Pontotoc,* an eventually unsuccessful employment discrimination case; and *Minor v. Starkville.* Brittain and Joseph suggest that the fact that the federal judges dismissed none of these suits demonstrates their merit.

145. They concluded that "the disparities in employment and incomes in Mississippi must be attributed to the phenomenon of racism, unfairness and inequality," citing a Mississippi Research and Development Center report, *Social and Economic Profile of Black Mississippians in 1977,* to support these conclusions. Brittain and Joseph to Terry, 25 September 1978, NMI, LSC.

146. They also responded to several of Lyon's specific questions involving the NMRLS's eligibility guidelines and the specific eligibility of the United League. North Mississippi's took its eligibility guidelines verbatim from LSC regulations §1611(5)(c), which stated, "A recipient may provide legal assistance to a group, corporation, or association if it is primarily composed of persons eligible for legal assistance under the Act and if it provides information showing that it lacks, and has no practical means of obtaining, funds to retain private counsel." As for the United League's eligibility, it relied on Skip Robinson's affidavit, which stated that roughly three-fourths of the organization's members had eligible incomes, their own ten-year association with the United League, and information about the social and economic makeup of northern Mississippi. Brittain and Joseph to Terry, 25 September 1978, NMI, LSC. In a third piece of correspondence with the LSC, the NMRLS further responded to specific charges against them, including the arrest of NMRLS paralegal Walter Stanfield and his representation by NMRLS attorney Leonard McClellan. Brittain and Joseph to Alice Daniel, 6 December 1978, NMI, LSC.

147. Michael Kerr, "KKK to Resume Patrol of Tupelo Streets," *DJ,* 12 May 1978, NMI, LSC.

148. Lewis Myers may have made such negotiations less likely by roundly criticizing a leading Tupelo businessman, George McLean, during court proceedings. McLean had been urging the city to begin talks with the United League but was also a supporter of the moratorium on protests. Joseph Shapiro, "League Ends Talks with Tupelo," *CA,* [11 May 1978]; Shapiro, "Tupelo Protest Ban Overturned in Court," *CA,* 24 May 1978; "Protesters in Tupelo Win Case," *CL,* 24 May 1978, 1A; Michael Kerr, "City-United League Talks Prospects Dim," *DJ,* 25 May 1978, 5; Michael Lollar, "Tupelo Loses Its Long-Lasting Shelter from Racial Strife," *CA,* 14 May 1978.

149. Fredric N. Tulsky, "Violence Mars Tupelo Protest," *CL,* 11 June 1978, 1A, in Tupelo Boycott, 1978 Subject File, MDAH; Warren Brown, "Black Protest in Tupelo Stirs Klan-Led Backlash," *Washington Post,* 26 June 1978, 1A; David L. Langford, "Rights Struggle, Klan Rallies . . . Tupelo," *Indianapolis Star,* 20 August 1978, sec. 5, 4.

150. Beyond the affirmative action plan Robinson's demands included setting aside the convictions of United League members whose charges stemmed from the league's protest activities, rehiring two sanitation workers, setting the affirmative action plan's racial quota of 25 percent for new hires, rather than the 21 percent agreed to initially, and instituting a similar plan for the Tupelo schools. Robinson to Mayor Clyde Whitaker, 20 November 1978, NMI, LSC; Whitaker to Robinson, 21 November 1978, and enclosed statement, NMI, LSC. "Civil Rights Opponents Meet; Terms Due Tonight," *JDN,* 8 September 1978, 1D, in United League Subject File, MDAH; "League, NAACP at Odds in Mediating Dispute," *CL,* 8 September 1978, 3A, in United League Subject File, MDAH; "NAACP to Stay Outside of United League Struggle," *JDN,* 12 September 1978, in United League Subject File, MDAH; "Evers Arranges Meeting for Two Groups," *JDN,*

28 September 1978, 10A, in United League Subject File, MDAH; "Tupelo Mayor Plans Second Meeting on Racial Problems," *JDN,* 29 September 1978, 12D, in United League Subject File, MDAH; "Newsman Charged for Klan Rally Coverage," *News and the Law,* October 1978, NMI, LSC, relating the experiences of the *Commercial Appeal*'s Joseph Shapiro; "United League to Continue White Merchants Boycott," *JDN,* 5 October 1978, 1C, in United League Subject File, MDAH; Johanna Neuman, "Evers Credited with Bringing Both Sides Together in Tupelo Dispute," *CL,* 5 October 1978, 3A, in Tupelo Boycott, 1978 Subject File, MDAH; "League Pledges Support," *JDN,* 23 October 1978, 6A, in United League Subject File, MDAH; "League Seeks Backing from around the Country," *CL,* 27 October 1978, 5A, in United League Subject File, MDAH; "Tupelo March to Climax League Drive," *CL,* 27 October 1978, 6B, in United League Subject File, MDAH; Elizabeth Fair, "Visitors Join League March in Tupelo Civil Rights Rally," *CA,* 26 November 1978, NMI, LSC; "United League to Continue Fight on Alleged Bias," *JDN,* 27 November 1978, 7A, in United League Subject File, MDAH; David Comer, "Bulk of Marches from Out of State," *DJ,* 27 November 1978, NMI, LSC; "Tupelo: A Freedom Campaign," *Worker,* December 1978, NMI, LSC; "A Tale of Two Cities," *JA,* 21 December 1978, in United League Subject File, MDAH, contrasting then-peaceful Tupelo with Okolona; Johnson, "Below Tupelo's Calm, a Residue of Tension," *NYT,* 30 January 1979; "Racial Unrest Still Churning Despite Silence in Tupelo Streets," *CA,* 4 March 1979, 1B, in United League Subject File, MDAH; "Tactics Changes in Tupelo Unrest," *CL,* 5 March 1979, 3A, in United League Subject File, MDAH.

151. The United League traveled to Okolona shortly after law enforcement officials beat Wardell Ford, a local black youth, on 4 July 1978. Okolona saw an outbreak of violence that included two shoot-outs, one of which involved Okolona's United League leader Howard Gunn, who served as chairman of the NMRLS Board of Directors from 1978 to 1980, succeeding Wayne Johnson. See Elizabeth Fair, "March in Okolona by Blacks Is Quiet," *CA,* 6 August 1978, 1B, NMI, LSC; Fair, "Curfew Calms Tension in Okolona," *CA,* 15 August 1978, NMI, LSC; *NMRLS Notes,* September 1978, NMI, LSC; "Boycott Continues," *JDN,* 16 September 1978, 7A, in United League Subject File, MDAH; "Okolona School Boycott Enters Its Eighth Day," *JDN,* 20 September 1978, 6D, in United League Subject File, MDAH; "Marching Permit Requirement Approved by Okolona Council," *JDN,* 22 September 1978, 8A, in United League Subject File, MDAH; "Tale of Two Cities." One example of NMRLS's involvement in Okolona was the legal services attorneys' argument before Federal District Judge Orma Smith that a local justice of the peace could not unilaterally create an ordinance governing the carrying of concealed weapons by peaceful demonstrators. Smith accepted their argument, declaring the law "null, void and unconstitutional," saying the justice of the peace had no authority to legislate. *NMRLS Notes,* September 1978, NMI, LSC. As for the United League activity in Lexington, see Anne Wetzel, "4 Nuns among 11 Protesters Arrested in Lexington Boycott," *CL,* 27 August 1978, 1B, in Lexington, 1970 Subject File, MDAH; "150 Demonstrators Show Support for Lexington Business Boycott," *CL,* 3 September 1978, 3A, in Lexington, 1970 Subject File, MDAH; "Police Brutality in Lexington," *CL,* 10 September 1978, 1C, in Police Brutality Subject File, MDAH; "Holmes County United League Taking Complaints on Brutality," *JDN,* 11 September 1978, 1D, in United League Subject File, MDAH; "League Demands Lexington Firings—Vows Boycott through Winter," *CL,* 24 September 1978, 1B, in Lexington, 1970 Subject File, MDAH; "Nuns Evicted from Home in Lexington," *CL,* 25 September 1978, 3A, in Lexington, 1970 Subject File, MDAH; "Prayer Day Spurs Hope in Lexington," *CL,* 13 November 1978, 1B, in United League Subject File, MDAH; "Embattled United League Attorneys File Motion to Move Holmes County Suit to Federal Court," *CL,* 8 December 1978, 1B, in United League Subject File, MDAH; "League Plans to

Defy Lexington March Ban," *CL*, 15 December 1978, 3A, in United League Subject File, MDAH; "League Marches in Lexington Despite Court Order Prohibiting the Demonstration," *CL*, 17 December 1978, 1C; "United League Seeks Order to Prevent Enforcement of Lexington Protest Ban," *CL*, 19 December 1978, 1B, in United League Subject File, MDAH; "Judge Refuses to Block Lexington Demonstration Ban," *CL*, 20 December 1978, 1B; "United League Chapter Planning to Keep Fighting Demonstration Ban," *CL*, 21 December 1978, 2B, in United League Subject File, MDAH; "Blacks Plan to Defy Order by Marching," *CA*, 22 December 1978, 22, in Lexington, 1970 Subject File, MDAH. For other NMRLS–United League activities, see "United League Protests at Goodman," *JDN*, 16 November 1978, 11A; and "Rights Group Opens Office in Indianola," *CL*, 22 March 1979, 3B, both in United League Subject File, MDAH.

152. Myers outlined this plan at a United League meeting in Okolona on 5 August 1978. Fair, "March in Okolona."

153. The following articles documented United League activities in Okolona during 1979, including their inability to overturn a parade ordinance but also the sanctioning of a protest at Okolona schools by Federal District Judge William Keady. "200 March through Okolona," *CL*, 18 March 1979, 3A, in Okolona Subject File, MDAH; "3 Charged in Incident at Protest," *CL*, 19 March 1979, 3B, in Okolona Subject File, MDAH; "115 Rights Marchers Arrested in Okolona," *CA*, 15 April 1979, 1A, in Okolona Subject File, MDAH; "Parade Ordinances Raise Legal Questions," *CA*, 22 April 1979, 15B, in Okolona Subject File, MDAH; "Okolona March Leads to Arrest," *JDN*, 29 April 1979, 3B, in Okolona Subject File, MDAH; "Okolona Arrests Draw Lawsuit," *CL*, 1 May 1979, 2B, in Okolona Subject File, MDAH, documenting Myers's attempt to win $200,000 in damages for 177 protesters arrested during a march; "United League Can Hold Protest at Okolona Schools," *CL*, 17 May 1979, 7B, in United League Subject File, MDAH; "Special Prosecutor Requested for Probe of Inmate's Death," *CA*, 8 June 1979, 13B, in Okolona Subject File, MDAH; "Group Asks for Special Prosecutor," *CL*, 8 June 1979, 3A, in United League Subject File, MDAH; "March in Okolona Hot, Peaceful," *CL*, 10 June 1979, 3A, in Okolona Subject File, MDAH; "United League Petition Rejected," *CL*, 4 July 1979, 3B, in United League Subject File, MDAH, relating Judge Keady's decisions that he did not have jurisdiction over Okolona's parade ordinance and his refusal to issue an injunction to stop alleged acts of harassment by Chickasaw County law enforcement officers; Elizabeth Fair, "League's Legal Aid in Jeopardy," *CA*, 21 July 1979, 11B, in North Mississippi Rural Legal Services Subject File, MDAH, relating NMRLS's consideration of ending its representation of three hundred protesters on criminal charges in Okolona. United League activities generated far less press coverage elsewhere in the state during 1979. See "Judge Orders Delay in Suit over Boycott," *CA*, 16 January 1979, 3, in United League Subject File, MDAH.

154. This reveals much about some of North Mississippi's attorneys' perception of the law: NCBL was not a party to the "liberal legality" that undergirded much of the support for legal services but, rather, viewed the law much more critically. That NMRLS attorneys, notably Lewis Myers, joined with such a group suggested that they (rightly) perceived law as highly political in nature—and often construed so as to discriminate against the poor and minorities.

155. Summary of the Conference on the First Amendment Rights of Legal Workers—A People's Program under Attack, 24 November 1978, and Resolution Unanimously Adopted at Conference on the First Amendment Rights of Legal Workers, 24 November 1978, NMI, LSC; Candace Lee, "Legal Service Attorneys Meet to Discuss Free Speech Right," *CL*, 23 November 1978, 15B, NMI, LSC; "Rights Attorneys Warned of Continued Pressure," *CL*, 25 November 1978, 8A, in Legal Services Corporation and Legal Ser-

vices Coalition Subject File, MDAH. Many of the delegates then joined the United League march held the last weekend in November.

156. That the protesters were cynical about the LSC investigation was evidenced by the flyer announcing the 15 January 1979 demonstration. Above the caption, "LSC: Which Side Are They On?" was a picture of a man wearing a suit and Klan cap. The group was in Washington for a conference on the First Amendment Rights of People's Lawyers and Legal Workers held 14 January 1979 at Antioch Law School. Antioch Law School was the brainchild of legal services founders Jean and Edgar Cahn. The National Organization of Legal Services Workers, a nascent national union for legal services employees, expressed its support for Myers and NMRLS in "Legal Services Workers under Attack," 22 November 1978, in NMRLS Investigation Files, LSC. The flyers announcing the conference and demonstration are also located in NMI, LSC. "Legal Services Group Faces 400 Protesters," *CA*, 16 January 1979, 3, in Legal Services Corporation and Legal Services Coalition Subject File, MDAH.

157. Statement of Legal Services Corporation Regarding the Investigation of Complaints Against North Mississippi Rural Legal Services, 15 January 1979; and Thomas Ehrlich to Members of the Legal Services Community, 23 January 1979, NMI, LSC.

158. Wilhelm Joseph does not recall seeing a final report but only that the investigation "petered out." Wilhelm Joseph, interview by author. The quotations here are from the consultant's report, Memorandum, James E. Coleman Jr. to Stephen S. Walters, 14 February 1979, NMI, LSC. Coleman had been assistant general counsel at LSC but left the corporation in 1978. Acting General Counsel Stephen S. Walters's final report was, inexplicably, not located in the NMRLS Investigation Files but was reported by Elizabeth Fair, "Legal Services Found 'Blameless' in Report," *CA*, 6 March 1979, 13; and "NMRLS Charges Dropped," *JDN*, 6 March 1979, in North Mississippi Rural Legal Services Subject File, MDAH.

159. "Subversion Hinted in League-NMRLS Rift," *JA*, 5 July 1979, 1A.

160. Joseph, interview by author.

161. Fair, "Myers' Resignation from Post 'Will Be Blow,' Gunn Laments," *CA*, 18 July 1979, 13, in North Mississippi Rural Legal Services Subject File, MDAH. This report was not included in NMRLS Investigation Files, LSC. According to *Commercial Appeal* reporter Elizabeth Fair, whose article was based on interviews with Wilhelm Joseph and Howard Gunn, the report on NMRLS suggested that too much time had been devoted to league activities and that Myers, as director of litigation, had provided "too little supervision" to remedy this problem. Gunn and Joseph said the program would spend more time on other issues.

162. Elizabeth Fair, "League's Legal Aid in Jeopardy," *CA*, 21 July 1979, 11B; "Legal Service Group Aid in United League Efforts May Soon Have to Halt," *CL*, 22 July 1979, 3A; Fair, "Myers' Resignation."

163. McClellan, interview by author.

164. "United League Seeks Ouster of Legal Director," *CL*, 19 June 1980, 3B, in United League Subject File, MDAH.

165. In 1981 Robinson announced that the United League would no longer be used to effect social change but, rather, to serve as a vehicle for Islam. "Skip Robinson to Proselytize for Islam," *CL*, 25 March 1981, 4A. Robinson had become jaded about the prospects of bringing about change through protest and legal action. See "League resumes marches in Lexington," *CL*, 1 March 1980, 3A, and "United League Plans Tupelo Protest March," *CL*, 22 April 1980, 6B, in United League Subject File, MDAH. Both articles announced the resumption of protests after United League leaders expressed dismay over the cities' failure

to abide by agreements made in 1978 and 1979. Regarding Tupelo, Robinson said that city officials "haven't done what they said they would. I didn't believe them all along. The only way we can get things done is to bring black people together." See also "Profile: Black Leader Makes Anti-American Comments," *North Mississippi Times*, 27 December 1979, in Alfred "Skip" Robinson Subject File, MDAH. United League leaders did not disappear. See "United League Back in Good Graces," *JDN*, 23 February 1985, 1C; and "Group Speaks Out for Poor," *CL*, 17 September 1987, 1A, in United League Subject File, focusing on Arnett Lewis of Lexington, Miss., and his renaming the United League as the Rural Organizing and Cultural Center, Inc.

166. This perception sometimes got North Mississippi lawyers into trouble, as when District Judge William Keady, whom many legal services lawyers considered fair, assessed thirteen thousand dollars in court costs against NMRLS and threw out a claim of racial discrimination against the Calhoun County Hospital. It was the first time that a judge assessed such costs to a legal services program nationwide, but Keady felt the program's lawyers were acting in bad faith and found no evidence of racial discrimination. See "Judge: Agency Wasted Court's Time in Discrimination Suit," *CL*, 12 December 1978, 2B; "Legal Group Ordered to Pay Attorney Fees," *CL*, 19 November 1980, 3A; "Civil Rights Lawyers Fear Court Ruling," *CL*, 1 December 1980, 3A, in Legal Services Corporation and Legal Services Coalition Subject File, MDAH; Guy Mitchell Jr. to Roy Coleman, 11 May 1978, NMI, LSC.

167. Partial Transcript of Non-Jury Trial, 13 August 1980, in *Kelsey v. Killebrew,* Case File No. 78-33-MAC (M.D. Ga.), FRC.

168. Owens prodded the parties to settle the case, which they apparently did. The judge made it clear that he wanted the streets paved and sewer system installed, among other changes, and set a timetable for the city to make the changes. He did so without issuing an opinion. The case file does not, however, document the specifics of the final settlement. See *Kelsey v. Killebrew,* Case File No. 78-33-MAC (M.D. Ga.), FRC.

169. *Deriso v. Cooper,* 246 Ga. 540 at 543 (1980); see also decision at 245 Ga. 786 at 791 (1980).

170. The Tattnall County cases *Anderson v. Banks* and *Johnson v. Sikes* sought to prevent the local school board from maintaining its requirements that students receive a certain score on the California Achievement Test (CAT) in order to graduate. GLSP attorneys fashioned a variety of arguments against the test's imposition and eventually convinced Judge Newell Edenfield to suspend the requirement in 1983. Edenfield found a causal link between the school system's tracking system, established when the system desegregated under court order in the early 1970s, and the disproportional failure of African-American students to earn the score required to graduate. Thus, GLSP achieved part of its objective, halting the use of the CAT and winning high school diplomas for the students who had been denied them. But, when GLSP appealed to the Eleventh Circuit to have the court declare the system inherently flawed because of its tenuous relationship to the school curriculum, the justices were unwilling to go along with them, saying the issues were not "ripe" for appeal given that Tattnall County had yet to reinstitute the requirement. *Anderson v. Banks,* 520 F. Supp. 472 (S.D. Ga. 1981) and 540 F. Supp. 761 (S.D. Ga. 1982); and *Johnson v. Sikes,* 730 F.2d 644 (11th Cir. 1984).

171. *Georgia State Conference of Branches of NAACP v. State of Georgia,* 99 F.R.D. 16 (S.D. Ga. 1983), 570 F. Supp. 314 (S.D. Ga. 1983), 775 F.2d 1403 (11th Cir. 1985). GLSP filed another education case in 1978 dealing with the educational provisions for the mentally retarded. The program won relief in 1981 then spent much of the 1980s in an ultimately unsuccessful attempt to win attorneys' fees. *Georgia Association*

of Retarded Citizens v. McDaniel, 511 F. Supp. 1263 (N.D. Ga. 1981), granting relief; 716 F.2d 1565 (11th Cir. 1983), affirming; *McDaniel v. Georgia Association of Retarded Citizens*, 468 U.S. 1213 (1984), vacating judgment of Eleventh Circuit; *Georgia Association of Retarded Citizens v. McDaniel*, 740 F.2d 902 (11th Cir. 1984), amending previous decision, still in favor of plaintiffs; *McDaniel v. Georgia Association of Retarded Citizens*, 469 U.S. 1228 (1985), denying certiorari to McDaniel's appeal; *Georgia Association of Retarded Citizens v. McDaniel*, 855 F.2d 794 and 855 F.2d 805 (11th Cir. 1988), overturning district court's award of attorney's fees to GLSP; and, finally, *Georgia Association of Retarded Citizens v. McDaniel*, 490 U.S. 1090 (1989), denying certiorari on the issue of attorney's fees.

172. Zimring, interview by author. Zimring noted a couple of elements of the case that do not appear in the official records. First, he said the clients' councils, local and statewide, urged GLSP to pursue these education cases. Second, he remembered that LSC, then under the influence of the Reagan administration, investigated GLSP because involvement in the *NAACP* case might have violated the LSC Act's prohibition on legal services representation of clients in school desegregation cases. The investigation had no serious impact on GLSP.

173. Even then, Chambliss's involvement did not end. The settlement was for $503 million to be contributed to Mississippi's historically black colleges over a period of ten years. Chambliss felt this was insufficient, so he challenged the settlement (which was primarily an agreement between the United States Department of Justice and the state of Mississippi). He lost another job, his teaching position at Texas Southern University's Thurgood Marshall School of Law, claiming that the university was pressured to release him by politicians upset with his continued involvement in the *Ayers* case. "Attorney Loses Job, Blames Involvement with *Ayers* Settlement," *Black Issues in Higher Education*, 26 September 2002, 12.

174. *United State v. Fordice*, 505 U.S. 717 (1992); Osborne, interview by author; Pennington, interview by author; Sara Hebel, "A Pivotal Moment for Desegregation," *Chronicle of Higher Education*, 27 October 2000, A26.

175. Halpern, *On the Limits of the Law*, 279–80. See also Dennis Hutchinson's account of the case in *The Man Who Once Was Whizzer White: A Portrait of Justice Byron R. White* (New York: Free Press, 1998). Another scholar has criticized *Fordice* for encouraging the closure of the historically black institutions in order to achieve integration; he argues that the Court should have forced the state to increase funding to the black colleges. Alex M. Johnson Jr., "Bid Whist, Tonk, and *United States v. Fordice*: Why Integrationism Fails African-Americans Again," *California Law Review* 81 (1993): 1401.

176. Osborne, interview by author; Pennington, interview by author. It is revealing that by the time Chambliss argued and won the 1992 round before the Supreme Court, he was no longer working for North Mississippi Rural Legal Services. During the 1980s LSC had instructed the program that it could no longer allot resources to this time- and labor-consuming case; Chambliss refused to quit the case or to quit his job, and the program was forced to fire him. He subsequently moved to Houston to assume a teaching position at the Thurgood Marshall School of Law at Texas Southern University. Such tension between local programs and the national office became increasingly common during the 1980s and 1990s.

177. The connections had also frustrated civil rights activists during the late 1960s. Witness Martin Luther King Jr. transitioning from pressing for voting rights for southern blacks to focusing on poverty in northern cities such as Chicago. The Poor People's Campaign, which King was planning before his assassination and which occurred during the summer of 1968, represented the next stage of protest addressing

economic stratification. King and other civil rights activists never enjoyed the success in the economic sphere that they did with respect to equal rights for African Americans. See Foner, *Story of American Freedom*, 282–85, among the many who have documented this transition.

178. Cullen, interview by author, 19 March 1999.

179. Walbert, interview by author.

180. Zimring, interview by author.

181. Pennington, interview by author.

182. Laurie Moran argues, quite persuasively, that poverty lawyers would do well to increase their cooperation with community groups to encourage economic development. Noting that narrow litigation strategies failed to eradicate poverty, she supports the "self-help" of building businesses in low-income areas. Laurie A. Moran, "Legal Services Attorneys as Partners in Community Economic Development: Creating Wealth for Poor Communities through Cooperative Economics," *University of the District of Columbia Law Review* (Fall 2000): 125–76. See also Ann Southworth, "Business Planning for the Destitute? Lawyers as Facilitators in Civil Rights and Poverty Practice," *Wisconsin Law Review* (1996): 1121–69.

183. Halpern, *On the Limits of the Law*, 3.

184. Qtd. in Jack Greenberg, *Crusaders in the Courts: How a Dedicated Band of Lawyers Fought for the Civil Rights Revolution* (New York: Basic Books, 1994), 213. See also Payne, *I've Got the Light*, chap. 13. Payne suggests that civil rights activism shifted from grassroots organization to more centralized, "top-down" models by the late 1960s and 1970s. In particular he documents the decline of what he calls the "organizing tradition" among African-American activists. Whether poverty lawyers contributed to this decline is unclear. As will be evident in later pages, poverty lawyers often served as allies of community organizers. On the other hand, one might argue that the trend toward legal solutions was itself evidence of weakness within the organizing tradition; i.e., activists risked becoming dependent on legal experts to solve problems.

185. See Mark Tushnet, *Making Civil Rights Law: Thurgood Marshall and the Supreme Court, 1936–1961* (New York: Oxford University Press, 1994). See also Purcell, *Brandeis and the Progressive Constitution*.

186. McClellan, interview by author.

187. See, e.g., Franz Fanon, *The Wretched of the Earth* (New York: Grove Press, 1965).

188. Osborne, interview by author.

189. See Bartley, *New South*, 417–54, regarding changes in the southern economy; and Black and Black, *Politics and Society in the South*, 3–72.

190. Although the Warren Court gave some indications that it might require strict scrutiny of laws imposing wealth classifications, the Burger Court retreated from this approach in *San Antonio Independent School Dist. v. Rodriguez*, 411 U.S. 1 (1973). In *Rodriquez* the Court assessed San Antonio's method of financing its public schools through local property taxes. The plaintiffs, who were Mexican-American parents of children in one of San Antonio's school districts, argued that the scheme violated the equal protection rights of children residing in districts having a low property tax base. Spending between districts varied significantly despite an attempt by the Texas legislature to reduce this disparity through a "minimum foundation school program." Justice Powell delivered the opinion of the Court that this scheme did not involve a suspect classification, nor the fundamental interests, of the plaintiffs. Regarding the suspect classification analysis, the Court asserted that previous decisions that held wealth classifications to be suspect involved statutes that rendered someone completely unable to pay for a desired benefit (such as obtaining a divorce

in *Boddie*) and thus absolute deprivation of an opportunity to enjoy that benefit. As for whether education was a fundamental interest, the Court held that it was not because it was not explicitly or implicitly guaranteed in the Constitution. Without having to submit the San Antonio school financing scheme to strict scrutiny, the Court had only to determine whether the scheme bore some rational relationship to a legitimate state purpose. Finding that it did, the scheme was constitutional.

An earlier Supreme Court case, *James v. Valtierra*, 402 U.S. 137 (1971), similarly rebuffed an attempt to convince the Court to recognize wealth as a suspect classification. *James* involved a challenge to a California law that required a local referendum before a state agency could develop a "low rent housing project." In his dissenting opinion Justice Thurgood Marshall, joined by Brennan and Blackmun, asserted that the statute was an example of "invidious discrimination," "an explicit classification on the basis of poverty—a suspect classification which demands exacting judicial scrutiny." By the time of *Rodriguez*, in 1973, even Marshall in his dissent from that opinion had let go of this claim that wealth was as suspect a classification as race, and in *Harris v. McRae*, 448 U.S. 297 (1980), the majority stated that "this Court has held repeatedly that poverty, standing alone, is not a suspect classification." The practical effect of this opinion is to reduce equal protection analyses of statutes that appear to discriminate against the poor to a determination of whether the statutory framework bears a rational relationship to a legitimate state purpose. See, generally, Frank I. Michelman, "Foreword: On Protecting the Poor through the Fourteenth Amendment," *Harvard Law Review* 83 (November 1969): 7–59. Michelman emphasized that American society, and hence American law, accepted the market distribution of resources. Indeed, "the risk of exposure to markets and their 'decisions' is not normally deemed objectionable, to say the least, in our society. Not only do we not inveigh generally against unequal distribution of income or full-cost pricing for most goods. We usually regard it as both the fairest and most efficient arrangement to require each consumer to pay the full market price of what he consumes." Michelman, "On Protecting the Poor," 28.

191. See Lisa A. Keister, *Wealth in America: Trends in Wealth Inequality* (Cambridge: Cambridge University Press, 2000); Edward N. Wolff, *Top Heavy: The Increasing Inequality of Wealth in America and What Can Be Done about It* (New York: New Press, 2002); Bernadette D. Proctor and Joseph Dalaker, U.S. Bureau of the Census, *Poverty in the United States, 2002* (Washington, D.C.: Government Printing Office, 2003).

7. POVERTY LAW, POLITICS, AND THE RATIONING OF JUSTICE, 1981–1996

1. Gottlieb, interview by author, 17 December 1998; Askew, interview by author, 21 March 2000.

2. Dennis Goldstein, when asked to characterize the opposition to his ALAS cases, focused on this immediate opposition, noting especially the often bitter reaction of landlords to Legal Aid representation of tenants. Goldstein, interview by author, 21 January 1999.

3. John W. English, "The Legal Services Crisis," *AC*, 5 April 1981, mag. 26–34.

4. See chap. 4.

5. From an October 1980 statement reported in the *ABA Journal* (October 1980): 52, qtd. in Houseman and Dooley, "Legal Services History," chap. 4, 33 n. 4.

6. "Reagan Is Moving to End Program That Pays for Legal Aid to the Poor," *NYT*, 6 March 1981, 1A.

7. Meanwhile, Houseman and Dooley wrote, in "Legal Services History," chap. 4, 3, that Howard Phillips, whom Nixon had appointed to dismantle OEO in the early 1970s, had "revitalized" the National Defeat Legal Services Committee, joining with the Conservative Caucus. The conservative Heritage Foun-

dation compiled a report calling for the abolition of the LSC written by Alfred S. Regnery and entitled *Mandate for Leadership, Project Team Report, The Poverty Agencies: Community Services Administration, Legal Services Corporation, Action* (22 October 1980). See "Legal Services History," chap. 4, 34 n. 6.

8. Legal Services History," chap. 4, 4–6.

9. Ibid. Congress last reauthorized LSC during the Carter administration. As of this writing, Congress still has not reauthorized LSC.

10. The Carter administration had asked Congress for nearly $400 million for FY 1982. "Legal Services Corporation," *CQA* 37 (1981): 366–67; "Legal Services Corp. Kept Alive Temporarily," *CQA* 37 (1981): 412–14; "Legal Services Corporation," *CQA* 38 (1982): 372; "LSC Kept Alive; Reagan Board Unconfirmed," *CQA* 38 (1982): 412–13; "Legal Services History," chap. 4, 6–9.

11. These restrictions were copied from the reauthorization bills that remained stalled in Congress. See Pub. L. 97-377 (21 December 1982) and Pub. L. 98-166 (28 November 1983); "Legal Services History," chap. 4, 7–8.

12. Wolfgang Saxon, "Legal Aid Agency Limits Its Funding," *NYT*, 2 January 1982, 9A; "Legal Services History," chap. 4, 9; Askew, interview by author, 21 March 2000; Houseman interview.

13. "Legal Services History," chap. 4, 10 and 43 n. 61; Askew, interview by author, 21 March 2000; Lyons, interview by author; Stuart Taylor Jr., "Legal Aid Executive Quits, Citing Differences with Reagan's Board," *NYT*, 3 December 1982, 18A, about Clint Lyons; Houseman, interview by author.

14. Askew, interview by author, 21 March 2000; Lyons, interview by author; Phil Gailey, "Homosexual Takes Leave of a Job and of an Agony," *NYT*, 31 March 1982, 24A, reporting on Bradley's leaving LSC and relief at not having to hide his sexual preference any longer.

15. Askew, interview by author, 21 March 2000.

16. "Legal Services History," chap. 4, p. 7. The history of Reagan's appointees is quite complicated. None of his forty-four board nominees gained confirmation by the Republican-controlled Senate until June 1985, primarily because of the nominees' apparent opposition to legal services (chap. 4, 13).

17. Ibid., chap. 4, 13–14.

18. Advocates of Legal Services, *An American Institution: The Legal Services Corporation* (N.p.: Advocates of Legal Services, 1981).

19. "Legal Services History," chap. 4, 14; Editorial Opinion and Comment, "Legal Services," *ABAJ* 67 (April 1981): 390; Thomas Ehrlich, "Save the Legal Services Corporation," *ABAJ* 67 (April 1981): 434–37; Askew, interview by author, 21 March 2000. See also Denton, "The LSC Survival Campaign," in Hatch et al., *Legal Services Corporation*, for a critical discussion of this campaign.

20. Under the LSC Act the corporation could not "undertake to influence the passage or defeat of any legislation by the Congress of the United States or by any State or local legislative bodies, *except that* personnel of the Corporation may testify or make other appropriate communication (A) when formally requested to do so by a legislative body, a committee, or a member thereof, or (B) *in connection with legislation or appropriations directly affecting the activities of the Corporation*" (emph. added). 42 U.S.C. §2996, Sec. 1006(c)(2). While legal services employees could not engage in certain prohibited political activities, they did not include legislative lobbying until Congress added further restrictions in 1983. See 42 U.S.C. §2996, Sec. 1006(b)(5); Orrin G. Hatch, "Myth and Reality at the Legal Services Corporation," in Hatch et al., *Legal Services Corporation*, 15. In fact, in *The Robber Barons of the Poor?* none of the authors support their

arguments that the LSC staff had actually violated the law by pointing to the LSA Act itself or LSC regulations. Isaac takes issue with the LSC staff's "creative" interpretation of the act's restrictions but suggests only that, in adopting such an interpretation, they fostered a "disobedience" to the law that was counter to the intentions of those who founded and supported legal services. This point, of course, is arguable. See Rael Jean Isaac, "Bringing Down the System through 'Training'—The LSC Manuals and Training Materials," in Hatch et al., *Legal Services Corporation*, 109–10. None of the other authors offered a detailed examination of the LSC Act itself, much less an argument based on the act.

21. Jeremiah Denton, "The LSC Survival Campaign: Manipulating against the Mandate," in Hatch et al., *Legal Services Corporation*, 21–22.

22. Orrin G. Hatch, "Myth and Reality at the Legal Services Corporation," in Hatch et al., *Legal Services Corporation*, 16.

23. Ibid., 16, 18. Like most politicians, Hatch believed that "there is justification for using federal funds to help poor citizens with their genuine legal needs" and "there is also justification for insuring that no citizen is denied access to our judicial system simply due to economic standing." "But," he continued, "there is no legal, moral or logical authority for having the federal government fund the political ambitions of a handful of self-appointed leaders of a movement so hidden that even the Congress has no idea what it is underwriting" (12).

24. Qtd. in ibid., 10; and Denton, "LSC Survival Campaign," 38. They quote a Transcript of Legal Services Corporation Meeting of Project Directors in Denver, Colo., January 1981, 5. At a GLSP conference held to plan for the "survival campaign," Houseman reportedly said: "Many social benefit and entitlement programs that have developed during the 1960s and 1970s to provide concrete benefits to poor people are threatened. We must continue to use our resources and energies to increase social benefits, improve housing and health care, prevent arbitrary private and public actions, improve job and educational opportunities, and eliminate discrimination." Qtd. in John W. English, "The Legal Services Crisis," *AC*, 5 April 1981, mag. 26–34.

25. Lucie White, "Specially Tailored Legal Services Programs for Low-Income Persons in the Age of Wealth Inequality: Pragmatism or Capitulation?" *Fordham Law Review* 67 (April 1999): 2576. While I agree with this assessment, I disagree with White's acceptance of the terms of the debate. She suggests that the debate over legal services is best understood within the context of the debate over the nature of welfare states in modern industrial societies. As should be clear from the following discussion, I believe this focus inhibits our understanding of the role of legal assistance programs for the poor within societies based on the rule of law. White's ultimate conclusion, however, is an intriguing suggestion for the future of legal services for the poor. She answers the question posed in the title of her article by suggesting that specialized legal services for the poor is a necessary, pragmatic response; i.e., as an incremental step toward equal justice, we might do well to accept a less-than-elite level of legal counsel in exchange for broader coverage of legal assistance programs.

26. Joan Mahoney, "Green Forms and Legal Aid Offices: A History of Publicly Funded Legal Services in Britain and the United States," *Saint Louis University Public Law Review* 17 (1998), 223, 226–29; Abel, "Law without Politics."

27. Abel, "Law without Politics," 544. See Nick Huls, "From Pro Deo Practice to Subsidized Welfare State Provision: Twenty-Five Years of Providing Legal Services to the Poor in the Netherlands," 5 *Maryland*

Journal of Contemporary Legal Issues 5 (1994): 333. Some form of government financing prevails throughout the West: in the Netherlands since 1957, Canada (beginning in Ontario) since 1967, France and Sweden since 1972, Finland since 1973, Australia since 1974, and Germany since 1981. See also Robert J. Rhudy, "Comparing Legal Services to the Poor in the United States with Other Western Countries: Some Preliminary Lessons," *Maryland Journal of Contemporary Legal Issues* 5 (1994): 223–46.

28. Congress has implemented programs, such as Medicare and Medicaid, that utilize market forces to deliver services to a target population. For a proposal in the context of legal services, see Andrea J. Saltzman, "Private Bar Delivery of Legal Services to the Poor: A Design for a Combined Private Attorney and Staffed Office Delivery System," *Hastings Law Journal* 34 (1983): 1165. Other scholars have stressed that the staff model should, if it continues to exist, join more closely with community institutions or even cede control to community groups. See Raymond H. Brescia, Robin Golden, and Robert A. Solomon, "Who's in Charge Anyway? A Proposal for Community-Based Legal Services," *Fordham Urban Law Journal* 25 (Summer 1998): 831–63; Moran, "Legal Services Attorneys as Partners."

29. Stephen Labaton, "Back from the Brink, the Legal Services Corporation Discovers It's in Danger Again," *NYT,* 31 March 1996, 28A.

30. NMRLS, *30th Year Reunion* (NMRLS, 1997), in author's possession.

31. Gottlieb reported that the society did not have to lay off lawyers; it simply did not hire replacements when staff members left. The cut may have been less deleterious for the ALAS because 25 percent of the society's funding came from sources other than LSC, a higher proportion than most other Deep South programs. "Legal Aid Office Closing Dec. 10," *AC,* 8 December 1981, 9A; Charles P. Smith-Williams, "Reagan Proposal Will Cripple Legal Aid for Poor, Agencies Warn," *AC,* 14 May 1981, 5C; Steve Gottlieb, interview, 17 December 1998.

32. English, "The Legal Services Crisis," *AC,* 5 April 1981, mag. 26–34; GLSP, *20th Anniversary,* 3; Cromartie, interview by author. The GLSP was still the largest program in the Deep South, with 175 people on staff after the Reagan cuts.

33. Gottlieb, interview by author, 17 December 1998.

34. Keith, interview by Cain.

35. See Martha Bergmark, interview by Harrison McIver, 28 July 1992, St. Petersburg, Fla., videotape at NEJL, discussing her leadership of Southeast Mississippi Legal Services.

36. McClellan, interview by author.

37. Gottlieb, interview by author, 17 December 1998. Gottlieb suggested that ALAS lawyers might have become better qualified, on average, after the Reagan cuts as a result of more selective hiring procedures and training.

38. He has since returned to the legal profession. Baird, interview by author.

39. Campbell, interview by author. See also Powell, interview by author, for another figure who left poverty law practice as a result, at least in part, of the Reagan cuts.

40. Friedman, *American Law,* 486, mentions the rising cost of legal education; increasingly, "students typically began their legal careers with a big burden of debt."

41. Stephen Wizner, "Can Law Schools Teach Students to Do Good? Legal Education and the Future of Legal Services for the Poor," *New York City Law Review* 3 (Summer 2000): 259–66.

42. On the turnover problem generally, a problem that preceded these political developments, see Jack

Katz, "Lawyers for the Poor in Transition: Involvement, Reform, and the Turnover Problem in the Legal Services Program," *Law and Society Review* 12 (1978): 286–97.

43. The Atlanta bar had a long history of supporting the society in word if not in deed; bar leaders had, after all, been instrumental in the organization's founding and development since 1924. Gottlieb is adamant that this response to budget cuts has made the society a much stronger, more stable institution. That first LSC grant came in the early 1980s in the midst of the corporation staff's "survival campaign." In Gottlieb's words the staff also "saw the handwriting on the wall" and was trying to encourage programs to nourish other sources of support. The society's strategies propelled Gottlieb into a leadership role among legal services programs seeking alternative sources of funding. Gottlieb, interview by Leanna Gipson, 22 July 1991, St. Petersburg, Fla., videotape at NEJL; and interview by author, 17 December 1998.

44. The Georgia Bar Foundation and State Bar of Georgia Campaign for Georgia Legal Services contributed over $1.1 million to the GLSP in 1996, or 14.6 percent of the program's budget. That same year GLSP received a gift of $1 million to establish an endowment administered by the Georgia Legal Services Foundation. Other major sources of funding included contracts for services to the elderly and the Georgia Department of Community Affairs; lesser sources, which totaled nearly a half-million dollars, included the cities of Augusta and Savannah; Christ Church of Savannah; United Way of Camden County and Glynn County; United Way of the Coastal Empire; Glynn County Board of Commissioners; Christian Renewal Ministries; Georgia Department of Human Resources; attorneys' fees; Stuckey Timberland, Inc.; and others. GLSP, *Annual Report, 1996*. Other programs developed similar, if less substantial, relationships with the private bar. Note the work of Phyllis Thornton in Mississippi. Thornton moved to Mississippi to head the state bar's pro bono program during the mid-1980s. Phyllis Thornton, interview by Victor Geminiani, 23 July 1992, St. Petersburg, Fla., videotape, NEJL.

45. Compared to other states, Mississippi and Alabama had the lowest percentage of non-LSC funding for their legal services programs. In Georgia 41 percent of funding for the ALAS and GLSP combined came from non-LSC sources. Center for Law and Social Policy, "Legal Services Funding," [n.d., late 1990s], in author's possession. As of the early 1990s, North Central Alabama Legal Services, e.g., enjoyed virtually no non-LSC funding; the program had lost state funding, and conservative Huntsville businessmen on the United Way board blocked that source of funding, leaving only attorneys' fees as alternatives to the LSC. Keith, interview by Cain.

46. See GLSP, *1995 Annual Report*, and *1996 Annual Report*. This diversification was not uniform, however. Dennis Goldstein pointed out that, due to budget limitations, ALAS eliminated its community education specialist, a position that had existed since the 1960s and helped publicize the society and provide modest preventative advice. Goldstein, interview, 21 January 1999.

47. ALAS had experimented with such programs as early as the 1960s, when it received a grant to fund Golden Age Legal Aid, but not until the Senior Citizens Law Project was such an initiative made a permanent part of institution. Often this occurred when the society received funding from one or more organizations to provide services to such a specified group. ALAS had, of course, long been organized into divisions dealing with broader areas of law such as family, housing, or consumer law. See ALAS, *Annual Report, 1969, Annual Report, 1976;* and *Annual Report, 1979*.

48. Kilgore, interview by author.

49. Gottlieb, interview by author, 17 December 1998.

50. Burge, interview by author. For discussion of how these issues affected other programs, see Kilgore, interview by author.

51. ALAS, *Annual Report, 1979*; Dokson, interview by author. Dokson left the ALAS in July, 1980.

52. Houseman and Dooley, "Legal Services History," chap. 4, 18–20.

53. Keith, interview by Cain; Kilgore, interview by author.

54. Houseman and Dooley, "Legal Services History," chap. 4, 20–31, esp. 20–24. The tension between the LSC and its grantees was not entirely new, of course; there had always been a lack of clarity about the relationship between Washington bureaucrats and field programs, as there had between program leaders and staff attorneys. See chap. 3.

55. McClellan, interview by author. McClellan recalled that from 1975 to 1990 "the major changes I saw involved the restrictions that were imposed by Congress as far as what legal services could and could not do. The first four or five years I was with the program, we pretty much operated under the same guidelines or restrictions as any other lawyer in private practice, meaning that we could do for our clients whatever a private lawyer could do for a paying client. There were not restrictions as far as the types of cases we could take on." Prior to McClellan's selection as the program's director, North Mississippi had experienced more than its share of internal strife as a result of bureaucratic limitations, beginning with the LSC's investigation of the Tupelo conflict and the departure of Lewis Myers.

56. Askew, interview by author, 21 March 2000.

57. McClellan, interview by author.

58. Keith, interview by Cain; Bergmark, interview by McIver, discussing Mississippi programs. Bergmark was particularly critical of the Mississippi programs' timidity by the 1990s. Bergmark, interview by author.

59. GLSP, *20th Anniversary*, 8.

60. GLSP, *1994 Annual Report*, 1; and *1995 Annual Report*, 2.

61. Gottlieb explained why he believed he was a good leader of the ALAS: "I'm very good at taking advantage of a situation. I'm opportunistic. And I think the way the program has developed . . . is not because I've had any grand scheme, but because there have been opportunities that have presented themselves to me, and they relate to funding or they relate to . . . having people who have a particular vision. And I'm smart enough to know that these are good people who have a valuable thing they can contribute. So out of that has grown things like the AIDS Project, Bill Brennan's work with predatory lending, Sue Jamieson on mental health. I'm smart enough to know that when we've got somebody who's passionate and I think can do a good job, that we can take advantage of that." Gottlieb, interview by author, 17 December 1998.

62. See Brennan, interview by author, 11 November 1998; Goldstein, interview by author, 19 and 21 January 1999; the series of articles by Bill Dedman entitled "The Color of Money" that began with "Atlanta Blacks Losing in Home Loans Scramble," *AC*, 1 May 1988, 1A; Dedman, "Despite 'Good Citizen' Image, Trust Company Finds Itself in a Battle," *AC*, 3 May 1988, 14A. Dedman won a Pulitzer Prize for the series. According to Brennan and Goldstein, they helped Dedman compile the data for the articles. Most of the banks changed their lending practices, among other things, although some were more willing than others to make such changes.

63. *Olmstead v. L.C. by Zimring*, 527 U.S. 581 (1999).

64. GLSP also represented men and women involuntarily committed to state mental health facilities after criminal trials in which juries acquitted them by reason of insanity. Similar to their work on behalf of J.L. and J.R., children committed by their guardians, GLSP attorneys hoped to establish a process by which these individuals could challenge their continued incarceration. The case was *Benham v. Edwards*, 501 F. Supp. 1050 (N.D. Ga. 1980) and 678 F.2d 511 (5th Cir. 1982); *Ledbetter v. Benham*, 463 U.S. 1222 (1980), granting certiorari and vacating Fifth Circuit decision in light of *Jones v. United States*, 463 U.S. 1222 (1983); *Benham v. Edwards*, 719 F.2d 772 (1983), remanding case to district court; and *Benham v. Ledbetter*, 609 F. Supp. 125 (1985), finding in light of *Jones v. United States* that Georgia's scheme was constitutional. See chap. 3 for discussion of similar Community Legal Services cases.

65. Barry Powell cited these changes as a reason for his return to private practice shortly after Reagan's election. Powell, interview by author. See, generally, Feldman, "Political Lessons," 1606: "the experience of representing the poor could be relentlessly demanding, frustrating far more than satisfying, and downright painful. Hard work and good intentions exerted little influence on case outcomes and did not diminish the staggering need for service. Occasional victories quickly evaporated. Tension and disappointment filled daily practice life far more than gratification and accomplishment."

66. GLSP, *20th Anniversary*, 4; Goldstein, interview by author, 21 January 1999.

67. Cromartie, interview by author, 16 March 1999. See also Rev. John Cromartie, Fr. Fred Kammer, and Ashley Wiltshire, "Spirituality and Legal Services?" *Management Information Exchange* (November 1994): 10–13.

68. Stephen Labaton, "Back from the Brink, the Legal Services Corporation Discovers It's in Danger Again," *NYT*, 31 March 1995, 28A.

69. Pear, "As Welfare Overhaul Looms, Legal Aid for Poor Dwindles," *NYT*, 5 September 1995, 1A. Likewise, Republicans Dan Burton and Bob Dornan complained that legal services lawyers "file lawsuits advancing a political agenda" and believed private groups could handle the legal problems of the poor. Dan Burton and Robert K. Dornan, letter to editor, *NYT*, 22 July 1996, 18A.

70. Pear, "As Welfare Overhaul Looms"; Labaton, "Back from the Brink."

71. Some scholars have approached this problem by discussing "poverty law advocacy as a medium of storytelling" and focusing on the ways in which attorneys and the legal process itself altered the meaning of clients' descriptions of their experiences and problems. "The daily turbulence of practice compels a discomfiting method of storytelling. Stories must be quickly heard, interpreted, and translated. Much of the client's story may be lost in the hurried acts of listening and retelling." Alfieri, "Reconstructive Poverty Law Practice," 2110 n. 9.

72. See, generally, Judith Resnik and Emily Bazelon, "Legal Services: Then and Now," *Yale Law and Policy Review* 17 (1998): 291–303.

73. LSC, *1996 Annual Report* (LSC, 1996), 3–5.

74. Gottlieb, interview by Gipson.

75. The Supreme Court has held that this restriction violates the First Amendment free speech rights of legal services attorney and their clients. *Legal Services Corp. v. Velazquez*, 121 S.Ct. 1043 (2001). It is unclear as of yet what effect this will have on legal services practice or the welfare reforms (which by 2001 were six years old). These restrictions applied not only to federal funds but also to most state, local, and

private funding utilized by LSC grantees. LSC, *1996 Annual Report*, 5. LSC imposed a "physical separation requirement" that authorizes LSC grantees to use non-LSC funds but only if they established a separate office with a separate executive director, separate staff, and separate equipment. 45 C.F.R. 1610.8; Memorandum and Order, *Dobbins v. LSC*, No. 97-CV-182 (E.D.N.Y., 20 December 2004). Congress also directed LSC to allow other entities to compete for LSC grants and to suggest priorities to local programs. At least one commentator has suggested that the various restrictions may be unconstitutional: J. Dwight Yoder, "Note: Justice or Injustice for the Poor? A Look at the Constitutionality of Congressional Restrictions on Legal Services," *William and Mary Bill of Rights Journal* 6 (Summer 1998): 827–83.

76. Over 95 percent of the work in which poverty lawyers had engaged prior to the restrictions could continue after the restrictions were in place. Alan W. Houseman and Linda E. Perle, Report prepared for the Center for Law and Social Policy, "What Still Can Be Done: Representation of Clients by LSC Recipients," 2 December 1997. See, more generally, LSC, *1996 Annual Report*.

77. This was in part a result of, as Todd Gitlin called it, the "twilight of common dreams" within the American Left, but also is related to an independently resurgent Right. See Todd Gitlin, *The Twilight of Common Dreams: Why America Is Wracked by Culture Wars* (New York: Henry Holt, 1995), esp. 223–37. Gitlin focuses on the divisive effect of identity politics, including white men's growing affinity for the Republican Party (233).

78. See Feldman, "Political Lessons."

79. These statistics are included in Legal Services Corporation, *Budget Request for Fiscal Year 2005* (Washington, D.C.: Legal Services Corporation, 2004), except for the inflation adjusted figures, which are based on statistics in this budget request.

80. ABA president Michael S. Greco delivered an address to the Alabama Law Foundation when he was president-elect urging lawyers to redouble their pro bono efforts and public service. He went further to promote a civil counterpart to the *Gideon* decision that would recognize a right to counsel in certain civil cases. His belief was that "the time has come for us to recognize, finally, that a poor person, whether facing either a serious criminal or civil matter, must have access to counsel if that person is to receive justice." Specifically, there should be a "right to counsel" in "matters where a poor person's family, sustenance, health or housing are threatened by a legal problem." Furthermore, "Such critically important assistance should not be measured out by the teaspoonful. . . . It should be available to all who qualify." Pro bono and public services efforts were necessary, but Greco also urged his audience to support adequate funding for LSC. Michael S. Greco, "An Address to the Fellows of the Alabama Law Foundation Annual Dinner," 28 January 2005 (on file with the Brennan Center for Justice at the NYU School of Law).

81. See Mauricio Vivero, "From 'Renegade' Agency to Institution of Justice: The Transformation of the Legal Services Corporation," *Fordham Urban Law Journal* 29 (February 2002): 1323–48.

82. Talbot "Sandy" D'Alemberte, "Tributaries of Justice: The Search for Full Access," *Florida State University Law Review* 25 (Spring 1998): 631–53. D'Alemberte discusses Johnson's multi-lane highway metaphor (631–32).

83. See the adverse Supreme Court decision, *Phillips v. Washington Legal Foundation*, 524 U.S. 156 (1998), holding that interest income generated by funds held in IOLTA accounts is the private property of the owner of the principle; and then *Brown v. Legal Foundation of Washington*, 538 U.S. 216 (2003), holding that, although the IOLTA plan in question constituted a "taking" for "public use" under the Fifth Amend-

ment, no payment of "just compensation" was required because nothing of value was taken from the owners of the principle, since it would cost more to distribute the interest than the amount of interest earned. Like many recent Supreme Court cases, the *Brown* decision was five to four.

84. Melanie D. Acevedo, "Client Choices, Community Values: Why Faith-Based Legal Services Providers Are Good for Poverty Law," *Fordham Law Review* 70 (March 2002): 1491–1534.

85. Leigh Goodmark, "Can Poverty Lawyers Play Well with Others? Including Legal Services in Integrated, School-Based Service Delivery Programs," *Georgetown Journal on Fighting Poverty* 4 (Spring 1997): 243–67.

86. Linda Zazove, "The *Cy Pres* Doctrine and Legal Services for the Poor: Using Undistributed Class Action Funds to Improve Access to Justice" (2001). Zazove suggests that lawyers negotiating class action settlements should specifically provide for the direct payment of residual funds to civil legal assistance programs in settlement agreements.

87. *In re Amendments to Rules Regulating the Florida Bar 1–3.1(a) and Rules of Judicial Administration 2.065 (Legal Aid)*, 573 So.2d 800, at 806 (Fla. Sup. Ct. 1990). See also the Florida Supreme Court's adoption of a comprehensive plan, *In re Amendments to Rules Regulating the Florida Bar 1–3.1(a) and Rules of Judicial Administration 2.065 (Legal Aid)*, 630 So.2d 501 (Fla. Sup. Ct. 1993); D'Alemberte, "Tributaries of Justice." For a discussion of the possibility of amending legal ethics requirements to promote the provision of legal services to the poor, see Bruce A. Green, "Foreword: Rationing Lawyers: Ethical and Professional Issues in the Delivery of Legal Services to Low-Income Clients," *Fordham Law Review* 67 (April 1999): 1713–48; Ronald H. Silverman, "Conceiving a Lawyer's Legal Duty to the Poor," *Hofstra Law Review* 19 (Summer 1991): 885–1111. See, generally, Alan W. Houseman, "Civil Legal Assistance for Low-Income Persons: Looking Back and Looking Forward," *Fordham Urban Law Journal* 29 (February 2002): 1213–43.

88. Campbell, interview by author.

89. "Legal Services Survives, Barely," *NYT*, 6 May 1996, 14A.

90. Friedman, "Rights of Passage," 665.

91. Audre Lorde, *Sister Outsider: Essays and Speeches* (Trumansburg, N.Y.: Crossing Press, 1984), 110. Lorde warned that the master's tools can "never" be used to dismantle the master's house.

92. See, e.g., the works of Piven and Cloward.

93. The term *civilizing* in this context is Katz's, from *Poor People's Lawyers in Transition*, 182–83. Alexis de Tocqueville wrote that Americans, like most citizens of democracies, "love change but they dread revolutions." *Democracy in America* (New York: Random House, Vintage Books, 1954), 2:270.

94. English, "The Legal Services Crisis," *AC*, 5 April 1981, mag. 26–34.

95. McIver went on to explain why legal services was controversial by saying, "when you're trying to change a system that disfavored poor and minority people, that's where the problem comes in." This comment suggests that McIver believed that poverty lawyers were somehow in, but not of, the legal culture. McIver, interview by author, 1998.

96. McClellan, interview by author.

97. 42 U.S.C. §2996 Sec. 1001(4). Uslaner suggested "that people are more likely to obey laws and pay taxes if they believe that laws are enforced fairly and if people trust government." Uslaner, *Moral Foundations*, 44.

98. See Uslaner, *Moral Foundations*, 44, noting that "trust in government is contingent." The legal system itself is essential to American democracy and the rule of law. As John Norton Moore has pointed out, "the rule of law inevitably requires a healthy and robust legal profession," including "a tradition of understanding and protection for the lawyer's role in representing unpopular as well as popular clients and causes." "The Rule of Law: An Overview," Paper presented to the Seminar on the Rule of Law 21, Moscow and Leningrad, USSR, 19–23 March 1990. A vibrant legal profession is essential to the rule of law because it facilitates and strengthens an independent judiciary, which helps protect the constitutional and other legal rights of the people, especially vis-à-vis governing authorities (10–18).

99. Hand's address took place on 16 February 1951. James B. Simpson, comp., *Simpson's Contemporary Quotations* (Boston: Houghton Mifflin, 1988), no. 1533.

APPENDIX

1. Sources for the data used to create the explanatory variables include: U.S. Bureau of the Census, *Congressional District Data Book, 93rd Congress (A Statistical Abstract Supplement)* (1973); and U.S. Bureau of the Census, *Statistical Abstract of the United States, 1974* (1974).

2. ACU's statement of principles is available at *Statement of Principles* (n.d.), at http://www .conservative.org/acucontents/about/principles.shtml (visited 22 November 2002). The group's ratings and vote preferences are available at *Annual Rating of Congress* (n.d.), at http://www.acuratings.com (visited 22 November 2002).

3. 119 *Cong. Rec.* 20717-23 (1973).

4. 119 *Cong. Rec.* 20736-40 (1973).

5. 119 *Cong. Rec.* 20746-47 (1973).

6. Albert H. Quie, Testimony before the House of Representatives, 21 June 1973, 119 *Cong. Rec.* 20736; Alphonzo Bell, Testimony before the House of Representatives, 21 June 1973, 119 *Cong. Rec.* 20736-37.

7. See tables 1 and 4.

Selected Bibliography

T HE fate of the Legal Services Corporation's official records is a story in itself. Many records perished during the 1980s and early 1990s, when the LSC board pored over them to determine whether local programs had violated the federal statutes governing poverty law practice. After storing these records for some time, apparently at a facility in northern Virginia, LSC either destroyed or lost most of them. Present-day LSC archivists know of no other records than those that exist at LSC, which include some useful material—especially regarding North Mississippi Rural Legal Services (NMRLS)—but do not include program reports or any examination of the actual work of legal services programs during the 1960s or 1970s. LSC did provide me with annual reports that surveyed the work of the national organization.

Local programs provided a different set of difficulties in researching the past work of poverty lawyers. These programs were not required to keep records for historical use and during the 1960s and 1970s kept very little internal documentation. Some of them produced reports of varying quality. The Georgia Legal Services Program (GLSP), for example, produced a monthly newsletter during the late 1970s, and Atlanta Legal Aid Society (ALAS) issued annual reports during the 1960s and 1970s (although I have not been able to locate one for every year, I found some at the Atlanta History Center and others at ALAS itself). North Mississippi Rural Legal Services produced a newsletter as well, but I have located only one of them, and the Legal Services Corporation of Alabama (LSCA) also produced annual reports during the late 1970s. These documents were quite helpful, and I owe a special debt of gratitude to Steve Gottlieb of ALAS, Phyllis Holmen of GLSP, and Sam Davenport of LSCA for making these materials available to me. Several individuals provided me with copies of documents in their personal files, including Barry Powell, John Cromartie, and Michael Trister. Unfortunately, legal services programs have either not kept case files from their early years, or, if they did, I was generally unable to see them because they remain protected by the attorney-client privilege. Thus, for information on cases and clients I relied primarily on published reports (including those in the *Clearinghouse Review*), newspaper articles, and official case records. The most severe limitation this placed upon the research was the difficulty of exploring cases that did not leave such records behind, including the vast majority of legal services cases from divorces to public benefits claims. Hopefully, the oral interviews help fill this gap in the documentary record.

SELECTED DOCUMENTS AND FILES

Atlanta Legal Aid Society. *Annual Report, 1963.* Atlanta: ALAS, 1964. ALAS, AHC.

———. *Annual Report, 1966.* Atlanta: ALAS, 1967. ALAS, AHC.

———. *Annual Report, 1967.* Atlanta: ALAS, 1968. ALAS, AHC.

———. *Annual Report, 1969.* Atlanta: ALAS, 1970. ALAS.

———. *Annual Report, 1972.* Atlanta: ALAS, 1973. ALAS, AHC.

———. *Annual Report, 1975.* Atlanta: ALAS, 1976. ALAS, AHC.

———. *Annual Report, 1976.* Atlanta: ALAS, 1977. ALAS, AHC.

———. *Annual Report, 1977.* Atlanta: ALAS, 1978. ALAS.

———. *Annual Report, 1978.* Atlanta: ALAS, 1979. ALAS, AHC.

———. *Annual Report, 1979.* Atlanta: ALAS, 1980. ALAS, AHC.

———. *Annual Report, 1980.* Atlanta: ALAS, 1981. ALAS, AHC.

———. *Annual Report, 1981.* Atlanta: ALAS, 1982. ALAS.

"Atlanta Legal Aid Society History." Atlanta: ALAS, [1974]. ALAS, AHC.

Georgia Department of Family and Children Services. *Adding Hope to Help II: Annual Report of the Georgia Department of Family and Children Services.* Atlanta: Department of Family and Children Services, 1969.

———. *Time of Change and Reform: Annual Report of the Georgia Department of Family and Children Services.* Atlanta: Department of Family and Children Services, 1971.

Georgia Legal Services Program. *20th Anniversary.* Atlanta: GLSP, 1991. GLSP.

———. *Annual Report, 1972.* Atlanta: GLSP, 1972. In author's possession.

———. *Annual Report, 1993.* Atlanta: GLSP, 1994. GLSP.

———. *Annual Report, 1994.* Atlanta: GLSP, 1995. GLSP.

———. *Annual Report, 1995.* Atlanta: GLSP, 1996. GLSP.

———. *Annual Report, 1996.* Atlanta: GLSP, 1997. GLSP.

———. "Directory of Reported Decisions and Unreported Decisions with Ongoing Impact." Atlanta: GLSP, December 1988. GLSP.

———. *The First Decade: A Special Report.* Atlanta: GLSP, 1981. GLSP.

———. *Toward Justice.* Atlanta: GLSP, 1984. GLSP.

Henry, Aaron Subject File, MDAH.

Legal Services Corporation. *Annual Report, 1976.* Washington, D.C.: LSC, 1976. LSC.

———. *Annual Report, 1977.* Washington, D.C.: LSC, 1977. LSC.

———. *Annual Report, 1978.* Washington, D.C.: LSC, 1978. LSC.

———. *Annual Report, 1979.* Washington, D.C.: LSC, 1979. LSC.

———. *Annual Report, 1980.* Washington, D.C.: LSC, 1980. LSC.

———. *Annual Report, 1981.* Washington, D.C.: LSC, 1981. LSC.

———. *Annual Report, 1996.* Washington, D.C.: LSC, 1996. LSC.

Legal Services Corporation of Alabama. *The First Year.* Montgomery, Ala.: LSCA, 1979. LSCA.

———. *What You Should Know about Legal Services.* Montgomery, Ala.: LSCA, 1980. LSCA.

———. *A Report.* Montgomery, Ala.: LSCA, 1981. LSCA.

Legal Services Corporation and Legal Services Coalition Subject File, MDAH.

Lexington, 1970 Subject File, MDAH.

Litigation Docket through December 20, 1974, CLS Mississippi Mental Health Project. [20 December 1974.] MSBA.

Legal Services Corporation of Alabama. *Legal Services Corporation of Alabama: The First Year.* Montgomery, Ala.: LSCA, 1979. LSCA.

———. *A Report.* Montgomery, Ala.: LSCA, 1980. LSCA.

———. *What You Should Know about Legal Services.* Montgomery, Ala.: LSCA, 1980. LSCA.

Lyman, Edward H. "Overview Report: Community Legal Services and Mississippi Bar Legal Services Programs, Jackson, Miss." Washington, D.C.: Office of Legal Services, 7 May 1974. MSBA.

Mississippi Bar Legal Services. *Annual Report, 1975.* Jackson, Miss.: MBLS, 1975. MSBA.

NAACP Subject File, MDAH.

NMRLS Office of Planning and Development. *An Analysis of the Attitudinal, Socioeconomic, County Expenditure and Federal Grant Characteristics of the North Mississippi Rural Legal Services Needs Assessment Survey.* Oxford, Miss.: NMRLS, 1981. NM, LSC.

North Mississippi Rural Legal Services Subject File, MDAH.

Okolona Subject File, MDAH.

Police Brutality Subject File, MDAH.

Powell, Barry. "CMLS Decrees, 1971–1983." In author's possession.

———. "Director's Report—1975, CLS." N.d. MSBA.

Proctor, Bernadette D., and Joseph Dalaker. U.S. Bureau of the Census, *Poverty in the United States, 2002.* Washington, D.C.: Government Printing Office, 2003.

Race Relations 2 Subject File, MDAH.

Robinson, Alfred "Skip" Subject File, MDAH.

Tupelo Boycott, 1978 Subject File, MDAH.

United League Subject File, MDAH.

United States Bureau of the Census. *U.S. Census of Population: 1980.* Vol. 1: *Characteristics of the Population.* Pt. 1: *United States Summary.* Washington, D.C.: Government Printing Office, 1973.

———. *U.S. Census of Population: 1980.* Vol. 1: *Characteristics of the Population.* Pt. 1: *United States Summary.* Washington, D.C.: Government Printing Office, 1983.

———. *U.S. Census of Population: 1970.* Vol. 1: *Characteristics of the Population.* Pt. 2: *Alabama.* Washington, D.C.: Government Printing Office, 1973.

———. *U.S. Census of Population: 1980.* Vol. 1: *Characteristics of the Population.* Pt. 2: *Alabama.* Washington, D.C.: Government Printing Office, 1983.

———. *U.S. Census of Population: 1970.* Vol. 1: *Characteristics of the Population.* Pt. 12: *Georgia.* Washington, D.C.: Government Printing Office, 1973.

———. *U.S. Census of Population: 1980.* Vol. 1: *Characteristics of the Population.* Pt. 12: *Georgia.* Washington, D.C.: Government Printing Office, 1983.

———. *U.S. Census of Population: 1970.* Vol. 1: *Characteristics of the Population.* Pt. 26: *Mississippi.* Washington, D.C.: Government Printing Office, 1973.

———. *U.S. Census of Population: 1980.* Vol. 1: *Characteristics of the Population.* Pt. 26: *Mississippi.* Washington, D.C.: Government Printing Office, 1983.

INTERVIEWS

(Unless otherwise noted, interviews by author are audiotaped and in the author's possession.)

Affleck, Tom. Interview by author, 31 March 1999, Decatur, Ga.

Askew, Hulett "Bucky." Interview by Thorns Craven, March 1990. Published in *Management Information Exchange* (March 1990): 385.

———. Interview by author, 4 March 1999, Atlanta.

———. Interview by author, 21 March 2000, Atlanta.

Baety, Edward L. Interview by author, 15 January 1999, Atlanta.

Baird, Charles. Interview by author, 27 March 1999, Atlanta.

Bamberger, E. Clinton. Interview by author, 26 May 1998, Baltimore, Md.

Bell, David. Interview by author, 15 July 1998, Oxford, Miss.

Bergmark, Martha. Interview by Harrison McIver, 28 July 1992, St. Petersburg, Fla. Videotape, NEJL.

———. Interview by author, 22 May 1998, Washington, D.C.

Bips, Virginia. Interview by author, 23 November 1998, Atlanta (by telephone). Handwritten notes.

Bowman, Tom. Interview by author, 10 December 1998, Conyers, Ga.

Brennan, Bill. Interview by author, 6 November 1998, Decatur, Ga.

———. Interview by author, 11 November 1998, Decatur, Ga.

Brent, John. Interview by author, 18 November 1998, Atlanta.

Brown, Tom Watson. Interview by author, 25 February 1999, Marietta, Ga.

Budnitz, Mark. Interview by author, 9 March 1999, Atlanta. Handwritten notes.

Burge, Marian. Interview by author, 21 January 1999, Atlanta.

Campbell, Marvin H. Interview by author, 1 August 2000, Montgomery, Ala. (by telephone).

Christian, Mattie. Interview by author, 26 January 1999, Atlanta (by telephone).

Clinton, Hillary Rodham. Interview by Victor Geminiani, 21 July 1991, St. Petersburg, Fla. Videotape, NEJL.

Cobb, William. Interview by author, 23 March 1999, Atlanta.

Condon, Aaron. Interview by author, 15 July 1998, Oxford, Miss.

Cooper, Clarence. Interview by author, 28 January 1999, Atlanta. Handwritten notes.

Cromartie, John. Interview by author, 16 March 1999, Cumming, Ga.

Cullen, Robert. Interview by author, 19 March 1999, Atlanta.

——. Interview by author, 30 March 1999, Atlanta.

Davis, Eva. Interview by author, 6 March 1997, Decatur, Ga. Handwritten notes.

Dokson, Robert N. Interview by author, 2 December 1998, Atlanta.

Elliott, James. Interview by author, 6 April 1999, Atlanta.

Ferguson, Gene. Interview by author, 2 March 1997, Atlanta. Handwritten notes.

Ford, Austin. Interview by author, 6 March 1997, Atlanta. Handwritten notes.

Froman, Michael. Interview by author, 23 March 1999, Atlanta.

Gardner, Ayers. Interview by author, 10 March 1999, Decatur, Ga.

Goldstein, Dennis. Interview by author, 19 January 1999, Atlanta.

——. Interview by author, 21 January 1999, Atlanta.

Gottlieb, Steve. Interview by Leanna Gipson, 22 July 1991, St. Petersburg, Fla. Videotape, NEJL.

——. Interview by author, 4 December 1998, Atlanta.

——. Interview by author, 17 December 1998, Atlanta.

Holmen, Phyllis. Interview by author, 4 March 1999, Atlanta.

Horowitz, Michael. Interview by author, 28 May 1998, Washington, D.C.

Houseman, Alan. Interview by Victor Geminiani, 21 October 1991, St. Petersburg, Fla. Videotape, NEJL.

——. Interview by author, 18 May 1998, Washington, D.C.

Ide, Bill. Interview by Sharon Rowen, n.d.. [Atlanta]. Videotape, Sharon Rowen personal collection.

——. Interview by author, 5 March 1999, Atlanta.

Jenkins, Bob. Interview by Michael Pritchard, 21 July 1991, St. Petersburg, Fla. Videotape, NEJL.

Johnson, June. Interview by author, 1 June 1998, Washington, D.C.

Joseph, Wilhelm. Interview by author, 26 May 1998, Baltimore, Md.

Kehrer, Bettye. Interview by Sharon Rowen, n.d., [Austell, Ga.]. Sharon Rowen personal collection.

Keith, Tom. Interview by Ken Cain, 26 July 1992, St. Petersburg, Fla. Videotape, NEJL.

Kilgore, Virginia. Interview by author, 14 July 1998, Oxford, Miss.

Kramer, Myron. Interview by author, 23 November 1998, Atlanta.

Lescault, Guy. Interview by Bucky Askew, 3 September 1991, Atlanta. Videotape, NEJL.

Loeb, Jay. Interview by author, 18 January 1999, Atlanta.

Lokey, Muriel. Interview by author, 26 February 1997, Atlanta (by telephone). Handwritten notes.

Lyons, Clint. Interview by Victor Geminiani, 23 July 1991, St. Petersburg, Fla. Videotape, NEJL.

———. Interview by author, 1 June 1998, Washington, D.C.

Mathews, Ethel Mae. Interview by author, 27 February 1997, Atlanta. Handwritten notes.

Maxey, John. Interview by author, 8 July 1998, Jackson, Miss.

McClellan, Leonard. Interview by author, 8 July 1998, Jackson, Miss.

McDougal, Luther. Interview by author, 2 July 1998, New Orleans, La.

McIver, Harrison. Interview by Susan Perrian, 24 July 1991, St. Petersburg, Fla. Videotape, NEJL.

———. Interview by author, 5 June 1998, Washington, D.C.

Moody, Maggie. Interview by author, 26 February 1999, Atlanta.

Morris, Carrie. Interview by author, 21 February 1997, Atlanta. Handwritten notes.

Oelkers, Joseph, III. Interview by Brian Leonard, 28 July 1992, St. Petersburg, Fla. Videotape, NEJL.

Oliver, Mary Margaret. Interview by Sharon Rowen, n.d., [Decatur, Ga.]. Sharon Rowen personal collection.

———. Interview by author, 10 March 1999, Decatur, Ga.

Osborne, Solomon. Interview by author, 10 July 1998, Greenwood, Miss.

Padnos, Michael. Interview by author, 11 January 2001, Vauvenargues, France (by telephone).

Pauley, Frances. Interview by author, 21 February 1997, Atlanta. Handwritten notes.

Pennington, Jesse. Interview by author, 8 July 1998, Jackson, Miss.

Powell, Barry. Interview by author, 6 July 1998, Jackson, Miss.

Raff, Michael. Interview by author, 7 July 1998, Jackson, Miss.

Remar, Robert. Interview by author, 7 April 1999, Atlanta.

Roesel, Richard. Interview by author, 1 June 1998, Washington, D.C.

Royals, Tom. Interview by author, 6 July 1998, Jackson, Miss.

Samuel, Don. Interview by author, 25 March 1999, Atlanta.

Sanders, Alix. Interview by author, 10 July 1998, Greenwood, Miss.

Shelton, Luther Rosser. Interview by author, 16 December 1998, Atlanta. Handwritten notes.

Smith, Kendric. Interview by author, 25 November 1998, Atlanta.

Sobelson, Roy. Interview by author, 23 March 1999, Atlanta.

Spriggs, Kent. Interview by author, 29 June 1998, Tallahassee, Fla.

Stevens, Francis, and Ann Stevens. Interview by author, 2 June 1998, Bethesda, Md.

Strickler, George. Interview by author, 2 July 1998, New Orleans, La.

Taylor, Stanley. Interview by author, 1 July 1998, Biloxi, Miss.

Thornton, Phyllis. Interview by Victor Geminiani, 23 July 1992, St. Petersburg, Fla. Videotape, NEJL.

Trister, Michael. Interview by author, 28 May 1998, Washington, D.C.

Walbert, David. Interview by author, 9 March 1999, Atlanta.

Walls, Johnnie. Interview by author, 13 July 1998, Greenville, Miss.

Ward, Columbus. Interview by author, 25 February 1997, Atlanta. Handwritten notes.

Webster, David. Interview by author, 5 March 1997, Atlanta. Handwritten notes.

———. Interview by author, 18 February 1999, Atlanta.

Williams, Hosea. Interview by author, 5 March 1997, Atlanta. Handwritten notes.

Zimring, Jonathan. Interview by author, 10 March 1999, Atlanta.

LEGAL CASES

(Unless otherwise noted, case files are located at the Federal Records Center, East Point, Georgia. *CR* indicates that the case was reported in the *Clearinghouse Review*.)

Abrams v. Commercial Credit Plan, Inc., 128 Ga. App. 520 (1973).

Adams v. Parham, No. 16041 (N.D. Ga. 1972), *CR*.

Adams v. Parham, No. 16042 (N.D. Ga. 1971), *CR*.

Addison v. Holiday, No. G76-163-K (N.D. Miss. 1978), *CR*.

Alabama Cooperatives Association v. Solomon, No. 78-1936 (D.D.C., filed 1978), *CR*.

Allen v. Alco Finance Inc., 131 Ga. App. 545 (1974).

American Federation of Government Employees, Local 2677 v. Phillips, 358 F. Supp. 60 (D.D.C. 1973).

Anderson v. Banks, 520 F. Supp. 472 (S.D. Ga. 1981), 540 F. Supp. 761 (S.D. Ga. 1982).

Anderson v. Burson, 300 F. Supp. 401 (N.D. Ga. 1968).

Anderson v. Schaefer, Case File No. C.A. 10443 (N.D. Ga., filed 1966).

Andrews v. Drew Municipal Separate School District (N.D. Miss. 1973), *CR*.

Anthony v. Marshall County Board of Education, 409 F.2d 1287 (5th Cir. 1969).

Anthony v. Wheat Street Gardens, Case File No. B-62717 (Fulton Co. Civil Court, filed 1971).

Armour v. England, No. C79-32G (N.D. Ga., filed 1979), *CR*.

Arrington v. City of Fairfield, Alabama (N.D. Ala.) and (5th Cir.), *CR*.

Atkinson v. Motz, Case File No. C.A. 13344 (N.D. Ga. 1970).

Atlanta Housing Authority v. Jones, No. 61041 (Fulton Co. Super. Ct., 1971), *CR*.

Baker v. Carr, 369 U.S. 186 (1962).

Barron v. Bellairs, 496 F.2d 1187 (5th Cir. 1974), *CR.*

Belton v. Columbus Finance and Thrift Company, 127 Ga. App. 770 (1972).

Benham v. Edwards, 501 F. Supp. 1050 (N.D. Ga. 1980) and 678 F.2d 511 (5th Cir. 1982); *Ledbetter v. Benham*, 463 U.S. 1222 (1980); *Benham v. Edwards*, 719 F.2d 772 (1983); and *Benham v. Ledbetter*, 609 F. Supp. 125 (1985).

Benson v. Schweiker, 638 F.2d 1355 (5th Cir. 1981); and 652 F.2d 406 (5th Cir. 1981), *CR.*

Billington v. Underwood, 613 F.2d 91 (5th Cir. 1980).

Blackburn v. Blackburn, 249 Ga. 689, 292 S.E.2d 821 (1982).

Blair v. City of Greenville, 649 F.2d 365 (N.D. Miss. 1981).

Blocker v. Blackburn, No. 26728 (Fulton Co. Super. Ct., Atlanta, 1971), *CR.*

Boddie v. Connecticut, 401 U.S. 371 (1971).

Bogard v. Cook, 60 F.R.D. 508 (N.D. Miss. 1973), 405 F. Supp. 1202 (N.D. Miss. 1975), and 586 F.2d 399 (5th Cir. 1978).

Boone v. Dennis, No. 72J-118(N) (S.D. Miss., filed 1972).

Bowen v. Neal, 277 So.2d 433 (Miss. Sup. Ct. 1973).

Boyd v. Harris, Case File No. CV 178-250 (S.D. Ga., 1979).

Bradford v. Byars, 302 So.2d 503 (Miss. Sup. Ct. 1974).

Brantley v. Califano, 478 F. Supp. 613 (M.D. Ga. 1979).

Brown v. Beck, 481 F. Supp. 723 (S.D. Ga. 1980), *CR.*

Brown v. Cantrell (N.D. Ga.), *CR.*

Brown v. Jaquith, 318 So.2d 856 (Miss. Sup. Ct. 1975), *CR.*

Brown v. Housing Authority of McRae, 784 F.2d 1533 (11th Cir. 1986); 804 F.2d 612 (11th Cir. 1986); and 820 F.2d 350 (11th Cir. 1987).

Brown v. Twin County Electric Power Association, No. GC69-35S (N.D. Miss. 1969), *CR.*

Brown v. Vance, 637 F.2d 272 (5th Cir. 1981), 1981 U.S. App. LEXIS 19148 (1981), *CR.*

Bryson v. Burson, 308 F. Supp. 1170 (N.D. Ga. 1969).

Buchanan v. Wheat Street Three, Inc., Case File No. 13183 (N.D. Ga., filed 1969).

Burns v. Alcala, 420 U.S. 575 (1974).

Burt v. Ramada Inn of Oxford, 507 F. Supp. 336 (N.D. Miss. 1980).

Callahan v. Callahan, 381 So.2d 178 (Miss. Sup. Ct. 1980).

Campbell v. Mincy, 413 F. Supp. 16 (N.D. Miss. 1975).

Cane v. Mississippi Employment Security Commission, 368 So.2d 1263 (Miss. Sup. Ct. 1979).

Carpenter v. Herschede Hall Clock Division, Arnold Industries, 77 F.R.D. 700 (N.D. Miss. 1977).

Carr v. Saucier, No. 16704 (N.D. Ga. 1973), *CR.*

Carter v. State of Mississippi, 334 So.2d 376 (Miss. Sup. Ct. 1976).

Cash v. United States, 571 F. Supp. 513 (N.D. Ga. 1983).

Chancey v. Department of Human Resources, 156 Ga. App. 338 (1980).

Chapman v. King, 154 F.2d 460 (5th Cir. 1946).

Cheley v. Burson, 324 F. Supp. 678 (N.D. Ga. 1971).

Clark v. Emerson Electric Manufacturing Company, 430 F. Supp. 216 (N.D. Miss. 1977).

Cloud v. Regenstein, Case File No. C77-599A (N.D. Ga. 1981).

Cody v. Community Loan Corporation of Richmond County, 606 F.2d 499 (5th Cir. 1979), *CR.*

Collier v. State of Mississippi, 299 So.2d 203 (Miss. Sup. Ct. 1974).

Consolidated Credit Corporation of Athens, Inc. v. Peppers, 144 Ga. App. 401 (1977).

Cook v. Conn, 267 So.2d 296 (Miss. Sup. Ct. 1972).

Crane v. Davis, No. C79-56G (N.D. Ga., filed 1979), *CR.*

Crane v. Mathews, Case File No. C75-2317A, 417 F. Supp. 532 (N.D. Ga. 1976), *CR.*

Crews v. Brantley County Department of Family and Children Services, 146 Ga. App. 408 (1978).

Crosby v. State of Mississippi, 270 So.2d 346 (Miss. Sup. Ct. 1972).

Cross v. Baxter, 604 F.2d. 875 (5th Cir. 1979), *CR.*

Crowe v. Heckler, Case File No. C84-355R (N.D. Ga. 1985).

Cullers v. Home Credit Company, 130 Ga. App. 441 (1973).

Curry v. Block, 541 F. Supp. 506 (S.D. Ga. 1982); 738 F.2d 1556 (11th Cir. 1984); and 608 F. Supp. 1407 (S.D. Ga. 1985).

Dailey v. Cawthon, No. 14546 (N.D. Ga. 1971), *CR.*

Dandridge v. Williams, 397 U.S. 471 (1970).

Daniels v. State of Mississippi, 315 So.2d 443 (Miss. Sup. Ct. 1975).

Davis v. Caldwell, No. 14973 (N.D. Ga. 1971), *CR.*

Davis v. Graham, No. 16891 (N.D. Ga. 1972), *CR.*

Deriso v. Cooper, 245 Ga. 786 (1980), 245 Ga. 786 (1980), and 246 Ga. 540 (1980).

Diggs v. Diggs, 158 Ga. App. 277 (1981).

Dixon v. GILS, 388 F. Supp. 1156 (S.D. Ga. 1974).

Dodson v. Parham, 427 F. Supp. 97 (N.D. Ga. 1977), *CR.*

Doe v. Bolton, 410 U.S. 179 (1973).

Doe v. Venable, Case File No. 15862 (N.D. Ga., filed 1971).

Dotson v. City of Indianola, 521 F. Supp. 934 (N.D. Miss. 1981); and 551 F. Supp. 515 (N.D. Miss. 1982).

Dropkin v. Dropkin, 237 Ga. 768 (Ga. Sup. Ct. 1976).

Dutton v. Lamb, Case File No. C78-582A (N.D. Ga., filed 1978), *CR.*

Eady v. General Finance Corporation of Augusta, No. 1726 (S.D. Ga. 1972), *CR.*

Ealy v. Littlejohn, 569 F.2d 219 (5th Cir. 1978).

Echols v. Auburn City Housing Authority, No. CV 79-035 (Ala. Sup. Ct. 1980), *CR.*

Eldridge v. Weinberger, 361 F. Supp. 520 (W.D. Va. 1973), 493 F.2d 1230 (4th Cir. 1974), *CR.*

Ellison v. Weinberger, No. C75-497A (N.D. Ga., filed 1975), *CR.*

Elrod v. Department of Family and Children Services, 136 Ga. App. 251 (1975).

Evans v. Liberty Cash, Superintendent, Mississippi State Penitentiary, 429 F. Supp. 681 (N.D. Miss. 1977).

Evans v. State of Mississippi, 273 So.2d 495 (Miss. Sup. Ct. 1973).

Fambro v. Fulton Co., Case File No. C82-2136 (N.D. Ga., filed 1982).

Fantroyal v. Caldwell (S.D. Ga. 1980), CR.

Farley v. Reinhart, No. 15569 (N.D. Ga. 1971), CR.

Ferguson v. Williams, 330 F. Supp. 1012 (N.D. Miss. 1971); 405 U.S. 1036 (1972); and 343 F. Supp. 654 (N.D. Miss. 1972).

Finch v. Weinberger, Case File No. 75-592A, 407 F. Supp. 34 (N.D. Ga. 1975), CR.

Flora v. Moore, 78 F.R.D. 358 (N.D Miss. 1978); and 461 F. Supp. 1104 (N.D. Miss. 1978).

Foy v. Lewis, 248 Ga. 234 (Ga. Sup. Ct. 1981).

Frazier v. Courtesy Finance Company, 132 Ga. App. (1974).

Frazier v. Jordan, 457 F.2d 726 (5th Cir. 1972).

Freeman v. Lynn, No. 18901 (N.D. Ga. 1973), CR.

Freeman v. Martin, Case File No. 15877 (N.D. Ga., filed 1971).

Freeman v. Parham, 475 F.2d 185 (5th Cir. 1973), No. 15877 (N.D. Ga. 1973), CR.

Freeman v. Rogers, Case File No. C76-141R (N.D. Ga., filed 1976).

Gaston v. Calhoun County Board of Education, 88 F.R.D. 356 (N.D. Miss. 1980).

Gates v. Collier, 349 F. Supp. 881 (N.D. Miss. 1972); and 501 F.2d 1291 (5th Cir. 1974).

Gay v. Gay, 149 Ga. App. 173 (1979).

Georgia Association of Retarded Citizens v. McDaniel, 511 F. Supp. 1263 (N.D. Ga. 1981), 716 F.2d 1565 (11th Cir. 1983); *McDaniel v. Georgia Association of Retarded Citizens*, 468 U.S. 1213 (1984); *Georgia Association of Retarded Citizens v. McDaniel*, 740 F.2d 902 (11th Cir. 1984); *McDaniel v. Georgia Association of Retarded Citizens*, 469 U.S. 1228 (1985); *Georgia Association of Retarded Citizens v. McDaniel*, 855 F.2d 794 and 855 F.2d 805 (11th Cir. 1988) and 490 U.S. 1090 (1989).

Georgia Investment Company v. Norman, 231 Ga. 821 (1974).

Georgia State Conference of Branches of NAACP v. State of Georgia, 99 F.R.D. 16 (S.D. Ga. 1983); 570 F. Supp. 314 (S.D. Ga. 1983); and 775 F.2d 1403 (11th Cir. 1985).

Gideon v. Wainwright, 372 U.S. 335 (1963).

Gill v. Woods, 226 So.2d 912 (Miss. S.C. 1969).

Givens v. Delta Electric Power Association, 572 F. Supp. 555 (N.D. Miss. 1983).

Glaze v. Atlanta Housing Authority, No. C79-246A (N.D. Ga. 1979), CR.

Goldberg v. Kelly, 397 U.S. 254 (1970).

Gomillion v. Lightfoot, 364 U.S. 339 (1960).

Gray v. Quality Finance Company, 130 Ga. App. 762 (1974).

Green v. Stanton, 364 F. Supp. 123 (N.D. Ind. 1973).

Grier v. Stovall, Case File No. C81-113N (N.D. Ga., filed 1981), *CR.*

Guthrie v. Evans, 93 F.R.D. 390 (S.D. Ga. 1981).

Gwinnett Nonprofit Housing Corporation v. Pruitt, No. 17602 (N.D. Ga. 1973), *CR.*

Hammond v. Russell, No. J77-0408(N) (S.D. Miss. 1978), *CR.*

Hannah v. Butz, 445 F. Supp. 503 (N.D. Miss. 1977).

Hardwick v. Parham, 141 Ga. App. 318 (1977).

Harrell v. Harris, No. 79-2935 (5th Cir. 1980), *CR.*

Harris v. Levi, 416 F. Supp. 208 (D.D.C. 1976); *Harris v. Bell*, 562 F.2d 772 (D.C. App. 1977), *CR.*

Harris v. Mississippi State Department of Public Welfare, 363 F. Supp. 1293 (N.D. Miss., 1973).

Heath v. D. H. Baldwin Company, 447 F. Supp. 505 (N.D. Miss. 1977).

Herring v. B. H. Moore and Son, Inc., No. B-8155 (Ga. Super. Ct. 1973), *CR.*

Hodge v. Dodd, Case File No. 16171 (N.D. Ga., filed 1972), *CR.*

Hodges v. Community Loan and Investment Corporation, No. 29643 (Ga. Sup. Ct. 1975), *CR.*

Hodges v. Hodges, 346 So.2d 903 (Miss. Sup. Ct. 1977).

Holland v. Steele, 92 F.R.D. 58 (N.D. Ga. 1981).

Holloway v. State of Mississippi, 261 So.2d 799 (Miss. Sup. Ct. 1972).

Hooks v. Jaquith, 318 So.2d 860 (Miss. Sup. Ct. 1975), *CR.*

Horton v. Horton, 235 Ga. 227 (1975).

Hudson v. Farmers Home Administration, 654 F.2d 334 (5th Cir. 1981), *CR.*

Huff v. Moore, 144 Ga. App. 668 (1978).

In re Amendments to Rules Regulating the Florida Bar 1–3.1(a) and Rules of Judicial Administration 2.065 (Legal Aid), 573 So.2d 800 (Fla. Sup. Ct. 1990).

In re Amendments to Rules Regulating the Florida Bar 1–3.1(a) and Rules of Judicial Administration 2.065 (Legal Aid), 630 So.2d 501 (Fla. Sup. Ct. 1993).

In re Christian, No. 19368 (M.D. Ga. 1973), *CR.*

In re Cooper (Alabama Medical Services Administration, 1980), *CR.*

In re DeKalb General Hospital (Ga. Dept. of Health and Human Services, 1981), *CR.*

In re Holmes (Ga. Real Estate Commission), *CR.*

In the Interest of M. A. C. et al., 261 S.E.2d 590 (Ga. Sup. Ct. 1979).

In re Pickett, 205 S.E.2d 522 (Ga. App. 1974).

In re R. R. (Miss. Youth Ct., Hinds Co., 1976), *CR.*

In re Randy Joe Watkins, 324 So.2d 232 (Miss. Sup. Ct. 1975).

Irving v. Hargett, 518 F. Supp. 1127 (N.D. Miss. 1981).

Irving v. State of Mississippi, 361 So.2d 1360 (Miss. Sup. Ct. 1978).

Ivey v. Garner, No. 74-200-MAC (M.D. Ga.1975), *CR.*

Jackson v. Indiana, 406 U.S. 715 (1972).

Jackson v. Riddell, 476 F. Supp. 849 (N.D. Miss. 1979).

Jackson v. State of Mississippi, 311 So.2d 658 (Miss. Sup. Ct. 1975).

Jackson v. Tupelo, No. EC 75-159-S (N.D. Miss., filed 1975).

Jeffries v. Georgia Residential Finance Authority, 503 F. Supp. 610 (N.D. Ga. 1980); 90 F.R.D. 62 (N.D. Ga. 1981); 678 F.2d 919 (11th Cir. 1982); and 459 U.S. 971 (1982).

Jenkins v. Allen Temple Apartments, 127 Ga. App. 611 (Ga. App. 1972).

J. L. and J. R. v. Parham, 412 F. Supp. 112 (M.D. Ga. 1976); *Parham v. J. L. et al.*, 425 U.S. 909 (1976), 427 U.S. 903 (1976), 431 U.S. 936 (1977), 434 U.S. 962 (1977), 442 U.S. 584, at 597 (1979).

Johnson v. Johnson, No. 74-11 Col. (M.D. Ga. 1975), *CR*.

Johnson v. Sikes, 730 F.2d 644 (11th Cir. 1984).

Jones v. Caldwell, No. B-81520 (Fulton Co. Super. Ct., 1973), *CR*.

Jones v. Consumer Remodeling Service, Inc. (M.D. Ala., 1981), *CR*.

Jones v. Mississippi, No. H925 (S.D. Miss. 1971), *CR*.

Jordan v. Allain, 619 F. Supp. 98 (N.D. Miss. 1985).

Jordan v. City of Greenwood, 450 F. Supp. 765 (N.D. Miss. 1978); and 477 F. Supp. 885 (N.D. Miss. 1979).

Jordan v. City of Greenwood, 534 F. Supp. 1351 (N.D. Miss. 1982); 541 F. Supp. 1135 (N.D. Miss. 1982); and 711 F.2d 667 (5th Cir. 1983).

Jordan v. Winter, 604 F. Supp. 807 (N.D. Miss. 1984).

Kaplan v. Sanders, 136 Ga. App. 902 (1975); 237 Ga. 132 (1972); and 139 Ga. App. 624 (1976), *CR*, Case File No. 30851 (Ga. Sup. Ct.), GDAH.

Kates v. Motz, Case File No. B-50919 (Fulton Co. Civil Court, filed 1969), Fulton Co. Civil Court.

Kelsey v. Holder, Case File No. 79-CV-196-MAC (M.D. Ga., filed 1979).

Kelsey v. Killebrew, Case File No. 78-33-MAC (M.D. Ga., filed 1978).

Keough v. Tate County Board of Education, 748 F.2d 1077 (5th Cir. 1984).

Kilgore v. Kennesaw Finance Company of Douglasville, No. 47586 (Ga. App., filed 1973), *CR*.

King v. Johnson (Miss. Chancery Court, Neshoba County, 1980), reported in *CR*.

King v. Smith, 392 U.S. 309 (1968); and *Smith v. King*, 277 F. Supp. 31 (M.D. Ala., 1967).

Kline v. Rankin, 352 F. Supp. 292 (N.D. Miss. 1972).

Kronlund v. Honstein, No. 14103 (N.D. Ga. 1971), *CR*.

Lambert v. Waynesboro Properties, Inc., Case File No. CV 181-71 (S.D. Ga. 1982) *CR*.

Lane v. Inman, 509 F.2d 184 (5th Cir. 1975), *CR*.

Langdon v. Drew Municipal Separate School District, 512 F. Supp. 1131 (N.D. Miss. 1981).

Lanning v. Mignon, 233 Ga. 665 (1975).

Lassiter v. Department of Social Services, 452 U.S. 18 (1981).

Law v. United States Department of Agriculture, 366 F. Supp. 1233 (N.D. Ga. 1973), *CR.*

Lawrimore v. Sun Finance Company, 131 Ga. App. 96 (1974).

Lee et al. v. G. A. C. Finance Corporation, 130 Ga. App. 44 (1973).

Leslie v. Mann, Case File No. C77-49N (N.D. Ga., filed in 1977), *CR.*

Lewis v. Delta Loans, Inc., 300 So.2d 142 (Miss. Sup. Ct. 1974).

Lewis v. Termplan, 124 Ga. App. 507 (1971).

Leyva v. Brooks, 244 S.E.2d 119 (Ga. App. 1978); and 249 S.E.2d 628 (Ga. App. 1978).

Lipman v. Van Zant, 329 F. Supp. 391 (N.D. Miss. 1971), *CR.*

Lodge v. Buxton, 639 F.2d 1358 (5th Cir. 1981); *Rogers v. Lodge,* 458 U.S. 613 (1982); and 459 U.S. 899 (1982), Case File No. CV176-55 (S.D. Ga., filed 1976).

Loe v. Smith, Case File No. C79-1176A (N.D. Ga., filed 1979).

Malone v. Ventress, No. CA-75G-1858-NE (N.D. Ala. 1976), *CR.*

Martin v. Saucier, No. 16955 (N.D. Ga. 1973), *CR.*

Mason v. Davis, No. 75-G-0348-NE (N.D. Ala.), *CR.*

Mason v. Service Loan and Finance Company, 128 Ga. App. 828 (1973).

Mathews v. Eldridge, 424 U.S. 319 (1976), *CR.*

Mathews v. Little, No. 18241 (N.D. Ga., filed 1973), *CR.*

McClain v. Lafayette County Board of Education, 673 F.2d 106 (5th Cir. 1982).

McFall v. Helton Enterprises of Jackson, Inc., No. 72J-120 (C) (S.D. Miss., 1972), *CR.*

McIntosh County NAACP v. City of Darien, 605 F.2d 753 (5th Cir. 1979), *CR.*

McLemore v. Cubley, 569 F.2d 940 (5th Cir. 1978).

McLemore v. Schweiker (5th Cir. 1981), *CR.*

McRae v. Board of Education of Henry County, 491 F. Supp. 30 (N.D. Ga. 1980).

Miller v. Hartwood Apartments, Ltd., 689 F.2d 1239 (5th Cir. 1982).

Milton v. Busbee, Case File No. C77-18A (N.D. Ga., filed 1977).

Mississippi Public Service Commission, et al. v. Mississippi Power Company, 429 So.2d 883 (Miss. Sup. Ct. 1983).

Mitchell v. Board of Trustees of Oxford Municipal Separate School District, 625 F.2d 660 (5th Cir. 1980).

Moore v. Beneficial Finance Company of Georgia, 158 Ga. App. 535 (1981).

Montgomery Improvement Association, Inc. v. HUD (M.D. Ala., filed 1977), *CR.*

Morgan v. Sproat, 432 F. Supp. 1130 (S.D. Miss. 1977).

Morris v. Alabama Department of Industrial Relations (N.D. Ala.), *CR.*

Morris v. Jefferson County Committee for Economic Opportunity (5th Cir.), *CR.*

Morris v. Richardson, Case File No. 15733, 346 F. Supp. 494 (N.D. Ga. 1972), 455 F.2d 775 (4th Cir. 1972), and 409 U.S. 464 (1973), *CR.*

Morrow v. Mississippi Publishers Corporation, 5 Fair Empl. Prac. Cas. (BNA) 287 (S.D. Miss. 1972).

Muller v. Oregon, 208 U.S. 412 (1908).

Murray v. Murray, 358 So.2d 723 (Miss. Sup. Ct. 1978).

Myers v. Douglas County Board of Election, No. C78-1837A (N.D. Ga. 1978), *CR.*

Nelson v. Taylor, 244 Ga. 657 (Ga. Sup. Ct. 1979).

Nicholson v. Choctaw County, 498 F. Supp. 295 (S.D. Ala. 1980), *CR.*

Norman v. St. Clair, 610 F.2d 1228 (5th Cir. 1980), *CR.*

Nunn v. Harris, No. CA 78-MO 1765 (N.D. Ala. 1978), *CR.*

Obadele v. McAdory, No. 72J-103N (S.D. Miss. 1973), *CR.*

Olmstead v. L.C. et al., No. 98-536 (U.S. Sup. Ct., decided 22 June 1999); and 138 F.3d 893 (11th Cir. 1998).

Owens v. DeLoach, 134 Ga. App. 783 (1975).

Paige v. Gray, 399 F. Supp. 459 (M.D. Ga. 1975); 538 F.2d 1108 (5th Cir. 1976); and 437 F. Supp. 137 (M.D. Ga. 1977), *CR.*

Palmer v. Mangum, 338 So.2d 1002 (Miss. Sup. Ct. 1976).

Parks v. Harden, 354 F. Supp. 620 (N.D. Ga., 1973); and 504 F. 2d 861 (5th Cir., 1974), *CR.*

Pate v. Parham, No. 75-46-MAC (M.D. Ga. 1975), *CR.*

Peacock v. Drew Municipal Separate School District, 433 F. Supp. 1072 (N.D. Miss. 1977).

Pickens v. Okolona Municipal Separate School District, 380 F. Supp. 1036 (N.D. Miss. 1974); and 527 F.2d 358 (5th Cir. 1976), *CR.*

Pickens v. Okolona Municipal Separate School District, 594 F.2d 433 (5th Cir. 1979).

Pinson v. Hendrix, 493 F. Supp. 772 (N.D. Miss. 1980).

Potter v. James (M.D. Ala. 1980), *CR.*

Prescott v. Judy, 157 Ga. App. 735 (1981).

Quarles v. North Mississippi Retardation Center, 455 F. Supp. 52 (N.D. Miss. 1978).

Quarles v. Oxford Municipal Separate School District, 366 F. Supp. 247 (N.D. Miss. 1972), *CR.*

Quarles v. St. Clair, 711 F.2d 691 (5th Cir. 1982).

Ramage v. Shell, 493 F. Supp. 718 (N.D. Miss. 1980); and 644 F.2d 33 (5th Cir. 1981).

Ramberg v. Porter, No. 72 J-43(N) (S.D. Miss. 1973), *CR.*

Ramsey v. Ramsey, 231 Ga. 334 (Ga. Sup. Ct. 1975).

Randle v. Indianola Municipal Separate School District, 373 F. Supp. 766 (N.D. Miss. 1974).

Ray v. Department of Human Resources, 270 S.E.2d 303 (Ga. App. 1980).

R.C.N. v. State of Georgia, 233 S.E.2d 866 (Ga. App. 1977).

Redditt v. Mississippi Extended Care Centers, Inc., 718 F.2d 1381 (5th Cir. 1983).

Reece v. Evans, Case File No. 1:CV-82:0001251 (N.D. Ga., filed 1982).

Reese v. Termplan, Inc., 128 Ga. App. 527 (1973).

Reyer v. Harrison County Department of Public Welfare, 404 So.2d 1023 (Miss. Sup. Ct. 1981), *CR.*

Rias v. Henderson, 342 So.2d 737 (Miss. Sup. Ct. 1977), *CR.*

Robinson v. McAlister, 310 F. Supp. 370 (N.D. Miss. 1970), *CR.*

Robinson v. Stovall, 473 F. Supp. 135 (N.D. Miss. 1979); and 646 F.2d 1087 (5th Cir. 1981).

Roe v. Wade, 410 U.S. 171 (1973).

Rush v. Parham, 625 F.2d 1150 (5th Cir. 1980); and 565 F. Supp. 856 (N.D. Ga. 1983).

Russell v. Harrison, 562 F. Supp. 467 (N.D. Miss. 1983); and 736 F.2d 283 (5th Cir. 1984).

Russell v. Savannah Housing Authority, No. CV477-254 (S.D. Ga. 1978), *CR.*

Rustin v. State of Mississippi, 338 So.2d 1006 (Miss. Sup. Ct. 1976).

Saddler v. Winstead, 332 F. Supp. 130 (N.D. Miss. 1971), *CR.*

Sagoes v. Atlanta Housing Authority, No. C76-1171A (N.D. Ga. 1976), *CR.*

Saine v. Hospital Authority of Hall County, No. 1478 (N.D. Ga., filed 1973), *CR.*

Sanks v. Georgia, 225 Ga. 88 (1969), *CR,* Case File Nos. 24992 and 24993 (Ga. Sup. Ct.), GDAH.

Sanks v. Georgia, 395 U.S. 974 (1969), 399 U.S. 922 (1970), and 401 U.S. 144 (1971).

Sapp v. Rowland, Case File No. CV176-94 (S.D. Ga., filed 1976).

Scott v. Housing Authority of Macon, Case File No. 2899 (M.D. Ga., filed 1973).

Scott v. Parham, No. C75-614A, 69 F.R.D. 324 (N.D. Ga. 1975); and 422 F. Supp. 111 (N.D. Ga. 1976), *CR.*

Sellers v. Alco Finance, Inc., 130 Ga. App. 769 (1974).

Shapiro v. Thompson, 394 U.S. 618 (1969).

Sheffield v. Cochran, No. CV 374-14 (S.D. Ga. 1974), *CR.*

Shenfield v. Prather, 387 F. Supp. 676 (N.D. Miss. 1974).

Simmons v. Parham, No. 15244 (N.D. Ga. 1971), *CR.*

Smith v. Allwright, 321 U.S. 649 (1944).

Smith v. Community Federal Savings and Loan Association of Tupelo, 77 F.R.D. 668 (N.D. Miss. 1977).

Smith v. Granberry, 349 So.2d 555 (Miss. Sup. Ct. 1977).

Smith v. Mississippi Employment Security Commission, 344 So.2d 137 (Miss. Sup. Ct. 1977).

Snowden v. Birmingham-Jefferson County Transit Authority, No. 75-G-330-S (N.D. Ala. 1975), *CR.*

Southern Discount Company v. Cooper et al., 130 Ga. App. 223 (1973).

Southern Discount Company of Georgia v. Ector, 152 Ga. App. 244 (1979); 246 Ga. 30 (1980); and 155 Ga. App. 521 (1980).

Steward v. Winter, 669 F.2d 328 (5th Cir. 1982), *CR.*

Stewart v. Bank of Pontotoc, 74 F.R.D. 552 (N.D. Miss. 1977).

Tate v. Mississippi Employment Security Commission, 407 So.2d 109 (Miss. Sup. Ct. 1981).

Tate v. State of Mississippi, 290 So.2d 263 (Miss. Sup. Ct. 1974).

Taylor v. Coahoma County School District, 581 F.2d 105 (5th Cir. 1978).

Thomas v. Burson, 398 U.S. 934 (1970).

Trice v. Weinberger, No. 74-208 (N.D. Ga. 1974), *CR*.

Triplett v. Cobb, 331 F. Supp. 652 (N.D. Miss. 1971), *CR*.

Trister v. University of Mississippi, 420 F.2d 499 (5th Cir. 1969).

Tucker v. Burford, 603 F. Supp. 276 (N.D. Miss. 1985).

Turner v. Colonial Finance Corp., No. 4821 (S.D. Miss., 1972), *CR*.

Turner v. Crider, No. EC 78-67-S (N.D. Miss., filed 1978).

United States v. Dimeo, No. 19021 (N.D. Ga. 1974), *CR*.

United State v. Fordice, 505 U.S. 717 (1992).

United States v. Garner, 567 F. Supp. 313 (N.D. Miss. 1983).

United States v. Henderson, 707 F.2d 853 (5th Cir. 1983).

United States v. White, 543 F.2d 1139 (5th Cir. 1976); and 429 F. Supp. 1245 (N.D. Miss. 1977), *CR*.

United States v. Wynn, 528 F.2d 1048 (5th Cir. 1976).

Vincent v. Payne (N.D. Ala.), *CR*.

Wade v. Carsley, 221 So.2d 725 (Miss. S.C., 1969).

Warren v. Tupelo, No. EC 78-71-K (N.D. Miss., filed 1978).

Watkins v. Mobile Housing Board, No. 79-0067-P (S.D. Ala. 1979), *CR*.

Webb v. Webb, 245 Ga. 650 (Ga. Sup. Ct. 1980) and 451 U.S. 493 (1981).

Wehunt v. Atlanta Legal Aid Society, No. B-94519 (Fulton Co. Super. Ct. 1974).

West v. Cole, 390 F. Supp. 91 (N.D. Miss. 1975).

White v. Butz, Case File No. C75-1511A (N.D. Ga., filed 1975), *CR*.

White v. Harris, 605 F.2d 867 (5th Cir. 1979).

White v. Regester, 412 U.S. 755 (1973).

White v. World Finance of Meridian, 653 F.2d 147 (5th Cir. 1981).

Whitehead v. Mississippi Employment Security Commission, 349 So.2d 1048 (Miss. Sup. Ct. 1977).

Williams v. Butz, No. J75-24(N) (S.D. Miss. 1976), *CR*.

Williams v. Butz, No. ÇV 176-153 (S.D. Ga., filed 1976), *CR*.

Williams v. City of Fairburn, No. C78271A (N.D. Ga., filed 1978), *CR*.

Williams v. Land-Hurst Furniture Company, No. EC 71-79-S (N.D. Miss. 1971), *CR*.

Williams v. Mississippi Employment Security Commission, 395 So.2d 964 (Miss. Sup. Ct. 1981).

Williams v. Phillips, 360 F. Supp. 1363 (D.D.C. 1973).

Williams v. St. Clair, 610 F.2d 1244 (5th Cir. 1980), *CR*.

Williams v. Weinberger, Case File No. 17128, 360 F. Supp. 1349 (N.D. Ga. 1973), 494 F.2d 1191 (5th Cir. 1974), *CR*.

Williams v. Winstead (N.D. Miss., filed 1970), *CR*.

Wilson v. Weaver, 358 F. Supp. 1147 (N.D. Ill. 1973).

Winningham v. HUD, No. 3237 (S.D. Ga., filed 1974), *CR*.

Winstead v. Kirkwood, 246 So.2d 557 (Miss. Sup. Ct. 1971), *CR*.

Woodes v. Morris, 247 Ga. 771 (Ga. Sup. Ct. 1981).

Wooley v. Mississippi Employment Security Commission, 368 So.2d 840 (Miss. Sup. Ct. 1979).

Yearby v. Parham, Case File No. C75-2532-A, 415 F. Supp. 1236 (N.D. Ga., 1976), *CR*.

Yinger v. Hutson, Case File No. 1:CV-81-785-MHS (N.D. Ga., filed 1981).

Young v. Young, 221 S.E.2d 424 (Ga. 1975).

Zimmer v. McKeithen, 485 F.2d 1297 (5th Cir. 1973).

ARTICLES, BOOKS, AND DISSERTATIONS

Abel, Richard L. "Law without Politics: Legal Aid under Advanced Capitalism." *UCLA Law Review* 32 (1985): 474–621.

Abramovitz, Mimi. *Under Attack, Fighting Back: Women and Welfare in the United States*. New York: Monthly Review Press, 1996.

Acevedo, Melanie D. "Client Choices, Community Values: Why Faith-Based Legal Services Providers Are Good for Poverty Law." *Fordham Law Review* 70 (March 2002): 1491–1534.

Achtenberg, Emily Paradise, and Peter Marcuse. "The Causes of the Housing Problem." In *Critical Perspectives on Housing*, ed. Rachel G. Bratt, Chester Hartman, and Ann Meyerson, 4–11. Philadelphia: Temple University Press, 1986.

Agnew, Spiro. "What's Wrong with the Legal Services Program." *American Bar Association Journal* (September 1972): 930–32.

Alabama State Bar Committee on Group and Prepaid Legal Services and Legal Services to the Poor. "Group and Prepaid Legal Services and Legal Services to the Poor." *AL* 36 (1975): 380–81.

Albert, Lee. "Choosing the Test Case in Welfare Litigation: A Plea for Planning." *Clearinghouse Review* 2 (November 1968): 4–6, 28.

Alfieri, Anthony V. "The Antinomies of Poverty Law and a Theory of Dialogic Empowerment." *New York University Review of Law and Social Change* 16 (1987–88): 659–712.

———. "Impoverished Practices." *Georgetown Law Journal* 81 (August 1993): 2567–2663.

———. "Reconstructive Poverty Law Practice: Learning Lessons of Client Narrative." *Yale Law Journal* 100 (1991): 2107–47.

Ambrose, Stephen E. *Nixon: The Triumph of a Politician, 1962–1972*. New York: Simon and Schuster, 1989.

Arnold, Mark. "The Knockdown, Drag-Out Battle over Legal Services." *Juris Doctor* (April 1973): 4–10.

Atlas, John, and Peter Dreier. "The Tenants' Movement and American Politics." In *Critical Per-*

spectives on Housing, ed. Rachel G. Bratt, Chester Hartman, and Ann Meyerson, 378–97. Philadelphia: Temple University Press, 1986.

Auerbach, Jerold S. *Unequal Justice: Lawyers and Social Change in Modern America.* New York: Oxford University Press, 1976.

Ayers, Edward L. *The Promise of the New South: Life after Reconstruction.* New York: Oxford University Press, 1992.

Bailis, Lawrence Neil. *Bread or Justice: Grassroots Organizing in the Welfare Rights Movement.* Lexington, Mass.: Lexington Books, 1974.

Bartley, Numan V. *The Creation of Modern Georgia,* 2nd ed. Athens: University of Georgia Press, 1990.

———. *The New South, 1945–1980.* Baton Rouge: Louisiana State University Press, 1995.

Bell, Derrick. *Race, Racism and American Law.* 3rd ed. Boston: Little, Brown, 1992.

Bellow, Gary, and Jeanne Charn. "Paths Not Yet Taken: Some Comments on Feldman's Critique of Legal Services Practice." *Georgetown Law Journal* 83 (April 1995): 1633–68.

Bellow, Gary, and Jeanne Kettleson. "From Ethics to Politics: Confronting Scarcity and Fairness in Public Interest Practice." *Boston University Law Review* 58 (1978): 337.

Bennett, Michael, and Cruz Reynoso. "California Rural Legal Assistance (CRLA): Survival of a Poverty Law Practice." *Chicano Law Review* 1 (1972): 1–79.

Besharov, Douglas J., ed. *Legal Services for the Poor: Time for Reform.* Washington, D.C.: American Enterprise Institute, 1990.

Bethel, Billie, and Robert Kirk Walker. "Et Tu, Brute!" *AL* 27 (1966): 17–31.

Black, Earl, and Merle Black. *Politics and Society in the South.* Cambridge, Mass.: Harvard University Press, 1987.

Boehm, Kenneth F. "The Legal Services Corporation: Unaccountable, Political, Anti-Poor, Beyond Reform and Unnecessary." *Saint Louis Public Law Review* 17 (1998): 321.

Braden, William. *Age of Aquarius: Technology and the Cultural Revolution.* Chicago: Quadrangle Books, 1970.

Branch, Taylor. *Parting the Waters: America in the King Years, 1954–1963.* New York: Simon and Schuster, 1988.

———. *Pillar of Fire: America in the King Years, 1963–1965.* New York: Simon and Schuster, 1998.

Brescia, Raymond H., Robin Golden, and Robert A. Solomon. "Who's in Charge Anyway? A Proposal for Community-Based Legal Services." *Fordham Urban Law Journal* 25 (Summer 1998): 831–63.

Brinkley, Alan. *The End of Reform: New Deal Liberalism in Recession and War.* New York: Vintage Books, 1995.

Brownell, Emery A. *Legal Aid in the United States: A Study of the Availability of Lawyers' Services for Persons Unable to Pay Fees.* Rochester, N.Y.: Lawyers Cooperative, 1951.

Bussiere, Elizabeth. *(Dis)entitling the Poor: The Warren Court, Welfare Rights, and the American Political Tradition*. University Park: Pennsylvania State University Press, 1997.

Cahn, Edgar S., and Jean C. "The War on Poverty: A Civilian Perspective." *Yale Law Journal* 73 (July 1964): 1317–52.

Cappelletti, Mauro, and James Gordley. "Legal Aid: Modern Themes and Variations." *Stanford Law Review* 24 (January 1972): 347–421.

Carson, Clayborne. *In Struggle: SNCC and the Black Awakening of the 1960s*. Cambridge, Mass.: Harvard University Press, 1981.

Carter, Dan T. *From George Wallace to Newt Gingrich: Race in the Conservative Counterrevolution, 1963–1994*. Baton Rouge: Louisiana State University Press, 1996.

———. *The Politics of Rage: George Wallace, The Origins of Conservatism, and the Transformation of American Politics*. New York: Simon and Schuster, 1995.

———. *Scottsboro: A Tragedy of the American South*. Rev. ed. Baton Rouge: Louisiana State University Press, 1979.

Chilton, Bradley Stewart. *Prisons under the Gavel: The Federal Court Takeover of Georgia Prisons*. Columbus: Ohio State University Press, 1991.

Cohodas, Nadine. *The Band Played Dixie: Race and the Liberal Conscience at Ole Miss*. New York: Free Press, 1997.

Cole, Luke W. "Empowerment as the Key to Environmental Protection: The Need for Environmental Poverty Law." *Ecology Law Quarterly* 19 (1992): 619–83.

"Committee on Law and Poverty Recommendations." *AL* 27 (1966): 142–43.

Cowley, John. "The Limitations and Potential of Housing Organizing." In *Critical Perspectives on Housing*, ed. Rachel G. Bratt, Chester Hartman, and Ann Meyerson, 398–404. Philadelphia: Temple University Press, 1986.

Cummins, Eric. *The Rise and Fall of California's Radical Prison Movement*. Stanford, Calif.: Stanford University Press, 1994.

Dallek, Robert. *Flawed Giant: Lyndon Johnson and His Times, 1961–1973*. New York: Oxford University Press, 1998.

Daniel, Pete. *The Shadow of Slavery: Peonage in the South, 1900–1969*. Urbana: University of Illinois Press, 1972.

Davis, Martha F. *Brutal Need: Lawyers and the Welfare Rights Movement, 1960–1973*. New Haven, Conn.: Yale University Press, 1993.

Delbanco, Andrew. *The Death of Satan: How Americans Have Lost the Sense of Evil*. New York: Farrar, Straus, and Giroux, 1995.

Dickstein, Morris. *Gates of Eden: American Culture in the Sixties*. New York: Basic Books, 1977.

Dittmer, John. *Local People: The Struggle for Civil Rights in Mississippi*. Urbana: University of Illinois Press, 1994.

DuBois, W. E. B. *The Souls of Black Folk*. 1903. Rpt. New York: Vintage Books / The Library of America, 1990.

Dunlap, Justine A. "I Don't Want to Play God—A Response to Professor Tremblay." *Fordham Law Review* 67 (April 1999): 2601–16.

Dunn, Charles W., and J. David Woodard. *The Conservative Tradition in America*. Lanham, Md.: Rowman and Littlefield, 1996.

Editorial Opinion and Comment. "Legal Services." *ABAJ* 67 (April 1981): 390.

Ehrenreich, Barbara. *The Hearts of Men*. New York: Anchor Books, 1983.

Ehrlich, Thomas. "Save the Legal Services Corporation." *ABAJ* 67 (April 1981): 434–37.

Failinger, Marie A. "Necessary Legends: The National Equal Justice Library and the Importance of Poverty Lawyers' History." *Saint Louis University Public Law Review* 17 (1998): 265–91.

Failinger, Marie A., and Larry May. "Litigating against Poverty: Legal Services and Group Representation." *Ohio State Law Review* 45 (1984): 1–56.

Falk, Jerome B., Jr., and Stuart R. Pollak. "Political Interference with Publicly Funded Lawyers: The CRLA Controversy and the Future of Legal Services." *Hastings Law Journal* 24 (March 1973): 599–646.

Feldman, Marc. "Political Lessons: Legal Services for the Poor." *Georgetown Law Journal* 83 (April 1995): 1529–1632.

Foner, Eric. *Reconstruction: America's Unfinished Revolution, 1863–1877*. New York: Harper and Row, 1988.

———. *The Story of American Freedom*. New York: Norton, 1998.

Foucault, Michel. *Discipline and Punish: The Birth of the Prison*. New York: Pantheon, 1978.

Friedman, Lawrence M. *American Law in the 20th Century*. New Haven, Conn.: Yale University Press, 2002.

———. *A History of American Law*. 2nd ed. New York: Simon and Schuster, 1985.

———. "Rights of Passage: Divorce Law in Historical Perspective." *Oregon Law Review* 63 (1984): 649–69.

Gabel, Peter, and Jay Feinman. "Contract Law as Ideology." In *The Politics of Law*, ed. David Kairys, 497–510. 3rd ed. New York: Basic Books, 1998.

Gans, Herbert J. *The War against the Poor: The Underclass and Antipoverty Policy*. New York: Basic Books, 1995.

Garrow, David J. *Bearing the Cross: Martin Luther King, Jr., and the Southern Christian Leadership Conference*. New York: Morrow, 1986.

———. *Liberty and Sexuality: The Right to Privacy and the Making of Roe v. Wade*. New York: Macmillan, 1994.

Gates, Henry Louis, Jr. *Colored People: A Memoir*. New York: Vintage Books, 1994.

Genovese, Eugene. *Roll, Jordan, Roll: The World the Slaves Made*. New York: Vintage Books, 1976.

George, Warren E. "Development of the Legal Services Corporation." *Cornell Law Review* 61 (June 1976): 681–730.

Giddings, Paula. *When and Where I Enter: The Impact of Black Women on Race and Sex in America.* New York: Morrow, 1984.

Gillette, Michael L. *Launching the War on Poverty: An Oral History.* New York: Twayne Publishers, 1996.

Gilmore, Glenda. *Gender and Jim Crow: Women and the Politics of White Supremacy in North Carolina, 1896–1920.* Chapel Hill: University of North Carolina Press, 1996.

Gitlin, Todd. *The Twilight of Common Dreams: Why America Is Wracked by Culture Wars.* New York: Holt, 1995.

Goldfield, David R. *Black, White, and Southern: Race Relations and Southern Culture, 1940 to the Present.* Baton Rouge: Louisiana State University Press, 1990.

Goodmark, Leigh. "Can Poverty Lawyers Play Well with Others? Including Legal Services in Integrated, School-Based Service Delivery Programs." *Georgetown Journal on Fighting Poverty* 4 (Spring 1997): 243–67.

Goodwin, Doris Kearns. *Lyndon Johnson and the American Dream.* New York: Harper and Row, 1976.

Goodwin, Joanne L. *Gender and the Politics of Welfare Reform: Mothers' Pensions in Chicago, 1911–1929.* Chicago: University of Chicago Press, 1997.

Goodwyn, Lawrence. *Democratic Promise: The Populist Moment in America.* Oxford: Oxford University Press, 1976.

Gordon, Linda. *Pitied but Not Entitled: Single Mothers and the History of Welfare, 1890–1935.* New York: Free Press, 1994.

Green, Bruce A. "Foreword: Rationing Lawyers: Ethical and Professional Issues in the Delivery of Legal Services to Low-Income Clients." *Fordham Law Review* 67 (April 1999): 1713–48.

Greenberg, Jack. *Crusaders in the Courts: How a Dedicated Band of Lawyers Fought for the Civil Rights Revolution.* New York: Basic Books, 1994.

Greene, Melissa Fay. *Praying for Sheetrock: A Work of Nonfiction.* Reading, Mass.: Addison-Wesley, 1991.

Gunther, Gerald. "Foreword: In Search of Evolving Doctrine on a Changing Court: A Model for a Newer Equal Protection." *Harvard Law Review* 86 (1972): 1–48.

Hahn, Steven. *The Roots of Southern Populism: Yeoman Farmers and the Transformation of the Georgia Upcountry, 1850–1890.* New York: Oxford University Press, 1983.

Hall, Kermit L. *The Magic Mirror: Law in American History.* New York: Oxford University Press, 1989.

Halpern, Stephen C. *On the Limits of the Law: The Ironic Legacy of Title VI of the 1964 Civil Rights Act.* Baltimore: Johns Hopkins University Press, 1995.

Hamby, Alonzo L. *Liberalism and Its Challengers: From F.D.R. to Bush.* 2nd ed. New York: Oxford University Press, 1992.

Handler, Joel F., Ellen Jane Hollingsworth, and Howard S. Erlanger. *Lawyers and the Pursuit of Legal Rights.* New York: Academic Press, 1978.

Harrington, Michael. *The Other America: Poverty in the United States.* New York: Macmillan, 1962.

Hatch, Orrin G., Jeremiah Denton, Rael Jean Isaac, James T. Bennett, and Thomas J. DiLorenzo, eds. *Legal Services Corporation: The Robber Barons of the Poor?* Washington, D.C.: Washington Legal Foundation, 1985.

Holmen, Phyllis. "Georgia Legal Service: Quality Justice for All." *Georgia Bar Journal* 3 (August 1997): 10–17.

Horwitz, Morton J. *The Transformation of American Law, 1780–1860.* Cambridge, Mass.: Harvard University Press, 1977.

———. *The Warren Court and the Pursuit of Justice.* New York: Hill and Wang, 1998.

Houseman, Alan W. "Civil Legal Assistance for Low-Income Persons: Looking Back and Looking Forward." *Fordham Urban Law Journal* 29 (February 2002): 1213–43.

———. "Political Lessons: Legal Services for the Poor: A Commentary." *Georgetown Law Journal* 83 (April 1995): 1669–1709.

Houseman, Alan W., and John A. Dooley. "Legal Services History." MS, November 1985.

Houseman, Alan W., and Linda E. Perle. *Securing Equal Justice for All: A Brief History of Civil Legal Assistance in the United States.* Washington, D.C.: Center for Law and Social Policy, 2003.

Huls, Nick. "From Pro Deo Practice to Subsidized Welfare State Provision: Twenty-five Years of Providing Legal Services to the Poor in the Netherlands." *Maryland Journal of Contemporary Legal Issues* 5 (1994): 333.

Ide, R. William, III, and Lawrence L. Thompson. "The Organized Bar—Yellow Brick Road to Legal Services for the Poor." *Vanderbilt Law Review* 27 (1974): 667–80.

Irons, Peter H. *The New Deal Lawyers.* Princeton, N.J.: Princeton University Press, 1982.

Isaac, Rael Jean. "War on the Poor." *National Review,* 15 May 1995, 32.

Jackson, Larry R., and William A. Johnson. *Protest by the Poor: The Welfare Rights Movement in New York City.* Lexington, Mass.: Lexington Books, 1974.

Jeffries, John C., Jr. "Lewis F. Powell, Jr. and the Birth of Legal Services." *Virginia Lawyer* (December 1998): 7–9.

Johnson, Alex M., Jr. "Bid Whist, Tonk, and *United States v. Fordice:* Why Integrationism Fails African-Americans Again." *California Law Review* 81 (1993): 1401.

Johnson, Earl, Jr. *Justice and Reform: The Formative Years of the OEO Legal Services Program.* New York: Russell Sage Foundation, 1974.

Johnston, Paul. "Legal Services to the Poor—Where Does the Alabama Bar Stand?" *AL* 27 (1966): 144–51.

Kairys, David. "Introduction." In *The Politics of Law,* ed. D. Kairys, 1–20. 3rd ed. New York: Basic Books, 1998.

—, ed. *The Politics of Law: A Progressive Critique.* 3rd ed. 1982. Rpt. New York: Basic Books, 1998.

Katz, Jack. "Lawyers for the Poor in Transition: Involvement, Reform, and the Turnover Problem in the Legal Services Program." *Law and Society Review* 12 (Winter 1978): 275–300.

———. *Poor People's Lawyers in Transition.* New Brunswick, N.J.: Rutgers University Press, 1982.

Katz, Michael B. *In the Shadow of the Poorhouse: A Social History of Welfare in America.* New York: Basic Books, 1986.

———. *The Undeserving Poor: From the War on Poverty to the War on Welfare.* New York: Pantheon Books, 1989.

Keister, Lisa A. *Wealth in America: Trends in Wealth Inequality.* Cambridge: Cambridge University Press, 2000.

Kelley, Robin D. G. *Race Rebels: Culture, Politics, and the Black Working Class.* New York: Free Press, 1994.

———. *Yo' Mama's Disfunktional! Fighting the Culture Wars in Urban America.* Boston: Beacon Press, 1997.

Kessler, Mark. *Legal Services for the Poor: A Comparative and Contemporary Analysis of Interorganizational Politics.* Westport, Conn.: Greenwood Press, 1987.

King, Richard. *Civil Rights and the Idea of Freedom.* Athens: University of Georgia Press, 1992.

Kotz, Nick, and Mary Lynn Kotz. *A Passion for Equality: George A. Wiley and the Movement.* New York: Norton, 1977.

Kluger, Richard. *Simple Justice: The History of* Brown v. Board of Education *and Black America's Struggle for Equality.* New York: Knopf, 1976.

Kull, Andrew. *The Color-Blind Constitution.* Cambridge, Mass.: Harvard University Press, 1992.

Lawrence, Susan E. *The Poor in Court: The Legal Services Program and Supreme Court Decision Making.* Princeton, N.J.: Princeton University Press, 1990.

Levitan, Sar. *The Great Society's Poor Law: A New Approach to Poverty.* Baltimore, Md.: Johns Hopkins University Press, 1969.

Lowenstein, Daniel H., and Michael J. Waggoner. "Note: Neighborhood Law Offices: The New Wave in Legal Services for the Poor." *Harvard Law Review* (February 1967): 805–50.

Lupsha, Peter A., and William J. Siembieda. "The Poverty of Public Services in the Land of Plenty: An Analysis and Interpretation." In *The Rise of the Sunbelt Cities,* ed. David C. Perry and Alfred J. Watkins, 169–90. Beverly Hills, Calif.: Sage, 1977.

Mahoney, Joan. "Green Forms and Legal Aid Offices: A History of Publicly Funded Legal Services in Britain and the United States." *Saint Louis University Public Law Review* 17 (1998): 223.

Margulies, Peter. "Political Lawyering, One Person at a Time: The Challenge of Legal Work against Domestic Violence for the Impact Litigation/Client Service Debate." *Michigan Journal of Gender and Law* 3 (1996): 493–514.

———. "Representation of Domestic Violence Survivors as a New Paradigm of Poverty Law: In Search of Access, Connection, and Voice." *George Washington Law Review* 63 (August 1995): 1071–1104.

Matusow, Allen J. *The Unraveling of America: A History of Liberalism in the 1960s.* New York: Harper and Row, 1984.

McAfee, Kathy. "Socialism and the Housing Movement: Lessons from Boston." In *Critical Perspectives on Housing,* ed. Bratt, et al., 405–27. Philadelphia: Temple University Press, 1986.

McCombs, Rufe, with Karen Spears Zacharias. *Benched: The Memoirs of Judge Rufe McCombs.* Macon, Ga.: Mercer University Press, 1997.

Melnick, R. Shep. *Between the Lines: Interpreting Welfare Rights.* Washington, D.C.: Brookings Institution, 1994.

Michelman, Frank I. "Foreword: On Protecting the Poor through the Fourteenth Amendment." *Harvard Law Review* 83 (November 1969): 7–59.

Moran, Laurie A. "Legal Services Attorneys as Partners in Community Economic Development: Creating Wealth for Poor Communities through Cooperative Economics." *University of the District of Columbia Law Review* (Fall 2000): 125–76.

Morgan, Edmund S. *American Slavery, American Freedom: The Ordeal of Colonial Virginia.* New York: Norton, 1975.

Moynihan, Daniel P. *Maximum Feasible Misunderstanding: Community Action in the War on Poverty.* New York: Free Press, 1969.

Murray, Charles. *Losing Ground: American Social Policy, 1950–1980.* New York: Basic Books, 1984.

Nadasen, Premilla. "The Welfare Rights Movement, 1960–1975." Ph.D. diss., Columbia University, 1999.

Nielsen, Leland C. "Three-Judge Courts: A Comprehensive Study." *Federal Rules Decisions* 66 (1975): 495–526.

Note. "The Legal Services Corporation: Curtailing Political Influence." *Yale Law Journal* 81 (1971): 231–86.

Oshinsky, David M. *"Worse than Slavery": Parchman Farm and the Ordeal of Jim Crow Justice.* New York: Free Press, 1996.

Parker, Frank J. *The Law and the Poor.* New York: Orbis Books, 1973.

Parker, Frank R. *Black Votes Count: Political Empowerment in Mississippi after 1965.* Chapel Hill: University of North Carolina Press, 1990.

Parmet, Herbert S. *Richard Nixon and His America.* Boston: Little, Brown, 1990.

Patterson, James T. *America's Struggle against Poverty, 1900–1994.* 3rd ed. Cambridge, Mass.: Harvard University Press, 1994.

——. *Grand Expectations: The United States, 1945–1974*. New York: Oxford University Press, 1996.

Payne, Charles M. *I've Got the Light of Freedom: The Organizing Tradition and the Mississippi Freedom Struggle*. Berkeley: University of California Press, 1995.

Phillips, Roderick. *Untying the Knot: A Short History of Divorce*. Cambridge: Cambridge University Press, 1991.

Pipkin, Ronald M. "Legal Aid and Elitism in the American Legal Profession." Introductory essay in *Justice and the Poor*, by Reginald Heber Smith, xi–xxvi. Montclair, N.J.: Patterson Smith, 1972.

Piven, Frances Fox, and Richard A. Cloward. *The Breaking of the American Social Compact*. New York: New Press, 1997.

——. *The New Class War: Reagan's Attack on the Welfare State and Its Consequences*. New York: Pantheon, 1982.

——. *Poor People's Movements: Why They Succeed, How They Fail*. New York: Random House, 1977.

——. *Regulating the Poor: The Functions of Public Welfare*. Updated ed. New York: Vintage Books, 1993.

——. "The Weight of the Poor . . . A Strategy to End Poverty." *Nation*, 2 May 1966, 510–17.

Platt, Anthony M. *The Child Savers: The Invention of Delinquency*. 2nd ed. 1969. Rpt. Chicago: University of Chicago Press, 1977.

Pope, Jacqueline. *Biting the Hand That Feeds Them: Organizing Women on Welfare at the Grass Roots Level*. Westport, Conn.: Praeger, 1989.

Powe, Lucas A., Jr. *The Warren Court and American Politics*. Cambridge, Mass.: Belknap Press, 2000.

Purcell, Edward A., Jr. *Brandeis and the Progressive Constitution: Erie, the Judicial Power, and the Politics of the Federal Courts in Twentieth-Century America*. New Haven, Conn.: Yale University Press, 2000.

Quadagno, Jill. *The Color of Welfare: How Racism Undermined the War on Poverty*. New York: Oxford University Press, 1994.

Reich, Charles A. "Individual Rights and Social Welfare: The Emerging Legal Issues." *Yale Law Journal* 74 (1965): 1245–57.

——. "The New Property." *Yale Law Journal* 73 (1964): 767–87.

Resnik, Judith, and Emily Bazelon. "Legal Services: Then and Now." *Yale Law and Policy Review* 17 (1998): 291–303.

Rosenblatt, Rand E. "Health Law." In *The Politics of Law*, ed. David Kairys, 147–71. 3rd ed. New York: Basic Books, 1998.

Rothman, David J. *The Discovery of the Asylum: Social Order and Disorder in the New Republic*. 1971. Rpt. Boston: Little, Brown, 1990.

Rhudy, Robert J. "Comparing Legal Services to the Poor in the United States with Other Western Countries: Some Preliminary Lessons." *Maryland Journal of Contemporary Legal Issues* 5 (1994): 223–46.

Sarat, Austin. "Going to Court: Access, Autonomy, and the Contradictions of Liberal Legality." In *The Politics of Law*, ed. David Kairys, 97–114. 3rd ed. New York: Basic Books, 1998.

Siegel, Fred. *The Future Once Happened Here: New York, D.C., L.A., and the Fate of America's Big Cities*. New York: Free Press, 1997.

Silver, James W. *Mississippi: The Closed Society*. New York: Harcourt, Brace and World, 1964.

Silverman, Ronald H. "Conceiving a Lawyer's Legal Duty to the Poor." *Hofstra Law Review* 19 (Summer 1991): 885–1111.

Skolnick, Arlene. *Embattled Paradise: The American Family in an Age of Uncertainty*. New York: Basic Books, 1991.

Smith, Reginald Heber. *Justice and the Poor: A Study of the Present Denial of Justice to the Poor and of the Agencies Making More Equal Their Position before the Law with Particular Reference to Legal Aid Work in the United States*. 3rd ed. Montclair, N.J.: Patterson Smith, 1972.

Southworth, Ann. "Business Planning for the Destitute? Lawyers as Facilitators in Civil Rights and Poverty Practice." *Wisconsin Law Review* (1996): 1121–69.

Stevens, Francis B., and John L. Maxey II. "Representing the Unrepresented: A Decennial Report on Public-Interest Litigation in Mississippi." *Mississippi Law Journal* 44 (1973): 348–54.

Stone, Michael E. "Housing and the Dynamics of U.S. Capitalism." In *Critical Perspectives on Housing*, ed. Rachel G. Bratt, Chester Hartman, and Ann Meyerson, 41–67. Philadelphia: Temple University Press, 1986.

Taub, Nadine, and Elizabeth M. Schneider. "Women's Subordination and the Role of Law." In *The Politics of Law*, ed. David Kairys, 328–55. 3rd ed. New York: Basic Books, 1998.

Tindall, George. *The Emergence of the New South: 1913–1945*. Baton Rouge: Louisiana State University Press, 1967.

Trattner, Walter I. *From Poor Law to Welfare State: A History of Social Welfare in America*. 5th ed. New York: Free Press, 1994.

Tremblay, Paul R. "Acting 'A Very Moral Type of God': Triage among Poor Clients." *Fordham Law Review* 67 (April 1999): 2475–2532.

——. "Rebellious Lawyering, Regnant Lawyering, and Street-Level Bureaucracy." *Hastings Law Journal* 43 (April 1992): 947–70.

——. "Toward a Community-Based Ethic for Legal Services Practice." *UCLA Law Review* 37 (August 1990): 1101–56.

Tushnet, Mark. *Making Civil Rights Law: Thurgood Marshall and the Supreme Court, 1936–1961*. New York: Oxford University Press, 1994.

——. *The NAACP's Legal Strategy against Segregated Education, 1925–1950*. Chapel Hill: University of North Carolina Press, 1987.

Uslaner, Eric M. *The Moral Foundations of Trust*. Cambridge: Cambridge University Press, 2002.

Van Alstyne, William W. "The Demise of the Right-Privilege Distinction in Constitutional Law." *Harvard Law Review* 81 (May 1968): 1439–64.

Vivero, Mauricio. "From 'Renegade' Agency to Institution of Justice: The Transformation of the Legal Services Corporation." *Fordham Urban Law Journal* 29 (February 2002): 1323–48.

Warren, Earl. *The Memoirs of Earl Warren*. New York: Doubleday, 1977.

Weinstein, Bernard L., and Robert E. Firestine. *Regional Growth and Decline in the United States: The Rise of the Sunbelt and the Decline of the Northeast*. New York: Praeger, 1978.

Weitzman, Lenore J. "The Economics of Divorce: Social and Economic Consequences of Property, Alimony, and State Support Awards." *UCLA Law Review* 28 (1981): 1181–1268.

West, Guida. *The National Welfare Rights Movement: The Social Protest of Poor Women*. New York: Praeger, 1981.

White, Lucie. "Paradox, Piece-Work, and Patience." *Hastings Law Journal* 43 (April 1992): 853–59.

———. "Specially Tailored Legal Services Programs for Low-Income Persons in the Age of Wealth Inequality: Pragmatism or Capitulation?" *Fordham Law Review* 67 (April 1999): 2573–80.

Wizner, Stephen. "Can Law Schools Teach Students to Do Good? Legal Education and the Future of Legal Services for the Poor." *New York City Law Review* 3 (Summer 2000): 259–66.

Wolff, Edward N. *Top Heavy: The Increasing Inequality of Wealth in America and What Can Be Done about It*. New York: New Press, 2002.

Woodward, Bob, and Scott Armstrong. *The Brethren: Inside the Supreme Court*. New York: Simon and Schuster, 1979.

Woodward, C. Vann. *Origins of the New South: 1877–1913*. Baton Rouge: Louisiana State University Press, 1951.

———. *The Strange Career of Jim Crow*. 3rd rev. ed. New York: Oxford University Press, 1974.

Yoder, J. Dwight. "Note: Justice or Injustice for the Poor? A Look at the Constitutionality of Congressional Restrictions on Legal Services." *William and Mary Bill of Rights Journal* 6 (Summer 1998): 827–83.

Young, Rosalie R. "The Search for Counsel: Perceptions of Applicants for Subsidized Legal Assistance." *Brandeis Journal of Family Law* 36 (Fall 1997–98): 551–83.

Zazove, Linda. "The Cy Pres Doctrine and Legal Services for the Poor: Using Undistributed Class Action Funds to Improve Access to Justice." *American Bar Association Center for Continuing Legal Education* (October 2001).

Index

ABA. *See* American Bar Association (ABA)

Abel, Richard L., 259n24, 263n45, 263n47, 264n49, 314n115

Abernathy, Ralph, 56

Abortion rights, 94–95, 133, 154, 292n107

Abrams v. Commercial Credit Plan, Inc., 306n30

Abuse. *See* Child abuse; Domestic violence

ACLU (American Civil Liberties Union), 22, 25, 38, 65, 170, 180, 201

ACU. *See* American Conservative Union (ACU)

Adams, Doris, 88

Adams v. Parham, 276n45

Addison v. Holiday, 311n74

Advocates of Legal Services, 228

AFDC. *See* Welfare programs

Affirmative action, 127, 192, 207, 333n150. *See also* Employment discrimination

Affleck, Thomas, 183–85

Affluent Society (Galbraith), 17

African Americans: and AFDC, 38, 40–53, 271n3; as community workers for poverty law programs, 88; as elected officials, 193; and law enforcement, 19–20, 89–90, 182–83, 204, 209, 327n101, 334n151; as lawyers, 8, 18–21, 76, 77–78, 87–88, 127, 204–5, 285n29; as legal services clients, 128–29, 179, 302–3n105; legal status of, 6–7; poverty of, 7, 17, 19, 128–29, 319n6; as teachers, 282n115, 290n81; violence against, 20, 89–90, 182–83, 206, 330n123, 334n151. *See also* Civil rights cases; Civil rights movement; Racial discrimination; Voting rights

Agnew, Spiro, 104, 234, 295n10

Aid to Families with Dependent Children. *See* Welfare programs

Aid to the Permanently and Totally Disabled. *See* Disability benefits

Aiyetoro, Sentwali, 213–14, 331n127

Alabama: average legal services grant per person in, 112; and Legal Services Corporation (LSC), 114–15; poverty law services in, during 1960s and 1970s, 10, 34, 68, 71, 76–77, 82–83, 101; poverty statistics for, 7, 128, 285n27, 319n6; statistics on poverty lawyers needed in, 112. *See also specific cities and poverty law programs*

Alabama Clients Council, 120–21

Alabama Consortium of Legal Services Programs, 118

Alabama Cooperatives Association v. Solomon, 326n90

Alabama State Bar, 77

Alaimo, Anthony, 185, 191, 193, 196–97, 324n73

ALAS. *See* Atlanta Legal Aid Society (ALAS)

Alaska, 112

Albany, Ga., election system, 96, 186–88, 193, 320n28

Alfieri, Anthony V., 260n29, 264n49, 301n73, 346n71

Allen, James, 107, 123

Allen v. Alco Finance Inc., 291n99

Allen v. State Board of Education, 320n27

Alston, Thurnell, 182–85, 192, 193, 322n51

American Bar Association (ABA), 27, 29, 70, 105, 106, 112, 227, 239, 240, 298n43, 300n67

American Civil Liberties Union (ACLU), 22, 25, 38, 65, 170, 180, 201

American Conservative Union (ACU), 245–46

American Federation of Government Employees, Local 2677 v. Phillips, 286n40

American Medical Association, 194, 195

American Trial Lawyers Association, 106

Anderson, Mary Bell, 40

Anderson v. Banks, 337n170

Anderson v. Burson, 273n15

Anderson v. Schaefer, 40, 41–42, 43, 276n52

Andrews v. Drew Municipal Separate School District, 290n80

Anthony v. Marshall County Board of Education, 63–64, 281n111

Anthony v. Wheat Street Gardens, 280n94

Antipoverty programs. *See* Poverty law and lawyers; War on poverty

Arkansas, 112

Armour v. England, 324n67

Arnold, David, 155

Ash Council, 105

Asher, Jonathan D., 10

Askew, Hulett "Bucky," 74, 114–16, 211, 212, 224, 227, 235, 299n54, 332n133

Atkinson v. Motz, 279n83, 280n92

Atlanta Housing Authority (AHA), 31, 53–56, 70, 143, 233, 270n72, 277nn65–66, 278n68, 278n70, 280–81n99–100

Atlanta Housing Authority v. Jones, 280n97

Atlanta Housing Code, 141

Atlanta Journal, 291n95

Atlanta Legal Aid Society (ALAS): and abortion rights, 94–95; and bureaucratization of legal services, 121–22, 234; caseload of, 29–30, 79, 84, 286n36, 301n75; and civil rights cases, 193–94; client survey by, 304n117; and community education, 83, 92–93, 304n117; and consumer law, 84, 92–94, 138–39, 236, 305n9; and correctional system, 94, 194–95; creation of, 4, 28–29; and domestic violence, 163; and family law, 159–60, 163, 314n106, 316n135; fire in Southside office of, 79, 286n37; and fiscal cutbacks of 1980s, 231, 232–34, 343n31, 343n37, 344n43; funding for and budget of, 29, 30, 70, 78–79, 113, 232–33, 239, 343n31, 344n45; and health services, 152–53, 154, 311n77; and housing, 53–62, 84, 92, 141, 142–43, 145–46, 278n68, 309n57; internal tension in, 126; law reform division of, 84; lawyers with, 8, 18, 20–21, 23, 31, 53, 73, 83–84, 267n13; mission of, 29; from 1970–1975, 78–79, 83–84, 91–95; prioritization of cases by, 233–34, 301n71, 301n75; and Reagan's election, 224; and salaries, 78–79; Saturday Lawyers Program of, 71, 72; and special units focusing on specific groups of clients, 233, 344n47; staff positions and staff size for, 29, 30, 79, 113, 269n52; staff training by, 118; telephone services of, 233; and voting rights, 94; and welfare rights, 45–48, 51–52, 84, 92, 157, 233–34, 273n21, 313n95

Atlanta Poverty Rights Office (PRO), 46

Atlanta Voice, 83, 92–93

Atlanta Welfare Rights Organization (AWRO), 46–48, 274nn31–32, 274n37, 324–25n76

Attridge, Byron, 56

Auerbach, Jerold, 258n16

Australia, 343n27

AWRO. *See* Atlanta Welfare Rights Organization (AWRO)

Ayers v. Fordice, 206, 220–21, 235

Bacon's Rebellion, 283n3

Baety, Ed, 58

Baird, Charles, 93, 96, 139, 231–32

Baker v. Carr, 266n2

Bamberger, Clint, 24, 111

Barnes, Gladys, 121

Barron v. Bellairs, 275–76n43

Bass, Jack, 272n4

Battered women. *See* Domestic violence

BCIA. *See* Burke County Improvement Association (BCIA)

Beacham, Marion, 194–95

Bell, Griffin, 41

Bell v. Anderson, 332n144

Bellow, Gary, 300n67

Belton v. Columbus Finance and Thrift Company, 291n99

Benham v. Edwards, 346n64

Benson v. Schweiker, 312n92

Benton, Reece, 316n139

Benton v. Mississippi State Department of Public Welfare, 287n56

Bergmark, Martha, 116, 200–202, 313n103, 327n96, 345n58

Billington v. Underwood, 308n54

Bining, Bob, 74

Birmingham Area Legal Services Corporation, 115, 142, 307n45, 326n93

Birmingham Legal Aid Society, 2, 4, 34, 68, 76, 82–84, 114–15, 285n25

Birth control, 25, 133

Bishop, Sanford D., 196

Black, Hugo, 60, 276n48

Black Power movement, 47, 48, 275n38

Blackburn v. Blackburn, 166–67, 316n137

Blackmun, Harry, 15, 276n48, 340n190

Blacks. *See* African Americans; Racial discrimination

Blackshear, Rev. Hosea, 324n67

Blair v. City of Greenville, 327n106

Blevins, Luvenia, 135–36, 140

Blocker v. Blackburn, 280n96

Boddie v. Connecticut, 60, 265n56, 279n87, 280n91, 339–40n190

Bogard v. Cook, 290n84

Boone, Joe, 278n72

Boone v. Dennis, 289n65

Borders, William Holmes, 280n95

Bowen v. Neal, 316n129

Bowman, Tom, 31, 267n13

Boycott against white businesses, 192

Boyd, Henry, 217

Boyd v. Harris, 309n57

Boykin v. Bremen Housing Authority, 308n54

Braboy v. Chatham County School Board, 323n58

Brackett v. Brackett, 314n109

Bradley, Dan, 74, 80, 116–17, 124, 227, 267n13, 341n14

Bradley, Norman, 76, 115

Bragg, Alfred, III, 125–26, 187, 322n53

Brantley v. Califano, 312n92

Brennan, Bill, 21, 22–23, 31, 58, 92, 141, 236, 287n51, 345n61, 345n62

Brennan, Justice William, 52, 173–74, 276n48, 340n190

Brent, John, 54, 279n84

Britain. *See* Great Britain

Brittain, John, 33, 64, 65, 78, 212–15, 281n114, 282n115, 332n140, 332–33n144

Brock, Bill, 107

Brooks et al. v. Leyva, 316n128

Broun, Paul, 99

Brown, Marcus, Jr., 139

Brown v. Beck, 324n66

Brown v. Board of Education, 19, 24–25, 178, 180, 222

Brown v. Cantrell, 324n67

Brown v. Housing Authority of McRae, 308n53

Brown v. Jaquith, 289n67

Brown v. Legal Foundation of Washington, 347–48n83

Brown v. Twin County Electric Power Association, 282n117

Brown v. Vance, 86, 289n65

Brownell, Emery, 258n16

Bryson v. Burson, 273n24

Buchanan v. Wheat Street Three, Inc., 280n93

Burge, Marian, 83–84, 234, 314n109

Burger, Warren, 51, 173, 276n48, 339n190

Burke County, Ga., 188–92, 193

Burke County Improvement Association (BCIA), 189, 190

Burns v. Alcala, 288n58

Burson, Bill, 46

Burt, Annie, 88

Burt v. Ramada Inn of Oxford, 327n106

Burton, Dan, 346n69

Burton v. Wilmington Parking Authority, 307n44, 309n59

Busbee, George, 97–100

Bush, George W., 240

Byhalia, Miss., 89–90, 206, 289n75

Cahn, Edgar and Jean, 2, 25, 26, 27, 336n156

Caldwell, Grady, 186

California Rural Legal Assistance, 35, 79, 103–4, 224, 225

Callahan v. Callahan, 315n123

Campbell, Marvin, 76, 82–83, 114, 115, 118, 119, 232, 242

Campbell v. Mincy, 328n109

Campbell, Will, 151–52, 157

Canada, 343n27

Cane v. Mississippi Employment Security Commission, 312n93

Capitalism, 13–14, 89, 133, 155

Cappelletti, Mauro, 263n44

Carden, Mary, 124

Carnes, Geraldine, 288n61

Carpenter v. Herscheded Hall Clock Division, Arnold Industries, 327n106

Carter, Dan, 297n28

Carter, Fannie Mae, 124

Carter, Jimmy, 10, 113, 225, 226, 234, 341nn9–10

Carter v. State of Mississippi, 317n143

Cash v. United States, 310n67

Center for Social Welfare Policy and Law (CSWPL), 10, 36–45, 49, 50, 63, 107, 272n5

Central Mississippi Legal Services (CMLS): black clients of, 179; and civil rights cases, 199, 203; creation of, 114, 299n54; and family law, 315n123, 315n127; and health services, 152; and housing, 309n57, 310n67; and institutionalization of children and adults, 170; and juvenile justice system, 168; possible expansion of, 299n57; and welfare rights, 157, 313n96

Chambliss, Alvin, 78, 150, 220, 235, 328n110, 338n173, 338n176

Chancey v. Department of Human Resources, 316n135

Charn, Jeanne, 300n67

Cheley v. Burson, 50, 51, 276n52

Chesser, Henry, 1

Cheves, Nancy, 21, 73

Chicago legal aid societies, 3, 258n9

Child abuse, 161, 162, 175

Child custody, 159, 163–66, 233, 235, 290–91n86, 314n109, 316nn128–29, 317n148, 327n96

Child support, 91, 233, 315–16n127

Children: institutionalization of, 159, 169–76, 317–18n153, 318n159, 346n64; legitimation of, 315n123; Medicaid for, 85, 311n79. *See also* Education; *and headings beginning with Child*

Children's Defense Fund, 66

Christian Coalition, 238

Christian, In re, 291–92n99

Civil Rights Act (1964), 16, 88, 178, 180, 189–90, 222

Civil rights cases: Albany, Ga., election system, 96, 186–88, 193, 320n28; and Atlanta Legal Aid Society (ALAS), 193–94; in Burke County, Ga., 188–92, 193; and community mobilization, 200; court decisions on, 218–23; and Georgia Legal Services Program, 85, 181–99, 200,

Civil rights cases (*continued*)
219–21, 319n8; and grand juries, 183, 184–85, 190;
and Legal Services Corporation of Alabama (LSCA),
200, 201, 319n8; in McIntosh County, Ga., 181–85,
190, 192–93; and NAACP Legal Defense Fund, 65,
180, 196–97, 201; and North Mississippi Rural Legal
Services (NMRLS), 32, 62–66, 85, 89–91, 199, 200,
203–18, 220–21; and poverty lawyers generally, 20, 21,
23, 25, 180–81, 221–23; and southern federal judges,
272n4; and Southern Poverty Law Center (SPLC),
170, 180, 201, 285n26; and students, 94, 202, 219–20,
322–23n58, 327n92; in urban areas, 326n93. *See also*
Correctional system; Voting rights

Civil rights movement, 7, 20, 62–66, 87–89, 179, 180,
186, 204, 266n7, 286n39, 319n7, 338–39n177

Clark, H. Sol, 72

Clark v. Emerson Electric Manufacturing Company, 327n106

Clark v. Housing Authority of Alma, 308n54

Clarksdale, Miss., 33, 82

Class action lawsuits, 239, 241

Clinton, Bill, 240, 268n25

Clinton, Hillary Rodham, 116, 242–43

Cloud v. Regenstein, 312n82

Cloward, Richard A., 262–63n42, 305n7

CLS. *See* Jackson, Miss., Community Legal Services (CLS)

Coahoma Legal Aid, Inc., Miss., 270n61

Cobb, Bill, 149, 169, 310n64, 322–23n58

Cody v. Community Loan Corporation of Richmond County,
306n24

Coen, Douglas C., 210

Coggins, Joseph, III, 196

Collier v. State of Mississippi, 290n83

Columbus, Ga., Legal Aid Society, 136, 137

Communist Party, 38

Community Action Program, 24, 34, 70

Community education, 83, 92–93

Community Legal Services of Jackson, Miss. *See* Jackson,
Miss., Community Legal Services (CLS)

Comstock Act, 25

Condon, Aaron, 32, 270n55

Connecticut, 25, 112

Connor, Bull, 20

Connor, Chuck, 211

Conservatism, 68–69, 109–10, 224–30, 237–38

Consolidated Credit Corporation of Athens, Inc. v. Peppers,
139–40, 306n34

Constitutional amendments. *See specific amendments*

Consumer law: and Atlanta Legal Aid Society (ALAS), 84,

92–94, 138–39, 236, 305n9; and bankruptcy, 291n99,
305n14; and Georgia Industrial Loan Act (GILA),
93–94, 135, 138–40, 232, 305n15, 306n31; and Georgia
Legal Services Program (GLSP), 85, 93–94, 134–39,
246, 291n95, 292n112, 313n100; and Legal Services
Corporation of Alabama (LSCA), 135, 136, 305n8; and
replevin statute, 306n21; and repossession, 291–92n99;
and Truth in Lending Act, 135, 136–38, 232, 305–6n19,
306n24, 307n35

Cook v. Conn., 290–91n86, 316n129

Cooper, Clarence, 8, 20–21, 268n25

Correctional system: and Atlanta Legal Aid Society
(ALAS), 94, 194–95; and Atlanta Welfare Rights Association, 324–25n76; desegregation of prisons, 196,
198, 324n70; end of legal services to prisoners, 239; and
Georgia Legal Services Program (GLSP), 96, 194–99;
and Jackson, Miss., Community Legal Services (CLS),
86; jail conditions, 86, 201, 202, 203, 288–89n64,
325n82, 328–29n113; jail construction, 192; and Legal
Services Corporation of Alabama (LSCA), 326n89;
and NAACP Legal Defense Fund, 196–97; and North
Mississippi Rural Legal Services (NMRLS), 91, 206,
328–29n113; personal injury case against prison, 91;
prisoners' legal complaints against, 323n62, 323–24n65;
state costs for court case on, 325n79

Cowley, John, 278–79n80

Cox, Archibald, 16

Cramton, Roger, 111

Crane v. Davis, 324n67

Crane v. Mathews, 97–100, 113, 152, 175, 293–94nn119–20,
295n135

*Crews v. Brantley County Department of Family and Children
Services,* 316n135

Criminal cases, 91, 188–89, 290n83, 327n108

Cromartie, John, 98–100, 118, 121, 143, 158, 175–76, 197,
231, 237, 243, 294n126, 302n99, 324n73

Crosby v. State of Mississippi, 290n83

Crowe v. Heckler, 312n82

Crumbley v. Housing Authority of Winder, 308n55

CSWPL. *See* Center for Social Welfare Policy and Law
(CSWPL)

Cuban refugees, 193

Cullen, Bob, 158, 164, 188–90, 196–99, 221, 321n44,
322–23n58, 324nn73–74

Cullers v. Home Credit Company, 306n32

Cumberland Schools of Law, 77

Cummins, Eric, 323n62

Curry v. Block, 310n67

Dailey v. Cawthon, 275n40

D'Alemberte, Talbot "Sandy," 241

Dallaire, Greg, 98, 100, 292n110, 294n126

Dandridge v. Williams, 50, 51, 158, 276n51, 276n54

Daniel, Alice, 33n133

Daniels v. State of Mississippi, 327n108

Davis, Eva, 45

Davis, Jamie, 323n58

Davis, Martha F., 273n20

Davis v. Caldwell, 275n40

Davis v. Graham, 292n104, 322n54

Davis v. Wynn, 323n58

Dedman, Bill, 345n62

Dees, Morris, 180, 285n26

DeKalb General Hospital, In re, 312n82

Delaney, Joseph, 125

Dennard, Tom, 74

Denton, Jeremiah, 226, 228–29, 234

Dependent individualism, 176

Deriso v. Cooper, 337n169

Desegregation: court cases on, 19, 24–25, 63–64, 178, 180; decline of white resistance to, 66; of higher education, 220–21, 338n173, 338n175; NAACP campaign on, 7, 24, 39, 64, 110, 205–6; and Nixon administration, 66; of prisons, 196, 198, 324n70; of public housing authorities, 308n55; of schools, 16, 19, 24–25, 31, 32, 62, 63–64, 66, 69, 88, 90, 110, 178, 222, 325n84, 338n172. *See also* African Americans; Civil rights cases; Racial discrimination

Devillers, Chester, 193

Diggs v. Diggs, 316n128

Disability benefits, 52, 85, 96, 124, 140, 157, 275–76n42, 281n107

Disabled students, 201, 322–23n58, 326n92, 337–38n171

Discrimination. *See* Employment discrimination; Racial discrimination; Sex discrimination

Dittmer, John, 285n23, 319n7

Divorce: bigamy as grounds for, 315n123; court cases on, 60, 315n123; court fees for, 60; domestic violence as cause of, 162, 233; government regulation of, 133; and male "emancipation" from family support, 315n122; in 1940s, 29–30; and poverty law practice, 62, 95, 134, 159–60, 233, 263n46, 292n112, 301n71, 313n100, 315n125; property disputes arising from, 315n123; rise in divorce rate, 163–64, 315n125; women lawyers' caseload including, 137. *See also* Family law

Dixon v. GILS, 294n128

Dobbins v. LSC, 347n75

Dodson v. Parham, 152–53, 311n75

Doe v. Bolton, 94, 292n106, 292n107

Doe v. Secretary of the Army, 322n57

Doe v. Venable, 292n108, 311n80

Dokson, Robert, 18, 31, 60, 81, 84, 121–24, 126, 227, 234, 267n13, 301n85

Domestic relations cases. *See* Family law

Domestic violence, 160–63, 233, 313n103, 314n109, 314n113, 314n117

Dooley, John A., 340n7

Dornan, Bob, 346n69

Dotson v. City of Indianola, 328n110

Douglas, William O., 44, 52, 276n48

Dropkin v. Dropkin, 316n128

Due process clause, 11, 39, 48–49, 51–52, 59, 60, 141–42, 149–50, 257n2, 276n47, 326n93

Dutton v. Lamb, 169, 317n148

Dylan, Bob, 22

Eady v. General Finance Corporation of Augusta, 306n24

Ealy v. Littlejohn, 289n75, 328n111

East Mississippi Legal Services, 116, 316n129

Eastland, James, 212

Ebbinghouse, Richard, 136

Echols v. Auburn City Housing Authority, 308n45

Economic Opportunity Act (1964), 1–2, 23–24, 30, 268–69n33

Economic Opportunity Act Amendments (1966), 268–69n33

Edenfield, Newell, 158, 337n170

Edmonson v. Leesville Concrete Company, 307n44

Education: and achievement testing, 337n170; and civil rights cases involving students, 94, 202, 219–20, 322–23n58, 327n92; community education on legal issues, 83, 92–93; desegregation of schools, 16, 19, 24–25, 31, 32, 62, 63–64, 66, 69, 88, 90, 110, 178, 180, 222, 325n84, 338n172; and disabled students, 201, 322–23n58, 326n92, 337–38n171; financing of schools, 339–40n190; firing of black teachers, 282n115, 290n81; historically black colleges, 220–21, 338n173, 338n175; legal education costs, 343n40; McIntosh County, Ga., school board, 183, 184; of poor, 130, 143; of poverty lawyers, 17, 19, 21, 22–23, 75, 269n52; and pregnant teenagers, 94, 202; racial discrimination in schools, 219–20, 323n58, 326n92, 337n170; segregation in higher education, 220–21, 338n173, 338n175

Ehrenreich, Barbara, 315n122

Ehrlich, Thomas, 111, 112, 216–17, 332n133

Eighth Amendment, 195
Einstein, Gloria, 162, 323n58
Eisenhower, Dwight D., 1, 222
Elderly, 194, 233, 344n47
Eldridge v. Weinberger, 52, 277n56
Elliott, Jim, 71
Ellison v. Weinberger, 293n117
Ellsworth, George, 31
Elrod, Jerry, 165
Elrod v. Department of Family and Children Services, 316n131
Employment discrimination, 86, 90, 192–93, 201, 202, 206, 207, 209, 288n63, 326n91, 331n129, 332–33nn144–145
England. *See* Great Britain
Equal access to justice, 110–17, 124, 131, 241, 302n88
Equal justice under the law, 124, 302n88
Equal protection clause, 11, 16, 33, 39, 40, 44, 50, 51, 52, 59, 141–42, 181
Evans v. Liberty Cash, Superintendent, Mississippi State Penitentiary, 327n108
Evans v. Newton, 307n44
Evans v. State of Mississippi, 290n83
Evers, Charles, 215
Evers, Medgar, 21

Fair, Elizabeth, 336n161
Fambro v. Fulton Co., 323n65
Family law: and child abuse, 161, 162; and child custody, 159, 163–66, 233, 235, 290–91n86, 314n109, 316nn128–29, 317n148, 327n96; and child legitimation, 315n123; and child support, 91, 233, 315–16n127; court cases on, 164–67; and domestic violence, 160–63, 233, 313n103, 314n109, 314n113, 31417; and institutionalization of children, 159, 169–76, 317–18n153, 318n159; and juvenile justice system, 167–69; and poverty lawyers, 13, 95, 134; and regulatory state, 133–34, 159–76; and termination of parental rights, 159, 164–67, 327n96. *See also* Divorce
Fantroyal v. Caldwell, 312–13n93
Farley v. Reinhart, 292n105
Farmers Home Administration (FmHA), 124, 148–50, 310n67
Federal National Mortgage Association (Fannie Mae; FNMA), 148–49, 310n64
Feinman, Jay, 307n38
Feldman, Marc, 300n67, 346n65
Ferguson v. Williams, 288n62
Fifteenth Amendment, 181, 187, 320n33
Fifth Amendment, 48–49, 276n47, 347–48n83

Finch, Ed, 182–83, 192
Finch v. Weinberger, 313n95
Finkelstein, James, 325n82
Finland, 343n27
Fiquette v. Harden, 275n41
First Amendment, 206, 213, 216, 276n51, 346–47n75
Floods, 235–36
Flora v. Moore, 327n106
Florida, 241–42, 348n87
Florida Migrant Legal Services, 35–36
FmHA. *See* Farmers Home Administration (FmHA)
FNMA. *See* Federal National Mortgage Association (Fannie Mae; FNMA)
Foner, Eric, 266n7
Food stamps, 83, 85, 96, 125, 128, 156, 313n94, 313n96
Ford, Gerald, 52, 295n137
Ford, Wardell, 334n151
Fortas, Abe, 276n48
Fortune, Porter, 32, 70
Foucault, Michel, 263n43
Fourteenth Amendment, 11, 16, 33, 39, 40, 44, 48–52, 59, 187, 257n2, 276n47, 276n51
Foy v. Lewis, 315n127
France, 343n27
Frazier et al. v. Courtesy Finance Company, 306n32
Frazier v. Jordan, 292n102
Freedman, Sheriff, 19–20
Freeman v. Lynn, 280–81n99
Freeman v. Martin, 292n101, 323n63
Freeman v. Parham, 275n43, 311n77
Freeman v. Rogers, 308n55
Friedman, Lawrence M., 257–58n6, 261nn35–36, 264n53, 278n74, 304n6, 305–6n19, 312n89, 315n125
Froman, Mike, 160, 163, 292n112, 313n100

Gabel, Peter, 307n38
Galbraith, Kenneth, 17
Gambrell, E. Smythe, 29
Garbus, Martin, 43–44, 50, 272n10
Gardella, Lawrence, 326n90
Gardner, Ayres, 143–45, 308n55
Gaston v. Calhoun County Board of Education, 327n107
Gatekeeping function of lawyers, 119–20, 301n73
Gates, Henry Louis, Jr., 267n22
Gates v. Collier, 91, 290n84
Gault, In re, 317n151
Gay v. Gay, 316n135
Geminiani, Victor, 195
Georgia: average legal services grant per person in, 112;

and Legal Services Corporation (LSC), 113–14; poverty law offices in, during 1960s and 1970s, 10, 34, 35, 68; poverty statistics for, 7, 128–29, 283n10, 319n6; statistics on poverty lawyers needed in, 112. *See also specific cities and poverty law programs*

Georgia Association of Retarded Citizens v. McDaniel, 338–39n171

Georgia Clients Council, 120

Georgia Indigents Legal Services (GILS), 72–74, 79, 98, 99

Georgia Industrial Loan Act (GILA), 93–94, 135, 138–40, 232, 305n15

Georgia Investment Company v. Norman, 291n99

Georgia Legal Services Program (GLSP): affirmative action policy of, 127; black clients of, 179; black employees of, 127, 302n99; branch offices of, 74, 95, 123–24, 294n126; and bureaucratization of legal services, 118, 121; case histories from, 123–24; caseload of, 74; and civil rights cases, 181–99, 200, 219–20, 319n8, 322–23n58–59; client participation in, 120; and consumer law, 85, 93–94, 134–39, 246, 291n95, 292n112, 313n100; and correctional system, 96, 194–99; creation of, 71–75; criticisms of, 97–101, 224–25, 295n132; and domestic violence, 160–62; and education cases, 337–38nn170–71; and family law, 95, 159, 160–61, 164, 165–67, 235, 316n128, 317n148; and fiscal cutbacks in 1980s, 231–32, 233; and floods (1994), 235–36; funding for and budget of, 74–75, 81, 98–101, 113, 233, 284n12, 284n17, 344nn44–45; and health services, 151–55; and housing, 95, 124, 143–50, 292–93nn112–13, 308nn53–55, 313n100; and institutionalization of children and adults, 169–76, 316n139, 318n159, 346n64; investigation of, 338n172; and landlord-tenant hotline, 233; lawyers with, 123–24, 126–27; and Medicaid, 97–101, 152–53; from 1970–1975, 95–101; personnel policies of, 126–27; prioritization of caseload by, 119; social composition of clients of, 128; staff positions and staff size for, 74, 84, 95, 231; staff training by, 118; support staff at, 126–27; and unemployment compensation, 312–13n93; and voting rights, 96, 184–92; and welfare rights, 85, 96–101, 157–58, 292n112, 313n94, 313n100

Georgia Residential Finance Authority (GRFA), 147–48, 309–10nn60–61

Georgia State Bar, 35, 71–72, 271n69

Georgia v. McCollum, 265n60

Gerald, Martha, 80–81

German Legal Protection Society, 2–3

Germany, 343n27

Gideon v. Wainwright, 19, 73, 257n2

Giese, Kay, 160, 161, 162

GILA. *See* Georgia Industrial Loan Act (GILA)

Gilbert, Spencer, 76

Gill v. Woods, 281n109

GILS. *See* Georgia Indigents Legal Services (GILS)

Gingrich, Newt, 237

Gitlin, Todd, 347n77

Givens v. Delta Electric Power Association, 328n109

Glasbrenner, Wendy, 162

Glaze v. Atlanta Housing Authority, 308n47, 308–9n57

GLSP. *See* Georgia Legal Services Program (GLSP)

Godee, Ellis, 191

Goldberg v. Kelly, 49, 51, 52, 61, 72, 91, 147, 149, 150, 156, 276n48, 276n51, 313n96

Goldenfarb, Sondra, 278n68

Goldstein, Dennis, 141, 142–43, 236, 237, 286n37, 344n46, 345n62, 390n2

Goldwater, Barry, 69

Gomillion v. Lightfoot, 320n32, 321n34

Gordley, James, 263n44

Goren, David, 169–70, 316n139

Gorman, Mark, 183, 192

Gottlieb, Steve, 31, 57, 58, 67, 98–99, 224, 230–34, 239, 343n31, 343n37, 344n43, 345n61

Government regulations. *See* Regulatory state

Gramm, Phil, 237–38

Grand juries, 183, 184–85, 190

Gray v. Quality Finance Company, 306n31

Great Britain, 5, 111, 230, 240

Greco, Michael S., 347n80

Green Amendment, 107, 108, 109–10, 113, 246–49, 296–97n25, 297n27

Green, Edith, 109

Green v. Stanton, 288n58

Greenberg, Jack, 272n10

GRFA. *See* Georgia Residential Finance Authority (GRFA)

Grier, Christine, 235

Grovner, Nathaniel, 183, 184, 192

Gunn, Howard, 89, 208, 211, 213, 217, 218, 334n151, 336n161

Guthrie v. Evans, 196–99, 324n71

Gwinnett Nonprofit Housing Corporation v. Pruitt, 280n98

Hall, Kermit L., 264n53

Hames, Margie, 94

Hammond v. Russell, 309n57

Hand, Learned, 244

Hannah v. Butz, 310n67

Hardwick v. Parham, 317n143

Harlan, John M., 52, 60, 276n48, 276n51
Harmon v. Brucker, 273n18
Harrell v. Harris, 312n92
Harrington, Michael, 17
Harris, Joe Frank, 268n25
Harris, Richard, 92
Harris v. Bell, 322n52
Harris v. Levi, 322n52
Harris v. McRae, 340n190
Harris v. Mississippi State Department of Public Welfare,
  288n58
Harvard Center for Law and Education, 110
Harvey, William, 227
Harvey, Woodrow, 191
Hatch, Orrin, 226, 228–29, 234, 342n23
Havighurst, Clark, 310–11n70
Hays v. Mississippi State Department of Public Welfare,
  287n56
HCBLS. See Hinds County (Miss.) Bar Legal Services
  (HCBLS)
Head Start, 24, 32, 66, 88
Health care, 90–91, 130, 150–55, 311n81. See also Medic-
  aid; Medicare; Mental health services
Health, Education and Welfare Department (HEW), 72,
  81, 97, 99, 195, 294n121
Heiner, Philip, 71
Heller, Louella, 50, 51
Helms, Jesse, 107
Henretta Young v. Morris Hanna et al., 290n78
Henry, Aaron, 329n118
Herring v. B. H. Moore and Son, Inc., 292n100
HEW. See Health, Education and Welfare Department
  (HEW)
Hewatt, Amy, 141
Higher education. See Education
Hill-Burton hospitals, 130, 151–52, 154, 202
Hinds, Lennox, 216
Hinds County (Miss.) Bar Legal Services (HCBLS), 75, 80
Hispanics, 303n105, 339n190
Hodge v. Dodd, 323n64
Hodges v. Community Loan and Investment Corporation,
  306n24
Hodges v. Hodges, 315n123
Hoffman v. HUD, 310n64
Holland v. Steele, 324n67
Hollings, Ernest "Fritz," 107
Holloway v. State of Mississippi, 290n83
Holmen, Phyllis, 303n109
Holmes, Oliver Wendell, Jr., 264n53

Holmes, In re, 322n55
Holmes v. Housing Authority of Brunswick, 308n55
Homosexuality, 193
Hood, John, 278n68
Hooks v. Jaquith, 289n66
Hope, Camille, 196
Horowitz, Michael, 270n55
Horton v. Horton, 315n127
Horwitz, Morton J., 264n51
Hospitals, 90–91, 130, 151–52, 154, 328n109. See also
  Health care
Houseman, Alan W., 227, 229, 258n16, 261n37, 300n67,
  340n7, 342n24
Housing: and Atlanta Legal Aid Society (ALAS), 53–62,
  84, 91; conditions of public housing complexes,
  145–46; court cases on, 54, 58, 59–61, 147–50; and
  evictions, 61, 141, 146–48; federal subsidies for home
  purchases, 148–50; foreclosures on homes, 91, 149–50;
  and Georgia Legal Services Program, 95, 124, 292–
  93nn112–13, 313n100; Georgia's landlord-tenant law,
  54, 58; government regulation of, 140–50; and HUD
  regulations, 56, 271n62; and Legal Services Corporation
  of Alabama (LSCA), 307n39, 326n90; list of tenants'
  grievances, 277n65; means test for public housing, 128;
  and public housing authorities, 142–48; racial discrimination in, 95, 145, 146, 193, 271n62, 309n57; and rent
  strikes, 58, 279n82; and rent subsidies, 146–47; and repair cases, 57–58; Section 8 housing, 146–47, 192, 202,
  309nn57–58, 321n46; subsidized housing for lower- and
  middle-income families, 141–42; and Tenants United
  for Fairness (TUFF), 55–56, 277nn65–66; treatment of
  public housing residents and their rights, 142–45
Housing and Community Development Act (1974), 146
Housing and Urban Development Department (HUD),
  56, 61, 142, 146, 271n62, 292–93n113
Houston v. Prosser, 292n105
HUD. See Housing and Urban Development Department
  (HUD)
Hudson v. Farmers Home Administration, 310n67
Huff v. Moore, 316n128
Huie, Stell, 99–100, 295n132
Humphrey, Hubert, 69
Huntsville, Ala. See Madison County (Ala.) Legal Aid
  Society
Hutchinson, Guy, 182

Ide, Bill, 71, 73, 287n45
Immigration and Naturalization Service, 193
Indian Child Welfare Act (1978), 316n129

Institutionalization of children and adults, 159, 169–76, 316n139, 317–18n153, 318n159, 346n64

Interest on Lawyers' Trust Accounts (IOLTA), 241, 347–48n83

IOLTA. *See* Interest on Lawyers' Trust Accounts (IOLTA)

Irving v. Hargett, 327n108

Irving v. State of Mississippi, 290n83, 327n108

Isaac, Rael Jean, 342n21

Ivey v. Garner, 293n114, 322n52

J. J. v. Ledbetter, 317n148

J. L. and J. R. v. Parham, 169–76, 317n150

Jackson, Charles, Jr., 92–93

Jackson, Evelyn, 97

Jackson, Jesse, 48

Jackson, John, 89–90

Jackson, Maynard, 141

Jackson, Miss., Community Legal Services (CLS): civil rights cases of, 85–86; and consumer law, 306n21; and correctional system, 86; creation of, 71, 75–76; funding for, 80, 105; and health services, 153; and justice system, 85, 86; and justices of the peace, 86; and mental health services, 82, 85, 86, 87; and merger with Mississippi Bar Legal Services (MBLS), 80–81, 114; opposition to, 79–80; and voting rights, 86; and welfare rights, 85, 156. *See also* Central Mississippi Legal Services (CMLS)

Jackson, Miss., Legal Aid Society, 75

Jackson v. Indiana, 293n115

Jackson v. Riddle, 328n110

Jackson v. State of Mississippi, 327n108

Jackson v. Tupelo, 332n143

Jackson v. Winstead, 281n105

Jails. *See* Correctional system

James v. Valtierra, 340n190

Jamieson, Sue, 236, 345n61

Javins v. First National Realty Corporation, 278n74

Jefferson County (Ala.) Legal Services, 34, 76, 270–71n62

Jeffries v. Georgia Residential Finance Authority, 147–48, 309nn59–60

Jelinek, Donald, 43

Jenkins v. Allen Temple Apartments, 280n95

Job Corps, 24

Johnson, Earl, 241

Johnson, Earl, Jr., 258n16, 261n37, 266n10, 271n70, 271n71

Johnson, June, 217

Johnson, Lyndon: on poverty, 257n3; Supreme Court appointments by, 16, 276n48; and Vietnam War, 35, 70; and war on poverty, 10, 17, 20, 23–24, 26, 177, 239

Johnson, Wayne, 88–90

Johnson v. Greenwood, 332n144

Johnson v. Johnson, 306n23

Johnson v. Sikes, 337n170

Joiner, Bill, 204

Jones, Cecil, Jr., 166

Jones, Chatham, 183

Jones, Frank, 286n39

Jones v. Caldwell, 275n42

Jones v. Consumer Remodeling Service, Inc., 305n19

Jones v. Mississippi, 288n57, 312n88

Jones v. United States, 346n64

Jordan v. Allain, 328n110

Jordan v. City of Greenwood, 328n110

Joseph, Wilhelm, 203–5, 207, 212–15, 217–18, 327nn100–101, 332n133, 332n140, 332–33n144

Justice Department, 28, 64, 90, 180, 325n88, 338n173

Justices of the peace, 86

Juvenile cases, 317n142

Juvenile justice system, 167–69, 289n64, 317n143

Kaplan v. Sanders, 307n41

Kates v. Motz, 278n77

Katz, Jack, 262–63nn39–43, 285n28, 297n37, 319–20n11, 348n93

Katz, Michael B., 128, 302n104

Katzenbach, Nicholas deB., 266n8

Keady, William C., 64, 150, 335n153, 357n166

Kehrer, Bettye, 53–55, 73–75, 94, 284n19

Keith, Tom, 235

Kelley, Robin, 260n26, 264n52

Kelly, John, 49

Kelsey, Terry, 195–96

Kelsey v. Holder, 325n80

Kelsey v. Killebrew, 322n53, 324n68, 337n168

Kennedy, John F., 16, 17, 22, 276n48

Kennedy, Leon, 154, 311n81

Kennedy, Robert F., 1, 2, 20, 26, 27, 257n2

Keough v. Tate County Board of Education, 327n107

Khrushchev, Nikita, 38

Kidd, Culver, 99

Kilgore, Virginia, 162, 313n103, 313n117

Kilgore v. Kennesaw Finance Company of Douglasville, 306n24

Kimbrell, Vicky, 236–37

King, C. B., 40, 272n10

King, Martin Luther, Jr., 6, 7, 20, 23, 56, 179, 186, 208, 266n7, 319n7, 338–39n177

King v. Smith, 43–44, 50, 273n18, 312n88, 318n165

KKK. See Ku Klux Klan

Kline v. Rankin, 282n118

Kronlund v. Honstein, 292n103, 322n54

Ku Klux Klan, 180, 183, 208, 209–10, 215, 216, 331n127

Laden, Ellen, 125

Lafayette County Legal Services. See North Mississippi Rural Legal Services (NMRLS)

Lake v. Winder Housing Authority, 308n54

Lambert v. Waynesboro Properties, Inc., 309n57, 321n46

Land v. Cockrell, 287n48

Lane v. Inman, 322n55

Langdon v. Drew Municipal Separate School District, 327n106

Lanning v. Mignon, 315–16n127

Lasch, Christopher, 318n163

Lassiter v. Department of Social Services, 257n2

Law. See Poverty law and lawyers

Law, Bud, 150

Law Day, 1, 26

Law enforcement: and African Americans, 19–20, 89–90, 182–83, 204, 209, 327n101, 334n151; in McIntosh, Ga., 182; and police brutality, 89–90, 182–83, 206, 209, 215

Law v. United States Department of Agriculture, 310n67

Lawrence, Alexander A., 98–99

Lawrimore v. Sun Finance Company, 306n33

Lawyers: Carter on, 113; and cost of legal education, 343n40; residency requirements for, 64–65, 282n118; salaries of, 79, 299n50; statistics on, 231, 258n16, 298n41. See also Poverty law and lawyers

Lawyers' Committee for Civil Rights Under the Law (LCCRUL), 25, 65, 78, 85, 180, 201

Lawyers' Constitutional Defense Committee (LCDC), 25, 33, 43, 65, 180, 201

LCCRUL. See Lawyers' Committee for Civil Rights Under the Law (LCCRUL)

LCDC. See Lawyers' Constitutional Defense Committee (LCDC)

LDF. See NAACP Legal Defense Fund

LeClercq, Fred, 50, 51

Ledbetter v. Benham, 346n64

Lee et al. v. G. A. C. Finance Corporation, 291n99

Legal aid societies, 2–5, 24, 28, 34, 68, 75, 258n16. See also Poverty law and lawyers

Legal culture, definition of, 261n36

Legal Defense Fund. See NAACP Legal Defense Fund

Legal reform. See Poverty law and lawyers

Legal Services Corp. v. Velazquez, 346n75

Legal Services Corporation Act (1974), 101, 102–10, 244, 246–53, 296n24, 325n84, 341–42n20

Legal Services Corporation (LSC): and average legal services grant per person, 112; board of directors for, 106, 108, 110, 113, 226–27, 341n16; and bureaucratization of legal services, 117–27, 234–35; and Bush administration, 240; and Carter administration, 10, 113, 225, 226, 234, 341nn9–10; and client participation in local programs, 120–21; and Clinton administration, 240; congressional investigation of, 228; and consumer law, 305n9; creation of, 102–10; Delivery System Study of, 297n35; and equal access, 110–17, 124, 131; and Ford administration, 295n137; funding for and budget of, 112–13, 225–28, 237–38, 240–41; investigation of North Mississippi Rural Legal Services (NMRLS) by, 212–18, 332n138, 332n140, 333n146; "minimum access" objective of, 111–12, 116–17, 205, 225, 240, 298n42; and national support centers, 108, 296–97n25; and Nixon administration, 102, 106, 108, 239; opposition to and criticisms of, 106–7, 113, 122–23, 224–30, 237–38, 298n48, 340–41n7; and passage of Legal Services Corporation Act (1974), 101, 102–10, 246–53, 296n24; political support for, 105, 227–28, 240, 245–53, 347n80; and prioritization of caseloads, 118–20, 200; purpose of, 102–3, 110; Quality Improvement Project of, 118; and Reagan administration, 10, 224–30, 232, 234–35, 239, 341n16; Republican restrictions on, in 1990s, 10, 239, 240; resignations of staff from, in 1980s, 227. See also Legal Services Program (LSP); Poverty law and lawyers

Legal Services Corporation of Alabama (LSCA): black clients of, 179; board members for, 121; and bureaucratization of legal services, 118; case histories from, 125, 135–36; caseload of, 298n43; and civil rights cases, 200, 201, 319n8; and consumer law, 135, 136, 305n8; and correctional system, 326n89; creation of, 115; and education cases, 326n92; and employment issues, 326n91; and family law, 160, 314n109; and fiscal cutbacks of 1980s, 231; funding for and budget of, 115; and health services, 152, 154; and housing, 307n39, 307–8n45, 326n90; newsletter of, 118; prioritization of caseload by, 119; socioeconomic characteristics of clients of, 303n105; staff positions and staff size for, 115; and voting rights, 325n88; and welfare rights, 125, 156, 200

Legal Services Program (LSP): creation of, 2, 23–28; creation of, in Deep South, 28–36, 268–69n33; criticisms of and opposition to, 34–35, 72, 104–5, 315n125; funding for, 2, 10, 66, 70, 283n127; and law reform, 271n71; local initiative for, 34, 35, 36; and Nixon administration, 10, 66, 68–71, 72, 79, 104–5, 122; publications of, 271n64; statistics on, 2, 28, 70. *See also* Legal Services Corporation (LSC); Poverty law and lawyers

Lenzner, Terry, 79, 286n39

Leslie v. Mann, 308n50

Levin, Joseph, 180, 285n26

Levin, Kenneth, 311n77

Lewis, David and Viola, 138

Lewis, Jim, 89

Lewis v. Delta Loans, Inc., 306n21

Lewis v. Housing Authority of Augusta, 308n54

Lewis v. Termplan, 93, 138, 306n28

Leyva, Barbara, 164

Leyva v. Brooks, 316n128

Liberal legality, 297–98n38

Linda Hill v. A. B. Johnson, 323n58

Lipman, David, 33, 64–65

Lipman v. Van Zant, 282n118

Lister, Joey, 170–76

Loans, 93–94, 135, 136–40, 236. *See also* Consumer law

Lockett, Willie, 161

Lodge, Herman, 188–91

Lodge v. Buston, 190–91, 193, 321n40

Loe v. Smith, 323n65

Loeb, Jay, 31, 46, 51, 52, 94–95, 277n55

Logistic regression method, 245–53

Lokey, Muriel, 274n32

Long, Russell, 107

Lorde, Audre, 348n91

Lott, Trent, 212

Louisiana, 4, 34

LSC. *See* Legal Services Corporation (LSC)

LSP. *See* Legal Services Program (LSP)

Lyons, Clint, 115–16, 212, 227, 332n142

M. A. C. et al., In the Interest of, 316n132

Maddox, Lester, 72, 74, 195, 284n12

Madison, Isaiah, 220

Madison County (Ala.) Legal Aid Society, 34, 76, 77, 82–83, 114–15

Malden, Arthur, 309n58

Malone v. Ventress, 312n93

Mann, James, 143–44, 145

MAP. *See* Mississippi Action for Progress (MAP)

Marshall, Thurgood, 39, 52, 174, 276n48, 340n190

Martin v. Saucier, 275n42

Mary Holmes Junior College, 33, 70

Maryland, 50, 276n51

Mason v. Service Loan and Finance Company, 291n99

Massachusetts, 112

Mathews, David, 97

Mathews, Ethel Mae, 48, 274n37, 324–25n76

Mathews v. Eldridge, 48, 52, 277n56

Mathews v. Little, 322n54

Maxey, John, 33, 62, 63, 64, 76, 86, 114, 285n23, 288n61, 327n96

Mayfield, Rev. R. B., 289n73

Mayfield, Thomas, 65, 89

MBLS. *See* Mississippi Bar Legal Services (MBLS)

McAfee, Kathy, 279n80

McClain v. Lafayette County Board of Education, 327n107

McClellan, Leonard, 78, 207, 222, 231, 235, 244, 319n4, 327n108, 345n55

McCombs, Rufe, 134, 136–38, 305n15

McDaniel v. Georgia Association of Retarded Citizens, 338–39n171

McDonald, Laughlin, 190

McFall v. Helton Enterprises of Jackson, Inc., 306n21

McGowen, Beth, 123–24

McIntosh County, Ga., 181–85, 190, 192–93, 322n51

McIntosh County NAACP v. City of Darien, 321n49

McIver, Harrison, 202, 207, 243, 348n95

McLean, George, 333n148

McLemore v. Cubley, 317n143

McLemore v. Schweiker, 312n92

McRae v. Board of Education of Henry County, 322n52

Means test, 128, 302n103

Medicaid: and abortions, 94–95; for AFDC recipients, 63; beginning of, 24; for children, 85, 311n79; court cases on, 63, 85, 97–101, 152–54, 275n43, 292n109, 311n77; denial of Medicaid benefits, 236–37; and Georgia Legal Services Program (GLSP), 97–101, 152–53, 293n119, 294n121; means test for, 128; and poverty law practice, 63, 85, 94–95, 97–101, 151–54; for sex changes, 311n77

Medicare, 24, 151

Medicine. *See* Health care; Medicaid; Medicare

Medlock, Rufus and Mary, 236

Melikian v. Avent, 289n65

Mental health services, 82, 85, 86, 87, 169–76, 236, 289nn66–67, 293n115, 312n84, 316n139

Meredith, James, 31, 66, 204

Merkel, Phil, 151, 323n58

Michaels, David, 87

Michelman, Frank I., 340n190

Middleton v. Jackson Housing Authority, 308n54

Miller v. Hartwood Apartments, 309–10n61

Milliken v. Bradley, 110

Milton v. Busbee, 311n76

Minor v. Starkville, 333n45

Mississippi: average legal services grant per person in, 112; and Legal Services Corporation (LSC), 114, 115–16; monitoring of poverty lawyers in, 65; poverty law services in, during 1960s and 1970s, 10, 33–34, 68, 71, 75–76, 76, 79–81, 101, 270n61; poverty statistics for, 7, 128, 319n6; statistics on poverty lawyers needed in, 112. *See also cities and poverty law programs*

Mississippi Action for Progress (MAP), 76, 285n23

Mississippi Bar Legal Services (MBLS), 75, 80–81, 82, 114, 159, 299n54, 299n57, 317n142. *See also* Central Mississippi Legal Services (CMLS)

Mississippi Public Service Commission et al. v. Mississippi Power Company, 327n96

Mississippi Sovereignty Commission, 65, 89, 204, 205

Mississippi State Bar, 35, 64–65, 79, 116, 271n68

Mitchell, Guy, Jr., 211, 215

Mitchell v. Board of Trustees of Oxford Municipal Separate School District, 327n107

Mizell, Wilmer, 110

Mizell Amendment, 110, 246–49, 252

Mobile, Ala., legal aid society, 2, 68, 77

Mobile County (Ala.) Legal Aid Society, 77

Mobilization for Youth, 25, 38

Mondale, Walter, 228

Montgomery, Cleveland, 204

Montgomery Improvement Association, Inc. v. HUD, 326n90

Moore, George, 14–15

Moore, Howard, Jr., 272n10

Moore, John Norton, 349n98

Moore v. Beneficial Finance Company of Georgia, 306–7n35

Moore v. Stewart, 323n60

Moran, Laurie, 339n182

Morgan v. Sproat, 317n145

Morris, Carrie, 47

Morris v. Richardson, 274n33

Morrow v. Mississippi Publishers Corporation, 288n63

Morse, Joshua, 31, 32–33, 204

Moss, Erma, 186

Moye, Charles, 97

Mozley, Otis, 140

Murphy, George, 103

Murray v. Murray, 315n123

Myers, Lewis, 89–90, 209, 211, 212, 217, 218, 235, 331nn128–29, 332n133, 333n148, 335n153, 335n154, 336n161, 345n55

Myers v. Douglas County Board of Elections, 322n58

"Myth of legal efficacy," 264n49

"Myth of rights" versus "politics of rights," 13, 263n44

NAACP in Mississippi, 329n118, 329–30n121

NAACP Legal Defense Fund: and civil rights cases, 65, 180, 196–97, 201; and correctional system, 196–97; creation of, 7; desegregation campaign of, 7, 24, 39, 64, 110, 205–6; impact cases of, 38; and local lawyers, 276n50; and racial discrimination in housing, 271n62; and welfare rights, 40, 272n5

Nadasen, Premilla, 271n3

National Association for the Advancement of Colored People. *See headings beginning with NAACP*

National Clients Council, 14–15, 120

National Conference of Black Lawyers (NCBL), 216, 335n154

National Consumer Law Center, 93, 107

National Housing Act, 24, 148

National Housing and Economic Development Law Project, 150

National Juvenile Law Center, 170

National Legal Aid and Defender Association (NLADA), 27, 106, 228, 235, 258n16, 284n19

National Organization of Legal Service Workers, 336n156

NCBL. *See* National Conference of Black Lawyers (NCBL)

Neely, Betsy, 71

Neighborhood law offices, 25

Nelson v. Taylor, 316n128

Netherlands, 343n27

New Deal, 133, 141, 155, 177

New York, 2–3, 25, 38

Newman, Bob, 54

Newsome, Lansom, 199

Newton, Demetries, 271n62

Nicholson v. Choctaw County, 326n89

Nixon, Richard: appointment of federal judge by, 196; and conservatism, 69; and dismantling of war on poverty, 66, 70; and Legal Services Program/Corporation, 10, 66, 68–71, 72, 79–80, 102, 104–6, 108, 122, 234, 239; and Office of Legal Services, 70, 110; resignation of, 102, 108; and school desegregation, 66, 69; southern strategy of, 69, 178; Supreme Court appointments by, 52, 276n48

NLADA. *See* National Legal Aid and Defender Association (NLADA)

NMRLS. *See* North Mississippi Rural Legal Services (NMRLS)

Norman v. St. Clair, 311n76

North Central Alabama Legal Services, 115, 231, 344n45

North Mississippi Rural Legal Services (NMRLS): black clients of, 179; black leadership of, 127; board members of, 121; branch offices of, 33, 231; and bureaucratization of legal services, 121; caseload of, 289n68; and child custody, 290–91n86; and civil rights cases, 32, 62–66, 85, 89–91, 199, 200, 203–18, 220–21; client survey by, 129–30, 304n118; community workers, paralegals, and support personnel at, 88, 114; and consumer law, 136; and correctional system, 91, 206, 328–29n113; creation of, 31–33; and criminal cases, 91, 290n83; and domestic violence, 162; Elder Law Project of, 233; eligibility guidelines of, 333n146; and employment discrimination cases, 90; and family law, 162, 313n103, 316n129; and fiscal cutbacks of 1980s, 231, 235; funding of, 20, 32, 33, 70, 78, 113–14; and health services, 90–91, 152, 153–54; and housing, 91, 310n61; and impact cases generally, 84; investigations of, 65, 90, 121, 125, 210–18, 332n138, 332n140, 333n146; lawyers with, 18, 20, 22, 33, 77–78, 87–88, 207, 267n13, 288n60; and Mary Holmes Junior College, 33, 70, 88–91; from 1970–1975, 77–78; opposition to, 78; Sanders as director of, 77–78; and school desegregation, 32, 62, 63–64, 90; social composition of clients of, 128; staff positions and staff size for, 33, 77, 88, 114, 231; Trister as director of, 62, 65–67, 125; and United League, 200, 203, 208–19; and University of Mississippi, 28, 31–33, 70; and voting rights, 206; and welfare rights, 32, 45, 63, 91

Nunn v. Harris, 307n45

Obadele v. McAdory, 288–89n64

Office of Economic Opportunity (OEO): and American Bar Association, 239; and California Rural Legal Assistance, 104; and Center for Social Welfare Policy and Law (CSWPL), 36; creation of, 23, 26; funding for, 283n127; and Georgia Legal Services Program, 74; and governor's veto of OEO funding, 32, 79; and legal services programs, 26–28, 30; and "maximum feasible participation" by poor, 120; and Nixon administration, 66, 70, 79–80; Office of Legal Services of, 70–71, 72, 79–81, 110; Phillips as director of, 79–81, 104–5. *See also* Legal Services Program (LSP)

Office of Legal Services, OEO, 70–71, 72, 79–81, 110

Oliver, Mary Margaret, 126, 161

Olmstead v. L. C. by Zimring, 346n63

Osborne, Solomon, 78, 87–88, 202, 220, 223

Otis Mozley v. Ford Motor Credit Company, 307n36

Overton, Ben F., 242

Owens, Wilbur D., Jr., 170–71, 187, 188, 219, 320nn32–33, 337n168

Owens v. DeLoach, 315n126

Pack, Lagrone, 290n81

Packard, Ron, 238

Padnos, Michael, 22, 23, 30–31, 54, 55, 59, 66, 67, 73, 92, 93, 269nn51–52, 278n68

Paer, John, 31

Paige v. Gray, 96, 186, 193, 293n114, 320nn31–32

Palmer v. Mangum, 315n127

Paralegals, 2, 88, 114, 118, 126–27, 231. *See also* Poverty law and lawyers

Parental rights, 159, 164–67, 327n96

Parham, Jim, 72, 74

Parham v. J. L. et al., 317–18n153

Parker, Frank J., 277n58, 320n27

Parker, Frank R., 328n110

Parks, Rosa, 7

Parks v. Harden, 276n46, 288n58

Pasto, Eugene, 209, 213

Pate v. Parham, 293n115

Payne, Charles M., 282n124, 319n7, 339n184

Peacock f. Drew Municipal Separate School District, 290n80

Pearson, James B., 228

Pegues v. Oxford, 332–33n144

Penal system. *See* Correctional system

Pennington, Jesse, 18–20, 33, 63, 220, 222

Peppers case, 139–40, 306n34

Perkins, Willie, 328n110

Perle, Linda E., 258n16

Perryman, Mattie, 56

Persells, Lester H., 56

Pettigrew, Harry, 93, 96, 137

Phillips, Howard, 79–81, 104–5, 340n7

Phillips v. Washington Legal Foundation, 347n83

Pickens v. Okolona Municipal Separate School District, 281n115, 290n81, 327n106, 328n111

Pinkney, Sammie, 183, 184, 192

Pinson v. Hendrix, 327n106

Piven, Francis Fox, 262–63n42, 305n7

Plessy v. Ferguson, 24

Police. *See* Law enforcement

Pollota, Mary, 31

Poor People's Action Committee, 270n62

Poor People's Newspaper, 47, 48, 92, 324n76

Poppell, Tom, 182, 184, 185, 322n51

Potter v. James, 311n73

Poverty: of African Americans, 7, 17, 19, 128–29, 131; African Americans as legal services clients, 128–29, 302–3n105; attitudes of legal services clients, 129–30; and average legal services grant per person, 112; and education, 130; L. Johnson on, 257n3; R. Kenney on, 1; and lawyer-client relationship, 8, 9–10, 14–15, 260nn29–30; and legal problems, 4, 8–9, 13, 37, 83–84, 123–25, 127–30, 143, 242–43; and means test for public services, 128, 302n103; "minimum access" to legal services for the poor, 111–12, 205, 225, 240, 298n42; and poverty level/rate/threshold, 128, 259n21, 302n103, 303n108; and race, 221–23; social impact of legal services on the poor, 11–13; socioeconomic characteristics of legal services clients, 128–31, 143, 302–3n105, 303–4nn111–12; statistics on, 6–7, 128–29, 258n16, 285n27, 303n108, 319n6; women as as legal services clients, 129, 303n109; women's poverty, 129, 303n109. See also African Americans; Poverty law and lawyers; War on poverty

Poverty law and lawyers: African Americans as lawyers, 8, 18–21, 76, 77–78, 87–88, 127, 204–5, 285n29; attrition rate of lawyers, 84, 299n50; broad significance of, 243–44; and bureaucratization of legal services, 117–27, 234–35; and capitalism, 13–14, 89, 133; characteristics of and backgrounds of lawyers, 16–23, 81–101, 125–27; and client-lawyer relationship, 8, 9–10, 14–15, 260nn29–30; and client participation, 120–21; conclusion on, 239–44; criticisms of, 34–35, 263n46; decision to leave poverty law, 231–32, 237; disempowering assumptions of, 264; education of lawyers, 17, 19, 21, 22–23, 75, 269n52; and empowerment of poor clients, 7–8, 11; and equal access, 110–17, 124, 131, 241; and equal justice under the law, 124; and fiscal retrenchment in 1980s-1990s, 231–35, 238–39; hierarchies among attorneys in larger organizations, 84; and legal problems of poor clients, 4, 8–9, 13, 37, 83–84, 123–25, 127–30, 143, 242–43; and legal reform, 10–13, 45, 82, 84–85, 180, 200, 232, 236, 239, 262n40, 262n42, 271n71; legal strategies and doctrines available to, 10–11; "minimum access" to legal services for the poor, 111–12, 205, 225, 240, 298n42; monitoring of activities of lawyers, 65; moral discourse of lawyers, 17, 21–23, 84, 125–26, 129, 237; and "myth of legal efficacy," 264n49; and "myth of rights" versus "politics of rights," 13, 263n44; from 1970–1975, 81–101; and prioritization of caseloads, 118–20, 200, 233–34; and regulatory state, 176–77; residency requirement for lawyers, 64–65, 282n118; rewards for, 84; salaries of lawyers, 78–79, 266n10, 299n50; social impact of, on the poor, 11–13;

specialists in, 86–87; statistics on, 2, 28, 29–30, 34, 70, 74, 79, 111–12, 116, 123, 128–29, 238–39, 240, 283n10, 298n42; and welfare state, 229–30, 238, 241; women as lawyers, 18, 73–75, 123–24, 126–27, 137, 143, 302n101. See also specific lawyers and legal services programs; and specific types of cases, such as Welfare rights

Powell, Barry, 75, 85, 86, 114, 153–54, 168, 288n61, 299n57, 309n57, 346n65

Powell, Lewis F., Jr., 27, 227, 339n190

Prescott v. Judy, 316n128

President's Advisory Council on Executive Organization, 105

Pressel, Wayne, 9, 96, 158, 294n121

Pressley, Mary Lee, 40, 42

Price, LaNita, 121

Prisons. See Correctional system

Public welfare. See Welfare programs

Quarles v. North Mississippi Retardation Center, 327n106

Quarles v. Oxford Municipal Separate School District, 281n114

Quarles v. St. Clair, 315n127

Quie Amendment, 110, 246–50

R. C. N. v. State of Georgia, 316n135

R. R., In re, 317n144

Race relations. See African Americans; Civil rights cases; Civil rights movement; Desegregation; Racial discrimination

Racial discrimination: and Albany, Ga., election system, 96, 186–88, 193; in Burke County, Ga., 188–92; court cases on, 218–23; difficulties in addressing, 178–80; in employment, 290n81; family law involving interracial intimacy, 166–67; in housing, 95–96, 145, 146, 193, 271n62, 292n113; and legal system generally, 6–7, 19; in McIntosh County, Ga., 181–85, 192–93; in Mississippi, 203–5, 220–21, 329n119; in public housing, 309n57; in schools, 219–21, 323n58, 326n92, 337n170; and vote dilution, 187–88; and welfare rights, 44. See also African Americans; Civil rights cases; Desegregation; Employment discrimination

Raff, Michael, 116

Ramage v. Shell, 310n67

Ramberg v. Porter, 85–86, 168, 288n61

Ramsey v. Ramsey, 315n127

Randle v. Indianola Municipal Separate School District, 290n81

Randy Joe Watkins, In re, 289n64

Randy Joe Watkins, In the Interest of, 317n143

Ray, Wilma Nix, 166

Ray v. Department of Human Resources, 316n135

Reagan, Ronald: as California governor, 103–4, 224, 225, 234; and Legal Services Corporation (LSC), 10, 224–30, 232, 234–35, 239, 341n16

Redditt v. Mississippi Extended Care Centers, Inc., 327n106

Reece v. Evans, 324n67

Reed, Ralph, 238

Reese v. Termplan, Inc., 306n32

Regnery, Alfred S., 341n7

Regulatory state, 132–33, 176–77, 305n7. *See also* Consumer law; Family law; Health care; Housing; New Deal; Welfare programs

Rehabilitation Act (1973), 323n58

Reich, Charles, 39, 41, 49

Remar, Robert, 98–99

Republican Party v. The City of Blue Ridge, 323n59

Reyer v. Harrison County Department of Public Welfare, 316n134

Rias v. Henderson, 315n127

Rindskopf, Elizabeth, 94

Riots, 66, 69, 178, 266n7

Roberts, Elizabeth Madox, 257

Roberts, Eva Mae, 148–49

Roberts v. Cameron Brown Company, 310n64

Robinson, Alfred "Skip," 89, 90, 203, 208–13, 215, 217, 218, 329n118, 332n138, 333n150, 336n165

Robinson v. Ensley, 290n77

Robinson v. McAlister, 291n87

Robinson v. Stovall, 328n111

Roe v. Wade, 94, 107, 292n107

Roosevelt, Franklin, 6

Rothman, David J., 317n140

Roy, Ruby, 31

Rush, Carolyn, 311n77

Russell v. Harrison, 327n106

Russell v. Savannah Housing Authority, 309n57

Rustin v. State of Mississippi, 290n83, 327n108

Saddler v. Winstead, 291n88

Sagoes v. Atlanta Housing Authority, 308n47

Saine v. Hospital Authority of Hall County, 312n82

San Antonio Independent School Dist. v. Rodriguez, 339–40n190

Sanders, Alix, 33, 65, 77–78, 328n110

Sanger, Margaret, 25

Sanks v. Georgia, 54, 58, 59–61, 279n84, 279n88

Sapp v. Rowland, 190, 321n42

Satterfield, M. B., 55, 56, 70

Savannah Legal Aid Society, 2, 34, 74

Scheingold, Stuart A., 263n44, 302n88

Schools. *See* Education

Schwartz, Tobiane, 31, 94

SCLC. *See* Southern Christian Leadership Conference (SCLC)

Scott v. Housing Authority of Macon, 292n113, 308n54

Scott v. Parham, 293n117, 313n94

Segregation. *See* Desegregation; Racial discrimination

Seiler, Frank W. "Sonny," 98

Sellers v. Alco Finance, Inc., 291n99

Sex change, 311n77

Sex discrimination, 5–6, 86, 94, 190, 288n63. *See also* Women

Shapiro v. Thompson, 45, 51, 273n24, 276n53

Shaw, Pink, 148

Sheffield v. Cochran, 293n114, 322n52

Sheldon, Andrew, 195

Shelley v. Kraemer, 307n44

Shenfield v. Prather, 282n118

Sheriffs. *See* Law enforcement

Shriver, Sargent, 26

Siegel, Fred, 266n7

Simmons v. Parham, 276n44

Simms, Kathryn, 165–66

Small Business Administration, 63

Smith, Kendric, 306n34

Smith, Orma, 85, 91, 215, 334n151

Smith, Reece, 227

Smith, Reginald Heber, 4–5, 111, 258n7

Smith, Sylvester, 42–43

Smith v. Allwright, 320n30

Smith v. Community Federal Savings and Loan Association of Tupelo, 327n106

Smith v. Granberry, 328n110

Smith v. King, 43–44

Smith v. Mississippi Employment Security Commission, 312n93

SNCC. *See* Student Nonviolent Coordinating Committee (SNCC)

Snowden v. Birmingham-Jefferson County Transit Authority, 326n93

Sobelson, Roy, 163, 292n112

Social Security Act, 44, 47, 63, 275n43

Social Security benefits, 47, 48, 51–52, 96, 129, 234, 275n42, 276n43

South Carolina, 34

South Mississippi Legal Services, 116, 166, 200

Southard, Reggional, 156

Southeast Mississippi Legal Services, 116, 162–63, 200–202, 313n103

Southern Christian Leadership Conference (SCLC), 56, 89, 186

Southern Discount Company of Georgia v. Ector, 306n35

Southern Discount Company v. Cooper et al., 306n32

Southern Poverty Law Center (SPLC), 170, 180, 201, 285n26

Southwest Mississippi Legal Services, 78, 116, 202

Soviet Union, 38

Sparer, Edward, 25, 37–38, 41, 43, 272n10, 273n26

Spellers v. Saucier, 275n43

SPLC. *See* Southern Poverty Law Center (SPLC)

Spousal abuse. *See* Domestic violence

Spriggs, Kent, 33, 64, 148

Spruell, Billy, 324n65

Spruill, Nancy, 161–62

Stalin, Joseph, 38

Stanfield, Walter, 217

Stanley, Raiford, 323n58

Stanley, Rosita, 120

Starkville, Miss., 89

Starr, Kenneth, 220

State v. Sanks, 279n86

Steiner, Allison, 163, 309n57, 313n103

Stennis, John, 212, 331–32n133

Stevens, Francis, 75–76, 285n23

Stevens, John Paul, 174

Steward v. Winter, 328n113

Stewart, Potter, 276n48, 276n51

Stewart v. Bank of Pontotoc, 281n115, 290n81, 327n106

Stewart v. Pototoc, 333n144

Stoddard, Harry and Joan, 302n100

Stovall, Sam, 144–45

Strickler, George, 31–33

Student Nonviolent Coordinating Committee (SNCC), 186, 319n7, 329n118

Supremacy Clause of U.S. Constitution, 10–11, 86

Supreme Court, U.S.: and at-large election system, 191; Burger Court's decisions, 51, 173–74, 339n190; and Civil Rights Act (1964), 16; on desegregation of higher education, 220–21; on desegregation of schools, 16, 19, 24–25, 178, 180, 222; on First Amendment rights, 346n75; on housing issues, 54, 59–60; on incompetence to stand trial, 293n115; on institutionalization of children, 172–74; and intent to discriminate, 187; on Interest on Lawyers' Trust Accounts (IOLTA), 347–48n83; Johnson appointees to, 16, 276n48; on legal counsel for indigent defendants, 19, 73, 257n2; on legal system, 265n56; on mental health services, 236; Nixon and Ford appointees to, 52, 276n48; and "overbreadth" concept, 276n51; on separate but equal accommodations, 24; on Social Security, 47; and voting rights, 16, 288n62; Warren Court's decisions, 16, 19, 51, 52, 59, 222, 339n190; and welfare rights, 10, 43–44, 45, 48–53, 273n23, 318n165. *See also specific cases and Supreme Court justices*

Swann decision, 107

Sweden, 343n27

Talmadge, Herman, 107

Tarutis, Gerald, 172

Tate v. Mississippi Employment Security Commission, 312n93

Tate v. State of Mississippi, 290n83

Taylor, Ken, 135

Taylor, Stanley, 21–22, 33, 62, 64, 91, 136, 149–50, 153–54, 166, 200, 202, 268n26, 290n86, 327n96

Taylor v. Coahoma County School District, 328n109

Taylor v. St. Clair, 309n61

Temple, Arlo, 210

Tenants United for Fairness (TUFF), 55–57, 277nn65–66

Terry, Michael, 67, 94–95, 195, 212

Thomas v. Burson, 273n23

Thomas v. Clements, 287n48

Thomas v. Mathews, 288n56

Thompson, Lawrence L., 287n45

Thornberry, Homer, 148

Thornton, Phyllis, 344n44

Three-judge courts, 41–42, 272–73n14

Till, Emmett, 20, 66, 87

Tinker v. Ussery, 287n48

Tocqueville, Alexis de, 265n57, 348n93

Tremblay, Paul R., 260n30, 301n74

Trice v. Weinberger, 275n42

Triplett v. Cobb, 63, 85, 153, 281n108, 291n88, 311n78

Trister, Michael, 31–33, 62, 65–67, 77, 125, 282n120

Truth in Lending Act, 135, 136–38, 232, 305–6n19, 306n24, 307n35

Truth in Lending Simplification and Reform Act, 307n35

TUFF. *See* Tenants United for Fairness (TUFF)

Tupelo, Miss., 209–11, 213–15, 218, 329n119, 331–32n126, 331n129, 337n165

Tucker v. Burford, 328n110

Turner v. Colonial Finance Corp., 306n21
Turner v. Crider, 332n143
Twenty-sixth Amendment, 288n62

Unemployment compensation, 156, 157, 275n42,
    312–13n93, 313n95
United League, 89, 90, 121, 200, 203, 208–19, 289n75,
    329n118, 329–30nn121–22, 331n127, 333n146, 333n148,
    333n150, 334n151, 335n153, 336–37n165
United States v. Fordice, 220–21, 338nn174–76
United States v. Garner, 310n67
United States v. Henderson, 310n67
United States v. White, 149–50, 310n66
United States v. Wynn, 310n65, 310n67
University of Alabama, 77
University of Mississippi, 28, 31–33, 65, 70, 178, 204–5,
    207, 282n118, 282n120
Urban law, 53, 277n58
Urban riots. See Riots
Uslaner, Eric M., 265n59, 348–49n97–98

Vietnam War, 18, 20, 35, 70, 107, 126, 184, 267nn12–13,
    268n25, 283n127
Vincent v. Payne, 326n93
VISTA, 24, 269n52
Vocational rehabilitation, 157–58
Volunteers in Service to America (VISTA), 24, 269n52
Von Briesen, Arthur, 2–3
Voting rights: in Alabama, 201, 325n88; and at-large
    election system, 185–91, 328n110; in Barbour County,
    Ala., 325n88; in Burke County, Ga., 189–91, 193; of
    convicted felons, 94, 193; of eighteen- to-twenty-year-
    olds, 86, 288n62; and equal protection clause, 181;
    and Fifteenth Amendment, 181, 187; and Fourteenth
    Amendment, 187; and Georgia Legal Services Program
    (GLSP), 96, 184–92; in McIntosh County, Ga., 181,
    184–85, 193; in Mississippi, 202; and North Mississippi
    Rural Legal Services (NMRLS), 206; of senior citizens,
    194; and voter registration, 186
Voting Rights Act (1965), 16, 66, 178, 180, 181, 186,
    325n88

Wade v. Carsley, 281n115
Walbert, David, 96, 149, 184–87, 190, 192, 221, 310n64,
    321n44
Wallace, George, 69, 178, 215
Waller, William, 79
Walls, Johnnie, 88

War on poverty, 10, 17, 20, 23–24, 26, 66, 70, 177, 239.
    See also Legal Services Program (LSP); Office of Eco-
    nomic Opportunity (OEO); Welfare rights
Ward, Columbus, 275n38
Ward v. Village of Monroeville, 289n65
Warren, Earl, 16, 19, 51, 52, 59, 222, 266n2, 339n190
Washington, D.C., Neighborhood Legal Services
    Project, 25
Washington Research Project, 66
Watergate scandal, 102, 107
Watkins v. Mobile Housing Board, 309n58
Webb v. Webb, 316n128
Webster, David, 31, 46, 138, 267n13, 274n31, 277n55
Wehunt v. Atlanta Legal Aid Society, 294n128
Welfare programs: and African-American women, 38,
    40–43, 271n3; in Alabama, 42–44; eligibility for, 44,
    48, 50–51, 273n18; in Georgia, 40–42, 46–48, 50–51,
    273nn23–24, 275n40, 312n91; and labor market, 155;
    and local legal services programs, 44–45; in Maryland,
    50; means test for, 128; in Mississippi, 44, 49, 63, 85;
    public assistance versus social insurance, 302n104;
    reform of, in 1990s, 240; and regulation of labor
    market, 262–63n42; residency requirements for, 45;
    and standard of need, 312n91; and "substitute father" or
    "man-in-the-house" rule, 42–44, 273n23, 318n165; and
    termination of benefits, 49. *See also* Disability benefits;
    Food stamps; Medicaid; Welfare rights
Welfare rights: and Atlanta Legal Aid Society (ALAS),
    45–48, 51–52, 84, 92, 157, 233–34, 273n21, 313n95;
    and Atlanta Welfare Rights Organization (AWRO),
    46–48, 274n37, 274nn31–32; and Center for Social
    Welfare Policy and Law (CSWPL), 36, 37–45, 49,
    50, 63, 272n5; court cases on, 40–53, 63, 85, 157,
    273nn23–24, 275nn40–41; and Georgia Legal Services
    Program (GLSP), 85, 96–101, 157–58, 292n112, 313n94,
    313n100; and Jackson, Miss., Community Legal Ser-
    vices (CLS), 85, 156; and Left and Black Power move-
    ments, 47–48, 275n38; and Legal Services Corporation
    of Alabama (LSCA), 125, 156, 200; and NAACP Legal
    Defense Fund, 40, 272n5; and North Mississippi Rural
    Legal Services (NMRLS), 32, 45, 63, 91; and poverty
    lawyers, 10, 261n35; and racial discrimination, 44;
    and right to live, 39, 44, 50, 157; and state violations
    of federal regulations for public aid, 156–57. *See also*
    Welfare programs
Welke, 318n164
West, Larry, 153–54
West v. Cole, 85, 153–54, 288n59, 311n79

Whitaker, Clyde, 210, 215, 331n127
White, Byron, 276n48, 276n51
White, Garney and Margie, 149–50
White, Lucie, 229, 301n73, 342n25
White v. Butz, 96
White v. Harris, 312n92
White v. Regester, 320n34
White v. World Finance of Meridian, 305n19
Whitehead v. Mississippi Employment Security Commission, 312n93
Williams, Carolyn, 51–52
Williams, John Bell, 79, 204
Williams, Osgood, 59, 294n128
Williams v. Butz, 310n67, 313n96
Williams v. Land-Hurst Furniture Company, 306n20
Williams v. Mississippi Employment Security Commission, 312n93
Williams v. Phillips, 286n40
Williams v. St. Clair, 311n76
Williams v. Weinberger, 52, 277n56
Williams v. West Point, 332n144
Williams v. Winstead, 281n106
Wilson, Gary, 215
Wilson v. Kelley, 324n70
Wilson v. Weaver, 288n58
Winningham v. HUD, 292–93n113
Winstead v. Kirkwood, 281n107

Wisdom, John Minor, 86
Wizner, Stephen, 272n10
Women: African-American women and AFDC, 38, 40–43, 271n3; African-American women as community workers, 88; education of pregnant teenagers, 94, 202; as lawyers, 18, 73–75, 123–24, 126–27, 137, 143, 302n101; as legal services clients, 129, 303n109; legal status of, 5–6; and Poor People's Action Committee, 270n62; and sex discrimination, 5–6, 86, 94, 190, 288n63. *See also* Child custody; Domestic violence; *and specific women*
Woodes v. Morris, 315n127
Woodward, C. Vann, 6
Wooley v. Mississippi Employment Security Commission, 327n106
Wright, Edward L., 105
Wrightsville Housing Authority, In re, 308n55

Yearby v. Parham, 157, 312nn90–91
Young, Andrew, 101
Young, Butler, Jr., 89
Young, Mary, 186, 187
Young v. Young, 315n127

Zacker, Ed, 183
Zazove, Linda, 348n86
Zimmer v. McKeithen, 321nn34–35
Zimring, Jonathan, 220, 221, 338n172